TEXAS

1971

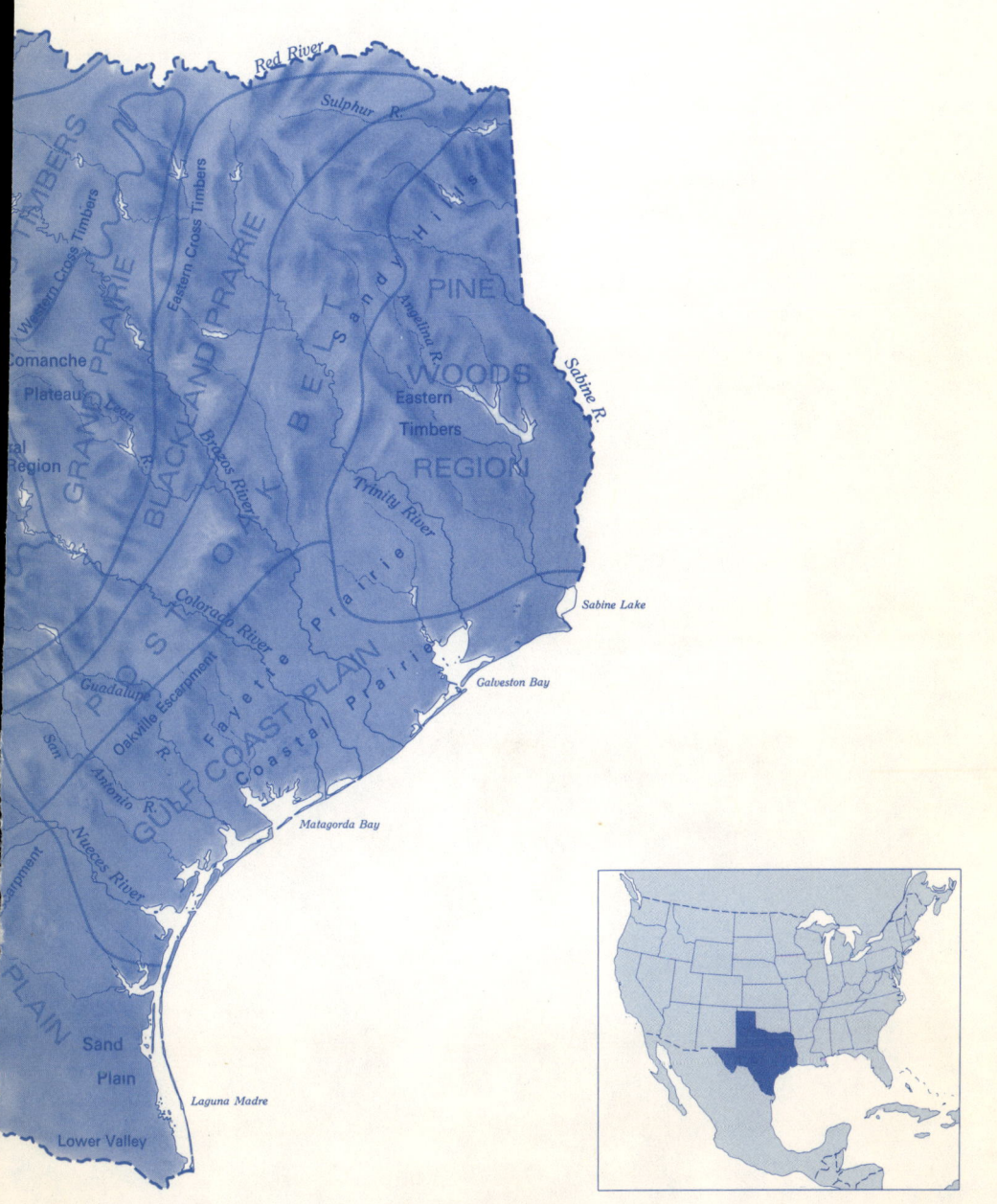

Drawn by Miklos Pinther

TEXAS

A History

TEXAS

SEYMOUR V. CONNOR
Texas Tech University

A History

Harlan Davidson Inc.
Arlington Heights, Illinois 60004

Copyright © 1971
Harlan Davidson, Inc.

All rights reserved

This book, or parts thereof, must not be used or reproduced in any manner without written permission. For information address the publisher, Harlan Davidson, Inc., 3110 North Arlington Heights Road, Arlington Heights, Illinois 60004.

ISBN: 0-88295-724-4
(Formerly 0-630-80937-9)

Library of Congress Card Number: 71-136037

PRINTED IN THE UNITED STATES OF AMERICA

84 85 86 87 88 EB 10 9 8 7 6

Preface

It has long been my conviction that history in general should be written in as interesting a manner as the author is capable of and that history textbooks in particular should be lifted from the dry-as-dust stereotypes that too often stunt rather than enlarge a student's perspectives. This book is intended for use as a college and university text; I hope that it is sufficiently well written to merit the attention of serious adult readers as well as students.

Although Texas is the book's central point of focus, an attempt has been made to avoid the platitudes of provincialism and to place the state in national and even international perspective. This has led to slight emphases on Texas' role in the exploration of North America, in the conquest of colonial empires, in the turbulence of Mexican revolution, in the causes of the United States' war with Mexico, in the development of the Compromise of 1850, in the movements of agrarian reform and later progressivism, and in the emergence of an energy-oriented national economy. Several unusual interpretations are offered to explain the causes of the Texas Revolution, the secession movement in Texas, the ethnic flavors of the state's heritage, the Reconstruction era, and the essential progressivism of Texans until quite recent times.

Although much of the work has grown out of my own research, vastly more of it (as evidenced in the bibliography) is drawn from the published investigations of several generations of scholars. If I have misrepresented their conclusions or otherwise misused their work, it has certainly been inadvertent and unintentional, and I am sorry.

In addition to the gratitude I owe to those researchers, I have a number of more specific debts. Many of my colleagues in history throughout Texas criticized one or more chapters of the manuscript. Their suggestions not only have greatly improved the book but also have removed a number of the pesky errors inevitable in a work of this kind. No onus for the errors that remain can attach to them. I would like to acknowledge here my appreciation of the help of Allwyn Barr of Texas Tech University; Roy Sylvan Dunn of Texas Tech; Odie B. Faulk of Oklahoma State University; Earl Green of Texas Tech; William C. Pool of Southwest Texas State University; James V. Reese of Texas Tech; Wilbert H. Timmons of the University of Texas at El Paso; and David M. Vigness of Texas Tech. My special thanks go to Billy Mac Jones of Southwest State University, who read the entire manuscript; to J.M. Skaggs of Wichita University, who was of particular help with the section on trail drives; and to Senator A. M. Aikin and former Attorney General John Ben Shepperd, who scrutinized the last chapter. The staff of the Southwest Collection at Texas Tech rendered unflagging aid, and the Graduate School, with a small research grant, assisted in the preparation of the bibliography. Finally, I wish to thank Mrs. Gale Webber for her loyal assistance, which went far beyond the call of duty.

S. V. C.
Lubbock, Texas

Contents

1/ The Beginning   1

The Land and the People   1
     Geological Development · Topography
     Early Man · The Indians

Spanish Beginnings   9
     Charting the Gulf Shores · Cabeza de Vaca · The Coronado Entrada De Soto and Moscoso · The Establishment of New Mexico

The Lure of the Conchos   15
     Father Salas and the Jumanos · The River of Nuts · The Mendoza-López Expedition

2/ The Missionary Era   20

The First Mission Wave   20
    Fort St. Louis · De León's Expeditions · The First Missions

The Second Mission Wave   26
    French Intrusion · The Ramón-St. Denis Expedition · The Alarcón Expedition · The Chicken War

The Third Mission Wave   31
    Reoccupation by Aguayo · Canary Islanders · Pedro de Rivera · The Indian Dilemma

The Fourth Mission Wave   36
    The Establishment of Nuevo Santander · The Western Missions Renewed Activity on the Coast · The Transfer of Louisiana and the Shift in Spanish Policy

3/ Spain's Last Years   45

Reorganization   45
    East Texas · The *Provincias Internas* · The New Indian Policy

Spanish Colonial Life   50
    The Missions · The Presidios · The Settlements · The Cattle Industry Texas in 1800

Alarums and Excursions in the Wings   58
    Spain's New Neighbor · The Independence Movement in Mexico Filibusters and Patriots · The Adams-Onís Treaty

The Beginnings of Anglo-American
Settlement   68
      Miller County   ·   Moses Austin

4/ The Mexican Years   73

The First Colony   73
      Stephen F. Austin   ·   The Mexican
      Revolution   ·   The Old Three Hundred

Colonization under the Republic of Mexico   80
      The Legal Structure   ·   The Empresario
      Contracts   ·   The Fredonian
      Rebellion   ·   Colonial Life

The Change in Mexican Policy   87
      Terán's Recommendations   ·   Political
      Upheaval in Mexico   ·   The Law of
      April 6, 1830   ·   The Later Colonies

Political Chaos and Confusion   92
      Anahuac and Velasco   ·   The Removal
      of Mexican Garrisons   ·   The Convention
      of 1832   ·   The Convention of 1833

5/ The Texas Revolution   97

The Outbreak of Resistance   97
      The Downfall of Federalism
      Resistance in Texas

The Federalist Rebellion against Tyranny   105
      The Organization of Provisional
      Government   ·   The Siege of Béxar
      Confusion in Texas   ·   The Fall of the
      Alamo

The War for Independence   112
      The Convention of 1836   ·   The Loss of

South Texas · The Campaign and
Battle of San Jacinto

A Brief Analysis of Causes of the
Revolution   118

6/ The Republic of Texas   123

The Establishment of Government   123
Problems of the Ad Interim Government
The Election of 1836 · The Question
of Recognition · Stability · Later
Political Events

Domestic Affairs   133
Problems of National Defense ·
Financial Affairs · The Establishment
of Colonies · Indian Affairs · Other
Domestic Programs

Foreign Relations   146
Texas in the Family of Nations
Mexican Relations · Annexation

7/ Statehood, 1846–1860   156

Early Years   156
The Mexican War · The Boundary
Controversy · The Compromise of
1850 · The Settlement of the Texas
Debt · Political Developments

The Frontier   165
Exploration · The Indian Problem
Expansion of the Frontier

The People of Texas   172
The Population · Social and Cultural
Aspects

The Economy   178
Transportation · The Basic Economy
Slavery and the Plantation System

8 / Secession and Civil War   186

Secession   186
    The Constitutional Issue · Secession Sentiment in Texas Politics · The Mounting Tempo of Secessionism
The Secession Convention

Military Affairs   195
    Early Offensives · The Defense of the Coast · Texans at the Other Fronts

Domestic Affairs   202
    State Politics · The Military Board and the Effort to Finance the War
Union Sentiment in Texas · Domestic Hardships

9 / Reconstruction and Reaction   212

Reconstruction   212
    Analysis · Presidential Reconstruction
Congressional Reconstruction · Radical Rule

Reaction   223
    The Election of Coke · Coke and the New Constitution · The Status of the Negro

Lawlessness   230
    The Aftermath of War · Feudin' and Fightin' · The Texas Rangers

10 / The Frontier   240

Indian Wars and Buffalo Hunters   240
    The War Years · The Postwar Decade
The Buffalo Hunters

The Rise of the Cattle Industry   249
        The Antecedents of the Boom   ·   The Era of the Great Trail Drives   ·   The Spread of the Cattle Kingdom

Frontier Settlement   257
        The Advance of the Frontier   ·   Frontier Conflicts   ·   The Closed Range

11/ Recovery and Reform   267

Economic Developments   267
        Introduction   ·   Railroad Construction Industrial Developments   ·   Farming

Recovery and Protest   275
        The Politics of Recovery   ·   The Voices of Protest

The Politics of Reform   282
        The Beginnings of Reform   ·   "Hogg and Commission"   ·   The End of the Century

Social Developments   290
        Demographic Changes   ·   Educational Developments   ·   Cultural Developments   ·   The Texas Statehouse

12/ Progressivism and the New Freedom   297

Progressivism in Texas   297
        Campaigns and Candidates Progressive Measures   ·   Jim Ferguson

World War I and the Twenties   307
        Watching and Waiting on the Border Texas in the War   ·   Postwar Developments

Social and Economic Changes   317
    The Oil Industry · Educational Advances · Women, Prohibition, and the New Freedom · The New Ku Klux Klan in Texas

13/ *Depression and War*   328

The Depression Strikes   328
    The Politics of Prosperity · The Crash of 1929 · The East Texas Oil Boom

The Roosevelt Years   337
    The Deepening Depression · State Politics · World War II

The Changing Scene   347
    Population Growth · The Texas Mexicans · Industrial Growth

14/ *Flamboyant Texas*   356

Political Affairs   356
    A Period of Controversy · The Political Career of Allan Shivers · Legislation and Scandal

Recent Skirmishes on the Political Fronts   367
    State Politics and More Scandal · Political Battles, 1958–1962 · A Texan Becomes President

Social and Economic Developments   376
    Civil Rights in Texas · Texas Today · The Wheeler-Dealers

A Selective Bibliography of Texas History   387

Index   447

Maps

Physiography of Texas	front endpaper
Early Spanish Exploration	10
The Missionary Era	22
Spain's Last Years	46
Principal Towns in Colonial Texas about 1835	74
The Texas Revolution	98
The Republic of Texas	124
Statehood: The Frontier Forts	158
Civil War in Texas	188
The Proposed State of West Texas	214
The Frontier	242
Railroad Construction in Texas	268
Major Oil Fields to 1940	298
Distribution of Foreign-Born Population in 1940	330
Urban Texas	358
Counties of Texas	back endpaper

1

The Beginning

The Land and the People

Geological Development In the geologic age identified as the Pennsylvanian, some two hundred fifty million years ago, the Llanorian Mountains snaked across Texas in a giant crescent from the Big Bend through the sites of the present cities of San Antonio, Austin, and Dallas. To the northwest of this large range lay a wide and shallow sea that covered most of the area of modern West Texas. There, teeming marine life, of a form long since extinct, multiplied, died, and sank to the floor of the sea to form the gigantic oil reserves discovered in the twentieth century. To the southeast of the Llanorian Mountains a land mass extended far into today's Gulf of Mexico. Primeval reptiles, amphibians, and giant insects, in scores of now vanished species, mindlessly crawled and fought in swamps and forests made weird by rank and fantastic growths of vegetation which have also ceased to exist.

Time passed. Sea and land changed places. Through the aeons the continental shelf sank slowly, the waters of the Permian Sea drained off

The Beginning / 2

into the ocean, and the mountains eroded and covered the dry seabed with the sediment of the Permian Age. Finally the mountains themselves, mere roots and nubs of former grandeur, were covered by later alluvial deposits. This was one hundred million years ago, in the Cretaceous Age, and Texas was but a ball-shaped peninsula of the mainland, with its center near present San Angelo, surrounded by shallow seas. Vegetation had evolved to species of a modern appearance, but for animals it was the time of the dinosaurs. Most of those monsters were vegetarian, ponderously tramping through oozing marshes in incessant forage to fill their gargantuan bellies. Some animals were killers and flesh eaters. Some flew and preyed on insects. Most were reptilian, but in this land of horrors a few small mammals struggled for survival. Fossil remains of this world and a few rock-hardened tracks of the great dinosaurs have been found in various places in Central Texas, in what were once swampy morasses and shallow gulfs and bays.

Time passed. The waters of the shallow seas that had surrounded Texas in the Cretaceous Age receded. A low plain extended across all of West Texas, and where the Llanorian Mountains once stood a coastline formed, almost along the same crescent, holding back the ocean waters which had washed over the sinking land. Reptilian life waned, dinosaurs disappeared, true birds began to soar through the air, and early forms of modern mammalian life scampered over the vast grassy prairies and lurked in the shadows of the aboriginal forests—tiny monkeys, camels no larger than jack rabbits, the three-toed eohippus, forerunner in other parts of the world of the modern horse, and similar little beasts.

Time passed. Earth convulsed and shuddered in a global era of mountain building. In Asia the Himalayas thrust upward; in Europe, the Alps; in South America, the Andes; and in western North America, the great Rocky Mountain chain was extruded to incredible heights of two to three miles above the plains. All of Texas rose slightly, and the water of the Gulf backed off to the southeast, where after several advances and retreats it settled at about the present coastline.

Rains and winds began anew the inevitable erosion of the mountains, and new rivers cascading off the steep slopes of the Rockies carried debris toward the Gulf. As these raging torrents hit the flat lands and decelerated, they dropped the sediment from the mountains and began to create a giant plain, sloping southeast to the receding Gulf. In the aeons that followed, a high, featureless plain was deposited across West Texas—and then itself was tormented by eroding rains and winds into a phantasmagoria of canyons, cliffs, rugged hills, and flat-topped "outliers." In the present Panhandle and South Plains the rainfall was insufficient to wash away the grass covering and the plain remains intact.

Thus was the basic topography of modern Texas formed during the last fifty million years, and thus did the three major geographic provinces of North America—the western mountains, the central prairies and plains, and the eastern woodlands—find a rendezvous between the Sabine and the Rio Grande. Anyone who would understand Texas and its history must become familiar with this widely varying topography.

Topography The mountains, southern extensions of the Rockies, rise in a half-dozen small chains in the region known as the Trans-Pecos, between the Pecos River and the great bend of the Rio Grande. There, near the New Mexico boundary, stand Guadalupe Peak, 8,751 feet above sea level, and the photogenic El Capitan, the highest elevations in the state. North and east of the Pecos, the Great Plains province of North America rolls down across the central portion of Texas to the Rio Grande. One part of this province is the High Plains, the remnant of the early debris plain, which covers the Panhandle and South Plains. The jagged edge of the plains, called the Caprock, looms two to three hundred feet above the eroded country to the east. Here is another major subdivision of the Great Plains province in Texas, for convenience known as the North Central Plains. South of this region and east of the Trans-Pecos, stretch the rolling, semiarid grasslands of the Edwards Plateau. The eastern edges of these two regions follow approximately the Balcones Escarpment, a zone of geologic faulting that curves from Del Rio northward across the state, roughly coincident with the great crescent of the lost Llanorian Mountains. The southern portion of this vague demarcation is the lovely hill country of South Central Texas. The northern portion, where the Balcones fault zone is almost entirely subsurface, is a fertile belt of blackland prairie. And along this broad sweep from Del Rio to the Red River, the semiarid lands of Central Texas merge with the undulating meadows of the Coastal Plains, which on the southeast flatten toward the Gulf and on the northeast become low hills heavily forested with a variety of timber, mostly yellow pine, in all respects no different from the woodlands of the southern United States.

Because the entire surface of the state tilts slightly to the east and south, the major drainage systems spill from West Texas to the Gulf. The Rio Grande, annually freshened by melting snows from the mountains of Colorado and New Mexico, flows restlessly along the boundary between Texas and Mexico, curving back almost 180 degrees in the Trans-Pecos region east of El Paso to form the Big Bend. Also snow-born in New Mexico, the Pecos River dives southeast to disembogue into the Rio Grande a few miles above present Del Rio. The Nueces River flows east from springs in the hills along the Balcones Escarpment into the Gulf at

Corpus Christi. The San Antonio and Guadalupe rivers, north of the Nueces, run similarly from the hill country to the Gulf. The upper tributaries of the turbid Colorado, the next major river emptying into the Gulf, head far to the west. These are the Llano, the San Saba, and the Concho rivers of the Edwards Plateau and the upper Colorado proper, which carries some of the runoff from occasional rains on the South Plains. The once-frequent floods of the Colorado are checked today by a series of dams, and the resulting man-made lakes in the hills west of Austin have become vacation spots.

To the north of the Colorado the twisted tributaries of the Brazos River drain most of the South Plains, cutting deep canyons into the Caprock and winding through the North Central Plains to converge in the river the Spaniards called Los Brazos de Dios, The Arms of God, which flows into the Gulf near Freeport just south of Galveston Bay. Northeast is the Trinity River, whose three major forks come together near modern Dallas before running into Galveston Bay. East of the Trinity River, the piney woods are drained by myriad streams that ultimately form the Neches River or run into the Sabine River, both of which conjoin in Sabine Lake near the coast. Last of the major rivers, the Red runs like the Colorado and the Brazos off the High Plains, forming the northern boundary of Central Texas, and debouches into the Mississippi in Louisiana.

These drainage systems, however, do not impose as significant a natural influence on the state as rainfall. Precipitation varies from a dankly humid annual average of fifty-five inches in East Texas to a witheringly arid seven to ten inches in the Trans-Pecos. Although the rivers traverse the state roughly from west to east, the lines of constant rainfall run roughly north and south, creating a loose homogeneity of flora and fauna in broad north-south belts. Texans themselves tend to divide their land into East Texas and West Texas along an axis defined only by point of view. It is mythically a division between the humid and the arid, between molly cottontails and jack rabbits, between stately oaks and stunted shinnery, between lush meadows and sparse, short grass, between snap-brimmed fedoras and high-crowned Stetsons.

Early Man The same loose division into East and West characterized the cultural emergence of early man in Texas. Through thousands of years and countless generations an agricultural society developed in the east, while in the west nomadic hunters wandered the western prairies and plains. But because of numerous exceptions archeologists prefer a time and cultural-level subdivision for early man. The earliest,

5 / *The Land and the People*

the Paleo-American Stage, began with man's first appearance and ended about 4000 B.C., a period of very primitive, stone-age hunters. The next, the Archaic Stage, includes approximately the years 4000 B.C. to A.D. 1000. After this comes the Neo-American Stage, from A.D. 1000 to 1600, followed by the Historic Stage, A.D. 1600 to the present. The dates at which a particular cultural group emerged from one stage to another varied in different localities and with different peoples.

The earliest human remains found in Texas were the partially fossilized bones of a woman located in a sandhill near Midland. Dubbed Midland Minnie, she has, like a proper female, refused to reveal her true age. By such techniques as radiocarbon dating, archeologists have estimated the remains at 10,000 B.C. Abilene Man, the next oldest human skeleton, found near Abilene, has been dated at about 5000 B.C.

The absence of human remains between these dates and in the millennia after Abilene Man does not indicate that early man existed in Texas only sporadically or for short periods. It merely means that early man sites are rare. In fact, many archeologists postulate a migration of peoples from Asia as long as forty thousand years ago. It may be presumed that there was continuity of human life in Texas from about 10,000 B.C. to the present. Bits and scraps of other evidence, such as man-made flint points embedded in the bones of prehistoric bison and other extinct Pleistocene mammals, have been gleaned in various places in West Texas, especially the South Plains. The most important of these sites are a gravel pit near Plainview and the Lubbock Lake Site, sources of a panorama of human culture across a wide geological spectrum. All over the surface of the South Plains, Clovis and Folsom arrow points (named for sites in New Mexico) have been discovered, indicating the presence of stone-age hunters for many thousands of years.

Just as the chronological skips in the evidence do not indicate a discontinuity of life, so the fact that these finds have all been in West Texas does not preclude the existence of man at a very early time in East Texas. It simply indicates that the semiarid environment has preserved the remains better than the humid eastern regions. Certainly, as various groups of peoples emerged into the Archaic Stage, all of Texas was sparsely populated with aboriginal men.

This transition was marked by the development of better weapons and more efficient hunting practices, as well as the beginnings of crude agriculture in some areas. Several discrete cultural groups of the Archaic Stage have been identified in the area of the Falcon Reservoir and the Rio Grande, around Aransas Bay, on the Edwards Plateau, and in the Trans-Pecos. This last, the Hueco Phase, is the best known, the people being commonly called the Big Bend Cave Dwellers and the Big Bend

Basket Makers in the later part of the period. These people lived in caves on sides of the mountains and hills, wove mats and baskets from the fibrous plants of the region, hunted with an *atl-atl* (a spear-throwing device), and sometimes practiced a primitive agriculture, growing squash and maize. That they held some kind of religious belief is indicated by burials in caves, rock cairns, and crevices in which weapons, ornaments, baskets of seed, and perhaps food, were placed with the body apparently for its use in life after death. Many of the bodies were buried in a flexed rather than a prone position.

Archaic Stage life was similar on the Edwards Plateau, but its chief archeological feature was the burnt rock midden: a campsite where countless fires charred and split the rocks stacked up around them and where piles of refuse accumulated such as flint chips, grinding implements, and bones split to permit voracious appetites to fare on the tasty marrow. Some of these sites cover several acres along streams and creeks, often to depths of four and five feet. In the Aransas area the middens are burnt shell rather than burnt rock, but reveal similar characteristics.

Much more evidence of life in the Neo-American Stage has been found in many parts of Texas. The transition is usually marked by extension of agriculture, manufacture of pottery, and improvement of tools and weapons. In the eastern woodlands, the Neo-American people (the Caddo and their predecessors) lived in villages, farmed a large variety of crops, domesticated animals, and tended a few orchards. In the western part of the state, where nature generally prohibited farming, the Neo-Americans improved their hunting skills, made pottery, and developed tribal organizations. In the Panhandle, along the Canadian River, there appeared the greatest enigma in Texas' prehistory: a highly advanced people commonly called the Canadian River Puebloans and identified by archeologists as the Antelope Creek Focus of the Neo-American Stage. These people seem to have migrated into the area about A.D. 1100 and to have left quite suddenly (over a period of very few years). Where they came from, why they left, and where they went cannot be determined, although current archeological opinion holds that their culture derived from that predominant on the upper Republican River in Nebraska. They were competent farmers, planting mostly maize and beans with a variety of other crops, and they built community apartment dwellings similar to the pueblos of New Mexico and Colorado. But their architecture and method of construction exhibited a characteristic unlike any ruins in North America. Instead of building walls in horizontal courses of rocks or sun-dried bricks stacked one atop another, they embedded flat stones vertically in the dirt some distance apart to form two parallel rows. Between these they heaped rubble and upended another line of stones just inside the first, then more dirt and rubble and a smaller pair of retaining walls, and then another, until a substantial enclosure was completed. The square and rectangular buildings were roofed by *vigas* (large timbers laid like rafters from the top of one wall to the top of another) crossed at right angles by smaller logs, then by twigs and sticks, and finally covered by sod blocks, mud, and dried grass.

Sometime about the year 1400 these people abandoned their communities and disappeared. Perhaps they were struck by disease and pestilence. Perhaps they migrated to avoid attacks of more hostile enemies. Or, more likely, perhaps they sustained two or three years of severe drought and were forced to move for subsistence. They not only were gone but had passed from the memories of other peoples in the region by the time the first Spaniards crossed the plains.

The Indians With the arrival of Europeans and their written records, the story of early man passes to the Historic Stage. Columbus and his crew, expecting to reach fabled Cathay in the East Indies in 1492, mistakenly called the New World inhabitants Indians, and the name persisted. The Texas Indians at the beginning of this Historic Stage were not unlike their immediate Neo-American ancestors. Across the plains and prairies of the western part of the state scores of separate bands roamed on a perennial hunt. They especially followed the enormous herds of buffalo. They moved on foot for horses were not native to North America. (The Plains Indians did not become mounted until a century or more after the arrival of the Spaniards with their strange and wonderful beasts.) These nomads eked out a precarious existence, feast or famine depending on the fortune of the hunt. They lived in skin tepees that could be folded and rolled for easy carrying—usually by the women. Likewise their ornaments, pottery, tools, and weapons had to be transportable, small, and few.

To the south, other bands, more primitive and less skilled than these hunters, roamed on both sides of the Rio Grande. Taken together, they are called Coahuiltecans. More rooters and diggers than hunters, they subsisted largely on cactus fruit, worms, bugs, nuts, and roots. On the coast lived even more primitive Indians, ancestors of the cannibalistic Karankawa, fishermen and beachcombers who scoured the shallow waters of the coast for all types of marine life and scavenged from the flotsam washed ashore by the Gulf. But to the north of these coastal savages flourished a branch of the great Caddoan Confederation.

Indians of the Caddoan linguistic family lived in East Texas, Louisiana, and Arkansas. Most of the Texas Caddoans belonged to a loose confederation of tribes called Hasinai. Their villages were scattered between

The Beginning / 8

the Neches and Sabine rivers, where their ancestors apparently had lived since the late Archaic Stage. Typical Neo-American farmers, they also hunted in the forests of their own region and from time to time sent parties west to hunt buffalo on the prairies and plains. They tanned skins, made tools, weapons, and pottery, and wove baskets and mats. Their houses were comfortable thatched dwellings, usually circular in shape, with conical roofs and colorful mat "rugs" over the dirt floors.

The various tribes of the confederation, such as the Anadarkos, Natchitoches, Nacogdoches, Adaes, Neches, and Nazoni, as well as several other Caddoan-speaking tribes that seem to have been independent, lived in village communities of eight to a dozen families. Each tribe, some comprising several villages, had its own political chief (*caddi*) and high priest (*chenesi*). The society was well organized, with great emphasis on oratory at tribal councils. Women enjoyed virtually equal status with men, not as in most primitive societies, and many of them rose to prominent positions. Religion seems to have been fairly complex, with a priest group and ceremonial holidays. The most important holiday was for the annual rekindling of a perpetual temple fire, in a New Year's Day recognition. Some of the Caddoans were mound builders at one stage or another, and atop these mounds some of them built their grass temples to house the religious fires.

Sporadic trade existed between these advanced Indians of East Texas and the wandering nomads of the plains. By the seventeenth century a West Texas tribe, the Jumanos, began to specialize in trade, and toward the end of that century Jumano Indians were trading regularly with other peoples, from the Caddoans in East Texas to the Puebloans in New Mexico. The Jumanos seem to have originated in the Trans-Pecos, where their villages and semipermanent camps have been found principally in the vicinity of present Presidio, but they also hunted regularly on the Edwards Plateau and camped with some permanency on the Pecos and Concho rivers.

Thus, at the beginning of the Historic Stage, Texas was sparsely occupied by Indians of cultural levels ranging from the settled farmers of East Texas to the primitive coastal and Coahuiltecan bands of South Texas. Most of the Indians throughout West and Central Texas were wandering hunters, many just developing into the Neo-American Stage. During the sixteenth century Spanish explorers began to make contact with these native groups, whose friendliness, acquiescence, or hostility influenced the later advance of the Spanish frontier.

Spanish Beginnings

Charting the Gulf Shores Spanish horizons in the New World widened rapidly after discovery by Columbus in 1492. Columbus himself in later voyages charted several Caribbean islands and portions of the coastline of Central and South America. His captains mapped the Yucatan peninsula, explored the lower coast of Mexico, and circumnavigated Cuba. The islands of Haiti, Jamaica, and Puerto Rico were taken, the natives killed or enslaved, and Spanish colonies established. Then Cuba was conquered. Cortéz and his avaricious band overran the Aztec empire on the mainland, occupied Montezuma's capital, and wrested an incredible treasure in gold and silver from these hapless natives. The conquerors looked north and south, and Pizarro stormed the Incan stronghold in Peru.

As the rewards to the north were less exciting, exploration and conquest were slower. In 1513 Ponce de León, searching for a fountain of youth of Indian legend, explored the coastline of the Florida peninsula, which he thought was an island. For several decades many Spaniards continued to believe that they had only found outlying islands of Cathay and were confident of finding a water route through the islands to the Asian mainland. The governor of Jamaica, in 1519, sent a navigator to the west coast of Florida to follow up Ponce de León's exploration and, by sailing westward, to chart the coast or islands there and report on a possible route westward. The navigator was Alonzo Álvarez de Piñeda, the first European to set foot on Texas soil.

Piñeda sailed up the west coast of Florida, discovered it was not an island, and turned to tack his way west, preparing as he went a sketchy map of the coastline, bays, and rivers. He charted, somewhat inaccurately, the shore of the Gulf of Mexico all the way to Tampico. On his return he landed at the mouth of a river generally believed to be the Rio Grande, which he called Rio de las Palmas and on which he camped for six weeks to take on supplies and fresh water. He found the land delightful and recommended the establishment of a permanent colony there. Like other Spaniards of his time who had seen strange sights and incredible wealth in the New World, his credulity was not strained by anything the Indians told him, and, also like his followers, he may have embroidered his report from his imagination. He said that the region, which he called Amichel, was occupied by a race of pygmies and a race of giants.

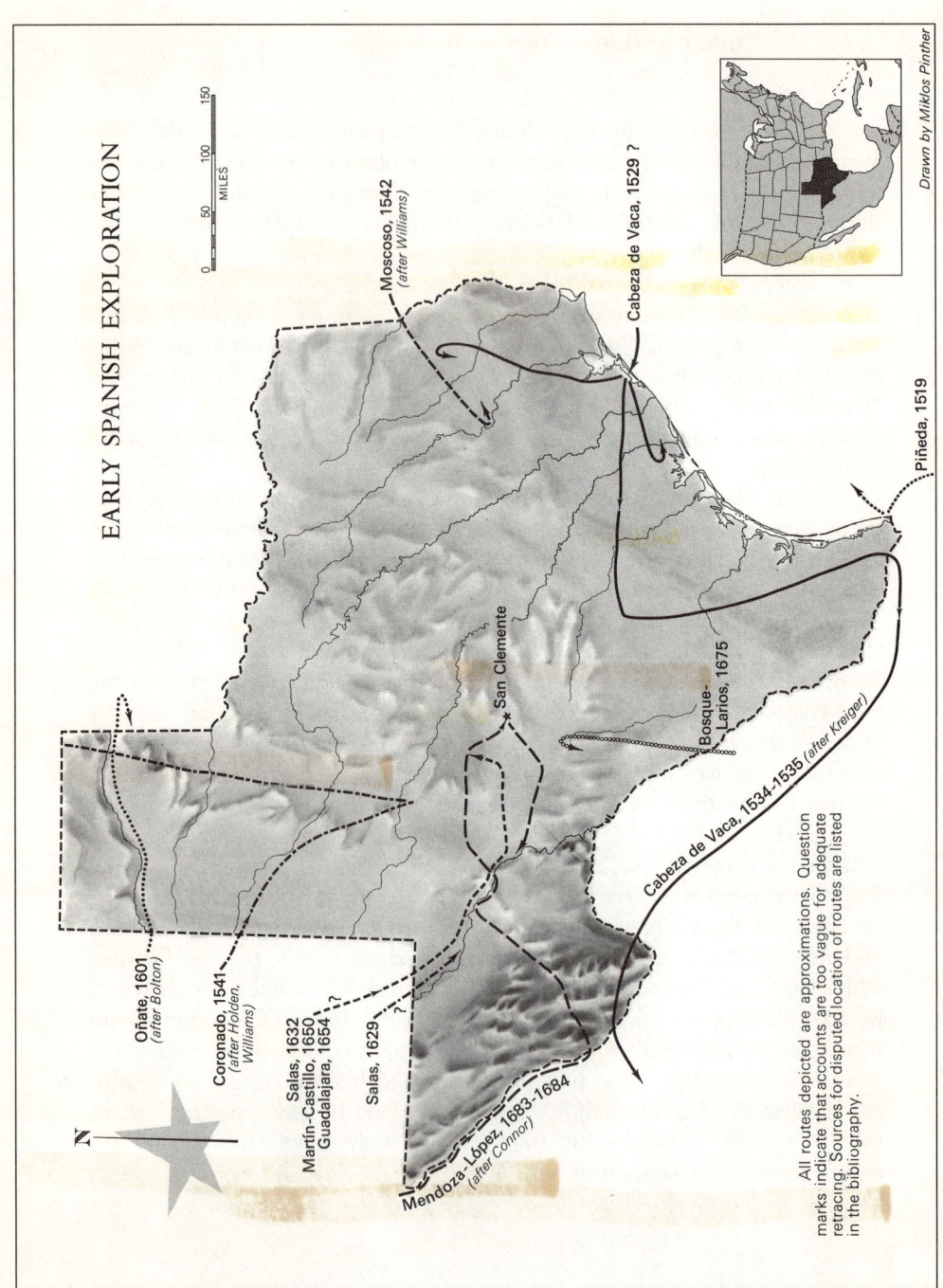

Cabeza de Vaca   No action was taken on Piñeda's recommendation for a colony, and the next Spaniard to come to Texas did so entirely by unhappy accident, a survivor of the storm-tossed Narváez expedition. In 1528 Pánfilo de Narváez was commissioned to conquer Florida. He took a large expedition, landed on the northwest coast, sent his ships to a rendezvous point up the coast where he intended to lead the overland force. Plagued by mosquitoes, hostile Indians, swamps, rain, and heat, the land party worked their tortuous way northward to the meeting point. When they arrived, the ships were nowhere to be seen. The captain in charge, after waiting twice the prescribed time, had sailed back down the coast looking for the overland force and, failing to find it, had headed back to Cuba.

In desperation, Narváez and his men built jury-rigged rafts and boats from logged trees and launched themselves bravely toward Mexico. A hurricane blew across the Gulf, swamping most of the craft. Two boats with about eighty dying men were washed ashore days later on a sandy, low-lying island hundreds of miles to the west. The Spaniards called it Malhado; it was present Galveston Island on the Texas coast. A band of Indians first succored and then enslaved them. By the spring of 1529 there were only fifteen survivors, among whom were a Negro named Estevanico and a nobleman named Álvar Núñez Cabeza de Vaca. De Vaca, treasurer and second in command of the Narváez expedition, was one of the hardiest and most resourceful adventurers in New World history.

Breaking away from one tribe, he was captured by another. For several years he enjoyed increasing status as a medicine man and then as a trader. His freedom less restricted, he moved about the coastal and East Texas areas until 1535, when he began, in the company of Estevanico and two other Spaniards, the escape to Mexico that he had long been planning. He knew only that Spanish colonies lay somewhere to the southwest, and in this direction he set off. The route of his incredible journey across nearly half a continent is not known with certainty. Many historians have tried to establish it by an account De Vaca wrote after his return to Mexico, but there is little consensus among these authorities. It is not improbable that from the vicinity of present San Antonio, De Vaca went south across the Rio Grande, whose course he paralleled in northern Mexico to cross back into present Texas in the Big Bend, then turned southwest following the Concho River of Mexico to its source, and struck across the mountains to the Pacific coast of Mexico.

There he encountered a detachment of Spanish troops on a slaving expedition who could hardly believe that the emaciated, half-naked men who ran up, shouting and sobbing, were truly Spaniards. Only their beards saved them from being shot as demented Indians, and eventually De Vaca was able to convince the soldiers of his identity. He and his companions were then escorted back to the viceregal court at Mexico City with the curious awe that might be given those welcomed back from the dead.

What tales they had to tell! Among other yarns, De Vaca related an Indian legend of a golden city somewhere to the northwest of his travels that was richer in treasure than Mexico City itself. Immediately, every able-bodied Spaniard in Mexico clamored to be off for the conquest. Had not fantastic fortunes been acquired by the men with Cortéz and Pizarro? Who knew what wealth might lie in the legendary city in the north, ripe for looting and plundering?

The Coronado Entrada The viceroy prudently decided to send a reconnaissance party to determine the strength and exact location of the city of gold before he ordered out an eager expedition of conquest. De Vaca, the logical man to lead the reconnaissance, understandably refused to return, but in 1539 the Negro, Estevanico, was sent in the company of a Franciscan monk, Father Marcos de Niza, and several friendly Indians. Father Marcos's party did not reach Texas but instead crossed into the present United States somewhere in eastern Arizona. Estevanico was murdered by Indians, and the padre scampered back to the safety of Mexico. A man of more imagination than De Vaca, Father Marcos reported that he had seen the fabled city from a distant hill, that it had walls of gold blocks, gates studded with precious jewels, streets paved with silver—wealth beyond any man's dreams.

Nothing could hold back the tide of conquest. Hundreds of Spain's finest young men vied for places on the expedition to be commanded by Francisco Vásquez de Coronado. It was to be Spain's grandest entrada in the New World. Over a thousand men, fifteen hundred horses and mules, herds of cattle and sheep, several priests, and scores of (inevitable) laundresses and cooks passed in review before the viceroy at Compostela and set off for the land of Quivera, as it later came to be known.

After weeks of slow progress northward, Coronado impatiently plunged ahead with a hundred horsemen. He too crossed into the present United States in Arizona and in 1540 encountered the city the friar may have seen: a Zuñi pueblo called Hawikuh near the present border of Arizona and New Mexico. After a hard fight, the Spaniards overcame the Indians and entered the village, greatly disgusted at finding only sun-dried brick, sand, and crude pottery. Not yet disillusioned, Coronado split his force when the main body arrived, sending two groups west, which discovered the Grand Canyon and the head of the Gulf of California, and one group east, which located the pueblo villages on the Rio Grande in New Mexico.

Winter headquarters were established at the pueblo of Tiguex on the Rio Grande. In the spring, following an Indian "who looked like a Turk" and who promised to guide them to the city of gold, the Spaniards searched eastward into Texas. Coronado's route is no better known than De Vaca's. The most recent study suggests that Coronado proceeded to the Pecos Pueblo, crossed the New Mexico desert, and entered the Texas Panhandle west of present Lubbock. He may have passed near Lubbock as he crossed the High Plains that the Spaniards named the Llano Estacado. He probably went southeast to a canyon north of present Sterling City, but the reported canyon may have been, as many historians think, the Palo Duro Canyon near Amarillo. From the canyon, with a small detachment of mounted men, Coronado traveled "north by the needle" to the land of Quivera, somewhere on the Canadian River in present Oklahoma or farther north on the Arkansas River in present Kansas. They found nothing but prairies, herds of buffalo, and primitive Indian encampments.

Disappointed and utterly disillusioned, the Spaniards returned to New Mexico, wintering again at Tiguex on the Rio Grande. The expedition returned to Mexico in the spring of 1542. Its chief significance, beyond the marvelous breadth of its explorations in the American Southwest, was its negative report. There was nothing in these lands to the north to interest the gold-seeking Spaniards. Yet the legend of the golden city persisted and merged with an earlier myth as the Seven Cities of Cíbolo.

De Soto and Moscoso Even while Coronado rode across the grassy plains of Texas and into the land of Quivera in the summer of 1541, another party of Spaniards was trudging westward, weariness increasing at every step, through present Oklahoma. The two expeditions, unknown to each other, may at one time have been not more than a few hundred miles apart. According to legend, an Indian woman carried into Quivera by Coronado's men fled east from one group of Spaniards only to fall into the clutches of the other.

The second group of Spaniards was the expedition led by the indefatigable Hernando de Soto, which had landed in Florida in 1539 and had been wandering across the southeastern part of the continent for over two years. After penetrating a short distance into present Oklahoma, the expedition returned to the Mississippi River, where De Soto died and command devolved upon Luis de Moscoso. The men pleaded to return to Mexico instead of continuing the futile search for wealth, a program heartily endorsed by the new leader. Off to the south they marched, entering Texas in the vicinity of present Texarkana.

During the summer of 1542 this pitiful remnant of De Soto's original six hundred struggled across East Texas to a broad river where, discouraged, they turned back to the Mississippi, built crude ships, and with more luck than Narváez and his men rowed, sailed, and drifted down the coast to a Spanish settlement at the mouth of the Panuco River in Mexico. Their route through East Texas and the site of their later two-week stay at some inlet on the Texas coast is debated by historians as inconclusively as the routes of De Vaca and Coronado. After crossing the Sabine and the upper reaches of the Angelina and the Neches rivers, they probably reached the Brazos River, possibly no further than the Trinity, before turning back.

Moscoso and his men rendered a report on Texas little more favorable than Coronado's. Moscoso had visited some of the Caddoan villages but had found no riches there. He had seen oil seeps in East Texas, the crude petroleum used for medicinal purposes by the Indians, but Moscoso could not possibly have envisioned the enormous wealth it was to bring later. His account, rather than awakening Spanish interest in Texas, delayed it.

The Establishment of New Mexico As the years passed and men of another generation matured hoping to emulate the conquests of their fathers and grandfathers, the Spanish frontier was pushed northward in Mexico. Silver mines were opened in Durango; missions were built in Chihuahua, Coahuila, and Nuevo León; large estates, *encomiendas*, were established in the central valley of Mexico; and slaving parties carried bewildered Indians into peonage in the mines and on the ranches. By the close of the century the tentacles of empire had reached New Mexico.

Several previous expeditions of priests and soldiers, interested in the salvation of the souls of the Puebloan Indians as well as in the legend of the Seven Cities, had penetrated the upper Rio Grande before the viceroy commissioned Juan de Oñate in 1598 to establish a permanent settlement there. Oñate crossed into the United States at El Paso del Norte, passing through present El Paso, and followed the Rio Grande to an Indian village a few miles north of present Santa Fe, where he established his headquarters. More eager to seek gold than to colonize, Oñate led several expeditions into the unknown regions. On one of these, in 1601, he crossed the present Texas Panhandle, continued parallel to the course of the Canadian River, and reached the land of Quivera. Like Coronado before him, he found nothing of value.

Oñate was soon replaced as governor of New Mexico, and the capital was shifted south in 1609 when Santa Fe was established. Priests, supported by troops, flooded into the pueblo villages along the upper Rio Grande to bring salvation to the heathens, who a few years earlier the Pope had declared to be possessed of souls. The establishment of the province of New Mexico and its occupation by Spaniards was to lead to further exploration of Texas and almost, but for a quirk of history, to establishment of a permanent settlement on the Edwards Plateau. This activity was chiefly caused by a band of importuning Jumano Indians.

The Lure of the Conchos

Father Salas and the Jumanos   In 1629 a party of Jumano Indians, painted and tattooed with jagged stripes across their bodies, pounded on the door of a little mission church near present Albuquerque, New Mexico. They had been directed to go there, the priest in charge later related, by a mysterious Lady in Blue, who had several times appeared suddenly in their village for short visits. She had told them the story of Christianity with such fervor that the whole tribe had become eager to embrace the new religion. But since she was not ordained, she had sent them to the nearest priest for baptism. Moved by this remarkable report, Father Juan de Salas sent a messenger to the father-superior in Santa Fe to beg for permission to return with the Jumanos to their village many miles to the southeast in order to bring salvation to those eagerly receptive savages. Usually the missionary fathers encountered in the Indians a varying degree of resistance to the Spanish-Christian path.

While Father Salas awaited this permission, the Jumanos fell into a profitable trade in pueblo pots and Spanish metal tools. In the summer of 1629 the small party of native Texas entrepreneurs returned home, accompanied by Father Salas and Father Diego León, both Franciscan missionaries. Salas reported that they traveled one hundred leagues (about three hundred miles) southeast. The padres remained several months at their ranchería, or village, distributing gifts and baptizing the natives. Although they did not see the Lady in Blue themselves, they became convinced of her existence because of the Indians' frequent stories of her visits. The precise location of this initial missionary activity in Texas cannot be determined. The reported distance would place it somewhere in the Trans-Pecos, possibly on the Pecos River.

The following year, after the priests had returned to New Mexico, their father-superior, Alonso de Benavides, visited Spain, where he heard of a pious young nun who was experiencing the miracle of transportation. From time to time she would slip into a catatonic trance from which she would return to consciousness with marvelous stories of a strange land peopled with savages whom she had instructed in the fundamentals of Christianity. Father Benavides went to interview the nun, Sister María Jesús de Agreda. Under his skillful interrogation she revealed that the dusky, red-skinned peoples she visited painted themselves with striped patterns and lived in a semiarid region of rocky mountains and plateaus. Furthermore, she frequently wore a blue cloak over her habit. There was no question in Father Benavides' mind about the miracle. Sister Agreda had been transported to West Texas. He and a devout following claimed she should be canonized, but the church never officially recognized the miracle.

Word of this soon reached Benavides' successor in the New Mexico missions. In 1632 Father Salas, with Father Juan de Ortega and a few soldiers was sent back to the Jumano country. This time the Spaniards traveled two hundred leagues (about six hundred miles) southeast and may have penetrated the Edwards Plateau to the junction of the Concho Rivers at present San Angelo. There Salas left Ortega for six months to distribute presents and baptize the Indians.

The River of Nuts During the next two decades there was desultory trade between the Jumanos in Texas and the Spaniards in New Mexico. Parties of Jumanos frequently bartered buffalo hides for Spanish tools and weapons and traded these later to Indians to the east. Parties of Spaniards occasionally visited the Jumano country to hunt buffalo for themselves, but none of these excursions was an official entrada. In 1650, however, the governor of New Mexico ordered an expedition to the river known at this time as the Rio de los Nueces, or the River of Nuts.

This party, primarily for exploring rather than evangelizing, was commanded by Hernán Martín and Diego del Castillo. Although their exact route is not known, there is some evidence that they crossed from Santa Fe to the Pecos, then followed it downstream to the vicinity of present Iraan, where they turned east to the head of the South Concho River. A profusion of magnificent pecan trees (known to the Spaniards by the generic term *nueces*, their language having no word for pecan since it was indigenous to North America) grace the banks of all three branches of the Concho. In this lovely region, filled with game, berries, wild fruit, and nuts, the expedition remained for about six months. A reconnaissance party sent eastward rode about fifty leagues (about one hundred fifty miles) to what they reported was the border of the land of the Tejas Indians. Since this Caddoan-speaking tribe lived far away on the Neches River, it seems more likely that the Spaniards encountered a hunting party of Tejas or were informed by their Jumano guides that they were near the Tejas country. More important than this eastward reconnaissance was the discovery of pearls in the Concho River. The streams abounded in fish and mussels; many of the latter, cracked open by heat, exposed fresh water pearls, mostly of poor quality. It may be supposed that the expedition returned to Santa Fe with enough of these not only to show a small profit on the trip, but also to stimulate further exploration of the area.

On learning of the pearls, the viceroy of New Spain himself ordered a second expedition. Diego de Guadalajara left Santa Fe in 1654 in command of thirty soldiers and some two hundred friendly Indians. The Spaniards again harvested the mussel beds of the Concho and again attempted to reach the land of the Tejas. Some seventy-five leagues (a little over two hundred miles) east of the main encampment on the Concho, a reconnaissance party was attacked by a band of Indians they called Cuitaos. Defeating them, the Spaniards took about two hundred prisoners, but turned back without visiting the Tejas.

Again Spanish interest in Texas waned. In 1675 a missionary expedition commanded by Fernando del Bosque, accompanied by Father Juan Larios, briefly penetrated the Edwards Plateau to a river that Bosque called the Rio Nueces, but nothing of particular interest was found. Originating at Monclova, on the northern Spanish frontier in Mexico, the party crossed the Rio Grande somewhere between present Eagle Pass and Del Rio and may have reached either the upper Nueces River in Edwards County or, somewhat more likely on the basis of Bosque's journal, the North Llano River in Sutton County. The expedition returned to Mexico by a different route. Father Larios baptized several hundred Indians on the journey.

The Mendoza-López Expedition If the next expedition into West Texas, in 1683, had been successful, it would have significantly changed the course of Texas history. It was commanded by Juan Domínguez de Mendoza, who had been with the Guadalajara party of 1654 and who believed that Spain should establish a permanent mission settlement on the Edwards Plateau. With him was the aging Hernán Martín and no less a personage than the father-superior of the New Mexico missions, Father Nicolás López. The time seemed especially propitious for the establishment of a new mission, for the Spaniards had been driven out of New Mexico by the bloody Pueblo Revolt of 1680. But nearly two decades were to pass before they were able to return permanently.

A cluster of refugees fleeing from the vengeance of the aroused Puebloans had settled on the Rio Grande near present El Paso. Most of them chose to live on the south side of the river, but a few Franciscans and some loyal Indians established on the north bank a mission community called Corpus Christi de Isleta. Founded in 1681, Isleta is the oldest settlement in Texas, although it was not considered part of Texas until 1849.

It was to the relocated Spaniards in this area that a crafty Jumano chief named Juan Sabeata appealed in 1683, sparking the Mendoza-López expedition. Sabeata sought relief from the encroachment into his people's hunting grounds of a hostile and bellicose tribe called Apaches. A southern branch of the numerous Athapaskan linguistic family which stretched from Mexico to Alaska, the Apaches hunted throughout the Southwest in numerous tribes and bands. The most important of these were to become known as Chiracahua in Arizona, Mescalero in New Mexico and Texas, and Lipan in Texas. Apparently the Apaches invading Jumano country came from the north, possibly from a ranchería in southern Colorado that the Spaniards called Cuartelejo. The Apaches were among the first of the Plains Indians to mount Spanish horses, and it takes little imagination to share the thrill of these footsore wanderers who suddenly, on climbing aboard a Spanish pony, found themselves the equal of the buffalo, deer, and antelope, game that they had pursued on foot for untold generations. Not only did they become masters of the hunt, but they quickly developed into the fiercest of warriors and began raiding the less militant bands of hunters and the northern pueblos.

For several years these Apaches had been troubling the Jumanos and the associated bands of the Edwards Plateau and Pecos valley. Chief Sabeata believed that only the establishment of a Spanish settlement, with its guns and soldiers, would deter the aggressors. But he was not so naive as to think that the Spaniards would come to the Jumano defense without reason. Therefore, he tried the trick of asking for a mission and a padre. He told the Spaniards that his people had several times seen a cross in the sky over their camp, that many Jumanos were already Christians, and that the rest were anxious to be saved. He begged the officials to send priests and establish a church.

Sabeata's plea, combined with the temporary inactivity of the refugees on the Rio Grande and Mendoza's personal interest in the Concho country, resulted in the expedition of 1683–1684. Thirty or more soldiers and three priests traveled down the south side of the Rio Grande from the vicinity of present Juárez, Mexico, to the mouth of the Concho River of Chihuahua, a place called La Junta, where they crossed into Texas. Father López left one priest with the Jumano village there to build a chapel, and guided by Sabeata he proceeded with Mendoza across the Trans-Pecos, by way of present Fort Stockton, to the Pecos near present McCamey. There they fell in with another band of friendly Indians affiliated with Sabeata's tribe.

The expedition went eastward to the Middle Concho River and followed it to the juncture of the three Conchos at San Angelo. On the way they were joined by scores of Indians of a dozen different bands. Father López and the other priest were kept busy baptizing the heathens while Mendoza and his men killed thirty to fifty buffalo a day to feed the accumulating mob. From the junction of the Conchos, the entrada journeyed three days to a river Mendoza called San Clemente, where a mission was built. Mendoza described it in his journal as a "bastion" in which the lower room was used by the priests for services and the upper room by the soldiers for a guard post. This first Texas mission was probably on the San Saba River between present Menard and Ft. McKavett, although ambiguous evidence indicates that it may have been on the Colorado River just below the mouth of the main Concho River.

Some two or three thousand Indians gathered about the Mission San Clemente, and during the Spaniards' brief stay approximately ten thousand buffalo were slaughtered. After sustaining three attacks by the Apaches and dismissing Sabeata for his treachery, Mendoza decided to withdraw to Mexico for more support. Neither he nor Father López intended to abandon the endeavor. Returning by a slightly different route, both men importuned Spanish officials for authorization to take a stronger force back to San Clemente. Mendoza claimed that with only two hundred men he could conquer the entire region for the crown and that the province would be self-supporting because of the bountiful game, fish, and wild fruits. López maintained that the natives were eager for salvation, unlike the Puebloans at the time, and that they provided a more fertile evangelical field than Spain had yet seeded with the true faith.

But as promising as Mendoza and López made the region seem, officials refused to grant their requests. Another matter of greatest moment demanded immediate attention. All the resources of the northern frontier might be needed, for the French were rumored to have landed somewhere on the coast of Texas!

2

The Missionary Era

The First Mission Wave

Fort St. Louis   Somewhere on one of the countless bayous of the Mississippi delta at the great river's disemboguement into the Gulf of Mexico, a tiny party of Frenchmen beached a canoe one day in 1682. Their leader, a hard-countenanced man of nearly forty years, unfurled a banner on which were sewn three fleur-de-lis and planted its staff in the soggy ground. So doing, he claimed all of the lands drained by the Mississippi and its tributaries for his king, Louis XIV of France. Only one explorer had been more audacious: when Balboa crossed the isthmus of Panama in 1513, he claimed all lands touched by the Pacific Ocean for Spain!

These two, the mightiest nations of Europe, were engaged in a race for empire during the sixteenth and seventeenth centuries. Although the Pope had divided the unknown world between Spain and Portugal, France refused to be excluded and launched her own explorers and settlers into the New World. A French colony in present South Carolina had been crushed by starvation and another in Florida had been cruelly massacred by Spaniards before the French began to expand their claims to the St. Lawrence River far to the north. Quebec, Montreal, and then a score of trading posts in the Great Lakes area came into being. Two priests, following a portage from the Fox to the Wisconsin rivers, discovered the upper Mississippi. A young man named René Robert Cavelier established Fort Frontenac at Niagara and opened such a fur trade in the Great Lakes area that he was given the title Sieur de la Salle.

It was this same man, commonly called La Salle, who portaged from the Illinois River, floated down the Mississippi to its mouth in 1682, and claimed the heartland of North America for France. Returning to Canada and then across the Atlantic to the court of Louis XIV at Versailles, he received permission to colonize the mouth of the Mississippi. With four ships and over two hundred colonists, he left France in the summer of 1684. A series of misadventures plagued the expedition. One of the ships sank in a storm in the Gulf with many of the supplies, although most of the personnel were saved; La Salle became ill; he quarreled with his principal ship captain; the expedition missed the mouth of the Mississippi, landing instead in Matagorda Bay at the mouth of the Lavaca River in Texas; two other ships sank in Matagorda Bay; and finally, after the landing, the last ship and its crew deserted the colonists and sailed back to France, leaving them to the mercy of the wilderness.

La Salle, partially recovered, ordered the construction of a fort several miles inland, either on the Lavaca River itself or on Garcitas Creek, which drains into the Lavaca, and then set out ostensibly to locate the Mississippi River. Strangely, this man of the woods who had found his way across half of North America, headed *west* from his base, which he called Fort St. Louis. After several forays in this wrong direction in 1685 and 1686, during which time his followers became increasingly restive, La Salle decided to return to Canada for desperately needed supplies. Unerringly, he then led a small party northeast across Texas—in the right direction!

What could have been the reasons, first, for La Salle's failure to land at or near the mouth of the Mississippi and, second, for his westward reconnaissance? There is some evidence, not fully substantiated, that La Salle never intended to colonize the mouth of the Mississippi but rather planned to locate as near to the Spanish mines in northern Mexico as possible, either for trade or plunder or both. Such an hypothesis, at the least, explains the great explorer's otherwise erratic behavior.

Many of his men, resentful of his arbitrary leadership and alarmed at the rapid diminution of the scant store of supplies, turned from surly disobedience to outright mutiny. On La Salle's last trip from Fort St. Louis,

THE MISSIONARY ERA

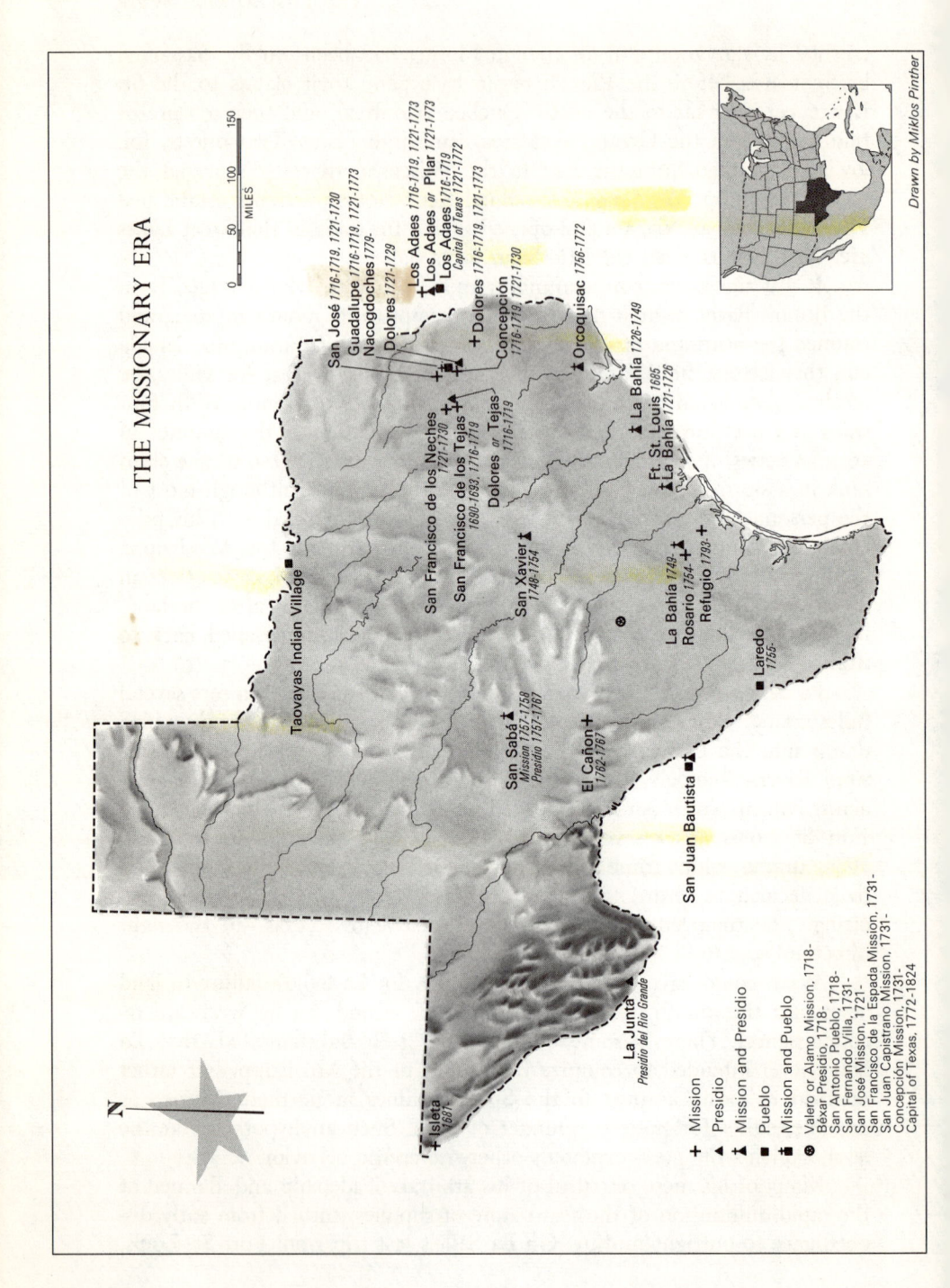

Drawn by Miklos Pinther

- **+** Mission
- **▲** Presidio
- **▲+** Mission and Presidio
- **■** Pueblo
- **■+** Mission and Pueblo
- **⊙** Valero or Alamo Mission, 1718-
  Béxar Presidio, 1718-
  San Antonio Pueblo, 1718-
  San Fernando Villa, 1731-
  San José Mission, 1721-
  San Francisco de la Espada Mission, 1731-
  San Juan Capistrano Mission, 1731-
  Concepción Mission, 1731-
  Capital of Texas, 1772-1824

Los Adaes 1716-1719, 1721-1773
Los Adaes or Pilar 1716-1719, 1721-1773
Los Adaes 1716-1719, 1721-1773 Capital of Texas 1721-1772
San José 1716-1719, 1721-1730
Guadalupe 1716-1719, 1721-1773
Nacogdoches 1779-
Dolores 1721-1729
Concepción 1716-1719, 1721-1730
Dolores 1716-1719, 1721-1730
Orcoquisac 1756-1772
San Francisco de los Neches 1721-1730
San Francisco de los Tejas 1690-1693, 1716-1719
Dolores or Tejas 1716-1719
St. Louis 1685
Ft. St. Louis
La Bahía 1726-1749
La Bahía 1721-1726
Taovayas Indian Village
San Xavier 1748-1754
La Bahía 1749-
Rosario 1754-
Refugio 1793-
Laredo 1755-
San Sabá
Mission 1757-1758
Presidio 1757-1767
El Cañon 1762-1767
San Juan Bautista
La Junta
Presidio del Rio Grande
Isleta 1681

22

in March 1687, headed for Canada and succor, a group of his own men waylaid and assassinated him at an overnight camp somewhere in East Texas, possibly in present Navasota County. After much discussion the murderers permitted Henri Joutel, with La Salle's brother, who was a priest, and several others who had had no part in the affair, to continue to Canada. Joutel wrote a fascinating narrative of the entire affair. The assassins scattered, some to live with the Indians or to die in the woods and one, Jean L'Archeveque, to make his way to a frontier Spanish outpost and finally to settle in Santa Fe.

Back at the unhappy little post on Matagorda Bay the remaining colonists grew desperate as they waited in vain for La Salle's return. When winter came, they were almost entirely without food, ammunition, and other essentials. Many succumbed to illness, starvation, and Indian attacks. A remnant fled to live with a friendly band of coastal Indians. The French colony thus ended in complete and dismal failure, but it had given France a vague, although later very important, claim to Texas.

De León's Expeditions Meantime, wandering Indians had carried the news of the French landing to the Spaniards, who had become suspicious of their presence by the capture of one of the French ships in the Gulf. If there was anything that could move the cumbersome machinery of Spanish bureaucracy faster than the discovery of gold, it was the alarm of foreign invasion. The French post must be destroyed! Immediately every effort was bent to locate it. Eleven different expeditions were sent, five by sea and six by land. Although at least one of the sea expeditions entered Matagorda Bay, they failed to spot the post, secluded a few miles inland. Four of the six overland expeditions were led by Alonso de León. On the last, in following one of the Frenchmen who had been captured a few months earlier, De León crossed the Rio Grande from his base at Saltillo, turned up the coast, and arrived at the ruins of Fort St. Louis on April 22, 1689.

A few more Frenchmen were found living among the Indians, but the threat of invasion was past, if it had ever existed at all. De León's expedition was a large one (some evidence indicates that he may have planned to colonize the area), and before returning to Mexico he led it northeast to at least the border of the Tejas Indian country. There the priest who accompanied him, Father Damian Massanet, was welcomed by emissaries of the tribe, but no attempt was made to establish a mission, and the Spaniards turned back to Mexico.

The following year, they returned to the land of the Tejas, this time intending to plant a permanent mission among the settled, agrarian Indians of East Texas. The search for Fort St. Louis and the decision to establish this mission diverted Spanish attention from the Edwards Plateau and the Concho country, which they were not to reenter for three-quarters of a century. Again Alonso de León was in command, and again he was accompanied by Father Massanet, who brought along several other Franciscans. The expedition left Mexico in the spring of 1690. The decaying ruins of Fort St. Louis were burned to the ground, in hopes of obliterating forever any trace of France in lands claimed by Spain. De León continued into East Texas to support Father Massanet's attempt to establish a mission for the Tejas Indians.

The decision to occupy East Texas was motivated by several reasons. First, of course, the alarm caused by the appearance of the French made Spanish officials anxious to establish a permanent claim to hold Texas against future intrusions of other European powers. Also, by this time the Tejas people had been recognized by the Spaniards as the most civilized and advanced Indians in the area; their farms and gardens would provide more support for enduring missionary effort than would the scant resources and ravenous appetites of the nomadic hunters in the west. And, furthermore, the Tejas' expressed desire to become Christians had aroused the zeal of the Franciscan fathers, ever anxious to expand the faith.

The First Missions   In May 1690, De León and Father Massanet selected a mission site on a small creek a few miles west of the Neches River in present Houston County. Tejas from the nearby village helped the Spaniards erect a roomy log building and a small chapel with a large cross near its entrance. The mission was named San Francisco de los Tejas. The friendliness of the Indians, their willingness to be baptized and to participate in services, and their ready assistance persuaded De León that the little outpost would be successful. He struck out for Mexico in July, leaving three soldiers and three priests behind. Father Massanet returned with him in order to make recommendations to the authorities for the expansion of the apostolic effort among these friendly and civilized Indians.

Acting on Massanet's suggestions, the government ordered the establishment of six additional missions. Gregorio de Salinas Varona was sent by sea in charge of about forty soldiers and a quantity of supplies to rendezvous at the site of Fort St. Louis with a larger overland party commanded by Domingo Terán de los Rios. Terán, a man of considerable experience, was named governor of this new province and was instructed to explore the country and to investigate rumors of other Frenchmen in the area. Father Massanet accompanied the Terán overland party on the journey to Texas, bringing nine additional Franciscans. The two parties missed contact at Matagorda Bay but were later reunited.

Governor Terán named the province Nuevo Reyno de la Montaña de Santander y Santillana, but this ponderous appellation was soon discarded in favor of Texas (pronounced *Tay-has* in Spanish as was *Tejas*). During the latter part of 1691 and for several months of the following year, Terán explored the regions of eastern Texas and western Louisiana, visiting a number of Caddoan villages. In April he embarked on the ships brought by Varona, intending to land at the mouth of the Mississippi, but bad weather caused him to sail on to Vera Cruz.

Meantime, Father Massanet was facing discouragement. During his absence one of the priests at the San Francisco mission had taken it upon himself to initiate the expansion program. In September 1690 he had established a second little mission a few miles away on the Neches River, calling it Santísimo Nombre de María. An unidentified epidemic struck a number of the Indians who had visited the new chapel, and the natives grew restive. Then in January 1692 María was washed away by a sudden flood.

At the San Francisco mission the Indians likewise became intractable and then openly hostile. They would neither assist in establishing more missions nor work at the one already built. They even refused to help clear fields and plant crops. Consequently provisions grew short, and six of the priests were sent back with Governor Terán. When Terán arrived in Mexico in the summer of 1693, he sent Captain Varona to East Texas with supplies. On his return Varona's report was so unfavorable that the government decided to abandon the missionary field.

But before the order to do so reached Massanet, the priest came to the same conclusion himself. In the face of increasing antagonism from the once-friendly Tejas, there was little else the Spaniard could do but leave. On October 25, 1693, the three remaining priests, aided by the nine remaining soldiers, packed as many religious articles as they could carry, set fire to the building, and left for Mexico.

The first effort at the mission settlement of Texas had failed. It would be a quarter of a century before Spain tried again.

There were several reasons for the abandonment of East Texas. First, no Frenchmen were found in the area, so the motive for the earlier activity dissipated. Second, because of the length of the supply line from the nearest post in northern Mexico, support of the missions was almost prohibitively expensive. And, finally, the hostility of the Indians made the position altogether untenable without the support of troops. Massanet himself had noted this in his last letter from Texas. But the cost of maintaining a garrison, called a presidio, would have been even more burdensome.

Only one of the traditional three arms of Spanish colonization had been extended into Texas, and permanent settlement required the other two. These three symbiotic Spanish frontier institutions were the mission, the presidio, and the civil settlement. The soldiers of the presidio subdued the Indians and protected the mission while the padres taught the natives Christianity and the arts of civilization. Near the presidios families of the soldiers and other settlers congregated in villages, planted crops, and raised livestock. The Indians then worked in the mission fields to help these civil settlers make the community virtually self-sustaining.

The Second Mission Wave

French Intrusion It took a second intrusion by the French to provoke the Spanish empire into investing in a full-fledged effort at settlement. In 1698 the Le Moyne brothers, natives of the French province of Quebec, received a patent from the crown for the settlement of Louisiana. The Le Moyne family were prominent fur trappers and traders, and both of the brothers had titles in France's New World nobility: the Sieur d'Iberville and the Sieur d'Bienville. During the summer of the following year, the brothers established a post at Biloxi and in 1702 another on Mobile Bay. The French *couriers d'bois* (woodsmen) spread rapidly through the watercourses of the Mississippi, founding during the next decade a number of trading posts and building a friendly rapport with most of the Indian tribes.

In 1712 a commercial enterprise headed by Antoine Crozat, a Parisian merchant, received a fifteen-year trading monopoly and other rights in Louisiana. Crozat was confident that fantastic treasures of gold and silver would be found in Louisiana, equal to those discovered by Spain in Mexico and South America, but this was a vain illusion, as the only metal located was lead in the southeastern part of present Missouri. Although he believed his principal profits would come from mining, Crozat did not overlook the commercial potential. This meant trade with the Indians, of course, because no matter how longingly the French eyed the northern Spanish colonies, Spain's empire was closed to foreign commerce.

All trade and communication in Spain's far-flung northern provinces had to flow through channels to Vera Cruz. The cost of transportation and various taxes made manufactured goods enormously expensive in such distant outposts as Santa Fe, El Paso, and San Juan Bautista, the recently established outpost on the Rio Grande. Had it not been for the rigid imperial restriction against foreigners, French traders could have undersold the competition with a very handsome profit. Frenchmen hoped for an opportunity for illicit trade to present itself, and it soon did.

One of the priests who had been at the San Francisco mission, Father Francisco Hidalgo, was apprehensive about the spiritual lives of the baptized Tejas Indians. Their souls would be lost without a priest to administer the other sacraments. Father Hidalgo begged his superiors to reopen the mission or even to authorize him to return alone, but to no avail. Finally, in 1713 he wrote a letter to Governor Lamothe Cadillac in Louisiana. Since the French were Catholic, would they please send a priest over to East Texas to tend the souls of his charges? According to the traditional account, Father Hidalgo made three copies of the letter, sending each by different Indian couriers. One of them ultimately reached Cadillac.

The French governor was delighted with what he interpreted, perhaps with tongue in cheek, as an invitation to enter Spanish domains. In response he sent a young Frenchman named Louis Juchereau de St. Denis not to East Texas but to San Juan Bautista. And St. Denis was perhaps more devil's advocate than priest, for the French interest in Texas was in commercial expansion rather than Indian salvation.

St. Denis, a native of Quebec, had come to Louisiana with the Le Moyne brothers. He was placed in charge of Iberville, a small post at the mouth of the Mississippi; later he entered into a profitable trade with the Indians. Entrusted by Cadillac to open trade with the Spaniards, St. Denis went first to the Indian village of Natchitoches on the Red River, where he enjoyed good relations and where he apparently cached a large supply of trade goods. From there during the summer of 1714 he made his way across Texas to San Juan Bautista.

Exactly what happened after his arrival is not known. Instead of being arrested and sent immediately to Mexico City, he was welcomed as an honored guest in the home of the commandant of the presidio, Diego Ramón. Ramón only wrote to the viceroy in Mexico City of the unauthorized presence of a Frenchman at his post and asked for instructions. Before these arrived, St. Denis exercised the magnetism of his personality to charm the Spaniards at San Juan Bautista. He won the affection of Ramón's granddaughter, Manuela Sánchez, but also acquired the enmity of one of her suitors, whose jealous wrath resulted in St. Denis's arrest. The Frenchman was then sent directly to Mexico City. On the journey, he gained the friendship of his guards, and on his arrival he was granted a prompt audience with the viceroy, more as an ambassador than a prisoner.

Again his compelling personality had remarkable results. Rather than being tried and possibly executed, St. Denis was named co-commander of an expedition to establish a Spanish settlement in East Texas! Somehow he had artfully persuaded the viceroy not only to build a substantial mission field in East Texas but also to permit him to assist. Officially he was listed as the expedition's guide, with the same salary and rank as the commander. The French adventurer had succeeded where the ardent supplications of Fathers Massanet and Hidalgo had failed. Six missions and a presidio were to be founded among the Hasinai.

The Ramón–St. Denis Expedition Returning to San Juan Bautista, St. Denis married Ramón's granddaughter and in the spring of 1716 led a Spanish expedition back to East Texas. The military commander of the expedition was Domingo Ramón, son of the post commandant and uncle of St. Denis's bride. The force consisted of nine priests including Father Hidalgo, twenty-five mounted soldiers, and about thirty settlers. It was well supplied with the materials needed for permanent settlement and, in addition, carried flocks of chickens and herds of cattle, sheep, goats, and horses into East Texas. Thus encumbered, the Spaniards traveled slowly and arrived at the Neches River in June after about two months.

Presents were distributed among the Indians, who once again professed friendship for the Spaniards, and the mission San Francisco de los Tejas was rebuilt. Leaving Father Hidalgo in charge, Ramón and St. Denis proceeded eastward to establish a second mission, Nuestra Señora de la Purísima Concepción, at the village of the Hasinai Indians about twenty-five miles away in the eastern part of present Nacogdoches County. Turning southeast to the Nacogdoches village, where the town of Nacogdoches is today, the Spaniards established a third mission, Nuestra Señora de Guadalupe. Then, a few miles farther north at the Nazoni village, near present Cushing in northern Nacogdoches County, a fourth mission was built, San José de los Nazonis.

At this point St. Denis suddenly remembered his affiliations with the French and led the expedition to the Natchitoches village on the Red River, where he opened his cache of merchandise and established a trading post. It is a reflection of his charm that this disloyalty cost him neither his bride nor his friendship with the Spaniards. Indeed, in December 1716 he helped Ramón establish two more missions in East Texas, San Miguel de Linares at the Adaes village about twenty miles southwest of Natchitoches, and Nuestra Señora de los Dolores at the Ais Indian village near present San Augustine, Texas. Ramón constructed a presidio named Nuestra Señora de los Dolores de los Tejas on the Neches River across from the San Francisco mission. Some of the civilians with the expedition settled near the presidio, but some apparently began to carve wilderness homes near the San Miguel mission and the Adaes village in present western Louisiana. This site later became the capital and most important settlement of East Texas. St. Denis had more than fulfilled his instructions from Cadillac: not only had he found a Spanish market for French goods but he had brought the Spaniards to within a half-day's ride of his trading post at Natchitoches.

It was inevitable that the new mission field would depend on the nearby French for supplies unless adequate provision was made to supply it from Mexico, and even then illicit trade would be impossible to prevent. The viceroy called a special council in Mexico City that decided to establish a halfway station on the route to East Texas in order to shorten the supply line. Martin de Alarcón, governor of Coahuila, and Father Antonio de San Buenaventura Olivares were to establish what was later the most important Spanish post in Texas, the present city of San Antonio.

The Alarcón Expedition The Alarcón expedition of about seventy persons crossed the Rio Grande in April 1718, driving herds of livestock and carrying bountiful supplies, for Alarcón was instructed to succor the East Texas missions as well as to establish a mission and a presidio on the route. The site selected for the halfway station on the San Antonio River was one of the most beautiful in Texas, but it was only about one third of the distance from San Juan Bautista on the Rio Grande to San Francisco on the Neches.

On May 1 Father Olivares formally dedicated the San Antonio de Valero mission, and on May 5 Captain Alarcón established the presidio of San Antonio de Béxar about a half-mile away. The chapel of the mission, built several years later, was to become famous as the Alamo, and the five or ten families that settled around the presidio were the nucleus of the village that became San Antonio.

Alarcón made a quick trip to the coast to inspect the site of Fort St. Louis on present Matagorda Bay, known to the Spaniards as La Bahía del Espíritu Santo. Although the French post had long since been obliterated, the Spaniards still thought of it as an unhealed pox that might suddenly eruct a plague through the northern empire. Finding nothing, Alarcón returned to the new mission and went back to San Juan Bautista for more supplies. In the fall of 1718 he reached the East Texas mission field and the following spring returned to Coahuila. The supplies and provisions he brought were desperately needed, but they gave only temporary relief to the East Texas missions.

The Indians of the Hasinai villages where the six missions had been located were no more helpful than the Tejas Indians had been two decades earlier. Initially eager to work for the Spaniards in return for presents, they soon refused to submit to mission life or regulation and direction by the priests. Consequently, the missions had a most tenuous existence, which the slightest storm might end. And such a storm was brewing.

The Chicken War At that time in Europe, the aggressive Spanish monarch, Philip V, had attacked the islands of Sicily and Sardinia, which were claimed by France. France, then under a regency, promptly declared war. Word of the hostilities reached the French colonies on the Gulf of Mexico long before the Spaniards were alerted, for French communications were direct whereas Spanish communication had to follow the bureaucratic channels from Vera Cruz and Mexico City. In May 1719 Frenchmen from Louisiana easily surprised and captured the Spanish post at Pensacola, Florida, and turned their attention to their Spanish neighbors in Texas.

St. Denis sent a Corporal Blondel with six soldiers to reconnoiter the settlement at Los Adaes. Blondel found it virtually unsupported, took possession of the mission, and imprisoned a lay brother and a Spanish soldier he found there. Then, as his men were plundering the mission, some of the chickens escaped from their pens and set up such a clamor of squawking that Blondel's horse was startled and the Frenchman thrown from its back. In the ensuing confusion one of the Spaniards slipped away and fled precipitately to the Dolores mission, where he reported that the French were invading with a large force.

The padres at Dolores rushed west to the presidio, where Captain Domingo Ramón had remained in charge. Enhanced by rumor and supported by fear, with each retelling Blondel's detachment grew from a company to a battalion to a regiment. Ramón decided that his position, already weakened by the unfriendliness of the Indians, who were predisposed toward the French, was now untenable. A hasty withdrawal was begun in near panic. Word was sent to the other missions, and a motley caravan of frightened Spaniards trekked back to San Antonio, reaching the halfway post in October 1719.

Thus was enacted the farce known as the "Chicken War." It exposed the Spaniards to the ridicule of French and Indians alike, shook the morale of the priests, and vacated the Spanish claim to East Texas. Although the

French made no attempt to move into the area, other than to quicken their trade with the Indians, more than mere territory was at stake: Spanish honor must be redeemed. To this end, the viceroy appointed the Marquis de San Miguel de Aguayo to lead a major force into East Texas to reestablish Spanish control so that it would be forever unshakable.

The Third Mission Wave

Reoccupation by Aguayo Aguayo, scion of a prominent Spanish family who had married a wealthy heiress, underwrote the entire cost of the reoccupation of Texas from his own purse. He was made governor and captain-general of the provinces Coahuila and Texas and was ordered to drive out the French who were presumed to have occupied East Texas, to reestablish the missions, and to quarter enough troops in the area to prevent any possibility of a recurrence of the "invasion."

Recruiting from various posts of Coahuila and Nuevo León, Aguayo assembled some five hundred men, acquired between four and five thousand head of horses and other livestock, and purchased ample supplies. It was the largest force Spain had yet sent into colonial Texas, and Aguayo was one of the most competent leaders Spanish Texas ever had. After careful planning he crossed the Rio Grande on March 20, 1721, and marched up the well-marked route to San Antonio. Domingo Ramón was detached at the head of a small party to occupy La Bahía del Espíritu Santo where the ghost of La Salle still haunted Spanish memory.

When he reached San Antonio, Aguayo found that the priests from the East Texas missions, perhaps chagrined by their undue haste in leaving their posts, had built a new mission and sheepishly named it in his honor: San José y San Miguel de Aguayo. The plan to establish it had earlier received his blessing, and the mission had been placed under his patronage. Located on the San Antonio River about five miles from San Antonio de Valero, it was to enjoy the greatest success of any of the Spanish missions in the present limits of the United States.

Within a few years San José had a chapel accommodating two thousand people, quarters for a large number of friars, offices, a refectory, a granary, a mill, a carpenter shop, and rooms for spinning and weaving. A stone wall to which were attached cells for Indian charges surrounded the church and the other buildings except the mill, and fairly elaborate irrigation works watered adjacent fields. The present chapel, begun in 1768, is considered by many to be the finest example of Spanish mission architecture in the New World. It is graced by an exquisitely carved window known as the Rose Window. Today, faithfully restored, the entire mission is a National Historic Monument.

The founding of this mission meant little to the Marquis de Aguayo; his concern was the rebuilding of the East Texas field. After resting his men for several weeks, Aguayo set out on the trail accompanied by most of the Franciscans who had been in East Texas. Unusually heavy rains delayed the expedition by flooding the creeks and rivers and necessitating frequent detours. When at last the Spaniards reached East Texas in midsummer, they found the area unoccupied by French troops and the Indians once again professing friendship.

Aguayo relocated the San Francisco mission on the Neches River a few miles away and renamed it San Francisco de los Neches. Then at each of the remaining five missions he left priests and supplies and attempted to impress the Indians with the strength of Spanish arms. At Los Adaes he built a new presidio, Nuestra Señora del Pílar, where he mounted six brass cannon and garrisoned a hundred troops.

Venturing over to the French post at Natchitoches, he learned what St. Denis had known for months: the hostilities between the mother countries had ended the year before by the Treaty of London. The versatile Frenchman convinced Aguayo of the lack of animosity of the French colony and readily agreed to confine his Indian trade to the east side of the Red River. As a surety of French intentions, however, Aguayo reestablished the Dolores presidio on the Angelina River near the Concepción mission, garrisoning it with about fifty men.

The Marquis returned to the settlement on the San Antonio River in January 1722 and had the presidio there, San Antonio de Béxar, reconstructed of stone and adobe brick. In March, with the undispersed remainder of his expedition, he moved across to join Domingo Ramón at La Bahía. There Ramón had established the presidio Nuestra Señora de Loreto, allegedly on the very site of Fort St. Louis. A short distance away priests who had gone with Ramón had founded a mission, Nuestra Señora del Espíritu Santo de Zuñiga. Both were commonly called La Bahía even after the two were moved a hundred miles inland. In April Aguayo began construction of a permanent fortification in the form of an octagon with four bastions and a tower and surrounded by a moat. He left ninety soldiers under Ramón's command and returned to San Antonio and thence to Coahuila.

This period was the crest of Spanish occupation during the eighteenth century. Four presidios, adequately manned and provisioned, were located at strategic points on the frontier, and nine missions—six in the East Texas field, two at San Antonio, and one on Matagorda Bay—were functioning, if not thriving. There were civil settlements at San Antonio and in East Texas, with Los Adaes the capital of the province. Aguayo felt that Texas was well-secured for the Spanish empire, but in his report to the crown he suggested that the civil settlements be augmented by the transportation of two hundred colonial families from Galicia, Cuba, or the Canary Islands to Texas.

Canary Islanders The bureaucratic machinery of the empire turned ponderously. Seven years later provision was made for transporting one hundred families from the Canaries by way of Havana, Vera Cruz, and Mexico City. But only twenty-five families had been shipped out before the order was canceled, and only ten reached Vera Cruz, the others remaining in Cuba. From Vera Cruz the colonists journeyed overland to San Antonio, marriages enroute increasing the number of families to fifteen—a total of fifty-six persons.

Each family head was granted a town lot near the Alamo (Valero mission), a tract of agricultural land in the country, and the minor title of hidalgo. Also, the government provided the colonists with seeds, equipment, supplies, and further support for a year. Shortly thereafter, the Canary Islanders organized a village government, the first in Texas to have legal status as a villa with a degree of self-government. On the viceroy's recommendation it was named in honor of the king's son, Villa de San Fernando de Béxar. In time comfortable stone houses were built, the first school in Texas established, and a parish church erected. The church evolved into the modern San Fernando cathedral; the village has been largely restored and as La Villita is today a major tourist attraction in downtown San Antonio.

Pedro de Rivera Even as one agency of the crown was undertaking this modest expansion of settlement in Texas, another was advocating attenuation. In the interest of economy, the viceroy had ordered Brigadier Pedro de Rivera y Villalon in 1724 to inspect the northern frontier and make recommendations for reducing government expenditures. Rivera spent four years preparing his report. He traveled some eight thousand miles through northern Mexico and present New Mexico and Texas, visited all the frontier posts, mapped the coast from La Bahía to the Sabine Pass, and made extensive notes on the Indians. His report included three recommendations that affected Texas: (1) a consolidation of the East Texas missions, (2) the transfer of the mission and presidio of La Bahía to the Medina River near San Antonio, and (3) a war of suppression against the Apache Indians. None of the recommendations was adopted.

Rather than consolidating the missions in East Texas, church authorities simply moved three of them in 1730: San José de los Nazonis, San Francisco de los Neches, and Purísima Concepción de los Hainai. Transfer of the missions did not, of course, mean moving the buildings. Rather, mission records, religious articles, tools, supplies, and other items were packed, and the priests and the few converts living in the mission arduously journeyed by caravan back across Texas. They did not return all the way to San Antonio but stopped on the Colorado River near the present city of Austin. The effort to establish a mission field there was unsuccessful, and the next year, 1731, the missions were moved to San Antonio.

Each of the three missions located near San José, and the padres and their charges soon began permanent construction. The beautiful buildings they erected during the following decades remain today a monument to their industry and a permanent record of Spanish achievement in Texas. Because of the move, the names of the missions were changed. San José de los Nazonis became San Juan Capistrano; San Francisco de los Neches became San Francisco de la Espada; and Purísima Concepción de los Hainai became Purísima Concepción de Acuña. After this move, the San Antonio area included five missions, a presidio, and the Villa de San Fernando, and the East Texas field had been reduced to three missions and one presidio at Los Adaes, the Dolores garrison having been closed in 1730.

Rivera's recommendation to move La Bahía to the vicinity of San Antonio was ignored. On his visit to the mission and presidio of La Bahía in 1727, he had found that the two had been moved the year before from the unfavorable location on Matagorda Bay, at the site of Fort St. Louis, to a better location on the Guadalupe River near the present city of Victoria. Rivera felt, however, that this site was too isolated and suggested moving back to the San Antonio area. The priests disagreed; La Bahía remained on the Guadalupe River until 1749, when it was transferred to its permanent location on the San Antonio River at present Goliad, some ninety miles below the city of San Antonio.

The Indian Dilemma The third of Rivera's suggestions for Texas was not as blatantly ignored as the first two but it was equally unrealized, for the recommended war of suppression against the Apaches could not possibly be fulfilled. In the first place, no army—Spanish, Mexican, Texan, or American—could force the mounted nomads of the plains into pitched battle in their home territory. At the approach of a substantial

35 / *The Third Mission Wave*

force the Indians simply scattered and regrouped later. They had no permanent villages that could be attacked, no supply lines to be cut, and no commissary to be destroyed. Elusive as the wind, they needed only a herd of game and a water hole to perpetuate their way of life.

A second reason for the failure of the proposed war was the failure of Rivera and the Spaniards to understand fully the situation then developing in the Great Plains area. They had noticed that Apache raids and depredations were increasing; they failed to recognize the cause. A new and irresistible force from the north was driving a wedge into the plains Apaches, pressing them south against the Spaniards in northern Mexico and splitting them east and west against Texas and New Mexico. This powerful force was the sudden intrusion of the fierce Comanche Indians on the plains.

The Comanches were a Shoshone-speaking people that had lived for generations in the foothills of the Rockies along the Yellowstone and Platte rivers. Small, squat, and coarse-featured, they had subsisted on grubs, roots, nuts, and small game, in incongruous contrast to the fearsome tribe they became about the beginning of the eighteenth century. At that time they acquired horses and virtually overnight became the terror of the plains. In a few decades they swept south, driving all other tribes away and establishing undisputed dominion over the South Plains, from the Arkansas River to the Rio Grande and from the mountains of New Mexico to the hills of Central Texas. Pawnee, Wichita, Waco, and other tribes were forced east in present northern Texas and Oklahoma. Utes and Piutes were crowded into the mountains in Colorado and northern New Mexico. Lipan and Mescalero Apaches were sundered and driven into northern Mexico, southern Texas, and eastern New Mexico. Virtually alone among all the bands previously ranging the South Plains, the Kiowa made a loose alliance to live in relative peace with the implacable Comanches.

The Apaches tried to resist. According to unsupported Indian legends, a seven days' battle was fought about 1725 somewhere on the Red River near the eastern boundary of the Texas Panhandle. After the Comanches' victory, the Apaches never again dared confront their bitter foes. Whether such a fight actually took place is immaterial; the Comanches did take over the South Plains hunting grounds, and the consequent pressure of the Apaches was noted by the Spaniards.

Had Rivera understood the reasons for the increase in Apache marauding, he might have recommended instead an alliance with the Apaches against the Comanches, but it is only remotely possible that combined Spanish and Apache maneuvers might have turned the Comanche tide. For the remainder of the century this was the dilemma that Spain faced on the Indian frontier in Texas: whether to ally themselves with the

Apaches against the Comanches or to join these northern bands to eliminate the immediate nuisance of the Apaches. In the years that followed Spanish policy oscillated between the two courses.

The Fourth Mission Wave

The Establishment of Nuevo Santander During the middle eighteenth century Spain made several half-hearted attempts to expand both her settlements and her influence among the Indians in Texas. But these endeavors were largely unsuccessful: they were inadequately supported, the Texas Indians were too wild for mission assimilation, and increasing friction between the military and religious arms of the empire hamstrung efficient operations. In the south along the Rio Grande a vast civil colonization project directed by José de Escandón was to leave a weak but permanent mark on Texas. In the east new missions among the coastal tribes met with only meager rewards. And in the west the missionary effort to solve the Indian dilemma ended in costly tragedy.

At the beginning of this era of expansion the Spanish frontier hopscotched through the wilderness north of the valley of Mexico in small and often stagnant regions of semicivilization. There were substantial centers of population at Monclova, Saltillo, and Monterrey; there were two settlements on the Rio Grande, one in the present Juárez-El Paso area and the other, San Juan Bautista, located across from present Eagle Pass; farther up the Rio Grande, of course, were the settlements in New Mexico; and there were the three mission fields in Texas—San Antonio, La Bahía, and East Texas. Between these scattered outposts were vast stretches of land occupied only by wild game and roving bands of Indians. But much of this unclaimed land was habitable, and a glance at a map of the northern frontier at the time reveals the strategic weakness of the coast. There was not a single Spanish settlement from Tampico north and eastward along the entire Gulf shoreline to the French posts in Louisiana. Not even La Bahía remained on the coast, having been moved in 1726. The important region between Tampico and Matagorda Bay (or Espíritu Santo), known as the *Seno Mexicano,* was totally unsettled.

Its vulnerability was highlighted during the War of Jenkins' Ear, between Spain and Great Britain, and during the resultant War of the Austrian Succession, also known as King George's War, in which the British demonstrated an aggressive acquisitiveness for colonial territory. Apprehensive of foreign intrusion and even settlement in the *Seno Mexi-*

cano, the viceroy ordered an inspection of the area. José de Escandón, a brilliant career officer in the Spanish Army in Mexico, was commissioned to lead the undertaking.

With seven divisions Escandón entered the *Seno Mexicano* in January 1747 and spent nearly a year and a half in an intensive investigation, especially along the twisted courses of the lower Rio Grande. He submitted a plan for the colonization of the region, and even before its approval he began selecting sites for villages and missions. In June 1748 the territory, present Tamaulipas, was renamed Nuevo Santander and Escandón was made its governor general. The colonization project approved, Escandón began the process of settlement early in 1749. His careful organization and competent leadership resulted in one of the most successful and enduring Spanish ventures on the northern frontier.

At the head of a caravan of 2,500 settlers, 750 soldiers, and a score of priests, he moved into his province and founded in almost rapid-fire succession during the next seven years twenty-three towns and fifteen missions. The first two villas on the Rio Grande were Camargo and Reynosa, established on the south bank in 1749. The next year one of Escandón's captains built the town of Dolores in present Zapata County on the north bank at the mouth of Blancas Creek, and also that year the town of Revilla was founded on the south side of the river above Camargo. There followed Mier in 1753 on the south bank and Laredo in 1755 on the north bank. Although only Laredo and Dolores were within the present boundaries of Texas, residents of the towns on the south bank received land grants and established ranches north of the river. Laredo, if not prospering in the course of years, at least survived; Dolores failed. Thirty years later Laredo's population was about 700, and by that time Dolores had disappeared.

Escandón's original territory extended to the San Antonio River. The northern boundary of Nuevo Santander was later set at the Nueces River, and the state of Tamaulipas, created later from the old province, inherited the same frontier. Hence the region of Escandón's activities is usually not considered a part of Spanish Texas.

The Western Missions While Escandón labored in the *Seno Mexicano*, three mission fields were begun on the western frontier of Texas: San Gabriel, San Sabá, and "El Cañon." The San Gabriel field was established by Father Mariano Francisco de los Dolores y Viana, a Franciscan who came to San Antonio in 1733 to take charge of San Antonio de Valero, the Alamo. While there he often visited the Indian tribes along the frontier west of the road to Nacogdoches. On the San Gabriel

River, called by the Spaniards San Xavier, he formed a friendly relationship with the leaders of a large ranchería of Tonkawa Indians.

The Tonkawas were a Central Texas band of hunters often described as fierce and warlike and occasionally as cannibalistic. In truth, they were no fiercer than other bands of the period, and their cannibalism seems to have been limited to ceremonial purposes. Many primitive societies believed like the Tonkawas that devouring the heart or brain of an especially brave or cunning enemy might impart some envied qualities. But the Tonkawas were never especially troublesome either to the Spaniards of the eighteenth century or the Anglo-Americans of the nineteenth, and many individual Tonkawas acted as guides and scouts when the newcomers ventured into Comanche country.

The Tonkawas were enemies of both the Comanches and the Apaches, and they were involved in essentially the same dilemma as the Spaniards. In 1745 four Tonkawa leaders rode into San Antonio to request that missionaries and soldiers be sent to their ranchería and to San Gabriel. Undoubtedly they were looking for aid against depredating Comanche war parties, but Father Viana was gratified to believe that his visits among them had borne fruit. He fired off a petition to the viceroy for authorization of a mission field, but without waiting for an answer he went to the ranchería in the spring of 1746 to begin planting a crop, aided by friars and neophytes from the San Antonio missions.

The government, under Viana's almost incessant importuning, finally acceded to the request, and in the spring of 1748 the mission San Francisco Xavier de Horcasitas was formally dedicated. It was located on Brushy Creek two or three miles above its juncture with the San Gabriel River in present Milam County. A few soldiers were garrisoned nearby, and in March 1751 the presidio of San Francisco Xavier was built about two miles from the mission and manned by a complement of fifty troops. Meantime, two more missions had been added to the settlement in 1749: San Ildefonso and Nuestra Señora de la Candelaria.

The ever-present antagonism between priests and soldiers flared into open hostility at San Gabriel. A quarrel between the presidial captain, Felipe de Rábago y Terán, and Father Juan José Ganzábal of the San Francisco Xavier mission culminated in 1752 in the friar's murder. The captain was implicated and removed from command although his guilt was never established. But the tragedy bore stark witness to the fact that, at San Gabriel if not elsewhere, the padres were under more danger from the soldiers than from their Indian charges. The affair caused all but one of the friars to abandon their posts.

Father Anda y Altamirano kept the San Francisco Xavier mission open for a handful of neophytes, and a skeleton force of soldiers remained at the presidio until 1755, when a brief effort was made to reopen the mission. When this failed after a few months, the new presidial commander, without authority, ordered the missions and presidio removed to the springs at the head of the San Marcos River, one of the missions being relocated on the Guadalupe near present New Braunfels. But the move proved temporary, and the San Gabriel missions and presidio were soon closed forever and their properties assigned to a new venture, a mission to the Apaches.

Spanish policy had shifted. Officials became aware of the northern pressure on the Apaches and began to dare forming an alliance rather than pursuing Rivera's hopeless war of suppression. At this time, a wealthy mine owner in northern Mexico, Pedro Romero de Terreros, offered to finance building a mission to the Apaches and maintaining it for three years—if the government provided troops for protection and if his cousin, Father Alonso Giraldo de Terreros, was placed in charge of the mission.

The friar may have aroused his cousin's interest in the scheme, for he had earlier tried to work with the Apaches. Following a vague treaty made with them in 1749, Father Terreros had established a mission for them below the Rio Grande in Coahuila, and when the treacherous Apaches burned it to the ground, the priest fatuously argued that their knavery was caused by the fact that the mission was not located farther north.

In 1756, through the philanthropy of his cousin, Father Terreros and four other Franciscans headed into Apache country on the San Saba River. They were accompanied by nine families of Christianized Indians from Coahuila and one hundred troops under the command of Colonel Diego Ortiz de Parilla. With the properties formerly belonging to the San Gabriel missions, Father Terreros founded the mission San Sabá de la Santa Cruz in April 1757 on the south bank of the San Saba River near present Menard. Upstream about two miles and across the river, Colonel Parilla built the massive stone presidio San Luis de las Amarillas. When the remnant of troops from the defunct San Gabriel presidio were assigned to it, its total population reached nearly four hundred persons, including Indian servants and wives and children of the soldiers.

The Lipan Apaches did not come immediately into the mission as they had promised, but the priests, by traveling through their hunting grounds to distribute presents, were able to persuade many to visit the mission. In June 1758 some three thousand Lipans were encamped around Santa Cruz, but they would not enter mission life. Before the end of the summer, most of them had left on a buffalo hunt. Through the winter a few returned for brief visits, bringing rumors of a Comanche plan to attack the Spaniards in the spring. The priests became discouraged not so much by the fear of attack as by the fickle nature of the Apaches pretending to accept Christianity. Nevertheless, when Parilla, preparing the presidio defenses against the alleged attack, urged the Franciscans to seek safety in the presidio, they refused.

In March a war party of two thousand Comanches suddenly surrounded the mission. Under a pretext of friendship the Indians easily gained admission into the wooden stockade, where they began a massacre. Defense was impossible. The Comanches burned the buildings and killed all of the mission personnel except nine men who barricaded themselves in a room. That night a scouting party from the presidio found only four of them still alive in the smoldering ruins. Soon thereafter the Comanches attacked the presidio, which the Spaniards defended successfully.

In this first encounter, Spanish leaders were taken aback by the violence and treachery of the Comanches. A council of war in San Antonio decided that to sustain Spanish prestige among the other bands it would be necessary to maintain the presidio on the San Saba and to send a massive punitive expedition against the Comanches. Led by Colonel Parilla, a force of over five hundred soldiers and Indian allies set out the following summer, in 1759, to chastise the Comanches. Ten times that many could not have succeeded.

Parilla went north from the San Saba presidio, captured a Tonkawa village on the Brazos that had allied itself with the Comanches, and chased a small band of Comanches to the Red River, where, to the amazement of the Spaniards, stood a fortified town. This Taovayas village, in present Montague County, surrounded by a crude moat and stockade, flew a French flag and was defended by French guns. Behind the palisade were hundreds of Indians who screamed with laughter at the ineffective volleys from the Spaniards. Parilla decided to charge the fort, a disastrous error that ended in a rout as Comanches sallied from the village and nearly outflanked the Spaniards. Parilla and his men fled south, abandoning their supplies and a cannon they had laboriously dragged from San Antonio. According to Parilla's report, the battle was an inconclusive victory for the Spaniards, who had lost eleven dead, fourteen wounded, and nine deserted, as well as most of the horses, stolen by the fickle Apache allies. Victory or no, Spain never again attempted a military expedition against the Comanches.

The Taovayas village that had been Parilla's nemesis was a center of Indian commerce for French traders from Louisiana and Plains Indians from the buffalo grounds. Even the Comanches visited it in cautious neutrality. Despite possible exaggeration by Rivera, there can be little doubt that Frenchmen had supplied guns and ammunition to the Taovayas. The site, after its abandonment by the Indians in the next century, was incongruously named Spanish Fort by pioneer settlers who knew nothing of its history.

41 / *The Fourth Mission Wave*

Parilla led his force back to the presidio on the San Saba and went himself to San Antonio for treatment of a wound. The presidio was not closed for another decade, and it is of passing interest to note that Felipe de Rábago y Terán, who had been accused of murdering the priest at San Gabriel, was placed in command. Under pressure of Comanche raids he abandoned it in 1768, retreating to a mission on the upper Nueces River that he had helped establish six years before.

This little mission field, in present Edwards County, was Spain's last effort to missionize the Lipan Apaches in Texas. San Lorenzo de la Santa Cruz, the first of two missions, can be considered in only the loosest sense a successor to San Sabá de la Santa Cruz. About ten miles south of it the second mission, Nuestra Señora de la Candelaría del Cañon, also established in 1762, was connected equally vaguely with the Candelaría mission on the San Gabriel. The two missions, together with a detachment of soldiers, were commonly referred to as El Cañon. They were dismally unsuccessful in attracting Lipan Apaches to Christianity and were abandoned in 1771.

In fact, the whole Spanish effort among the Plains Indians was a failure, and as a result Spain's status with these nomadic bands probably diminished. But a new shift in frontier policy was soon to be made.

Renewed Activity on the Coast While these ventures on the San Gabriel, the San Saba, and the Nueces were moving to their dreary ends, other padres were trying, with only slightly better success, to tame the primitive coastal bands. In 1749, seeking a more advantageous location, the La Bahía mission and presidio moved from the Guadalupe River to a permanent site on the San Antonio River, about a hundred miles below the city of San Antonio. The move was authorized by José de Escandón, then governor-general of Nuevo Santander, who desired to bring the settlement under his jurisdiction. The village that developed at the new location was named Goliad almost a century later. Here a new attempt was made to induce the Karankawa Indians to adapt to mission life, but instead the Karankawas persuaded converts from northern Mexico to run away from the mission fathers.

To meet this problem, a second mission, Nuestra Señora del Rosario, was established in 1754 about four miles away. Its purpose was to serve as a focal point for the restless Karankawas and to free the parent mission of this nuisance. Rosario was not a grand success, although it clung to existence tenaciously, suffering a brief period of abandonment from 1781 to 1789. Despite numerous vicissitudes, it was still functioning as late as 1830. Both Rosario and the La Bahía mission of Nuestra Señora del Espíritu Santo de Zuñiga were secularized in 1831.

Up the coast from the Karankawa Indians, just off Galveston Bay near Anahuac in present Chambers County, a mission and a presidio were established in 1756 at a village of Orcoquisac Indians. The year before a French trader had been arrested in this area by a party of Spanish scouts. Hence, the principal purpose of the settlement, which included fifty families of civilized Indians from Mexico, was strategic: to guard the approaches from the coast to East Texas. The mission was named Nuestra Señora de la Luz and the presidio, San Agustín de Ahumada. A full-fledged civil settlement was authorized but never established, and the mission and presidio known collectively as Orcoquisac had a tenuous existence for the next fifteen years. A Gulf storm in 1766 destroyed the presidio, which was rebuilt in a more favorable location. But this was an undertaking hardly worth the effort, since by 1771 Orcoquisac consisted of only three soldiers at the presidio to guard the two priests at the mission. The settlement was withdrawn the following year.

The Transfer of Louisiana and the Shift in Spanish Policy Underlying the debilitation and final abandonment of Orcoquisac was a shift in Spanish frontier policy resulting from changes in the international scenery painted by the 1763 Treaty of Paris. The Treaty of Aix-la-Chapelle in 1748 had been merely a recognition of the stalemate of the European powers after the War of the Austrian Succession. Conflict broke out anew in the Seven Years' War, also called the French and Indian War, which originated as a colonial war between the French and the English in western Pennsylvania in 1754. Fighting became worldwide in 1756, and once again Spain was dragged into the melee by her cornered ally, France. The invincible eighteenth-century British Navy soon occupied the key Spanish ports of Havana in Cuba and Manila in the Philippines, choking the flow of Spanish commerce.

As the war drew to an end, France recognized that she had been defeated and would be routed out of her colonial possessions. Spain, although not threatened with such catastrophe, knew that she would have to give some territory to Britain in order to break the British Navy's stranglehold on imperial marine traffic; she would have to trade something at the treaty table for the peaceful restoration of Havana and Manila. Thus, just prior to the Treaty of Paris of 1763, which ended the war, Spain and France concluded a territorial agreement. Because France knew she would lose her entire North American empire, because she did not want Britain to have it all, and because she desired to compensate Spain for the certain loss that Britain would require for the restitution of the two ports, France ceded western Louisiana to Spain. Spain now possessed all territory west of the Mississippi. In the following negotiations, Britain confirmed this transfer but demanded that Spain relinquish Florida, a rather large price, in exchange for the vital ports.

Therefore the Treaty of Paris not only closed the curtain on the last act in the century-long contest for empire between Spain and France but also made Britain and Spain neighbors along the length of the Mississippi River. Britain quickly established government in Canada and drew a line along the ridge of the Appalachian Mountains to contain the restless colonists on the seaboard. Two years later, in the Stamp Act of 1765, she took the first major step in alienating those same colonists. The shift in British policy that followed the Treaty of Paris was soon to lose her the thirteen (actually sixteen at that time) colonies on the Atlantic; the shift in Spanish policy was less catastrophic.

To accommodate the new acquisition, Spanish government was established in New Orleans, Frenchmen living in Louisiana were invited to remain and become Spanish citizens, and many entered the service of the Spanish crown. Encumbered by red tape and an ever-burgeoning bureaucracy, however, Spain shifted more slowly than Britain. It was nearly ten years before the effects were felt in Texas.

In 1764 a Spanish field marshal, the Marquis de Rubí, was appointed to inspect the entire northern frontier. Rubí arrived in Mexico in February 1766, crossed into present Texas in August the next year, and rapidly toured the western outposts as he moved toward the east, reaching Los Adaes in September 1767. He returned to Mexico in November and filed his report in April 1768. Despite the relative haste of his inspection, Rubí's investigation was surprisingly thorough, his recommendations were logical, and his report and the resultant royal order were of great significance to Texas.

Passing through the Nueces valley, he had first visited the little establishment known as El Cañon in Apache country, which he recognized could be supported only at excessive expense. Then at the undermanned presidio on the San Saba, he concurred with Captain Rábago y Terán's conclusion that this place, caught between Apaches and Comanches, was indefensible. At San Antonio he was impressed by the flowering of the Franciscan missions; in East Texas he was dismayed by the deterioration. Orcoquisac he found virtually worthless, with only three soldiers in the partially destroyed presidio and the mission practically extinct. Escandón's revitalized settlement of La Bahía on the San Antonio River, consisting of two missions, a presidio, and an informal civil settlement, met with his approval.

He assessed accurately two general flaws in frontier policy, as well as a number of specific problems, and made several recommendations directly bearing on Texas. The flaws were the army's pay system and the futile attempt of the previous decade to placate the Lipan Apaches. Soldiers in the frontier presidios received less than one-fourth of their meager wages in cash; the remainder was carried on the presidial commandant's books and charged off against the individual soldier for clothes, supplies, and equipment, inferior merchandise often being sold to the troops at exorbitant prices to the profit of the commandant. The result was growing resentment and insubordination. Such petty corruption had to be ended if the frontier army was to be effective.

Rubí believed the policy toward the Apaches was fatuous. The Apaches were the immediate menace on the frontier, and their enemies, the Comanches and the associated "northern tribes," were obviously stronger. Spain should unite her frontier forces with the Comanches in warfare against the troublesome Apaches. Both Texas and New Mexico, as well as the interior provinces of Coahuila and Chihuahua, would profit.

These two general recommendations together with the specific ones affecting Texas were ultimately incorporated in a royal decree known as the New Regulations for the Presidios of the Frontier, promulgated in 1772. The army pay system was to be revised and a closer audit of presidial accounts maintained; an alliance was to be sought with the "northern tribes" and a war of extermination waged against the Lipan Apaches; the posts on the San Saba, at El Cañon, and at Orcoquisac were to be closed; the capital of Texas was to be moved from Los Adaes to San Antonio; the East Texas mission field was to be abandoned; and the civil settlers in East Texas were to be relocated at San Antonio. East Texas was no longer important. Its function as a buffer against the French in Louisiana was obsolete; now Spain needed to strengthen Louisiana as a buffer against the far more aggressive British across the Mississippi.

3

Spain's Last Years

Reorganization

East Texas   Spain's acquisition of Louisiana made the maintenance of East Texas unnecessary, as the Marquis de Rubí had been quick to recognize. As soon as the New Regulations for the Presidios of the Frontier reached the viceroy in Mexico, he issued orders to abandon the missions and settlements in East Texas, thus relieving the treasury of an expense that had been a small but nearly constant drain. It fell to the governor of Texas, the Baron de Ripperdá, to execute the withdrawal from the area; he faced an unpleasant task.

There were about five hundred civilians living around the former capital of the province, Los Adaes, and perhaps a score or so at the other missions. These people did not want to abandon their homes and crops and move to San Antonio, despite the promise of land titles there. When Ripperdá arrived at Los Adaes in May 1773 to oversee the evacuation, they prevailed upon him to allow them a little more time to pack their belongings and prepare for the migration. Reluctantly in July with a last,

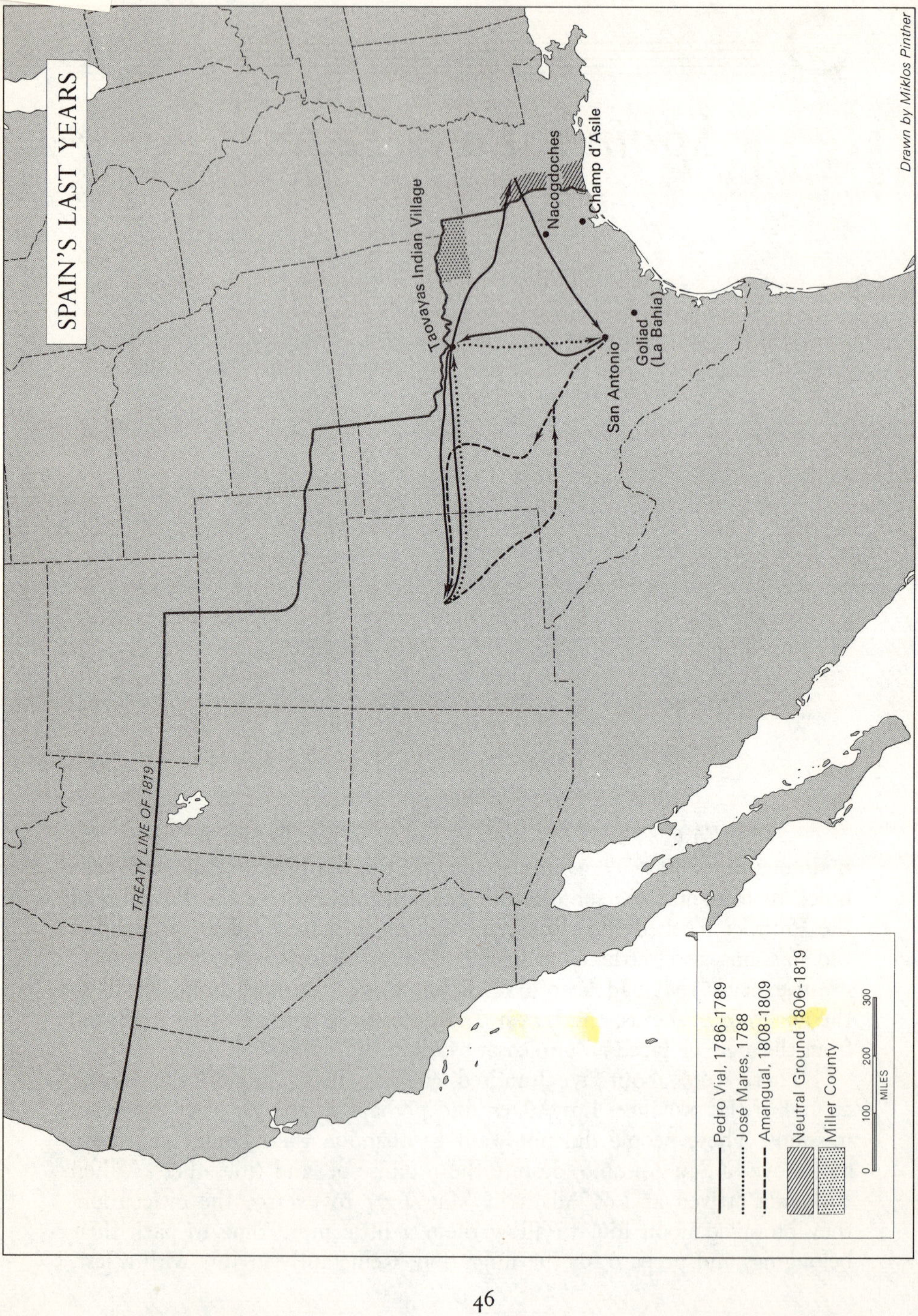

SPAIN'S LAST YEARS
TREATY LINE OF 1819
Taovayas Indian Village
Nacogdoches
Champ d'Asile
San Antonio
Goliad
(La Bahía)
Pedro Vial, 1786-1789
José Mares, 1788
Amangual, 1808-1809
Neutral Ground 1806-1819
Miller County
0
100
200
300
MILES
Drawn by Miklos Pinther

sad look at their unharvested crops, they began the long trek down the *Camino Real* to San Antonio.

Ripperdá had much less difficulty with the fathers and their few converts at the three remaining missions. The missionaries had received instructions from their superiors and had almost eagerly accompanied the governor back to San Antonio, where they and their charges were amalgamated into the mission establishments. Of the three missions, San Miguel at Los Adaes, Dolores at the Aís village, and Guadalupe at the Nacogdoches village, the latter appears to have been the most successful, and that the buildings were in good repair and were not destroyed indicates that the priests may have hoped to return later. They never did, but the civilians from Los Adaes were soon to put the abandoned buildings to use.

As soon as these people arrived in San Antonio, they petitioned the viceroy for permission to return to their former homes. Neither the lands Ripperdá proposed to grant them nor his genuine efforts to alleviate their distress lessened their desire for their woodland homesteads. They selected Antonio Gil Ybarbo, a forty-four-year-old native of Los Adaes, to carry their petition to the viceroy.

Ybarbo left San Antonio with the sanction of Ripperdá in December 1773; in February the viceroy acceded in part to their request. Fearing the possibility of smuggling, he permitted them not to return to Los Adaes but to move as far east as the Trinity River. Somewhat surprisingly, the refugees accepted this witless compromise and eagerly prepared for another migration. In August 1774 they established a village, under Ybarbo's leadership, on the San Antonio Road at the crossing of the Trinity River. The settlement, named Bucareli in honor of the viceroy, contained about three hundred fifty of the five hundred settlers who had left Los Adaes.

Bucareli was ill-fated and short-lived. The unhealthful Trinity bottom was infested with insects. A Comanche raid in 1778 evidenced that the location was too far west. And the next year a raging flood that wiped out the village showed that the site had been chosen unwisely. Then as the villagers tried to regain their self-possession in a temporary camp, they were surrounded by a war party of Comanches that entrapped them for the night and stole away the next morning with most of their horses. It was too much; without asking permission from anyone, Ybarbo led his followers farther east.

They resettled in 1779 at the abandoned buildings of Nuestra Señora de Guadalupe de los Nacogdoches and with the old mission as a nucleus laid out another town, calling it by the logical name of Nacogdoches. There is reason to believe that the government's apprehensions were justified and that very soon they were busily engaged in trading contraband goods from Natchitoches with the local Indians. In any event, Nacogdoches became a permanent settlement and in a few years received legal recognition.

The Provincias Internas   The New Regulations with the consequent though indirect founding of Nacogdoches was of no more importance than another plan affecting the frontier: the *Provincias Internas* (Interior Provinces). This was a military-administrative unit, independent of the viceroy, which subsumed all the provinces of the northern frontier, including, of course, Texas. Its purpose was to make more efficient the administration of the far-flung outposts. The great distances to Mexico City and the viceregal court had made it most difficult for the frontier governors to render prompt decisions on important matters since the protocol of the Spanish bureaucracy required the viceroy's approval for most actions.

In the long run, however, the new agency did not facilitate frontier affairs but only complicated them. The *Provincias Internas* was created in 1776 after a trial operation began in 1772; within ten years the viceroy had regained control, and the *Provincias Internas* had become just one more link in the chain of imperial bureaucracy. Soon the viceroy subdivided the *Provincias Internas* into first three and then two districts. Texas was included in the eastern division with Coahuila, Nuevo León, and Nuevo Santander. In 1792 the crown attempted to restore the original scheme, reuniting the *Provincias Internas* and separating it again from viceregal jurisdiction. Within another few years, however, the viceroy restored his authority and in 1813 again effected the division into eastern and western halves. Thus, from 1776 until the end of the Spanish period in 1821, the government of Texas was subject to the *Provincias Internas* in one form or another.

The first commandant of the Interior Provinces was Teodoro de Croix, a competent Frenchman who spent his life in the service of Spain's Bourbon monarchs. A member of the personal guard of the Spanish king, he had served five years in Mexico, 1766–1771, and perhaps for this reason he was given the new post in 1776. Shortly after his arrival at Vera Cruz he set out, accompanied by Father Juan Agustín de Morfí, to inspect the northern frontier. Father Morfí used his diary of the trip to write during 1779 and 1780 the first history of Texas. De Croix's inspections became the basis for a new Indian policy for Texas and New Mexico.

In January 1778, De Croix held a council in San Antonio for the purpose of expanding Rubí's recommendation of a war of extermination against the Apaches. Out of this conference grew a plan to split the Mescalero and Lipan Apaches, to war against the Lipans, and to seek alliances with the "northern tribes," primarily the Comanche bands. Actually, parts of this plan had already been put into effect by Hugo Oconór, a former governor of Texas, who served as commandant of presidios in the *Provincias Internas* before De Croix's arrival.

Oconór was an Irishman in Spanish service, one of many such "wild geese" as they were called who fled Catholic Ireland after one or another revolt and consequent persecution by protestant England. These Catholic refugees found succor under the Spanish banner and generally migrated to Spain's colonies in the New World, many of them like Oconór rendering valuable service on the frontier. Another wild goose, Alejandro O'Reilly, became governor of Louisiana after the Treaty of Paris of 1763. Perhaps it was this background that enabled O'Reilly to persuade many of the Louisiana French also to enter Spanish service.

The New Indian Policy One such Frenchman, Athanase de Mézières, son-in-law of St. Denis, French army officer at Natchitoches and part-time Indian trader, was enlisted by O'Reilly and made deputy-governor of Louisiana. De Mézières' chief service, however, was to win for Spain the friendship of the Indian tribes along the Red River. He was a capable man who could speak several Indian tongues and could read and write fluently in Spanish, French, and Latin. In 1770, 1771, and 1772, he made trips up the Red River for O'Reilly, cementing the allegiance of a number of the non-Comanche "northern tribes."

Then in 1778 De Croix appointed him governor of Texas and assigned him the difficult task of making alliances with the Comanche bands. Although De Mézières died in 1779 before he officially assumed the governorship, he made two trips into northern Texas with substantial success. Inspired largely by De Mézières, the Comanches took the warpath against the Lipans early in 1779, and De Croix's strategy began to function. Reports of fierce battles between Lipans and Comanches reached the commandant during 1779 and 1780, and in 1780 Lipan leaders began to seek peace in San Antonio, representing themselves as friends of the Spaniards. An uneasy truce ensued on the frontier, as Spain's fickle Comanche allies vacillated between peace and war during the next several decades. But De Croix's basic policy of alliance with the northern tribes continued until the end of the Spanish period.

Another Frenchman, Pedro Vial, was almost as effective as De Mézières. Because of his knowledge of the Plains Indians, Vial was commissioned to travel through their country, to distribute gifts. He was also instructed to explore a route between the frontier capitals San Antonio and Santa Fe. Vial left San Antonio in 1786 and spent several weeks first at a Tawakoni village in Central Texas and later at the Taovayas village on the Red River. Then he traveled across the plains with a Comanche band and arrived at Santa Fe in May 1787. The following year he explored a route from Santa Fe to Natchitoches, and another party, under José Mares, returned to San Antonio along his first route. Vial returned to Santa Fe by way of San Antonio in 1789, and in 1792 he opened communications between Santa Fe and St. Louis.

Their activity increased Spanish officials' information about the frontier area and the Indians if it did not prompt peace. But despite sporadic Comanche raids, the closing decades of the eighteenth century were quieter than they might have been without De Croix's intelligent policy and the work of such Frenchmen in Spanish service. By the turn of the century, the frontier settlements in both New Mexico and Texas enjoyed comparative security.

Spanish Colonial Life

The Missions Of the three branches of Spanish civilization on the Texas frontier—the mission, the presidio, and the civil settlement—the principal was the mission, from the humble thatch hut on the Rio Grande at La Junta to the magnificent grandeur of San José at San Antonio. Whatever the mission's outward form, the purpose remained, at least ostensibly, the same: to Christianize the Indians; to teach them the basic arts of civilization such as farming, leathercraft, weaving, spinning, and dyeing; to make them good citizens and loyal subjects of the crown; and to lead them pacifically to their destination for generations to come, a life of peonage on the large estates. In each area when this goal was achieved, the mission was secularized, or transferred from the jurisdiction of the "regular" clergy to the "secular" clergy and converted into a parish church. Perhaps because it was the age of the Inquisition or perhaps because force was occasionally necessary to persuade the natives of the advantages of the Spanish way, the term *indios reducidos* (reduced Indians) was customary to refer to Christianized Indians.

Across the frontier, many Indian bands resisted such reduction. The fierce Yaqui people of western Mexico did not succumb to the white man's rule until, surprisingly, the present century. The proud Puebloans of New Mexico had revolted in 1680 against their subjugation, had driven the Spaniards from the upper Rio Grande, and had enjoyed a brief respite from domination until the reconquest under Pedro de Vargas in 1692.

None of the Indians in Texas, from the agrarian Caddoans in the eastern woodlands to the warlike nomads of the plains ever accepted reduction gracefully, and only a few of them ever accepted it at all. Never were Spanish missions anything but dismal failures among the Apaches or Comanches, and a century of effort was expended futilely on the Karankawas and associated coastal bands. Although a few Texas Indians in East Texas and around San Antonio came into the missions and adjusted to the priests' routines, even they did not go all the way toward reduction and peonage. In the main, the missionary fathers had to resort to importing Indians from Mexico to staff the Texas missions and act as bellwethers for the local peoples.

Spanish Catholic evangelism was carried out primarily by the monastic orders of Jesus and St. Francis. The Jesuits did not missionize in Texas, and in the latter part of the eighteenth century they were expelled from the empire, their missions devolving upon the "Little Brothers of Assisi." The first major Franciscan convent north of Mexico City was the colegio at Querétaro. From it was formed in 1704 the colegio at Zacatecas. The two houses participated almost equally in the missionary activity in Texas. Queretaran fathers established three (or four if the short-lived María is included) of the six East Texas missions—San Francisco, Concepcion, and San José, later San Juan Capistrano—the Alamo, the three missions in the San Gabriel group, and the missions on the Nueces known as El Cañon. Zacatecans founded the other three East Texas missions, La Bahía and its two later subdivisons, Rosario and Refugio, the mission to the Orcoquisacs, and the "Queen of Spanish Missions," San José in San Antonio. In 1772, after the Queretaran group assumed control of the Jesuit properties in Mexico, all of the Queretaran missions in Texas were transferred to the colegio at Zacatecas.

Wearing thonged sandals and brown robes tied loosely by a white, knotted cord, Franciscan friars from both these convents trudged on foot over most of South and East Texas. Their vows of poverty were interpreted then to require them to walk, and if any footsore and weary padre ever sneaked up on the back of a horse for a short distance or rode a wagon at an icy stream crossing, it was not recorded. No words can adequately describe their apostolic zeal, nor can any amount of historical cynicism detract from their accomplishments.

But despite the restriction of their vows, the discipline of their creed, and the rigors of the Texas frontier, they had a good life. Their work was creative if not always rewarding, and in the well-established missions the hard labor was done by the Indian converts. In later missions along the

Spain's Last Years / 52

California coast, the Franciscans, accused of an unchristian exploitation of the natives, rejected secularization and clung tenaciously to their missions to resist conversion to parish churches until after the Mexican revolution for independence. In Texas secularization was almost welcomed, and in 1794 it was complete at the Texas missions, except for the three in the La Bahía group.

The third mission in this group, Nuestra Señora del Refugio, was an anachronism. It was not established until 1793, a year before the secularization decree and long after the missionary fires in Texas had been banked. And its purpose was not to expand the frontier or carry Christianity to savages but merely to provide a third mission for deserters from Rosario and the original La Bahía mission, Espíritu Santo de Zuñiga. Padres had worked for years among the Karankawa and associated bands of coastal Indians with only the smallest measure of success. Five years after La Bahía had been moved to the San Antonio River in 1749, the Rosario mission had been established to care for its deserters. Rosario functioned sporadically with frustrating futility and then settled into a complacent routine supported by reduced Indians from Mexico. Refugio's history was much the same. Established at the junction of the San Antonio and Guadalupe rivers, it was moved upstream in 1795. Because of the primitive condition of the local Indians, the three missions in this group were not secularized until 1830 and 1831.

Life in a functioning mission, even those in the La Bahía field, was in many ways a pastoral idyll. Each mission attempted to support itself by farming and maintaining herds of cows, sheep, and pigs. San José, the archetype, had a granary and a grist mill. Most missions processed the clip from the flocks of sheep, and the padres taught Indian women to spin, weave, and dye. Indian men were taught to farm and were used as herdsmen. The fields of the missions at both San Antonio and La Bahía were irrigated with water from the San Antonio River by an ingenious system of ditches. The principal crops were corn and beans, but a wide variety of garden produce was grown, orchards were planted, and fruits such as cantaloupes, watermelons, and pumpkins were regularly harvested.

The general plan of the average mission can be inferred from the following 1785 description of Purísima Concepción de Acuña, translated by J. Autry Dabbs:

> The mission is square in shape and enclosed by a stone and mud wall, low in parts, and provided with three ample openings, one on the east, another on the west, and a third on the south. These have gates of carved wood with good locks. This rampart serves as a wall for houses of the same material. These furnish ample shelter for the Indians. In fact, there

are twenty-three rooms, with flat roofs; and although some of them are in a ruinous state, they are not difficult to restore or repair. In the present year all or nearly all will be rebuilt. On the east side stands the roomy house of the missionaries, and the offices of the community, all made of stone and lime, nearly all provided with arched roofs. This is a one-story building except for one room built above. The sacristy and the church adjoin the main stone and lime structure; they are both very notable for this country because of the two towers and the beautiful cupola. The church and sacristy together are valued at 30,000 *pesos*, and their furnishings and ornaments at three or four thousand. East of the church is a spacious granary about fifteen or twenty *varas* in length, and eight or nine *varas* in width, with walls of stone and lime, and a flat, wooden roof.

The Indians' routine in the missions revolved around prayers, classes, and agricultural labor. Since living at the mission was in essence a trade of freedom for security, desertion was a serious problem for the padres. Indians would come in, stay a few months, and leave. Many returned only when they were hungry, especially in the wintertime when hunting was poor. The Indians may have recognized that the security of the mission was somewhat illusionary. Food and shelter were to be found, but so were the European diseases that often spread like wildfire through the densely inhabited mission communities.

Many of the Indians who accepted Christianity and remained at the missions married and established homes on small plots in the vicinity. A number of these marriages were mixed, primarily between Indian women and mestizos, people of mixed Indian and Spanish lineage, from nearby presidios and villages. Negro slaves and mulatto servants had been brought to Texas by the Spaniards, and unions produced curious mixtures of Hispanic, Negro, and Indian blood. In the passage of generations, around the missions grew up unorganized civil settlements called pueblos, which were permitted some self-government under the close supervision of the mission fathers.

The Presidios It was the soldiers from the presidios, of course, who provided the security for these motley communities. Life in the frontier presidios was usually dull, unattractive, and underpaid. Troops were present primarily for defense purposes, but offensive raids against hostile Indians were rare and the presidios did not often suffer direct attacks. Thus soldier duties were principally escort and patrol; soldier life was an unvaried monotony.

In the presidios discipline was irregular but harsh, and equipment was poor and often neglected. Soldiers were required to buy their clothes and other necessities from the presidio commissary at exorbitant prices, as noted by the Marquis de Rubí. Their meager wages often did not cover their accounts, and rarely could a soldier jingle two silver pesos together at the end of a month. As many of the officers were more interested avariciously in personal profits than in efficient military garrisons, guns and ammunition invariably were in poor supply and antique to the point of uselessness. Indeed, at one time it was reported that the soldiers at the Orcoquisac presidio had no arms at all.

The forts themselves also reflected this dilapidation although their initial construction was usually well done. Several ground plans had been used in building the presidios but all involved a wall or stockade surrounding a group of buildings, usually including a barracks, officers' quarters, a storehouse or two, and a headquarters building. The log presidios in East Texas slipped rapidly into varying states of decay, but the stone and adobe presidios at La Bahía and San Antonio were usually kept in better condition. Several artillery pieces were brought into Texas and mounted on presidial walls, but they were mostly ineffective from lack of repair.

Although the presidios were established to give protection to the missions, which to some extent they did, there was an almost inherent antagonism between the priests and the soldiers. Sometimes this friction reached a point of combustion as at the San Xavier mission, but more often it created a smoldering bitterness. The soldiers, largely despised by the priests and regularly cursed and exploited by their officers, were rarely happy with frontier duty. Many of them, however, at the expiration of their enlistment settled in the pueblos with their Indian or mestizo wives.

The Settlements   Life in the pueblos or villages was probably as routine as that in the missions and presidios. It was subject to nearly as much regulation. Gubernatorial decrees were issued on such minute matters as the cutting of an excessive amount of firewood, and royal taxes were levied in every conceivable form and collected punctually. Fee-paid permits were required to go fishing, to gather nuts, to kill unbranded cattle, and to hunt bears. Spanish bureaucracy seemed to know no limits. Nevertheless, the peoples' lives were not unpleasant. They amused themselves by gambling, drinking, dancing, and horse racing, and since the basic necessities were easily procured, most settlers relaxed into a sort of happy indolence. The climate, especially at San Antonio and La Bahía, was mild. The soil was fertile; crops could be grown almost untended; livestock ran wild and multiplied rapidly; the woods and countryside held abundant game; and the streams were full of fish.

The basic economy of Spanish colonial Texas was naturally agrarian. At both missions and villages a surprisingly wide variety of farming was practiced successfully. Pigs, chickens, cattle, and sheep were raised, the latter more for wool than meat. Settlers were able to sell eggs, beef, garden produce, and homespun cloth to the presidios, although for scant profit. The major source of income and the principal measure of wealth—for coins were extremely scarce—were the large and ever increasing herds of cattle owned by the missions as well as by the settlers. A secondary source of income was illicit trade with the French and the Indians.

The Cattle Industry South Texas was a highly suitable habitat for cattle, and from the first the small herds brought by Alarcón and Aguayo prospered and multiplied. Neither the occasional droughts nor the ravages of Apache and Comanche raiders could check their growth. By the middle-eighteenth century the cattle had increased so greatly that most of them roamed wild through the brush country south of San Antonio. Originally, it is supposed, of Andalusian stock, the animals adapted themselves to the Texas environment through scores of cattle generations, developing longer and longer horns, leaner and tougher bodies, rangier legs, and meaner dispositions. By the mid-nineteenth century they had become the longhorns of today's legend, and in incredibly vast numbers they were the resource for the great cattle industry of Texas, which did not come into its own until after the American Civil War.

The hardy vaqueros of Spanish colonial Texas, however, used, if not invented, all the basic and stylized practices of this industry: working cattle from horseback, roping, branding, gathering in a roundup, and even trail-driving to market. The vaqueros' horses were mustangs, which were nearly as plentiful as the cattle and nearly as wild. And like the cattle they too had changed, from the original Spanish stock to a small, wiry animal capable of great bursts of speed over short distances, eventually to develop into the modern quarter horse. Properly trained, it could outmaneuver longhorns in the rough brush country and carry its rider to roping position.

Supple horsehair lariats, intricate brands so large that they sometimes covered half the side of a cow, roping saddles, and annual roundups to identify and brand calves were all in use before the transfer of Louisiana to Spain in 1763. This event produced the first known trail drives from Texas. In 1779 beef became scarce in Louisiana, and the governor requested the governor of Texas to permit his agent to buy fifteen to twenty hundred head of cattle and drive them back to New Orleans. The trail drive was made along the old road to Nacogdoches, through forests and over rivers that might have caused a nineteenth-century trail boss to turn back. But the drive was successful and, more important, profitable. The next summer three herds of twelve hundred, two thousand, and fifteen hundred respectively were trailed to Louisiana. It has been estimated that from then until the transfer of Louisiana to the United States some fifteen thousand head a year were driven eastward. As late as 1802 the commandant at Nacogdoches reported that ten thousand animals had passed through bound for Louisiana. Shortly afterward the industry died, apparently because of trade restrictions, and was not revived for over half a century.

Cattle sales accounted for the principal revenue in Texas; smuggling may have been second. From the time of the first settlements in East Texas, illicit trade between Frenchmen and Spaniards had thrived. Goods from Louisiana were cheaper than those brought overland from Mexico City, and all decrees and regulations were unenforceable. Presidial captains and even governors were from time to time implicated in contraband trade.

Although farming, ranching, and smuggling were the main occupations—often combined in one man—a 1795 census reveals the presence of merchants, tailors, shoemakers, cart drivers, fishermen, carpenters, mule drivers, blacksmiths, barbers, notary publics, factors for the presidios, and servants. This latter class was large and consisted of regular domestic labor, indentured servants, and slaves, little distinction being made among these types in Spanish Texas.

Texas in 1800 During the last quarter of the eighteenth century both the missionary and the civilian populations of Texas declined. By the close of the century there were not five thousand people in the state, counting troops and civilized Indians as well as civilians. Since the new century was to bring many changes, it will be worthwhile to pause to review the centers of settlement in 1800 and to survey Spanish achievements after a century of occupation.

Far to the west on the Rio Grande near present El Paso, the little mission settlement of Isleta continued to survive. Located in present Texas, it was then considered a part of New Mexico. Down the Rio Grande there was a small military outpost in the Big Bend near present Presidio under the jurisdiction of Chihuahua. Known generally as Presidio del Norte and occasionally as El Fortin de San José, this post had been established in 1759, abandoned in 1767, and reoccupied in 1773. Rarely were as many as fifty men stationed there although it was operative as late as 1814.

57 / *Spanish Colonial Life*

Near modern Eagle Pass, across the river from San Juan Bautista, a few ranchers raised herds of cattle, but there was no settlement on the Texas side above Laredo. With its scant two or three hundred people Laredo was one of the most isolated villages on the frontier and was subject to incessant Apache and Comanche raids. Its sister village of Dolores, also founded by Escandón, had disappeared by 1800. Laredo, of course, was not at that time under the jurisdiction of the governor of Texas. From Laredo to the mouth of the river there were scattered haciendas on the Texas side, but no settlements.

Texas proper consisted of three major centers of population: Nacogdoches, La Bahía, and San Antonio. Nacogdoches contained a church, a small military garrison, and a population of about five hundred. La Bahía included the three missions, the old presidio, and the pueblo that had evolved at present Goliad. The population was approximately twelve hundred. San Antonio was without question the seat of Spanish culture in Texas. It comprised five missions, the only authorized villa, San Fernando, the adjacent pueblo of Béxar, San Fernando church, a governor's palace, and a military garrison. The population was about twenty-five hundred.

Following the secularization of the mission, all but Concepcíon and San José were closed, and these became small parish churches. The Alamo (San Antonio de Valero) was converted to a military hospital and was occasionally used to quarter troops. The governor's home and office on the west side of the plaza was probably the most elaborate building in town, although some of the more substantial citizens had built a few stout and roomy houses.

Small as it was, the population of Texas was cosmopolitan—a fact not often recognized. In addition to families of Hispanic origin, criollos and native Spaniards, there were numerous mestizos, Negroes, mulattoes, *indios*, and varying mixtures of these. There were also traces of Irish and French background. To this conglomerate were soon to be added English, Dutch, German, and Anglo-American strains.

It is a baffling and futile task to attempt to assess Spanish achievements in Texas or to answer the often-posed question, Was Spanish Texas a failure? In a little over a century Spaniards had explored most of Texas, named most of the rivers and bays, pacified some of the Indians, established permanent and durable settlements, and contributed the basis for the cattle industry. (The large proportion of the modern population of Texas that calls itself Latin American, speaks the Spanish language, and worships at the Catholic church descends not from the early Hispanic population, being composed principally of more recent immigrants to the state.)

On the other hand, Spain failed to populate Texas sufficiently to hold it, and during the latter period of Spanish rule the population declined. Spain failed to develop the economy of the area or to utilize the vast fertile acres that were so inviting to later homesteaders. But she did maintain her jurisdiction over the area until 1821, when Texas was wrested from her in the Mexican Revolution. And she did accomplish her primary objective: to hold Texas against foreign intrusion.

Alarums and Excursions in the Wings

Spain's New Neighbor Shortly after the turn of the century two major factors interacted to change the somewhat complacent course of Texas and point it toward a new destiny. One of these was the acquisition of Louisiana by the United States; the other was the independence movement in Mexico. Together they were to produce a little over a decade of excited confusion and nearly a score of expeditions, filibusters, and insurgencies. They each had roots in intrigue and international politics and to some extent in the success of the American Revolution against Britain.

Aristocratic officials of the Spanish empire could not help being appalled at the principle of separatism, the principle that colonies could declare their independence from their mother country and establish their own government. Such a thought was, of course, abhorrent to the masters of the greatest colonial empire in the world. Yet, incongruously, Spain profited from the American Revolution, for by the Treaty of Paris of 1783 Britain returned Florida to her, a result of the alliance between Spain and France known as the "Family Compact." In this same treaty, Britain gave to the new United States all the territory south of the Great Lakes and west to the Mississippi River, making her Spain's neighbor on the borders of both Florida and Louisiana.

In the Pinckney Treaty (San Lorenzo) of 1795, Spain adjusted the Florida boundary and gave the United States the right to use the Mississippi River. But secretly Spanish officials began to conspire to split off the territory west of the Appalachians and establish a Spanish protectorate over it. Their tool was James Wilkinson, former general in the Revolutionary Army, who became a secret agent of Spain in 1787 and remained in Spanish pay for many years thereafter despite his position of trust for the United States. When an initial conspiracy to bring Kentucky under Spanish influence failed, Wilkinson reentered the United States Army and fought in the Indian wars in the old Northwest. In 1800 he was given command of United States troops in the South, a position he held until 1812.

An isolated incident suggests that Wilkinson may have been only an opportunist playing both sides or even a double-agent. His clerk and bookkeeper, Philip Nolan, moved from the Wilkinson home in Kentucky to Nacogdoches in 1790 with a Spanish passport apparently secured for him by the general. Thereafter until his death Nolan divided his time between Texas and the United States, capturing wild horses to sell in Louisiana and living among the Indians in northeastern Texas. Among other things that hint he was something more than a renegade, he visited the governor of Texas in 1795 or 1796 and had an interview with Thomas Jefferson in 1799! On his last trip into Texas in December 1800, his passport was canceled by the Spanish government, and he was killed on March 4, 1801, while resisting a Spanish force sent to arrest him. Neither Philip Nolan nor his activity has any bearing on the mainstream of Texas history; the affair has been magnified out of all proportion by romanticists who credit him with a greater role in the intrigues of the time than he probably had or who anachronistically associate him with the westward surge of American frontiersmen into the Louisiana Purchase.

In any event, the failure of the conspiracy in Kentucky to establish control over the trans-Appalachian country led Spanish officials to reassess their position in Louisiana. They greatly feared intrusion by Anglo-American frontiersmen, but as one Spaniard said, "You can't lock up an open field." Decadent Spain was not strong enough to fortify and defend the entire Mississippi River. Therefore, when Napoleon developed fleeting illusions of reestablishing the old French colonial empire, Spain unprotestingly transferred Louisiana to him in the Treaty of San Ildefonso in 1800, which was kept secret for several years while Spain continued to govern Louisiana.

But the secret came out, and Thomas Jefferson, newly inaugurated as president of the United States in 1801, determined to acquire New Orleans from France so that Mississippi River commerce could continue unmolested. He commissioned James Monroe and Robert R. Livingston to negotiate with Napoleon's government for the purchase of New Orleans. For months, the negotiations seemed futile, but suddenly, in April 1803, through his ministers, Napoleon asked what kind of a bargain the Americans would strike for all of Louisiana. Hard-pressed by a revolution in Haiti and an imminent war with Britain, the emperor had abandoned his imperial schemes. The Americans quickly negotiated an unauthorized treaty for the purchase of Louisiana for sixty million francs.

Jefferson overcame his constitutional scruples about the agreement and pushed its ratification through the senate. On December 20, 1803, Louisiana was officially transferred to the United States. Spanish officials found themselves in a worse dilemma than before, for now the young United States was its neighbor along an undetermined boundary that touched much closer to the heart of the empire.

The western boundary of Louisiana had never been defined because when Spain acquired Louisiana in 1763 it adjoined her other possessions in North America. When she returned it to France in 1800, the treaty merely specified that it had the same boundary as when France had ceded it to Spain. Consequently, the United States acquired the same vague line and with it all of the old French claims to western North America. Many in the United States, including Jefferson, considered Louisiana to extend southwest to include La Salle's Fort St. Louis. Others claimed its limits were the drainage area of the Mississippi River. After a decade and a half negotiations to settle this boundary culminated in the Treaty of 1819.

While diplomats parlayed the question, Jefferson's insatiable curiosity had led him to send explorers to determine the nature of the land and the people. The famous Lewis and Clark expedition braved the upper Missouri; Dr. John Sibley made two trips on the Red River and reported to Jefferson on the Indian tribes he visited; and in 1806 Thomas Freeman searched for the headwaters of the Red River and Captain Zebulon Pike reached the headwaters of the Arkansas. Spanish officials viewed these explorations and the independent influx of American frontiersmen with trepidation and alarm. Once more they tried to mount a conspiracy to wrest the Mississippi Valley from the United States. The leading figure in this episode was Aaron Burr, who in 1806, after long conferences with General James Wilkinson led a small group of armed men down the Mississippi on purposes that never became clear. He was arrested for treason but was acquitted. His accomplice, and perhaps the mastermind of the plot, James Wilkinson, was not touched although he was apparently still receiving pay as a Spanish agent. As soon as the warrant was issued for Burr's arrest, Wilkinson did an about-face, exposed the plot, fortified New Orleans, and prepared to defend Louisiana against an imagined Spanish attack.

His activities caused the Spanish commandant at Nacogdoches, Simón de Herrera, to call for reinforcements and move his men toward the Sabine. Herrera may have believed that the Burr intrigue was aimed at an invasion of Texas and that Wilkinson and the United States Army would participate.

Had not many in the United States publicly declared that the Louisiana Purchase extended to the Rio Grande? Shortly after the American occupation of New Orleans, Spain regarrisoned the old presidios at Orcoquisac and Los Adaes. Orders were issued to stop the Freeman expedition bound up the Red River and to arrest Pike if he entered Spanish territory. Freeman was turned back in July 1806 by a detachment of Spanish troops near the present boundary of Arkansas. Pike, having reached the upper Arkansas in November and having turned south to find the source of the Red River, was arrested by a company of Spanish dragoons in present New Mexico and escorted to Chihuahua. Hostilities between Spain and the United States seemed imminent.

Wilkinson demanded that Spanish troops evacuate Los Adaes; Herrera demanded pledges of assurance against invasion of Texas. The two met in November 1806 and concluded an informal agreement that prevented an armed clash along the border. This Neutral Ground Agreement provided that Wilkinson would keep American troops east of the Arroyo Hondo, a stream in western Louisiana, and that Herrera would limit Spanish activity to west of the Sabine River. Between these two streams and for an undetermined distance north, there would be no settlement and no jurisdiction until the joint boundary commission established the Louisiana border.

Despite the inability of these diplomats to agree, this unofficial arrangement was scrupulously honored by the two military men and their successors. The absence of law in the Neutral Ground, however, made it a sanctuary for brigands and outlaws, and twice, in 1810 and 1812, the two commanders sent joint military expeditions into the area to try to expel the outlaws. The Neutral Ground Agreement prevented international conflict, but it created an area that for years later was tainted as a haven of thieves. And in part the unsavory reputation was deserved.

Meantime, Spanish officials turned their anxieties to the northern frontier, where Pike and Freeman had created alarm. They feared not invasion from the north but possible American intrigues with the Indians. For nearly a generation there had been something approaching peace with the northern tribes. Was the United States trying to break the Indians' loose allegiance to Spain? Although Pike had been thoroughly interrogated before he was allowed to return, suspicious Spanish minds could not believe that he and other Americans who had penetrated the region were free of duplicity.

In 1808, therefore, the commandant of the *Provincias Internas* ordered an expedition to travel from San Antonio to Santa Fe to distribute presents among the Indians, especially the Comanches, to renew their pledges of allegiance, and to try to discover what the machinations of the Americans had been. It was Spain's last expedition in the Southwest. Francisco Amangual, a career officer in the army, assembled five companies from Texas, Coahuila, and Nuevo León in San Antonio and set out on a leisurely trip across West Texas. He journeyed first to the old presidio on the San Saba, where he fell in with a friendly band of Comanches, then to the Concho rivers, out to the foot of the Caprock, north along its edge to one of the canyons penetrating the High Plains, and then across to New Mexico and Santa Fe. He could discern no evidence that there had been any Americans operating among the many Comanche bands that he encountered. In 1809 he returned by way of the Pecos River to San Antonio. His report, however, did little to allay the mounting Spanish suspicions of the United States, suspicions that in fact were unwarranted.

The Independence Movement in Mexico Royal officials would have done better to look for trouble within the empire, for in Mexico ferment and unrest were seething. Indeed, all the colonies and Spain itself evinced dissatisfaction with the old autocratic regime. In the light of the exciting philosophies and successful examples of the American and French revolutions, Spanish colonials began to consider independence, and the lower classes throughout the empire began to dream of Liberty, Equality, and Fraternity. Although officials tried to exclude the literature of the Age of Reason from Mexico, it was futile. Secret clubs and "literary societies" met, discussed, and waxed enthusiastic over the new ideas. This intellectual infiltration proved to be far more dangerous to the empire than the mere appearance on the frontiers of an occasional American trapper or explorer. And in Mexico, where a small class of wealthy criollos dominated the great mass of peasants and peons, the situation was explosive.

At a little village church in Dolores, north of Mexico City, a parish priest named Miguel Hidalgo y Costilla was to ignite the powder keg. Greatly touched by the hopeless plight of the lower orders in Mexico and thoroughly indoctrinated with the inflammable ideas of democracy, Father Hidalgo organized a conspiracy to overthrow the despotic government. It was for the most part a movement of the lower classes, but a few rich mestizos and criollos participated, intent not on republican government but on separation from troubled Spain, where in 1808 Napoleon's brother Joseph had been placed on the throne.

When the plot was prematurely exposed by royalist spies, Father Hidalgo hastily issued on September 16, 1810, the *Grito de Dolores*, exhorting his followers to rise and overthrow their Spanish rulers. Initial successes turned soon to disastrous losses as persons in power in Mexico began to suspect that the Hidalgistas desired more than mere separation from Spain. The entire socioeconomic order was at stake. A series of reverses sent Hidalgo fleeing northward, the first of an almost constant succession of Mexican liberals to seek refuge in Texas. He was captured by royalist troops in March 1811 and executed in Chihuahua.

Although Hidalgo did not reach Texas, his ideas and many of his followers did. On January 22, 1811, Juan Bautista de las Casas, with a small band of men, took the royalist military headquarters in San Antonio, succeeding largely by surprise. He imprisoned Governor Manuel de Salcedo and Colonel Simón de Herrera and proclaimed himself the chief executive of Texas under the revolution. Quickly he sent detachments into La Bahía and Nacogdoches and there repeated his easy victory. Royalist officials were replaced with revolutionaries, and Las Casas notified Father Hidalgo that the revolution was successful in Texas.

But the triumph was short-lived, besides being of no help to the priest. On March 2 a counter-revolution led by Juan Zambrano deposed Las Casas as easily as he had taken Salcedo. Zambrano, a native Texan, a landowner and a rancher, a one-time army officer, and a subdeacon in the Catholic Church, had quickly organized resistance with the aid of such prominent Texans as Juan Veramendi, Erasmo Seguín, and Francisco Ruiz. The counter-revolutionists repeated Las Casas' performance in La Bahía and Nacogdoches, and Texas was soon back in the royalist camp. Zambrano's military junta turned the government back to civil authorities on July 22, 1811, and the episode ended. But it was only a precursor.

Filibusterers and Patriots From Nuevo Santander, present Tamaulipas, a landowner and merchant named Bernardo Gutiérrez de Lara had met in Saltillo with Father Hidalgo before his capture and had plotted the overthrow of his native province. When the Hidalgo uprising collapsed, Gutiérrez fled across Texas to Louisiana where he took up residence in Natchitoches. He was to prove to be guileful with a hardy instinct for survival as he schemed and conspired for Mexican independence during the next decade. He was one of a substantial number of Mexican liberal leaders who found sanctuary in the United States, but more than the others he focused attention on Texas.

Gutiérrez believed as did Las Casas and Ignacio Aldama, Hidalgo's special representative who was captured with Las Casas, that Texas could be made the key to Mexican independence. It was isolated from Mexico City; it was already noted for liberal attitudes; and it was adjacent to the United States, from which volunteers could be drawn. Gutiérrez was able with little difficulty to capture the imaginations of many Americans. In Washington, with a letter of introduction from Dr. John Sibley, Gutiérrez explained his plan for the establishment of an independent republic in

Texas. Despite a lack of official support, he may have drawn some encouragement from his reception. He returned to Louisiana with letters of introduction to Governor W. C. C. Claiborne and William Shaler, a consular agent in Natchitoches. Shaler was to become one of his principal advisers.

With Shaler's aid, Gutiérrez persuaded Lieutenant Augustus W. Magee to resign from the United States Army and take military command of his filibustering expedition into Texas. Scores of eager volunteers gathered in Natchitoches, some idealistically imbued, others mere soldiers of fortune bent on plunder, and still others seeking the thrill of adventure. With a combined force of Mexicans and Americans totaling about one hundred thirty men, Gutiérrez and Magee crossed the Sabine on August 8, 1812, and four days later easily routed the royalist troops at Nacogdoches.

Volunteers, both Mexicans and Americans, continued to flock to the standard as Gutiérrez had predicted. When the expedition attacked a royalist post on the Trinity, it had swelled to about seven hundred men, and again it won an easy victory. From there the invaders took the old La Bahía presidio on November 7. But they were soon surrounded by a royalist army under Governor Salcedo. Magee died, according to many, by suicide, and command of the insurgents devolved upon another American, Samuel Kemper. Kemper drove the royalists off, winning two small skirmishes on February 10 and 13, 1813, and a month later followed Salcedo to San Antonio. On March 29 he defeated a force of twelve hundred men commanded by Simón de Herrera and took possession of San Antonio.

Gutiérrez now assumed leadership. He either ordered or condoned the execution of fourteen royalist officers, including Herrera and the governor. This cruelty so disgusted the Americans that nearly a hundred men under Kemper abandoned the expedition and returned to the United States. Gutiérrez organized a revolutionary junta to govern Texas and issued a declaration of independence. In August, José Álvarez de Toledo arrived in San Antonio and with Shaler's backing assumed command of the insurgency. Gutiérrez retired to Natchitoches just ahead of a punitive royalist invasion.

Under Joaquín de Arredondo, the royalist army reached the outskirts of San Antonio on August 15 and three days later on the Medina River ambushed the now demoralized revolutionary army under Toledo. The Battle of Medina ended the revolution. Once again Texas was under the Spanish banner, and once again the liberals fled pell-mell for the safety of the American border. Not all escaped; Arredondo was more revengeful than the insurgents and in a bloody purge, known as the *noche trieste,* he executed many citizens believed to have collaborated with Gutiérrez.

In Louisiana the Mexican patriots, for so they may be called, regrouped and began anew plans for the invasion of Texas and the *Provincias Internas*. An organization for a paper Republic of Mexico was perfected by a New Orleans group, and a French naval officer, Luis Aury, was named governor of the province of Texas and commissioner of the port of Galveston. All he had to do was to occupy Texas and open the port of Galveston! But Aury was a man of experience in the fine art of privateering. With several privateers, he occupied Galveston Island in July 1816. After quelling a mutiny in his own forces, he built a shanty town on the end of the island. The rebels' flag was raised there on September 13, 1816. Success followed rapidly as the privateers captured and hauled into port a succession of Spanish prize ships. Their cargoes were divided among Aury and the ships' captains, and then the rebels' share was smuggled into Louisiana and sold at a mercantile establishment in Natchitoches operated by none other than Gutiérrez de Lara!

This sudden prosperity did not endure, however, for the New Orleans associates whom Aury represented insisted on an invasion of Mexico. General Francisco Mina arrived in Galveston and planned a joint operation with Aury to land a filibustering expedition on the Tamaulipan coast. The expedition left Galveston in April 1817 but was decisively defeated in short order by a royalist force. Aury escaped and returned to Galveston to resume operations.

But to his consternation a professional pirate had moved in during his absence. Jean Lafitte (sometimes spelled Laffite), long known for his nefarious adventures around the mouth of the Mississippi, had made the island the headquarters of his illicit operations. Aury could not dislodge him, and after temporarily shifting his base to Matagorda Bay, he left Texas. Lafitte organized a government on Galveston Island allegedly loyal to the Mexican Republic, but he seems also to have been employed as a secret agent for Spanish royalists. Intrigue was piled upon intrigue, while Lafitte and his brother built a small fortune from the capture and illegal sale in New Orleans of Spanish cargoes. The population on the island increased to about a thousand buccaneers and their associates. Lafitte's infestation on Galveston Island was ended in May 1820, when a U.S. Navy cutter sailed into the harbor, and Lafitte and his gang meekly sailed away to Yucatan to continue for six more years his raids on Caribbean shipping.

During his occupation of the island, however, he nearly became involved in two other filibustering schemes. One was headed by a French general, Charles Lallemand, more a colonist than a freebooter, and the other by an American physician, James Long, more a misguided patriot than an adventurer.

Following Napoleon's defeat at Waterloo, Lallemand, one of his most trusted commanders, fled to the United States. He seems to have developed a vague scheme to establish a military colony in Texas, possibly with the purpose of winning Mexico for Joseph Bonaparte, the then deposed king of Spain. With about one hundred fifty men Lallemand reached Galveston Island in January 1818. Lafitte refused to become embroiled but helped the Frenchmen move up the Trinity River to a location near present Liberty. There Lallemand erected fortifications and several log buildings, naming the settlement Champ d'Asile. Although he issued a manifesto that stated it was one of the natural rights of men to seek homes in the wilderness, he later claimed to have sought the permission of the Spanish government for the settlement. That he actually planned a coup in Texas on behalf of Bonaparte may be seriously doubted.

Whatever its ultimate purpose, within six months the venture ended in a rout. Apprised by Indians of the unauthorized presence of the French, Governor Antonio Martínez in San Antonio sent troops to expel them. Long before even advance units reached Champ d'Asile, the French learned of the movement and fled back to Galveston. A few enlisted with Lafitte, but most were transported by the pirate to New Orleans in July 1818.

Dr. James Long, who next came to plague Lafitte for aid, headed a group of filibusterers whose purpose was to make Texas a part of the United States. They had been spurred to action by a treaty between the United States and Spain in which the long disputed western boundary of Louisiana was fixed at such a line as to cause a storm of protest in the United States. This was the Treaty of 1819, otherwise known as the Adams-Onís Treaty or the Florida Purchase Treaty.

The Adams-Onís Treaty   This treaty was among the most important foreign negotiations in American history. It established a boundary line visible on the map of Texas today; it secured Florida for the United States; and it established a significant precedent in the handling of foreign claims. Drafted by John Quincy Adams, then United States secretary of state, and Luis de Onís, Spanish ambassador in Washington, the treaty provided that Spain would transfer Florida to the United States if the American government would assume the claims of United States citizens against Spain for the losses incurred from depredation by Florida

Indians. International code held that Spain was responsible for the Indians under her jurisdiction; and the raids had reached such proportions as to create serious international incidents, not the least of which was Andrew Jackson's illegal penetration of Florida and hanging of two Englishmen who were instigating some of the attacks. The amount of the American claims was estimated to be five million dollars, the figure specified in the treaty as the purchase price for Florida. This procedure was to be followed later in an attempt to trade claims against Mexico for Texas, to buy California, and finally to pay for the Mexican Cession after the Mexican War.

As a sop to Spain, the treaty set the boundary of Louisiana well within the area that the United States might have claimed. The boundary was defined as follows: from the mouth of the Sabine River up the west bank of the Sabine to the 32nd parallel, thence directly north to the Red River and up it to the 100th meridian, thence up that line to the Arkansas River and up its south bank to the headwaters, thence directly north to the 42nd parallel, and thence along the 42nd parallel to the Pacific. Spain was unconcerned that north of the 42nd parallel Russia and Britain as well as the United States had established valid claims in the Pacific Northwest.

Along the southeastern part of this line, the United States had given up territory that many believed was rightfully a part of Louisiana, including particularly the drainage area of the Red River and the upper Arkansas. Others, of course, resented the assignment of a vague claim to the Rio Grande. At an especially vehement protest meeting in Natchez, Mississippi, Dr. James Long was selected to lead a filibustering expedition to restore Texas to the United States. Long and his associates had deluded themselves that the people of Texas were ripe to rebel against Spanish despotism and link their future to the American flag. There are two interesting sidelights in the organization of this expedition. One is that Long's wife, Jane Wilkinson, was a niece of General James Wilkinson, who actively lent his support to Long's plan. The other is that Gutiérrez de Lara quickly associated himself with the venture and assured Long that he could win the support of the people of Texas.

The expedition, of about one hundred twenty men, crossed the Sabine in June 1819 and occupied Nacogdoches with ease on June 21. There, Long, Gutiérrez, and various citizens of Nacogdoches organized a provisional government and on June 23 declared the independence of Texas. Because of a scarcity of supplies, Long scattered his forces, grown to about three hundred, to live off the country and went to Galveston Island to try to persuade Lafitte to join him, but Lafitte refused. During October and November, while Long was absent from Nacogdoches, an army of about five hundred men from San Antonio drove the fragmented force of filibusters from Texas. Long slipped back into Nacogdoches and then fled to New Orleans.

In New Orleans he fell in with a group of Mexican liberals headed by José Trespalacios who were planning another invasion of Texas. They joined forces temporarily and in April 1820 established a headquarters on Point Bolivar opposite Galveston Island. Soon Long broke with Trespalacios and leading about fifty men sailed down the coast to the San Antonio River and proceeded upstream to La Bahía in September and October 1821. The town and poorly defended presidio fell quickly to the invaders on October 4, but four days later a royalist army invested the site and Long was forced to surrender. Long was imprisoned in Mexico, where he was killed by a guard six months later in what was reported as an accident but was believed by many to have been instigated by Trespalacios.

Long had left his wife on Point Bolivar when he sailed for La Bahía. There she gave birth to a daughter in December 1821 and remained encamped until she learned of her husband's capture and death. She returned to Natchez, but reentered Texas as one of Austin's colony in 1824. Known affectionately as the Mother of Texas, she operated a boarding house in Brazoria and was closely acquainted with most of the prominent Texans of later years. The Mexican government denied her petition for a pension in which she claimed her husband had died for the cause of Mexican independence.

The Beginnings of Anglo-American Settlement

Miller County The Treaty of 1819, which Long and his followers so disastrously refused to accept, defined the boundary between Spanish and American territory with precision, using Melish's 1818 map as a reference. But describing a line in words and locating it on the ground are two entirely different things, and a serious problem arose because of misinterpretation and the lack of an official survey. Two rivers flow southward into Sabine Lake near the Gulf: the Neches on the west and the Sabine on the east. Despite the fact that the Sabine was well identified and that it was accurately depicted on Melish's map as the eastern of the two rivers, some Americans immediately claimed that the western river, the Neches, was in fact the Sabine River intended in the treaty. The contention, supported in the United States mainly by land speculators, was without basis and cannot be justified, although there were doubtlessly a few sincere but misinformed people who also advocated it. The Neches River claim was never taken seriously by either the United States or Mexico; however, Andrew Jackson on several occasions expressed his belief in its possible validity, simply because no less an authority than Dr. John Sibley of Natchitoches, who had described the Red River country to Jefferson in 1803 and 1804, had first advanced the theory.

More perplexing than the Neches River claim was the location of the 32nd parallel. Until an official survey was made, no one would know for practical purposes where the boundary was. And because of political turmoil in Mexico, a survey was long delayed. About a half-degree north of the 32nd parallel, the Sabine describes a sharp bend and in its upper courses runs nearly east and west. Consequently, a slight northerly mislocation of the 32nd parallel would cause a considerable western displacement of the line due north from the junction of the river and the parallel. Melish's map showed the river's curve even more exaggerated and farther south than it is. It is not surprising, therefore, that in the absence of a survey much misunderstanding should arise over this section of the boundary.

Acting unquestionably in good faith, the Territorial Legislature of Arkansas in 1820 created Miller County in its southwest corner adjacent to the treaty line. Almost immediately settlers began moving into what they believed was Miller County, north and east of the Sabine River. Lands were located and filed on, and the land office soon began to issue titles to those few who could afford the purchase price of $1.25 an acre. Probably the first settlement in the area was near a bend in the Red River that had been known for many years as Pecan Point. There George and Alex Wetmore had established an Indian trading post in 1815. The following year at least three settlers, Walter Pool, Charles Burkham, and Claiborne Wright, had moved to the site, and when Miller County was created in 1820, there were at least twelve families and five Indian traders calling the Pecan Point settlement home. In 1825 Jacob Black patented the land in the loop of the river at the actual Pecan Point. The Pecan Point settlement, in present northeastern Red River County, Texas, continued to grow slowly.

More prosperous was nearby Jonesborough, also in present Red River County at the site of the present town of Davenport. It was named for Henry Jones, a trapper and hunter in the region, but the first permanent settlers were probably Adam Lawrence and William Hensley. When Miller County was created, there were at least a dozen families at Jonesborough, and in 1821 a large number of settlers moved in from across the Red River in Indian territory. In 1832 Jonesborough became the county seat of Miller County.

Miller County was thus a legitimate, if inaccurately located, American settlement. That most of it was later proved to be within Texas does not, as has been often intimated, imply that the people who moved there were unscrupulous poachers on Spanish and later Mexican soil. In any case, when in 1834 a Mexican official, Juan N. Almonte, visited the area, believing it within Mexico, he assured the settlers that they would receive land titles from the Mexican government if it indeed proved to be Mexican territory. Almonte noted then that Johnsburg, as he called it, had a population of two thousand. By that time, although no official survey had yet been made, the people themselves were in serious doubt about their location, and because the land policy of Mexico was far more generous than that of the United States, many applied for Mexican land titles. An excellent example of the ambivalence among the settlers is that Richard Ellis in 1836 represented the area in the Texas convention at Washington-on-the-Brazos (and was elected its president) while his son was duly representing Miller County in the Arkansas legislature.

Moses Austin While Miller County was being created, a more important Anglo-American settlement had begun. In that year, 1820, a scheme for colonizing Anglo-Americans in Spanish Texas was born in the enterprising mind of a man named Moses Austin, a native of Connecticut, then fifty-nine years old. At the age of twenty-two he had moved to Philadelphia to enter his brother's mercantile firm, and a few years later he had opened a branch store in Richmond, Virginia. In 1791 he became interested in lead mining in the southwestern part of that state. Persistent rumors of incredibly rich deposits of lead in Spanish Louisiana led him in 1798 to move his family to what is now southeastern Missouri.

He obtained a grant of a league of land from the Spanish government, built smelter furnaces and a shot tower, established a general store, and founded the town of Potosi. The venture was apparently successful from the beginning, and after the United States acquired the territory in 1803, Austin's affairs prospered greatly. His business suffered during the War of 1812, and in an attempt to stimulate the economy of his region he helped in 1816 to found the Bank of St. Louis. To do so, he hypothecated most of his property and assets, and the bank's failure in the Panic of 1819 virtually wiped him out. Under the stress of financial ruin he developed the plan to colonize Texas.

How the plan came to evolve in his mind, or even precisely what it was, is not known. Three elements, however, as Austin was probably aware made it feasible: (1) Since he had previously received a grant from Spain and had lived under her laws in Missouri, Texas officials would look favorably on his proposal. (2) Thousands of others had also been hurt or bankrupted by the Panic and would welcome an opportunity for a new start in a foreign land. (3) Public land in the United States was priced too high for the average settler, and some believed that the major cause of the Panic was the credit feature of the Land Act of 1816, which by permitting payment in four annual installments had encouraged many homesteaders as well as land speculators to overextend themselves. So prevalent was this idea that in 1820 congress passed a new land act requiring that the full cost be paid at the time of purchase. Although the Land Act of 1820 lowered the minimum price to $1.25 an acre, it was still too expensive for the average pioneer farmer.

Thus Austin no doubt believed that if he could obtain lands in Texas to sell at lower prices than the minimum in the United States, he would have no difficulty in attracting settlers and could turn a handsome profit. In December 1820 he arrived in San Antonio to lay his project before the governor, Antonio Martínez. But Martínez, sharing the jealous suspicions his superiors had of Americans, refused to listen and ordered Austin out of the province. As Austin was dejectedly returning to his lodgings, there occurred, in the words of the great Texas historian, Eugene C. Barker, "one of the fortuitous accidents of history." Austin encountered an old acquaintance, Baron de Bastrop. Bastrop was an influential man in the northern Spanish provinces and was supposed to have been at one time immensely wealthy. Austin had met him in Louisiana when Bastrop was involved in land speculation there.

Bastrop was an enigma on the Spanish frontier. He was not a Spaniard and spoke the Castilian tongue with a thick accent. Because he kept his origin and personal history a closely guarded secret, there was much speculation about his antecedents. But because he was a large and powerful man and an expert swordsman and pistoleer, there was no one to gainsay him his title. Furthermore, when he first appeared in Spanish territory, he possessed a substantial quantity of gold and spent it freely on land purchases in Louisiana. Some said he was a runaway member of Frederick of Prussia's private guard; others guessed he was a Prussian soldier of fortune in the secret service of the Spanish crown; a few believed him a French nobleman; and members of the Spanish foreign office seem to have been convinced he was an adventurer from the United States. On his death in 1827 his will revealed his true name as Felipe Enrique Neri and his birthplace as Holland. But not until quite recently did historical researches stumble upon his whole story. He had been a respected family man and a tax collector until he suddenly disappeared from Holland with most of the annual revenue from his jurisdiction.

It was, however, on that wintry day in 1820 in San Antonio, Texas, that he made his greatest mark in history. After his chance encounter with Austin he promptly interceded on Austin's behalf, and it is evidence of Bastrop's status as well as Martínez' inconsistency that the governor then agreed to a conference. Giving the project tacit, if not direct, approval, Martínez forwarded Austin's petition to Joaquín de Arredondo, the commandant of the Eastern Interior Provinces at Monterrey. This was the same Arredondo who had crushed the mixed force of Americans and Mexican liberals under Toledo in the Battle of Medina in 1813, who had ordered the Long expedition expelled from Texas, and who had coped with other filibustering efforts organized by the Mexican liberals in the United States. He could hardly be expected to approve the establishment of a colony of Americans within his jurisdiction.

As unexplainable as the chance that threw Austin into Bastrop's path is the illogical fact that Arredondo approved the proposal. Arredondo was influenced perhaps by Bastrop's intercession, perhaps by Austin's previous contributions to Spanish Louisiana, and perhaps by the hope that legally colonized, law-abiding Americans might somehow affect the filibusters in Texas. In any case, on January 17, 1821, he gave Austin permission to introduce three hundred families into an area of two hundred thousand acres. The terms of the grant were as ambiguous as Arredondo's approval was anomalous. Nothing was stated about the location of the two hundred thousand acres; presumably it would have to be in an unoccupied region. Nor was anything said about how the grant would be administered or the land subdivided or the titles conferred. Presumably Austin was to handle these details, and he no doubt thought that he himself had received the two hundred thousand acres although his title was not stipulated in Arredondo's permission.

Austin had remained in San Antonio and did not learn of the grant until March. Despite the vagueness of the terms, he was elated and hurried back to his home in Potosi to organize the project and begin active colonizing. But tragedy awaited him, and a series of cataclysmic events in Mexico nearly prevented the culmination of the scheme. Nonetheless, this plan was the beginning of a deluge of American migration to Texas during the next decade, and to Moses Austin must go the credit for opening the floodgates.

4

The Mexican Years

The First Colony

Stephen F. Austin Death mounted Moses Austin's saddle as he returned home from Texas in the spring of 1821. Weakened by the unaccustomed rigors of his long journey and beset by spring rains and cold winds, Austin contracted pneumonia and died after a lingering illness on June 10, 1821. Before his death he had persuaded his eldest son, Stephen Fuller Austin, to join him in the Texas enterprise. Young Austin, then twenty-seven years old, had been somewhat reluctant, having left Potosi after the collapse of his father's business to make a new start as an attorney. But, more to help his father than from any conviction that the venture would be successful, he agreed and to finance the project arranged a loan from a New Orleans friend, Joseph H. Hawkins, with whom he had planned to read law. Stephen Austin was in Natchitoches, awaiting his father to accompany him to San Antonio, when he learned of his death. He decided to proceed with the colonization scheme if the Spanish government would recognize him as his father's heir, and so he rode to San Antonio in the summer of 1821 with Erasmo Seguín and Juan Veramendi.

PRINCIPAL TOWNS IN COLONIAL TEXAS
about 1835

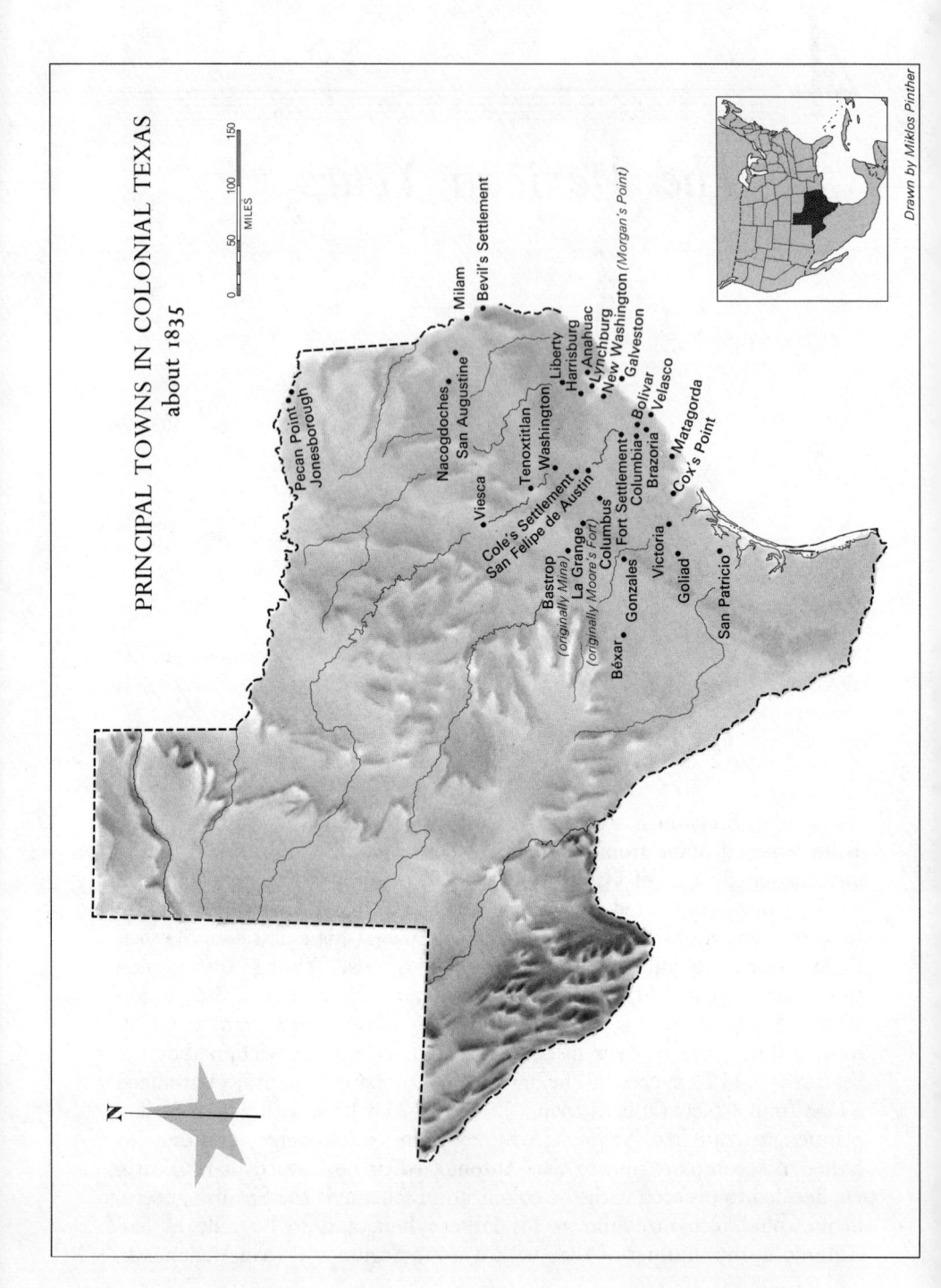

Governor Martínez gave him permission to take over the Moses Austin grant and helped him work out the details. Austin was to offer land to colonists for a twelve and a half cent per acre fee, which he could retain for his services. Each head of a family would receive six hundred forty acres, an additional three hundred twenty acres for each member of his family, and eighty acres for each slave. Austin was to be responsible for the good conduct of the colonists and to administer the government of the colony as an agent of the governor. He would also be required to organize a militia among the settlers for protection from Indians, as Martínez would not provide troops. The final problem was the selection of a site. Martínez authorized Austin to explore the coastal plains between the San Antonio and Brazos rivers and to choose the best location. While returning to New Orleans, Austin made a careful reconnaissance and decided to settle his colonists on the rich bottomlands along the Colorado and Brazos rivers.

Advertising the generous terms of the grant through newspapers, Austin received enthusiastic responses from hundreds of prospective colonists. With funds from his friend and partner Hawkins, Austin bought supplies and chartered a schooner, the *Lively*, to carry the supplies and some colonists to the mouth of the Colorado. He himself proceeded overland in December 1821 to meet other settlers who had already begun moving to the colony. Several families were there when he arrived, including that of Josiah H. Bell, who was to become his deputy. By the end of 1821 there were settlers located at present Columbus on the Colorado and at present Washington-on-the-Brazos. Most prominent of the first arrivals was Jared E. Groce, a wealthy planter who had earlier moved from Georgia to Alabama seeking better land. He came overland with a caravan of fifty wagons and ninety slaves and established Bernardo Plantation in present Waller County. Men usually came alone to look over the colony and select their land before sending for their families. During the first three months of 1822, one hundred fifty such "prospectors" arrived to locate their tracts.

Just as everything seemed to be going well, Austin was dealt two disappointing blows. The *Lively* did not arrive at the Colorado rendezvous. Austin waited there for days and searched the area thoroughly but could find no trace of his supply ship. Later he learned that the *Lively* had landed at the mouth of the Brazos instead, unloaded its cargo, and returned to New Orleans for more supplies. The schooner was wrecked on Galveston Island in June with a complete loss of the crew and the second cargo.

When he gave up looking for his ship at the mouth of the Colorado, Austin rode to San Antonio to confer with Governor Martínez. There he received the second shock. Martínez informed him that Mexico had overthrown Spanish authority, had declared its independence, and had established a provisional government in Mexico City. Martínez had conveniently turned his coat wrongside out, proclaimed himself a patriot, and remained in office. But, he informed Austin, the provisional officials at Monterrey did not recognize the Austin grant because it had been made by Spain. But the new government, he said, was greatly interested in colonization, and it was probable that in time the congress then meeting in Mexico City would pass a general colonization law under which Austin could continue his project. Meantime, the colonists would have to leave Texas or move to San Antonio, which was the nearest established government. Martínez agreed to delay enforcing this regulation if Austin would try to persuade the central government in Mexico City to overrule the provisional deputation at Monterrey and confirm his grant.

However much he may have desired to abandon the project then and there, Austin persisted because of a deep sense of responsibility to the colonists who had already settled in Texas. At the end of March he left on the long and arduous overland journey to Mexico City, putting Josiah H. Bell temporarily in charge of colonial affairs. Not the least of his problems were the expense of the journey and the fact that he knew virtually no Spanish. Had he known of the vexing instability of the Mexican political situation, he might never have made the trip.

The Mexican Revolution Much misinterpretation of Texas history has resulted from a failure to relate events in Mexican Texas to those in politically tumultuous Mexico. Complex as the shifting political scene was, it influenced the development of Texas and the revolution there fifteen years later. Consequently, at least a superficial knowledge of Mexican politics is vital to the understanding of Texas' past.

The Hidalgo Revolution had not died with the priest's execution; others carried on sporadic guerrilla warfare in many parts of Mexico. Lacking support from the wealthy and powerful criollos, however, the movement was notably unsuccessful and by 1820 had nearly lost its force. The criollos feared the Hidalgistas, who as social reformers would undermine their privileges, more than they despised the gachupins, who as native Spaniards merely displaced them in governmental authority. But when in 1820 the Spanish crown was forced to establish the liberal constitution originally promulgated in 1812, the criollos concluded that their position could be protected only under an independent monarchy in Mexico. They found a leader in Agustín de Iturbide, a criollo army officer who persuaded the viceroy to place him in command of an army to quell the last of the Hidalgo forces led by Vincente Guerrero and a remarkable Indian named Guadalupe Victoria. Iturbide then betrayed the royalist government by making a pact with the revolutionaries to join forces for the independence of Mexico. The *Plan de Iguala*, the covenant between these two basically disparate groups, signed on February 24, 1821, provided for the establishment of a limited monarchy in Mexico separate from Spain.

Iturbide turned his combined armies against the remaining royalist armies and forced the recognition of Mexican independence on September 27, 1821. Appointing an interim junta of five regents, he called for a congress in Mexico City in February to draft the frame of government for the new nation. Discord was immediately apparent. Liberal leaders, political heirs of Father Hidalgo, wanted to form a republic instead of the limited monarchy of the *Plan de Iguala*; criollo leaders split over whether to back Iturbide's pretension to the new throne or to invite a Bourbon prince from Europe.

The revolutionary coalition was about to disintegrate when Austin arrived in Mexico City on April 29. He had traveled disguised as a beggar to avoid being robbed in that troubled land where law and order had nearly disappeared. Having acquired a little Spanish by that time, he submitted a petition to the revolutionary congress. In this first encounter with Mexican political leaders in congress, Austin demonstrated the courtesy, tact, and diplomacy that were to win him many friends in Mexico and enable him to accomplish what few other Americans could. But even though congress seemed favorably disposed—not so much toward Austin's immediate relief as toward a general colonization law—it was soon rendered powerless.

On May 18, three weeks after Austin's arrival, Iturbide staged a coup d'etat by having one of his sergeants begin a chant for "Agustín I" in a throng in the city. With an appearance of reluctance reminiscent of Caesar's refusal of the diadem, Iturbide accepted the demands of the crowd and with the army behind him proclaimed himself emperor of Mexico. Austin's petition was forgotten in the petty quarrels that arose between congress and Iturbide, and in October the emperor dismissed congress and replaced it with his own junta. Austin transferred his petition to the junta and began cultivating influential men in the imperial court, an elegant travesty of those in Europe.

The junta, like the congress before it, was less interested in Austin's problem than in a general colonization law. There had arrived in Mexico on the heels of the revolution a large number of foreigners, many of them Americans and some of them associated with the earlier independence movement. These men pressed for the passage of a law to permit them to speculate in the unoccupied lands of Texas. A general authorization of

American colonies would give them this opportunity. Among these men of daring imagination and enterprise were General James Wilkinson, former commandant of Louisiana; General Arthur Wavell, an English soldier of fortune who had lately left the revolutionary furor in South America to become a brigadier general in the Mexican Army; Green DeWitt, an American from Missouri; and Joseph Vehlein, a German merchant. Austin, staying at Wavell's home in Mexico City and borrowing money from him to support himself, imparted a small tone of practical reality to the fanciful schemes bruited by these men. Their enthusiasm was contagious, and several Mexican leaders such as Lorenzo de Zavala were soon caught up by their ideas.

The junta consequently passed a general colonization law on January 4, 1823, which Iturbide approved on February 18. The act permitted these men to enter colonization contracts with the imperial government and allowed Austin to continue his colony in Texas. But Austin feared that the law would be short-lived and so delayed leaving for Texas. His alarm was justified as the kaleidoscope of Mexican politics was about to turn again. A month later, on March 19, 1823, Iturbide was forced to abdicate and his junta to give way to a reassembled congress, which promptly nullified all the acts of the imperial government, including the Imperial Colonization Law.

Hastily Austin reinitiated his petition, this time asking for permission to continue his colony under the terms of the Imperial Colonization Law. Since he had been in Mexico a year and was well known to many of the members of congress, since his cause was justified, and since congress intended to establish a colonization program eventually, it authorized a special contract for Austin in accordance with the annulled law. On April 11 the contract was signed by the acting president.

The Old Three Hundred Although the interminable delays had been exasperating, the contract was far more generous than Austin could have hoped for. Based on the Imperial Colonization Law, it offered a league (4,428 acres) and a labor (177 acres) of land to heads of families who settled in Austin's colony, engaged in farming and stock raising, and became Roman Catholics and Mexican citizens. Single men would receive a third that amount. As empresario of the colony Austin would receive approximately one hundred thousand acres from the government for introducing the three hundred families stipulated in the contract. Furthermore, certain duties and taxes were waived for the six-year period of the contract.

As these provisions were greatly more advantageous than the previous arrangement with Martínez, Austin expected the colonists to be as highly pleased as he was. He hastened back to Texas with the news, only to find his colony in a serious state of debility. His long absence and the rumors that the colony would not be validated had badly affected morale. The loss of the *Lively* had made seed and other supplies scarce. Further, the summer of 1822 had been droughty, and many of the first crops had failed. Karankawa Indians had begun stealing livestock and now threatened more serious depredations. Many of the settlers gave up and left.

Recognizing that the principal allure of the colony was land, Austin brought with him the Baron de Bastrop, who had been named land commissioner and who began issuing titles as rapidly as Horatio Chriesman could complete the surveys and draw the field notes. News of the land bonanza raced through Louisiana and most of the apostate colonists returned. A few settlers from Miller County moved in, and some persons who had stopped at Nacogdoches on the way into Texas proceeded to the settlement. By the end of the following summer Bastrop had issued two hundred seventy-two of the allotted three hundred titles; later, additional titles brought the number to two hundred ninety-seven. Austin abandoned his twelve and a half cent fee and charged a flat fee of fifty dollars for administering the paper work, although he felt he was entitled to a greater compensation because of his original cash expense and debts. The land given him by the government was not salable, and he was hard pressed financially.

These first settlers came to be known as the Old Three Hundred. They were justly recognized by those who came later as the pioneers of Anglo-American Texas. By organizing a militia to chastise the Karankawas and by making a treaty with the Tonkawas, they secured relative freedom from Indian attacks. They cleared fields, planted crops, built homes initially of logs, and quite literally tamed the wilderness. They founded a town on the Brazos named San Felipe de Austin and divided the colony into six administrative units. Grist mills and even a cotton gin were erected, and in San Felipe several stores and a newspaper were established. Officials in San Antonio, accustomed to the easygoing indolence of the native Hispanic population, which was comprised mostly of mestizos of more Indian than Spanish extraction, looked on this rash of aggressive industry with amazed bewilderment. And later when the general colonization program then being contemplated by the government got under way and a flood of Anglo-Americans swept into Texas, this bewilderment was to turn to concern.

Colonization under the Republic of Mexico

The Legal Structure In Mexico City, the congress that granted Austin special and exclusive permission to colonize under the Imperial Colonization Law proceeded with the business of organizing a government. The liberals held the upper hand, temporarily to be sure, and created a republic. In August a new congress drafted a constitution based chiefly on that of the United States to form a federated republic. It was an excellent instrument of government, providing for the three branches of judicial, executive, and legislative authority, guaranteeing the natural rights of man, and embodying a democratic philosophy within a republican structure. The document was written by a committee headed by Miguel Ramos Arispe, for whom Austin had translated the United States Constitution, into Spanish, and it was adopted as the *Acta Constitutiva* on January 31, 1824. Recast in a more appropriate form, it was approved as the Federal Constitution of the Republic of Mexico on October 4, 1824. It was only natural that this constitution accepted Roman Catholicism as the state religion and based the judicial structure on Roman Law, and the Anglo-Americans in Texas at the time considered these two aspects of the constitution but minor weaknesses. More important, the *Acta Constitutiva* joined Texas to Coahuila as one state to be called Coahuila y Texas, a measure reaffirmed by a federal act in May 1824.

The new state government was quickly organized, with Saltillo as the capital. Two years of debates produced a state constitution under which Texas was made one of twelve subdivisions of the state called departments. The structure of local government modified earlier Spanish patterns. The basic unit was the municipality, a jurisdictional area with its center in a town or village. Few of the Texas municipalities that later came into existence had definite boundaries, each of the outlying ranches simply being affixed to the nearest municipality. Large municipalities were further subdivided into districts. Thus San Felipe became a municipality with six districts comprised of Austin's colony.

The state government had executive, legislative, and judicial branches. The governor had more authority than chief executives in the United States, and the legislature, called a congress, was smaller, consisting of one deputy from each department. The judiciary was centralized and even trials at the lowest level in the municipalities had to be reviewed and approved by the state court in Saltillo, a process that restricted and badly hampered the administration of justice. Each department had only one administrative official, called a political chief, but the municipalities had a full panoply of officials. The principal officer was an alcalde, who combined the American functions of mayor and county judge. He presided over an *ayuntamiento*, or combination court and council, which was made up of *regidores*, or councilmen, and a *sindico*, or public prosecutor. All these officials were locally elected. The ayuntamiento chose an *alguacil*, who served as sheriff and tax collector, and a *secretario* to handle its records and correspondence. *Comisarios*, or sub-alcaldes, were elected in each district in the municipality.

Thus a framework was provided in which the Anglo-Americans could easily exercise their passion for self-government, and Austin promptly organized his colony as a municipality to relieve himself of the burden of administration. Later, as other municipalities were formed in the area settled by Anglo-Americans, the ability of the colonists to make local government function became pronounced. In 1834 Texas was divided into three departments, Béxar, Brazos, and Nacogdoches, but this action did not materially affect the operation of the municipalities. Most of the Anglo-American municipalities were placed in the Department of Brazos, of which Henry Smith was named political chief.

Before the structure of government was fixed or the constitution written, demands by land speculators and would-be empresarios for a colonization law became incessant. After restudying the problem, congress decided not to hamper the federal government with the administration of such a program and instead passed that duty to the state governments in a law of August 18, 1824, called the Federal Colonization Law.

This statute's main provision was the assignment of the public domain to the states in which it was located, a procedure diametrically opposite that of the United States, where the states had turned over the public lands to the central government. Though each state was to develop its own programs, the Federal Colonization Law provided some basic guidelines. State laws had to conform to the Constitution of 1824; no lands could be granted to foreign-born persons within ten lineal leagues of the coast or twenty of an international border; grants could not be made to foreigners unless they became Mexican citizens; and no individual could own more than eleven leagues, a special exemption being made for empresarios. Congress also promised in this law that it would make no major changes in immigration policy until 1840, unless immigration from a particular nation had to be stopped in the interests of national security.

It was thrown, then, to the state legislatures to devise colonization programs. Each state drafted its own acts, with variations on the Federal Colonization Law. In California, for example, settlers were offered a total of eleven leagues: one of irrigable farm land, four of "seasonable" farm land, and six of grazing land. To be eligible, they had to be native or naturalized citizens, had to live on the property and make improvements, and had to file an application accompanied by a *diseño,* or scenic map. The government of the newly formed state of Coahuila y Texas was slightly less generous.

On March 24, 1825, it passed an act called the State Colonization Law, which offered a league of land to settlers who would reside on the land and make improvements. They were required to pay the government several small fees, totaling less than two hundred dollars, which could be remitted in installments over a six year period. Native Mexicans could purchase for nominal fees additional lands up to the total of eleven leagues. Foreigners were invited to become settlers but were required to become naturalized citizens, join the Catholic church, and give evidence of good character. No changes were to be made in the law for six years, and state taxes were waived for ten years. Although colonists did not need to obtain land under the auspices of an empresario, the law provided for colonization contracts with such agents. The contracts were to run for six years and become void if less than one hundred families were introduced into the colony in that time. Empresarios would receive five leagues of grazing land and five labors of farming land for each one hundred families they settled.

The Empresario Contracts Immediately after the passage of the law there was a rush to sign colonization contracts with the governor, some thirty or more being issued. In the haste with which they were drawn many careless mistakes were made, especially in the location of the colonies. Boundaries of the grants often overlapped or were poorly defined, many of the colonies were located in semiarid and then uninhabitable lands in West Texas, and one, granted to Haden Edwards, included the already populated region around Nacogdoches.

Few of these contracts caused problems, however, as the empresarios who received them often did not actually bring in settlers. Those who did included Stephen F. Austin, who signed several additional contracts, Green DeWitt, Martín de León, Haden Edwards, E. S. C. Robertson, John Charles Beales, Ben Milam (for Arthur Wavell), James Power and James Hewetson, and John McMullen and James McGloin.

Without question, Austin was the most influential of the empresarios and was responsible for bringing the greatest number of colonists into Texas. As his original contract was substantially fulfilled by 1825, Austin obtained a second contract for five hundred more families to be settled in the same area as his first colony. In 1827 he signed a third contract for the settlement of one hundred families east of the Colorado in present Bastrop County. This was known as the Little Colony and its headquarters town, founded in 1832, was named Bastrop. Austin's fourth contract, in 1828, was somewhat unusual. He requested and received special permission from the president of the republic to settle three hundred families in the ten-league coastal reserve established by the Federal Colonization Law. As a matter of fact, however, many of the Old Three Hundred had already established themselves there. Prior to 1830, the four Austin contracts called for the settlement of a total of twelve hundred families: three hundred in the original contract and nine hundred more under the State Colonization Law. For all practical purposes, the contracts were fulfilled.

Green DeWitt received a grant to settle four hundred families west of Austin's first colony. DeWitt, who had been in and out of Mexico since 1822, was one of the first to sign a contract under the State Colonization Law. James Kerr, DeWitt's surveyor, laid out the colony town of Gonzales in December 1825. Erastus (Deaf) Smith, who became famous later as a scout, was among the first settlers in DeWitt's colony. About thirty or forty families were living in Gonzales in July the following year when it was attacked by a Comanche war party. Fearing another raid, the colonists moved to DeWitt's post called Old Station on Matagorda Bay through which he planned to bring colonists by sea. As this was within the restricted coastal zone and as a quarrel had arisen between these colonists and Martín de León, another empresario, the political chief ordered Old Station abandoned in August 1827. By July 1828 the colonists had all returned to Gonzales. DeWitt moved his own family to the colony that year. The colonists repeatedly petitioned the government for protection against the Indians, but they received little aid. In 1831 they were given the six-pound cannon that their refusal to return four years later sparked the Texas Revolution.

The De León colony, DeWitt's neighbor on the southeast, was actually initiated prior to the State Colonization Law. Martín de León, a native Mexican and stock raiser in Tamaulipas, received special permission in April 1824 to settle forty Mexican families on the Guadalupe River. These families were granted the same amount of land as that given in Austin's first contract. De León laid out the town of Victoria in October 1824. He was later authorized to settle an unlimited number of Mexican families between the Lavaca and Guadalupe rivers but without either specific boundaries or time limits. In 1829 he received a contract to settle one hundred fifty families in the restricted areas, some from the United States, some from Ireland, and the rest from Mexico. De León's quarrel with the DeWitt colonists at Old Station arose because he suspected they were smuggling tobacco, a contraband trade item, and because he felt they were encroaching on his colony.

The Fredonian Rebellion A more serious quarrel was provoked by the grant given Haden Edwards in 1825. The Edwards Colony was located in the already populated Nacogdoches area and included the town of Nacogdoches itself. Many of the people living in the region did not have titles to their land, and although some of them were illegal squatters, others were bona fide settlers, descendents of Gil Ybarbo's plucky band. When he brought in some fifty colonists in the summer of 1825, Edwards ran into trouble. He peremptorily ordered all persons living in the region to produce a title to their land or to secure one through him as empresario. The older settlers resented this demand and petitioned the government in November 1825 to relieve them of Edwards' interference. During the next six months Edwards quarreled with several officials of the government, and then while he was in the United States to raise funds for his operation, his brother, Benjamin Edwards, inaugurated an armed uprising.

This Fredonian Rebellion, as it was called, was a minor episode more illustrative of a very significant problem of unrest in East Texas than of Mexican-American friction as it is so often misinterpreted. The area contained, in heterogeneous juxtaposition, early Hispanic settlers, a few European immigrants, renegades and outlaws who had moved from the Neutral Ground when it became part of the United States, the families Edwards had brought in, the remnant of the Caddoan tribes, several relatively peaceful bands of Indians recently crowded out of the United States such as the Alabamas and Coushattas, and a powerful branch of Cherokee Indians who were trying to secure a title to lands they had occupied in the 1820's.

Benjamin Edwards rode into Nacogdoches on December 16, 1826, with a banner reading "Independence, Liberty, and Justice." He had with him about thirty armed men, some of whom were undoubtedly from the old Neutral Ground crowd. They captured the virtually undefended Old Stone Fort, declared the independence of the Republic of Fredonia, and imprisoned the alcalde, Samuel Norris, who had quarreled with one of the Fredonians, a fractious man named Martin Parmer. Norris had previously been expelled from Texas by Joaquín Arredondo; Parmer was expelled later on two separate occasions. Parmer was elected president of the Republic of Fredonia, and five days later, on December 21, he signed a pact with two representatives of the Cherokees—John Dunn Hunter, a white renegade, and Richard Field, a half-breed chief. According to this agreement, for joining the rebellion the Cherokees would be granted half of Texas.

Since the Cherokee Indians refused to support the alliance and since both Anglo and Hispanic settlers scorned to participate, the uprising was short-lived. On January 22, 1827, learning of the approach of troops from San Antonio and militia from Austin's colony, the Fredonians fled. Edwards' contract was canceled, but both Haden Edwards and his brother, who was later pardoned, returned to make their homes in Nacogdoches. Stephen F. Austin, who had counseled Edwards to be more prudent and circumspect with government officials, was concerned that many in Mexico would make the wrong interpretation of Anglo-American immigration. The Cherokee Indians, also anxious about their image in Mexican eyes, reported that Field and Hunter were tried and executed.

Colonial Life The ridiculous and confusing affair neither abated nor disturbed the process of colonization. During 1827 the movement of Anglo-Americans into Texas was significant, increasing in 1828 and 1829 to hundreds of families. Colonists who were pleased with the Texas prospect wrote to hometown newspapers and sent for friends and families. Most of the immigrants headed for Austin's colonies, the best publicized. By 1830 the population in those colonies exceeded four thousand, and other colonies had grown proportionately. Many immigrants came on their own, some settling in Nacogdoches, La Bahía, and San Antonio, and others homesteading where there were no actual colonies. One such area north of Galveston Bay came to be called Liberty. Ben Milam, agent for Arthur Wavell, brought about a dozen families into Wavell's grant on the Red River, north of the defunct Edwards Colony, but then abandoned the venture for more speculative personal pursuits.

Everywhere Texas was taking on the appearance of a civilized state. Roads were built, ferries installed at major river crossings, towns established, cotton gins and grist mills erected, a few homes of elegant dimensions constructed—plantations functioned profitably, and all in all Texas began to prosper.

Frontier conditions with the usual frontier hardships still prevailed, however. Luxuries were scarce, and money—hard cash in specie—was virtually nonexistent. Austin and the other empresarios resorted to the collection of fees in barter. Merchants did the same, and much business was done on credit. Most of the settlers were nearly self-sufficient on their farmsteads, where corn was the all-important crop, to be eaten, ground into meal and baked, distilled in liquor and drunk, or held in cribs to feed livestock during the winter. Cotton and to a less extent sugar cane were the money crops, but neither provided very much revenue during the early years.

The typical colonial family lived in a two-room log house called a double log cabin because the rooms were separated by a breezeway, or "dog run," where dogs lolled almost perennially. Most of the cabins were windowless, and where no stones were available they had a "stick and mud" chimney for heating and cooking. In most cabins the floors were dirt and the furniture homemade. Rarely was more than one bed available, and since families averaged six to eight persons, the children customarily slept on pallets in the attic.

There were no schools in the rural areas, but occasionally an itinerant teacher was hired by a community for a few months. English-speaking grammar schools were established in Jonesborough, Nacogdoches, and San Felipe in the early period, and a few of the wealthy planters retained tutors. Religion was even more scarce than education. Almost all the colonists had Protestant backgrounds, but the law had required them to be Roman Catholic. This wrought little difficulty since few of the pioneers had strong religious inclinations and the archbishop in Monterrey did not bother to send a priest until 1831. Even this created no difficulty, for the priest was a jovial Irishman named Michael Muldoon who, it was said, took great delight in marrying couples joined by common law and in the same ceremony baptizing the children of the union. A few evangelical protestants were secretly active from time to time. The first, a Baptist preacher named Joseph E. Bays, was arrested in San Felipe and expelled. Austin issued several warnings to protestant ministers that their activities were illegal. In 1829 Thomas J. Pilgrim, a schoolteacher in San Felipe, was forced by the ayuntamiento to close a Sunday school he had tried to operate.

Although a good many slaves were brought into the colonies—some estimates say that over a third of the total population was Negro—most of them were on the large plantations such as Groce's. Few colonists could afford to own slaves, and most of those who did had only one or two. The state constitution of Coahuila y Texas prohibited the introduction of slaves and declared that children born of slave parents were free. But an 1828 decree permitted lifetime work contracts, a dodge that perpetuated the importation of slaves. In 1829 Vincente Guerrero, then president, abolished slavery in the Republic of Mexico, but the decree was not promulgated in Texas, and the general interpretation considered Texas exempt. Nonetheless, the Guerrero decree caused a flurry of excitement in the colonies, and some believed it an attempt to slow down American immigration. In 1830 the further introduction of slaves was absolutely forbidden, and in 1832 labor contracts were limited to ten years' duration.

If Mexican officials were amazed in 1824 at the industry of the first Austin colonists, they were astounded and nearly overcome by the teeming, restless energy throughout the colonies five years later. Alarmed by reports that Texas was becoming completely Americanized, the government sent an agent to Texas to investigate the condition. He was Manuel de Mier y

Terán, whose recommendations were to be distorted into the objectionable Law of April 6, 1830, that marked a major shift in Mexican policy in Texas.

The Change in Mexican Policy

Terán's Recommendations Terán entered Texas at Laredo in February 1828 and traveled northward through San Antonio and thence by way of the Anglo-American settlements to Nacogdoches, which he reached in June. From there he commented in a letter to the president that Mexican influence in Texas had decreased as he moved northeast. He noted that the Hispanic settlers around Nacogdoches were in the lowest class and were greatly outnumbered by Anglos, who even maintained an English speaking school. He also commented on the strange diversity of the population: Indians, Anglos, outlaws, and Negro slaves in his view on the point of rebellion. The Anglos, he said, traveled "with their political constitution in their pockets" and knew more about the constitution and the operation of government than most native Mexicans. "Texas could throw the whole nation into revolution," he warned the president, unless "timely measures" were taken. Terán made a series of recommendations that included the creation of a separate political department of Nacogdoches and the settlement of more industrious and progressive native Mexicans. He was not opposed to American immigration; he merely wanted to offset it with a better quality of colonists from Mexico.

There is something ironical in Terán's fear that Texas could throw Mexico into revolution, for Mexico had enjoyed only superficial stability for a brief four years, and at the very time he made his recommendations a major revolution was brewing in the capital. The Law of April 6, 1830, based on his recommendations, was not passed until two successive coups had placed the Centralist elements in illegal control of the government.

Political Upheaval in Mexico During the liberal ascendancy after the abdication of Iturbide and the establishment of a republic, the conservative criollo forces had chafed increasingly at the institution of such preposterous doctrines as natural rights, elections of officials, and the other paraphernalia of a democratic government. Too small a group to win a national election, they lighted upon the most devastating tactic one political party can use against another: instead of naming a candidate for president in the election of 1828, they threw their support behind the less liberal of the opposition forces. At this time the conservatives, the old

Iturbidists and monarchists, were known as Escoceses because many of them had joined the Scottish Rite branch of the Masonic order; later they were called Centralists because their basically unvaried demands were for a centralized, autocratic dictatorship. The liberals, the old Hidalgistas and revolutionaries, were known as Yorkinos, from the York Rite to which many of them belonged, including Vincente Guerrero, who had headed the last of Hidalgo's armies; later the Yorkinos were called Federalists because they supported a federal republic as established by the Constitution of 1824.

In the national election of 1828, the Escoceses-Centralists supported Gómez Pedraza, a criollo associated with the liberal government of Guadalupe Victoria. The Yorkino-Federalists supported Guerrero, grand master of the York Rite. Although Pedraza appears to have won by electoral votes, the Yorkino-Federalists claimed that the count was fraudulent and that Guerrero had a plurality of the popular vote. They promptly took up arms to force Guerrero's inauguration, and just as promptly Escoceses-Centralist troops chased them into the mountains. But while the two armies were away from the capital, another Federalist insurgency quite illegally and unconstitutionally hastened to inaugurate their man, Guerrero, as president. Thus in the first election after the establishment of the republic, the party purporting to defend the constitution rejected the results of the election and resorted to arms. It would be over a hundred years and nearly as many revolutions before the people of Mexico came fully to recognize the necessity of accepting the dictates of the polls.

The action of Guerrero and the Federalists threw Mexico into a turmoil of armed camps during the summer of 1829. Then an unusual opportunity let the Centralists steal the government. Spanish troops bent on reconquest invaded Mexico at Vera Cruz. When Guerrero sent the government's forces to defend the nation, a Centralist army of several thousand took Mexico City by the dark of night and deposed and executed Guerrero. The Centralist leader in this coup, Anastacio Bustamente, assumed dictatorial powers as chief executive. The Spanish invasion being easily repelled, the Federalists turned to fight Bustamente and the Centralists. A new leader had emerged during these revolutions to head the Federalist faction: Antonio López de Santa Anna. From the latter part of 1829 through most of 1832 fighting raged across Mexico. And Terán had feared *Texas* might "throw the whole nation into revolution."

The Law of April 6, 1830 Terán's recommendations concerning Texas, however, came into the hands of the Centralist government. No friend of Americans or their liberal political philosophies, the

Centralists determined to stop American immigration. Thus, to put an end to the increasing American influence in Texas, the Law of April 6, 1830, was drafted, chiefly by Lucas Alamán, mastermind of the Centralist coup. The law was unquestionably harsher than what a Federalist government would have enacted on Terán's recommendations. That the revolutionary changes in the Mexican government during 1829 greatly affected relations between Texas and Mexico has been often overlooked by Texas historians, with a result of gross misinterpretations of both Texan and Mexican attitudes during this period.

The Centralists' sharply anti-American law forbade all foreigners whomsoever to cross the northern border without a passport from an agent of the Mexican government. It forbade all further immigration of Americans into Mexico, and it canceled all empresario contracts. It provided for constructing military garrisons in Texas and manning them with convict soldiers (men fulfilling a penitentiary sentence by military service). These men were to be allowed to settle in Texas when their term was finished. It created the post of commissioner of colonization to oversee enforcement of the law and regulation of the colonies. On the positive side, and directly traceable to Terán's recommendations, the law authorized the establishment of an open port on the Texas coast to encourage trade with Tampico and Vera Cruz, and it provided for certain government subsidies to Mexican families migrating to Texas.

Although apparently not an ardent Centralist, Terán was a personal friend of Bustamente and was named to the post of commissioner of colonization. He also succeeded Bustamente as commander of the Eastern Interior Provinces. Many Texans feared him as a tool of the Centralists, but Austin believed him to be a reasonable man and at once set to work to alleviate the drastic law through amiable interpretation. He found Terán helpful and cooperative. Terán once wrote him, "The affairs of Texas are understood by only you and me, and we alone are able to regulate them." Terán benignly interpreted the suspension of contracts to apply only to those in which fewer than a hundred settlers had already been introduced, thus permitting Austin and DeWitt to continue colonizing. He also ordered troop commanders in Texas particularly to restrain soldiers from annoying the settlers, and in other small ways he prevented the law from bearing as heavily as it might have on Texas. Nonetheless, military garrisons were built, convict soldiers were imported, and American immigration was stopped. On the other hand, the positive provisions of the law, such as those for free ports and a better quality of Mexican immigrants, were never implemented. Americans who had moved to Mexican Texas to make their homes in a new land naturally resented being surrounded by soldiers and cut off from their friends and relatives. The reaction to this law marks the beginning of sentiment for war against Mexico, but the prudent majority of the stable colonists counseled, with Austin, for patience.

The Later Colonies The colonization program did not end completely, as immigrants from Europe were introduced during the ensuing years. Some Germans and a few French and Swiss trickled in, and on the coast two small colonies of Irish Catholics developed. The first was established by John McMullen and his son-in-law, James McGloin, both natives of Ireland who were in the mercantile business in Matamoros when the State Colonization Law was passed. Receiving an empresario contract for two hundred families of Irish Catholics, they introduced the first shiploads from New York on the *Albion* and the *New Packet* in October 1829. These families settled around the mission Refugio but in 1831 obtained permission to establish the town of San Patricio on the north bank of the Nueces River just above Corpus Christi Bay. Other immigrants arrived later, and eighty-four titles in all were issued in the colony. Both McMullen and McGloin made their homes in Texas after the founding of the colony.

Slightly more successful was the colony also for Catholic Irish settlers in the littoral reserve between the Lavaca and Guadalupe rivers established by James Power and James Hewetson, both natives of Ireland. The first groups of three hundred fifty Irish immigrants arrived in 1833 suffering from a severe epidemic of cholera. Some of these early arrivals in the McMullen and McGloin Colony settled around Refugio mission; others founded the village of Cópano on Cópano Bay. Power acquired Hewetson's interest in the venture and made his home in the colony. Some two hundred titles were ultimately issued to Irish settlers in this area.

At about the same time an English physician, John Charles Beales, established a colony on the Rio Grande in present Maverick County. In December 1833 he landed a shipload of German, English, Spanish, and American immigrants at Cópano Bay and led them overland to the site of his colony, where he founded a town named Dolores on Las Moras Creek. The next year he brought a second group of immigrants although he himself did not remain at Dolores. The colonists built crude homes, erected a sawmill, a grist mill, and a church, and planted crops. But Beales' Rio Grande Colony was in a semiarid region, and their efforts at farming were unsuccessful. Harassment by Comanche Indians culminated in a raid in the spring of 1836 that destroyed the town, and they abandoned the settlement. The survivors scattered, but many apparently remained in Texas and later received land titles from the Republic of Texas.

There was some activity in two other colonization ventures after the Law of April 6, 1830: the Galveston Bay and Texas Land Company, and the Texas Association of Nashville. The first was formed by a group of New York promoters led by the notorious Samuel Swartwout that ostensibly acted as agent for three contracts granted to Joseph Vehlein, a merchant in Mexico City, David G. Burnet, an Ohio attorney who had spent much time in Texas, and Lorenzo de Zavala, one of the leading liberals in Mexico. These three grants were in the vicinity of the former Edwards Colony, but they extended east to the international boundary and south to the coast, comprising many thousands of acres in East Texas. The company issued and sold meaningless certificates entitling immigrants to settle in the area, and in December 1830 a shipload of colonists was dispatched to Galveston Bay. A few months later a second boatload followed. Although these immigrants purported to be from Switzerland and Germany, Mexican officials were reluctant to permit them to colonize and delayed granting authority until many became discouraged and left. Company agents were active in Europe during the next several years, and ultimately over nine hundred titles were issued, not all to Europeans, for the Liberty area north of Galveston Bay. Much about this company's activities was considered bogus and fraudulent. Since immigrants were permitted by law to settle in Texas without an empresario's services, the certificates sold by the company were of no value to the colonists. Furthermore, the company issued and sold land scrip at five cents an acre, as if it owned the land in the colony reservation, to unsuspecting buyers who were never able to redeem it. Such a grandiose operation was it that at one time the company offered to buy all the vacant land in Texas for ten million dollars. Neither the company nor the original grantees received premium lands for the services alleged to have been performed, but Lorenzo de Zavala later made his home in the area. At least two Texas towns, Swartwout and New Washington, were established by company agents.

The Austin-Williams Colony derived from the cancellation of a contract granted to Robert Leftwich as agent for the Texas Association of Nashville. This company had attempted to colonize a large area north of Austin's Little Colony along the watershed of the Brazos River. Eight hundred families were authorized, and the colony's area was the largest granted in a single contract. Later Hosea League and then Sterling C. Robertson became agents for the company. The contract was invalidated under the Law of April 6, 1830, but Stephen F. Austin and his secretary, Samuel May Williams, received permission in 1831 to settle European families in the colony. Robertson appealed to the governor in Saltillo to revoke the grant to Austin and Williams on the grounds that the Nashville company had settled over a hundred families prior to the Law of

April 6, 1830, and should have been allowed to continue in possession of the grant. In 1834 the contract was taken from Austin and Williams and awarded to Robertson; the following year it was returned to Austin and Williams; and finally after much litigation Texas courts decided in 1847 that Robertson's claims were valid. More than eight hundred families were settled and the towns of Salado, Viesca (later Milam), and Nashville had been established before the outbreak of the Texas Revolution.

Political Chaos and Confusion

Anahuac and Velasco   After Antonio López de Santa Anna put himself at the head of the opposition following the Centralist takeover in 1829 and 1830 by Bustamente and Lucas Alamán, the Federalists slowly gained strength. In 1831 they erupted into outright rebellion. For over a year bloody revolution seared the face of Mexico as armed forces contested for power in first one and then another village, town, and district. This fighting did not reach Texas, but it was almost comically reflected in the affairs of Anahuac and Velasco.

Anahuac, a settlement on Trinity Bay, was the major port of entry for East Texas. There a customs house and a military garrison were built pursuant to the Law of April 6, 1830. John Davis Bradburn, an adventurer from Kentucky and a colonel in the Mexican Army, was placed in command of the fort; and George Fisher, a Serbian immigrant, was named customs collector. Almost immediately after assuming command, in November 1830, Bradburn began antagonizing the colonists by his haughty attitude and high-handed tactics. He confiscated supplies and commandeered slaves belonging to settlers for the construction of his post. He captured some runaway slaves and, instead of returning them to their owners, put them to work at the garrison. He aroused bitter resentment when he closed the newly organized ayuntamiento at Liberty and arrested Francisco Madero, land commissioner of Coahuila y Texas, and his surveyor, José María Carvajal. Madero had been sent to issue long-delayed titles to settlers who had come without benefit of an empresario's services. Among these no doubt were some of the Galveston Bay and Texas Land Company colonists. Madero had also been authorized to establish the municipality of Liberty and organize local government. Bradburn considered both activities to be violations of the national Law of April 6, 1830, and after warning Madero to desist he arrested and imprisoned him. If this were not enough to arouse the settlers' wrath, Bradburn next assisted the conscientious customs collector by closing all Texas ports except that at Anahuac. Fisher had made the unreasonable and unenforceable demand that all vessels bound for or from any port in Texas had to receive clearance at Anahuac—an insufferable inconvenience, for example, for a ship entering or leaving Velasco at the mouth of the Brazos.

In the spring of 1832 Bradburn arrested Patrick C. Jack and William Barrett Travis, attorneys who were trying to secure the release of some runaway slaves he was holding. He held Jack and Travis without trial and refused to remit them to civil authorities. This outrage was followed by similar arrests of other citizens and in May 1832 by his declaration of martial law for the entire border reserve. This was more than the irate colonists could stand. Already thoroughly enraged by Bradburn's arrogance, they organized a militia force under the leadership of William Jack, who was a brother of Patrick C. Jack and who had tried in vain to secure Jack's and Travis's release. They were joined by an armed group from Brazoria led by John Austin. Early in June they encamped on nearby Turtle Bayou and demanded the release of the prisoners and respect for their rights under the Mexican constitution.

While Bradburn negotiated with the leaders and delayed by indications of concurrence, he hastily improved the fortification at the post. Then he broke his tentative agreement, refused to deliver his prisoners, and ordered the militia to disperse. The colonists decided to attack, but the consensus was that they needed to get an artillery piece from Brazoria. John Austin and some companions left for it. In the interim the colonists adopted the Turtle Bayou Resolution, in which they declared that their actions were in no way an uprising against Mexico but only a resistance to tyranny and an attempt to reestablish their constitutional rights. They went a step further and stated that they had merely taken up arms on the side of Santa Anna and the Federalists.

Austin and his cohorts loaded the cannon on a vessel in the Brazos River, but the military commander at Velasco, Domingo de Ugartechea, advised them that he could not permit them to leave the mouth of the river. Although he was not in sympathy with Bradburn, Ugartechea could not in good conscience allow the insurgents to arm themselves with cannon against a Mexican garrison. The colonists insisted, and on June 26 the Battle of Velasco was fought with a loss of ten colonists and five Mexican troops. Ugartechea surrendered the garrison. This action was to no avail, however, for meanwhile the affair at Anahuac had been settled.

Colonel José de las Piedras had rushed from Nacogdoches to Anahuac as soon as he learned of the disturbance. Quickly he realized that Bradburn's and Fisher's unlicensed actions were the roots of the trouble, and he agreed to replace the two troublemakers, to turn the prisoners over to civil authorities for trial, to remit the martial law, and to try to arrange indemnification for the lost property. The colonists dispersed; Bradburn and Fisher went to New Orleans but later returned to Mexico; the customs house was closed; and shortly the garrison at Anahuac also declared for Santa Anna and returned to Mexico to join the general melee against Bustamante.

This clash can properly be considered no more a revolution against Mexico than any of the dozen armed uprisings against Centralism in Mexico. And it is similarly an error to interpret it as an indication of Anglo-American hostility against Mexicans, as the source of the trouble was the Kentuckian John Davis Bradburn.

The Removal of Mexican Garrisons   Within months after this affair Texas was cleared of Mexican troops, most of them leaving to join Santa Anna in Mexico. Piedras, who had aided the colonists at Anahuac, refused to take the Federalist side, however, and in an affair sometimes called the Battle of Nacogdoches he surrendered his garrison to a group of Anglo and Hispanic settlers in August. Thirty-three soldiers and three settlers, including the Hispanic alcalde of Nacogdoches, were killed. After Piedras surrendered, his troops declared for Santa Anna and he was escorted to Matamoros in the custody of James Bowie and Stephen F. Austin.

Shortly before the Battle of Nacogdoches, the Anahuac disturbance provoked another minor reaction. Centralist and Federalist forces were fighting for control of Matamoros when they learned of the uprising at Anahuac. Fearing that it was a general Anglo-American uprising, they arranged a truce, and the Federalist general, José Antonio Mexía, set out for Texas with five hundred troops. Austin, returning from Saltillo, traveled with him. As Mexía entered Texas, he was everywhere met with protestations for the Federalist cause. At San Felipe a gala banquet and dance was held in his honor. Santa Anna was toasted, the Turtle Bayou Resolution was read, and Federalism and the constitution were cheered. Encouraged by such strong avowal of the Texas colonists' support of Federalism, Mexía returned to Mexico to continue the fight against Centralism.

Before the end of 1832 the *santanistas*, as the Federalist followers of Santa Anna called themselves, forced the resignation of Bustamante and ousted the Centralists. Santa Anna then installed as president Gómez Pedraza, who had been declared elected in 1828, and postponed the 1832 elections until January 1833. Encouraged by Santa Anna's successes, the Texans decided that the time was ripe to protest officially the Law of

April 6, 1830. The ayuntamiento at San Felipe called for a general convention of delegates from all the municipalities to assemble in San Felipe in October 1832.

The Convention of 1832 This Convention of 1832, consisting of fifty-eight delegates from sixteen municipalities, elected Austin its president and addressed itself efficiently to the business of drawing petitions and memorials to the central government for an alleviation of the problems in Texas. The most important request, of course, was for the repeal of the anti-immigration section of the Law of April 6, 1830. Next a lengthy petition asked for separate statehood for Texas: it had sufficient population, it had traditionally been a separate province under Spain, and it would benefit both Texas and Coahuila as well as the entire nation if Texas were a separate state. The convention also requested a school system, exemption from certain tariff duties for another three years, and land titles for settlers who had not yet received them. Delegates discussed the problem of Indian depredations and decided that committees of "safety and correspondence" should be established in each municipality to maintain communication about Indian affairs. An ulterior purpose was, of course, to keep posted on political events in Mexico. A committee was appointed to investigate the Cherokee Indian situation in East Texas, but there is no evidence that the committee functioned. With strong expressions of loyalty to the Republic of Mexico the convention adjourned, having accomplished its work in the remarkably short time of five days, and forwarded its petitions through the political chief in San Antonio.

Ramón Músquiz, the political chief, actually favored the colonists' requests, especially the one for separate statehood, but he was appalled by the procedure. Accustomed as he was to the highly centralized autocracy that Spaniards had experienced for uncounted generations, this freewheeling convention of citizens seemed not only illegal but frighteningly near treason. To his mind, requests and protests should originate only in the ayuntamientos. He therefore refused to forward the petitions and remonstrated with the colonists, warning them that their meeting was a "disturbance of good order."

Meantime, the postponed national elections were held, and Santa Anna was elected president of Mexico. The colonists felt assured that the ills in Texas would now be remedied. Had they not declared for Santa Anna? Had they not forced the closure of Centralist garrisons in Texas and sent troops to Mexico to support Santa Anna? They attached little blame to Músquiz for his timidity, but with Federalism so plainly victorious it was obvious that the government would accede to any reasonable requests they might make. The central committee of safety and correspondence called another convention to meet in San Felipe on April 1, the day Santa Anna was to be inaugurated in Mexico.

The Convention of 1833   The Convention of 1833 was attended by fifty-five delegates, but only about a third of them had been at the previous meeting. Two new members were Sam Houston, lately arrived in Nacogdoches from the exile in Indian Territory that he had imposed upon himself after his resignation as governor of Tennessee, and William H. Wharton, young son-in-law of Jared E. Groce and an important Brazos River planter. This convention is customarily considered more radical than the previous delegation as though a cleavage had occurred between the "moderates" led by Austin and the "radicals" led by Wharton. There is little evidence, however, that such factionalism existed anywhere but in the minds of later historians. Austin was the head of the central committee that had called the convention, and rather than opposing it, as has been suggested, he made a lengthy address the first day of the meeting on the necessity for the convention. Wharton was then elected president, Burnet was appointed to draft the petition for statehood, and Houston was made chairman of a committee to draft a proposed constitution for Texas.

Despite the differences in members and the greater confidence of the meeting, the requests were almost identical with those of the Convention of 1832. But this group went one step further. Convinced that Santa Anna would approve statehood for Texas, it submitted the proposed constitution with the petition for statehood to facilitate the organization of state government. And not trusting Músquiz to forward the petition the convention appointed a committee of three men to deliver its memorial directly to Santa Anna's government in Mexico. Austin, Erasmo Seguín, who was a rancher southeast of San Antonio and had been a member of the congress that drafted the federal Constitution of 1824, and Dr. James B. Miller, who was a physician at San Felipe, were selected for this committee, but only Austin was able to make the journey. He left Texas late in April and arrived in Mexico City in July, with high hopes of success. Little did he suspect the fate that awaited him.

5

The Texas Revolution

The Outbreak of Resistance

The Downfall of Federalism Carrying the petition of the Convention of 1833, Austin made his second trip to Mexico City and found as great a political confusion as he had during his first visit in 1823. Santa Anna, on whom Texas had pinned its ambitions for statehood and the renewal of immigration, had embarked upon a secretive and complex voyage into the turbulent waters of Mexican politics. Although elected president in the deferred elections of January 1833, he had refused to be inaugurated in April and had installed instead as acting chief executive his vice-president, Gómez Farías, on the pretext of retiring to his estate of Manga de Clavo to "recruit his health." Actually, he knew Farías to be a devoted Federalist and a dedicated reformer, and he planned to be safely on the sidelines when the new government exploded its changes over Mexico. If these changes were not welcomed, as indeed they were not, he would remain prudently uninvolved—the champion of law and order, not reform and agitation.

THE TEXAS REVOLUTION

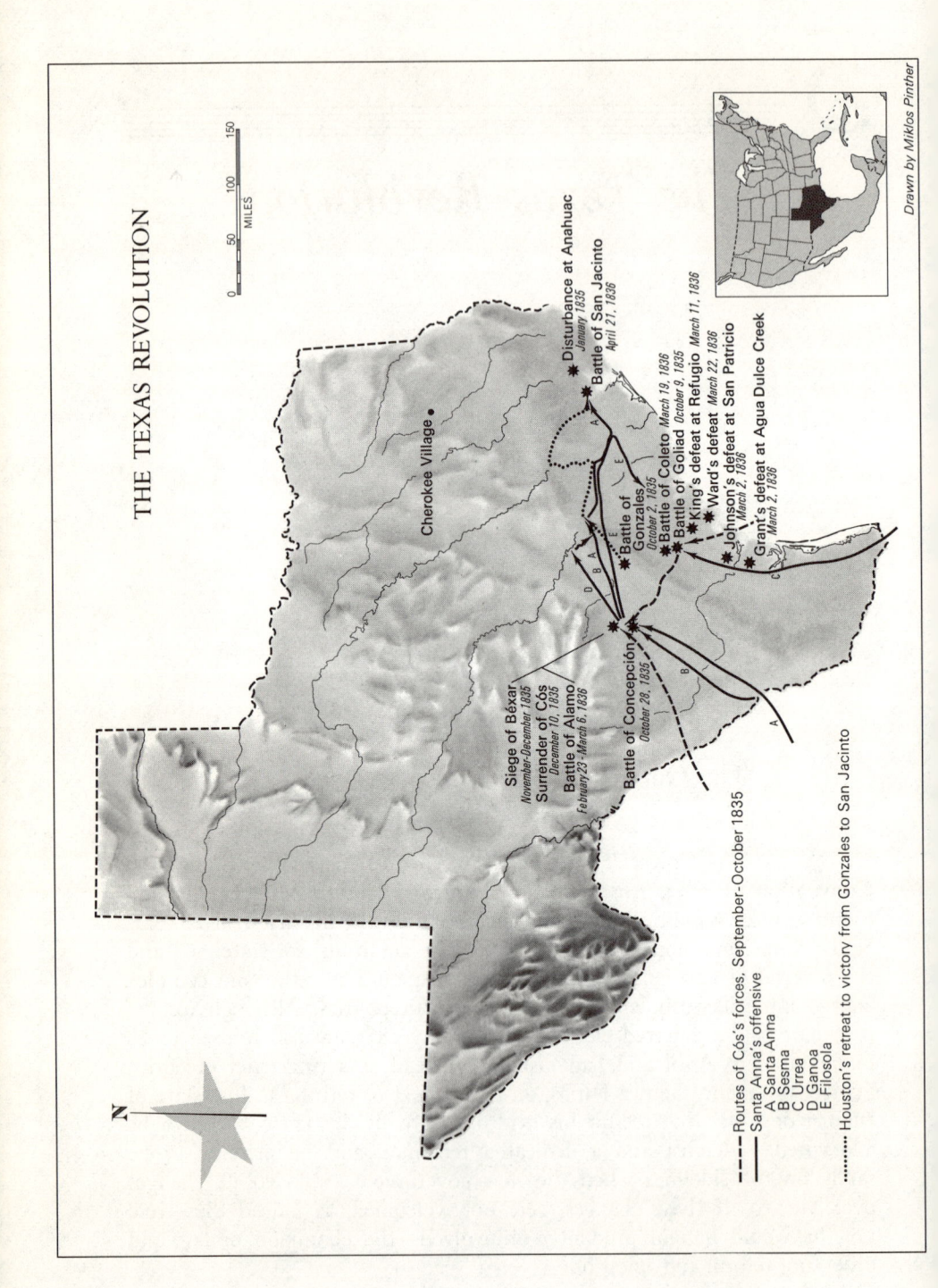

The first Farías reform, directed principally against the entrenched hierarchy of church and army, immediately provoked a new revolution. Six weeks after the inauguration Santa Anna returned to Mexico City, assumed the presidency, and marched off to put down the uprising. In what seems a remarkable farce of beautifully staged events, he was "captured" by the conservative insurrectionists, who proposed that he become their leader in the restoration of established privileges. Farías reassumed the presidency, but Santa Anna effected an "escape" from his "captors," returned to the capital in June 1833, and took over the executive power again. He nullified the reforms and returned once more to his hacienda in December, leaving Farías with free rein to initiate other reforms. Chief among these was a law for the separation of church and state, which prompted another uprising. Eventually, in April 1834, the astute Santa Anna, aware that the great majority of Mexican people were exasperated with an overdose of liberalism, stepped back into the presidency, but this time donning the cloak of conservatism. He would soon exchange it for the mantle of Centralist dictatorship.

He forced the hapless Farías into exile and in May dismissed the cabinet, dissolved congress, repudiated the government's reform measures, and began disbanding state legislatures and even local ayuntamientos that supported the Farías programs. In the comic opera of the preceding year he had exchanged the executive power with his scapegoat vice-president five times while he sampled the taste of reform and the waning strength of Federalism around the nation. He now began to move toward dictatorship, a complete apostate from the cause he had once led.

Austin observed the opening scenes of this frenetic drama in frustrated bewilderment. He arrived in Mexico City just as Santa Anna seized power the first time and was puzzled, if not a little skeptical, at the subsequent "capture" and "escape." During this period he submitted the Texan memorials to Farías but was not cordially received by the acting executive, who professed not to understand the nature of the Texans' demands. Discouraged, Austin wrote a fateful letter to the ayuntamiento in San Antonio, urging the Hispanic element of that city to take the lead in establishment of the separate state government in Texas. The national government in Mexico City would accept, he felt, a fait accompli, especially if it had been effected by the people of San Antonio.

After this letter, which was to embroil Austin in grave difficulty, had been sent on its way, Santa Anna returned to the presidency and directed governmental affairs for six months, from July to December 1833. Austin found him receptive and even friendly, and he soon accomplished the major portion of his mission. Only the petition for statehood was denied. The Law of April 6, 1830, was repealed, and the other measures the

Texans proposed were promised. Pleased by his achievements, and with the hasty letter forgotten, Austin set out overland for Texas. When he reached Saltillo in December he was arrested without warning and transported back to an old Inquisition prison in Mexico City.

For six months Austin was held in confinement in a narrow cell, thirteen feet by sixteen feet. During the first month he was allowed to speak to no one except the guard who served his meals through a slot in the door. Later he was given writing materials, and some friends in Mexico City were permitted to send books to him. A small skylight admitted during the middle of the day enough sunlight to read. Although he had to pay his own expenses in prison, he was neither allowed bail nor even informed of the charges against him. His confinement, ordered by Gómez Farías on the recommendation of Vicente Filisola, commanding general of the Eastern Interior Provinces, made a mocking travesty of the avowed liberalism of Federalist leaders.

Filisola, an Italian who had fought first in the Royalist ranks in Mexico, then with Iturbide, later with the Federalists, and finally for the Centralists, believed that Austin's letter to the ayuntamiento at San Antonio was tantamount to treason. The ayuntamiento had referred the letter to Músquiz, the political chief, who immediately sent it to the governor, who in turn passed it to Filisola. Farías, hopelessly entangled in the imbroglios of Santa Anna, saw it only as a precursor of revolution and, disregarding all principles of justice, clapped Austin into prison. When General Santa Anna reassumed the presidency for the last time in April 1834, he ordered Austin removed from solitary confinement. But still no charges were made. In June Austin was transferred to a city jail, and in December, thanks principally to the efforts of two attorneys from Texas, Peter W. Grayson and Spencer H. Jack, he was released on bail. Six months later, in July 1835, a court decided that Austin was eligible for freedom under the terms of a general amnesty law previously passed for the benefit of political prisoners. During his entire eighteen months travail he had never been charged or tried. But it was clear that at least some in Mexico believed that the gentle, ever-patient Austin was fomenting rebellion in Texas.

Before he was ousted from office, Farías sent Juan N. Almonte, an educated, English-speaking army officer, to make a tour of inspection in Texas in the spring of 1834. Almonte's observations are valuable, not only for his description of Texas but also for his conclusions regarding the people's intentions. He found the settlements in an almost thriving prosperity, with a total population of twenty-one thousand. Nowhere did he discern unrest or disloyalty toward Mexico. Rather he reported that a wholesome spirit of cooperation prevailed and that Texas could be expected to support the general government in Mexico.

One reason for the apparent satisfaction in Texas was the remission of immigration restrictions that was approved by Santa Anna in the fall of 1833 to become effective in May 1834. At once a stream of settlers poured over the American border into Texas. Although there is no basis for a statistical estimate, contemporary observations indicate that hundreds, perhaps even thousands, of people settled in the province during the following twelve months. Few of them, it should be noted, had substantial ties with the Mexican government, and many did not receive titles to their lands until well after the Texas Revolution.

So Texas was satisfied by the renewal of immigration and the implementation of other promised reforms by the state legislature. In March 1833 a liberal legislature had transferred the capital to Monclova. There the government had instituted measures for dividing Texas into three departments and for reshaping the judicial procedures. The changes in the judiciary were never accomplished, but the establishment of departments was quickly done. The new department of Nacogdoches comprised the settlements east of the Trinity and Brazos. The second new department, called Brazos, encompassed the Anglo-American area of Texas between the Colorado and the Trinity. The department of Béxar was reduced to the settlements south and west of the Colorado, including Goliad and San Antonio.

The tendency of the liberal deputation at Monclova toward generosity in the granting of lands also gratified Texans, at least in the beginning. By 1835 this generosity was suspected to have grown into corruption, and in later years Texas courts refused to recognize some of these grants. But while the state government was evidencing its friendliness toward Texas, the pace of events quickened to a stampede that trampled the Monclova government.

For condemning Santa Anna's banishment of Farías and dismissal of congress, it was soon to suffer his displeasure. The ayuntamiento at Saltillo, restive ever since the removal of the capital, took advantage of the situation and declared in July 1834 that by failure to support Santa Anna the Monclova government had lost legal jurisdiction. The people of Saltillo then chose their own governor. Both sides raised militia forces, but the impending clash was averted in December when Santa Anna recognized the Monclova government. He appointed his brother-in-law, Martín Perfecto de Cós, commandant of the Eastern Interior Provinces and ordered new elections to be held.

Cós, however, resented the annoying Federalist tendencies of the

Monclova government and the new deputation elected in the spring of 1835. Furthermore, he favored the pretensions of Saltillo. After additional quarrels between the two cities he intervened with force. While he was leading a small army toward Monclova, the legislature adjourned on May 21, 1835, authorizing the governor, Agustín Viesca, to move the capital wherever he saw fit. Vacillating too long, Viesca, led by Ben Milam, headed across the mountains toward San Antonio. He was captured by Cós on June 8, but Milam eluded the army and cautiously made his way back to Texas.

By this time all of Mexico was in a turmoil. Santa Anna's open espousal of Centralism after his return to the presidency had taken many Federalists by surprise. His dismissal of congress and several state legislatures in the summer of 1834 was quickly followed by the bogus election of a new congress entirely subservient to his demands. Before the Federalists had time to regroup, decree after decree undermined the federal structure and devastated the rights of individuals under the Constitution of 1824. Finally, in October 1835, the federal constitution itself was abrogated and replaced by a new document known as the *Siete Leyes*, which provided a completely centralized government and converted the states of the erstwhile republic into departments ruled by governors appointed by the president—for which, read dictator.

The dictatorship of Santa Anna began, however, months before this act, which merely bore witness to his power. With it began anew the struggle between Centralists and Federalists for control of the Mexican nation. Most of the Mexican states soon became embroiled in the general insurrection against the dictatorship, either directly, as Yucatan, or indirectly, as those nearer the capital, but in the beginning only California, Zacatecas, and Coahuila y Texas dared to resist. Although California was much too far away to be reached by force, pressure within ultimately forced the Federalist government there to accept the *Siete Leyes* in 1839. Zacatecas was near, and the wrath of Santa Anna fell on it before his disastrous attempt to crush Texas under his heel. The stalwart people of Zacatecas, led by their governor, resisted a decree calling for reduction of the militia and for surrender of excess arms and ammunition to the central government. Santa Anna himself headed the army that defeated the Zacatecans on May 10 and extracted a bloody vengeance.

This same month, Cós harried the state government of Coahuila y Texas from Monclova, and resistance became centered in Texas. At first the reactions in Texas were mixed: many were disgusted with the speculations of a horde of land speculators who had engulfed the government at Monclova; others were unaware of the naked implications of Santa Anna's apostasy. Trouble began in Anahuac (again!), but in the general ambivalence of public opinion, resistance did not crystallize until fall.

Resistance in Texas The post at Anahuac had been reoccupied by Captain Antonio Tenorio in January 1835. Soon he fell afoul the colonists by arresting Andrew Briscoe and DeWitt C. Harris, who had refused to pay customs duties because of the awkward procedures that had been reinstituted. Cós, learning of the trouble, wrote Tenorio that reinforcements were on the way. This message was intercepted at San Felipe, where a hotheaded citizens meeting hastily organized a militia force under William Barrett Travis to drive Tenorio out of Texas. On June 30 Travis and his men invested the post, and Tenorio meekly surrendered without an exchange of shots.

But Texas was not yet ready for an open break with Santa Anna. In most of the towns, committees of safety and correspondence had been organized or reorganized. Some of these expressed approbation of Travis's action, but not those anxious to avoid entanglement in Mexican political quarrels. San Felipe sent an apology to Cós in mid-July, and a week later a joint action of the committees of Mina (Bastrop), Columbia, and San Felipe sent a special messenger on a mission of conciliation. For several months Texans had been dividing into the so-called peace party, which favored support of Santa Anna, and the war party, which urged armed resistance and even a declaration of independence from Mexico.

General Cós refused to accept the offer of peace. He ordered the arrests of Travis for his attack on Tenorio, of R. M. "Three-Legged Willie" Williamson for an inflammatory speech on the Fourth of July, of Francis W. Johnson for his involvement with the Monclova land speculators, and of Lorenzo de Zavala, the Mexican liberal leader who had fled to Texas. The colonists were not prepared to fulfill this demand. Even before the trouble at Anahuac several of the committees had suggested another convention; on August 15 the committee at Columbia sent out a general call for the municipalities to elect delegates for a General Consultation at Washington-on-the-Brazos in October to consider Texas' position. It appeared to be a step toward outright resistance and toward war.

Whatever hopes the peace party had for conciliation were dashed when Austin returned to Texas the last week in August, freed at last from his long imprisonment. In a notable speech at Brazoria describing the situation in Mexico he is reported to have declared, "War is our only recourse." Austin endorsed the call for the Consultation, and the way was paved for resistance.

And resistance came with the demand from Colonel Domingo de Ugartechea at San Antonio that the people of Gonzales return the cannon given them in 1832 for defense against Indians. Andrew Ponton, the alcalde, put off with excuses the detachment sent for the cannon and meanwhile dispatched a call for aid from the other municipalities. The cannon was buried in a peach orchard, but as volunteers began to arrive in Gonzales, it was dug up and mounted on an ox cart over which a hastily contrived banner read: COME AND TAKE IT. When his men returned emptyhanded, Ugartechea ordered a hundred dragoons to Gonzales to take the cannon by force. The detachment was met on October 2 by one hundred and sixty volunteers headed by John H. Moore across the Guadalupe River about four miles above the town. The volunteers fired; a dragoon fell, killed; the lieutenant in charge, Francisco Castañeda, ordered a retreat; and the Texas Revolution began.

Word of the Battle of Gonzales spread through Texas like a grass fire across the prairie. Already alerted by the committees of safety and correspondence, many men were under arms. A number had headed toward the coast to intercept General Cós, who was reported to have arrived to take command in Texas. But all volunteers now rushed to the defense of Gonzales. Cós, hastening toward San Antonio, left a small detachment at the presidio at Goliad, where on October 9 occurred the Battle of Goliad. One company of Texan volunteers, led by George M. Collinsworth, had refused to be diverted toward Gonzales. At Victoria Collinsworth learned that Cós had passed through Goliad, and he and his men resolved to attack. They were joined by Ben Milam, then returning from Mexico. At eleven o'clock that night they reached the presidio, forced open the doors of the chapel where the Mexican soldiers were quartered, and after a brief skirmish accepted the surrender of the defenders. In the melee three Mexican soldiers were wounded and one was killed. The Texans had one man wounded, the first of the Revolution, a free Negro named Samuel McCullough.

The capture of Goliad was important for two reasons. First, it placed in Texan hands a large quantity of lead and powder and other military supplies that Cós had deposited there. Second, the Texan occupation of Goliad and the subsequent accumulation of volunteers there denied Cós access to the coast.

Cós arrived at San Antonio with four hundred men. Reinforcements that arrived from Coahuila about the same time and the troops under Ugartechea raised Cós' command to approximately twelve hundred men. Alarmed by the colonists' activity, he decided to fortify San Antonio as best he could and defend himself there.

Meanwhile volunteers from all over Texas continued to converge on

Gonzales. The Consultation was unable to meet at Washington-on-the-Brazos because most of the delegates were under arms at Gonzales, so it was rescheduled for San Felipe in November. There was great confusion over leadership among the volunteers encamped at Gonzales, for each group vied with the others for the election of its own captain as commander in chief, and a dozen such captains claimed ascendancy. The contest, which might have stymied the war effort, was resolved when Stephen F. Austin arrived and was unanimously elected the commanding general. He quickly organized the men into companies, appointed a general staff, and accepted the overwhelming verdict of men and captains that San Antonio should be attacked. The march there from Gonzales began on October 12.

Two weeks later the still somewhat disorganized Texans, styling themselves the Volunteer Army of Texas, reached the missions on the outskirts of the city. James Bowie and James W. Fannin were sent with a detachment of ninety men to reconnoiter the Mexican position. On October 28 they were attacked near the Mission Concepción by about four hundred Mexican cavalry troops. During the thirty minutes of fighting one Texan and some sixty Mexicans were lost. The Mexicans hastily withdrew to San Antonio, abandoning several artillery pieces and some supply wagons. The Battle of Concepción was the first and probably the most important of a series of skirmishes outside San Antonio during the next month while the Texans kept Cós under siege. Austin and his staff established headquarters at the Old Mill between Concepción and San Antonio. They hoped to force surrender from Cós by the attrition of his supplies. The siege of Béxar culminated in an attack on San Antonio, but before the assault a decisive political action gave it meaning and purpose.

The Federalist Rebellion against Tyranny

The Organization of Provisional Government Delegates to the Consultation of 1835 assembled a few at a time in San Felipe during the exciting days of October. The committee of safety there with a few delegates from other municipalities organized a temporary governing body on October 11. Called the Permanent Council, it undertook to handle the nonmilitary affairs of Texas until a quorum arrived for the Consultation. Although its real effectiveness is a matter of debate, it was a focal point for the incipient Revolution and a central clearing house for information. Through Thomas F. McKinney, a Texas merchant whose credit was quite strong in New Orleans, it borrowed $100,000, bought supplies for the army, issued appeals for volunteers from the United States, and initiated other vital measures. After three weeks it turned the institution of government over to the Consultation on November 3 when a quorum finally arrived at San Felipe.

The Consultation quickly organized to elect Branch T. Archer president and proceed at once to a lengthy discussion of the objectives of the war effort. For several months a sentiment had been building among Texans for separation from the unstable government of Mexico with the ultimate aim of joining the United States, not an unnatural feeling for most of the colonists. These advocates of independence were called the independence party or the war party. Among the most outspoken were Henry Smith and John A. Wharton. Austin, who on his return from Mexico had argued for the necessity of war, was the principal voice of what has incongruously been called the peace party, the second faction at the Consultation. This group had consistently supported the Constitution of 1824, opposed the rising tide of centralism, and advocated cooperation with the Federalists in Mexico. Although he did not attend the meeting, Austin sent a lengthy statement of his views. Archer, Sam Houston, and others represented this faction at the Consultation, and in a keynote address Archer proposed that Texas establish itself as a provisional state in the now-defunct Republic of Mexico to serve as a nucleus for the Federalist insurrection.

Two and a half days were spent debating a declaration "setting forth to the world the causes that impelled us to take up arms and the objectives for which we fight." On November 6 the issues were put to a vote, and on the critical question of a declaration of independence the vote was thirty-three to fifteen against it. The following day a declaration in support of the federal Constitution of 1824 was formally adopted, and the delegates turned their attention to the establishment of a provisional government.

The Organic Law, behind the provisional government, provided for a governor, a lieutenant governor, and a general council consisting of a delegate from each municipality. But the document inadequately defined the executive and legislative powers and was wholly unsatisfactory as an instrument of government. Henry Smith, a competent man but a contentious proponent of independence, was with a similar lack of foresight elected governor, and James W. Robinson was chosen lieutenant governor.

Before it adjourned on November 14, the Consultation ordered all land operations halted; authorized the provisional government to borrow money for the war; appointed Sam Houston commander of all troops except those then at San Antonio; commissioned Austin, Archer, and William H. Wharton to appeal for aid in the United States; endorsed the work of the permanent council; made an ambiguous and misleading offer of friendship to the Cherokee Indians; and passed several other resolutions of lesser significance.

The Siege of Béxar   On November 25 Austin turned command of the army at San Antonio over to Edward Burleson and left to make preparations for his journey to the United States. The siege of the city, then beginning its second month, was growing wearisome to the volunteers, despite occasional skirmishes outside the city, and sentiment was developing for abandonment of the effort. The following day one of the best-known incidents of the campaign took place when James Bowie and about one hundred Texans intercepted a Mexican pack train making its way toward San Antonio carrying what was believed to be silver to pay Cós' troops. When Bowie attacked, Cós sent out reinforcements, and the fighting became general until the Mexicans effected a withdrawal. Some fifty Mexicans were killed, and two Texans were wounded. On ripping open the captured packs, the Texans discovered they contained grass and forage for Cós' animals rather than money for his troops. The affair was promptly labeled the Grass Fight.

That Cós was in need of fodder for his livestock indicated the effectiveness of the siege, but Burleson and his staff ignored it and a few days later decided to lift the siege and retire the army to winter quarters at Gonzales. Before this decision was acted upon, however, three Texans, including Samuel A. Maverick, who were prisoners in San Antonio escaped and made their way to the Texan camp on the evening of December 3. They reported the decay of morale and the shortage of supplies in the city, and Ben Milam took it upon himself to negate the order to withdraw. Calling for volunteers to follow him into San Antonio, he found the entire army disposed to attack.

An assault was organized with Milam in command of one column, Francis W. Johnson of another, and Burleson of a third. At dawn on December 5 Milam's and Johnson's forces attacked, with Burleson's in reserve and James C. Neill's company making a diversionary attack from a different direction. The fighting was intense, as Cós was well prepared. Barraged by artillery fire, the Texans literally fought their way from house to house and street to street for five days. Milam was killed on the third day of the fighting. On December 9, Cós raised a flag of truce and the next day accepted the terms of surrender offered him by Burleson and his staff.

Taking their cue from the November 7 declaration of the Consultation, the Texans required Cós and his officers to vow not to interfere with the restoration of the Constitution of 1824 and to withdraw across the Rio Grande. Convict soldiers serving in the army were also required to leave Texas, but others were allowed to remain if they declared their loyalty to the constitution, which a number did. Permitted to retain sufficient arms and ammunition to protect themselves from Indians, Cós and his army of some twelve to fourteen hundred men crossed the Rio Grande on Christmas day, defeated and disgraced. It must have been especially embittering that the Texans had humbled them in the name of their own constitutional government. And it was especially fatuous of the Texans to think that Cós and his officers would honor their pledges.

It was a substantial triumph for Texas, and in short order the few remaining Mexican troops were evacuated from other small garrisons. But the victory was soon to be tragically marred by confusion and dissension. An early evidence of this confusion was a resolution passed by the council on December 10, the same day Cós capitulated, calling for a new convention to meet at Washington-on-the-Brazos in March to draft a constitution for a new government. The move seemed to presage complete independence from Mexico, but its intent is not completely clear. Smith, staunch proponent of independence, vetoed the measure, and it was passed over his veto on December 13.

Confusion in Texas Before long Smith and the council were at complete odds, and the governor, grandly exercising the ancient prerogative of British kings, dissolved the council. In rejection of this arrogance the council impeached Smith and continued to meet, with James W. Robinson as acting governor. But their efforts were ineffective, and by the end of January not enough delegates were left at San Felipe for a quorum, and Texas no longer had a government.

The chief quarrel between Smith and the council concerned a rather preposterous plan to invade Mexico through Matamoros. The initial scheme was suggested at the Consultation and approved by that body. After the victory at San Antonio and the expulsion of Mexican troops from Texas, the idea was urged again by several persons, and many of the volunteers streaming in from the United States were eager for an expedition against Matamoros. Governor Smith approved at first and ordered James Bowie to organize and command the scattered volunteer forces. Houston did not sanction the harebrained proposal and apparently failed to deliver the order to Bowie. Smith swung over to Houston's view, but the council then espoused the invasion and advised Houston to lead it. When he declined, the council commissioned Francis W. Johnson to take command and later approved his plans for the proposed expedition. Johnson with the aid of James Grant gathered volunteers at Refugio and Goliad and sent to San Antonio for additional men. James C. Neill, in command there, objected to the weakening of his defensive force and wrote Smith advising against his campaign. Smith, who had vetoed the council's action, then wrote the council admonishing the delegates in haughty and apparently vituperative language not to meddle in military affairs. His letter and the council's equally violent reply caused the open break on January 10.

While the dissonance between the governor and council mounted, conditions approaching chaos arose among the Texas military forces. Believing that Johnson had abandoned the Matamoros campaign, the council ordered James W. Fannin to undertake it. Fannin moved his command from the coast to Refugio and finally to Goliad, garnering about four hundred volunteers. Johnson and Grant, giving only tacit acceptance to Fannin's command, moved to San Patricio with about sixty or seventy men. Houston attempted to dissuade the volunteers from the movement and was rejected by them. Because of the discordant posture of his "army," Houston furloughed himself until March 1 to fulfill another duty assigned him, that of treating with his friends the Cherokee Indians in East Texas. Before he left, he sent orders by Bowie to Colonel Neill in San Antonio to destroy the fortifications there and draw back to Gonzales with all the military supplies he could move.

By this time no one doubted that Santa Anna intended personally to lead an army into Texas in the spring to avenge Cós' defeat and force Texas to submit to his dictatorship. Even then, in January, the Mexican leader was reported to be gathering his forces at Saltillo. If, while he attacked from the south, the Cherokee Indians fell upon the Texans' rear from the northeast, the fate of the Revolution would be sealed. Houston, forced to give up the futile attempt to organize the volunteers, turned his attention to securing if not the aid at least the neutrality of the Cherokees.

No man was better suited to this vital task. Houston had first come to Texas on behalf of the Cherokees in 1832, had lived with them in Indian Territory after his resignation as governor of Tennessee, and had visited Washington in 1834 as the self-appointed ambassador of the Cherokee Nation. In a resolution on November 13 the Consultation had authorized a treaty with the Cherokees, and the council appointed Houston, John Forbes, and a third man, who refused to serve, to negotiate the agreement. On February 23 in the Cherokee village northwest of Nacogdoches a treaty was signed assuring the Cherokees the peaceful possession of their lands and promising the Texans the friendship and alliance of the Indians. It was a remarkably futile and ill-starred document. Houston and Forbes signed as representatives of a government that had passed out of existence by that time. Chief Bowles signed as representative of the Cherokees and of twelve associated bands of East Texas Indians who later claimed he had no right to speak for them. The treaty was never ratified by any responsible Texas government, and it was ultimately disavowed on the grounds that it had been ignored and even violated by the Cherokees. Although Chief Bowles' duplicity was later credibly established, the Cherokees were constrained from taking the warpath against the Texans in that fateful spring of 1836. Houston had at least accomplished this.

But the Texas military forces were hopelessly unprepared for Santa Anna's invasion. While the volunteers on the coast and around Goliad and Victoria quarreled over the futile Matamoros campaign, the defense of San Antonio continued to deteriorate. Neill disobeyed the order to withdraw, and when he took a leave to visit his family, Bowie also refused to instigate the retreat. Governor Smith ordered William Barrett Travis to San Antonio to take command, apparently intending the city's evacuation, but Travis too became enamored of the idea of defending the ancient capital "so dearly won," as he wrote, by the fighting in December. A potential dispute between Bowie and Travis over the command of San Antonio was resolved when Bowie, already too ill and emaciated by tuberculosis to be effective, was crippled by the fall of an artillery piece on the eve of the Mexican attack.

To the great surprise of the Texans at San Antonio, the vanguard of the Mexican Army was sighted on February 23. None had expected it so early, and the outcome was disaster at San Antonio and Goliad. Sending some fifteen hundred men under José Urrea from Matamoros up the coast, Santa Anna had crossed the Rio Grande at Laredo at the head of about six thousand troops. On his left marched Joaquín Ramirez y Sesma with over one thousand. The numerical advantage was overwhelming, and if the courage of the convict soldiers left something to be desired, the apparent discipline and organization was impressive. Furthermore, many of the Mexican troops were seasoned veterans of Santa Anna's earlier revolutionary successes. Egotistically styling himself the Napoleon of the West, Santa Anna was confident of victory. He reached San Antonio a few days before Urrea, who, advancing more cautiously, had first engaged the volunteers in the southeast; he effected a costly and bloody triumph at the Alamo nearly two weeks before Urrea defeated Fannin at Coleto Creek.

The Fall of the Alamo

At the first sight of the advancing Mexican Army, Travis withdrew his men into the walls of the Alamo and answered Santa Anna's demand for surrender with a cannon shot. He drove several head of cattle into the old mission courtyard, and he found corn in deserted houses nearby with which to feed them. The Texans, about half of whom were recently arrived volunteers from the United States, responded eagerly to Travis' heroic intention to defend the post. Among these newcomers was James Butler Bonham, who had organized the Mobile Grays for service in the Texas Revolution, and David Crockett, a former United States congressman from Tennessee of picturesque manner and speech, who had said that he went to Texas "to fight for my rights."

As the first units of the Mexican Army were investing San Antonio, Travis was able to send out several dramatic appeals for aid. One reached Fannin at Goliad, but while he vacillated over a decision, the Alamo was lost. Another reached the new convention assembled at Washington-on-the-Brazos, but there the delegates' initial urge to rush to Travis' aid gave way to the sobering necessity for the creation of a stable government. A third reached Gonzales, and thirty-two men marched to their deaths in the Alamo, the only response to Travis' appeals.

The men from Gonzales raised the strength of the defense to one hundred eighty-seven; by March 4 Santa Anna had between five and six thousand of his army in San Antonio. Between February 24 and March 5 he subjected the tiny band of defenders to almost constant cannonades and ordered several forays against the walls, which were turned back with mercilessly accurate rifle fire. At dawn on March 6 the final assault was made, and twice the Texans repelled waves of attack before the walls were breached and the horde of Mexican soldiers, prodded into action by the bayonets of their officers, drowned the Texans in a sea of blood. There is no history of the last hours of the defense: "Thermopylae had its messenger, the Alamo had none." The defenders were killed to a man, and on Santa Anna's orders their bodies were stacked and burned in a savage funeral pyre. Mexican losses were estimated at sixteen hundred.

Actually there were about fifteen noncombatants variously reported as survivors of the Alamo, none of whom was present in the last minutes of the battle. Among them were Victor Rose and Madame Candelaria, whose stories were disputed; two Negro servants, who were able to give little or no information; and Mrs. Almaron Dickenson, whose husband was killed in the fight and who bore the sad news to Gonzales. Several other aspects of the Alamo defense are but question marks on the pages of history. Not the least of these is Travis' unexplained remark in a letter of February 24 that "our flag still waves proudly over the walls." Was this merely literary license or was it the battle flag of the Mobile Grays, which Santa Anna himself noted was "found at the Alamo"? Or was it the flag of Coahuila y Texas, which Juan N. Almonte, Santa Anna's aide, said he saw when he approached San Antonio on February 23? Or was it the flag of the Republic of Mexico, which the martyrs believed they were defending? It was probably the latter, for the heroes of the Alamo died without hearing of the Texas Declaration of Independence adopted on March 2.

The convention had assembled on schedule at Washington-on-the-Brazos on March 1, and immediately after electing Richard Ellis of Jonesborough president it had passed unanimously a resolution stating that Texas should declare its independence of Mexico. The resolution was supported by Lorenzo de Zavala, the former Mexican liberal, and two other Mexicans who were delegates. George Childress headed the committee that drafted the Declaration of Independence, which on the following day, March 2, was unanimously adopted.

The War for Independence

The Convention of 1836 With the March 2 Declaration of Independence, the Texas Revolution passed into its final phase. No longer a mere insurrection against tyranny or a Federalist rebellion to save the Mexican Constitution, it was thenceforth a war for the independence of the Republic of Texas. The declaration was only a necessary precursor of the chief business of the convention: framing a constitution for the new republic and establishing a temporary government to prosecute the war. On March 4 it became the business of Sam Houston to win this war against desperately hopeless odds, for on that day he was reaffirmed as the commander in chief of all Texas forces in the field.

This convention was one of the ablest ever assembled in Texas, and the delegates rose to the challenge of the time. Most of them were young, under forty. Most of them were from southern states, nine coming from Virginia, but there was also a surprising heterogeneity in their origins— England, Wales, Vermont, Mexico, New York, Canada, Ohio, and Connecticut. Many of them had had legislative experience, and several had served on constitutional conventions in their home states. In less than three weeks they wrote a constitution for the Republic of Texas and created the ad interim government.

The constitution was an excellent one (and will be discussed briefly in the next chapter); the ad interim government was probably as effective as could have been managed at the time. It consisted only of an executive department. David G. Burnet was elected president; Lorenzo de Zavala, vice-president; Samuel P. Carson, secretary of state; Thomas Jefferson

Rusk, secretary of war; Bailey Hardeman, secretary of treasury; Robert Potter, secretary of navy; and David Thomas, attorney general. These men, all of some political experience and of considerable competence, were empowered to borrow money, issue promissory notes, commission privateers, purchase supplies, charter ships for a navy, recruit and enlist volunteers for the army, and do all things necessary to coordinate the war effort.

On the day the convention adjourned, March 17, the chances of a Texas victory appeared at the least precarious, if not altogether hopeless. Eight thousand or more Mexican troops were by this time across the Rio Grande. Most of these were yet at San Antonio, where the Alamo had fallen on March 6, but Santa Anna had three armies marching toward the settlements: one of about four or five hundred men under Goana was headed for Bastrop; a second of six to eight hundred under Ramirez y Sesma was approaching Burnam's Ferry on the Colorado; and a third of about fifteen hundred under Urrea was on its way to Goliad. The meager Texan forces consisted of four to five hundred men under Fannin's command in the Goliad area and a little over three hundred under Houston, then in retreat from Gonzales.

Shortly after his reappointment as commander in chief, Sam Houston had ridden from the convention at Washington-on-the-Brazos to Gonzales, where he found three hundred seventy-four poorly armed and disorganized volunteers. He quickly established the First Regiment of Texas Volunteers with Edward Burleson in command. On hearing of the fall of the Alamo from Mrs. Dickenson and learning from his scouts of Sesma's advance from San Antonio, Houston decided to retreat to the Colorado River after burning Gonzales to prevent its use by the enemy. He ordered Fannin to withdraw to Victoria, and in a series of forced marches he reached Burnam's Ferry and crossed the Colorado on March 17, the day the convention adjourned. During the withdrawal, recruits increased his force to about six hundred men.

The Loss of South Texas Fannin was perhaps the most incompetent leader of the revolutionary period; his greatest fault was indecision. When he received Houston's order to retreat from Goliad, he had already exhibited this tragic quality that was to doom the men under his command. Late in February he had decided to go to Travis' relief at the Alamo and had evacuated Goliad, but about two miles down the road he changed his mind and marched his men back to the old presidio of La Bahía. Renaming it Fort Defiance, he mounted cannon on the walls and put his volunteers to work digging trenches and throwing up earthworks.

As noted earlier, Frank W. Johnson and James Grant had begun in defiance of Fannin a raid toward Mexico and were wiped out by Urrea's advancing forces—Johnson with about forty men at San Patricio on February 27 and Grant with about thirty at Agua Dulce Creek on March 2. Learning of these disasters, Fannin ordered Amon King with most of his wagons to evacuate the civilians around Refugio. King encountered detachments of Urrea's cavalry, fled to the Refugio mission for cover, and sent for reinforcements. Fannin foolishly dispatched William Ward with nearly a hundred men to Refugio, and Ward, with equal lack of wisdom, attacked Urrea's army. Neither Ward's nor King's forces were able to rejoin Fannin. After several futile maneuvers and skirmishes both were finally trapped by the Mexicans—King on his return to the Refugio mission on March 11 and Ward as he tried to retreat to the coast on March 22.

Meantime in Goliad, weakened by this separation of his command, Fannin vacillated over whether to retreat as Houston had ordered or to remain until Ward and King returned. Finally on the evening of March 17 he and his staff decided upon retreat. The next day the remaining wagons were loaded, oxen and mules harnessed, horses saddled, and men readied for withdrawal. Then, Fannin postponed the retreat until the morning of March 19, and when he finally began, his men and animals were already fatigued. Furthermore, his delays had given Urrea time to move most of the units of his army into the vicinity. One additional mistake by Fannin sealed his fate. He halted his caravan for noon on Coleto Prairie, about three miles from Coleto Creek and the protective woods along its banks. There he and his men were surrounded by the Mexicans.

The ensuing Battle of Coleto lasted through the afternoon and night. Without food or water the Texans were forced to surrender the next morning, on March 20. Nine of Fannin's men had been killed and over fifty wounded; he surrendered an additional two hundred thirty-four troops. He and his staff believed that they had given up their arms as honorable prisoners of war, but the vindictive Santa Anna had decreed that all foreigners found under arms in Texas were to be executed, and he intended that his orders be obeyed. Urrea herded his prisoners back to Goliad and wrote Santa Anna seeking clemency for them. Santa Anna denied this and viciously reiterated the death sentence. On Palm Sunday, March 27, the prisoners were marched out of Goliad in three columns between lines of Mexican guards and brutally massacred. About two dozen managed to escape through the woods after the firing began.

It is impossible to estimate accurately the losses to Urrea during this campaign. Including the detachments under Grant, Johnson, Ward, and King with the hapless victims of Fannin's leadership, the total was probably over five hundred. Significant, although not as important, was the loss of most of the supplies that had been arriving on the coast and were stored at Goliad and nearby places.

The Campaign and Battle of San Jacinto Houston was on the east bank of the Colorado, facing Sesma's army approaching from the west, when he learned of Fannin's defeat. He had indicated his intention of defending the Colorado, but because of this disastrous loss he retreated once more, deeper into Texas. His small force now stood alone to defy Santa Anna, and he dared not risk it in a pitched battle. He pulled back to San Felipe and thence up the Brazos to Groce's Plantation near present Hempstead. There he remained encamped for nearly two weeks, reorganizing his units and drilling his undisciplined men incessantly.

Houston was severely criticized for his retrograde movements. Literally hundreds of his men deserted, and he would have had no army at all had there not been an offsetting arrival of volunteers during the retreat. Two companies, under Moseley Baker and Wiley Martin, flatly refused to withdraw from San Felipe, whereupon Houston calmly ordered them to remain and defend the crossing. The ad interim government urged Houston to fight, and Burnet scornfully wrote him to stop retreating and face the enemy. More telling than mutiny, desertion, and criticism was the settlers' panic caused by Houston's movements. Since he had begun the withdrawal at Gonzales, the evacuation of frightened civilians had grown to the hysterical exodus called the Runaway Scrape. With each retreat of the army, fear mounted and more settlers fled their homes. Soldiers who deserted to aid their families in the rout added to the terror. Thousands of refugees were plunging toward the safety of the United States border when Houston established camp at Groce's.

Almost constant rain made conditions miserable for soldiers and refugees alike. Rivers and streams overran their banks and made every crossing treacherous. Carts loaded with family possessions were often overturned in raging creeks or washed irretrievably downstream by the torrents. The army's wagons had to be partially unloaded and half-floated, half-carried across the major streams. Roads turned to quagmires pocked with bogholes. Men, horses, and wagons floundered through rather than over them. Everything remained thoroughly covered with mud, and people were wet to the skin most of the time. Chilling north winds from time to time changed discomfort to dangerous exposure and created a near epidemic of colds, influenza, and pneumonia among both refugees and troops. Groce's plantation home, Bernardo, was converted to a temporary hospital for the scores of men too ill to remain in their crude tents and shelters.

But disheartening as this inclement weather was for the Texans, it also not only delayed the Mexican advance but caused, at least in part, the fragmentation of Santa Anna's army and the dictator's own isolation finally from the major part of his army. Santa Anna had rushed from San Antonio to join Sesma on the Colorado when Sesma had reported Houston's presence at Burnam's. By the time the Mexicans crossed the Colorado River to chase Houston to San Felipe, it was already swollen with rain. At San Felipe, because the flood conditions of the Brazos made a crossing under the guns of Baker's and Martin's men almost impossible, Santa Anna abandoned pursuit of Houston to attempt to catch Burnet and the ad interim government at Harrisburg. Ordering Urrea at Goliad, Goana at Bastrop, and the main army en route from San Antonio to converge on the lower Brazos, he turned downstream to try to cross near present Richmond. There high water forced him to leave Sesma behind to construct large rafts for the heavy equipment while he lunged toward Harrisburg with fewer than six hundred men. It was this last move that brought his destruction.

Learning of Santa Anna's movements from his able scouting corps, led by Henry Karnes and Deaf Smith, Houston left Groce's and headed for Harrisburg. Despite numerous conflicting accounts and later variations in historical interpretation, there can be little doubt that Houston had by this time decided to attempt an engagement. He reached the smoldering ruins of Harrisburg on April 18 to discover that Burnet and the ad interim cabinet had fled to Galveston Island, with Santa Anna in pursuit as far as New Washington on the coast after putting Harrisburg to the torch. Leaving the army's baggage and the men incapacitated from illness in camp across the bayou from Harrisburg, with seventy-five men to guard them, Houston set out after Santa Anna on April 19 with about nine hundred troops eager for the battle.

Santa Anna had missed capturing the government at Harrisburg by a scant twelve hours, and a company of fifty dragoons that he sent racing to the coast came within rifle range of Burnet and his associates as they boarded a small boat and rowed toward a waiting schooner in the bay. Santa Anna followed at a leisurely pace and dawdled for a day and a half in the comfort of James Morgan's plantation at New Washington before he turned to try to intercept Houston's army at Lynch's Ferry across the San Jacinto River. From garbled intelligence of Houston's movements Santa Anna believed the Texas Army was planning to cross at Lynch's and retreat again toward the Sabine.

Houston had received much more accurate information about Santa Anna's strength and plans from two couriers captured by Deaf Smith outside of Harrisburg. He marched his weary but enthusiastic troops down the road toward Lynch's through the night of April 19 and in the morning bivouacked near the confluence of Buffalo Bayou and the San Jacinto River for breakfast. That afternoon the vanguard of Santa Anna's army was sighted as it too moved into the flood-surrounded peninsula that was to become the battlefield of San Jacinto. The time of decision was at hand.

There was an exchange of artillery fire in which both sides suffered men wounded. Then Sidney Sherman impetuously attempted to capture the Mexican cannon in a cavalry charge and was trapped by mounted Mexican dragoons. A general battle was averted only by the Texans' heroic efforts to extricate themselves. When they reached safety behind the Texan lines in a hollow along Buffalo Bayou, the fighting ceased, and the two armies prepared for battle. The Texans' position was the stronger, so Houston wanted Santa Anna to take the offensive. Nevertheless, Santa Anna, realizing he had needlessly jeopardized his force, desperately feared a Texan attack. Exact strengths cannot be authenticated. Houston later reported nine hundred eighteen men present, and the Mexican Army was probably about the same size or smaller.

During the night of April 20 Houston permitted his men to prepare a hot meal and to sleep. Santa Anna kept his forces on the alert and busy piling their baggage into protective breastworks. At dawn Santa Anna anxiously awaited a charge and his men stood hungry and sleepless at their posts. The Texans breakfasted and wondered what their general would decide. A council of war in the Texan camp was about equally divided on the question of offense versus defense. Houston himself remained uncommitted. During the morning four or five hundred reinforcements led by Martín Perfecto de Cós reached Santa Anna. This brought the Mexican strength to between twelve and fourteen hundred men and lulled Santa Anna into a sense of security. Convinced that now the Texans would not attack, he ordered the preparation of a hot meal, authorized his exhausted troops to relax under a skeletal guard, and retired to his tent. Houston, after sending Deaf Smith to cut Vince's Bridge across the overflowing bayou east of the battlefield, both to restrict a Mexican retreat and to hamper further reinforcements, called the Texans into formation at three thirty in the afternoon.

Noiselessly the Texans advanced across the prairie between the two camps to, incredibly, within two hundred yards of the Mexican lines before they were discovered. Then bedlam broke loose. A drum and bugle corps began playing a lively though somewhat incongruous tune popular at the time, "Will You Come to the Bower?" The Twin Sisters, a pair of cannons donated by the citizens of Cincinnati, belched shrapnel, nails, and broken horseshoes into the Mexican center. The cavalry stormed over the right side of the Mexican barricade, and the infantry broke into the left flank. Someone shouted, "Remember the Alamo! Remember Goliad!" and the phrases became an awe-inspiring battle cry. Caught utterly by surprise, the Mexicans attempted a brief rally, returned the opening fire, and then disintegrated into a frightened, bewildered mob. In less than eighteen minutes the Battle of San Jacinto was over.

An uncontrollable carnage followed as the Texans with wrathful vengeance slaughtered the demoralized Mexican troops by the hundreds. During the next several days the scattered, fleeing Mexicans were rounded up and brought into a hastily constructed prisoner of war compound. The Mexican losses were estimated at about six hundred fifty killed and about seven hundred fifty prisoners. The Texans suffered nine dead and thirty wounded, one of whom was Sam Houston, shot in the ankle. This almost unbelievable victory was made complete the second day after the fighting when Santa Anna was captured fleeing ignominiously in the tattered uniform of a private.

Thus, despite the remaining six thousand Mexican soldiers in Texas, the capture of Santa Anna meant that the Texans had not merely won a battle; they had won the war. Fearing that his life would be forfeit for his butchery at San Antonio and Goliad, Santa Anna readily agreed to order his armies out of Texas. Had Filisola, to whom the order was addressed, and the other generals elected to ignore their captured commander and continue fighting, the future of Texas would have been entirely different. For with Houston incapacitated by his wound and the Texan army utterly disorganized by its amazing victory, it would not have been difficult for the Mexicans to have routed them. The odds were still six or seven to one. But the Mexican generals crossed the Rio Grande as ordered, grouping their forces uncertainly at Matamoros to await further instructions.

Texas independence was won; it had yet to be sustained.

A Brief Analysis of the Causes of the Revolution

Because of changes in the interpretation of events in Texas under Mexican rule, a brief examination of the causes of the Texas Revolution might prove worthwhile. Four general theories have been advanced: (1) that the Revolution was a conspiracy by the slavocracy of the Old South to wrest Texas from Mexico and bring it into the United States as a slave state; (2) that the Revolution was an expression of Manifest Destiny, a reflection of United States imperialism, and a conspiracy of some kind between Andrew Jackson and Sam Houston; (3) that the Revolution was merely the inevitable result of the conflict in cultural background between Hispanic and Anglo; and (4) that it was primarily a constitutional conflict against the rising waters of Centralist tyranny in Mexico.

The first of these interpretations was the earliest, and as advanced in a preposterous book by the abolitionist leader Benjamin Lundy in 1836 the conspiracy of the slavocracy concept found ready acceptance among anti-slavery elements in the United States. The propaganda tract, entitled *The War in Texas*, was skillfully written, combining ignorance, half-truths, and fancied facts with beautiful logic. According to the theory, which was quickly elaborated on by others, the vast conspiracy to grab Texas for slavery began with the first Anglo-American colonists who came into Texas. True, a majority, although not an overwhelming one, of the Anglos in Texas were from the southern states. A number were slave owners, and many who were not aspired to be, and certainly southern leaders tended to be expansionists. But beyond this there is not a shred of evidence to support the idea of a conspiracy. Such an idea implied, of course, the existence of an omniscient group of southern leaders who masterminded the whole plot. The paranoid invention of powerful leaders and sinister plans is an intrinsic part of radical thought; the entire fabric of the theory is so implausible that it needs little discussion.

But the theory was important at the time, not only because it was espoused by abolitionists but also because it was integrated into the mishmash of Whig policies to linger in the minds of Americans until the Civil War. Such historians as Van Holst, who endeavored to interpret all of American history in terms of the slavery conflict, revived it and flung it once more into the current of historical interpretation. But since the beginning of modern American scholarship, the conspiracy thesis has hardly been given a creditable glance.

The second interpretation, focusing on United States imperialism, is in part a modification of the slavocracy thesis. Here too one often finds the image of evil masters and insidious plots, this time for the expansion of the United States rather than merely the South. An additional element is the notion that Manifest Destiny was (rather than the original idea of the spread of the American system of government more than the expansion of United States territory) a driving, incorrigible force that turned American homesteaders into greedy beasts intent on territorial rapine in the national interest. Another piece of fancy in this interpretation is that Sam Houston came to Texas as Jackson's secret agent to help provoke the Revolution.

The concept of United States imperialism in Texas emerged slowly around the turn of the century and was then given inadvertent substance by the eminent historians George P. Garrison and Eugene C. Barker, who focused attention on the westward movement of Anglo-American settlement. These men, influenced by Frederick Jackson Turner's thesis of the significance of the frontier in American history, were by no means blind to other historical forces and were certainly not deprecators of the American motive, but in their emphasis on the advancing frontier they contributed grist to the mills of those who have chosen to portray the United States as an imperialist aggressor.

This theory is based on much more logic than the slavocracy interpretation, for American people generally had a sense of mission concerning the virtues of their institutions. But in addition to the paranoid delusion of conspiracy, this theory entails the sophistry of semantic perversion and the fallacy of anthropomorphism: the expository concept of Manifest Destiny cannot logically be twisted to mean a source of motivation in individual action, and the combination of individual and discrete motives cannot logically be ascribed, even if there were considerable homogeneity in them, to a government that was not at all a unitary personality. Furthermore, the theory runs roughshod over readily available facts, as traced in this chapter. Yet nonetheless in watered-down form it has found its way into a number of surveys of American history.

The third interpretation of the origins of the Texas Revolution grew out of research in Texas history but was molded by the preconceived notion that prior to the Revolution a basic antipathy existed between Anglos and Hispanics. That such animosity existed later cannot be denied, but that it existed in the 1820's and 1830's is an untenable proposition, except for that shown by ardent Centralists toward the United States. It would be a lengthy but easy task to demonstrate that, to the contrary, there was a marked amount of tolerance between these groups. The evidence exists in the Anglo settler's ready acceptance of Mexican laws and religion, in the large number of Anglo-Hispanic marriages, in the many business partnerships, and above all in the almost total lack of friction traceable to racial problems during the colonial period.

The essence of the cultural conflict interpretation is the assumption that the cultural differences inevitably meant conflict. The differences existed, but conflicts because of them were surprisingly rare. The Anglo settlers were Protestants whereas the Mexicans were Roman Catholics, but not a trace of trouble arose because of this, partly because few Anglo settlers were strongly interested in religion and partly because the Catholic church did not establish parishes among them. It is claimed that the two peoples were linguistically separated and therefore irresistibly drawn into misunderstandings. But in fact the language barrier caused no serious problems. Many of the Anglo leaders, like Austin, quickly learned Spanish, and many Hispanic officials spoke English with some fluency. The constitution and the important decrees were published in English in such colonial newspapers as the *Gazette* and the *Telegraph*. The Anglo ayuntamientos conducted their business in English and communicated with the state government in acceptable Spanish. None of the difficulties of the colonists can be laid to the language barrier.

It is asserted, more to the point, that the two groups differed in political heritage. The Anglos had a long background of self-government and the English common law whereas the Hispanics had been for generations accustomed to governmental autocracy and the trying peculiarities of Roman law. Without question these differences caused problems, but not problems serious enough to produce war. Because a criminal trial without a jury was inconceivable to most of the Anglo settlers and because the judicial system of Coahuila y Texas was extremely complex anyway, they regularly subverted it with extralegal procedures such as letting the ayuntamiento sit as a trial jury. They governed themselves fairly skillfully at local levels and had few dealings with government at higher levels. When they held the conventions of 1832 and 1833, they acted in keeping with their heritage and did not understand the government's objections to the assemblies. But neither of these meetings was in the least warlike. There were a score of other examples of friction from differences in political tradition, but all of them together were insufficient to cause a revolution. The Mexican Constitution of 1824 and the Republic that it created were in the best republican and democratic traditions of the times. The Anglos were dissatisfied not with the framework of government and only occasionally with the interpretations of officialdom.

It is further asserted quite seriously by historians that the Anglos were energetically aggressive, blunt, and straightforward whereas the Hispanics were indolently passive, secretive, devious, and otherwise different in character. In a general way such a gulf did exist, but more because the difficulties of migration screened out lazy and unenterprising Anglos than because the differences were inherent in the people. Many of the Hispanics had drifted in during the century of Spanish domination and had settled into a pattern of subsistence living. Few had the benefit of any education at all. On the other hand, such men as Lorenzo de Zavala and Juan Veramendi, father-in-law and business partner of James Bowie, had outstanding energy and ambition. The differences in the two groups should be attributed to economic and social factors rather than inherent racial characteristics.

This cultural conflict is often argued to be the cause of the Revolution by an emphasis on the half-dozen outbreaks during the colonial period rather than on the surprising peace that normally prevailed. Besides, these few outbreaks were not really seated in cultural friction. The Fredonian

Rebellion was caused less by the Haden Edwards conflict with Hispanic settlers than by the Nacogdoches election quarrel between Anglo factions led by James Norris and Martin Parmer. The disturbance at Anahuac was brought on entirely by the arrogance of Kentuckian John Davis Bradburn, not by Anglo-Hispanic friction. The quarrel between Martin de León and Green DeWitt was over land boundaries and smuggling, not racial background.

The most recent interpretation of the cause of the Revolution is the one followed in this chapter: that the Revolution resulted from the overthrow of the Republic of Mexico and the abrogation of its constitution by Centralist forces that substituted a dictatorship for democracy. The insurrection that followed shook Mexico for years and created in many Mexican states a general movement of separatism too complex for evaluation here. The Texas Revolution began as one of these efforts to restore the constitution and only later became a fight for separate existence. The chief difference between it and the later Republic of the Rio Grande in northern Mexico or the insurrection in Yucatan or other uprisings is that it was successful. It is of secondary although vital importance that most of the rebels in Texas were from the United States and that their plight drew ready sympathy and quick aid from the adjacent nation. Without such aid and without the incredible good fortune of the entrapment and capture of Santa Anna, the Texas Revolution would unquestionably have failed.

The outbreak of hostilities in Texas can be satisfactorily explained only as a reflection of the constitutional conflict in Mexico. And the participants consistently reiterated this, from 1832 and the Turtle Bayou resolutions to 1835 and the November 7 declaration of the Consultation, and ultimately in 1836 with the Declaration of Independence itself. But to discount the other interpretations of the Revolution is not to deny that some individuals were excited to rebellion by the themes of those interpretations. Unquestionably some slave owners yearned to bring Texas into the union as a slave state. Undeniably some settlers when they first entered Texas hoped for the future absorption of the area by the United States. And indisputably some Anglos felt strong racial aversion to the Hispanic-Indian. But these were individual motivations, among a minority of settlers, and not cause for concerted rebellion.

6

The Republic of Texas

The Establishment of Government

Problems of the Ad Interim Government On receiving Houston's report of the victory at San Jacinto and the capture of Santa Anna, President David G. Burnet and the ad interim government moved from Galveston Island to Velasco at the mouth of the Brazos. There on May 14 the two treaties of Velasco were signed by Burnet and Santa Anna. One, to be made public immediately, declared that hostilities between Texas and Mexico had ended, that Santa Anna would not again make war on Texas, that all Mexican troops were to withdraw south of the Rio Grande, that restitution would be made for property confiscated or destroyed by the Mexicans, that prisoners would be exchanged on an equal basis (the Texans, however, now held many more prisoners than did the Mexicans), and that Santa Anna would be returned to Mexico as soon as possible. The other treaty was to be kept secret until both treaties were fulfilled. It offered Santa Anna his immediate release and return to Mexico provided that he promised to secure from the Mexican government recog-

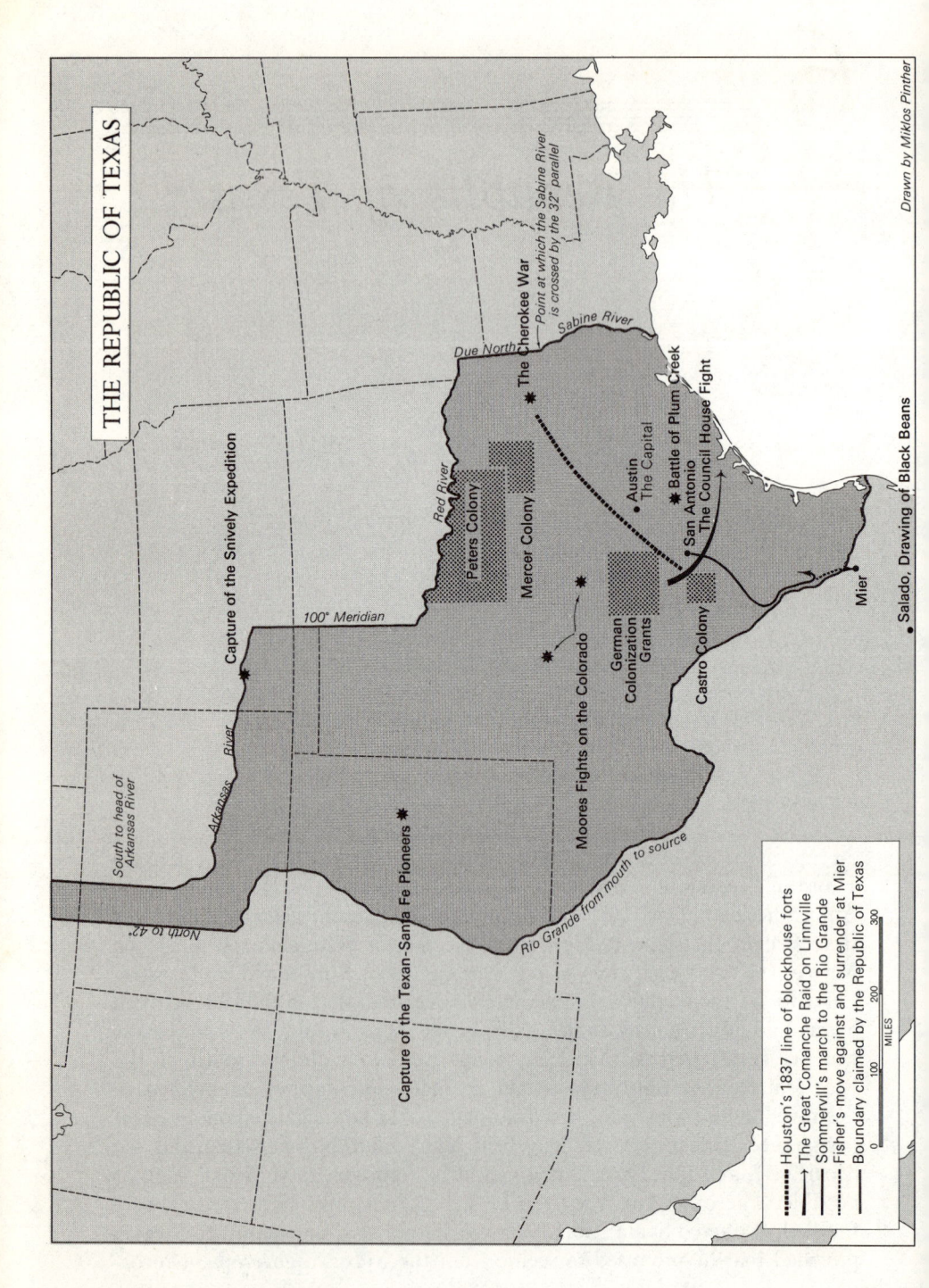

THE REPUBLIC OF TEXAS

Drawn by Miklos Pinther

Point at which the Sabine River is crossed by the 32° parallel

Due North

Sabine River

The Cherokee War

Red River

Peters Colony

Mercer Colony

Austin — The Capital

Battle of Plum Creek

San Antonio — The Council House Fight

100° Meridian

German Colonization Grants

Castro Colony

Moores Fights on the Colorado

Capture of the Snively Expedition

Arkansas River

South to head of Arkansas River

North to 42°

Capture of the Texan–Santa Fe Pioneers

Rio Grande from mouth to source

Mier

Salado, Drawing of Black Beans

Legend:
- Houston's 1837 line of blockhouse forts
- The Great Comanche Raid on Linnville
- Sommervill's march to the Rio Grande
- Fisher's move against and surrender at Mier
- Boundary claimed by the Republic of Texas

0 100 200 300 MILES

124

nition of Texas and a guarantee of the Rio Grande as the southern boundary.

Burnet was severely criticized for making this secret treaty. The argument was that it was fatuous to expect the Mexican dictator to keep his promise after he had been freed; not only had he signed the treaty under some duress but he was notorious for faithlessness. Particularly vehement in objecting to Santa Anna's release was Mirabeau B. Lamar, who had taken Rusk's place in the cabinet as secretary of war, Rusk having relieved Houston in command of the army when Houston went to New Orleans for treatment of his wounded leg. Lamar argued that Santa Anna should be held prisoner until the public treaty was fulfilled and until Mexico recognized the independence of Texas. Santa Anna should serve as a hostage for his own and his government's good faith. Because of the objections to the secret treaty, it did not remain secret, and a public outcry was raised against the immediate release of Santa Anna.

Valid as the idea of holding him hostage might seem at first glance, it was impractical for two reasons. First, the sentiment was so strong against him that it would have been difficult if not impossible, so Burnet thought, to protect him from assassination by someone who had a kinsman or friend slaughtered at the Alamo or Goliad. Second, probably no one is as powerless to influence a government as an imprisoned dictator. Burnet and those familiar with the Centralists in Mexico were convinced that if Santa Anna remained long away from the capital he would soon lose place to another ambitious tyrant who would be happy to see Santa Anna always a prisoner in Texas. His value to Texas would depreciate rapidly if he was not returned soon; better, advocates of the treaty pointed out, to risk the uncertainty of his honor than the presumed certainty of his displacement in power. And, as a matter of fact, this was an accurate assessment, for no sooner had word of the dictator's capture reached Mexico than Anastacio Bustamante seized the government again as "acting president," and on May 20 repudiated all Santa Anna's acts since his imprisonment.

In an attempt to fulfill the secret treaty Burnet put his prisoner aboard the *Invincible* of the Texas Navy with orders to the captain to deposit Santa Anna at Vera Cruz. Before the ship left port, however, an irate volunteer commander, Thomas Jefferson Green, on June 2 boarded the vessel and returned Santa Anna to custody. The army had taken the law into its own hands in defiance of the civil government but with the approval of the public. Thus did both Mexico and Texas reject the treaties of Velasco.

Filisola had withdrawn the Mexican armies to Matamoros, where almost immediately he was ordered by Bustamante to reinvade Texas. He vacillated and was replaced by Urrea, but the invasion never matured. In June, however, an ingenious Texan leader learned of the invasion plans: Major Isaac Burton and twenty mounted men celebrated thereafter as the Horse Marines effected by guile and disguise the capture of three Mexican vessels in Copano Bay. Aboard was some $25,000 worth of supplies for the proposed invasion. General Rusk promptly alerted the army, canceled all furloughs, and enlisted additional volunteers. By the end of June fear of imminent invasion mounted in Texas, and once again the volunteer forces showed themselves unable to cope with the situation.

The Texas Army was a shambles of confusion. Almost all of the approximately twenty-five hundred men had arrived from the United States too late to participate in the battle of San Jacinto. There was a score of separate companies and battalions, each with its own commander. These leaders acknowledged only the loosest allegiance to Rusk's overall command. Green, who had kidnapped Santa Anna from the *Invincible*, was particularly defiant, as was Felix Huston, a capable man who had brought several hundred men to Texas at his own expense. Both Green and Huston wanted to invade Mexico and attack Matamoros rather than prepare for defense. They were infected by the same spectre that had divided the troops disastrously at Goliad six months earlier.

Believing that Lamar might be able to control the nearly rebellious army better than Rusk and also wanting him out of the cabinet where his opposition had been a disturbing influence, Burnet promoted the meteoric Georgian to Rusk's place. But the army leaders liked Lamar even less than Rusk and flatly refused to accept him. Until early 1837 the army was without a leader, hovering on the brink of complete disobedience to the civil government.

This and other problems convinced Burnet that the ad interim government should be replaced by a permanent government under the constitution as soon as possible. He sent out a call in July for a general election to be held in September. The election was to accomplish three purposes: (1) ratification of the constitution, (2) election of constitutional officers and congressmen, and (3) ascertainment of public opinion on whether Texas should seek annexation to the United States. While awaiting the results of the election, Burnet did his best to manage the government's affairs in the face of a constantly deteriorating situation.

Besides the fractious army and the demoralizing threat of a Mexican invasion, Texas was also beset with financial problems. Two of the four navy vessels were being held in dry dock, one in New Orleans and one in New York, pending receipt of repair charges. One was sold to meet the bill; the other was released in September when friends of Texas raised the necessary funds. Texas promissory notes, issued by both the provisional and ad interim governments, were nearly worthless in American cities and of little more value in Texas. Indeed, both the Texas government and the Texas people were destitute and nearly bankrupt. Furthermore, hard times were in the immediate offing because few families had returned to their homes in time to plant. The fall harvest promised to be meager, and much of the livestock had strayed during the fighting.

The Election of 1836 In the September election, the voters overwhelmingly expressed a desire for annexation to the United States and with equal affirmation ratified the constitution. Both results were easily predictable, as most of the Texans were from the United States and virtually all had been disillusioned with Mexico since the overthrow of the Federalists. Juncture with the United States would secure protection and stable government. The adoption of the constitution was natural because it was a solid instrument of government based on republican principles and derived from the United States Constitution and the constitutions of several states. It provided for a president who would serve three years, except the first term which was two years, and who could not succeed himself but who could run again for an alternate term. It created a two-house congress and a supreme court but left to later congresses the establishment of supplementary courts and local governments. It recognized Negro slavery but otherwise included all of the traditional guarantees of individual liberty. So much was made of separation of church and state that ministers of the gospel were not allowed to hold public office. In general, it wisely provided authority to the three branches but did not attempt to detail specific procedures. In the first draft, for example, the framers had attempted to regulate land policy by requiring congress to sell the public domain, but in the final version congress was given complete discretion in the matter. The document has always been considered faultless.

The principal interest in the election was the choice of a president. The three candidates were Henry Smith, who had been the contentious head of the provisional government, Stephen F. Austin, who had returned from the United States in the summer, and Branch T. Archer, who had been president of the Consultation. Sam Houston, who had been treated for his wound in New Orleans and was recuperating in Nacogdoches, refused to let his name be considered despite innumerable requests from his friends. Archer withdrew from the campaign, and just eleven days before the election Houston changed his mind. He won by a landslide majority, receiving over four times as many votes as the other candidates together; Austin gleaned only 587 votes from approximately 6,500 votes cast. Houston's easy victory, despite his late entry in the race, was due to the tremendous popularity he enjoyed as the hero of San Jacinto. Austin's weak showing probably resulted from a combination of factors. His recent absence as Texas agent in the United States failed to identify him with the Revolution, although next to Houston he may have rendered the greatest single service by arousing American sympathy for the cause. In addition, many voters were such newcomers to Texas that they either had not heard of Austin or knew of him only by vague reputation. And in many minds he was branded as a friend to Mexico.

It is well for Texas that Sam Houston decided to run and that he was elected, because it seems likely that no one else had the experience and ability to handle the vexatious problems of establishing a strong government. Houston, then forty-three years old, had held several offices in Tennessee prior to his election to the United States Congress for two consecutive terms in 1823 and 1825. In 1827 he had been elected governor of Tennessee, an office which he resigned before the expiration of his term because of marital difficulties. His bride, Eliza Allen, whom he married on June 1, 1829, had returned from the wedding trip to her father's home, and her family had accused Houston of mistreating her. He refused to answer any of the accusations, and under increasing public pressure he resigned. He spent most of the next six years in the Indian country with his Cherokee friends, whom he represented on his first trip to Texas in 1832 before a short period in Washington as the self-styled ambassador of the Cherokee Nation. Houston was a large, well-proportioned man with a magnetic charm, a keen humor, a powerful intellect, and a deep sense of humanity. He was also flamboyant, ribald, often drunk, occasionally morose, and always self-contained. He refused to explain his nuptial problems just as he refused to explain his retreat to victory at San Jacinto and just as he refused to give his reasons for resisting before belatedly accepting the nomination for president of Texas. With all of these faults and virtues, he was a natural leader.

He dramatized his inauguration, as he did many events in his public life, by taking the oath of office in writing in an impressive ceremony in the small frame building in Columbia that served as the first meeting place for congress. After Lamar had been installed as vice-president, Houston urged the members of both houses of congress to address themselves seriously to the problems of organizing constitutional government. To reconcile possible factions, Houston appointed his campaign opponents to the chief cabinet posts, Austin as secretary of state and Smith as secretary of the treasury. He named Thomas J. Rusk secretary of war, William H. Wharton minister to the United States, and equally prominent men to the other appointive offices.

The Question of Recognition Before annexation, Texas had to be recognized as an independent nation; consequently, Wharton's first objective was to secure recognition. Recognition was also necessary if Texas currency and bonds were to be acceptable in the United States and if Texas land grants were to attract immigration. To everyone's surprise, Andrew Jackson, president of the United States, refused to grant recognition to Texas. During the Texas Revolution he argued that the United States must remain neutral. Then after San Jacinto he continued to delay on the grounds that it would be an unfriendly act to recognize Texas before Mexico did. When it became evident that Mexican recognition was not forthcoming, he withheld recognition because Texas had not yet established a firm government. In July he succumbed to pressure from congress and appointed Henry Morfit as special agent to investigate affairs in Texas. Morfit reported in a series of ten letters during August and September, but the unsettled condition of Texas at that time did not permit him to wax enthusiastic about Texas' future.

The true reason for Jackson's delay of recognition was twofold. He was engaged in delicate negotiations with Mexico over the claims question and did not want to disturb the volatile Mexicans by premature recognition of Texas. Also, 1836 was an election year, and he did not want to turn abolitionists and northern voters against his chosen successor, Martin Van Buren. The first of these reasons, the United States relations with Mexico, is complex and difficult to explain. For nearly a decade United States diplomats had been attempting to negotiate the settlement of claims of various American citizens against the Mexican government. Some of these claims, from the period of the Mexican independence movement, were for money and supplies advanced the revolutionists. Others were for confiscated goods, false imprisonment in Mexico, and even death. But United States ministers had found it impossible to reach an agreement with Mexico because of the frustrating rise and fall of so many successive revolutionary governments. The Centralists had absolutely refused to enter negotiation, and in the spring of 1836 the United States minister to Mexico had called for his passports and left Mexico in disgust, recommending that the only way to deal with the Mexican government was by force. It was the second time during Jackson's presidency that war or force had been recommended for the collection of the claims, but Jackson was determined to settle the issue peacefully. In October 1836 the Mexican minister to the United States had left Washington, ostensibly because of United States aid to Texas during the Revolution but probably to avoid further discussion of the claims. Thus, while he was engaged in trying to restore diplomatic negotiations with Mexico, Jackson did not want to antagonize Bustamante's government by recognizing Texas independence. Houston hoped to soften Jackson's position against recognition by sending Santa Anna to Washington to speak on Texas' behalf, but Jackson refused to see the ex-dictator, who was returned to Mexico to temporary retirement. Few failed to see the irony in his visit to Washington.

The second reason for Jackson's delay, the election, is much simpler. Abolitionists, who were charging that the Texas Revolution was a conspiracy of the slavocracy, screamed that recognition must be blocked because it was only a prelude to annexation. That the election was of less importance than the Mexican negotiations is suggested by Jackson's refusal even after Van Buren won in November. Not until congress passed a bill authorizing the salary of a minister to Texas did Jackson act. On March 3, 1837, the last day of his term, he appointed Alcée La Branche, a Louisianian, chargé d'affairs in Texas and thus gave the republic diplomatic recognition.

Stability Meantime, while he fought for recognition on the international scene, Houston struggled to achieve stability on the domestic front. The greater part of the legislation of the First Congress of the Republic resulted from his recommendations and admonitions. Until Houston exercised some leadership in legislative affairs, congress threatened to fritter its session away in dissension and meaningless debate. Under Houston's guidance, congress dealt with such problems as finance, land legislation, and military affairs (matters to be discussed in later sections of this chapter). Among a score of worthwhile achievements, two deserve special attention here: the Boundary Statute and the establishment of local government.

Passage of a boundary act was necessary because of Mexico's failure to ratify the public Treaty of Velasco. The loose code of international law held it to be the right of a revolting people to claim such territory as they could defend and exercise jurisdiction over. A definition of the limits of Texas' jurisdiction therefore was required. But the Boundary Statute, passed in December 1836, overstepped both prudence and common sense by claiming the Rio Grande from its mouth to its source, thence north to the 42nd parallel, and thence east and south to the coast along the treaty line of 1819, which had established the boundary between Spain and the United States. Not only was the Texas claim ambitious; the western boundary split the old province of New Mexico and included Santa Fe, Taos, and Albuquerque. Despite later arguments, for the most part advanced by historians a century after, Texas had a valid claim to the lower reaches of the Rio Grande accepted without equivocation by both Cós and Santa Anna in their surrender terms. But in the upper courses of the river, through El Paso and New Mexico, the Texas boundary claim was apparently motivated by geographical ignorance, land greed, and a vague and entirely erroneous belief that New Mexico would welcome Texas jurisdiction as an escape from Mexican Centralism. Yet the shape and the size of Texas today is directly traceable to this boundary act, preposterous as the western part was.

Internal boundary problems were inherent also in the establishment of local government. The Constitution of 1836 provided for the creation of counties but left the machinery of county and city government to congress. The First Congress passed a series of acts that converted the old Mexican municipalities to county units. Each county was to elect a chief justice and two associate justices to serve as the county court. Meeting with justices of the peace from each precinct, this court would act as a board of commissioners for legislative purposes. A coroner, a sheriff, a county clerk, a district clerk, and constables in each precinct were also to be elected to county office. The first problem of each county was to establish its boundaries, as they were virtually nonexistent under Mexico. It required years of legislation, litigation, and adjudication to establish contiguous county boundaries without overlapping or creating vacancies.

The twelve functioning municipalities in Texas in 1835 had been carved by the end of 1836 into twenty-two counties. In 1837 congress subdivided some of these to create five new counties; between 1838 and 1841 six additional counties were brought into existence; in 1841 and 1842 fifteen "judicial" counties were fragmented from older counties but were then declared unconstitutional; and in the next three years only three new counties were created. Thus by the end of 1845 congress had created and defined the boundaries of thirty-six counties, all of which were located east of the 98th meridian.

Houston and his first two congresses accomplished much during his first term in office, which ended in December 1838 according to the constitutional schedule. His positive, sometimes dogmatic, and always unexplained stands had created political enemies, however, and for the next quarter century the principal factions in Texas politics were pro- or anti-Houston. There were no political parties during the period of the Republic —only Houston's friends and the opposition. Vice-president Lamar headed the opposition and early in 1838 announced his presidential candidacy. Since the constitution prohibited Houston from running, his friends sought to persuade him to endorse a successor. But this he refused to do, and the election of 1838 was won by Lamar.

Later Political Events The election was one of the wildest in Texas political history. Lamar began campaigning months before the Houston party found, after much discussion and some dissension, a candidate in Peter W. Grayson. Grayson, one of the attorneys who had gone to Mexico City on Austin's behalf in 1834, had served as attorney general in both Burnet's and Houston's cabinets and was a strong supporter of Houston's regime. Shortly after his nomination, however, he committed suicide on a visit to Tennessee. Similarly, the next candidate named by the Houston faction, James W. Collinsworth, drowned on a return voyage from Galveston Island. Then, just a few weeks before polling time, a third candidate, Robert Wilson, was chosen, but he was not well known and was overwhelmingly defeated.

The new president, Mirabeau B. Lamar, was unlike Sam Houston in many respects, although both were southerners, politicians, men of action, and dynamic leaders. Lamar was a native of Georgia and had served in his state legislature. He was well educated and, besides being a fairly accomplished poet, was keenly interested in history. He collected extensive notes about Texas and planned later in life to write a definitive history of the Republic, which although never finished is valuable source material. His poems were published in a number of southern newspapers and literary magazines. Poet, dreamer, and idealist, Lamar tended to be precipitate in decision, rash in judgment, and impractical in planning. Nevertheless, or perhaps because of these qualities, he made many enduring contributions to the development of Texas, which are discussed later in this chapter. Lamar mistakenly interpreted his landslide victory in 1838 as a public rejection of Houston's conservative policies rather than the result of a disastrous campaign by the Houston faction. He promptly launched an expansive and expensive program of increased governmental activity and was invariably surprised whenever opposition arose in congress.

The principal leader of this opposition was Sam Houston himself, who had been elected to the house of representatives from Nacogdoches. So dissatisfied was he by the Lamar administration that he became a candidate for the presidency in 1841. The Lamar faction nominated Burnet, who had served as Lamar's vice-president, and the ensuing campaign sank to disgraceful vituperation and invective. Francis W. Moore, the caustic editor of the *Telegraph and Texas Register*, took the lead in characterizing Houston as a drunkard, but his friends rejoined that "Houston, drunk and in a ditch, is worth a thousand of Burnet and Lamar." Subjected to Houston's scathing ridicule, Burnet challenged him to a duel, and Houston's response, "I never fight downhill," must have added immeasurably to his frustration. Houston, of course, won an easy victory and, as if to give the lie to his detractors, was inaugurated in what a disappointed contemporary described as a "cold water doin's." After three eventful and constructive years in office, Houston picked Anson Jones as his successor, and Jones soundly defeated the anti-Houston candidate in the election of 1844.

Thus the affairs of the Republic were dominated by two men with policies in sharp contrast. As the following section shows, where Houston was conservative in domestic affairs Lamar was expansive, and where Houston was cautious in foreign relations Lamar was almost reckless. But both men were constructive, and some of their domestic policies endure in modified form to this day.

Domestic Affairs

Problems of National Defense The defense of the Republic against both the Indian depredations and the threatened Mexican invasion was one of the primary concerns of each administration. To meet them, congress maintained the army, still in existence since the battle of San Jacinto, and created a new navy and a corps of rangers.

The army, as has been seen, was a mixed blessing. Aggressive and self-confident, it was without question a strong deterrent to Bustamante's bellicose posturing south of the Rio Grande, but many of its officers, such as Thomas Jefferson Green, who had kidnapped Santa Anna, and Felix Huston, who had brought three or four hundred volunteers to Texas at his own expense, were openly rebellious to executive authority. Under such leaders the army had rejected Lamar as commandant in May 1836 and had insistently demanded an invasion of Matamoros. Shortly after he was inaugurated, Houston visited the principal camp and tried to instill a semblance of obedience. He did not remove Felix Huston, who then held the rank of brigadier general, but apparently he made a little headway at quieting the unrest. The post of major general was created by congress, and late in 1836 Houston appointed Albert Sidney Johnston to fill it. Johnston was one of the most capable officers ever trained at West Point and was to become one of Texas' greatest military figures. When he went to the army camp to assume command, however, Huston found a pretext to challenge him to a duel. In the exchange of shots Johnston was wounded in the thigh and was forced to abandon active command for treatment and recuperation. The army was now becoming a distinct nuisance.

Houston solved the problem neatly. In May 1837 when the doughty Felix Huston visited congress to promote his plan for an invasion of

Mexico, Houston slipped down to the army's main camp to reduce the strength of the army. He offered indefinite furloughs with free transportation to New Orleans to soldiers who desired to leave Texas and Second Class Headrights of twelve hundred eighty acres to those who preferred to be discharged and become settlers. In this way, much to the unruly officers' chagrin, over half the army was dispersed.

Houston received serious criticism for virtually dissolving the army in the face of a Mexican invasion, but he explained laconically, then and later, that he placed his faith in the militia for the defense of Texas. One of the first acts of congress had required that every able-bodied man between the ages of twenty-one and fifty belong to a militia company in his justice precinct and spend one day a month in company drills. A militia captain was appointed in each of the justice precincts, and the companies were organized into battalions and regiments. Thus on almost a moment's notice the president could call to active duty all or any part of the militia to meet emergencies. It was indeed the surest defense Texas had.

There was much sentiment in congress for the reestablishment of a navy. By the end of 1837 the first navy had gone out of existence—two of the ships wrecked, one sold for repair charges that the Republic was unable to pay, and one captured by the Mexican Navy. The Second Congress in 1838 voted an appropriation in promissory notes to purchase a new navy. It consisted of six sailing vessels built expressly for Texas in a Baltimore shipyard and one steam packet that was purchased and rechristened. Edwin Ward Moore resigned his commission in the United States Navy to assume command of the Texas fleet as commodore. He was an excellent seaman and attracted the enlistment of exceptionally fine crews. In 1840 he took his flagship, the *Austin*, on a record-breaking run from New York to New Orleans. The last of the six ships was completed in April 1840, and the scrappy little navy was ready for a fight.

Moore believed that by blockade and bombardment the navy could force Mexico to recognize Texas and ratify the Treaty of Velasco. He may have been right, but he was not given the opportunity because Lamar was then involved in a more delicate negotiation. Moore was ordered to patrol the Gulf, to open friendly relations with the Federalist rebels in Yucatan, and not to fire unless he was fired upon. In October 1840 a shore battery shelled one of his ships, and Moore, thinking hostilities had commenced, quickly accepted an offer of $25,000 from the Yucatan rebel government to help in the reduction of the key city of San Juan Bautista, eighty miles inland up the broad Tobasco River in Yucatan. This he accomplished easily with three ships: the day after he turned his guns on the city, it surrendered.

But the victory was an uncertain one. Tropical fever laid out Moore and a high percentage of the crews, and a Gulf storm wrecked the *San Jacinto*. Moore sailed back to Galveston in the spring of 1841 to discover that congress, lulled by the apparent truce with Mexico, had decommissioned all the fleet save two vessels, and these two were ordered to make a survey of the coast!

The third arm of Texas defense was the Texas Rangers. The name Rangers was first applied to volunteer groups organized in the colonies for protection against Indians, the best known of which was Tomlinson's Rangers. In May 1837 the first official corps of Rangers was created by congress, which appropriated $100,000 and granted Sam Houston a thirty-day leave of absence to organize the corps. He established six companies and ordered the construction of several blockhouse forts along the frontier, from Fort Houston in present Houston County to Walnut Creek in present Travis County. The Texas Rangers developed a unique spirit and attracted the most bold and daring young men in Texas. Among these were John Coffee "Jack" Hays, Ben McCulloch, Samuel H. Walker, W. A. "Bigfoot" Wallace, Tom S. Lubbock, and George Thomas Howard, whose names have become commonplace synonyms for "hero" in Texas. The Rangers' fearless exploits during the period of the Republic earned a reputation for bravery that has never been exceeded. During the Mexican War, 1846–1848, Hays' regiment of Texas Rangers became the leading element in first Taylor's and later Scott's armies. The corps was then in abeyance until after the Civil War, when it was reestablished as the Frontier Battalion.

Financial Affairs   Defense is expensive, as every taxpayer knows; the army, the navy, and the Rangers cost Texas in excess of $500,000 at a time when there was less than $500 in specie in the public treasury. Financing this and other costs of government was Texas' most serious problem, and it was a consistent and perennial one that was never solved. Since the Texas government had no gold and silver reserve, it had to resort to the issuance of paper money for which it pledged both its public honor, which was of little value, and its public land, which was of only slightly more value.

The process had begun with the provisional government. As governor, Henry Smith signed $66,000 worth of drafts and warrants to pay for supplies for the Revolution. Some of these were hand drawn entirely, but most were on forms printed in San Felipe. Burnet and the ad interim government continued the practice, issuing approximately $1,000,000 worth of drafts and warrants. As none of these could be redeemed until there was money in the treasury, the analogy to "hot" checks is striking. The constitutional government continued to issue treasury warrants throughout the period of the Republic, but the First Congress resorted primarily to three other forms of financial paper. One was interest-bearing promissory notes issued as currency to be redeemed at the end of a year. Another was land scrip, also a form of currency redeemable in land but not paying interest. The third was most ambitious: a five million dollar bond issue at an interest rate of 10 per cent. To redeem these bonds, congress pledged all the revenue from the sale of Texas public domain.

When the time arrived to redeem the promissory notes in 1837, there was still no money in the treasury, so congress appropriated land for their redemption at the rate of fifty cents an acre. In 1838 a new form of non-interest-bearing promissory notes was initiated, at first limited to $100,000 but later increased. Lamar's government spent nearly three million dollars of this currency. The first issue of these bills was called "star money" because of the small star on the face; a later issue was called "redbacks" because the obverse side of the bills happened to be printed in red ink. Two other forms of currency were also used: 'change notes and exchequer bills. The 'change notes were small denomination bills that could be exchanged in the treasury for larger denominations of promissory notes; the exchequer bills, a desperate attempt by Houston's second administration to restore the credit of the Republic, were limited to $350,000. By that time the profligate expenditures of the Lamar administration had so cheapened Texas money that it was circulating at ten to fifteen cents on the dollar.

Furthermore, purchasers could not be found for the bonds, the Five Million Dollar Loan, on which the First Congress had pinned its hopes of solvency, nor for a later one million dollar bond issue pledged directly against the public domain. Therefore congress took a step that had significant ramifications: it hypothecated the customs revenue to redeem the moneys.

The customs revenue was the only real money the Republic received, for taxes and other fees were paid in the government's own worthless paper. But merchants importing goods into Texas were required to pay the tariff in specie. The Customs Act was passed in December 1836 and was later amended and extended. A schedule of import tariffs and tonnage duties was established, and customs houses were erected at the principal ports of entry. Gail Borden, founder of the Borden Dairy Company, established the first customs post on Galveston Island in 1837. Customs revenue constituted fifty per cent of the government's income during the first half of the Republic's existence and over eighty per cent the last five years.

In 1836 the government of the United States not only was free of debt (!) but also had a surplus in the treasury (!!), a condition resulting from the sale of the public domain. Texas hoped to emulate this, and the Convention of 1836 seriously considered writing into the constitution certain provisions for the sale of the public lands. At the last minute, however, the formulation of a land policy was relegated to congress, and the convention established by ordinance the First Class Headright. This guaranteed a league and a labor of land to anyone who had settled in Texas prior to March 2, 1836, and had not received a grant from the Mexican government.

The First Congress then extended the First Class Headright to October 1, 1836, and established the Second Class Headright, which expired October 1, 1837, and which offered twelve hundred eighty acres to each family and six hundred forty acres to each single man who would settle in Texas. Congress also granted land to veterans of the battle of San Jacinto, to the heirs of the men killed at the Alamo and at Goliad, and to all soldiers as a bonus for services at the rate of three hundred twenty acres for three months' service, six hundred forty for six months', nine hundred sixty for nine months', and twelve hundred eighty for a year or longer. Both the convention and congress thought of these grants, especially the Headright Acts, as temporary measures designed to prime the pump of immigration. As soon as a regular flow of immigration began, the public lands, it was hoped, could be sold. But this was a vain hope, and in 1837 it became necessary to pass a new inducement, the Third Class Headright of six hundred forty acres for a family and three hundred twenty acres for a single man. This act was twice extended, but congress terminated it on January 1, 1841, and turned to the empresario system.

It should be noted that none of these grants was for specific tracts of land; they were merely entitlements. The recipients were required to locate the specified amount in some unclaimed area of the public domain, have it surveyed, and send the field notes to the General Land Office, whereupon a title to the land would be issued. There were two interesting results of this procedure. The first was the rise of speculation in this land paper. Merchants, surveyors, and others began to buy the unlocated paper in order to "lay," as the contemporary phrase went, a group of certificates together. The second result was that often the tract selected by a settler or a veteran was smaller than the amount of his entitlement, so the Land Office was forced to issue remainder certificates, most of which also passed into speculation. Few speculators in this land paper profited greatly, and many lost money because in the early years the costs of surveying, filing, and patenting the land exceeded its resale value.

The Establishment of Colonies The need to encourage immigration had prompted the three Headright measures, but their lack of success was so notable that the Fifth Congress killed a bill to take a public census for fear its results would be damaging. This same congress, meeting at the midpoint of the Republic, 1840–1841, abandoned the Headright grants and instituted the empresario system. Its origin was a curious memorial that arrived in the winter of 1840 while congress was debating the request of a French company, the Franco-Texienne Company, for authorization to establish a colony of a thousand French yeomen on the western frontier. Because there were serious objections to the French request, the timing of the memorial from a Louisville group headed by W. S. Peters was particularly good. Peters and nineteen associates requested permission to plant a colony of American settlers on the frontier, which was far more to the congress's liking than the idea of a large body of Frenchmen. It immediately dropped the Franco-Texienne proposal and passed a statute authorizing President Lamar to make an empresario contract with a representative of the Peters group. This act of February 4, 1841, applied only to the Peters Colony; a year later congress passed a general colonization law that authorized other contracts.

The Peters group was an odd mixture to be applying for colonization rights in Texas, and the timeliness of the petition seems to be completely coincidental. The group was made up of eleven Louisville musicians—organists, piano makers, and music teachers—and nine English acquaintances of W. S. Peters who had migrated to the United States from London and who probably did not know their names were on the petition. The Louisville musicians were so startled at the success of their memorial that it took them over six months to send an agent to Texas, Samuel Browning, who signed the colonization contract in August 1841. The business affairs of this group are unbelievably complex. After several reorganizations and three new contracts the Peters Colony was expanded as an operation of the Texas Emigration and Land Company in a vast area in northern Texas that extended over a hundred miles south of the Red River to about the center of present Ellis County and westward one hundred sixty miles into present Callahan County, the line then running north back to the Red River near the western boundary of present Wilborger County.

Despite innumerable vicissitudes the Peters Colony was the largest and most successful colonization enterprise in the history of Texas. The first settlers reached the area in December 1841 and soon founded the city of Dallas. The settled area of the colony was confined to its eastern border, in present Ellis, Dallas, Collin, Denton, Grayson, Wise, and Tarrant counties. In all the company claimed to have settled twenty-three hundred families prior to the expiration of the fourth and last contract on January 1, 1848, but the state legislature granted premium land to the company on the basis of seventeen hundred families. These premium lands, 1,066,000 acres, were located by company surveyors in the western portion of the colony reserve and then deeded to stockholders in the company on a proportionate basis. This was the largest single grant of land made by Texas up to that time and the third largest ever made. The actual settlers in the colony represented a homogeneous addition of about ten to twelve thousand people, who were of a slightly different background from that of most of the rest of the Texans. The Peters colonists came largely from the Ohio River valley (Kentucky, Ohio, Indiana, and Illinois), were nonslaveowners, were on the whole somewhat more prosperous than most immigrants, and included many skilled artisans and professional men. Under the empresario law they received a Third Class Headright free of charge with the company paying for surveying and other costs; consequently, they had funds available for commerce and capital investment, not for the purchase of slaves but for the development of the area, a circumstance that accounts for the quick growth of Dallas.

Three other colonies were established under the general law of 1842: the Mercer Colony, the Castro Colony, and the German colonies. The Mercer Colony was the least successful. Charles Fenton Mercer, a former congressman who associated himself with the Peters group, signed a contract for an area southeast of the Peters Colony. After a boundary dispute due to inept wording in his contract, he made a few desultory attempts at settlement that involved only fifty to seventy-five families. Therefore the state legislature refused to award him any premium lands, and after years of litigation the Texas Supreme Court ruled against his heirs in 1882.

The Castro Colony, established by Henri Castro, was more successful. Castro, an Alsatian and French citizen, received two contracts for the settlement of six hundred families in an area southwest of San Antonio. Between 1843 and 1847 he brought into his grants approximately five hundred families and a number of single men. Most of these emigrants were from the Rhine provinces of Europe, many being French and French Swiss. The result was that the towns in the Castro Colony—Castroville, D'Hannis, Quihi, and others—had a distinctly French atmosphere for many years. Castro did not profit greatly from his premium lands as he was something of an idealist and had spent a good deal of money supporting the colonists and transporting them from Europe.

More significant in the long run than either the Peters or the Castro colonies was the German colonization in Texas. A German group called the *Adelsverein*, a society for the promotion of emigration to Texas, acquired contracts issued to Henry Francis Fisher and Burchard Miller for the settlement of six thousand European emigrants in a three-million-acre reserve southwest and west of Austin. Under the leadership of Prince Carl of Solms-Braunfels, a small flood tide of Germans began arriving at Indianola, where Solms-Braunfels established a receiving station to settle them quickly and efficiently in the vicinity of present Comal County. Their most important town was New Braunfels, surrounded by villages like nearby Solms. In 1846 Solms-Braunfels turned the directorship of the company over to Baron Ottfried von Meusebach, who unlike the prince became a Texas citizen as plain John O. Meusebach. He founded the town of Fredericksburg on the western frontier in present Gillespie County, which became another center of German settlement.

The German immigrants might have contributed more significantly to the development of Texas had they not isolated themselves by clinging tenaciously to their language and culture. Primarily from the intellectual class in Germany, which was then painfully undergoing nationalization, they were more in the nature of political refugees than typical immigrants. The early German immigration included scholars, musicians, scientists, artists, and others of a generally higher educational level than the average Texan of the time. They were industrious and thrifty, and they prospered on lands that were far from being the most fertile in Texas.

Indian Affairs The establishment of these three major frontier colonies brought some relief to the rest of Texas from the depredations of the western Indians. The Republic had two sources of Indian trouble: in East Texas the Cherokees and a dozen or more smaller bands, and in the west the Plains Indians, chiefly the Comanches and the Lipans. The western problem was resolved by continued frontier settlement of hardy pioneers supported by Rangers and later by the United States Cavalry. That Indian threat did not end until well after the Civil War.

The Cherokee problem was long in development. In 1819 when their people were expelled to the Indian Territory by the United States, a segment of the Cherokee tribe had come into Texas and located northwest of Nacogdoches. They petitioned the Mexican government for a grant of land, but although their presence in Texas was accepted by Mexican officials, no grant was made. The Cherokees desired not only land but also the right to govern themselves as a quasi-independent nation within the borders of Mexico. This request was impossible for Mexico to comply with, and it was equally impossible for the Republic of Texas. In 1826 some Cherokee leaders, later disowned by the tribe, were involved in Benjamin Edwards' Fredonian uprising. In February 1836 Bowles signed a treaty with Sam Houston promising Cherokee allegiance in the Revolution in return for the grant of their lands. This treaty was ill-starred in almost every respect. Bowles did not represent the dozen or more East Texas bands he claimed were associated with the Cherokees, including the remnant of the Caddos and other migrant tribes from the United States such as the Delawares and the Anadarkos. Houston represented no government at all since the provisional government had become defunct by the time he made the treaty. The Cherokees did not aid in the Revolution and later evidence indicated that in the spring of 1836 at least some of them participated in an abortive conspiracy organized by Vicente Cordova. Furthermore, so fractious did the East Texas Indians become that General Edmund P. Gaines, in charge of United States forces in Louisiana, felt constrained to cross the Sabine and occupy Nacogdoches in August 1836 on the grounds that there was no government in Texas, Mexican or Texan, that could control the Indians. And finally, if all this was not enough to invalidate the Houston-Bowles treaty, the Texas senate refused to ratify it.

Initial sentiment against the treaty arose because of a suspicion of Cherokee hostility during the Revolution and because the Cherokees demanded that their lands be granted to the tribe. Had they asked for separate land grants and had they abandoned the idea of maintaining separate tribal government within Texas, Houston might have succeeded in the ratification of the treaty, for he was ever a staunch friend of the Cherokees. In October 1837 the senate rejected the treaty after an investigating committee reported that the Indians had not kept peace during the Revolution. It was also true, of course, that they had not launched an organized attack on the Texans' rear as they might have when the Texas Army faced Santa Anna. The senate report stated that there was *"notorious* evidence that part at least of the tribes . . . have been the most savage and ruthless of our frontier enemies ever since and even at the very date of the signing of this Treaty. . . ."

Cherokee hostility over the rejection of the treaty led a number of the Indians in 1838 to participate again in the machinations of Vicente Cordova. Cordova, a second generation Hispanic Texan of Nacogdoches, was a respected citizen of that community, had served as its alcalde, and in 1835 was elected primary judge under the provisional government. It was then that he secretly aligned with Santa Anna and the Centralists in Mexico and plotted an uprising in Nacogdoches. Later evidence indicates inconclusively that Bowles agreed to furnish him twelve hundred Cherokees for the relief of Cós in San Antonio, but Cós' surrender ended that. Then before he could mature new plans, Santa Anna was defeated at San Jacinto, and Cordova bided his time. In the spring of 1838 when General Filisola, then in command at Matamoros, commissioned him to enlist East Texas Indians as auxiliaries in the Mexican Army, he recruited mostly Cherokees. Compelled in August 1838 to reveal his conspiracy, he established headquarters on an island in the Angelina River with a force of six hundred Indians and Mexicans.

The militia was quickly called out, and the Cordova Rebellion ended almost before it began, Cordova and a small band fleeing westward and into Mexico while the Indians scattered into the prairies. Texans were aghast at this apparent perfidy by the Cherokees, but Bowles disavowed any knowledge of Cordova and claimed that the Cherokees involved were renegades from the tribe. The depths of his duplicity were discovered the following spring when the Mexican Indian agent, Manuel Flores, was killed by Ranger James O. Rice in an Indian battle on the San Gabriel River. Flores' saddlebags held letters from Cordova and several other documents that seem fully to implicate Bowles from as early as 1835.

President Lamar and Secretary of War Albert S. Johnston agreed that it was necessary to expel the Cherokee Indians and their associates from East Texas. Special commissioners supported by a force of five hundred men went to Bowles' village with an offer to buy the Indian crops and livestock and to pay the costs of removal to the Indian Territory. Bowles accepted but stalled repeatedly while mobilizing his forces. On July 15 he attacked the Texans in the Battle of the Neches. The Cherokee War had begun. In battle the next day Bowles was killed. A third fight occurred near the Grand Saline before the Cherokees precipitately retreated across the Red River. When the Cherokee power was broken, the other East Texas bands scattered, some to the Indian Territory and some to the west. Two bands that had consistently kept the peace remained: the Alabamas and the Coushattas. They were later granted the lands where they were settled as a reservation by the Texas government, and they are supported there today in the only Indian reservation in Texas.

Along the western frontier Indian raids and depredations had pounded almost incessantly, especially savage Comanche attacks on isolated farmsteads. The Comanches, who rarely attacked unless they had overwhelming superiority, had adopted the policy of killing the men and enslaving the women and children who fell prey to their cruelty. Occasionally a Comanchero trader from New Mexico was able to ransom a captive white woman who would then be returned to her friends or family via merchants in Taos or Santa Fe. The Texas government knew that various Comanche bands were holding an undetermined number of white women, but it was helpless to recover them. Suddenly one day in January 1840 three Comanche chiefs rode boldly into San Antonio and demanded a treaty as representatives of a general council of Comanche bands. A meeting was arranged for March in the Council House at San Antonio, to which the Comanches agreed to bring all captured white women for sale to the Texas peace commissioners. Neither the Indian party nor Henry Karnes, who made the negotiations, was completely candid with one another. The Indians had no intention of bringing all their prisoners, and Karnes, who suspected this, was prepared to hold them as hostages when they arrived for the conference if they did not.

On the day appointed for the conference some sixty-five Indians, with a dozen prominent chiefs and one white teenage girl, rode into San Antonio. The girl was Matilda Lockhart, in pitiable and emaciated condition, the flesh burned from her nostrils by live coals and her body covered with bruises. Sobbing, she told of fifteen other women held in the hills west of town and of the Indians' plans to ransom one at a time. The sight of the poor girl combined with the pernicious tactics of the Comanches were more than the Texans could stand. After a brief interchange of words, the Texans began to execute Karnes' plan to hold the chiefs hostage. A fight broke out in which several Rangers and most of the Comanches were killed.

Both Indians and whites were outraged by the other's violation of the truce. In retaliation the Comanches were said to have tortured a dozen prisoners to death, but more important they organized an immense raid into South Texas. That this raid was more than mere revenge is evidenced by three facts: (1) documents later taken from an Indian revealed that the Comanches were in communication with Mexican agents who may have been the instigators of the raid; (2) the raid was primarily for loot and plunder rather than blood, relatively few lives being lost; and (3) the Indians attacked not San Antonio but warehouses at the coastal town of Linnville. In August 1840 a war party estimated at a thousand warriors swooped out of the west, bypassing San Antonio and other settlements, to race into Victoria and thence to Linnville. Reaching Victoria on the afternoon of August 6, they ravaged the town while surprised and frightened citizens attempted a defense and watched from hastily barricaded windows. The Comanches gathered between two and three thousand head of livestock there and the following afternoon moved toward Linnville. On the morning of the eighth they rode boldly into the thriving town, whose citizens fled in panic to boats and paddled into the bay out of range. Every building in town was sacked, including a bulging warehouse, and to the citizens' helpless fury the Comanches donned various bits of finery and paraded up and down the beach. Firing the town, the Indians withdrew that evening. Although several people were killed or wounded at Victoria and Linnville, the raid was clearly made for plunder.

Ben McCulloch and a company of Rangers intercepted the Indian vanguard in a skirmish at Casa Blanca. Burdened by hundreds of pounds of plunder and several thousand head of livestock, the Indians moved slowly enough to give McCulloch, General Edward Burleson, and General Felix Huston time to muster about two hundred men and cut off the Indians' withdrawal at Plum Creek on August 12 in one of the few pitched battles between Comanches and whites. Between seventy and eighty Indians were killed and several hundred horses and mules were recovered, but the majority of Indians slipped around the Texans and headed west. John H. Moore, possibly the most experienced Indian fighter in Texas, at the head of two hundred seventy-five men tracked the Indians to their encampment on the upper Colorado somewhere in present Mitchell County. In this fight one hundred thirty Indians were killed, and much of the remaining plunder and livestock was regained. The great raid on Linnville and the subsequent battles at Plum Creek and on the Colorado were the largest between Comanches and Texans in a half-century of hostility. Implacable foes of the white settlers, the Comanches continued hit-and-run raids on the frontier until 1876, but never again was there such a major engagement.

When Houston became president in 1841, he initiated a new, friendly policy of making peace treaties with the western Indians. He sent agents with presents for the principal men in all the tribes. In order to provide the Indians with the kind of supplies they had been getting in raids, Houston encouraged trading posts in the Indian country. In 1842 and 1843 the three Torrey brothers and George Barnhardt established trading posts near present New Braunfels, near present Waco, on the Navasota River, at the falls of the Brazos, and on the upper Trinity. And Houston's agents held peace conferences with representatives of the various tribes and began to make treaties of peace and friendship. The most important of these conferences, at Tehuacana Creek in October 1844, was attended by representatives of all the bands, including the Comanches, and by Sam Houston himself. The resultant peace treaty brought relative quiet to the frontier for a few years.

Other Domestic Programs During the ten years of the Republic there were, of course, many other internal problems such as the establishment of a postal system, the construction of a military road along the frontier, the survey of the coast, the levying of taxes, the status of the free Negro, the chartering of cities and businesses, and the legitimatizing of children born to couples whose marriages had not been properly solemnized. The four presidential administrations and nine different congresses acted in domestic affairs with varying degrees of success. Among the most significant legislation were two unique statutes suggested and advocated by Lamar: the Homestead Act and the Education Act.

The Homestead Act, passed in 1839, permitted a man to hold his homestead and the tools of his trade or profession free from judgment for the collection of debts. The act had antecedents in a decree of Coahuila y Texas suggested by Stephen F. Austin. It was especially helpful to immigrants who after the Panic of 1837 had left considerable indebtedness in the United States. It was unquestionably progressive legislation for its time, as it assured a man the possibility of earning a living despite burdensome debts. Some other states have copied this law, which has been modified a number of times since 1839, but in recent years it has been criticized because bankrupts occasionally abuse it and because it impedes the movement of capital funds.

Because of the mid-twentieth-century image of Texas as a stronghold of conservatism, it may come as a surprise that in the nineteenth century Texas was for over fifty years a leader in progressive legislation. As discussed later in this book, Texas produced the nation's first true homestead act, its first workable antitrust act, its earliest railroad regulation and one of its first effective railroad commissions, one of its first popular referendums on election of senators, one of its first woman suffrage measures and its first major reform in city government, and one of its first bureaus of labor statistics, insurance regulation, stock and bond laws, and alien land laws. Texans introduced in the federal congress a workable though not adopted antitrust bill, the interstate commerce bill, and the Sixteenth and Eighteenth Amendments to the Constitution with sponsorship of the Seventeenth.

Texas was ahead of most states in the support of public schools. Lamar's 1839 Education Act laid the foundation for public education in Texas and served as a model for a later federal act establishing land-grant colleges. This act set aside two leagues of the public domain (later increased to four) for each county in Texas for the support of a public academy. It also reserved fifty leagues of land to finance the future establishment of two universities. Most counties acted fairly promptly to utilize this generous donation of over sixteen thousand acres. Some county courts sold all of the land at once; some sold part and retained part; some have derived great advantage from rents and royalties on the land retained. The university land grant was first located in the blackland prairies near present Waco and later moved to West Texas, where in the twentieth century the discovery of oil made the university endowment one of the largest in the world.

Another important domestic matter was the location of the capital. Since Columbia, the first capital, was too small, the capital was reestablished in 1837 in Houston, newly established by the Allen brothers. There a commodious two-story frame building was built and leased to the government with several smaller structures, including a two-room White House for the presidential residence. In 1839 Lamar proposed setting aside a tract of the public domain for the capital. The government laid out a town and constructed its own buildings on the Colorado River at the edge of the hill country. Lots in the town and larger tracts on the outskirts were sold to individuals. The city of Austin, like Washington, D. C., earlier and Brasilia in more modern times, came into existence under government sponsorship. The capital was moved there in 1839 and remained until 1842, when the threat of Mexican invasion gave Houston, then president, the opportunity to return the capital to his namesake town. But in 1843 swelling criticism caused him to compromise on Washington-on-the-Brazos as the capital. Not all of the government offices were moved out of Austin, and it again became the seat of government with the inauguration of state officials there in February, 1846.

Foreign Relations

Texas in the Family of Nations In immediate response to the United States recognition of Texas in the spring of 1837, the Texan ministers in Washington, Memucan Hunt and William H. Wharton, made proposals for annexation, but their overture was rejected. Disappointed, Houston attempted to secure recognition in Europe in order to broaden the possibilities for the sale of bonds and land scrip. He appointed James Pinckney Henderson minister to England. Henderson, a member of an aristocratic family in North Carolina, was ideally suited for the diplomatic post and served Texas for nearly three years in England and France. On his arrival in London in October 1837, he received a surprisingly warm welcome from government officials. The British foreign office wanted to recognize and encourage Texas' independence both to create a balance of power in North America against the burgeoning growth of the United States and to develop a new area for British trade. But, as in the United States, abolitionist sentiment in England delayed recognition. Henderson astutely overcame the difficulty by negotiating in July 1838 a trade agreement rather than a formal treaty. Formal recognition by Britain was yet to be obtained.

Henderson soon went to France, where he first spent several months acquiring a working knowledge of the language. In November he secured a commercial agreement similar to the one he had drawn with Britain. Almost a year later, in the summer of 1839, Henderson was able to begin negotiations of a formal treaty of recognition, which with some modifications suggested by James Hamilton was concluded on September 25, 1839.

France thus became the second nation to extend official recognition to Texas.

James Hamilton, a former governor of South Carolina, had been appointed by President Lamar to attempt to sell the Texas bonds in Europe. With sophistication and broad personal contacts, Hamilton first sold $400,000 worth of the bonds to Nicholas Biddle in Philadelphia—a major triumph for Texas. He arrived in Paris while Henderson was negotiating the treaty and suggested modifications to facilitate the bond sales. Thereafter Hamilton was an extremely busy man. He sailed for Texas before the end of the year to persuade congress to create a sinking fund for the bonds and to hypothecate the customs revenue for their redemption. He then went to England, where he saw that British investors desired formal recognition before speculating in Texas financial paper, so he reopened negotiations with the foreign office. While the British cabinet delayed, Hamilton dashed to Holland, where he secured Dutch recognition of Texas in September 1840. From Amsterdam he went to Brussels and began negotiations for Belgian recognition, which were successfully concluded in 1841. While this was in progress, he returned to England and finally obtained the all-important British recognition in November 1840.

British recognition was handled in three separate treaties. One was formal recognition, a treaty of friendship and commerce. The second authorized Britain to negotiate in Mexico for Texas. The third, which was not published, provided that the British Navy could search Texas vessels to suppress the slave trade, a policy to which Britain had been committed since 1815. This third treaty was considered necessary to secure ratification in the British Parliament but was kept secret for fear it would prove unpopular in Texas, where the senate ratified it in closed session.

European recognition had necessarily to precede the sale of the bonds; Hamilton had not forgotten his main objective. In February 1841 he secured a contract with a large French banking house for the purchase of the bonds if the French government would back them. The minister of finance at first agreed to it but backed out in the summer of 1841 because of a controversy in Texas that prompted the new French minister to Texas, Count Alphonse de Saligny, to leave his post and break off diplomatic relations. Saligny, a pompous dandy, had been offended by an innkeeper named Richard Bullock, who had used abusive language when the count failed to pay his hotel bill. Saligny moved out of the inn into a small frame house, later glorified as the French Embassy in Austin, and soon had a second altercation with Bullock because some of the innkeeper's pigs were killed while rooting in Saligny's corn crib. Although Bullock was arrested under a law passed at Saligny's insistence that made it illegal to speak disrespectfully to foreign diplomats, he was never brought to trial. The people of Austin sympathized with Bullock, and his bond was posted by none other than the secretary of the treasury. This Saligny considered the final insult and stormed out of Texas carrying the dreams of prosperity with him. His hopes of success dashed, Hamilton made one final attempt to dispose of the bonds in London in the fall of 1841. He estimated that he spent $280,000 from his own purse in his efforts to aid Texas.

While Texas diplomats worked to secure recognition, congress authorized the establishment of a consular service under the secretary of state. The first Texas consuls were Thomas Toby in New Orleans, David White in Mobile, and John Woodward in New York. New appointments were made regularly in such major United States cities as Baltimore, Philadelphia, Boston, and Charleston, and in such unlikely places as Bangor, Detroit, and Key West. After European recognition, consular agents were appointed in London, Liverpool, Plymouth, and a half-dozen smaller English towns, and in Paris, Bordeaux, Cette, Rouen, Bayonne, Glasgow, Dublin, Antwerp, Bremen, Amsterdam, and Rotterdam. Texas consuls did not draw salaries but were entitled to fees and commissions on the sale of land scrip or bonds and on the notarization of legal documents for use in Texas.

Another important and often overlooked matter of foreign affairs was the Sabine Boundary Convention of 1837 between Texas and the United States. The eastern boundary of Texas was that of the Treaty of 1819–1821 between Spain and the United States. The constantly shifting Mexican governments refused to recognize that line until 1828 and did not ratify the agreement until 1832. Before a joint survey could be made, however, Santa Anna overthrew the constitutional government and refused to accept the boundary. Meantime, Arkansas had created Miller County, and the United States had made land grants in an area that was later determined to be part of Texas. Immediately following United States recognition of Texas, the United States State Department urged that the boundary line be settled. The Sabine Boundary Convention was ratified by both governments in 1837, and in 1838 a joint commission surveyed the Sabine River and located the 32nd parallel. Texas accepted United States land titles that fell within its territories, and the United States responded in kind. Thus was this critical problem finally laid to rest after being delayed for nearly two decades by the Mexican governments' instability and their unaccountable refusal to negotiate even the simplest matters.

Mexican Relations Relations of the Republic of Texas with Mexico were never simple, and they were made more complex by Mexican instability and recalcitrance. The major problem was Mexico's refusal to recognize Texas independence even after it was clearly evident that she could never reestablish jurisdiction in Texas. Part of the reason for this was the adamant stubbornness of Bustamante's Centralist government and its belief that Texas was still in league with the Federalists of northern Mexico. In hopes of dispelling this notion, Lamar virtually turned his back on a Federalist separatist movement in Nuevo León, Coahuila, and Tamaulipas. A representative convention declared the independence of the Republic of the Rio Grande in January 1840, established a provisional government, and fielded an army. After an initial disastrous defeat in March, the provisional government fled for sanctuary to Victoria, Texas, and pleaded with Lamar for support.

Lamar, involved with James Treat in delicate negotiations with the Mexican government, had to decline, but he permitted General Antonio Canales to recruit volunteers in South Texas. In June 1840 Canales returned across the Rio Grande, having increased his army with about one hundred fifty men from the settlements around Victoria. (Is it any surprise that the Centralists' Indian agent had urged the attack on Victoria?) After losing one battle, in which part of his troops defected to the enemy, Canales capitulated in November 1840 to the Centralists.

James Treat, authorized by Lamar to work for a Mexican treaty, was a British subject thoroughly familiar with the intrigues of Latin American governments. Quite candidly he proposed on Texas' behalf to influence officials with funds, underwritten by Britain—the inevitable and traditional *mordido*. He might have succeeded had not the Bustamante government been fighting for its life against an uprising led by Santa Anna. Santa Anna had become active again in the defense of Vera Cruz in the "Pastry War" of 1838, when France sailed several gunboats into the harbor and unloaded a contingent of marines. The French purpose, which was fulfilled, was to collect the claims of French citizens against Mexico, which France had finally tired of trying to negotiate. Santa Anna lost a leg in the fighting and rose immediately to the stature of public hero. Soon he was at the head of a motley opposition to Bustamante, which included both Federalists and dissatisfied Centralists.

By 1841 Santa Anna was restored to power. Texans assumed that he would now recognize Texas as he had promised, but Texans, and many Mexicans, were to be disappointed. In June Santa Anna established an even more stringent Centralist constitution and dismissed the recently elected constitutional assembly. For the next three years Mexico was under a more virile dictator than Bustamante, and Texas had even less hope for recognition. The following year Santa Anna ordered two separate invasions of Texas, provoked only in part by the Texas naval alliance with the Yucatan rebels and by the unfortunate Texan–Santa Fe expedition.

After Santa Anna's refusal to negotiate, Lamar had recommissioned

Commodore Moore's fleet and authorized him to seek an alliance with the Yucatan rebels. In September 1841 the Yucatecos agreed to pay $8,000 a month for the use of the Texas Navy, and in December Moore sailed with three ships from Galveston. He patrolled the coast of Yucatan in the service of the rebel government until May, refusing to heed Houston's orders to return to Galveston. Houston, who had been inaugurated the day Moore sailed, did not approve of this naval activity, and finally in order to bring Moore to heel he proclaimed him a pirate and ordered his seizure by any navy of the world. When Moore returned on his own, he and Houston became involved in a lengthy quarrel that ended with the disbanding of the navy in 1842.

Santa Anna's other excuse to renege on his promises to Texas involved the Santa Fe expedition. In the spring of 1841 Lamar had proposed sending a commercial expedition to Santa Fe to divert the Santa Fe trade with Missouri to the Texas coast, with a secondary objective of establishing Texas political jurisdiction there. The former was clearly the primary reason, for Texas was destitute and the Santa Fe trade could bring in thousands of dollars in customs revenue. When congress refused to have anything to do with the scheme, Lamar proceeded on his own. He appointed Hugh McLeod as commander of the expedition, which was armed since it would cross the hostile Comanche region. Lamar named William G. Cooke, José Antonio Navarro, Richard Brenham, and George Van Ness as commissioners to offer to extend the Texas government to the people of Santa Fe if they wanted it. Merchants were invited to join the expedition with trade goods to sell in Santa Fe, and in June over three hundred men in a caravan of twenty-one wagons set out across West Texas.

They did not know the route and after a number of hardships divided into two parties. As they came down off the Caprock in New Mexico in the vicinity of present Tucumcari, Manuel Armijo, the Centralist governor of New Mexico, was waiting for them with a force of dragoons. By a ruse persuading the Texans to lay down their arms, he easily captured both parts of the expedition and confiscated the wagons. The prisoners were marched on foot to Santa Fe and then to Mexico City, where they were incarcerated in the dungeons of Perote Castle. Many died of privation along the way. The cruelty of Santa Anna's minion was soon exposed to the world by George Wilkins Kendall, a New Orleans newspaperman, and Thomas Falconer, a British writer, both of whom were on the expedition. United States and British ministers in Mexico eventually secured the release of their nationals, but the Texans remained imprisoned until Santa Anna's overthrow in 1844. Then a general amnesty freed them and several groups of Texans captured during 1842.

Inspired primarily by his hatred for Texas and provoked by the navy and the Santa Fe expedition, Santa Anna ordered General Rafael Vásquez at Saltillo to invade Texas. Vásquez crossed the Rio Grande with a force variously estimated at eight to fourteen hundred men, sent detachments to Goliad and Victoria, and himself entered San Antonio on March 5, 1842. He caught those cities utterly by surprise and occupied them with no difficulty. He only raised the Mexican flag, proclaimed sovereignty over Texas, and inspected the defenses. He and his troops withdrew from San Antonio two days later, on March 7. Jack Hays, in command of a Ranger company west of San Antonio, pursued and skirmished with Vásquez' rear guard on the Nueces.

Word of the invasion spread with fierce rapidity, and volunteers rushed to San Antonio. Houston ordered out part of the militia, and to the disgust of his vice-president, Edward Burleson, who wanted the command, he placed Alexander Somervell in charge. He then called a special session of congress. Within two weeks after Vásquez' departure there were thirty-five hundred armed men encamped in and around San Antonio. Many of them wished to rush pell-mell into Mexico but were prevented by some of the leaders. When it became apparent that Vásquez was not returning, the volunteers and the militia disbanded.

But the nation was rocked by the invasion. War fever swept like a plague across Texas, and once again a Matamoros expedition was projected. It was all Houston could do to control the situation. The special session, meeting in Houston because of Austin's exposed position, voted a declaration of war against Mexico, but Houston vetoed it and was barely able to prevent congress from overriding him. His position against war compounded by his recall of the navy at this point evoked a great public outcry against him, but he made his position clear: Texas could afford only to act on the defensive and must rely primarily on the militia for that. A war against Mexico would have been the utmost folly.

Just as Houston had begun to dispel the war talk, Santa Anna invaded a second time. General Adrian Woll appeared suddenly in San Antonio at the head of fourteen hundred men. He too caught the city by surprise, raised the Mexican flag, and proclaimed Mexican jurisdiction over Texas. But unlike Vásquez, Woll was prepared to stay. Jack Hays and his Rangers rushed once more to the outskirts of the town, and arriving volunteers placed themselves under his command. On September 18, when he had collected a force of about six hundred men, he decoyed Woll out of the city and ambushed a substantial portion of the Mexican force on Salado Creek. At the last minute Matthew Caldwell, an old Indian fighter, assumed command of the Texans, and the young Hays, only twenty-five years old, deferred to him gracefully. Losing sixty men to the

The Republic of Texas / 152

Texans' one, Woll withdrew across the Rio Grande with an assortment of prisoners. He had captured the Fayette County militia company under Nicholas Dawson and had imprisoned the entire district court then sitting at San Antonio, including attorneys and the jury.

Command of the troops at San Antonio was again given to Somervell, whom Houston ordered not to cross the Rio Grande but to drive Woll out of Texas and then patrol the river until he was certain the danger was over. Because of resentment of Somervell, the force of about seven hundred was not organized for the march until late November. The Texans reached Laredo on December 8, and in accordance with his orders Somervell decided to return to camp at Gonzales late in the month. The command to return was met with open dissension by about three hundred men who wanted to invade Mexico. Somervell led the rest back to Gonzales; those who remained elected W. S. Fisher commander and moved downstream opposite the Mexican town of Mier.

Disaster awaited them. Fisher demanded a ransom and supplies from the alcalde at Mier. When these were refused, he attacked the town on Christmas afternoon. He struck a hornet's nest. Some two thousand Mexican troops, unknown to the Texans, were temporarily garrisoned at Mier. The Texans battled furiously through the night and into the next day. At noon the Mexican general, his powder almost exhausted and his men broken by hunger and thirst, sent out a flag of truce. Although he intended to capitulate, he first boldly demanded that the Texans surrender themselves. Fisher, knowing his situation to be desperate, accepted the ultimatum. His chagrin and that of his followers when they learned the truth can well be imagined.

The Texans had been started down the long trek to Mexico City and Perote Castle when they overpowered the guards, and most of them escaped. But it was winter, and they were in strange mountainous country. Cold and lack of food forced most of them to surrender within a few weeks. Santa Anna sent orders to Salado, Mexico, where the recaptured men were held, that one out of ten was to be executed as an example. There were one hundred seventy-six men; seventeen black beans were placed in a pot with one hundred fifty-nine white. Prisoners drawing black beans were summarily executed, another example of Santa Anna's inhumanity. The rest were marched on to Perote Castle, where they joined the Santa Fe prisoners and the Woll prisoners.

When Santa Anna was overthrown and exiled in 1844, Houston was able to obtain the release of all the prisoners. With the aid of Lewis Pakenham, British minister to Mexico, and Charles Elliot, British chargé in Texas, he also arranged a truce with the Herrera government and expected with reason that a treaty of recognition might soon be negotiated.

But José Herrera lasted less than eighteen months before he too was overthrown. During the latter part of his regime he dared not antagonize any of his support by recognizing Texas or, as will be seen in the next chapter, by dealing with the United States, with which diplomatic relations had been broken a second time. Herrera's principal opponent was Mariano Paredes, a staunch Centralist and a violent anti-American.

Annexation But the truce of 1844 was welcome, as was the British mediation, for this created the illusion that Texas might become a British protectorate. Houston needed something of this sort to reawaken annexation sentiment in the United States. United States annexation had always been Houston's major goal. The Texas offer to be annexed was withdrawn in 1838 in the face of mounting opposition in the United States Congress, where aging abolitionist John Quincy Adams filibustered for three weeks to prevent the passage of an annexation bill. Lamar was not interested in annexation, believing Texas destined for a magnificent future among the family of nations. Shortly after Houston began his second term in 1842, he instructed the Texan minister in Washington to feel out the state department on the question of annexation. But New Englander Daniel Webster, who was secretary of state, refused to consider the matter. In July 1843 Houston withdrew the offer a second time to embark on a "coy" policy. He reasoned, correctly, that if Texas did not appear anxious and that if British interests in Texas, especially trade, could be magnified, perhaps some of the American opposition to Texas might be weakened. It worked.

When Webster resigned, John Tyler replaced him with a Virginian, Abel P. Upshur, who invited Isaac Van Zandt, the Texan minister in Washington, to reopen the question. Houston immediately sent Texas' leading diplomat, James Pinckney Henderson. The negotiations were completed on April 11, 1844, with John C. Calhoun, who had succeeded Upshur after his death. This Treaty of Annexation was promptly ratified in Texas although Houston was displeased with some portions of it. The treaty provided that Texas would enter the union as a territory and would pass through the various stages leading to statehood. It also stipulated that the vast public domain in Texas would be turned over to the federal government, which accepted Texas' boundary claims but reserved the right to negotiate with Mexico. The only favorable portion of the treaty was the federal agreement to assume the public debt of Texas.

It proved fortunate for Texas that the United States Senate failed to ratify the treaty in June and that the annexation of Texas became the major issue in the presidential election of 1844. The Whigs espoused the abolitionists, nominated Henry Clay, and opposed Texas. The Democrats picked James K. Polk, who entered the campaign crying expansion slogans: "Fifty-four-forty or fight," alluding to the northwestern boundary of the United States, and "The reoccupation of Oregon and the reannexation of Texas," alluding to the former claim derived from the Louisiana purchase. "Polk and Dallas [his running mate]—Texas and Oregon" swept the country and gave the Democrats a substantial victory.

To John Tyler, who would not leave the office until March 3, the election was a clear mandate from the people to proceed with the annexation of Texas. Since the two-thirds senate majority needed to ratify a treaty was not forthcoming, Tyler's advisers suggested the passage of a joint resolution, which required only a simple majority of both houses. He proposed this in a special message to congress in December 1844. The joint resolution offering annexation to Texas passed, and Tyler signed it on March 3, 1845.

There was no question whether Texas would accept the offer, which was much more generous than the earlier treaty. Under its terms Texas would be admitted directly as a state, would retain its public lands, would pay its own public debt, would deed established defense installations to the United States, and would have the option of dividing itself into as many as five states if it wished, providing that any created north of the parallel of 36°–30′ would be free states. Texas would, of course, submit a republican constitution for the approval of congress.

Texas had also had an election in 1844, and the Houston candidate, Dr. Anson Jones, became president in December. Jones later called himself the Architect of Annexation, but in truth all he did was mark time and follow Houston's program. The acceptance of the terms was delayed for three and a half months: first, to give Elliot and Pakenham an opportunity to work out a treaty with the Herrera government in Mexico (the British had become anxious for Texas to remain independent!), and second, to try to secure even better terms from the United States, for Houston wanted the United States to assume at least part of the Texas debt, that for which the custom revenue had been pledged.

The British agents came through with a curious treaty: Mexico would recognize Texas independence on the condition that Texas would not join the United States. The logic of this was as baffling and the offer as petulant as many other Mexican actions. It was, however, in keeping with British desires. Jones called a special session of the Ninth Congress to meet on June 16, 1845. The senate promptly rejected the Mexican treaty, and both houses accepted the United States offer and also approved a convention that Jones had called to meet in Austin to draft a state constitution. On July 4 the Convention of 1845 adopted with one dissenting vote an ordinance of annexation. For the next two months the delegates worked on the constitution. On October 13, 1845, both the ordinance and the constitution were submitted to popular vote and overwhelmingly approved. In short order the United States Congress passed the Texas Admission Act, which Polk signed on December 29, 1845.

According to a later Supreme Court decision, this was the day Texas became a state, but a state government did not replace the government of the Republic until February 19, 1846. Then when state officials were inaugurated in Austin with James Pinckney Henderson the first governor, Anson Jones lowered the Lone Star flag of Texas and raised the Stars and Stripes over the little capitol building.

7

Statehood, 1846–1860

Early Years

The Mexican War   Soon after the passage of the joint resolution offering annexation to Texas, Juan N. Almonte, then the Mexican minister in Washington, called for his passport and broke off diplomatic relations with the United States. He claimed that annexation was an act of hostility toward Mexico because Texas was Mexican territory. Almonte's belligerent posture, however, was not a true index of his government's attitude and was, in fact, almost contradictory to it: his government had already signed a truce with the Republic of Texas and was preparing to negotiate the rather illogical treaty recognizing its independence.

The reason for this contradiction was that Almonte did not represent the government then in power in Mexico. Santa Anna had been overthrown and exiled in the summer of 1844, and a moderate (although not Federalist) government had been installed in December under José Herrera. Extremists in Mexico, who attacked Herrera's willingness to negotiate with both Texas and the United States, were quick to seize upon the annexation of Texas as a point of further contention. Almonte, Santa Anna's Centralist appointee in Washington, undoubtedly expected to be replaced by the new government, and his tantrum was an attempt to embarrass Herrera. In this it was very effective, for Herrera's vacillating efforts to reopen diplomatic relations with the United States enabled his enemies to oust him from power.

Almonte's withdrawal was also a face-saving response to the United States minister in Mexico, who had previously broken off diplomatic relations over the perennial claims issue. The claims were debts owed by Mexico to citizens of the United States as well as of France and Great Britain. All three nations fruitlessly attempted to negotiate for payment with the successive Mexican governments. France finally collected hers after sending gunboats and marines to Vera Cruz in the Pastry War of 1838, and then Britain only had to threaten force to collect hers. But the United States continued to try negotiation, despite repeated recommendations from United States ministers in Mexico that a show of force was the only solution. In 1836 Powhatan Ellis left Mexico in disgust at the treatment he had received, and he did not return until 1839, after Mexico had agreed to an arbitration convention. Bustamante's government, however, like the governments before and after it, had no intention of paying the claims. It broke the arbitration agreement and then renegotiated it, stalling at every point. When finally the commission met in August 1840, presided over by a Prussian nobleman, the Mexican delegation wrangled over procedures for four months and then created one delay after another as the claims were taken up. After suffering through fifteen months of these tactics, the commission adjourned. Of the approximately eleven million dollars in claims, only six million had been allowed to reach the conference table, and of these, only two million had been decided.

It then became the unpleasant task of the United States ministers to collect the two million dollars as well as to negotiate a new arbitration agreement. Ellis resigned and was replaced by Waddy Thompson, who was instructed in 1842 to offer to accept territory in lieu of the claims. Though this offer was rejected, he did secure from the Santa Anna government in 1843 a new arbitration convention and an agreement to pay the two million dollars by installments. But Santa Anna, hard pressed by the rising tide of revolution in 1844, reneged on both agreements, having paid only one installment. In the summer, William Shannon, who was then the United States minister, in complete exasperation refused to deal further with the crumbling Santa Anna government. He was the third American diplomat to recommend that the collection of the claims was a matter for congress and could only be accomplished by force.

STATEHOOD: THE FRONTIER FORTS

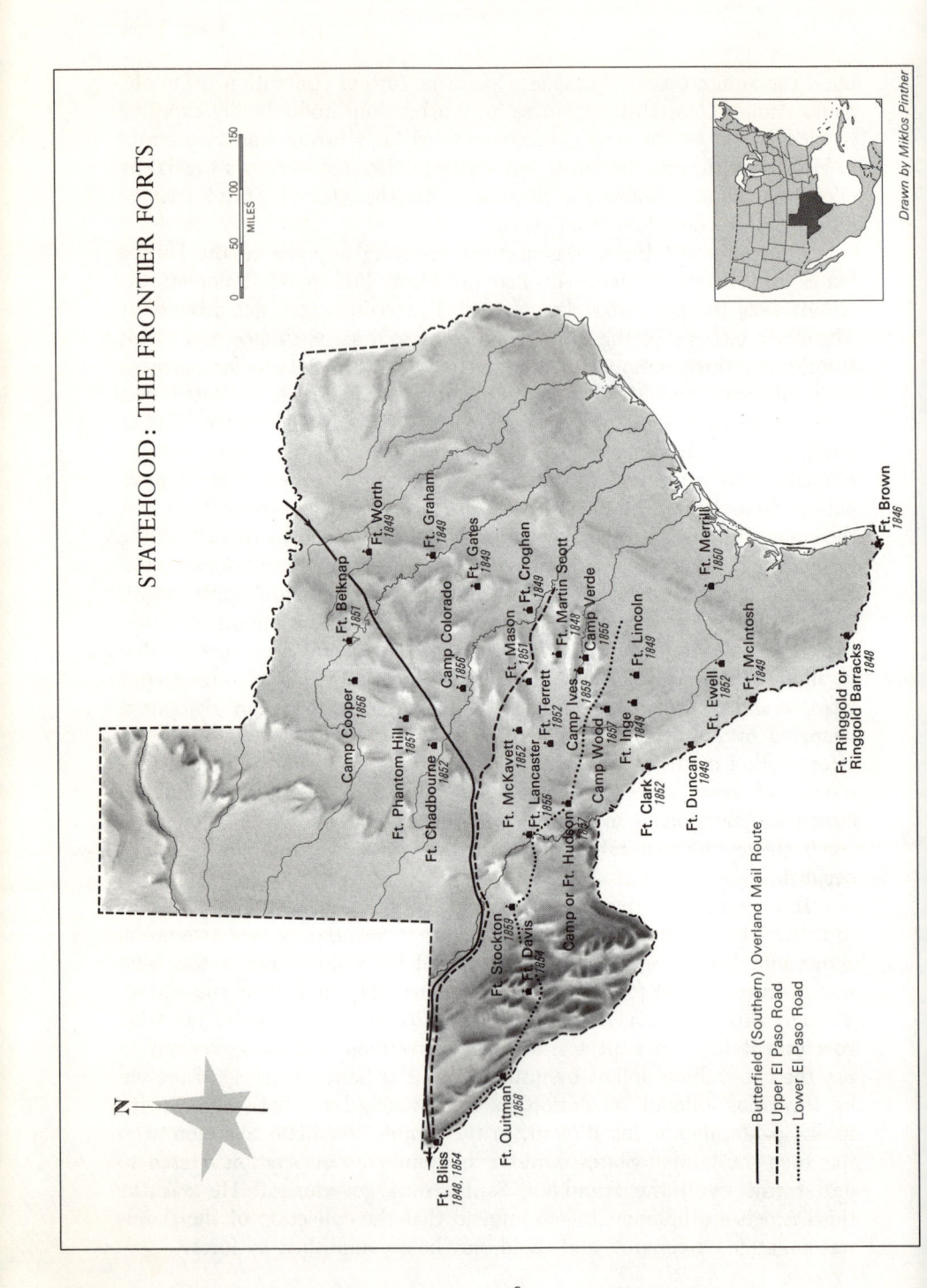

158

Thus did matters stand when Herrera was inaugurated in Mexico and Polk in the United States a few months later. Polk sent William Parrott to Mexico as a secret agent to determine whether Herrera would receive a new minister; Herrera replied through an American consul that he would accept an agent from the United States who had "full power to settle the present dispute." Dispatches from Parrott bore this out, and Polk appointed John Slidell to handle the delicate negotiations. Slidell was to secure Mexican acceptance of Texas annexation and to settle the pesky claims question in any way he could. He was authorized to trade the claims for recognition of the Rio Grande boundary and to offer additional funds for the rest of New Mexico. He was empowered alternatively to settle on a different boundary for Texas and to accept California in exchange for the claims and as much as $40,000,000. Polk hoped Slidell could get the Rio Grande boundary and New Mexico and California.

Meantime, the process of annexation was slowly moving to conclusion. When Texas accepted the United States' offer, Polk felt obligated to assume the defense of the country, and he ordered General Zachary Taylor to move his small command from Louisiana to a position on or near the Rio Grande. Taylor chose instead to encamp at the mouth of the Nueces near present Corpus Christi, arriving there in the summer of 1845.

Slidell reached Mexico in December 1845 only to be informed coldly that Herrera would not receive him and that no friendly relations could exist between the two nations until the United States returned Texas to Mexico! The cause of Herrera's reversal was the mounting pressure of rabid criticism by the ultra-Centralists, now led by the violently anti-American Mariano Paredes. In January 1846 Paredes overthrew Herrera and assumed control of the government. When Polk learned of the Paredes revolution and the warmongering threats to retake Texas, as well as the Herrera government's rejection of Slidell, he ordered Slidell to stay on and try to deal with Paredes, and he ordered Taylor to move his army to a defensive position on the Rio Grande. Slidell patiently petitioned for an interview, but in March he was insultingly rebuffed and ordered out of the country. Taylor complied with his orders and on March 23 took up a position near present-day Brownsville on the north bank of the Rio Grande a few miles above its mouth.

On April 4 Paredes ordered General Ignacio Mexia, who was in command at Matamoros, to attack Taylor. The following week Paredes replaced him with a more aggressive commander, General Pedro Ampudia, and sent several thousand additional troops. On April 23 Paredes' obedient congress declared war on the United States, and the next day

Mexican troops crossed the river and attacked a detachment of American dragoons commanded by Captain William A. Thornton. On May 8 and 9 Taylor's forces were attacked again in the massive battles of Palo Alto and Resaca de la Palma, both fought on the north side of the river. As soon as he received word of the attack on Thornton, Polk asked congress for a declaration of war. Despite abolitionist and Whig objections, war was approved on May 13, 1846, by a large majority of votes.

The Texas Legislature authorized Governor Henderson a leave of absence to take command of Texas volunteers, who rushed to enlist. A half-dozen companies of Rangers were the first to reach Taylor, and they formed a regiment under the command of Colonel John Coffee Hays. Approximately five thousand Texans were in federal service during the war.

There were three major campaigns: Taylor's, from the mouth of the Rio Grande to Monterrey and Buena Vista; a second led by Winfield Scott, who landed at Vera Cruz and marched into Mexico City; and the bloodless occupation of Santa Fe by Stephen W. Kearny, who split his force, sending Colonel William Doniphan into Chihuahua and going himself into California. In the first campaign, the hardest fought, Texans distinguished themselves for bravery. As scouts, Hays and the Rangers were the eyes and ears of Taylor's advance, and as assault troops, they were in the forefront of every battle. But Taylor quarreled with Henderson over trifles and despised the Rangers for their lack of military discipline. After the war, when Taylor became president, his antipathy for Texas was a significant factor in the New Mexico controversy.

When the Monterrey campaign ended, Henderson returned to Austin, but many of the Texans, including Hays and his Rangers, reenlisted and participated in Scott's conquest of Central Mexico. Again the Rangers were useful scouts and assault troops. No organized Texas units participated in Kearny's campaign in the west, although former Ranger George Thomas Howard, with secret orders from the war department, entered Santa Fe in advance of the American army and helped bring about the peaceful occupation of New Mexico.

In Mexico, Paredes had been forced to restore the Constitution of 1824 as a sop to the Federalists and compelled by public opinion to permit Santa Anna to return from exile to command the armies. In a December 1846 election under the Constitution of 1824 Santa Anna won the presidency. But the government collapsed during Scott's drive from Vera Cruz, and the American peace commissioners had difficulty deciding which to recognize of several groups claiming to be the legitimate government. (Ultimately the Herrera government was restored.) On February 2, 1848, the war was ended by the signing of the Treaty of Guadalupe Hidalgo. Its chief points were the recognition of the Rio Grande as the boundary of Texas; the cession of the territory occupied by Kearny west of the Rio Grande, including California; the nominal payment to Mexico of $15,000,000; and the assumption by the United States of the Mexican claims.

The Boundary Controversy The treaty seemed to establish the Texas claim to the upper Rio Grande, together with eastern New Mexico—if it did not vindicate it—on the basis of a technicality. The United States federal government had stipulated at the time of annexation that it would adjust the boundary claimed by Texas in 1836 *with other nations*. This had been done; Mexico had accepted the Rio Grande and had ceded the territory to the west of it; there was no reservation in the annexation agreement about adjusting internal boundaries; ergo, Texas owned eastern New Mexico. As early as June 4, 1847, Governor Henderson had notified the United States State Department that Kearny's military government in Santa Fe intruded on Texas' jurisdiction. Secretary of State James Buchanan replied that the temporary government there would not prejudice the Texas claim, which would, however, have to be settled by congress after the war's end.

Texas did not wait for congress to act. On March 15, 1848, the Texas Legislature created Santa Fe County and commissioned Judge Spruce M. Baird to organize civil government there under Texas statutes. Baird was coldly received by Colonel John M. Washington, who was in charge of the military government and who informed Baird that neither he nor the people of Santa Fe would consider permitting Texas to govern New Mexico. Furthermore, he would not even admit that Texas had a claim to the area.

Baird's rejection angered many Texans. Governor George Thomas Wood announced in November 1849 that Texas should assert its claim "with the whole power and resources of the state." The legislature created Santa Fe County anew, along with three other counties: Worth, Buchel, and El Paso. Ex-Ranger Robert S. Neighbors was appointed to organize government in those counties. Neighbors proceeded to the little settlement of Franklin, which had recently grown up around the Magoffin brothers' trading post across the Rio Grande from the old Spanish settlement of El Paso del Norte. There he had no difficulty in organizing a county government, an act which was to be of major consequence in the settlement of the boundary dispute. But in Santa Fe he found both the citizens and the military forces antagonistic.

President Zachary Taylor, who was nurturing a grudge against Texas, had encouraged New Mexico to hold a constitutional convention to petition for statehood. This had been done, and New Mexico claimed a large part of Texas. When Neighbors reported his failure to the governor in June 1850, a great public outcry arose—angry editorials, mass meetings, and talk of secession. Governor Peter H. Bell called a special session of the legislature and made a fiery address on what by that time most Texans considered a federal usurpation of Texas' jurisdiction.

The summer of 1850 was a critical time in American history. Not only Texas but the entire South was threatening to secede. For Texas the issue was the New Mexico boundary controversy; for the rest of the southern states the issue was the admission of California as a free state. California, whose population had swelled overnight because of the discovery of gold, had also held a convention and petitioned for immediate statehood. Since both California and New Mexico were excluding slavery and since congress seemed intent on making the entire Mexican Cession free soil, rebellious southern leaders called a secession convention in Nashville. Secession of the southern states would probaby have come at this time had not elder statesmen such as Henry Clay and Daniel Webster worked out an effective compromise.

The Compromise of 1850 Two major Texas problems influenced the details of the compromise: the boundary claim and the Texas debt. Ever since the joint resolution a strong contention had been advanced that the United States should be responsible for payment of the Texas "revenue" debt, or that portion of the public indebtedness of the Republic of Texas for which the customs revenue had been hypothecated. The argument was not without merit, because after annexation the federal government and not Texas collected the tariff duties in Texas ports. Most of this revenue debt was in the form of bonds, and most of the bondholders were investors and speculators in the major cities of the United States. Not surprisingly, a number of these men joined together, employed an agent, and lobbied for federal assumption of the Texas revenue debt.

The Texas bondholders threw their support behind the Compromise of 1850 because this solution combined the Texas problems with those of the Mexican Cession. The principal points of the compromise were immediate admission of California as a free state; territorial status for New Mexico and Utah, accounting for the remainder of the Mexican Cession; establishment of the Texas boundary; and the payment to Texas of $10,000,000 for the loss of territory, half of which sum would be retained in the United States Treasury for the settlement of the revenue debt. The Texas boundary was to run west from the 100th meridian along the parallel of 36°–30′ to the 103rd meridian, thence south to the 32nd parallel, and thence west to the Rio Grande. Had it not been for the organization of El Paso County, the line would probably have continued down the 103rd meridian to the river, thus placing most of the Trans-Pecos region in the New Mexico Territory.

The Settlement of the Texas Debt Texas agreed to the "sale" of its New Mexico claim on November 25, 1850, with a promptness born of financial desperation. Texas would not only be relieved of payment for the bonds but would receive five million dollars with which to settle its other debts. In 1849 the legislature had adopted the principle of adjusting the various forms of indebtedness to par or market value; an auditorial board, by "scaling" the debt from 100 per cent for treasury drafts to 12½ per cent for some of the paper money, had scaled the total debt of $12,436,991.34 to $6,827,278.64. Of this, $4,467,756.41 was considered revenue obligations, but under pressure from the Texas bondholders the United States Treasury refused to accept the reduced valuation and estimated the revenue debt at $10,078,703.21. After considerable controversy, the United States Congress appropriated an additional $2,750,000 in 1855, calling it interest, and settled the revenue debt at 76.9 cents on the dollar.

Meantime Texas began the payment of its other creditors as quickly as claims could be filed and adjusted. A total of only $1,575,366.59 was paid on these debts because some of the claims were never filed and some were disallowed. There remained, therefore, of the $5,000,000 Texas received directly, nearly $3,500,000. Two million of this was set aside in 1854 as a permanent endowment fund for public education in one of the most significant and far-reaching measures of the period. To this permanent school fund was added half the unsold public domain in 1876 and the remainder of the public lands in 1899. Revenue and other additions have brought the potential value of this endowment to approximately $500,000,000, making it the backbone of public education in Texas.

Political Developments The Mexican War, the New Mexico boundary controversy, and the settlement of the debt were the most important matters confronting the early state government, but there were, of course, a score of less significant developments. Not the least of these was the emergence of the Democratic Party to dominance of Texas politics and the consequent perfection of party machinery.

Originally there had been no political affiliations in Texas other than the pro- and anti-Houston forces. In the first state election, James Pinckney Henderson, a Houston man, had easily won the governorship, and the First Legislature had sent Houston, himself, and Thomas Jefferson Rusk, another Houston man, to the United States Senate.

Because of the long-standing Whig opposition to Texas, most Texans were nominally Democrats in national elections, but there was virtually no party organization. In state and local elections, after Houston transferred his influence to Washington, contests were largely decided by personal popularity. Henderson declined to run for reelection in 1847. His lieutenant governor, Albert Clinton Horton, who had served as governor during Henderson's absence in the Mexican War, also declined to run. Both J. B. Miller and George T. Wood offered themselves to the public in newspaper announcements, since not even a state convention of the Democratic Party was held. Wood was elected, with John A. Greer as his lieutenant governor.

In 1848 Wood called for a party convention to meet in Austin, but delegations from only a few counties presented themselves. A public quarrel with Henderson over Wood's actions in the Monterrey campaign lost Wood the support of the Houston faction, and in the election of 1849 he was defeated by Peter H. Bell. Again the voters' choice was based on personal rather than political issues. Both men were Democrats, planters, slave-owners, and inclined toward secession sentiment. John A. Greer was reelected lieutenant governor.

In 1851 the Whig Party made its first formal appearance in Texas politics when it supported the gubernatorial candidacy of B. H. Epperson. Democrats Greer, Thomas Jefferson Chambers, and M. T. Johnson also opposed Bell's reelection, but he won handily over all four candidates. His lieutenant governor was James W. Henderson. In 1853 Bell was elected to the United States Congress, and he resigned the gubernatorial office on November 23. Henderson then served as governor until December 21. He had entered the contest for the governor's office that fall along with Chambers and M. T. Johnson, and along with them had withdrawn from the race to support Elisha M. Pease. For in that election of 1853 personalities began to give way to politics. The Whig candidate, W. B. Ochiltree, had such strong support that the Democrats feared he might be elected if the Democratic vote was fragmented among several candidates. Interestingly, at that time the issue of secession had subsided, and both Pease and Ochiltree were known as being pro-union. Pease was elected with David C. Dickson, who was also identified as a unionist.

During Pease's first term a new party entered Texas politics: the American or Know Nothing Party. This semisecret organization opposed

Catholicism, foreign-born persons in office, and secession, although it professed to support slavery. In 1854 Know Nothing candidates captured local offices in the two most important Texas cities, Galveston and San Antonio. Its influence spread rapidly through the state, sundering the Whig Party and alarming the Democrats. In 1855 the Know Nothings held a statewide convention at Washington-on-the-Brazos (calling it a River Improvement Convention) and announced the candidacy of David C. Dickson for governor.

A few weeks earlier Dickson had been accepted by a lackadaisical Democratic convention as the running mate for Pease, who had been nominated for governor a second time. The peculiar anomaly of having endorsed the opposition candidate thoroughly aroused Democratic leaders from their lethargy. A meeting was hastily called in Austin, and Hardin R. Runnels, a planter and staunch secessionist, was chosen to run for lieutenant governor. County delegates pledged themselves to organize party support for the Pease-Runnels ticket at the precinct level, throwing themselves into the defense of Democratic control of the state. The election of 1855 was the most hotly contested election in Texas up to that time. Dickson and the Know Nothings, who implied they had the support of Sam Houston, lost by only four thousand votes. But the Know Nothings did win twenty-five seats in the legislature and a number of local offices. More important, their strength in this election caused the Democrats to tighten their organization in preparation for the next election.

The Frontier

Exploration While outside pressures were forcing a semblance of organization upon the Democrats during the decade after the Mexican War, the burgeoning state was experiencing prosperity and a constant stream of immigration. In 1849 Texas found itself on the route of many caravans of gold seekers bound for California. To aid the forty-niners and to attract others to cross Texas, the United States Army, the Texas Legislature, and the citizens of San Antonio and Austin authorized surveys to determine practical routes across semiarid West Texas.

The earliest survey was made in the late summer and fall of 1848 by Jack Hays, who went west from San Antonio and across Devils River to the lower Pecos, led by Indian guides who confessed themselves lost somewhere in the mountains west of the Pecos. Suffering from a shortage of supplies and water, the Hays party struggled back to San Antonio by a route somewhat to the north. A second survey, jointly sponsored by the citizens of Austin and the United States Army, was undertaken by John S. Ford, Hays' adjutant during the Mexican War, and Robert S. Neighbors, also a former Ranger. Ford and Neighbors traveled northwest from Austin to the head of Brady Creek in McCulloch County, crossed the South Concho below present-day Cristoval to strike the Middle Concho in present Irion County. From there they followed the Middle Concho and Centralia Draw west through Castle Gap to the Horsehead Crossing of the Pecos and reached Franklin by way of Comanche Springs at present Fort Stockton. They returned by way of the Hueco Tanks and Guadalupe Pass back to the Pecos. On the Middle Concho they veered southeast to find a route to San Antonio. On their return, Ford and Neighbors encountered several parties of gold seekers who were blindly but eagerly trying to follow the surveyors' exploratory route. Guides were detailed to lead them to El Paso. Neighbors himself returned to El Paso that fall to organize the county government there.

While Ford and Neighbors were locating what came to be called the Upper California Road, Captain W. H. C. Whiting of the United States Topographical Engineers was exploring a more southerly route to El Paso. On his return from El Paso he outlined the Lower California Road, which ran southeast from El Paso through the Davis Mountains to the mouth of Live Oak Creek on the Pecos, thence down Devils River almost to its mouth, and thence almost due east to San Antonio. Whiting and the Ford and Neighbors party arrived in San Antonio within a few weeks of each other in May and June 1849.

Since two practical routes were available, a more thorough reconnaissance was made by the Topographical Engineers. From June to December 1849 Lieutenant Francis T. Bryan traced the Ford and Neighbors trail to El Paso and back. He mapped the route and kept a fairly detailed log. Lieutenant Colonel Joseph E. Johnston, in charge of the Topographical Engineers in Texas, led a large and elaborate expedition along Whiting's return route from El Paso. This lower road was practical for wagon trains and was probably used more extensively than the upper road. It was estimated that as many as five thousand emigrants passed along both routes during the following year.

Two more routes were located across Texas in 1849, both by Captain Randolph B. Marcy, who escorted a party of emigrants from Fort Smith, Arkansas, to Santa Fe following the Canadian River across the Texas Panhandle. On his return Marcy explored the country from the Emigrants Crossing of the Pecos northeast to the Red River in present Grayson County, and he recommended a road that was soon followed by hundreds of emigrants and later became the approximate route of the Texas and Pacific Railroad. A different route was explored in November 1849 by Lieutenant Nathaniel Michler from Fort Washita in the Indian Territory to Marcy's Trail in the vicinity of present Big Spring.

The Corps of Topographical Engineers was perhaps the most brilliant group of officers developed by West Point in the nineteenth century, and their explorations in Texas were vital to the development of the frontier. One of these officers, Lieutenant William H. Emory, conducted in 1852 and 1853 an extensive survey of the Rio Grande from El Paso to its mouth, and Marcy returned to Texas twice, once in 1851 to explore the headwaters of the Red River and again in 1854 to assist in the location of an Indian reservation on the Brazos.

The Indian Problem With annexation the United States Army not only assumed the burden of exploring routes across West Texas but also the defense of the Texas frontier, the subjugation of hostile Indians. But few measures were taken until after the end of the Mexican War, and during the first two years of statehood Texas had to rely on state troops to defend frontier settlements. In the summer of 1846 five companies of mounted militia (commonly called Rangers, but not the same body of men as the Rangers of the earlier Republic period) were stationed respectively at Castroville, San Antonio, on the Little River in Bosque County, at Torrey's trading post in Johnson County, and on the West Fork of the Trinity in Tarrant County. The following year four additional companies were distributed between San Antonio and Laredo. After the close of the war, in 1848, seven companies of infantry from the United States Army replaced these state troops, and Texans began to hope that the federal government would remove the Indians to reservations in Indian Territory. Such reservations were not established, however, until well after the Civil War.

In 1849 military authorities decided to build a line of forts, similar to the line of Ranger posts, for the protection of the frontier. Ten were established that year: Worth, Gates, Graham, Croghan, Martin Scott, Lincoln, Inge, McIntosh, Duncan, and Bliss (originally the El Paso Post). Two other forts had been located on the lower Rio Grande earlier, Fort Ringgold in Starr County and Fort Brown, but these were not greatly involved in the defense of the Indian frontier. In 1849 this line of eight posts from Eagle Pass to Fort Worth marked the frontier. So rapidly did settlers push west, however, that a second line of forts was soon needed further west, and in the early 1850's forts Belknap, Phantom Hill, Chadbourne, Concho, McKavett, Terrett, and Clark were built. During the same period, partially to protect the routes to El Paso, it was necessary to build forts Lancaster, Stockton, Davis, and Quitman.

The principal Indian menace came from the roving bands of marauding Comanches who depredated the frontier settlements almost incessantly. The first line of posts halted Comanche raids for a short time. In 1850 some thirty Comanche chiefs and the United States Indian agent in Texas made an agreement that the Indians would remain west of the military line. But the army failed to support the second line of forts adequately, and by 1852 Comanches had again begun attacking settlements and isolated homesteads all along the frontier.

Although the ruthless ferocity of their raids cannot be condoned, there was some justification for the Indians' attacks. The white man was advancing westward inexorably, crowding the Comanches out of the hunting grounds from which a few generations earlier they had driven the Apaches. Neither Texas nor the United States was prepared to reserve all, or the greater part, of West Texas for the exclusive use of a few hundred nomadic hunters. The only solution lay in the reservation system long since established in Indian Territory.

Eager to help quiet the frontier, the Texas Legislature authorized the Indian Bureau to select one to three proposed reservations in the unoccupied public domain. Robert S. Neighbors, who had been appointed Indian agent shortly after his return from El Paso, and Randolph B. Marcy of the U.S. Topographical Engineers, who had already explored much of West Texas, located two reservation sites during the spring of 1855. One, for the remnant of the sedentary tribes of Central and East Texas who were now roaming the plains, was located near present Graham. A second, for the Penateka Comanches, was situated on the Clear Fork of the Brazos. Neighbors faced the almost impossible task of persuading the Comanches to move into the reservation and, once there, to stay. From among the estimated 1,200 Penetekas, the number on the reservation varied from 250 to 550, most of the time averaging about 350.

Thus the Comanche reservation in Texas proved to be unsuccessful. The majority of the Indians refused to enter the reservation, and many who did soon left. Frontier citizens believed that some of the raids were made by reservation Indians, who sought refuge on the reservation after pillaging nearby. So intense did feeling become over this issue that both reservations were closed in 1859, and Neighbors transferred his charges, at that time 384 Comanches and 1,112 sedentary Indians, to the Indian Territory. On his return, he was murdered by an irate man who incorrectly believed that he had aided some of the marauders by giving them reservation sanctuary. The failure of the reservations in Texas may be attributed both to Comanche recalcitrance and the inadequacy of the measure.

Other more stringent efforts to protect the frontier enjoyed not much greater success. Albert Sidney Johnston, who had rejoined the United States Army after annexation, was ordered to Texas to organize and command the Second Cavalry. Second in command was none other than Robert E. Lee. Beginning in 1856, elements of the Second Cavalry were stationed in the forts along the western line. These mounted troops deterred but did not stop the Indian attacks. In 1858 John S. Ford was sent on a punitive expedition by the Texas government. With a force of some two hundred Rangers and friendly Indians, he won a decisive victory over a band of northern Comanches on the Canadian River, killing 76 and capturing 18. For a time this stopped the raids from the northwest. That fall Major Earl Van Dorn of the United States Army and a young Ranger captain named Lawrence Sullivan Ross, who was later governor of the state, surprised and defeated another band of northern Comanches in present-day Oklahoma. In May 1859, in a second surprise attack on the same Indians, Van Dorn destroyed the entire band.

The following December young Ross, leading twenty United States troops and about seventy inflamed citizens of Palo Pinto County, pursued a Comanche raiding party to the Pease River in present Foard County. A large Nokoni camp was destroyed, the plundered property was regained, and—to the amazement of the Texans—Cynthia Ann Parker was found. Captured by Comanches at the age of nine, she had grown up among the Indians and married Chief Peta Nocona, by whom she had a son, Quanah Parker. Her reunion with her original family was not a happy one, however, because of her long years with the Indians, and she died at her brother's home in 1864 after having attempted several times to return to the Indian way of life.

The efficacy of these military tactics is uncertain. Many historians believe that they only stirred the Comanches into bitter revenge, for it was in 1858 and 1859 that the raiding became serious. It may be, however, that the westward movement of the frontier, more than the punitive expeditions, was the true source of the Indian trouble.

Expansion of the Frontier   The principal reason for the expansion of settlement in Texas was the availability of cheap land on the western and southwestern frontier. Although most land was not free in Texas, in general it was cheaper than in the other frontier states. The United States still charged a minimum of $1.25 per acre for land in the public domain. In Texas, even after the expiration of the Third Class

Headright in 1843, land was free to settlers in the empresario colonies established by the Republic as late as 1848. In 1854 the legislature passed a preemption act granting 160 acres to homesteaders on the public domain. This, a true homestead act in the popular sense, was a revision of previous statutes, which had required preemptors to file a valid certificate to complete the title to their land.

Such land certificates were plentiful before the Civil War. They consisted of land scrip issued by the Republic and a half-dozen other forms of land entitlement. Such certificates, of course, had to be "located" on vacant public land and proper field notes had to be filed before a title was issued by the land office. It was the pressure to "lay" (in the terminology of the time) the unlocated certificates that gave the initial impetus to western expansion. Surveying crews, led by such indefatigable frontiersmen as Neil McLennan or such avid speculators and promoters as Jacob de Cordova, penetrated the Indian country to establish land boundaries and lay claim to western land. Sometimes the surveyors worked on commission, but they also purchased unlocated paper for thirty to fifty cents an acre, filed in their own names on extensive tracts, which they then sold to settlers in smaller parcels at seventy-five cents to a dollar an acre. The surveying parties were always armed and often attacked by the Comanches, who recognized them as the first wave of the white man's advance.

Settlers soon followed the land locators. They established homesteads, brought herds of livestock, cleared fields for planting, organized local government, and built towns, schools, and churches. Many such frontier farmers, after perfecting their land titles and making minimal improvements, sold their land and plunged further west. Some of these inveterate pioneers moved three or four times, riding like a modern surfer with the crest of the wave of settlement. These men were as much land speculators as the locators who preceded them. Without question, land speculation was the prime motivation of the western advance.

At the time of annexation the frontier line of settlement extended roughly from the coast up the Nueces River just beyond the Irish colony at San Patricio and then north to the San Antonio River and upstream to the town of San Antonio. Southwest of the river lay a few scattered ranchos of the older Hispanic settlers, and some Anglo settlers had spilled over north of the river from DeWitt's former colony. From San Antonio the frontier line turned northeast through the German colony and New Braunfels, passing Austin, which was still on the western edge of civilization, and then made a wide curve to the east of present-day Waco and swung back to pass west of Dallas, continuing north to the Red River around the settled portions of the Peters Colony.

In 1846 the legislature subdivided several of the larger, older counties and created new counties along this frontier line. The creation of functional local governments along the frontier line was of vital importance to the pioneer settlers and serves better than any other measure to indicate the movement of civilization westward in Texas. Thus, from 1846 to 1850, the line had been uniformly pushed westward approximately the width of one county. South of the San Antonio River, however, only one new county, Nueces at the mouth of the Nueces River, had been organized. Settlement had jumped down the coast to the mouth of the Rio Grande, moved upstream to Laredo, and leaped far across West Texas to El Paso County.

During the next decade the population of Texas increased from 212,592 to 604,215, nearly 200 per cent, and the line of settlement marched westward through three tiers of new counties. The westernmost organized governments at this time ran from Maverick County on the Rio Grande to Clay County on the Red River, bulging northwest through the counties of Mason and McCulloch and continuing north through Brown County. Individual settlers, many of them stock raisers, had of course advanced here and there many miles west of the line of civilization, and small towns had developed around several of the army posts.

But it is inaccurate to think of the frontier line as unbroken through the western posts. To the south of the Nueces River there was as yet little settlement, although along the Rio Grande county governments had been organized from Maverick County to Cameron County. The curious pocket of unsettled land between the Rio Grande and the Nueces was due partly to the inhospitable natural environment and partly to problems with land titles. Much of this land lay within former Spanish and Mexican grants of the vaguest boundaries and often the most tenuous legality. Furthermore, with the passage of generations, many of these grants were held in common by scores or even hundreds of heirs and descendants, few of whom realized they had any claims at all and others of whom thought they owned the entire grant. There were no records of ownership or transfer, and consequently a man who purchased a tract from an alleged owner did so at some risk, for he might be confronted with a half-dozen other "owners" of the land. Occasionally the same piece of property was sold by different heirs to different purchasers. The legislature eventually created a special investigating committee to settle land claims in this region.

This area was a natural habitat for cattle, and for over a century strays from Hispanic ranchos to the north and south had wandered into it, had thrived, and had multiplied. There were uncounted thousands of these wild longhorns in this unsettled pocket, which was later to become the birthplace of the western cattle industry.

The People of Texas

The Population The expansion of the frontier created a remarkable increase in the state's population during the decade and a half after annexation. There was no census in 1845, of course, nor any reliable estimate of the population. But there is good reason to believe that between annexation and the census of 1850 the state's population nearly doubled. Since there is also reason to believe that the 1850 census count of 212,592 was an underenumeration, the Texas population in 1845 may be estimated at between 125,000 and 150,000. In 1860 it was enumerated at 604,215. The growth rate was five times that of the United States during the same period—a remarkable increase by any standard.

Even more remarkable, although much less often remarked upon, was the unusual heterogeneity of the population. Contrary to general opinion, Texas has one of the most cosmopolitan heritages of any state in the union.

This wide variety of peoples in Texas has been characteristic of the region from the earliest times. Of the first native Texans, the Indians, the differences between the sedentary, agrarian Caddoan and the wandering plains hunter were greater than the differences between Greek and Swede in Europe. Another great dissimilarity was that of the Coahuiltecans—short, dark, and coarse-featured—and the coastal bands of which the Karankawa were the best known—tall, copper-skinned, and quite primitive.

It was into this widely varied base that in the seventeenth century Europeans began to mix their blood and heritage: the French among the coastal Indians after the failure of La Salle's Fort St. Louis and later the Spanish among the Caddoans in East Texas. Some of the original civil settlers at Los Adaes and Dolores were mestizos of central Mexico origins, and the native mestizos at San Antonio were different from East Texas mestizos.

The eighteenth century added more Spanish settlers, a nucleus of Canary Islanders, a few Irish and more Frenchmen in Spanish service, more Indians and mestizos from central Mexico, and a not unsubstantial number of Negroes and mulattoes. The native population at the beginning of the nineteenth century was of much wider diversity than that of most of the states in the United States at the time. Men of greatly varying ethnic origins now began to play roles in the development of Texas: Richard Fields, renegade Englishman living with the Cherokees; Bowles, a Cherokee chief; Philipe Neri, the "Baron" Bastrop, a Hollander; Joseph Durst, a German-American merchant; José Antonio

Navarro, a native Spaniard, and his Corsican wife; Jean Lafitte, Luis de Aury, Charles Lallemand, Frenchmen all; Juan Bautista de las Casas, a San Antonio mestizo; Juan Zambrano, a Spanish creole—the list could be expanded almost indefinitely. Texas by 1820 had already become a melting pot of cultural, national, and ethnic groups. Spanish culture predominated, but it had been tinted even then with hues of native Indian, Negro, mestizo, English, French, Irish, Dutch, Italian, and Anglo-American.

During the decade and a half of rapid Anglo-American colonization the bulk of the immigrants were from the United States, and the majority of these from the "southern" states, but a good-sized minority of the settlers came directly from Europe. At least two shiploads from northern Europe—British, German, and Scandinavian—were landed by the Galveston Bay and Texas Land Company. Arthur Wavell interested a handful of Englishmen in Texas; John Charles Beales brought English and German settlers to his Rio Grande Colony. And several hundred Irish Catholics moved into the two colonies on the coast. If the civilized population of Texas at the time of the Revolution was 50,000, as has been estimated, the Anglo-Americans may have constituted less than half of that total.

During the period of the Republic the population more than doubled. Although no reliable data are available, most of the immigrants, perhaps more than sixty per cent, came from the United States. Nevertheless, the mixture of ethnic and cultural groups in Texas continued. Germans from all parts of central Germany and from Bavaria and Austria poured into the Republic. Henri Castro brought in French, Alsatians, and Swiss. Peters induced a few Englishmen and the ill-fated French Icarian group to settle in his colony. Texan consuls persuaded individuals from various other parts of Europe to migrate. The blending of all of these elements into a fairly homogeneous society continued. The Germans, however, who settled around New Braunfels and later in Fredericksburg, maintained an isolated ethnic identity for nearly a hundred years. On the other hand, many of the German immigrants who settled in the coastal plains, in Houston, and in the counties of Austin and Washington became a part of and contributed to the increasing cosmopolitanism of Texas.

The census of 1850 revealed that Texans were indeed a varied people. There were 58,000 Negroes and 154,000 persons classified as "white." The white population was almost thirty per cent native Texans and included, of course, the mestizos of early Hispanic origin, as well as the mixture of European nationalities represented in Texas. Approximately sixty per cent had been born in the United States, and a little over ten per cent had come from foreign countries. The nativities of these "foreigners" were remarkably widespread; almost every European nation, from Portugal to Russia and from Italy to Norway, had sent migrants to Texas. The greatest number had come from the German principalities; the British Isles were second, with most of this group from Ireland; France ranked next, and then the Scandinavian countries, with Norway leading. At that time Texas ranked fourth among the states in the number of passengers arriving from abroad—a significant figure if the relative size of the Atlantic ports such as New York and Boston is considered. Foreign migration and assimilation continued. In 1860 there were 43,422 foreign-born persons in Texas, again just over ten per cent of the "white" population of 421,649. And the list of nations from which these people had come had lengthened; there were even two immigrants from Sardinia and three from Turkey.

The significance of these figures is that by the time of the Civil War, the Texas population was by no means typical either of the other southern states or of the other frontier states. Over 40,000 persons were foreign-born, and a conservative estimate is that there were two or three times that number of first-generation Americans. Furthermore, the early population of Texas, before the coming of the Anglo-Americans, was a varied mixture. Texas, although not urban, was one of the most cosmopolitan areas in the world. One can only speculate on the result in the development of social and religious tolerance, in the availability of varied cooking and exotic dishes, in the general acceptance of foreign tongues and heavy accents, and in the countless social effects of a mixing of diverse cultures. And this was only the beginning, for in the century that followed, the influx of foreign immigrants continued, molding the Texan not in the image of Uncle Sam but in a distinctive character of his own. It should be remembered, however, that most Texans were white, Anglo-American, and Protestant. This majority was influenced by the cosmopolitan nature of the minority, but it remained the primary force in the state.

As the population increased from 1845 to 1860, so did the size and number of towns. Galveston was the largest in 1850 with 4,177 people; San Antonio was first in 1860 with 8,235. In 1850 only 7,665 persons lived in towns as enumerated on the census, but by 1860 this figure had jumped to 26,615. The number of incorporated towns more than doubled during the same decade. In addition, there were probably three or four times that many communities that were usually referred to as towns. None, not even the largest, could have been considered a city. Yet every major occupation was represented from brick mason to lawyer, with some minor ones: one man in Dallas gave his occupation as "floating trader"; the enumerator in another county listed one man as the county's "S.O.B." And of course some occupations of 1850 and 1860 have virtually passed out of existence, for example, that of wheelwright and blacksmith. Among the professions, physicians were most numerous; lawyers, second. Clearly, most Texans at this time lived in the country and farmed for a livelihood. The census of 1850 classified 96.4 per cent of the population as rural, and that of 1860 classified 95.6 per cent rural.

Social and Cultural Aspects Despite the rural and essentially frontier nature of society in Texas, there were considerable cultural developments prior to the outbreak of the Civil War. Perhaps literary endeavor has proved the most enduring. Texans during this period wrote histories, travel accounts, descriptions of Texas, and journals of personal adventure. Henderson Yoakum's documented *History of Texas*, published in two volumes in 1854, is useful reading even today, as is Thomas Jefferson Green's *Journal of the Mier Expedition*, issued in 1845. Less readable but of historical value are the many descriptions of Texas such as Mary Austin Holly's *Texas* (1831) and Melinda Rankin's *Texas in 1850* (1851). There were also descriptions of travelers through Texas, the most important of which were Frederick Law Olmsted's account of Texas in the 1850's, Ferdinand Roemer's work first published in German in 1849, and George Wilkins Kendall's and Thomas Falconer's separate accounts of the Texan Santa Fe expedition. Mirabeau B. Lamar, who published a number of creditable poems, planned but did not finish a comprehensive history of Texas.

There were several good newspapers published in Texas during that time. The best known was the *Telegraph and Texas Register*, which changed hands several times. Its most articulate editor was Francis W. Moore. Charles DeMorse established the *Northern Standard* in Clarksville in 1842 and continued as its editor and publisher until his death in 1887. The files of this paper are among the most valuable contemporary documents. The Galveston *News*, established in 1842 and piloted by Willard Richardson from 1843 until the Civil War, was another influential early paper. More important, possibly, than the newspaper was its offspring, the *Texas Almanac*, first published in 1857 under the editorship of David Richardson (who was not related to Willard Richardson). Another long-lived and significant newspaper was the New Braunfels *Zeitung*, established in 1852 by Ferdinand J. Lindheimer. The number and variety of the early Texas newspapers—in 1860 there were over 70, with a total circulation of nearly 100,000—bears witness to the literacy of the prewar Texans.

Certain newspaper advertisements indicate an interest in cultural entertainment. Many touring theatrical, including Shakespearean, companies played in the chief cities and towns. Scores of literary and musical societies were organized all over the state. Operas were staged from time to time—of what merit can only be speculated on—and innumerable recitals were given. Such cultural activities were not, however, the main form of entertainment. Modern puritans would be appalled at the range in early Texas of such "sinful" amusements as gambling, drinking, and horse racing. Barbecues, balls, and any occasion for heated oratory—the Texans loved to talk—always drew large crowds. And the Texans were a rowdy lot, given to brawling, dueling, and "shooting affrays," but none of these activities was altogether atypical of the American frontier anywhere.

Also quite definitely of frontier mold was the principal form of architecture: the double log cabin. Probably over half the Texas population lived in log houses, most of which consisted of two square rooms ten to twelve feet apart but connected by a common roof. The open breezeway between the cabins was called a "dog run." By modern standards these cabins could hardly be considered fit habitations. Each cabin usually was a mere twelve to sixteen feet square and had dirt floors. Most were windowless, but cracks between the logs where chinking and calking had fallen out admitted more than ample ventilation. In areas where stone was not available they were heated by stick and mud fireplaces and chimneys. Rarely were they furnished with more than one bed per family; the children slept on pallets in the loft under the eaves. Cooking was sometimes done in the fireplace but more often in a separate cook shack or in a lean-to annex to the cabin.

Most settlers began their home with a single cabin, later adding a dog run and second cabin, then a lean-to in back and a "gallery" in front. It was not uncommon for the basic log structure to be boarded later with milled lumber. Prosperous families tended to move into new frame and sometimes brick houses. Wealthier Texans succumbed to the Greek and Georgian styles popular in the old South, and a few houses were quite pretentious. Among the finest was the governor's mansion in Austin, finished in time for occupancy by Elisha M. Pease. Even finer perhaps was the house Pease bought later from James Shaw, originally named Woodlawn after Shaw's estate in Ireland, built in 1854 and considered by many to be the most striking example of antebellum architecture in Texas. In the 1930's the Historic American Buildings Survey included nearly fifty old Texas homes in its measured drawings series.

More interesting to architects than the white-pillared mansions are the surviving German stone buildings in such towns as Fredericksburg and some of the French houses in Castroville. Few public buildings in Texas at this time had anything to recommend them. The capitol buildng, for example, erected in Austin in 1856 and now used as a museum, was designed by a German architect after a Rhine castle.

The ruins of Baylor University at Independence are interesting, not so much for their architecture as for evidence of Texans' devotion to education. As early as 1832, in the resolutions of the convention of that year, Texans had begun talking about the need for education. This awareness was repeated in 1833 and again in the Declaration of Independence. In 1839 congress made land donations to each county to support public schools, and in 1854 the Pease administration established the permanent school fund. Meantime several dozen institutes, academies, and colleges were chartered, although few survived very long. The first of these was Rutersville College, established in 1841 near LaGrange, followed shortly by McKenzie College in Clarksville the same year and by San Augustine University in 1842. Several survived: "Old Baylor," founded in 1845 and now located in Waco; Austin College, a Presbyterian school established in 1849 and now located in Sherman; the Ursuline Academies at Galveston (1847) and San Antonio (1851); and St. Mary's University (1852), also in San Antonio. In 1858 the legislature created the University of Texas, but no action was taken for another thirty years. Despite this dereliction, Texas was far ahead of most states in the support of public education, the school laws of 1839 and 1854 being among the most generous of their time.

However generous pioneer Texas was toward education, it was parsimonious toward religion. Churches had a difficult time making ends meet, and preachers were commonly paid in produce. The frontier expression "pound the preacher" meant to give him a pound of some farm product. Early Texans appeared to take little interest in organized religion, and as late as 1840 there were no churches at all in Houston or Galveston. In 1850 there were only a few, church services customarily being held in town halls, school houses, courthouses, and even saloons and blacksmith shops by a largely itinerant ministry. By 1860 most of the standard denominations were represented in Texas, from Methodism (the largest) to Congregationalism (the smallest). Fundamentalist and evangelical sects were growing rapidly, however, and in a few decades were to claim the most adherents.

In those days there were nearly as many physicians as preachers, and they were of nearly as wide a variety of persuasions. The medical profession was by no means standardized: its practitioners included herbalists, climatologists, bleeders, purgers, massagers, and so on. There were neither laws nor professional regulations governing the practice of medicine, and any man who wanted to could call himself "doctor" and give treatment.

Many of these were purely and simply quacks who eked out a living selling an assortment of concoctions for which every cure imaginable was claimed. When the foundation of modern medical science was laid during the mid-nineteenth century, however, Texas had its share of skilled physicians. Foremost of these was Yale-educated Ashbel Smith, who constantly pressed for regulatory statutes and who founded the Texas Medical Association in 1853. The lack of regulations at first naturally created a plethora of home cures and patent medicines. Purgatives were invariably given for any illness; sulphur and molasses were used for spring tonics; whiskey was the usual anaesthetic, although chloroform was introduced in San Antonio in 1854; and turpentine was a common disinfectant. Yet despite such remedies—sometimes called "heroic medicine," for obvious reasons—Texans as a whole were healthier than people elsewhere, and it has recently been demonstrated that a principal motivation for settlement was the belief that Texas offered not only a healthy but also a curative climate.

The Economy

Transportation   With the increase in migration after the Mexican War, Texas began to prosper, but the size of the state and the lack of adequate transportation facilities made economic development slow. For example, from Jefferson, then a thriving town on Caddo Lake linked by steamboat to the all-important Mississippi River, it was a tortuous three hundred miles to the seat of government in Austin. Even as late as 1860 travelers usually made the trip by horseback rather than in a buggy because of the poor condition of the roads and the lack of bridges across creeks and streams. There was no single or direct stage line available for the journey; to go by stage, a traveler had to take two to a dozen different lines through various major towns, increasing the distance traveled as well as the time spent.

Commercial transportation would probably have improved had there been a central agency responsible for roads and highways. But instead each county was responsible for developing and maintaining its own roads. Consequently there was much unevenness in roads from one county to another —to the ridiculous extent that in some cases roads stopped at county lines and were not continued by the adjacent county. The principal roads linked the county seats and the larger towns, but even the best of these roads were rutted washboards in dry weather and boggy mires when it rained. Only a few bridges existed in Texas. Major rivers were crossed by ferry;

streams were forded. There were no road maps, and only a few counties bothered to put up signs. A stranger making a trip of any distance could expect to become lost at least once and to receive incorrect or confusing directions several times.

There were numerous small stage lines in operation between major points, but there were few of any length. The great Butterfield Overland Mail Company crossed the western part of the state on a road built and maintained by the company. This line entered Texas by Colbert's Ferry across the Red River in Grayson County, ran southwest to Tom Green County, where it turned west along the Middle Concho to the Horsehead Crossing of the Pecos, and then ran on to El Paso by way of Guadalupe Pass in the shadow of El Capitan. Service through Texas began in 1857. At that time another transcontinental line, derisively known as the "jackass mail" because of the donkeys used for crossing the mountains, began operating from San Antonio to San Diego along the southern route across the Edwards Plateau. Both lines ceased to function regularly during the Civil War, and afterward they were broken up into smaller companies.

Stages carried passengers and mail but little freight. Freight was hauled by much slower mule- or ox-drawn wagons. Freighting was an important business, and some freighters regularly contracted for long distances inland from the coast. One of the most prominent of these contractors was George Thomas Howard of Texas Ranger fame. Howard's reliable wagons and teams rolled from Indianola to San Antonio and, on special contracts, to points west and north. It was one of his teamsters who precipitated the incident in 1857 known as the Cart War. This man, actually a subcontractor for Howard, hired only Mexican drivers, who worked for lower wages than Americans. The resultant resentment broke out in a rash of attacks and even murders. There were reputed to have been seventy Mexican drivers killed—probably an exaggerated figure. Governor Pease sent a special company of Rangers to protect the vital freight wagons from continued pillage and the drivers from harassment. Howard replaced the subcontractor and employed Texan teamsters. By the end of the year the Cart War was over and commerce was moving smoothly again.

Although some of the inland traffic from the coast was carried on river boats, Texas never developed an important river trade. Most Texas rivers, even the large ones, were too shallow in many places to permit a regular steamboat operation. Furthermore, many were blocked by extensive jams of logs and debris called "rafts." Such a raft, some ten or fifteen miles in length, choked the mouth of the Colorado River. There remained several on the Red River even after Henry Shreve blasted the largest one open to permit his boats upriver from Shreveport, Louisiana. The mouth of the Brazos was nearly blocked by a large sand bar, and similar deposits made navigation of the Trinity treacherous.

Despite such difficulties, however, there were a few steamboats on some of the Texas rivers. Several small boats were operated on the Brazos between Velasco and San Felipe after 1840, and at least one was of sufficiently shallow draft that it could cross the bar. In the spring of 1845 a boat, constructed especially for the Colorado River trade, made a successful trip from above the raft as far upriver as Austin. Thereafter there was some navigation on the Colorado, but seldom was the river high enough for Austin to be reached by large boats. The Trinity was navigable in high water as far as the little town of Cincinnati in Madison County, but the river was frequently too low, and many boats foundered in mud banks. The Rio Grande was navigable, also only during times of high water, as far as Starr County, and Richard King, founder of the King Ranch, operated a steamboat there before the Civil War.

All in all, river navigation was a significant factor in the antebellum economy of Texas, but it was almost as difficult and trying as overland traffic. Boats were often grounded in the shallows, where they had to be unloaded while crews and passengers tugged on ropes from the shores to put them afloat again. Some remained aground until the spring floods, and others became hopelessly mired and were left to rot. Barges and flat-keeled craft were occasionally used to float cotton downriver, but because of the difficulty of returning them upstream, this did not become a common method of transportation.

Texas desperately needed, therefore, in addition to adequate highways, a system of rail transportation. Because of the expense of construction, some form of public aid was necessary. In 1850 San Antonio and Bexar County issued $100,000 in bonds to aid the San Antonio and Mexican Gulf Railway Company, a locally organized group. Construction was not begun until 1858, however, and by 1861 only twenty-one miles of track had been laid from Port Lavaca to Victoria. Meantime a Massachusetts firm, encouraged by Houston and Galveston businessmen who subscribed to its stock, began construction in 1852 of the Buffalo Bayou, Brazos, and Colorado Railroad. The following year, when operation began on twenty miles of track from Harrisburg to Stafford's Point, it became Texas' first functioning railway. The road reached Alleyton in Brazoria County in 1861 and ran irregularly during the war.

The state government began offering aid for railroad construction in 1852, and a general law in 1854 provided land grants of sixteen sections for each mile of track constructed. This brought about the chartering of a large number of companies, but only ten actually built any trackage before the war. Houston became the center for most of these early railroad lines, being connected before the war to Galveston, to Orange, to Millican, and to Columbia. By 1861 a total of 492 miles of track had been laid. It was a beginning, but it was hopelessly inadequate for the state's needs. The era of railroading was then delayed for over a decade, and the people of Texas continued to struggle with unsatisfactory transportation facilities.

An unusual experiment in transportation was tried in 1856 in West Texas. Jefferson Davis, then United States Secretary of War, imported thirty-four camels, with drivers, from the Near East to Camp Verde outside of San Antonio. The army conducted a number of experiments with them in arid and semiarid West Texas, even making one trek into the Trans-Pecos. The camels could carry more than mules or horses, could go much farther without water, and could move faster on the trail, allowing greater distances between camps. But they could not be shod, and their soft feet, suitable for sand, were bruised and cut by the rocky Texas terrain. The camels were sold to individuals, and most of them were used by freighting contractors for a few years in Arizona and Nevada. Even had the camel experiment been successful, however, it would have provided no solution to the growing transportation problem.

The Basic Economy   Without an effective transportation system, commerce and industry in Texas lagged behind many of the other states. The principal business was retailing, carried on in "general mercantile" stores, which handled everything from toothpicks to church pews. There was a general store in every community, and the large towns had dozens of them. The modern department store had not yet begun to develop, but today's large discount stores are almost a reversion to the old general store. The larger antebellum towns supported specialized retail stores such as book stores, dress shops, shoe stores, millinery shops, clothing stores, lumber yards, hardware stores, and music stores. Although the general stores usually handled grocery staples, most towns had grocery stores, which were the principal dealers in whiskeys and wines. Needless to say, saloons were common in early Texas.

There was a wide variety of other business establishments. Some not common today were blacksmith shops, wagon yards, stables, buggy shops, saddleries, and harness shops. Such places not only made repairs but also built and sold wagons, wheels, buggies, saddles, and harnesses. The manufacturing industries were not significant in the economy of the time. Among those leading a somewhat precarious existence were liquor distilleries, furniture manufacturers, tin and sheet iron producers, cement makers, iron works (makers of boilers, kettles, and small steam engines), and weaving and spinning mills. More important were processing industries such as cotton gins, grist and flour mills, sawmills, and sugar cane processors.

Antebellum Texas had, quite obviously, an agrarian economy in which many small farmers achieved a measure of self-sufficiency. The average farmer raised pigs, chickens, milk cows, and beef cattle. He also had a vegetable garden and a few fruit trees. He usually did his own harness and blacksmith work, built his own house and outbuildings, and made by hand most of his equipment such as furniture, plows, hoes, and ax handles. Many wives had spinning wheels for making thread from cotton and wool fibers, and many wove these into a cloth called "homespun."

Just less than half of the adult males in Texas, according to both the 1850 and 1860 censuses, were farmers. In 1860 there were 51,569 farmers, 2,576 stockmen, and 265 planters among the 105,491 persons listed with occupations. The farms varied in size from small one-man operations to extensive plantations of hundreds of acres. The principal crop, as in the colonial era, was corn; the "money" crops were cotton and sugar cane. That cotton production in Texas increased ten-fold in the decade 1850 to 1860, whereas the number of farmers only doubled, evidences the rapidly increasing importance of cotton to the economy.

Although not of great economic significance at the time, cattle also increased during the same decade by nearly ten times—to about four million head—despite the profligate slaughter that supported the hide and tallow factories on the coast. Hundreds of thousands of head of wild cattle in the South Texas region were driven to slaughtering pens at Aransas Pass, Copano, Indianola, and other ports. The hides were sold to leather finders, and the carcasses were boiled in enormous vats until they were reduced to tallow for lamps and candles. The hide and tallow factories were not the only market for cattle. Before the Civil War stockmen had begun to ship live beef to New Orleans and Havana, and a few had trailed herds overland to market, although this did not prove profitable until after the war.

Slavery and the Plantation System   Negro slavery had existed in Texas from the time of the first Europeans. Negro slaves formed a small part of the laboring class during the Spanish era, when colonial law made little distinction between slaves and servants. Anglo-American colonists from states of the American South brought slaves with them, and a few of the early migrants entered into the slave trade. Because the importation of slaves into the United States was prohibited, there was a small traffic in smuggling slaves into the United States from the West Indies by way of Texas. After the middle 1820's, however, the flow of slaves was definitely from the United States to Texas. Although Mexican laws prohibited slavery, the colonists continued the institution by various dodges, particularly the lifetime labor contract. Under the Republic and later the State Constitution of 1845, slavery was permitted.

The number of slaves in Texas increased from an estimated 5,000 in 1836 to 182,566 in 1860, nearly a third of the total population. Surprisingly, despite the large number of slaves, slaveholding was not widespread among the white population. There were only 21,878 slaveholders in 1860, about 5 per cent of the white population of 430,891. Nearly 60 per cent of these slaveholders—that is, 12,781—owned fewer than six Negroes. Another 20 per cent owned from six to nine, and 15 per cent owned from ten to twenty. The remaining 10 per cent of the slaveholders owned nearly half of the slaves. To be exact: the 16,292 persons each with holdings from one to nine owned a total of 56,520 slaves; 3,423 persons with holdings between ten and nineteen owned 52,214 slaves; and 2,163 persons with holdings from twenty to three hundred owned 73,832 slaves (the latter two totals have been adjusted from data in the census of 1860).

These statistics have several significant implications. First, there were very few actual plantations in Texas and very few large slaveholders. Second, the majority of the slaveholders owned from one to five slaves, most of whom were employed as domestics and semiskilled artisans rather than as farm labor. Third, most Negro slaves in Texas lived in the larger slaveholdings and were used to operate farms and plantations. And fourth, since the slaveholders represented only 5 per cent of the white population, they must have exercised an influence far out of proportion to their numbers.

Only 265 men called themselves planters in 1860; each owned an average of sixty slaves. Their operations, consequently, were on the large scale of today's romantic concept of the antebellum southern plantation. The owner lived in a large, comfortable house, well staffed with domestic slaves. He usually operated several farms with Negro quarters on each place. The field hands were divided into crews supervised by an overseer. The planter also trained some slaves in specialized work. He would need leather workers, blacksmiths, masons, carpenters, butchers, cooks, seamstresses, and the like, and he might have a small brick kiln on his home place. The typical planter built a small school building for the education of his and the neighboring children. In addition to the "quarters," a half-dozen or more other outbuildings were needed as stables, harness rooms, storage sheds, barns, and cook houses.

The consensus among historians of the Old South is that anyone who owned over twenty slaves could be classed as a planter. In 1860 there were, as has been noted, 2,163 Texans in this class (including the 265 who actually called themselves planters). Over half of this group—that is, 1,095—owned between twenty and thirty slaves. Their operations were not on a grandiose scale. In *Journey Through Texas* (1856) Frederick Law Olmsted, the New Yorker who visited Texas in 1854 and 1855, described a plantation on the Red River, which was probably typical of this size:

> The house was a small square log cabin, with a broad open shed or piazza in front, and a chimney, made of sticks and mud, leaning against one end. A smaller detached cabin, twenty feet in the rear, was used for a kitchen. A cistern under a roof, and collecting water from three roofs, stood between. The water from the bayou was not fit to drink, nor is the water of the Red River, or of any springs in this region. The people depend entirely on cisterns for drinking water. It's very little white folks need, however—milk, claret, and whisky being the more common beverages.
>
> About the house was a large yard, in which were two or three China trees, and two splendid evergreen Cherokee roses; half a dozen hounds; several negro babies; turkeys and chickens, and a pet sow, teaching a fine litter of pigs how to root and wallow. Three hundred yards from the house was a gin-house and stable, and in the interval between were two rows of comfortable negro cabins. Between the house and the cabins was a large post, on which was a bell to call the negroes. A rack for fastening horses stood near it. On the bell-post and on each of the rack-posts were nailed the antlers of a buck, as well as on a large oak-tree near by. On the logs of the kitchen a fresh deer-skin was drying. On the railing of the piazza lay a Mexican saddle with immense wooden stirrups. The house had but one door and no window, nor was there a pane of glass on the plantation.
>
> Entering the house, we found it to contain but a single room, about twenty feet by sixteen. Of this space one quarter was occupied by a bed —a great four-poster, with the curtains open, made up in the French style, with a strong furniture-calico day-coverlid. A smaller camp bed stood beside it. These two articles of furniture nearly filled the house on one side the door. At the other end was a great log fire-place, with a fine fire. The outer door was left constantly open to admit the light. On one side the fire, next the door, was a table; a kind of dresser, with crockery, and a bureau stood on the other side, and there were two deer-skin seated chairs and one (Connecticut made) rocking chair.
>
> Three of the hounds, a negro child, and a white child, had followed us to the door of the cabin, three chickens had entered before us, a cat and kittens were asleep in the corner of the fireplace. . . .

One can imagine the lack of opulence in the farmsteads of the slaveholders who owned fewer than twenty slaves, the majority of the slaveholders in the state. Here the owners normally worked side by side with their slaves, plowing, chopping, and picking. It would not be unrealistic to think of the Negroes in such small farmsteads as co-workers and members of the family rather than as exploited laborers. They usually fared as well as, and sometimes better than, the owner's own family. Instances of mistreatment of slaves were rare. The average cost of slaves in 1850 was nearly $400, with good field hands bringing $500 to $600, and by 1860 the average cost had risen to nearly $700, with field hands often selling for over $1,000. Although discipline was occasionally required, no owner in his right mind would punish his slave severely enough to harm him or to cause him to run away. Instead, slaveholders were often more solicitous of their Negroes' health and well-being than they were of their own. To get a productive day's work, many forms of inducement were used such as time off, new clothes, a small share in the crop, and even cash bonuses. No defense of the degrading institution is intended here; nevertheless, it was to be many years after emancipation before the average Negro freedman was as well fed, clothed, sheltered, or cared for as the average slave.

The disproportionate influence of the planter class is understandable in terms of human nature and ambition. The principal, almost the only, crops that could be sold for cash revenue required extensive field labor for production. The average field hand in a good year on good land could produce about fifteen bales of cotton. In the period before mechanized and scientific agriculture, the ratio between the number of field hands and the size of a man's income was direct. Almost every nonslaveholding farmer, toiling alone in his fields, dreamed of making enough one year to buy some help. Farmers who worked four slaves wanted ten, and those with ten yearned for twenty, and so on. As all men desire success in their own fields, the majority of men who wrested a livelihood from the soil aspired to fortune in the only way then available—by the acquisition of Negro slaves. Therefore most nonplanters and even nonslaveholders identified with the numerically small planter class, made its needs and demands theirs, and even stood ready to fight for the protection of the institution of slavery.

The causes of the Civil War, however, were by no means this simple. Although in the final analysis slavery was the emotional issue that divided the nation, the underlying cause was the multifaceted conflict over the political rights of the state governments under the federal constitution, including the issue of the right to slavery. The people of Texas were not certain of where they stood in this conflict; Texas' secession with the Confederacy was not clearly predicated by the Texas past. Nonetheless, secession, war, and reconstruction were the state's immediate destiny.

8

Secession and Civil War

Secession

The Constitutional Issue Almost immediately after the formation of the union under the constitution framed in Philadelphia in 1787, there arose the question of the rights of the theoretically sovereign states within that union. The most basic issue, although few recognized it then (or recognize it now), was where resided the right to find an action of the federal government unconstitutional. During the convention itself the point was little discussed, though Alexander Hamilton suggested that as federal courts should test the constitutionality of state laws, a special court consisting of justices from each state should rule on the acts of the federal government. During the fight for ratification, proponents of the new system of government, including the authors of the famed *Federalist Papers*, remained vague on the subject. In 1798 Thomas Jefferson and James Madison, in protesting the Alien and Sedition acts, drafted for the legislatures of Kentucky and Virginia respectively resolutions that outlined the right, as well as the obligation, of state governments to protect the people when the federal government usurped unconstitutional authority. During the War of 1812, New England delegates to the Hartford Convention discussed but did not pass resolutions calling for the secession of the New England states in protest against the allegedly unconstitutional actions of the federal government.

In these instances, as in later ones, the issue of constitutionality arose because of locally or regionally unpopular measures of the federal government. A few years after the Treaty of Ghent, northern and southern states began to reverse their attitudes on the right to find a federal act unconstitutional. The Tariff of 1824 precipitated John C. Calhoun's famous protest outlining the theory of nullification. To Calhoun, who was a brilliant constitutional theorist, it seemed perfectly clear that the separate states needed a remedy against the supposed violations of the constitution by the federal government. This was theoretically found in the rather complex procedure by which a state could nullify a federal act. In 1828 a nullification was attempted, but Andrew Jackson proved, by force and threats of force, that the nullification procedure was, if not illegal, at least impractical.

Then came the series of crises over the existence of slavery in the south. At first southern leaders sought to curb the activities of the anti-slavery forces in the national congress. Here was hammered out the Missouri Compromise in 1820, which was expected to settle the conflict for all time. But in 1849 California's petition for admission as a free state reawakened interest in the right of the federal congress to legislate on slavery. Fearing a defeat by the abolitionists, southern leaders began to push Calhoun's nullification theories to their logical conclusion—secession. A secession convention was called to meet in Nashville in the summer of 1850, to which it was proposed that all slave states send representatives. This crisis was averted by the Compromise of 1850, which let in California as a free state, compensated Texas for its loss of territory to New Mexico, and pacified the rest of the south with a stringent fugitive slave law.

California's self-determination of its slavery policy rather than the federal government's fiat, as in the Louisiana Purchase under the Missouri Compromise (or the Northwest Ordinance of 1787), led ambitious northern Democrats such as Stephen A. Douglas of Illinois to propose "popular sovereignty" for Kansas and Nebraska. The Kansas-Nebraska Act of 1854, besides bringing bloody turmoil to Kansas, caused thoughtful southerners to begin to defend slavery as an institution protected by the federal constitution and therefore exempt from action by either states or federal administrations.

This development appeared in Justice Taney's decision in the Dred

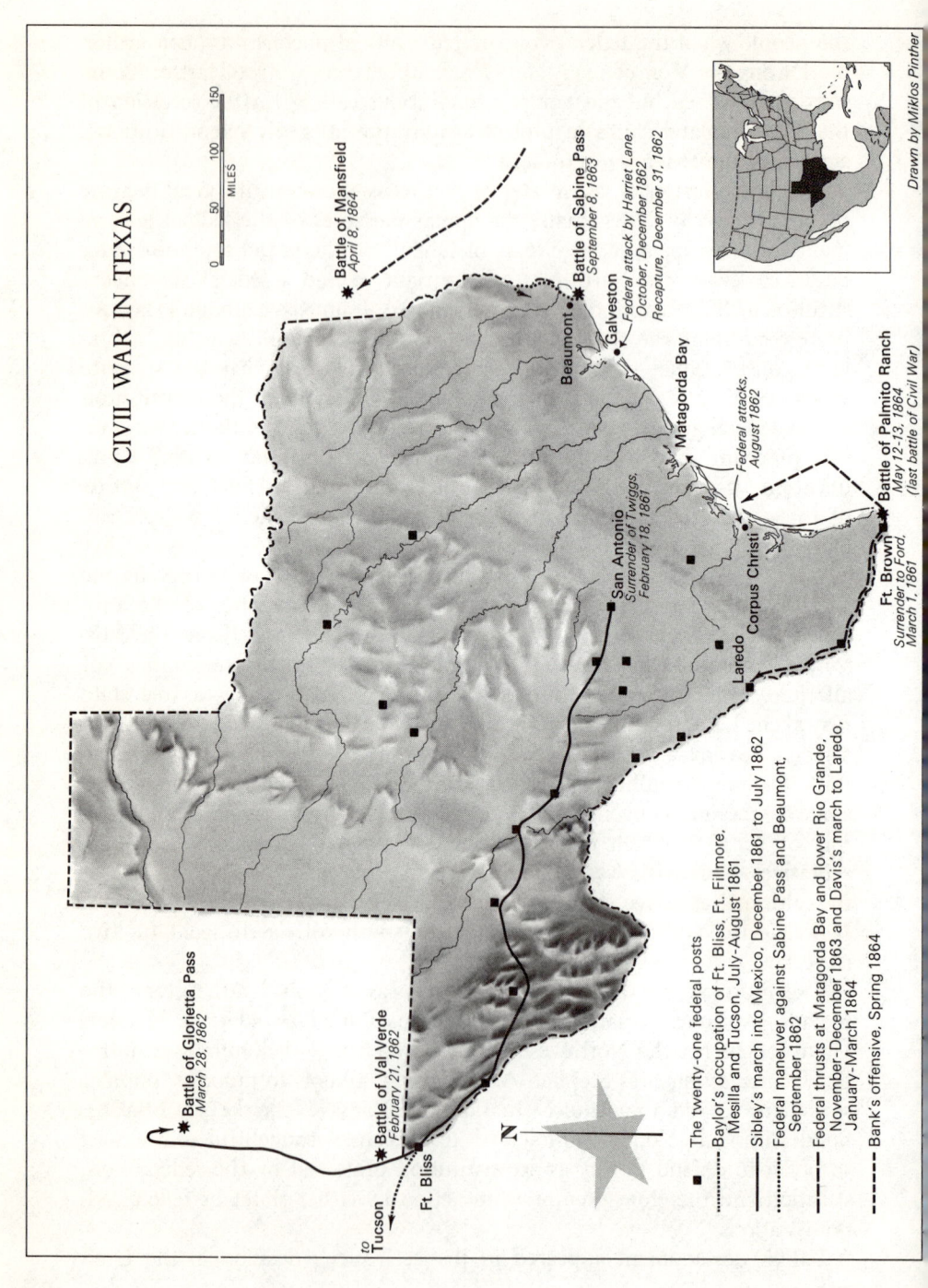

CIVIL WAR IN TEXAS

- Battle of Glorietta Pass, March 28, 1862
- Battle of Val Verde, February 21, 1862
- Ft. Bliss
- to Tucson
- Battle of Mansfield, April 8, 1864
- Battle of Sabine Pass, September 8, 1863
- Beaumont
- Galveston — Federal attack by Harriet Lane, October, December 1862; Recapture, December 31, 1862
- Matagorda Bay — Federal attacks, August 1862
- San Antonio — Surrender of Twiggs, February 18, 1861
- Laredo
- Corpus Christi
- Ft. Brown — Surrender to Ford, March 1, 1861
- Battle of Palmito Ranch, May 12–13, 1864 (last battle of Civil War)

Legend:
- ■ The twenty-one federal posts
- ········ Baylor's occupation of Ft. Bliss, Ft. Fillmore, Mesilla and Tucson, July–August 1861
- ——— Sibley's march into Mexico, December 1861 to July 1862
- ·········· Federal maneuver against Sabine Pass and Beaumont, September 1862
- — — — Federal thrusts at Matagorda Bay and lower Rio Grande, November–December 1863 and Davis's march to Laredo, January–March 1864
- ----- Bank's offensive, Spring 1864

Drawn by Miklos Pinther

188

Scott case, which in essence ruled that congress could not abridge a slaveholder's right to his property under the constitution. Thus the grounds were fully laid for secession as a constitutional remedy if the northern-dominated congress should pass a statute inimical to slavery. When secession came in 1861, however, it came as a reaction to the election of a minority president and the mounting fear of what he would do.

Secession Sentiment in Texas Politics Texas' attitude toward the rising tide of secession sentiment was ambivalent. Contrary to many assertions then and later, Texas' destiny was not irrevocably linked to the old South, and Texans were not characteristic southerners. True, the majority of Texans had been born in southern states, but many had migrated from Missouri and nonslave states north of the Ohio River. Recent historical investigations have revealed a considerable migration of nonslaveholding southerners northward to Ohio, Indiana, and Illinois during the decades before the Civil War. In the Peters Colony ninety per cent of the population had come from this area, although many of the colonists had been born in southern states. Furthermore, these settlers in the Peters Colony were almost all nonslaveholders, and many were opposed to slavery, as were both the foreign-born whites in Texas, who constituted about fifteen per cent of the state's population, and the scattered population from northern states. It must also be remembered that less than five per cent of the white population was slaveholding.

Nonetheless, southern ideas predominated, although not overwhelmingly. In 1849 and 1850 secession talk raged, but over the New Mexico boundary conflict, not slavery. The first three governors—Henderson, Wood, and Bell—were southerners and slaveholders, but the most significant executive of the antebellum era and the only one to be reelected was Elisha M. Pease, a native of Connecticut. Although the election of Pease in 1853 and 1855 did not necessarily mean that Texans were opposed to secession, it did mean that secession was not a major issue in Texas politics. It became so in the elections of 1857 and 1859, however, largely because Sam Houston decided to make it an issue. Houston was a southerner and a slaveholder but a staunch anti-secessionist. Representing Texas in the United States Senate, he had consistently spoken and voted against measures designed to upset the union, notably the Kansas-Nebraska bill. In the increasing tempo of secession activities, he was determined to keep Texas in the union. In the next few years he fought for his union convictions with all the political skills and cunning at his command, only to lose and die two years after secession, a broken man.

In the summer of 1856, the Democratic Party, which the year before had been organized and mobilized by the threat of Know-Nothingism, held a spirited state convention. Among other things, the convention denounced Houston's vote against the Kansas-Nebraska bill. The party machinery was in the hands of secessionist leaders. The next year the convention met in May and nominated for governor Hardin R. Runnels, an avowed secessionist and a Trinity River planter born in Mississippi. Francis R. Lubbock, an apostate supporter of Houston's who now stood firmly for secession, was chosen to run for lieutenant governor.

Within two weeks, Houston announced his candidacy for governor as an independent, running on his record and a union platform. His campaign was a personal one as he traveled about the state speaking to informal groups. The opposition, which controlled most of the newspapers, hounded him wherever he went and vilified him in print as a freesoiler, a traitor to Texas, and worse. Runnels won the election with 32,552 votes to Houston's 28,678. It was a small margin of victory due more to party organization than to a defeat of union sentiment.

Houston, who lost his seat in the senate as a result of the defeat, prepared for the next election. During 1858, while still a lame-duck member of the senate, he made a number of unionist speeches in Texas. His position was abundantly clear, and many unionists in Texas wrote to him expressing the hope that he would run again in 1859. In May that year the Democratic State Convention again took a "secesh" position and renominated Runnels and Lubbock, but an element of dissension was present. Houston announced as an independent, and the campaign issue was union versus secession. This time Houston won: 33,375 votes to 27,500.

It is difficult to arrive at a definitive analysis of these two elections beyond the surface interpretation that a slight majority of voters favored secession in 1857 and opposed it in 1859. However, Runnels' 1857 victory was partially due to the continued organization of the party after the Know-Nothing threat, and his 1859 defeat was due both to the disintegration of that machinery and his ineptness in handling frontier problems. Nonetheless, on the eve of secession Texas had taken a stand in favor of staying in the union.

The Mounting Tempo of Secessionism   In Sam Houston the union had a virile champion, but events conspired to strengthen the hands of the rabid secessionists. Increasing abolitionist radicalism throughout the nation caused a reactionary swing in Texas' public opinion. John Brown's fanatic raid on Harpers Ferry in October 1859 provoked fiery editorial denouncements in Texas papers. When Governor Houston's legislature assembled, instead of being led to a moderate posture, it promptly elected Louis T. Wigfall, an outspoken secessionist and an enemy of Houston, to the seat in the United States Senate made vacant first by Rusk's suicide and then by J. Pinckney Henderson's death. A few months later, the State Democratic Convention, once again under the control of the radicals, adopted an unrestrained secessionist platform.

More important was the bitterness and radicalism of the campaigns in the national election of 1860. The Democratic Party split at the national convention in April. The northern Democrats reassembled at Baltimore and nominated Stephen A. Douglas, the Illinois senator. The southern bolters met at Richmond and nominated John C. Breckinridge. Two new parties each entered the lists also with candidates: The Republican Party, representing abolition sentiment in the north, nominated Abraham Lincoln; and the Constitutional Union Party, hastily formed to save the union from division over the slavery issue, nominated John Bell, a unionist from Tennessee.

Houston had been seriously considered by the delegates to the Constitutional Union convention in Baltimore, and there can be little doubt that he desired the presidency. Several times he had seemed close to gaining it; now, when a compromise candidate, a unionist southern slaveholder, had a good chance of winning, he was especially eager to run. Nor can there be much doubt that Houston was convinced of his ability to save the nation from division. Disappointed by his failure to receive the nomination from the Constitutional Unionists, although he had run Bell a close second on several ballots, he let his name go before the people as an independent, and then withdrew it in August just before the election.

The summer of 1860 was a time of a high political excitement and variety of presidential candidates: Lincoln, who stood for immediate emancipation (and if he did not, did nothing to dispel the illusion); Breckinridge, who stood for secession if slavery or the Dred Scott decision was threatened; Douglas, who stood for popular sovereignty but against slavery; and Bell, who stood with equal ambiguity for slavery but against secession. Caught between radical dichotomy and ambiguous dilemma, Texan voters did not turn out in as large numbers as had been expected. At the polls in November, they gave Breckinridge 47,548 votes; Bell, 15,465; Douglas, 410; and Lincoln, none. Slightly more Texans voted than had in the state election of 1859, but only about half of the qualified electorate.

The overwhelming support given Breckinridge and the southern Democrats represented a clear shift, however, in Texas opinion toward secession. Two factors causing this have already been mentioned: (1) the increasing radicalism of the abolitionists, including the general belief that Lincoln and the Republicans would promptly pass an emancipation act;

and the control of the party machinery by secessionist leaders in Texas. A third factor is something of a mystery: the activities of a secret order called the Knights of the Golden Circle. Organized in South Carolina a decade earlier by the ubiquitous George Bickley, this society spread through the southern states. Its principal aim was the support and extension of slavery. In Texas it met with great success by advocating an invasion of northern Mexico. The ultimate destiny of slavery, so ran the Bickley line, was a great golden circle of cotton and slaves through Mexico, the Yucatan peninsula, Cuba and the Caribbean islands, back to the South through Florida.

Local chapters, called castles, were organized in many communities in Texas, and when the plan to invade Mexico from Texas gave him more members here than elsewhere, Bickley himself visited Texas. An "army" of filibustering Knights was actually fielded in the summer of 1860, but it was soon disbanded as interest shifted to the election. Despite the secrecy that shrouds from historical view the members and their activities, substantial evidence indicates that the Knights affected the outcome of the election. Perhaps even more than the political leaders, Bickley's followers generated fear and suspicion.

During the campaign an outbreak of violence was blamed on the abolitionists, but it was at least in part the responsibility of the Knights. Fires supposedly started by abolitionists broke out in Pilot Point, Denton, Gainesville, Waxahachie, and Kaufman. Three Negroes were hanged by a Dallas vigilante committee who held them responsible for the quarter of a million dollar conflagration at Dallas. In Fort Worth vigilantes hanged three men who were allegedly abolitionists who had incited the slaves to riot. Rumors of an impending slave insurrection spread rapidly through the state with unfounded tales of poisonings and assassinations of slaveholders.

The activities of the Knights and the radical secessionists did not slacken after the election. Was not Lincoln dedicated to immediate manumission of the slaves? Prompt action concerning secession was the only remedy. And so Texas, swept by the storm of radicalism and fear, soon joined the other southern states in the disastrous attempt to preserve their constitutional rights outside the union.

The Secession Convention Although Abraham Lincoln received less than forty per cent of the popular vote, his election was assured because of the split in the Democratic Party and the appearance of the Constitutional Unionists. Despite the fact that Lincoln was a minority president, neither he nor the jubilant Republican leaders took any action to alleviate the mounting fears of the South. Secession of the slave states began on December 20 with South Carolina; during January 1861, Mississippi, Florida, Alabama, Georgia, and Louisiana severed ties with the union. Efforts to save the union by compromise were made by Senator Crittendon in congress and by John Tyler, who called a special peace conference in Washington, but these moves were blocked by Lincoln and his advisers. Furthermore, Lincoln refused to consult with the lame-duck president, James Buchanan, who was futilely trying to halt the waves of secession. Fire-eaters in the North and the South were determined to test their theories.

In Texas, radical secessionists called mass meetings in towns throughout the state as soon as it was known that Lincoln was elected. Vehement speeches and impassioned editorials were followed by petitions to Governor Houston to call a special session of the legislature or to order an election of delegates to a secession convention. Houston urged patience, for Lincoln and the Republicans had not yet harmed the South, and advised that only after they passed some unconstitutional measure, if they did, would it be time to act. The governor reiterated his belief that remedies could be found within the union. But he was as helpless as Buchanan: the secessionists were moving too rapidly.

Two weeks after the national election, a mass meeting in Brazoria called upon each Texas county to elect on January 8 delegates to a secession convention, without waiting for Houston to order it. Early in December a group of secession leaders met in Austin, affirmed that date, and issued a further call for each county judge to order an election of delegates to the convention, which was to assemble in Austin on January 28, 1861. If the secessionists could not work through Houston, they would go around him.

Unable to prevent this election, Houston tried to negate its results by calling a special session of the legislature to assemble on January 21, a week before the convention. When the legislature convened, he pleaded for calm deliberation in the face of radicalism and asked that the forthcoming secession convention be ignored if not nullified. But the legislators, many of whom had been elected delegates to the convention, were in no mood to compromise. They promptly endorsed the secession convention with the stipulation that its work be submitted to a popular election for ratification.

The election of January 8 was extralegal, but it could not be described as illegal within the framework of a democracy, and it was certainly validated by the stamp of approval given by the legislature. It should be noted, however, that as a result of the procedure under which the convention was held, the Texas unionists tended not to participate. Therefore the secessionists controlled the polls, and it was a foregone conclusion that the delegates would be secessionists. In this sense, then, the convention was not fully representative.

At the opening session on January 28, Judge Oran M. Roberts of the Supreme Court was elected president by acclamation. The following day, a vote of 152 to 6 passed a resolution that Texas should separately secede from the union. Thereafter the convention worked quickly. The ordinance of annexation was repealed, a declaration of causes for secession adopted, a secession ordinance drafted, an interim Committee of Public Safety appointed, and the date for popular ratification set for February 23. When the convention passed the secession ordinance, by a vote of 166 to 8, J. W. Throckmorton, one of the eight, declaimed that he was "unawed by the wild spirit of revolution" around him and added this famous remark after he was hissed by the galleries: "Mr. President, when the rabble hiss, well may patriots tremble."

If the convention's work was approved at the polls, Texas would withdraw from the United States on March 2, the anniversary of its independence, and on that date the convention would reassemble to take all action necessary to implement secession. Anticipating a victory in the popular election, the convention sent seven delegates to Montgomery, Alabama, where the other seceding states were forming the Confederacy.

Although the election of February 23 was conducted in the midst of emotional intemperance, the results were clear. Secession was approved by 46,129 to 14,697, an overwhelming seventy-six per cent. It carried in all but nineteen of the organized counties. Eight of these were Central Texas counties, including Travis County; eight were in North Texas; two were on the southwest frontier; and one, unaccountably, was deep in East Texas, where there was a heavy concentration of slaveholders. The Central Texas vote against secession was influenced partly by the German population, but it is not true that Texas Germans as a whole disapproved of secession, since some German counties voted for it. The northern counties that opposed secession were mostly in the old Peters Colony region, and the two frontier counties were in the Castro Colony region. There was to be turmoil in these areas before the war was over.

Houston accepted the mandate of the people, but he was not prepared to follow secession leaders into the Confederacy. His alternative was for Texas to revert to its former status as an independent republic and to remain aloof from the maelstrom that was brewing.

When the secession convention reassembled on March 5 (a quorum not being present on March 2), it declared Texas independent of the union and approved the provisional government of the Confederate States, which had already acted to include Texas. Houston rebuked the convention: its work ended when secession was approved, and any further action was illegal. Implementation of secession was a task for the properly constituted authorities. The convention ignored him, modified the state constitution to conform with the Confederacy, and called upon state officials to take an oath of allegiance to the Confederate States of America on March 15.

This was too much for Houston, who refused to recognize the legality of the convention. The legislature was due to assemble on March 16; Houston hoped to make a last ditch fight there. But the convention declared the office of governor vacant, instructed Lieutenant Governor Edward Clark to assume the executive authority, and required members of the legislature to take the oath to the Confederacy. On March 23, after ratifying the constitution of the Confederacy, the convention adjourned, turning the reins of government over to Clark and the legislature.

The defeated Houston protested bitterly the usurpation of authority, but he ultimately submitted and retired to his home in Huntsville, where he died on July 26, 1863. Before he left Austin, he was given an opportunity to sustain himself by force. Lincoln sent a special messenger offering to put five thousand federal troops at his disposal. In the presence of a few unionist friends, Houston burned Lincoln's message, declining to accept aid that would bring bloodshed to his beloved Texas.

Military Affairs

Early Offensives   It is interesting that although Texas was not in the major theaters of operation during the war, the first, the last, and the most decisive battles were all fought in Texas and won by Texans. The first, the surrender of federal troops and military supplies in Texas, which began on February 18, was not exactly a battle, but it was an important victory. The last was the Battle of Palmito Ranch on May 12, 1865, when the victorious Texans learned from their prisoners of the surrenders of Lee and Johnston and the collapse of the Confederate government. The most decisive was the overwhelming defeat of the federal invasion at Sabine Pass on September 8, 1863.

At the beginning of 1861 there were twenty-one military posts in Texas, nearly three thousand troops, and many thousands of dollars worth of supplies and equipment. These placed in Texas for the defense of the border and the frontier, represented a very substantial proportion, perhaps ten per cent, of the military force of the United States. Both Governor

Secession and Civil War / 196

Houston and the Committee of Public Safety realized the significance of the force. Houston attempted as early as January to persuade Major General David E. Twiggs, commander of the Texas Military District, to surrender these forces to him. There was unwarranted speculation that had Twiggs done so, Houston would have used the army to prevent secession.

Twiggs, a Georgian in sympathy with the South, sent his resignation to Washington soon after his native state seceded, but was honor-bound to remain on duty until it was accepted and a replacement arrived. Texas commissioners, representing the Committee of Public Safety, opened negotiations with him for the surrender of the federal troops, forts, and military property on February 8. Negotiations were still pending when Twiggs' replacement arrived. Ben McCulloch, a former Texas Ranger, promptly raised a force of five hundred volunteers, including one hundred fifty Knights of the Golden Circle, and marched on Twiggs' headquarters at San Antonio. With only one hundred sixty troops at headquarters, Twiggs was forced to surrender on February 18 without a shot being fired.

Other state troops under John S. Ford and Henry McCulloch immediately set out to accept the surrender of the other federal garrisons in Texas. The only show of resistance was made at Fort Brown, where the commander refused to surrender and threatened to arrest Ford for treason. The arrival of several hundred reinforcements, however, persuaded the federal officer to accept Ford's terms on March 1. The surrender terms were simple. Forts and supplies were to be turned over to the Texans, and the federal troops were to evacuate the state. The troops from the western posts, who had not left the state by the time the war actually began, were interned and later exchanged.

Meanwhile, Colonel Earl Van Dorn had been named Confederate commander of Texas and had mustered into Confederate service McCulloch's and Ford's regiments, which had grown to ten mounted companies each. Ford sent Lieutenant Colonel John R. Baylor with four companies to occupy Fort Bliss and to establish Confederate control over New Mexico. With the backing of the Confederate government, Texas hoped to occupy New Mexico and even talked of a campaign to the west coast. When Baylor arrived at El Paso in July, he found Confederate sympathizers in full control, so he moved west to the nearby New Mexico village of Mesilla, across the Rio Grande from Fort Fillmore. When the federal troops attempted to withdraw, Baylor forced their surrender. On hearing this news, the federal commander at Fort Stanton retreated further upriver to Fort Craig, leaving southern New Mexico in the hands of the Texans. On August 1, 1861, Baylor proclaimed the formation of the Confederate Territory of Arizona, with a capital at Mesilla. He established a military government and sent a detachment to Tucson, where a mere handful of voters had signed their names to an ordinance of secession.

Henry H. Sibley, a brilliant but ill-starred graduate of West Point (and the inventor of the Sibley campaign tent), was then in command of the post at Taos in northern New Mexico. He resigned from the United States Army and offered his services to the Confederacy as commander of a campaign in the west. Commissioned by the government at Richmond as a Brigadier General in August 1861, he established headquarters at San Antonio and began recruiting volunteers. By November he had three regiments of thirty companies of mounted men, totaling thirty-five hundred troops. Sibley's brigade reached Fort Bliss in December and Mesilla in January 1862, where he assumed command of Baylor's troops. He then marched against Fort Craig, which was commanded by his brother-in-law, General Edward Canby.

Just before reaching Fort Craig, Sibley became ill or exhausted (some say he was drunk) and turned command of this engagement over to Colonel Tom Green (not to be confused with Thomas Jefferson Green). When Green learned that Canby had nearly four thousand men at Fort Craig, he decided to bypass it, but on February 21, 1862, Canby forced a battle at Valverde, across the river from the fort. The Texans captured the federal artillery and drove Canby back into the fort. The expedition then moved upriver and took Albuquerque on March 4. Shortly thereafter Santa Fe was occupied, but Sibley by no means controlled New Mexico, for Canby was still at Fort Craig, there was nearly a regiment at Fort Union, and a new regiment of volunteers was on its way from Colorado.

This latter regiment encountered Sibley's brigade at Glorietta Pass as Sibley was marching toward Fort Union. There, on March 28, a terrific battle ensued in which the Texans won the field but lost their supply train. This forced their withdrawal and ultimately Sibley's decision to abandon New Mexico. The retreat quickly became a confused rout, with stragglers stretched over a hundred miles along the way. New Mexico was finally evacuated on July 8, and during August and September contingents of the once-proud brigade found their way to San Antonio. This defeat, together with accusations of incompetence and drunkenness, broke Sibley's career. Command of what was left of the brigade devolved upon Colonel Tom Green.

While Sibley was pursuing his destiny in New Mexico, General Van Dorn authorized the enlistment of additional volunteer units and attempted to fortify the major coastal ports of Texas. During May 1861, a regiment of volunteers under W. C. Young crossed the Red River and occupied forts Cobb and Arbuckle to prevent invasion from the north. Van Dorn was soon transferred to Virginia and was replaced by an unpopular and less competent officer, Paul O. Hebert. Without consulting either the state or confederate officials, Hebert placed Texas under martial law on May 30, 1862. This enactment was quickly revoked by the authorities at Richmond, and Hebert was replaced in October by John B. Magruder, who was to command the Texas Military District until August 1864.

The Defense of the Coast The federal naval blockade reached the Texas coast during the summer of 1861, but for nearly a year it remained nothing more than a naval patrol. Then in August 1862 the lower coast was attacked at Matagorda Bay and Corpus Christi. Both attacks were repelled, but Corpus Christi sustained a severe bombardment from federal gunboats. In September 1862 federal troops struck Sabine Pass, slipped northward to Beaumont where they burned the railroad depot, destroyed the fortification at the Pass, and demolished a railroad bridge over Taylor Bayou. The next month the federal gunboat *Harriet Lane* entered Galveston harbor and demanded the surrender of the island. The handful of Texas troops at the fort resisted but were forced to evacuate under a flag of truce after heavy shelling from seven additional federal gunboats. Not until early December, however, did a federal landing party occupy Galveston.

Magruder, having replaced Hebert in command, determined to recapture Galveston, for it was the major port of Texas and a key to successful blockade running. The attack was made on New Year's Eve, 1862, Magruder himself leading the land operation by moving troops across to the island over the railroad bridge from Virginia Point, and Tom Green with his cavalry regiment from Sibley's brigade attacking the United States Naval fleet in the harbor. This was one of the most surprising operations of the war. Using several small ships and barges, Green hid his men on the decks behind cotton bales, for the compressed cotton made an unusually good armor. Green and his men boarded and captured the *Harriet Lane,* and a second gunboat was run aground. The remainder of the federal fleet evacuated under a flag of truce. Thus, with the capture of two ships and six hundred men, an important victory, Confederate control over Galveston was reestablished, not to be shaken again during the war.

The following month, using similar tactics, Magruder drove from the coast two gunboats commanding Sabine Pass, capturing one of them and taking more than one hundred prisoners. Confederate troops reoccupied the pass and constructed a rude earthwork for defense. Little did they realize that in a few months they would bear the brunt of a major federal offensive and that Sabine Pass would be the scene of what Jefferson Davis later called "the greatest military victory in the world."

In August 1863 federal authorities decided upon a major assault on Texas to cut it off from the Confederacy. It was to be a combined land and sea operation under General Nathaniel P. Banks and Admiral David Farragut. Four thousand federal troops boarded some seventeen transports at New Orleans and, protected by four gunboats, sailed for Sabine Pass. Against this formidable array stood Lieutenant Dick Dowling and forty-six men, most of them former Irish colonists, behind an unfinished earthwork about one hundred yards long. The federals opened the attack on the morning of September 8, 1863. A lucky shot from one of the Texan's six small cannon sank one of the gunboats in the channel. A second gunboat, loaded with five hundred sharpshooters, made for the fort; Dowling and his gunners held their fire until it was less than five hundred yards away, then took deadly aim, and a direct hit exploded its boiler amidships. Men and animals scrambled to save themselves as the Texas riflemen opened fire. The fighting lasted less than an hour. The federal loss was two gunboats, nineteen men dead, nine wounded, thirty-seven missing, and three hundred fifteen prisoners. Dowling and his hardy band, who had set something of a record by firing their artillery pieces over a hundred times during the brief engagement, had not a man injured. The incredible victory not only turned back the invasion but also lowered northern morale, caused a temporary drop in stock prices in New York, and reduced United States credit abroad by a reported five per cent.

Banks diverted his attack to South Texas, and sent some seven thousand men and three gunboats to take the lower Rio Grande. On November 6, 1863, a part of the force captured Fort Brown from the Texas defenders, who withdrew upriver. Colonel Edmund J. Davis, a Texas unionist in command of a mixed federal cavalry unit of Negroes and Mexicans, pursued them and took control of the river as far as Rio Grande City by the end of the month. During the same period a second detachment of this expeditionary force captured Matagorda Bay and Indianola.

Command of the Texas defense in South Texas was returned to John S. Ford, who had been assigned other duties. In the spring of 1864 Ford marched against Davis, who by that time had reached Laredo. He drove the federals from Laredo on April 15, and by April 30 he had forced them to evacuate Fort Brown. He lacked the means of attacking the union troops on the island of Brazos Santiago, but he held Fort Brown and the Rio Grande until the end of the war.

While Ford was retaking South Texas, Banks made his last thrust against Texas, moving up the Red River in Louisiana with an army of twenty-five thousand. In desperate haste, Magruder in Texas and E. Kirby Smith, Confederate commander of the Trans-Mississippi Department, tried to assemble an army to stop this assault. Every available man was sent to Louisiana. With troops from Texas, Louisiana, and Arkansas, the Confederate general Richard Taylor routed Banks at the Battle of Mansfield on April 8, 1864, less than fifty miles from the Texas boundary. Although hard fighting continued for some time in the region, the loss at Mansfield stopped Banks' operation against Texas.

As the war drew to its weary end in Virginia, Texas remained free of federal troops and suffered no further harassment. Robert E. Lee gave up his sword to Grant on April 9, 1865, and Johnston's surrender to Sherman on April 26 was followed by Taylor's on May 4, and finally Kirby Smith's on May 26. For a short time Smith seriously considered withdrawing to Texas and rallying the remnant of Confederate forces in the Trans-Mississippi to continue the war. He was supported by a few Texas leaders, but they abandoned the scheme when they discovered that most Texans were tired of the war and ready to return to peace.

Deep in South Texas, Colonel Ford and the Second Texas had not heard the news of war's end. The federals on Brazos Santiago had, and on May 12 Colonel T. H. Barrett landed three hundred troops, mostly Negroes, to take possession of Fort Brown. He encountered a detachment of Ford's regiment at Palmito Ranch near Brownsville, which withdrew after a brief skirmish. The next day, Ford arrived with reinforcements and artillery, and he routed the federal troops on the afternoon of May 13. Barrett's command was demoralized, and he suffered 30 killed or wounded and 113 captured. From these prisoners the Texans learned that they had won the last battle of the tragic war between the northern and southern states.

Texans at the Other Fronts Despite the ambiguity of the Texans attitude toward secession, when the war started, hundreds of Texans rushed to answer the call to arms. By the time of the first Confederate Conscription Act in April 1862, it was estimated that Texas had supplied over twenty thousand volunteers. Because of inadequate records and because of the confusion that attended the breakup of the Confederacy, it is impossible to determine accurately the number of Texans then in uniform. At the outset of the fighting, when the Confederate government was confident of an early victory, enlistment terms were brief: six months to a year. Most of the early volunteers reenlisted for longer periods of service. In all, probably over sixty thousand Texans saw military duty during the war. Over half of these remained in Texas, but those who fought on the other fronts distinguished themselves in battle. The Texas cavalry units were especially praised.

A number of famous Texas units were formed under Texas leaders. Among these were Ben McCulloch's brigade, Hood's Texas Brigade, and Terry's Texas Rangers. McCulloch's brigade, organized in the fall of 1861, consisted of eight regiments and two artillery batteries. Among these units were Elkanah Greer's Third Texas Cavalry, L. S. Ross's Sixth Texas Cavalry, and W. H. Parson's Twelfth Texas Cavalry. McCulloch's command saw action in Missouri in the spring of 1862, where McCulloch was killed in the Battle of Pea Ridge on March 8. The Texas units were later reorganized and assigned to the larger command of Albert Sidney Johnston.

Johnston without doubt was Texas' greatest single military figure in the war. After the annexation of Texas he had returned to duty in the United States Army, had commanded a regiment of Texans during the Mexican War, and later had organized the famed Second Cavalry Regiment for service in the west. A brigadier general stationed in San Francisco at the outbreak of the Civil War, he resigned his commission a second time and offered his services to the Confederacy. Jefferson Davis commissioned him a major general and assigned him to the command of the entire western division. On April 6, 1862, he was killed in the Battle of Shiloh.

In that engagement Terry's Texas Rangers won fame for their mobility and daring. Braxton Bragg, who succeeded Johnston, made extensive use of them in later action in Tennessee and Kentucky. Then, attached to Joseph E. Johnston's command, they protected his retreat to Atlanta. From the Battle of Woodsonville, Missouri, in 1861 to the Battle of Bentonville, North Carolina, in 1865, Terry's Texas Rangers were almost constantly in action. The organizing commander, B. F. Terry, was killed on December 17, 1861; Tom S. Lubbock, who succeeded him, died in January 1862 of illness; John A. Wharton was elected commander and led the unit until he was promoted to brigadier general in November 1862; Thomas Harrison, who followed, was replaced upon his promotion by Gustave Cooke, who was succeeded by J. F. Matthews, the last commander of the unit. In the four years of fighting the regiment lost 165 men killed, suffered 280 wounded, and had 38 captured. In the last charge at Bentonville there were only 150 survivors to follow Matthews against the enemy, at the last as gallant and daring as ever.

Hood's Brigade was organized in 1861 by Louis T. Wigfall from three Texas regiments and one each from Georgia and South Carolina. Although its composition was fluid, it remained principally a Texas unit commanded by Texans. John Bell Hood succeeded Wigfall in March

1862, and when he was promoted to major general and division commander, Jerome Robertson took charge of the brigade. Robertson was followed in 1864 by John Gregg, who was killed in October. Then the brigade had a series of temporary commanders until the end of the war. The brigade fought with the Army of Northern Virginia, participated in all the major engagements, and sustained heavy casualties. In the Battle of the Wilderness, Robert E. Lee himself led the Texans in one of the charges.

There was a score of other Texas units that distinguished themselves in the fighting on both sides of the Mississippi River, and hundreds of individuals won the praise of their commanders. Texas had not stinted in its supply of troops to the war. The best estimates give a total of 68,500 men in military service in two regiments of state troops, 28 infantry regiments, 30 artillery batteries, and 58 cavalry regiments, and two infantry legions, 13 infantry battalions, one artillery regiment, and 39 cavalry battalions—not all of which were in service simultaneously. Texas also furnished many high-ranking officers: one full general—Albert Sidney Johnston; three major generals—Sam Bell Maxey, John A. Wharton, and Tom Green; thirty-two brigadier generals, and nearly one hundred colonels.

Domestic Affairs

State Politics Edward Clark served out the remaining months of Houston's term in office and stood for reelection in August 1861. Against him ran two candidates: Francis R. Lubbock, brother of the Tom S. Lubbock who was at the time fighting in Missouri as assistant commander of Terry's Texas Rangers; and Thomas Jefferson Chambers, the nearly perpetual candidate. Francis Lubbock had been a vocal supporter of the secession movement, had served as lieutenant governor under Runnels, and no doubt felt that Houston's victory in 1859 had prevented his expected succession to the governorship. He won the election by a scant majority of 124 votes, with the outcome remaining in dispute for several weeks. His lieutenant governor was John M. Crockett. The race seems to have been based on personalities, as no major political issues arose.

The legislature in November elected to the Senate of the Confederacy Louis T. Wigfall, then commander of Hood's Brigade in Virginia, and W. S. Oldham. John H. Reagan had previously been named postmaster general of the Confederacy. Lubbock threw his administration wholeheartedly behind the war effort. He divided the state into thirty-three military districts, organized a battalion of mounted men for frontier duty, and sent fourteen regiments to training camps. In 1863 he persuaded the legislature to double taxes in support of the war effort, and he created the first Texas Military Board to supervise Texas participation in the war.

Lubbock, having announced that he would enter Confederate service when his term expired, enlisted first on Magruder's staff, later served under John A. Wharton, and finally became aide-de-camp to Jefferson Davis. Since he did not run for reelection, the campaign of 1863 was wide open. However, only T. J. Chambers and Pendleton Murrah were major candidates. The lack of interest in the race was reflected in the vote, the total being less than half that cast in either 1857 or 1859. Murrah was elected, with Fletcher S. Stockdale as lieutenant governor.

Murrah's administration marked the decline of the war effort and the deterioration of government at both the state and the Confederate levels. Murrah found himself in the unexpected position of defending the state rights of Texas against the Confederacy, which had been created to preserve the states' rights. The central government, desperate for men and supplies, made heavy and sometimes autocratic demands on the Texas government.

Texas had the special problem of defending its western frontier against hostile Indians and its southern border against bands of Mexican outlaws. When the United States Army had evacuated in the spring of 1861, it left a vacuum that Texas naturally expected the Confederacy to fill. But the government at Richmond was unable to help. Lubbock had worked out the compromise of establishing two regiments of state troops, one under Ford to defend the border and the other under J. E. McCord to protect the frontier. Men in these units were exempt from the Confederate conscription.

During Lubbock's administration the conscription quotas were met, usually by volunteer enlistments, but in the later stages of the war this became impossible. Murrah refused to transfer state troops to Confederate service on the eastern fronts and even demanded that Texans enlisted or drafted for Confederate service be stationed in Texas. The reason for his recalcitrance is obvious: Texas was under massive attacks from Banks, but because the major war effort of the Confederacy was in the east, the hard-pressed government there could not hope to defend Texas.

Dissatisfaction with the general government's attitude toward the west had arisen in complaints from the governor of Arkansas in 1862. Governor Lubbock had held a conference that year in Marshall with the governors of Missouri, Louisiana, Texas, and Arkansas, and the result was the creation of the Trans-Mississippi Military Department under the command of Edmund Kirby Smith. A second governor's conference, held in 1863 at Smith's request, availed little because of the increasing exigencies of the military situation. Murrah eventually had to accede to the general government and permit Texans to serve in the eastern armies, though with the exception of McCord's and Ford's regiments.

The Military Board and the Effort to Finance the War Probably the most important state agency during the war was the Texas State Military Board, created in 1862 and reconstituted in 1863. The board's chief purposes were to sustain foreign trade by supporting blockade running, to establish factories and munitions plants for the manufacture of military supplies, and to dispose of state indemnity bonds acquired by the Compromise of 1850.

The board, consisting of the governor, the comptroller, and the treasurer, was hampered by lack of appropriations and many other matters, but it did have partial success. A cotton trade overland to Brownsville and across the Rio Grande to Matamoros was established. There was created a boom port called Bagdad, which, being at the mouth of the river on the Mexican side, was secure under international law from the United States Navy. To Bagdad flowed hundreds of bales of Texas cotton for British and French markets, and from Bagdad came a trickle of money and military supplies. The Mexican bandit Juan Cortina temporarily interrupted the trade, as did the federal occupation of Fort Brown in 1863. Nonetheless, this trade was an important part of the war effort.

Among the most significant imports from France through Bagdad, although almost unnoticed at the time, were two Carré ice-making machines, one in 1862, the other in 1865. Installation at San Antonio in 1862 created the first ice factory in the United States and one of the first in the world, for the equipment had just been invented in 1860. This early experience with ice manufacturing was to make Texas the pioneer in that industry after the war.

The Military Board, under an incentive contract system, created a cannon foundry, a number of powder mills, and a small arms factory. None of these was highly successful, largely because of the lack of skilled labor and the inexperience of Texans in industry.

In its attempt to sell bonds the board was equally a failure, the fault of its agents more than of inept policy. There were over six hundred one-thousand-dollar United States bonds in the treasury at the beginning of the war. After many vicissitudes, the board turned them over to an agent in Monterrey, Mexico, who tried futilely to negotiate them in Europe. After the war the state was able to recover only some of these and other bonds scattered among various agents. A large portion, for example, was tied up in a chancery suit in England. The board met with questionable success in selling the eight-per cent "Texian" state bonds. Nearly a half million dollars worth of these were disposed of at heavy discounts to finance the operation of the state. Repayment of this issue was later canceled by the Fourteenth Amendment.

To finance the cotton trade, the board gave many bonds to planters for their crop and then traded the cotton at Bagdad for military supplies. Another major controversy arose between the state and the Confederate government over this practice. An act of the Confederate Congress allowed agents of the general government to "impress" cotton for sale or trade by the Confederacy. By a compromise scheme, worked out in the governors' conference in 1863, planters who exchanged half their crop for cotton certificates of the Confederacy would be exempt from impressment of the other half. Governor Murrah proposed a state plan, which substituted the Texas Military Board with its bonds for the Confederate cotton bureau. Because the terms of the state plan were more generous, Texans preferred to deal with the Military Board. The Confederate Congress then outlawed the exportation of cotton, and E. Kirby Smith in 1864 called a third governors' conference, at which an acceptable compromise was established.

An even more burdensome measure than such apparent usurpation of authority by the Confederate government was that of the heavy tax levies. From 1861 to 1864 Texans paid nearly forty million dollars in taxes to the general government, approximately five times the amount of state taxes during the same period. Texas' financial condition was precarious throughout the war. Lacking specie, Texans used Confederate notes as basic currency, bartered in cotton, used the bonds issued by the Military Board, and traded in treasury drafts and warrants. None of these had any intrinsic value, and consequently they all were sharply discounted, and they all became worthless at the end of the war. Texas found itself with a staggering eight-million-dollar debt in 1865.

Union Sentiment in Texas Unionist sentiment in Texas during the war was stronger than the vote on secession had indicated and probably grew during the later stages of the war in proportion to the South's reverses. In all likelihood, however, it was never as high as the one-third of the population that one historian estimated. And only a small percentage of the Texas unionists gave active support to the federal cause.

Of those who remained passive, most attempted to remain neutral and avoid participation on either side and some accepted the will of the majority and enlisted in the Confederate Army. Typical of the latter was J. W. Throckmorton, an outspoken unionist before the war who enlisted and rose to the rank of brigadier general in the Confederate service. Many of the older statesmen, such as Sam Houston, E. M. Pease, and David G. Burnet, tried to keep neutral. Because of the liberal deferment policy under Confederate conscription laws, many of the passive unionists were able to avoid military service. Some hired substitutes when they were conscripted, a device legally acceptable.

A small proportion of Texans were so strongly unionist that they moved north, many to enlist in the federal armies. One of the state's greatest losses for this reason was S. M. Swenson, the "father" of Swedish migration to Texas. Swenson attempted to remain neutral, but his unionist sentiments were so well known that he was virtually driven from the state in 1863. He spent the next two years in Mexico, as did a number of other unionists, and then moved to New Orleans and later to New York City, where he established one of the nation's most influential private banks. J. P. Newcomb, a staunch unionist newspaper publisher of San Antonio, also fled to Mexico after Knights of the Golden Circle destroyed his press. Edmund J. Davis, a district judge, organized a union cavalry regiment, and as noted earlier, reentered Texas with the federal invasion of 1863. Davis was not the only Texan to fight against his state; scores of others joined the federal forces.

There was much unionist sentiment in South Texas, partially because most of the Mexican population refused to take the oath of allegiance to the Confederacy and partially because unionists from elsewhere in Texas flocked there when Fort Brown was occupied by federal troops. Although three South Texas counties were placed under martial law in 1862, no violence occurred there, beyond renegade brigandage.

Fear of violence and treason, however, caused the formation of vigilante committees. In San Antonio such a group was formed because of the concentration of unionists there, and through a large part of the war the city was harassed by irrational southern patriots. It was similarly disturbed by the unionists' celebrations of northern victories, by plots to depreciate the currency further, and by an occasional placard calling on unionists to rebel.

In the German frontier counties to the northwest of San Antonio there was outright resistance to the Confederacy. Three militia companies of five hundred unionists, calling themselves the Union Loyal League, were organized in Gillespie, Kerr, and Kendall counties to resist conscription. Governor Lubbock sent two companies of Rangers to disband the organization. Most of the unionists fled to the hills, regrouped, and marched off to Mexico to enlist in federal service. En route on the upper Nueces a skirmish occurred with the Rangers on August 10, 1862. A number of the unionists in the area moved west to establish the community of Loyal Valley in Mason County. After 1863 overt unionist activity in that area died out.

In Central Texas defiance of the Confederacy was largely limited to mass meetings in protest of the conscription laws. Open resistance, however, in the form of militia organizations, appeared in Colorado, Fayette, and Austin counties, where there were large settlements of recent immigrants from Czechoslovakia (then Moravia and Bohemia) and Poland.

Travis County, where the seat of government was located, was about equally divided between unionists and Confederate supporters. No major conflict arose, although there were many minor episodes. Among the most comical of these was the refusal of the Episcopal bishop to attend Sunday services because the rector of the church was a Connecticut born unionist. The crisis was resolved with the organization of two parishes, one for the unionists and the other for the Confederates.

The greatest unionist activity occurred in North Texas, where conspiracy was mounted in 1862 to cooperate with an expected invasion. Known as the Peace Party, this group swore its members to secrecy, pledged to support a movement to restore federal control and to cooperate with an armed invasion, and proposed to establish a spy system for the North through members who were conscripted into Confederate service. Cooke County was the principal hotbed of this activity, although adjacent counties, chiefly Grayson, contained elements of the Peace Party. The plot was discovered and reported to the district military commander, who promptly declared martial law in North Texas.

Rumors spread through the area like wildfire, and panic soon pervaded the entire population. It was worse than the Salem witch hunts: neighbor accused neighbor; people's courts sprang into illegal existence; an uncontrolled militia made rampant arrests. Before the madness could be halted, forty accused men were hanged in Gainesville without proper trial, five were hanged in Decatur, and forty were sentenced in Sherman though all but one were released through the efforts of J. W. Throckmorton. A number of accused conspirators were jailed in Denton, where one was shot to death. The vigilante trials ended the conspiracy by October 1862, but perhaps at greater cost than was warranted.

Domestic Hardships   It was not long after the war started that the South's critical lack of industry was felt on the home front as well as in the military arena. By the end of 1861 many Texas homes were lacking such staples as sugar, flour, salt, and tobacco. Then as manufactured items began to wear out, cloth, leather goods (especially shoes), plows, wagons, and the like began to be in short supply. One of the first actions of the Military Board was to establish a textile mill at Huntsville, but its uncertain output could not meet the demand. Texas women began to revert to "homespun," and discarded spinning wheels were retrieved from attics and put back into use. A domestic problem typical of the many of the war arose when Texas women attempted to spin their own thread and weave their own cloth. Before the cotton fibers could be spun, they had to be separated by combing, or "carding." But such an insignificant item as a cotton card was not to be found. In 1863 the Texas Military Board requisitioned twenty thousand cotton cards through its purchasing agent in England.

Perhaps the most important shortage was medicine and hospital supplies. Herbal gardens were encouraged, and the Military Board in 1864 advocated the cultivation of poppies for the extraction of opium. The need for bandages at the front was so great that women sacrificed their dresses and petticoats to the purpose, thus increasing the shortage of textiles.

Privation followed shortage. The lack of manpower, especially on the small farms, meant lean crops followed by a decrease in livestock. Even corn and cornmeal were in short supply. On the larger farms and plantations women proved, as they so regularly do in emergencies, their ability to manage the operation without their husbands. But for a variety of reasons, including the breakdown of equipment and scarcity of seeds, production was below normal. Mrs. O. C. Connor, who supervised approximately fifty slaves, wrote her absent husband, bravely if a little plaintively, in 1862:

> As to home affairs, I am trying to do the best I can. I wove out the piece of cloth I had in the loom when you were here and 14 yds. in another piece and I warped 45 yds. this evening. Charley has been working on the little wagon. Got done this evening. He fastened the boxes and cut and welded the tyres. It is rough but perhaps it will do. He had nobody to help him but Frank. The other wagon is not fixed yet. They have no coal at town. I have to send for 4 bushels of coal and pay $4.00 for fixing it. I will perhaps send it up tomorrow. I had some of our wheat washed today to send to Will. It is very badly weavil eaten. I think I had better have it ground after a while. I do not think I can stay here longer than this year if you do not get home. But do not be uneasy about me.

I will do the best I can. Charley attends to the boys and other things very well. The Negroes appear glad to hear from you. Charley and Clariss particularly.

The paper shortage, which was to become acute later, was already evident in this letter, as she was forced to turn the paper and write sideways in the margin. Later correspondence between her and her husband utilized the trick of writing until the page was full and then turning it ninety degrees and writing across the preceding lines. Surprisingly, it can be read. The increasing lack of paper became one of the most serious problems of the entire Confederacy. Many newspapers were forced to suspend operations. Correspondence was necessarily limited, and even the government found difficulty in functioning. Few records were kept during the last months of the war.

The hardships from shortages were aggravated by the almost steady flow of refugees to Texas, especially in 1864 and 1865. Not only did men wish to remove their families from the dangers of the fighting in the other states but also there was a general belief that Texas was not suffering as great a deprivation. There is no way to estimate accurately the number of refugees, but many women and children, bringing domestic slaves with them, came to Texas to stay with kinfolks and friends. As federal troops occupied southern territory, slaveholders, who had no wish to risk the loss of their property, moved some two hundred thousand Negroes to Texas during the four years of the war.

Even more of a problem than the influx of refugees was the appearance in the late stages of the conflict of deserters from the Confederate army, outlaws, and renegades. In the latter part of 1863 a band of unionists and Confederate deserters that had been terrorizing Bell County was broken up. So serious did the problem of the "bush soldiers" become that Governor Murrah declared martial law in some counties in 1864. Desertion, a serious problem for the army as the South's loss became increasingly apparent, was even more menacing on the home front. The commander of the northern district of Texas reported in 1864 that disloyalty was widespread among his conscripted troops. Once, of a company of sixty-two men sent on a scouting expedition, only sixteen returned to camp; the remainder deserted, presumably for California. Such deserters, when they did not leave the state, turned outlaw. And because of its location Texas received more than its share of deserters from other states. Bands of Jayhawkers from Kansas were reported operating in North Texas just before the end of the war.

"Not with a bang but a whimper," wrote the poet Eliot allegorically of the end of the world; the phrase is an apt description also of the end of the Confederacy. During the spring of 1865, bands of war-weary soldiers, threadbare and emaciated, began heading home, usually on foot and often without benefit of discharge or orders. They knew that the cause was lost without having to be told.

Hungry, broke, and disgusted, many of these men resorted to lawlessness, apparently feeling that state or Confederate property belonged to any homeward-bound veteran who could take it. Governor Murrah called on local sheriffs to protect government property, but they were helpless to do so. The deterioration of law and order created throughout the state chaotic conditions for which there was no immediate relief.

Texas, the last of the southern states to be occupied by federal troops, suffered a total collapse of civil government in May and June of 1865. After Lee's surrender, generals Smith and Magruder, backed by Governor Murrah, issued a plea to continue the war in Texas, but to no avail. Everyone knew the war was over, and everyone but the die-hards was desperately thankful it was. Smith called another conference of the Trans-Mississippi governors to meet at Marshall in May, but the governors sent representatives who discussed only the terms of surrender and not the prolonging of the conflict. Smith sent peace commissioners to New Orleans to negotiate the surrender of the Trans-Mississippi, and on June 2 on a federal ship in Galveston harbor he signed the surrender terms, which were essentially those of complete capitulation. Men and officers were paroled and ordered to return to their homes. Confederate property was to be turned over to federal officers. No political disposition was made, for Lincoln had already appointed a provisional governor for Texas who would assume authority as soon as he arrived.

Immediately after the Marshall conference, some recalcitrant rebels began planning to seek refuge in Mexico and establish an independent nation along the Rio Grande or enlist in Maximilian's French-supported army. Among them were generals Joseph Shelby, A. W. Terrell, and William Preston. Shelby had nearly five hundred men who had sworn to follow him. The refugees were joined by a few other prominent citizens, including the governors of Louisiana and Missouri, the former governors of Missouri and Kentucky, former governor Clark of Texas, generals Magruder and Smith, and Governor Murrah of Texas. The offer of the exiles to fight for Maximilian was rejected, but they were welcomed as colonists. After Maximilian's fall, most of them returned home. The exact date Murrah abandoned the executive office is not known. He had been ill for some time, and apparently he left Austin in the company of General Terrell on June 18. He died in Monterrey on August 4.

Fletcher Stockdale, the lieutenant governor, tried futilely to cope with the collapsing government until the provisional governor arrived. He could do little to check the spreading lawlessness, which reached epidemic proportions during June and July. Civilians began to participate in plunder along with the returning soldiers, and soon the pillage was extended beyond the government supply depots to privately owned stores and warehouses. A special session of the legislature, which Murrah had called to meet in July, failed to assemble. There was no state law enforcement agency, and the harassed county sheriffs were nearly as helpless as Stockdale.

Thus it was that Texas awaited federal occupation and the restoration of law and order.

9

Reconstruction and Reaction

Reconstruction

Analysis The period from the end of the war to the time the South returned to what was more or less normalcy is usually called Reconstruction. Since the term was coined by northern Republicans to describe the process under which the South was punished after the war, most historians define the end of Reconstruction as the date political power was resumed by each vanquished state. For Texas this followed the election of Coke in 1873; for the South as a whole it followed the national election of 1876.

Southerners of that time considered the policies of their conquerors unnecessarily harsh. They also believed that a not-too-veiled implication of the term was the reconstruction of the southern states as political ramparts of the Republican Party by denying suffrage to many who had formerly exercised it and by extending it to those who had not, the recently freed slaves. In effect they believed that the radical Republicans, in control of congress after the election of 1866, intended to turn the social, economic, and political pyramid upside down in the southern states. They also believed that during the regime of radical Republican control in each state the government was infested with "scalawags" (local radicals) and "carpetbaggers" (transient radicals from the northern states come south for political advantage and economic gain). General southern opinion held that such governments were irresponsible and profligate as well as corrupt.

This belief was so deeply fixed in the southern mind that after the southern Democrats returned to political power the southern states rewrote the radical Republican constitutions under which they had been readmitted to the union. They undid as much of the radical legislation as they could, and for three generations or more they consistently refused to elect Republican candidates to office. They also came, in general, to despise and distrust the race that had once been their slaves. The preceding generation of American historians thought that Reconstruction was the greatest single factor in establishing racial prejudice in the South.

Modern historians, however, of the "revisionist" school of thought hold that the embittered southerners of the time were wrong, that Reconstruction was not bad for the South, that radical Republicanism was even beneficial in some areas, that there were few scalawags and fewer carpetbaggers, and that, of course, southern prejudice toward the Negro had always existed. The revisionists are right in many respects: the radical constitutions were for the most part good instruments of government; there were not many carpetbaggers and scalawags; and the antebellum southern attitude toward the Negro is evident in the slave codes and the statutes regulating the lives of free Negroes. Yet the residue of the Reconstruction era was the intense bitterness of most southerners who lived through the period, a bitterness that lasted nearly one hundred years and persists in rural pockets throughout the South today.

The period of Reconstruction has traditionally been subdivided on the basis of the political regimes. The first phase was Presidential Reconstruction under the terms of Lincoln's and Johnson's plans. The second was Congressional Reconstruction under the military rule established by the Reconstruction Act of March 2, 1867. The third was Radical Rule under the Republican constitutions and the Republican officials elected thereby.

Presidential Reconstruction Andrew Jackson Hamilton, a former United States Congressman from Texas and a unionist who had exiled himself in the North, was as early as 1863 appointed provisional governor of Texas by President Lincoln, who apparently believed that General Banks' thrusts would conquer the state. Hamilton went to New

THE PROPOSED STATE OF WEST TEXAS

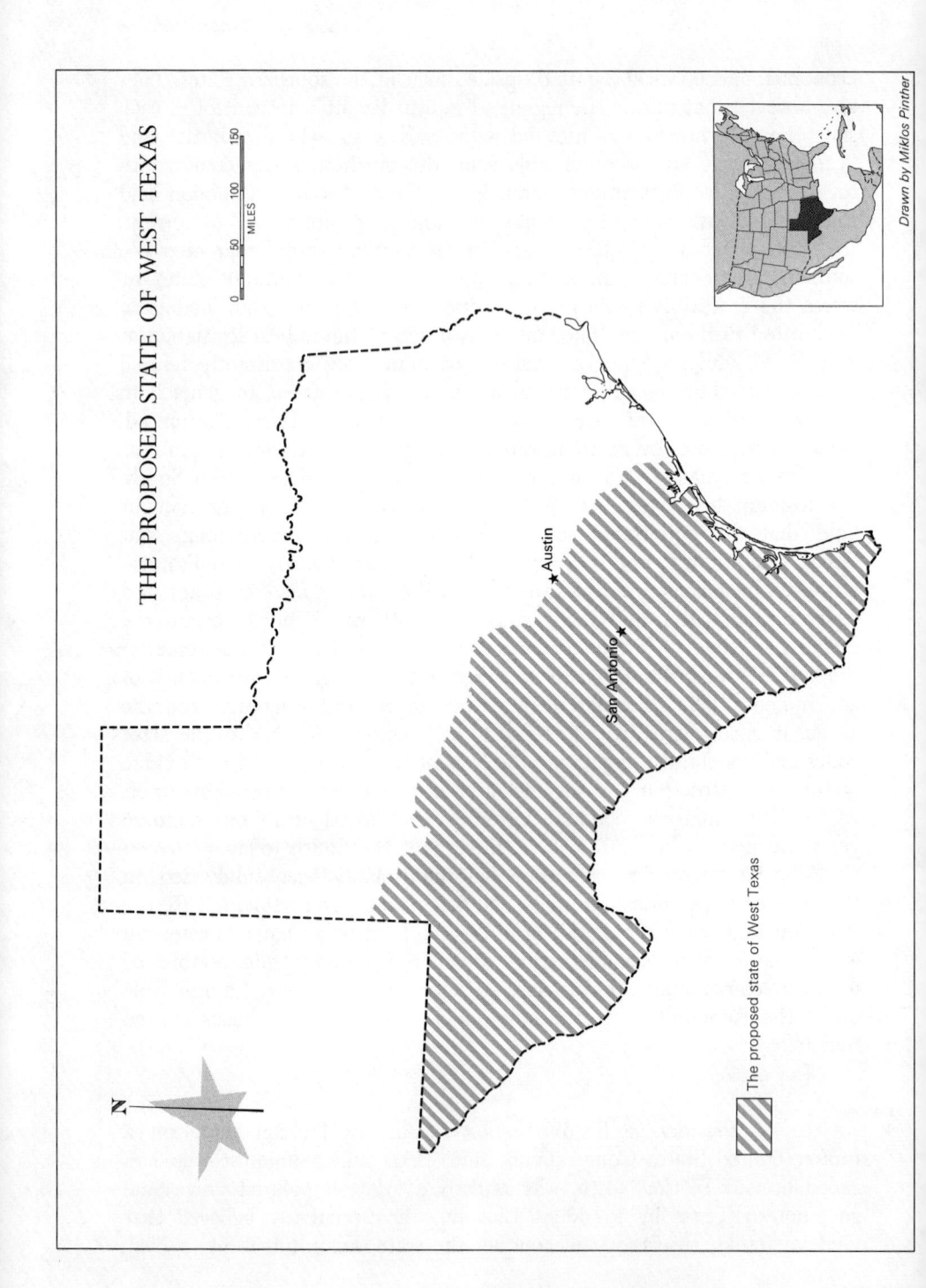

Orleans to await the occupation of Texas by federal armies. He had a long wait.

Even after Smith's formal surrender of the Trans-Mississippi Department, federal occupation was delayed. General Gordon Granger, deputized by General Philip H. Sheridan to take control of Texas, landed eighteen hundred men at Galveston on June 19, 1865. On that day he read Lincoln's Emancipation Proclamation. "June Teenth" was regularly celebrated by Texas Negroes as if it were a national holiday. Additional troops were soon sent to Texas, and Granger gradually dispersed them in the major population centers. Two detachments entered Texas overland from Louisiana, one commanded by General Wesley Merritt and the other by the flamboyant General George A. Custer.

Custer encountered little hostility on his march to the capital and in fact found many of the Texans friendly. His troops were the first to reach Austin, but he could do little toward establishing political stability before Hamilton arrived. Custer, out of deference to the citizens of the town, made his headquarters not in the capitol building but across the river in the nearly vacant school for the deaf and dumb. It is interesting to note in passing that from the children at the school Custer learned sign language, which he later found he could make use of with the Plains Indians, who had developed their own sign language. The yellow-haired general remained in Austin for several months.

A. J. Hamilton reached Galveston a month after Granger and proceeded immediately to Austin. His assignment was to make operative Lincoln's Reconstruction plan as modified by Andrew Johnson. But his first task was to restore law and order. He was supported by the military, and by the fall of the year there was a degree of stability in the local governments. He made provisional appointments to state and county offices as well as to the badly needed judicial system. It is debatable whether the military support was adequate. By the end of the year there were over fifty thousand troops in Texas, but most of these were stationed along the Rio Grande as a demonstration against the French in Mexico. Perhaps had more been dispersed into the settled portions of Texas there would have been less lawlessness, but certainly there would have been more resentment of the Yankees.

To be readmitted to the union under the presidential plan, a state had to repudiate secession, draft a new constitution excluding slavery, and cancel debts incurred during the war. A special convention would be required to take these actions. Before Hamilton could have delegates to the convention elected, he had to register the voters. In August he ordered the chief justices in each county to begin administering the general amnesty oath which simply required allegiance to the United States and acceptance of emancipation. Several classes of persons were not permitted to take this oath but had to secure special pardons from the President. Among them were high officials of the Confederacy and anyone who owned property valued at more than $20,000.

In November, Hamilton felt that registration of the voters was far enough along that he could call for the election to be held on January 8, 1866. The delegates were to convene in Austin the following month. The elections were peaceful, with a small turnout at the polls, chiefly because of bad winter weather. But the delegates when they reached Austin were far from tranquil. They tended to divide into two extreme factions that made a mockery of the northern victory: unionists and former secessionists. Fortunately a middle group was determined to face the reality of defeat. One of these, J. W. Throckmorton, was elected president of the convention.

The convention decided to submit its work to the voters as a series of amendments to the Constitution of 1845, which had been amended in 1861 for adherence to the Confederacy. The major questions debated were nullification of the ordinance of secession, status of the freedmen, and cancellation of the war debt. There was no need to debate emancipation; it was an accepted fact. Nullification of secession raised interesting constitutional questions. Lincoln had consistently maintained that secession was illegal and that consequently the secession ordinances were null and void *ab initio*. But if this opinion was held with logical consistency, then there was no need in the South for Reconstruction government, for the states would automatically revert to their previous status within the union. Since this clearly was not the case, it was argued in the Texas convention that secession had been legal and must be revoked, not nullified *ab initio*. The issue was temporarily settled by declaring secession void without any reference to time.

As did all the other southern conventions, the Texas convention refused to give freedmen equal rights with whites. It extended more privileges than most southern states did, such as the rights to testify in court and to sit on juries when Negroes were on trial. The convention also repudiated the entire state debt incurred during the war, not simply the war expenses, on the general grounds that it violated the Constitution of 1845. And although it rejected the Thirteenth Amendment to the federal Constitution, it did amend the state constitution to exclude slavery. A few other changes in the Constitution of 1845 were also made, such as lengthening the term of the governor.

The amendments were submitted to popular vote for ratification in June. At the same time a slate of officers under the constitution was to be chosen. The Democrats named J. W. Throckmorton, the unionist-turned-Confederate; the Texas unionists, now identified as both moderate and radical Republicans, nominated Elisha M. Pease, the unionist and former governor. In so doing, they widened the schism between moderate and radical Republicans. Pease, although not personally a radical, was identified with the radicals, and he lost the election by 12,168 votes to 49,277, an overwhelming endorsement of Throckmorton's policy of opposing Negro suffrage but supporting the presidential plan of reconstruction. The amendments carried by a vote of 28,119 to 23,400. The closeness of this vote may be explained by the fact that the amendments had to be voted on as a package rather than separately and that several amendments, especially one calling for higher salaries for state officials, were unpopular.

With the inauguration of constitutional government on August 9, 1866, and President Johnson's declaration on August 20 of the end of the insurrection in Texas, Reconstruction entered its second phase. This phase was to be short lived. In the national elections that year radical Republicans, who opposed the presidential plan of reconstruction, gained control of congress. It was probably the nastiest election in American political history. The Radicals abused and vilified Johnson, falsely accusing him of everything from chronic drunkenness to participation in Lincoln's assassination. They also "waved the bloody shirt," arguing that dead and wounded northern soldiers were being dishonored by the southern states' easy readmission to the union.

Unfortunately Texas and the other southern states played right into the hands of the Radicals by the adoption of Black Codes, which restricted the rights of freedmen, and by the election of former Confederates to their constitutional conventions, to posts in their new governments, and even to the United States Congress. Neither of the two senators whom the Texas Legislature elected could take the "ironclad oath," passed in 1862, that they had not abetted the Confederacy. Oran M. Roberts had been president of the secession convention, and David G. Burnet, although a prewar unionist, had accepted secession and the Confederacy.

Southerners maintained that secession was not treasonous and that congress should repeal the ironclad oath. The Radicals countered that the South had not learned its lesson and that the election of so many former secessionists was an insult to the union dead. In an open letter by John H. Reagan, who had been imprisoned with Jefferson Davis in Fort Warren at the war's end, Texans had been warned to abjure continued rebellion. It was good advice but unwelcome, and Reagan was almost ostracized as a traitor when he returned to Texas and again warned Texans of the North's attitude.

Congressional Reconstruction A contingent of Texas Radicals preceded the congressional delegation to Washington to urge that congress refuse to recognize the new government in Texas. When Roberts and Burnet arrived, with three of the four members of the house, they were not only denied their seats but prohibited from entering the halls. From the galleries they watched the fury of the Radicals unfolding against the South. Within months Radical leaders placed the South under military law, reestablished the Freedmen's Bureau with broader powers, impeached President Johnson, and harassed the southern states with further stringent regulations.

The first and most significant piece of legislation was the First Reconstruction Act of March 2, 1867, which divided the South into five military districts each under the absolute control of a general, declared the existing southern governments provisional and subject to military authority, and demanded that new state constitutions be drafted before congress would consider readmitting the states. The new constitutions were to establish Negro suffrage and were to disfranchise former Confederate leaders. The states were furthermore required to adopt the Fourteenth Amendment.

Texas was placed under the command of General Philip Sheridan in the Fifth Military District, which also included Louisiana and Arkansas. General Charles Griffin was named subcommander for Texas. A Reconstruction act in July 1867 authorized the generals to remove any state civil officers, and on July 30, Griffin removed Governor Throckmorton as an "impediment to reconstruction." Throckmorton had pledged himself to cooperate with the military authorities, but he found it impossible to do so when Griffin arbitrarily demanded that he pardon two hundred twenty-seven Negro convicts in the state penitentiary. Elisha M. Pease was named Provisional Governor in Throckmorton's place. Although Pease had consorted with the Radicals, he was the most moderate of them, and he was trusted by the military because of his political views and respected by most of the people because of his long service to the state.

Confusion returned to Texas, however, to a greater degree than before. Griffin's requirement that everyone serving on a jury must take the ironclad oath disqualified the majority of stable citizens. For several years many of the courts were in chaotic condition. Also, Griffin began removing other state officials and gave their places to "loyal men" who took the oath. Worse yet was the new registration of voters under still another Congressional Reconstruction act, which disfranchised anyone who had held any public office and had thereafter engaged in insurrection. "Public office" was interpreted to include even local offices such as mayor or school board. This act together with the registration of Negroes turned the political world upside down by withdrawing suffrage from many who had demonstrated civic responsibility and giving it to many who had no concept of such responsibility. When the voter registration was completed nearly six months later, there were 78,648 whites and 56,905 Negroes on the rolls.

An unusual five-day election of delegates to a new constitutional convention was called to take place from February 10 to 14, 1868. It was a mockery of the democratic system. Large numbers of whites stayed away from the polls in hopes of invalidating the results, for congress had ruled that a majority of the registered voters must participate in the elections. Both the southern whites and the Radicals made unethical efforts to control the Negro vote. The reconstituted Freedmen's Bureau, headed by E. M. Gregory, sought to influence the erstwhile slaves, and a new organization, the Loyal Union League, tried a variety of schemes to influence Negro voters. To compound the confusion in the freedmen's minds, the purpose of the Ku Klux Klan was to prevent the Negro from voting. Although a few groups became violent, most Klan riders simply played on Negro superstition by parading through Negro settlements after dark, clad in ghostlike white sheets and crying that dire events would follow if Negroes went to the polls. Possibly more effective was the technique of setting up a carnival at the edge of town and accepting voter registration slips for admission.

At the election a total of 56,129 votes were cast—a little over half of the registration. White leaders had lost faith in the plan to invalidate the results and at the last minute had urged Democrats to vote but against delegates who favored Negro suffrage. More than 37,000 Negroes and less than 19,000 whites voted. The new convention was to assemble in Austin on June 1, 1868. Of the ninety delegates, nine were Negroes, twelve were conservative or southern Democrats, six or eight could have been called carpetbaggers, and the rest were white Texas Republicans although—the candidates did not run specifically under those party labels.

Meanwhile, between the time of voter registration and the meeting of the convention, several changes in the military structure had occurred. At New Orleans Sheridan, considered overzealous, had been replaced by General George H. Thomas, who was himself replaced by General Winfield S. Hancock, a northern Democrat who distrusted and disliked the Radical Republicans and who in 1880 was to run for the presidency on the Democratic ticket. Hancock was followed by General Richard C. Buchanan, who was followed by General Edward R. Canby, a man who because of the New Mexico invasion during the war wasted no love on Texans. The Texas commander, General Griffin, died in a yellow fever epidemic in September 1867 and was succeeded by General J. J. Reynolds, who remained until the end of the congressional phase of Reconstruction.

The Constitutional Convention met in two separate sessions: June 1 to August 31, 1868, when it exhausted its funds and adjourned, and December 11, 1868, to February 8, 1869, after a special tax had been levied for its support. In direct expenditures the convention cost the taxpayers over $200,000 but spent less than ten days on the actual work of drafting a constitution, which it did not finish. Much of its time was frittered away in useless, although often fiery, debates. It also detoured into legislation to charter railroads, to create counties, to make land grants, to investigate lawlessness in the state, and to perform various near-legislative functions. The second session was not as well attended as the first, and only forty-five of the original ninety delegates signed the constitution. Most of the work on the constitution seems to have been done by a small *ad hoc* committee during the last days of the convention. The work was not actually finished until, under orders from General Canby, the fragments were assembled and printed.

Despite the inauspicious circumstances of its creation, the document has been considered (by later authorities, not by Texans at that time) as a sound instrument of government. It provided a much more centralized government than did previous constitutions. Several major elective offices were made appointive; all judicial positions became appointive; county courts were abolished; a centralized school agency and a centralized highway department were created; and terms of office were generally lengthened, including those of the governor and the senators. It provided for four-day elections, did not disfranchise former voters who could not take the test oath, and guaranteed suffrage to the freedmen. It also provided for a poll tax. In all respects it fulfilled the conditions established by the Radical Congress. Texas could rejoin the union if the proposed constitution were ratified by the electorate and approved by congress.

Meantime, the convention had considered a proposal to divide Texas and create a separate State of West Texas, encompassing the area south and west of the Colorado River. A group of Radical Republicans, believing perhaps that political control of the thinly populated area would be simple, drafted a Constitution for the State of West Texas. By a parliamentary trick they secured a resolution by the convention on January 18, 1869, to present this constitution to congress for approval. This group of Radical Republicans, increasingly dissatisfied with the work of the convention, focused its strength in support of the proposed new state. Led by Edmund J. Davis, they met in a rump session, adjourned three days before the main body of the convention, and rushed to Washington to try to persuade congress to approve division of the state and establishment of the West Texas Constitution. Congress was dissuaded from approving largely by testimony of a rival faction of Radical Republicans, led by A. J. Hamilton. These two Republican groups carried their fight for control of Texas into the election.

The state election was held November 30 to December 3, 1869. The constitution was adopted by a staggering vote of 72,446 to 4,928, for all factions recognized its necessity. The main contest was for the office of governor. A new leader of the Radicals had emerged: Edmund J. Davis, a former district judge who had settled in Texas in 1838, had joined the union army, had led the invasion of the lower Rio Grande, and had risen to the rank of brigadier general. A. J. Hamilton was forced into the role of leader of the moderate Republicans, and the historical images of these two men were cast: Davis as Radical, Hamilton as Moderate. It should be noted, however, that Hamilton's earlier actions were in tune with the Radical attitude and that Davis' later actions were often moderate. Davis was backed by General Reynolds, who seems to have stacked the voter registration boards with pro-Davis men and who refused to make public the election returns. Instead, he arrogantly certified to General Canby that there were 39,901 for Davis and 39,002 for Hamilton—one of the narrowest margins of victory ever in a Texas election.

Governor Pease resigned, and, over the anguished protests of Hamilton and his followers, General Reynolds exhibited further favoritism to Davis by appointing him to the governorship on January 8, 1870, before his constitutional term began, and by convening the legislature on February 8. In a disputed contest it elected Morgan C. Hamilton, who was A. J. Hamilton's brother, and J. W. Flanagan to the United States Senate. The legislature also ratified the Thirteenth and Fourteenth Amendments; on March 30, 1870, President Grant signed the act readmitting Texas to the union; and on April 16, Reynolds formally transferred all authority to the civil government.

Radical Rule The Twelfth Legislature, which convened in three separate sessions during 1870 and 1871, was dominated by Davis and the Texas Radicals, partially because of Reynolds' partisanship. Sixteen of the thirty senators, including two Negroes, were identified as Radicals; fifty of the ninety members of the house, including nine Negroes, were Davis supporters. A program of legislation, called by the Democrats the Obnoxious Acts, was pushed through. The Speaker, Ira Evans, was removed because of his opposition to them. Thirteen moderate senators left the chamber before the vote in order to break the quorum, but they were placed under arrest and four of them were returned to reestablish the quorum.

There were five basic acts in this series. One created a state police force directly under the control of the governor, who was authorized to declare martial law at his discretion in any area in the state. A second act created a state militia, also under the governor's control, to be composed of all able-bodied males between the ages of eighteen and forty-five. A third postponed until November 1872 the congressional elections, which by the Constitution should have been held in the fall of 1870, and the state elections, which should have been held in 1871. A fourth, called the Enabling Act, authorized the governor to fill all vacant offices by appointments. There were more than eight thousand such offices, from those of local officials to Supreme Court justices. The fifth Obnoxious Act empowered the governor to designate a newspaper as official state printer and award it all of the public printing.

These acts gave Davis extraordinary executive powers. One argument of the revisionists is that he did not abuse these powers, at least not to the extent generally believed. The still unsettled conditions in Texas warranted the existence of a militia and the power to call it out. Whether Davis needed to declare martial law the four times he did—in Hill, Walker, Freestone, and Limestone counties—is moot, but that martial law aroused intense resentment among the citizens of those counties is incontestable. There was also a need for a state law enforcement agency; lawlessness was rampant in Texas: in a little over two years the State Police made more than thirteen hundred arrests for murder or attempted murder. Although Davis' State Police did include a large number of inexperienced freedmen, it also included L. H. McNelly's Special Force of Rangers, which consisted mostly of Confederate veterans and which was a highly effective law enforcement body. The State Police appeared at election polls, but it did not always harass the voters—there were times when it was needed to keep order. And although some freedmen on the force were arrogant and provoked trouble rather than dispelling it, most of them were not disruptive. As for the third Obnoxious Act, Davis gave way to public pressure and called for congressional, state, and local elections in October 1871. The justification for the act had been to make all state elections simultaneous, but it also gave the Radicals an extra year in power. As a consequence of holding the elections in October, Davis limited the extent of his appointive power under the Enabling Act, but under it he had spread his influence at least temporarily. The printing act assured Davis of a subservient press and a range of accusations from favoritism and patronage to peculation and misuse of public monies.

The Radicals have been sharply criticized for their generosity toward railroads. This, too, is an open question. The state's need for railroad construction was desperate; elsewhere in the nation federal legislation supported railroad construction by land grants. But Texas itself owned its public domain and had to support its own program of railroad building. The Constitution of 1869 prohibited land grants to railroads, so the legislature issued state bonds to encourage construction. Fifty-two charter or relief bills were passed for specific companies. One company was offered a ten-thousand-dollar bond subsidy for each mile of track constructed. When this was declared unconstitutional in 1875, the company accepted twenty sections of land for each mile of track. Davis vetoed a number of the railroad acts, but he approved one authorizing county and city bond issues to railroads. Despite the criticism that Davis was bankrupting the state by the issuance of internal improvement bonds, the local governments, many under Democratic control, voted over one million dollars worth of bonds for the same purpose. In 1873 a constitutional amendment authorized land grants to railroads, and the nature of railroad support changed.

Although the Radicals did not bankrupt the state by railroad bonds, they increased the state indebtedness by more than two million dollars and at the same time increased taxation. Whether this expenditure was profligate is a relative question. A Taxpayers' Convention held in Austin in 1871 entered vigorous protests, and of course the burden of the increased debt fell on taxpayers' shoulders in later administrations. But even for that era, a two-million-dollar indebtedness was not enormous, as goodly parts of it were incurred for developing the state's resources. For the vital defense of the frontier three-quarters of a million dollars in bonds were provided. Only about half of them were sold, however, and whether the funds were used beneficially has been difficult to determine.

It is equally difficult to make an accurate appraisal of the Davis regime. Some measures were clearly detrimental; some were obviously good, such as the homestead law for granting land to frontier settlers and the measures taken to support education. The majority of citizens opposed Davis, however, and there was a strong reaction against Radicalism as soon as his power was broken.

Reaction

The Election of Coke   The beginning of the end of Radical power was marked by the election of 1872 when Texans supported Horace Greeley for president over the incumbent Grant, elected Democrats for all six seats in congress, and restored control of the state legislature to the Democratic Party. When this legislature assembled in January

1873, it promptly repealed everything that was left of the Obnoxious Acts. It then embarked on a program of undoing the effects of Radicalism and prepared for a Democratic governor by simplifying voter registration procedures and limiting the election to a single day. The next election was set for the second Tuesday of December 1873.

The Democratic State Convention that met in Austin that September was the best attended of any up to that time: eight hundred delegates came from every county in the state. Richard Coke, a former captain in the Confederate Army, and Richard B. Hubbard, a former colonel, were nominated for governor and lieutenant governor. The convention endorsed a platform of governmental economy and a new state constitution. The Republicans nominated Davis for reelection and denounced the recent Democratic legislature. The hottest electoral fight in the history of Texas had begun.

Neither side was scrupulous in its ethics, either during the campaign or at the polls. There was no rigorous investigation after the election, but there is a general belief that there were numerous incidents of fraud and intimidation. As Rupert N. Richardson phrased it, "the genius of legality had forsaken the people." The Democratic majority was determined to resume control of the state. Coke won by 85,549 votes to Davis' 42,663. The total vote cast was twice that of any previous election for several reasons: the population of the state had increased, there was an uncommon amount of interest and excitement, and some voters were underage and some voted twice. A very interesting legal case arose out of the last reason.

When Joseph Rodriguez of Houston was accused of voting twice, Davis and the Radicals sought to invalidate the election by bringing it before the Texas Supreme Court. There Davis' attorneys argued not about the double voting but about the constitutionality of the legislative act that limited the election to one day. The constitution called for four-day elections. On the basis of the location of a semicolon in the constitutional clause, the court struck down the one-day election, and it was thereafter popularly called the Semicolon Court.

When the decision of the Semicolon Court invalidated the election, Governor Davis notified Coke and the newly elected state officials that they were to make no attempt to assume office. Davis' position was somewhat incongruous since he himself had signed the act establishing a one-day election. In an appeal to President Grant for assistance, he requested the support of federal troops to keep him in office. He was well aware that the majority of Texans were determined to inaugurate Coke. From near and far people were streaming into Austin—excited, angry, and deadly serious. Davis alerted his state police and ensconced himself in the capitol building protected by guards. Negro troops took possession of the old arsenal building, kidnapped the mayor, and imprisoned him there. If the crisis had erupted, the violence might have condemned Texas to at least two more years of Reconstruction and military rule. President Grant denied Davis' request for military support, but everyone was aware that an outbreak of civil disorder would bring down the wrath of congress.

Before dawn on the morning of January 13 a party of Democrats slipped past the sleeping guards in the basement of the capitol and took possession of the second floor by means of a ladder. There the newly elected legislature organized, counted the election returns, and on January 15 officially declared Coke elected. Davis, from his basement bastion, thereupon called out the Travis County Militia and ordered it to break up the legislature. The militia reported instead to Coke's adjutant general and stood guard over the basement stairs while Coke and Hubbard were inaugurated. Tensions continued to mount and tempers became ugly. A mob threatened to force its way into the basement, and another headed for the arsenal, but calmer heads averted violence. On the night of January 17 Davis slipped out of the capitol. For the rest of his life his name was anathema to most Texans, but he continued to lead the Republican Party and to practice law in Austin.

Coke and the New Constitution True to their major campaign promises, Coke and the Democrats practiced economy and set to work to create a new constitution. They increased the Supreme Court to five justices and replaced the three who had ruled against them in the Semicolon Case. Oran M. Roberts was named Chief Justice of the new Supreme Court. Thirty-five district judges appointed by Davis were removed on one pretext or another and supplanted by Coke's appointees, and many other state officials were similarly replaced. The reaction against Davis and Radical Republicanism was to be quite extreme.

To achieve economy confronted by rising governmental expenses was a baffling task. As has been mentioned, the railroad bonds were declared unconstitutional by the new court, and grants of land from the public domain were substituted. Operating expenses of the government were soon cut almost by half, and the tax rate was reduced substantially. Marked reduction of the public debt, however, was not to come for several years.

The making of a new constitution during Coke's tenure received great attention from state officials and the public. In his first message to the legislature the new governor pointed out, without advocating either method, that constitutional change could be made either by extensive amendments or by a new convention. The legislature, both from a desire for haste and from a fear that Grant and the Radicals in Washington might be antagonized by a new frame of government, first decided upon amendment. A joint committee of both houses was appointed in March 1874, and within three weeks it drafted a system of amendments so extensive as to form virtually a new constitution. The senate approved, but the house voted to postpone consideration until the next session. The argument against the amendments was that they had not been drafted by the traditional convention.

When the next session of the legislature met, Coke urged the lawmakers to issue a call for a constitutional convention. The legislature did so, and the election was held in August 1875. The electorate overwhelmingly endorsed the convention and selected ninety delegates from the thirty senatorial districts. Of these, seventy-five were Democrats, and fifteen were Republicans, including six Negroes. There were more farmers than any other occupational group; lawyers were second; the other occupations represented included merchants, physicians, and newspaper editors. The capable and distinguished group included John H. Reagan, former postmaster general of the Confederacy; John Henry Brown, a diehard Confederate recently returned from self-exile in Mexico; two former United States congressmen; one former Confederate congressman; Charles DeMorse, the outspoken editor of the Clarksville *Standard*; and N. H. Darnell, a member of the Convention of 1845. Most important, over forty delegates belonged to the Grange, an agrarian protest movement then in its infancy which was to be the greatest influence, next to the reaction against Radicalism, in the shaping of the new document.

The Patrons of Husbandry, the proper name of the Grange, had been organized in 1867 by a clerk in the United States Department of Agriculture in order to alleviate through cooperative effort the economic conditions of poor farmers in the South and West. With many of the trappings of a secret fraternal order, it had a four-point program offering farm families happier home lives, more social contacts, better educational opportunities, and cooperation in financial affairs. The individual clubs or lodges called Granges had patron, matron, and juvenile memberships. The rapidly growing organization reached Texas in 1873. In 1876 the Texas State Grange claimed 40,000 members in 1,275 local affiliates. Although they disavowed partisan politics, naturally their size made them influential, and a few years later the Grangers organized the Greenback Party in Texas to express their political ideology. At the time of the Convention of 1875, however, their politics was just beginning to crystallize.

Another factor that influenced the attitudes of the delegates to the convention was the Panic of 1873, which struck the nation after the failure of Jay Cooke's banking firm and which wrought significant hardships in agrarian regions. The sum of the recent Radical expenditures plus the

Grangers plus the depression was a mandate for retrenchment and economy.

The delegates set their own stipends at $5 a day, which was $3 less than members of the legislature, refused to hire a stenographer to take the proceedings when one could not be found for less than $10 a day, and refused to print the proceedings because of the expense. In the new constitution they reduced the governor's annual salary from $5,000 to $4,000 and the principal state officers to $2,000, cut the legislators' salaries to $5 a day for the first sixty days and $3 a day thereafter to discourage extra sessions, and set Supreme Court justices' compensations at $3,500. Such parsimony was probably unwarranted and may have discouraged competent men from taking state jobs. The legislature was to meet in biennial rather than annual sessions, was not to incur an indebtedness greater than $200,000, and was not to exceed income in appropriation bills.

These last provisions were reflections more of the reaction to Radicalism than of economy. Further evidence of that reaction and the fear of centralized power were the severe restrictions placed on legislation in the constitution, the abolishment of the central education bureau and of the highway agency, the reduction in the governor's powers, and the increase in elective rather than appointive offices—all judges, from the Supreme Court down, were to be elected. In reaction against the centralized government created by the Constitution of 1869, many specific provisions of the new constitution should have been left to the discretion of later legislatures.

As a consequence, of course, the instrument was the longest in the state's history. It is indeed one of the longest state constitutions in the nation, is probably one of the worst, and, anomalously, has been longest in use. Constitutional legislation has continued for nearly a century, several amendments being submitted to voters at almost every election. By 1970 the constitution had been amended nearly two hundred times, with almost twice that many submitted. Despite consistent agitation during the twentieth century for a new constitution, Texas voters are satisfied with the much-amended patchwork that serves as their frame of government. One thing can be said to its credit: there is a popular referendum on almost every significant question.

The Constitution of 1876 contained, of course, many other important provisions: one-half of the public domain, about forty-two million acres of land, was added to the public school fund; one million acres of land, later discovered to be rich in oil, were granted as an endowment for the yet uncreated University of Texas; railroads were declared to be common carriers, and laws for their regulation were authorized; grants of money to aid railroad construction were prohibited, but grants of land were authorized; homestead grants of one hundred sixty acres to settlers were established; and a lengthy and explicit "bill of rights" specifically stated that the writ of habeas corpus could never be suspended (a reaction to Lincoln's autocratic suspension during the war, which had become an important Reconstruction issue).

Although there was some dissatisfaction with the finished document, ratification was a foregone conclusion, so great was the hostility toward the Radical constitution. The economy-minded convention was in session for only eleven weeks, and on February 15, 1876, the new constitution was adopted by a vote of 136,606 to 56,652.

The Status of the Negro   Emancipation came to Texas later and more suddenly than it had to the other southern states because there had been no federal occupation or control in any part of Texas until Granger's landing on June 19, 1865. Neither the Negroes nor their former masters were at all prepared for their new roles. There was confusion and misunderstanding on both sides. Many Negroes and whites believed that emancipation would not become effective until after harvest time, perhaps in December. A rumor circulated widely among Negroes that they would then each be given forty acres and a mule.

The Freedmen's Bureau, which had been created by congress in 1865 to aid in the adjustment, established headquarters in Galveston at the same time Granger did. During its first year it was a worthwhile organization. It gave aid to freedmen in a variety of ways and encouraged them to remain working on the farms, provided the former owners signed the required work contracts, but few of the former owners complied with this regulation.

The greater part of the freedmen did remain, however, in the service of their former masters, and it is to the credit of both groups that the confusion was kept to a minimum. Most Negroes were unprepared to assume responsibility for themselves. Not only were they without education and in the main illiterate, but also they were almost devoid of general information. They did not understand the value of the wages they received, had no idea of the cost of food or clothes or where to purchase either, and could not grasp the idea of paying rent for the quarters where they had always lived. Most Texans approached the transition with at least moderate patience. Many former masters simply carried the Negroes' wages and expenses in account books and introduced the freedmen to their responsibilities gradually. Many freedmen responded in their new roles with remarkable acumen and cooperated in the transition.

Some slaveholders simply turned the freedmen out and refused to provide their food, clothing, or shelter. Some did this out of petulance, others out of financial necessity. And some Negroes tried to burst into their new positions like bombshells, with little regard for the responsibilities entailed. Many Negroes left the farms and villages and either roamed the countryside or headed for the cities. Their hunger and lack of clothing and shelter created a major problem for the Freedmen's Bureau. In December 1865 two investigations of conditions among the freedmen were made. One, by an inspector general of the army, found that many Negroes did not know they were free and that conditions were worse than they had ever been. The other, by E. M. Gregory, chief of the Freedmen's Bureau in Texas, found that ninety per cent of the former slaves were under work contracts paying from eight to fifteen dollars a month plus room, board, and clothing, and that only sixty-seven freedmen were on full relief. Actual conditions were probably somewhere between these two extremes.

It was obvious that the major problem was a complete lack of education. Bureau agents held sessions in their offices and gave talks to explain some of the complications and responsibilities of freedom. Elementary schools and programs to teach reading were established. By the middle of 1867 there were over one hundred elementary schools with nearly five thousand pupils. Some freedmen did not understand that they had to continue working despite their freedom, and an educational campaign was directed at correcting this growing misconception.

The Convention of 1866 discussed extensively the legal status of the freedmen. Most of the delegates opposed Negro suffrage; a few believed it should be granted to literate freedmen only; and the Radicals, who planned to base political power on the Negro vote, demanded full suffrage and equal rights. Without consideration of the moral issues involved, it is clear that many of the freedmen were unable to exercise full responsible citizenship immediately after their manumission. All of the southern states during the period of Presidential Reconstruction adopted Black Codes, which abridged the freedom and the citizenship of the freedmen. In Texas they could own property (and be taxed) but could not vote. They could testify in court or serve as jurors only when other Negroes were involved in the circumstances of the case before the court.

Congressional Reconstruction swept away the Black Codes and assured voting privileges to all freedmen, first by congressional fiat, then by the Fourteenth Amendment. The voter registration of 1868 included almost as many Negroes as whites in Texas. But Negro suffrage became a major issue in the developing racial friction, and the whites who were determined to prevent it resorted to threats and acts of intimidation. Furthermore, the character of the Freedmen's Bureau began to change. Originally created for one year, in 1867 it was recreated by the Radical Congress on an indefinite basis, and many of the original agents were replaced. The political stepchild of the new Freedmen's Bureau was the Loyal Union League, designed to spread political propaganda among untutored Negro voters. The many white Texans and other white southerners who theretofore had regarded the new freedmen as children and wards now began to regard them as competitors and enemies.

During the Radical regime under Davis, Negroes in general exercised their right to vote. A few were elected to state offices, and Davis appointed others to various positions. The use of Negro troops in the United States Army and in Davis' state police added fuel to the racial fires. Nonetheless, during the half-dozen years after emancipation the freedmen began to adjust themselves to their new status and its problems. Predictably, most found themselves on the lowest rung of the economic ladder, a situation that has not improved rapidly over the last hundred years.

The 1876 constitution accepted the Thirteenth and Fourteenth Amendments and made no attempt to discriminate by race or to restrict suffrage. But after the overthrow of Radical rule Negroes tended to stay away from the polls because of local pressures acting upon apathy and disinterest. When they did vote, they usually cast ballots for Republican Party candidates and in effect thereby lost their votes. The more industrious and competent among the freedmen began slowly to establish themselves in fields other than farm labor. Some became skilled craftsmen, some went into business, and a few ventured north for professional educations. But most remained on the farms, where improvement in their condition was slow. Contract labor gave way to tenant farming and sharecropping. The last system made them somewhat more independent of white supervision but tended to keep them economically bound to the soil. A few Negroes became property owners, and during the next decade some moved west to homestead or work in the cattle industry.

Lawlessness

The Aftermath of War In the confusion after the Civil War there was an outbreak of disorder, which at times became complete lawlessness. The state government virtually collapsed when Murrah fled with other officials to Mexico. The ineffectiveness or lack of local law enforcement agencies encouraged the renegade bush soldiers, deserters who had begun to plague the state even before war's end. Many returning Confederate veterans who had lost all they possessed did not stick at outright larceny as they trudged in dreary groups back to their homes. A few reckless bands of freedmen began to roam the countryside for loot and plunder. And even ordinary citizens hazarded the wanton game of grab-what's-loose.

The first targets of theft were government warehouses where goods belonging to the state or the Confederacy were stored. Many returning veterans took the attitude that Confederate property belonged to them. County sheriffs were ordered to take possession of all government property in the state, but they were largely helpless to do so. Storehouse after storehouse was ransacked for clothes, food, and blankets. On May 23, 1865, a mob consisting mostly of former soldiers looted an ordnance storehouse in Houston. Before the day was over, a troop of soldiers who had missed out on the plunder threatened to sack the town, but the mayor finally placated them by arranging a free banquet. Soon the pillage spread from government depots to private warehouses. In San Antonio a band of former soldiers possessed themselves of a stock of luxury goods on the flimsy excuse that the storekeeper had profited excessively from cotton speculation. Equally weak was the excuse of a woman in Austin who joined in sacking a storebuilding because she "had never realized anything from the war." All through the demoralized state spread the disease. Perhaps the most flagrant case was the robbery of the State Treasury in Austin on June 11, 1865. Brigands stormed the old building during the night, hoping to steal a reported $300,00 in specie. An alarm was raised, and a group of vigilantes drove the thieves away before they had completed the burglary, although it was estimated that they made off with between $1,500 and $2,000.

When federal troops occupied Texas they took possession of what was left of military property. General Granger attempted to restore a semblance of order, as did the provisional governor Hamilton. But it was well over six months before the average citizen felt any sense of security. Meantime there were various outbreaks of violence and something of a degenerate Robin-Hood kind of lawlessness. A few bands of former soldiers, many of them recruited from the bush soldiers, found that their activities were condoned by some citizens because they were resisting federal authority. The most flagrant example of this occurred in East Texas. Cullen Baker, dubbed "the Swamp Fox of the Sulphur," was a deserter from the Confederate Army who joined the Federals in 1864 but was forced to flee after he allegedly killed a Negro freedman. He roamed in Arkansas with a plundering band of bush soldiers until the end of the war. Wanted for at least three murders, he returned to Texas to hide out in the swamps of the Sulphur River. When federal occupation forces tried to bring him to justice and posted rewards for his capture, he suddenly became a champion of the lost cause. Aided by many citizens of East Texas, Baker robbed federal wagon trains, shot at soldiers from ambush, and once taunted the Yankees in their East Texas headquarters. He evaded capture until 1869, when he was killed by an irate group of men who could no longer abide his arrogant lawlessness.

Activities like Baker's soon gave rise to another form of disorder and violence, almost inevitable under the circumstances: clashes between soldiers and civilians. In Bell County an alleged horse thief named Lindley persuaded military authorities to arrest two men who he feared would testify against him. Lindley's pretext was that he was a unionist and the two men were such violent secessionists that they had hanged his son. Then while the falsely accused men were under military guard, Lindley shot them in cold blood. Although he was indicted for murder, the military authorities refused to permit a trial by civilian courts for fear of prejudice, and they later acquitted him in a military tribunal. The resultant furor created a major rupture between the army and the citizens of the county. Another episode occurred in Brenham in September 1866, when a troop of drunken soldiers broke up a Negro dance and wounded two freedmen. The officer in charge arrested two citizens, and other troops under the pretext of investigation sacked a liquor store and set fire to a downtown building. Despite the evidence and an indictment by the local grand jury, military authorities exonerated all the federal troops involved and promoted the officer in charge. Little wonder civilian wrath began to mount!

The often arrogant activities of the Radical regime and E. J. Davis' State Police fueled the increasing disrespect for the law. According to W. C. Nunn, an historian of this period, members of the State Police murdered two men in DeWitt County, created a disturbance resulting in the death of another in Waco, and caused trouble in Brown, Nacogdoches, Smith, and Bastrop counties. Nunn wrote in the *Handbook of Texas*, "They broke up Democratic political meetings, patrolled election polling places, stuffed ballot boxes, entered private homes without warrant, made false arrests, and permitted prisoners to escape from the penitentiary at Huntsville." In 1872 the head of the State Police, James Davidson, absconded to Belgium with an estimated $37,430 of state funds.

Governor Davis did little to alleviate the explosive situation. In 1871 he expanded the size of the State Police force and exercised his powers under the Obnoxious Acts by declaring martial law on four separate occasions, none of which the citizens thought was warranted. A reexamination of the work of the State Police indicates that there were many things to their credit despite the popular belief. In the first place, lawlessness was rampant throughout the state, and a strong law enforcement agency was needed. Of the nearly four thousand arrests made not all were fraudulent. The State Police successfully quelled riots in the towns of Burton and Madisonville. And L. H. McNelly's famous Ranger force began as a company of the State Police. McNelly was a former Confederate captain from Washington County and a man of remarkable determination and daring. When the State Police force was created in July 1870, he accepted one of the four posts as captain and served until the force was disbanded in 1873. Much of his company was made up of former Confederates. McNelly's company aided greatly in stemming the tide of lawlessness in South and West Texas and could hardly be accused of Radical villainies.

So great was the lawlessness after the war that for several weeks the Convention of 1869 debated how to combat it. But for nearly a decade not the convention, nor the State Police, nor the local constabulary could bring it under control. Until there were a stable government and law officers respected and supported by the people, feuders and gunfighters flourished and captured the public imagination.

Feudin' and Fightin' It would be an error to blame the rise of violence, particularly the killing, solely on the lack of respect for law generated by the State Police, the federal occupation troops, and the Radicals. Texas, like most other frontier regions, had always had a reputation for brawling, dueling, and gunfighting, which the perversity of Texas humor tended to exaggerate. The several causes of the increase of lawlessness in Texas were the natural proclivities of a frontier region, the breakdown of government, the military and Radical rules, the development of widespread use of sidearms such as the revolver, and the great boom in the open-range cattle industry. But the bloodiest feud in Texas history was a direct result of Reconstruction: the Sutton-Taylor feud.

It began in a shooting affray in 1867 at a Mason saloon when Hays Taylor shot and killed a federal soldier who insulted him and then gunned down a Major Thompson who tried to arrest him. Hays and his brother Doboy hid from arrest. The following March, Deputy Sheriff William Sutton killed Charles Taylor, possibly a remote cousin, in Bastrop while searching for horse thieves, and later that year Sutton shot Buck Taylor in a dispute over the sale of a horse. In August 1869 Hays Taylor was ambushed and killed, and the feud was on, with nearly all of DeWitt County, where the Taylors lived, taking sides. Captain Jack Helm of Davis' State Police rode into the county and permitted his men to assassinate without reason the two Kelly brothers, both of whom were brothers-in-law to the Taylors. Helm was dismissed from the force and was replaced by William

Sutton. In 1872 Sutton's men killed Pitkin Taylor. Pitkin's son Jim revenged his death by shooting first one of Sutton's lieutenants and then Jack Helm. In the spring of 1874, after the State Police was disbanded, Jim and his brother Bill bushwhacked Sutton as he was preparing to leave the state. But this did not end the feud. The Sutton clan charged three of the Taylors with cattle theft and lynched them before the year was out. Shortly thereafter Bill Taylor gunned down the new leader of the Suttons. Then Jim Taylor was killed in December 1875. At this point the senseless slaughter came to an end, but it was only a nominal end to the feud, for the Suttons had gained control of the law enforcement machinery in DeWitt County. In 1876 eight people affiliated with the Suttons were arrested for the murder of a Dr. Phillip Brassell, and the litigation lasted twenty years.

Other feuds of the time, just as bitter if not as bloody, were the Early-Halsey feud in Bell County from 1865 to 1869, the Lea-Peacock feud in North Texas from 1867 to 1871, the Harrell-Higgins feud in Lampasas County in 1877 and the Hoodoo War in Mason County in 1875. The first two had roots in Reconstruction; the last two grew out of the cattle industry. During the same period other feuds broke out sporadically. Whatever the origins of these affairs, the inefficiency of the law enforcement machinery—officers and courts—was the catalyst. Soon after the organization of the Texas Rangers, the feuding was greatly reduced by these indefatigable men, although feuding continued in Texas into the twentieth century.

Possibly the bitterest of the feuds—not properly a feud but a small political war—was the Salt War. There are extensive dry salt lakes in northern El Paso County, where in 1863 a small commercial development began. In 1866 Samuel Maverick of San Antonio acquired title to the land and, under the Constitution of 1866, the minerals thereon. But his claim was found not to cover all of the salt lakes, and two opposing factions arose in El Paso: the Salt Ring filed claim to the remainder of the deposits, and the Anti-Salt Ring ostensibly sought to place them under the control of a public board of trustees. But actually the Anti-Salt Ring seems to have been trying to acquire the rights for a priest named Borrajo and a Republican state senator named A. J. Fountain. Intrigue and conspiracy led to the murder of a district judge, the resignation of Senator Fountain, and the reassignment of Father Borrajo. Control of the Borrajo faction passed to Charles H. Howard, who filed a counterclaim to the land and the deposits in his own name. Howard's announcement in 1877 that all trespassers on the property would be arrested was met with rioting and chaos. Howard was kidnapped by a mob and forced to sign a forfeiture of his claim, but as soon as he was free, he shot and killed the leader of his opponents. Arrested, then released on bond, he attempted with the aid of an inept Ranger lieutenant to reassert his claim. Howard and the Rangers were suddenly besieged at the Ranger station at San Elizario by a large band of men, many of them Mexicans from across the Rio Grande who by custom had been helping themselves to the salt. To save the Rangers, Howard offered himself as a hostage. He and two of his associates were placed before an impromptu firing squad and killed. In retaliation a posse of American citizens from El Paso attacked the Mexicans at San Elizario, killed four of them, and drove the remainder across the river. The denouement of the affair included a congressional investigation, a diplomatic exchange between the United States and Mexico, and the reestablishment of Fort Bliss in El Paso. Thereafter, no open attempt was made to subvert private ownership of the salt deposits.

During this post-war lawlessness several outlaws won enduring infamy as lone gunfighters, many of them becoming folk heroes. Among these killers were John Wesley Hardin, Bill Longley, Ben Thompson, and Sam Bass.

Hardin was probably the most ruthless of them all, although his murders have frequently been defended in the court of history as justifiable self-defense, and he has sometimes been interpreted as a good man who was misunderstood. The son of a Methodist preacher, he was fifteen years old when he killed his first man—in self-defense. Then and thereafter through some thirty killings, supposedly all in self-defense, it was his boast that he "never killed a man who didn't need killing." At the age of seventeen he left home with seven notches in his gun to join a trail herd to Kansas. He killed six men on the way north, three more in Abilene, and had added four more before he surrendered to the law in 1872. He broke out of jail, became involved in the Sutton-Taylor feud, and killed the deputy sheriff of Brown County in 1874. He fled to Alabama and then to Florida, killing six and possibly eight more men before he was tracked down by a Texas Ranger in Pensacola. He was convicted of the murder of Charles Webb and sentenced to a twenty-five year term in 1878, but he was pardoned in 1894. A year after his release he was shot in the back by a constable in El Paso.

William Preston Longley lacked Hardin's romantic aura. During 1867 and 1868 he killed four freedmen on one pretext or another, but he was arrested and hanged for cattle theft. He escaped death by faulty execution, joined Cullen Baker's gang, shot a soldier at Fort Leavenworth, escaped to join a gang of counterfeiters, and then returned to Texas, where he killed at least two more men. He was finally caught, tried, and executed in 1878 with a known record of thirty-two murders.

Ben Thompson may have been the most vicious killer of them all, yet his career captured the curious idolization of the public. He was a thirteen-year-old boy when he shot a playmate in Austin. Although the number of his killings is not definite, "Bat" Masterson, marshal of Dodge City, said of him, "It is doubtful if in his time there was another man living who equalled him with a pistol in a life and death struggle." Thompson was also a gambler and a cardsharp, and after a series of incredible adventures he returned to Austin, where he opened the celebrated Iron Front Saloon on Congress Avenue. In 1880 he was elected city marshal by the admiring citizens. In 1882 he killed the owner of a theater in San Antonio, was tried and acquitted, and was triumphantly welcomed back to Austin by a city-wide reception. Two years later he was assassinated in the same San Antonio theater.

More a folk-hero than even Ben Thompson was Sam Bass, a bold highwayman rather than a killer, who hit stagecoaches, trains, and banks, and whose free spending made him appear a nineteenth-century Robin Hood. In 1878 Bass was tracked down in Round Rock by John B. Jones, commander of the Texas Rangers, partially through the treachery of one of Bass' accomplices. This, of course, enhanced the false pathos of the Sam Bass legend, which has been crystallized in poem and song. Sam Bass, who died of wounds the day after the shoot-out at Round Rock, has found immortality, not as thief and killer but as a kind and generous person "of the type you scarcely ever see," according to an old folk song.

In Texas and on the cattle trails north, lesser gunmen and killers were pursued by their nemeses, fearlessly determined Texas Rangers such as John B. Jones and L. H. McNelly.

The Texas Rangers   The great historian Walter Prescott Webb wrote in the *Handbook of Texas*,

> Texas never needed the Rangers more than it did immediately following Reconstruction. Civil affairs were in chaos as a result of five years of war and nine of flagrant misrule. The Indians, though weakened, still threatened and harried the western settlements, while bandit raids and cattle theft kept the Mexican border in constant turmoil. Inside the state cattle and horse thieves formed organized gangs, while feudists carried on private war, and stage and train robbery flourished.

One of the first actions of Governor Richard Coke and the newly elected legislature of 1874 was the reestablishment of the Texas Rangers in two distinct commands: the Frontier Battalion under Major John B. Jones and the Special Force of Rangers under Captain L. H. McNelly.

Jones, with six companies, was sent to defend the western frontier; McNelly was sent to South Texas to stop cattle raids from across the border and to restore law and order in some of the South Texas counties.

McNelly, a frail and soft-spoken man, has become almost the archetype of the Texas Ranger as a law enforcement officer, in the same way that Jack Hays epitomized the Rangers of the Republic as an Indian fighter. McNelly was a Confederate veteran who had incongruously been a captain in Davis' State Police. He was thirty years old when he organized the Special Force, and three years later he died at his home in Washington County of tuberculosis, the debilitating effects of which he had apparently been suffering for some time. But the three years, 1874 to 1877, made him immortal.

His principal assignment was to break up the cattle rustling on the Rio Grande boundary. There gangs of Mexican thieves were regularly raiding Texas ranches and had driven hundreds upon hundreds of head across the river, the international line beyond which the bandits were safe from the wrath of the Texas ranchers. Such wholesale rustling could not have existed without a market and without the tacit protection of Mexican authorities. It had both in General Juan Flores of the Mexican Army and his partner Juan N. Cortina, former governor of Tamaulipas. This was the same Cortina who had caused the so-called Cortina War in 1859 by shooting a marshal in Brownsville and aiding a prisoner to escape. Although this episode was shrouded in the Mexican-American friction, Cortina had already established himself as a bad man, a murderer, and a thief. But he became a folk champion of the Hispanic element on both sides of the river around Brownsville, where his mother's family were wealthy landowners. And it was this same brigand whom John S. Ford had fought and finally come to terms with during the war. Joining the Juárez revolution, Cortina proclaimed himself governor of Tamaulipas in 1864 and retained the post for two years despite his twice changing his political allegiance.

Cortina and Flores operated their illicit cattle business from 1866 until 1875, but they met their match in McNelly and his thirty Rangers. In November 1875, angrily ignoring the international line, the Rangers chased a gang of thieves and seventy-five head of cattle across the river at Las Cuevas to raid what McNelly thought was Cortina's ranch headquarters but was actually Flores'. Greatly outnumbered, the Rangers ambushed Flores' troops near the river and forced the bandit leader to agree to return the stolen cattle. At the appointed time, the Mexicans showed up with seventy-five head, but they challenged McNelly to prove they were the stolen animals. Exasperated, the Rangers again crossed into Mexico and, although again outnumbered, threatened to kill every Mexican in sight if the cattle were not driven across immediately. Delivery was made within five minutes. Meantime, General O. C. Ord had been conducting an extensive investigation of the border lawlessness and had filed his report through diplomatic channels. Consequently, Cortina had been arrested by the Mexican government in July, before the Las Cuevas episode. McNelly's daring raid signaled the beginning of the end to organized rustling across the border.

More significant than McNelly's Special Force was the Frontier Battalion under Major Jones. Soon after the battalion was authorized, this unusually competent leader had six companies in the field. During the first year and a half of its existence, the Frontier Battalion had twenty-one skirmishes with marauding Indians on the frontier. It was largely due to the Frontier Battalion's efforts in cooperating with the United States Cavalry in West Texas that the Indians were finally placed on reservations. From 1876 to 1900 the Rangers of the Frontier Battalion were the principal law enforcement officers in the state. They settled the Mason County War, the Kimble County War, the Harrell-Higgins feud, the Salt War, and many other civil disturbances. They captured such notorious gunmen as Hardin, Longley, and Sam Bass. The Texas Rangers, like the Canadian Mounted Police, became known throughout the world as one of the most respected law enforcement agencies, admired to the point of adulation even today in story, movie, and television. But little that scriptwriters can dream up rivals the actual history of the brave men of the Frontier Battalion.

Although Jones and his men were expert with rifle and pistol, they quelled most of the disturbances by force of character. Jones and his men arrested forty bandits in Kimble County in 1877 without firing a shot—an almost incredible feat in view of the previous bloodshed there. That same year with only ten men Jones moved in on the Harrell-Higgins feud in Lampasas County and without firing a shot arrested fourteen leaders of the Harrell gang; and three days later Jones arrested the principals of the Higgins band without even drawing his gun. This kind of cool daring gave rise to the apocryphal tale of the West Texas town which after being terrorized for weeks by two gangs of desperadoes urgently wired the governor to send the Rangers. The anxious citizens who gathered at the depot to meet the promised assistance were dismayed when a single Ranger got off the train. Asked where the rest of his men were, the Ranger laconically replied, "You ain't got but one fight, have you?"

Major Jones became adjutant general in 1879 and died in 1881. Soon afterward his original captains—men like George Baylor and George W. Arrington, the Iron Man of the Panhandle—had resigned, but the Rangers lived on, their unique spirit and morale impressing itself upon later volunteers. By the mid-eighties the Rangers, as one man said, had made Texas "a relatively safe place to live." Because of the Rangers, the gunmen and fast-draw artists of the last part of the century avoided Texas whenever they could, and when they did visit the state, they stayed scrupulously out of trouble.

The way was clear for the settlement of the western frontier.

10

The Frontier

Indian Wars and Buffalo Hunters

The War Years At the onset of secession and war, the frontier line of organized counties ran northwest from Nueces County on the coast to Uvalde County west of San Antonio and then bent slightly to the northeast to Clay County on the Red River. The waves of mid-nineteenth-century civilization lapped along this line to the east, and a handful of hardy stock raisers had settled to the west of it under the meager protection of the chain of military posts. After the federal forces were withdrawn from these posts, the legislature authorized each of the thirty-seven frontier counties to establish its own militia company for the protection of the frontier. Since the greatest danger was from the Comanches, the Confederate Indian agent Albert Pike negotiated a treaty with them and their allies the Kiowas, promising to maintain an agency for them north of the Red River in return for the Indians' peaceful utilization of the hunting grounds in West Texas.

But before the year was out, Texans knew full well that there would be no peace on the frontier. To replace the militia companies, the legislature created the Frontier Regiment of ten mounted companies. James M. Norris, commissioned as colonel of this regiment in January 1862, was able to organize only nine companies, with a total strength of 1,089 men, who were usually called Rangers. After an inspection tour, Norris shortened the line of defense by moving it inside the former line of federal posts and establishing a chain of eighteen Ranger camps from the Rio Grande to the upper Trinity. Each company was assigned two camps, with approximately fifty men in each camp. A system of patrols between camps was intended to prevent Indian invasions. The effort was futile.

The Comanches, already aware of the weakened defenses, destroyed the Confederate agency in October 1862 and swept into West Texas, raiding and pillaging. It was easy for them to slip past the patrols and depredate isolated homesteads. The following year when J. E. McCord became commander of the Frontier Regiment, he replaced the patrols with sporadic scouting expeditions. This tactic was more successful, but it did not stem the tide: the frontier was pushed eastward by approximately one tier of counties. Throughout the troubled region, frontier families "forted up" in small groups for self-protection, as thousands of head of cattle and horses were lost and scores of farmsteads were burned.

Early in 1864 the Frontier Regiment was transferred to Confederate service, and the greater part of it was sent to East Texas. The legislature reverted to a reliance upon local militia companies. But the state was unable to equip or to supply these units, and there was considerable difficulty in recruiting men for them. In December 1864, James W. Throckmorton was named brigadier general with authorization to reorganize the northwest frontier. He successfully assembled about fourteen hundred men in twenty-six companies. In February 1865 Throckmorton tried to carry the fighting to the Indians' home ground by sending a force of five hundred into present Oklahoma, where the Indians had been gathering to make war against federal troops in New Mexico. A few months earlier, on November 26, 1864, a major battle had taken place between federal troops under Colonel Kit Carson and a large winter encampment of Comanches and Kiowas at Adobe Walls in the Texas Panhandle.

Adobe Walls, established in 1843 on the South Canadian River by William Bent, had been abandoned because of Indian hostility and had fallen into a ruin, which had become a well-known landmark on the plains. Two major Indian engagements were fought there: this one between Carson and the Indians known as the First Battle of Adobe Walls and one in 1874 between buffalo hunters and Indians known as the Second Battle of Adobe Walls. Carson, a prominent mountaineer, fur trapper, and guide, was ordered to attack the winter headquarters of the

THE FRONTIER

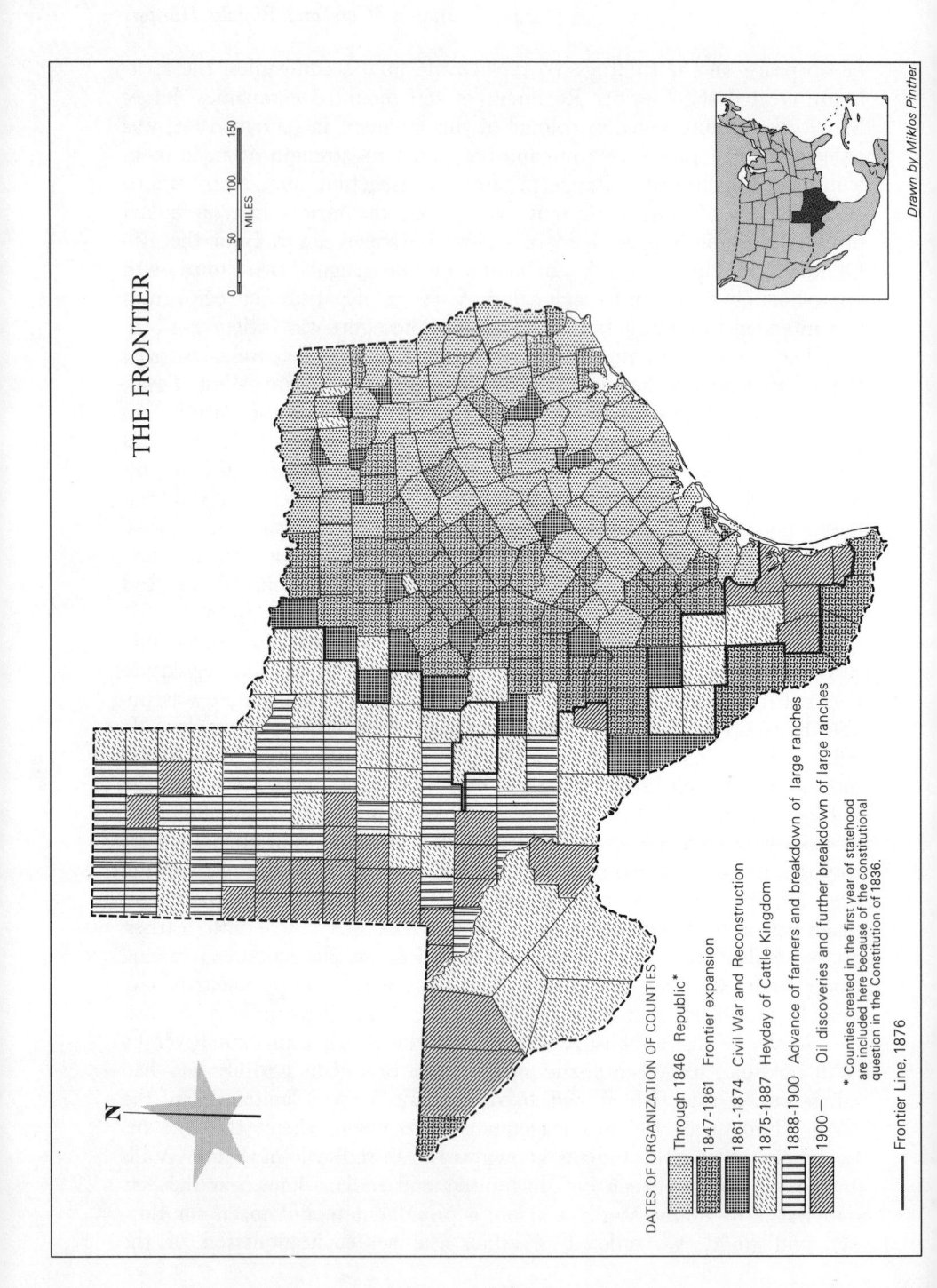

DATES OF ORGANIZATION OF COUNTIES

- Through 1846 Republic*
- 1847-1861 Frontier expansion
- 1861-1874 Civil War and Reconstruction
- 1875-1887 Heyday of Cattle Kingdom
- 1888-1900 Advance of farmers and breakdown of large ranches
- 1900— Oil discoveries and further breakdown of large ranches

*Counties created in the first year of statehood are included here because of the constitutional question in the Constitution of 1836.

——— Frontier Line, 1876

Drawn by Miklos Pinther

242

Indians who had been plaguing settlements in New Mexico. This little-known engagement was the most successful hit-and-run raid ever made on a large party of Plains Indians. Encamped in several villages along the breaks of the river were an estimated three to seven thousand Indians. Carson had fewer than four hundred men. After attacking a Comanche village, he ensconced his men with two mounted howitzers at the ruins of Adobe Walls, held off repeated forays, and slipped out the next morning, leaving a Kiowa village in flames and scores of Indians dead and wounded. The Indians were so taken aback by this startling defeat that they sued the Confederates for peace in February 1865 in order to avoid fighting on two fronts. The treaty, negotiated by Throckmorton, came to naught when the Confederacy collapsed.

A second major Indian battle during the Civil War was fought on Dove Creek, about sixteen miles southwest of present San Angelo. On January 8, 1865, Captain Henry Fossett with three hundred seventy militia men attacked a party of fourteen hundred nonhostile Kickapoo Indians under the impression that they were Comanches. The Kickapoos were skirting the settlements on their way from Indian Territory to Mexico. The routed Texans lost thirty-six killed and sixty wounded whereas the Indians lost eleven dead and thirty-one wounded.

The Postwar Decade After the war and the federal occupation of Texas, residents of the frontier expected the United States Army to reopen the frontier posts for protection against marauding Indians. Perhaps this was too much to ask of their erstwhile enemies; in any event, it was several years before peace came to the frontier. Federal troops were concentrated for the most part in posts along the Mexican border because France had disregarded the Monroe Doctrine during the Civil War in establishing Maximilian and Carlotta on a new throne in Mexico. Before the American government could take action, the Mexican people under the leadership of Benito Juárez deposed their foreign rulers.

Meantime, however, the western frontier of Texas was ravished as never before by savage Comanche and Kiowa raids. Complete data on the devastation were not gathered at the time, but a few examples suggest the situation. The population of Wise County was reduced approximately by half; a large group of citizens from Denton County threatened in October 1866 to abandon their homes; a report for twelve months of 1865 and 1866 stated that the Indians had killed seventy-eight Texans, wounded seven, and captured eighteen; a raid was reported on the outskirts of Gainesville; and the Waco paper in April 1866 warned that Comanches were roaming at will in the surrounding countryside. A government agent reported that a single encampment of Kwahadi Comanches near present Quitaque had in its possession some fifteen thousand horses, several hundred mules, and innumerable cattle. A later report made by Governor Throckmorton informed the legislature that between May 1865 and July 1867 Indians had killed one hundred sixty-two people, wounded twenty-four, and captured forty-three. Repeatedly and desperately the governor pleaded with federal Reconstruction authorities for help. The legislature even authorized a state force to be commanded by federal officers, but General Sheridan negated it.

In October 1867 federal agents with leaders of the Kiowa and Comanche Indians signed the important Treaty of Medicine Lodge Creek, which established a three-million acre reservation in present southwest Oklahoma and which promised the Indians annuities for their support. The treaty did not bring peace to the frontier because the government was slow to establish the agency and provide the promised supplies and because hundreds of the fiercest of the Comanches and Kiowas scorned to become wards of the government. They much preferred their nomadic existence on the western plains and prairies of Texas. Furthermore, they were enjoying a fairly lucrative barter commerce with New Mexico traders called Comanchéros, who traded trinkets, weapons, jewelry, and sometimes specie to the Indians for horses and cattle stolen from Texas farms and ranches. The scope of their illicit trade was fairly extensive, and it unquestionably spurred Comanche depredations. In 1872 one irate Texas rancher, John Hittson, with the permission of Governor E. J. Davis led a raid into the Mora Valley of New Mexico and recovered some six thousand head of stolen livestock. A later congressional committee, after an extensive investigation into their claims, awarded thousands of dollars in compensation to Texas stock raisers.

During the latter part of 1867 through the year 1868 the War Department reestablished a line of defense in Texas. A number of the older posts were reoccupied, and several new ones were built, the most important being Fort Concho and Fort Griffin. Scouting parties were sent out during the full moon, known to westerners as the "Comanche moon" because it was at this time that Comanches struck the heaviest. Despite these efforts, there was little abatement in the raids. The posts were too far apart to give real protection, and the troops were too inexperienced, most of them being Negroes called "buffalo soldiers."

Matters were not helped when in 1869 President U. S. Grant fatuously permitted the implementation of a new "Quaker peace policy" patterned after the method that William Penn had successfully practiced two centuries earlier with the eastern woodlands Indian. Quakers were employed as Indian agents throughout the West, and Lawrie Tatum, a sincere and devoted man, was made Comanche agent on the new reservation. Tatum discovered to his dismay that the Lords of the South Plains were hopelessly intractable and that only armed force would command their respect. Even worse, they used the reservation as a sanctuary after raids in Texas. The army was not permitted to pursue the marauders onto the reservation. But beneficial as this change in the rules was for the Indians, their game was soon to end.

Three factors finally quieted the frontier: a more aggressive federal policy, the restoration of autonomy to the state government permitting the use of state troops, and the extermination of the Indians' private commissary, the great buffalo herds, by the .50 caliber rifles of the buffalo hunters.

The end of the peace policy and the beginning of more vigorous military operations were foreshadowed by a visit to the Texas frontier by generals William T. Sherman and Randolph B. Marcy in April and May of 1871. When they nearly lost their lives in an episode known as the Salt Creek Massacre, they were convinced of the seriousness of the Indian menace. As their party proceeded from Fort Griffin to Fort Richardson, a Kiowa chief named Satanta led a band of one hundred fifty Kiowas into the region. The generals reached Fort Richardson just before the Indians fell on a wagon train of supplies on the same route. The Indians killed and scalped seven teamsters, one of whom was tied to a wagon wheel, indescribably mutilated, and burned alive. Five men escaped, and one of them, seriously wounded, made his way to Fort Richardson to gasp out the horrible story. Sherman and Marcy learned that their lives had been spared by only a few hours.

Prompt action followed. Sherman himself went to Fort Sill, arrested Satanta and two other chiefs on the reservation, and had them returned to Texas for trial as murderers. They were quickly convicted, but Governor Davis commuted their sentence from hanging to life imprisonment in the Texas penitentiary. As one of his last official acts, Davis paroled them in 1873. General Sherman wrote to Governor Davis indignantly and predicted the Indians would have revenge, adding, "if they are to take scalps I hope yours is the first. . . ." The general was right; the chiefs were soon leading raids into Texas, and on one of these Satanta was captured and returned to Huntsville, where he committed suicide in 1878. The narrow escape of the highest-ranking officers in the army and the spectacular trial of the Kiowa chiefs furnished wide publicity to the suffering of the Texas frontier. Quaker Tatum joined with Colonel R. S. Mackenzie in recommending an unconditional military effort to bring the Indians under control.

Mackenzie had arrived in Texas in 1868 and in 1871 was put at the head of the Fourth Cavalry. He was an aggressive leader and a brilliant tactician, and as soon as General Sherman permitted him to take the offensive, he initiated a major campaign on the plains. In the fall of 1871 he led an expedition of over six hundred men into the heart of the Comanche stronghold along the breaks of the Caprock. Although the mounted nomads eluded him, the next year a captured Comanchéro guided him to important Indian trails on the High Plains, where he surprised a large Comanche village on the North Fork of the Red River, killing twenty-three Indians, capturing one hundred twenty-four, and recovering hundreds of stolen horses. These punitive attacks reduced Comanche raids in 1873. Mackenzie was then ordered to the Rio Grande to stop the devastations of Kickapoos, Apaches, and Mexican bandits from south of the border. He and his Fourth Cavalry arrived at Fort Clark in April 1873, and a month later, with four hundred men, Mackenzie illegally crossed the international boundary and destroyed a Kickapoo and Lipan village eighty miles south of Eagle Pass. A flurry of protests over this violation of the international code quickly diminished when it was established that these uncontrolled raiders had inflicted damages amounting to nearly fifty million dollars north of the border.

The next year marked the last major campaign against the Indians in Texas. Word was sent to the wandering bands of Comanches and Kiowas that the deadline for entering the reservation was August 1874. The army then moved onto the Texas plains in a five-pronged campaign to mop up the recalcitrant diehards. Colonel Nelson A. Miles led one column south from Fort Dodge, Kansas, along the eastern edge of the Texas Panhandle; Major William Price led another east from Fort Union, New Mexico; Colonel John W. Davidson led a third west from Fort Sill; Lieutenant Colonel George P. Buell led a fourth northwest from Fort Griffin; and Colonel Mackenzie, who had been ordered to Fort Concho, led the veterans of the Fourth Cavalry up the eastern escarpment of the High Plains. The three thousand men thus fielded in mid-August easily ensnared the remaining Indians. Although several skirmishes occurred, the only significant engagement was between Mackenzie's troopers and a Comanche band camped in Palo Duro Canyon. Once again guided by a former Comanchéro, Mackenzie surprised the encampment and scattered the Indians after a brief fight. He captured their herd of about fifteen hundred horses, and then in perhaps the most unusual action of any Indian campaign Mackenzie had the horses shot. The Indians, thrown helplessly afoot, were rounded up with a minimum of casualties and taken to the reservation. Only a few hundred hostile Indians eluded this large pincer movement in the fall of 1874, and by the summer of 1875 all but an estimated fifty of them had reported dejectedly to the Indian agency on the reservation. The Comanche menace of the Texas settlements since the early eighteenth century had at last been ended.

The Buffalo Hunters   It was not the army alone that closed the curtain on this drama. The six companies of the Frontier Battalion, created by the Texas Legislature in 1874, had engaged in a score of Indian fights and had given substantial aid to the broader military effort. But more significant in the long run was the inadvertent assistance rendered by a handful of buffalo hunters, whose guns destroyed the Indians' source of food.

There were two great herds: one roamed the northern and the other the southern plains. Each divided into smaller groups in their forage through the short-grass country. Nor were the creatures limited to the plains. Sir Samuel Argall in 1611 sighted buffalo on Chesapeake Bay, and French fur traders (whose word for beef cattle, *bouefs*, gave them their name) found them in the forested Great Lakes region. It is impossible to make even a reasonable guess at the original bison population of North America.

Although the buffalo slaughter that nearly exterminated the American bison did not begin until after the Civil War, there were instances of unrestrained killing much earlier. According to Mendoza's report, the Mendoza-López expedition, with its hundreds of hungry Indians trailing along, shot almost twenty thousand head during its march across the Edwards Plateau. Spaniards from New Mexico conducted a fairly fruitful commerce in buffalo hides during the eighteenth century and into the nineteenth, and their expeditions occasionally ventured onto the Texas plains to harvest a seemingly inexhaustible crop. Plainsmen before the Civil War thought it impossible to diminish by even a small proportion the vast herds.

Slaughter of the northern herd began with the building of the transcontinental Union Pacific, for the railroad contractors employed hunters to provide the laborers with fresh meat. Soon the value of buffalo hides encouraged the hunters to kill not for meat but for hides, and wholesale hunting had begun in earnest by 1870. A professional hunting party usually consisted of one or two hunters armed with .50 caliber Sharps' rifles, which were too heavy to fire from horseback, and a team of skinners, whose unpleasant job was to strip the carcasses. The green hides were then taken to the hunters' camp, stretched and pegged to the ground for several days until the residual flesh had dried, and stacked in incredibly malodorous piles until the hunters were ready to haul them to market. The bones and meat of the animals were simply left where the carcasses were skinned. In the 1890's, a few years after the great buffalo hunt, a new business flourished briefly of gathering the bones that lay everywhere in the open plains and selling them for the extraction of calcium.

Among the first of the hunters to begin ravishing the southern herd were Bob and Jim Cator, who pitched camp in the northern Panhandle in 1872, the Mooar brothers, who hunted the breaks of the Canadian River in the spring of 1873, and George Causey, whose first stand was in the maw of Palo Duro Canyon. The Mooar hunt was so successful that a score of hunters was attracted to the Panhandle in 1874. A substantial expedition from Dodge City, including such youthful adventurers as Billy Dixon and Bat Masterson, established camp near the Adobe Walls ruins, where A. C. Myers planned to establish a store and James Hanrahan, a saloon. Charles Rath soon joined the Adobe Walls camp to establish a branch of his Dodge City store. But the community was short-lived. On June 27, 1874, in the Second Battle of Adobe Walls, a force of seven hundred Comanches and Kiowas incited by a medicine man attacked the buffalo hunters' camp of twenty-eight men and one woman. In the initial charge four men were killed, but the hunters repelled the attack. The Indians then held the camp under siege for four days during which time Dixon got off a shot from his buffalo gun that became legendary, killing a Cheyenne on horseback nearly a mile away. The Indians retired from Adobe Walls on the fifth day when a rescue party from Camp Supply and more than a hundred other hunters in the region converged on the battleground.

The rampant butchery of the buffalo had naturally incensed the Indians, whose leaders may have realized that it would soon put an end to their way of life, and the Second Battle of Adobe Walls was a main reason for the extensive campaign of 1874, which brought most of the Indians onto the reservation. During the next four years of the great buffalo hunt there were frequent skirmishes between the hunters and small bands of Indians, the last significant one in Yellow House Draw near present Lubbock in 1877. By 1879 the big hunt was over; the buffalo was almost extinct. The disappearance of the buffalo made possible the containment of the Indians on reservations, created several settlements in West Texas, and opened the North American plains to the cattle industry, as cattle could not have competed for grass with the larger buffalo.

The Rise of the Cattle Industry

The Antecedents of the Boom   The great range cattle industry of western America was born on the coastal plains of Texas, from whence it spread in an explosive boom during the quarter of a century after the Civil War. By 1890 Texas cows, Texas cowboys and cattlemen, and especially Texas methods of ranching were to be found in every state west of the Mississippi River and in several provinces of Canada. The range cattle business passed through two major phases: open and closed. The enclosure movement on the ranges caused as much turmoil as did the enclosure movement in seventeenth-century England. The enclosure movement also ended the long trail drives to market. Other characteristics of the Texas range operations, however, continued to mark the closed-range phase: working cattle from horseback; ranging the cattle in big pastures; rounding them up for branding, cutting, and marketing; roping them from agile cow ponies; and training the horses to aid in the operations. These features made Texas and western range cattle herding different from the raising of livestock in the wooded terrain east of the Mississippi.

As pointed out in an earlier chapter, the origins of the cattle industry are Spanish, and in Spanish colonial Texas after the transfer of Louisiana the long trail drive to market became an essential part of the industry. Had Spanish officials permitted free trade after Louisiana was transferred to the United States in 1803, the range cattle industry might have enjoyed a steady growth during the first half of the nineteenth century. But with markets shut off from them, Spanish cattlemen in Texas allowed their stock to multiply and roam freely into the brush country south of the San Antonio River, where they joined thousands of head of already wild cattle from the ranchos of the lower Rio Grande.

The country seems to have been a suitable habitat. The diamond-shaped area between the Nueces and the Rio Grande is usually considered the birthplace of the cattle industry. The cattle there increased phenomenally during the first half of the century. The population of wild cattle probably numbered several million by the time of the Texas Revolution.

The cattle business was revived during the period of the Republic. Texas ranchers mixed their own stock brought from the United States with the wild Spanish cattle, learned the techniques of the vaqueros, and were soon driving herds to market in Louisiana. James Taylor White, Texas' first cattle baron, trailed many animals branded JTW into Louisiana from his ranch in present Liberty and Chambers counties. Others rounded up wild cattle on the frontier to sell to farmers and planters in East Texas, and a few drives were made to river ports on the Red River for shipment further east. The wild cattle of South Texas also supported the hide and tallow industry of the 1850's.

Cattle were a "natural resource" requiring only a market to be exploited. After the gold rush to California, a few hardy drovers began daring the Indians and the desert to trail herds to the Pacific coast. As farms thickened in East Texas, drives to Louisiana were gradually replaced by coastal shipping from Indianola, Corpus Christi, and Aransas. The easy profit derived from rounding up wild stock, grazing them on public land, and selling them for cash revenue encouraged Texas cattlemen to seek out more markets. One of the first recorded major drives was by Edward Piper to Ohio in 1846. In 1856 a drive was made all the way to Chicago, and by that time thousands of head were being driven annually to various points in Missouri. This movement north was checked in 1858, when it was discovered that Texas cattle carried an epizootic disease that took heavy toll of other cattle. Not until many years later was it learned that the "Texas fever" was not carried by the cattle but by ticks that infested them.

The outbreak of war, with the reaction to Texas fever, brought a second and all-important hiatus in the development of the range cattle industry. Until 1863 Texas ranchers sold beef to the Confederacy by driving principally to ports on the Red River and the Mississippi, but after federal control of the rivers, this trade ended. Since the export of cattle during the 1850's had not dented the natural increase of the herds, the two to three years of almost no exports probably tripled or even quadrupled the already fantastic number of cattle on the southern Texas frontier. The agricultural schedules, which are of little value because most of the cattle were wild, unbranded, and unclaimed, indicate that in 1860 the cattle outnumbered the people in Texas by about six to one.

At this time Texas cattle were worth about three dollars a head when gathered, and a grown animal sold for thirty to forty dollars a head at northern and eastern slaughterhouses. It did not take much imagination for Texas ranchers or northern buyers to "figger up a fortune" based on the dearth of beef in the North and the plethora in Texas. During the winter of 1865–1866, a number of herds were gathered in preparation for a drive north as soon as the spring warmth had raised grass along the route. Several buyers from the North traveled to Texas, bought herds, outfitted a drive, and hired Texas drovers. One such drive to Iowa is recorded in the diary of George C. Duffield. Another important drive was made to a railhead market at Sedalia, Missouri, in the spring of 1866. It is estimated that over two hundred fifty thousand head were trailed north that year.

But these first post-war drives were somewhat less than profitable and were, indeed, disastrous to many drovers and their animals. Trailing through the timbered lands of Central Texas and eastern Oklahoma to the Kansas-Missouri border was difficult, and the herds had to cross creeks and streams swollen with spring floods. Then in Kansas and Missouri they encountered the same reaction, though perhaps more violent, to Texas fever. Furious farmers, declaring that anyone who drove Texas cattle into their area was worse than a horsethief, banded together, scattered and turned back many herds, killed hundreds of cattle, and, it was reported, even assaulted and murdered several drovers. Few of the animals that had been started north that spring reached the railhead at Sedalia, and those that were marketed did not bring great profits.

The Era of the Great Trail Drives In the spring of 1867 two attempts were made to solve the dilemma. The first were routes that bypassed the farmlands and forested regions by shipping on the Red and Mississippi rivers and by driving west of the trouble zone into western Kansas. The second solution, which proved eminently successful, was the brainchild of Joseph G. McCoy, an Illinois cattle buyer.

After negotiating for favorable freight rates, McCoy located his operation on the southern branch of the Union Pacific at the little village of Abilene, Kansas, where he built shipping pens, barns, livery stables, and a hotel. By midsummer 1867 he was ready to welcome drovers and their herds from Texas. The cattle could be shipped by rail directly to slaughterhouses in Chicago without danger of infecting other stock in the Midwest, and Abilene was far enough west that trail drivers not only could avoid the settlements but also could have a much easier journey over prairies and plains. He sent riders south to spread the news, and he marked a trail through Oklahoma and Kansas that had been blazed in 1865 by Jesse Chisholm, a half-breed Indian trader whose name was later given to this first great cattle trail. Only some thirty-five thousand longhorns reached Abilene in 1867 because the operation began too late to affect the spring drives. The following year the number more than doubled, and in 1869 an estimated three hundred fifty thousand Texas cattle were trailed to Abilene. McCoy had founded an industry, and the great cattle boom was on. The promoter sold his investments in Abilene at a profit. The town remained the center of the cattle business until 1872, receiving and shipping from 1867 to 1871 a total of approximately one and a half million head of cattle.

In the late 1860's, as the population of Texas began to shift westward, plowed fields gradually replaced the verdant grasslands in eastern Central Texas. In the early 1870's cattle herds on the Chisholm Trail were forced to make detours miles out of the way to avoid farm settlements. To the west, unmarked prairies were ideally suited to the cattlemen's needs, but marauding Indians made trailing through that region most hazardous. As early as 1874 a few venturesome stockers braved the Indian country under military escort and traced a new path along the ninety-ninth meridian; the majority, however, preferred farmers to Comanches and Kiowas.

When the hostile Indians were banished to the reservation in 1875, a new trail variously called the Western Trail or the Dodge City Trail immediately came into being. It ran north from San Antonio and Bandera through Kerrville, Coleman, Albany, Fort Griffin, Seymour, and Vernon, and left Texas at Doan's Trading Post on the Red River, a favorite stop for cattlemen. Its first and foremost terminus was Dodge City, Kansas, on the Santa Fe Railroad, but some herds were driven further north to the Union Pacific at Ogallala, Nebraska, and even to the open ranges of the Dakotas and Montana. The Western Trail, which lasted about fifteen years, gradually came to supplant the Chisholm Trail in the early 1880's. The towns along the Western Trail's route prospered apace directly from the spending that accompanied trail traffic. Although Texas communities benefited, Dodge City, with such legendary saloons as the Long Branch and the Lady Gay, received the lion's share of trail profits. Dodge City was the unchallenged cowboy capital of the world until its decline in 1885, by which time its stockyards had handled no less than three million bovines.

Trail drives to the railheads did not just happen; they were highly organized business operations. Each employee had a specific task. Herds invariably required a trail boss to command, a ramrod to oversee, a competent cook, a horse wrangler to care for extra mounts, a swamper to help the cook and to perform odd jobs about the camp, and the drovers to herd the cattle. On the trail the boss charted the way with the chuck and equipment wagons following. The movement of the herd was the responsibility of two men on point, a position of honor. Further back, the precise distance depending upon the size of the herd, swing men and, toward the rear, flankers prevented the beeves from spreading or wandering away. Bringing up the rear, several drovers, either for disciplinary reasons or because of inexperience, rode drag to pick up strays and to keep the animals moving for the usual ten or so miles a day. The monotony occasionally was punctuated by stampedes and by hazardous river crossings, but drovers preferred for variety to visit the saloons of nearby trail towns.

Since most Texas ranchers did not have sufficient manpower for the time-consuming deliveries, enterprising businessmen began in the late

1860's to contract for the delivery of herds to northern markets. These trailing contractors would agree to supply the necessary manpower and equipment, to supervise delivery, and to sell the herds—all for a set fee, usually $1.00 to $1.25 per head. This method increased the rancher's cost of transportation, but it allowed him to keep his men on the ranch, where they were needed, and avoid the burden of the drive as well. Contractors occasionally combined this phase of the cattle trade with another. For example, John Henry Stephens of Kansas City, Missouri, used his commission company and his trailing business to extract lucrative profits from both selling and trailing livestock. Others specialized. One of the largest contracting firms was organized in Texas by John T. Lytle and Charles Schreiner in 1874, and by 1888 it had handled approximately a half million beeves, about fourteen per cent of the total trail traffic. By 1890 similar companies had accounted for more than half the deliveries to northern railheads and ranges.

As the profitable Texas range cattle industry spread westward after the Civil War, new cattle trails were blazed. The Goodnight-Loving Trail, initiated in 1866 by cattlemen Charles Goodnight and Oliver Loving, ran west from the Middle Concho River to the Horsehead Crossing of the Pecos River and then north to Fort Sumner, New Mexico. This route was later extended through Raton Pass to provide West Texans with a path to Colorado. The Potter and Bacon Trail, sometimes called the Potter and Blocker Trail, was blazed in 1883 by A. J. Potter from the Western Trail at Albany, Texas, to Colorado by way of the Llano Estacado. Many other cattle trails splintered from the main paths, but most were of little significance.

The major exception was the proposed National Trail. By the early 1880's, northern cattlemen, as well as many Texas ranchers, had become distressed by the spiraling destruction of Texas fever. Stockers were calling for effective quarantine measures against the importation of infected Texas animals, and many states established quarantine lines over which Texas cattle could not cross. To thwart this movement, South Texans gained control of the national cattlemen's 1884 convention in St. Louis and passed a resolution that asked the federal government to create and maintain a National Trail from Texas to the northern railheads in order to guarantee Texans an outlet to the railheads. Although the measure was approved by the senate in 1886, failure to secure a quorum in the house stalled the issue. By then Arizona, Colorado, Kansas, Montana, Nebraska, New Mexico, Wyoming, and even Canada had quarantined Texas cattle. In 1885 trailing began to suffer a precipitous decline until by 1890 few herds were driven northward from Texas.

The problem posed by Texas fever and the quarantines was resolved in 1889, when it was proved that the disease was carried by ticks. This discovery explained why Texas cattle carrying the disease remained healthy themselves. Dipping vats with chemicals lethal to ticks were soon installed at shipping points, and cattle from Texas ceased to be anathema to northern ranchers. But trailing was not resumed. The westward advance of the frontier and the consequent fencing of the plains and prairies made trailing impossible, and the extension of railroad lines made it unnecessary.

The Spread of the Cattle Kingdom Although many Texans raised livestock prior to the Civil War, only a few had established ranches of any consequence. One of these early ones has become the best-known ranch in North America: the King Ranch. It was founded by Richard King in 1852, when he bought the large Santa Gertrudis land grant. At the time of the Mexican War, King had come to South Texas to operate a steamboat on the Rio Grande with his partner, Mifflin Kenedy. Kenedy joined King in the ranching venture in 1860, and the two acquired considerably more acreage during the Civil War. In 1868 they dissolved the partnership and divided their holdings. King and his son-in-law, Richard Kleberg, later expanded the King Ranch to its million acres. Kenedy sold his share of the ranch in 1882 and acquired another on the coast, which remains intact today, virtually coextensive with present Kenedy County. Another prominent early rancher was Thomas O'Connor, who was a nephew of James Power and who received a league of land in the Power and Hewetson Colony. From this he built extensive ranch holdings in five counties, which totaled at his death in 1887 more than a half million acres.

The boom in the cattle business created by the railhead market at Abilene encouraged people to go into ranching. Some purchased land, but many simply acquired a herd of cattle and drove them west into the unoccupied public domain. Often called free rangers because they utilized the free grass of the public lands, they generally headquartered at a stream or spring or permanent water hole. The free rangers pushed into West Texas immediately after the containment of the Indian and the slaughter of the buffalo. Indeed, a number of buffalo hunters themselves turned to free ranging. Among the earliest of the ranchers who established themselves on the public domain were Charles Goodnight, Thomas Sherman Bugbee, C. C. Slaughter, John Hittson, former buffalo hunter J. W. Mooar, another buffalo hunter Jim Cator, D. H. Snyder, Abel H. "Shanghai" Pierce, and Oliver Loving. Free-grass ranching, the open-range phase of the cattle business, quickly spread from Texas into New Mexico and Colorado and then into other western states. As the available ranges in

Colorado and New Mexico filled up, cattlemen penetrated Arizona, Wyoming, and Montana. By the end of the trail-driving era, ranches in the Texas style were operating on free grass all the way into Saskatchewan and Alberta.

When land in the public domain was put on the market, most of the free rangers began acquiring titles to their headquarters and as much good pasture as possible. In Texas this was awkward because of the state's policy of reserving each alternate section of land in a checkerboard pattern for the permanent school fund. Ranchers bought alternate sections and grazed their cattle on the school land as well as their own. Two legislative movements eventually permitted ranchers to solidify their ranges. One was a series of land acts that made the school lands available to settlers and the other was the granting of five year grass leases on the school lands whereby cattlemen could for a few cents an acre graze their stock on the state-owned alternate sections in their pastures.

As a consequence, ranching became less speculative and more attractive as a permanent investment. Eastern and British capital by the thousands of dollars flowed into Texas during the late 1870's and early 1880's to back Texas cattlemen or to buy land and cattle outright. Companies and syndicates were formed, usually with the words "land and cattle company" in their titles, and ranching became big business. Exact figures are not available, but by 1885 well over half the land and cattle in West Texas was controlled by out-of-state owners, and much of that portion by Britons. Most of the foreign owners lost money, and the ranches tended to revert to Texas owners, but the influx of capital had important effects on the state's economic development. Hundreds of ranches were established during this period, ranging in size from a few sections to many thousands of acres. Among the well-known spreads, commonly referred to by their brands, were the JA, the Spur, the Matador, the Four Sixes, the IOA, the Spade, and the XIT.

The JA Ranch was established by Charles Goodnight in the Palo Duro Canyon under the frowning cliffs of the Caprock. Goodnight, who had been free-ranging in Colorado, became acquainted with a wealthy Irishman, John Adair, who wished to invest in ranching. The two formed a highly successful partnership utilizing Goodnight's experience and Adair's capital. Goodnight decided to establish the operation back in Texas, purchased a substantial herd, registered the brand as his backer's initials, JA, and drove his animals into Palo Duro in 1875. It was nothing less than a stroke of genius to use the canyon walls to contain the herd before the advent of barbed wire fencing. Most large ranches had to surround their land with line camps and line riders to keep the stock from straying, but Goodnight needed only a few camps at the mouth of the giant canyon. Goodnight, whose name soon became a household word, was the epitome of Texas cattle barons. Under his capable management the JA Ranch prospered. Twelve years later, when he and Adair dissolved the partnership, the spread included some seven hundred thousand acres, forty thousand cattle, hundreds of miles of roads and fences, fifty houses, and numerous corrals, pens, and water tanks.

Goodnight had bought pasture land as quickly as it became available and had leased grazing rights on the alternate sections. He became the champion of other ranchers in the cause célèbre known as the Panhandle Grass Lease Case, in which many cattlemen lost the right to renew their grass leases on the school land in their pastures. Goodnight loaded a wheelbarrow with money and trundled it from an Austin bank to the General Land Office several blocks away, demanding that the state honor its contract as he saw it. Goodnight again made national news when he established his famous "Winchester quarantine" of the JA pastures. He advised other cattlemen, particularly trail drivers, that his cattle were free of the Texas fever and he would not permit herds from the south to be driven through his pastures. The quarantine was to be enforced at the points of Winchester rifles.

The Matador Ranch, perhaps the greatest ranching venture in American history, had its inception almost casually when a free ranger named Joe Browning in 1878 made his headquarters at an abandoned buffalo hunter's dugout near a spring in present Motley County. Browning sold his range rights to A. M. Britton and H. H. Campbell, who purchased land and cattle and organized the Matador Cattle Company. In 1882 the entire operation, then consisting of approximately three hundred thousand acres and sixty thousand head of cattle, was sold to the Matador Land and Cattle Company of Dundee, Scotland, which had been organized to purchase the property. From 1882 to 1952 the Scottish firm operated the ranch, never failing a single year after 1885 to pay dividends to its stockholders. It is the only major ranch in the state to have survived the vicissitudes of panic, drought, and depression without benefit of oil revenue or land colonization. At its height shortly after the turn of the century, the company maintained five pastures: three hundred thousand headquarter acres in Motley, Cottle, and King counties; five hundred thousand acres leased from the White Deer Ranch in Carson County; two hundred thousand acres purchased from the XIT Ranch on the Canadian River; five hundred thousand acres leased on the Sioux Reservation in North Dakota; and one hundred fifty thousand acres in Saskatchewan, Canada. At times the firm operated a farm in Iowa and owned or leased ranches in Colorado and Wyoming. Its American offices were maintained in Trinidad, Colorado, by Murdo Mackenzie, the Scottish manager.

Unlike the JA and Matador ranches, the Four Sixes was owned and operated by a Texas cattleman—Samuel Burk Burnett. According to apocryphal tradition, this famous brand derived from a poker hand that won Burnett his start in the cattle business. He began ranching in Denton County in 1867, moved his operations west to Wichita County in 1874, expanded onto grass leases in Oklahoma, and acquired the Old Eight Ranch in King County when the grass leases expired in 1900. After the discovery of oil on the Wichita Ranch, which made Burnett extremely wealthy, he shifted his ranch headquarters to Guthrie, Texas.

The XIT Ranch was the largest contiguous spread in North America, containing over three million acres and extending along the western boundary of the Panhandle for over one hundred fifty miles. An unfounded story explains the brand as representing the ten counties in Texas included in the ranch, that is, the X (roman numeral for 10) I(n) T(exas). This ranch derived from the grant of three million twenty-five thousand acres made by the State of Texas to the Capitol Syndicate, the firm that built the Texas statehouse. Desiring the grandest state capitol in the nation but lacking sufficient funds, the legislature used the public domain to entice a building contractor to erect the imposing structure in Austin. Control of the firm passed to the Farwell family of Chicago, who sold bonds to British investors to finance the building. The Capitol Syndicate spent a little over three million dollars on the building; in effect it had paid one dollar an acre when most such raw land was selling at fifty cents an acre. Unable therefore to recover the investment by immediate sale, the syndicate embarked upon large-scale ranching, which it continued for nearly a decade before beginning to sell the lands. Most of the ranch was sold in very large tracts to other ranchers, but some was subdivided into smaller tracts for sale to settlers as the frontier moved west. The Capitol Syndicate became one of the biggest promoters of West Texas settlement but is best remembered for its "six thousand miles of fence," its hundreds of windmills, its purchases of supplies in boxcar quantities, and its other trappings of immense size.

Frontier Settlement

The Advance of the Frontier   A number of factors contributed to the westward movement of the Texas frontier after the containment of the Indian and the slaughter of the buffalo. These included particularly the rapid alienation of the public domain in West Texas and the development of what has been called the "great plains techniques" for pioneering the semiarid lands of western America.

The fairly complex history of Texas land policy has largely been ignored by historians, although the alienation of the public domain was fundamental to the advance of western settlement. It needs also to be understood that Texas, unlike the other states, owned its public lands, developed its own land policies, and without aid from the federal government supported the construction of railroads in the state. Public land sales were suspended in 1863, and, except for a feeble attempt to raise revenue in 1866 by issuing land scrip at two dollars an acre, the process of alienation was virtually dormant until 1873. At that time a constitutional amendment permitted special land grants by the legislature to encourage internal improvements such as the building of railroads. The feature was part of the Constitution of 1876, which provided for grants to railroad companies of sixteen sections of land for each mile of track built. The need for railroad transportation was pressing, and the desire to induce companies to build in Texas was strong, so the state merely followed the example of the federal government. Legislators of the time and later historians are in general agreement that Texas needed railroads more than vacant land and that on the whole the policy of granting land as a subsidy was well advised. Over thirty million acres of public domain were thus granted to railroad companies.

Few if any of the companies profited from these subsidies for three reasons: first, laws required the companies to dispose of the land within eight years; second, the state undermined the value of the land by later acts that priced the public domain as low as fifty cents an acre in 1879; and third, the companies were required to locate the amount granted to them in the vacant areas of West Texas, to survey the land, and to submit field notes before receiving title. Furthermore, they got titles only to the alternate sections, the other sections being reserved for the school fund. Almost all of West Texas was thus surveyed at the expense of the railroad companies. And as the cost of surveying, mapping, and patenting was estimated to be nearly fifty cents an acre, the hapless companies were lucky if their "subsidy" did not actually cost them money. Many were forced to make premature and unprofitable sales, and a number of companies, having plunged into construction without sufficient capital, went bankrupt when their subsidies proved to be of little value. Other companies resorted to the subterfuge of establishing land-holding subsidiaries, instead of alienating the land as required by the law, and then began costly programs of advertising and development in order to sell the land to settlers.

In 1874 the state placed the alternate tracts on the market at a dollar and a half an acre but found few purchasers. The price was reduced in 1879 to a dollar an acre for school land and fifty cents an acre for the unappropriated public domain in a large group of unorganized counties in West Texas. In 1883 a major revision in land policy stopped the granting of lands to railroads and raised the basic price to two dollars an acre for unwatered pasture land and three dollars an acre for watered or arable lands. At the same time the provision for grass leases was made. Generous terms of thirty years at five per cent interest were offered, and settlers were given priorities to purchase. These terms were expanded to forty years in 1887, and in 1895 the minimum price was reduced to a dollar an acre and the interest rate to three per cent. This act is often called the Four Section Settler Act because bona fide settlers were authorized to purchase as many as four sections. It was amended in 1905 to allow eight sections in the Trans-Pecos and the sandy counties of the South Plains. Obviously few land companies were able to compete profitably until the vast public domain had been largely appropriated to settlers after the turn of the century. The Texas land policies were consistently more generous to settlers than the land policies of the United States.

The land alienation acts had three primary results. First, there was a flurry of activity among land speculators who hoped to make quick fortunes in Texas land. But the low prices established by the state continued into the early years of the twentieth century, and many of the speculators lost money. Second, the land passed into the ownership of ranchers who bought railroad lands as they became available and then filled in their holdings with fifty-cent land or by filing on the alternate school sections. After 1887 many ranchers had their employees file on the lands as settlers and then sell to them. Third, the "farmers' frontier" began, a movement of settlers and homesteaders into West Texas. This movement, however, could not have been made without the development of the "great plains techniques."

In a brilliant historical thesis the late Walter Prescott Webb pointed out that the American pioneer, accustomed for generations to the well-watered, woodland regions east of the Mississippi, found difficulty in establishing himself in the semiarid and arid prairie grassland and high plains country of the west. Webb attributes the success of western settlement to three revolutionary techniques: pumping underground water to the surface by windmills, fencing with barbed wire, and evolving special ways of farming arid land.

In the eastern woodlands pioneers found many streams and springs and usually needed to dig only a few feet to reach the water table. Wells were dug by hand, and water was brought to the surface by buckets. In the West subsurface water was deeper; there were few springs; and the streams were brackish and "gyppy." But nearly always there was plenty of wind. By 1875 a method of drilling deeper wells by mechanical augers had been linked to the development of pumping equipment operated by great wheels turned by the wind. Life-giving water could then be obtained at relatively low cost. In another ten years windmill towers with their large revolving fans, some wooden, some steel, and their monotonously squeaking sucker rods had been erected throughout West Texas. The first users were ranchers who created scattered wells so that their animals would not have to walk too far to water and so that pastures far from waterholes could be utilized. Soon homesteaders, moving under the state's generous land terms onto the plains and prairies, used the windmill to supply domestic water and to irrigate small garden plots.

Fencing, however, was a major problem, not only to keep wild game out of plowed fields but also to keep cattle from roaming into adjacent pastures. The eastern rail fence could not be adapted to the West, where there were no trees, and a multitude of wire fence patents were applied for during the 1870's. The most successful was patented by J. F. Glidden and put into production in 1880 by Isaac L. Ellwood. Two of Ellwood's salesmen, H. B. Sanborn and John W. "Bet-a-Million" Gates, quickly popularized the product in Texas. Gates flamboyantly put up a section of barbed wire fence on the San Antonio plaza and bet curious ranchers they could not drive a cow through it. By 1890 barbed wire fences, usually three or four strands stapled to posts fifteen to twenty feet apart, had sprung up throughout the ranch country. Few ranchers at first enclosed their entire ranch with fences. They built drift fences on the southern lines of their pastures to halt the cattle that drifted south in the winter with their rumps to the north winds. A great "die-up" was recorded by range chronicler Don Biggers in the winter of 1886, when hundreds of cattle drifting in front of a ferocious blizzard struck such a fence and died from cold, immobility, and crushing. Homesteaders were as quick as ranchers to adopt the new wire to fence off their fields. And almost as quickly the range began to erupt in fence-cutting wars.

The settler found to his disappointment that the cheap lands of West Texas were unsuited to farming, at least as it had been practiced for generations in the East. There simply was not enough rainfall. Dry-farming techniques were developed in the late 1880's and early 1890's to compensate for the insufficient moisture. Deep plowing loosened the soil to prepare it for any rain that might fall, and a light mulching of the surface after a rain formed a cover to hold the moisture in. In time other practices such as terracing evolved, and plants were adapted to the wind and semi-aridity.

Before the turn of the century the farmers' frontier was crowding into the big ranch country. The cattleman's frontier had reached the Pecos River and the Caprock edge of the plains by 1880. In the next decade, supported by the windmill, ranchers had climbed onto the remarkably fertile high plains and had begun to penetrate the forbidding land west of the Pecos. The farmers were close behind. The line of settlement, as indicated by organized county government, moved westward approximately two tiers of counties in the decade of the 1870's. In the next decade it entered the northern Panhandle, reached the foot of the South Plains, and penetrated the Trans-Pecos. In the 1890's, sixteen additional county governments were organized, leaving unsettled only a few areas where the soil was too sandy for the nineteenth-century agriculturalist. Only twenty-four out of Texas' two hundred fifty-four counties remained to be organized after 1900, and some of these new counties were merely taken from counties organized earlier. Hence, for all practical purposes, the Texas frontier was gone at the turn of the century.

Frontier Conflicts Motion picture and television scripts as well as western novels have exaggerated frontier conflicts between cattlemen and sheepmen and between ranchers and homesteaders. From the earliest days of Spanish colonial ranching, individual ranchers have run both sheep and cattle. Today on the Edwards Plateau, one of the greatest natural ranching areas in the world, sheep, goats, and cattle are to be found on many of the ranches, although rarely, of course, grazing in the same pasture at the same time.

Sheep and goat ranching never went through the boom that cattle ranching did, but there has been sheep ranching in Texas as long as cattle ranching. Its greatest early sheep rancher was George Wilkins Kendall, the editor of the New Orleans *Picayune*, who established a sheep ranch in 1857 in the area of the present county named after him. Sheep raising expanded rapidly during the era of the cattle boom, and some cattlemen, such as trailing contractor John Lytle, supplemented their incomes with sheep. There were an estimated 1,223,000 head in 1870 and 6,024,000 a decade later. Despite the increase in the number of sheep, many ranchers switched to cattle during the boom because of the greater profits. Typical was John Scharbauer, founder of the great Scharbauer Cattle Company, who began sheep ranching in Eastland County, moved his flocks to Mitchell County in 1884, acquired his first cattle in 1888, and sold his sheep in 1895 in order to concentrate on cattle. His nephew, Clarence Scharbauer, one of Texas' greatest cattlemen, also gained his first ranching experience as a sheepherder.

The conflicts that gave rise to the so-called Sheep War and to the special legislation on grazing sheep were questions of range rights and not of any special animosity between cattlemen and sheepmen. And there was just as much friction among cattlemen for the same reason. The principal problem was that many sheep raisers, instead of staying in one area, drifted their herds on the open range and came into conflict not only with cattle ranchers but also with settled sheepmen. Laws were passed against this drifting, and in 1884, because many sheepmen had acquired grass leases in separated areas, an interesting statute attempted to regulate the speed at which a flock must move when crossing the range.

The alleged conflict between ranchers and homesteaders is equally exaggerated. Its basis was also a question of land rights, especially titles to watering places, and not of any natural antagonism. Actually most ranchers welcomed and encouraged homesteaders for several reasons. The homesteaders' gardens were a source of fresh vegetables; his chickens were a source of eggs; he and his family were a source of labor when extra hands were temporarily needed; and above all the homesteaders heralded the coming increase in the value of land and were a potential market for it.

Over half the big ranches were organized as "land and cattle" companies with the objective of running cattle on the land until land values had appreciated. Many of these companies actively promoted settlement and competed with the state by selling small tracts to settlers on easy terms.

Friction between settler and rancher did arise, however, during the transition from the free grass of the open range to the owned or leased pastures of the closed range. When a settler filed on a tract of school land in the middle of a pasture that a rancher had been using, a certain amount of conflict was inevitable. When a settler filed on a section that contained the only waterhole for miles around, or when a settler fenced a rancher's cattle away from water, or when a rancher did the same thing to a settler, conflict was certain.

The greatest disturbance to the frontier was fence building. The principal clash was between landless cattlemen who wished to continue using the free grass and cattlemen who had bought and leased pastures and who began fencing them when barbed wire became available. Sometimes ranchers completely enclosed the homestead of a settler, and, less often, homesteaders blocked ranchers with their fences. In the first flush of fence building, much rampant and unwarranted fencing occurred. Fences blocked access to rivers and watering places and, strung across public roads, cut off schools and churches and even interfered with mail deliveries. It was especially frustrating for a man to be cut off by another man's wire from one section to another of his alternate sections of school land. The result was a rash of fence cutting in the early 1880's, which reached a peak in 1883. The cutting was usually done at night and often by groups who gave themselves such names as the Owls or the Blue Devils and who left warnings to the owner of the fence not to rebuild it. The feeling was so intense that the fence cutters even set pasture fires. The fence cutters were both ranchers and homesteaders, but most of the cutting seems to have been done by rival stockmen.

A special session of the legislature was called in 1884 to enact legislation on fence cutting. Estimates at that time of the financial loss caused by fence cutting ran as high as twenty million dollars. After heated debates, criminal statutes were enacted against fencing across public roads, fencing public land not under grass lease, and enclosing land belonging to another. It was even made a felony to carry wire-cutting tools on one's person—a ridiculously unenforceable statute still on the books. Special laws also provided that no one could be denied ingress to or egress from his property: ranchers whose pastures surrounded a settler had to permit him right-of-way to his property. Fence builders were also required to install gates every three miles.

These laws, enforced by Rangers, ended the fence-cutting wars, although there were sporadic outbreaks of trouble. One such occurrence in Navarro County in 1888 produced Ranger Ira Aten's famous "dinamite boom racket." Aten, exasperated by the elusiveness of the fence cutters and wishing to be relieved of the Navarro assignment, proposed an ingenious scheme for booby-trapping a fence line with a combination of shotgun and dynamite, which when detonated would be heard as far away as Austin and would scatter pieces of shotgun all over Navarro County. He ended his proposal: "Well if it don't kill the parties that cuts the fence, it will scare them so bad they will never cut another." Alarmed officials promptly ordered Aten not to construct his "dinamite boom" and transferred him to another assignment.

A problem even more serious than fence cutting was cattle rustling. The stealing of cattle in the vast and thinly settled ranch country was a perennial plague to ranchers. Cattlemen adopted several measures to reduce the rustling, if they could not effectively halt it. They prevailed upon the legislature to pass stringent acts against cattle theft and to establish district offices to inspect the hides of animals for evidence of brand running and of reported theft. They formed organizations such as the Texas Cattle Raisers Association to employ their own brand inspectors and detectives. They called upon the Texas Rangers to run down rustlers, and a few big ranches hired former Rangers. The giant XIT had such a problem that it employed Ira Aten and several other former Rangers as a special force of its own.

The practice of branding, so useful during the open range era, was continued after the fencing of the ranches, and ear crops were often used for further identification. Branding, which appears to have originated in Spain, was common in Spanish colonial Texas. Hispanic ranchers designed elaborate and even decorative brands, made with a running iron, with an infinite variety of curves and curlicues, which sometimes covered the entire side of a cow. Anglo ranchers, who called the Spanish brands "quien sabes" (who knows), adopted simpler and more practical brands, which often incorporated the rancher's initials. Three different types of branding irons came into general use: an iron made by a blacksmith with the brand symbol reversed in a mirror image so that the entire brand could be burned into the hair at one time, a bar iron of one single strip of metal that burned a straight line, and a running iron with a circle at its end that could be rolled over the hair in any direction. The running iron was often used by rustlers to change or obliterate the owner's brand.

The Closed Range   The enclosure movement, begun in 1881 with the introduction of barbed wire, had brought an end to the open range by 1890—an end accelerated by the state's liberal land policy, which made the public domain easily available to ranchers and land speculators (often one and the same person or firm) as well as to homesteaders and settlers. The investment in land, fencing, wells, and windmills, however, reduced sharply the margin of profit in the cattle business. This, combined with a drought in 1886, a severe winter in 1886–1887, and a sharp drop in cattle prices in 1887, brought disaster to many ranchers. There can be little doubt that the Texas ranges had become overstocked by 1885, despite the great number of longhorns sold in Kansas. Then, when spring precipitation was below average in most parts of the state, forage was markedly reduced. Cattlemen began selling their beeves at distress prices, and the cattle market soon declined seriously. The drought and the hard winter that followed have been described by Don Biggers, who witnessed them:

> In the spring of 1885 began the awfullest drought ever known in western Texas. On the fifth day of June there was a pretty general rain, but from that day until the 18th of August, 1886, there was scarcely a shower throughout the western part of the state. The winter of 1886 was very severe, and in the spring of 1887 occurred beyond a doubt the awfullest die-up ever known in the United States. From the Canadian borders to the Rio Grande the range country was covered with carcasses. By that time many big pastures had been completed, most of them on the staked plains, and in these pastures one could see sights almost too pathetic and revolting to contemplate. When the blizzards came the

cattle would drift south until they came to the southern line of fence. Unable to go further they would move back and forth, pressing close to the fence or stand in clusters, suffering from cold, hunger and thirst and trampling out every vestage [sic] of grass. One would fall or lie down and others would tumble over it, and soon there would be a heap of dead along the line of fence. I saw one instance and heard of many others, where, for a distance of two and three hundred yards, the heaps of dead bodies were higher than the fence. Over these bodies the snow drifted and sifted between them soon forming a solid, frozen mass, over which hundreds of living cattle walked, tumbled over the fence and drifted away.

One typical example of an unsuccessful ranch-land speculation operation will illustrate the situation in West Texas in the late 1880's and the extent to which speculation in Texas ranches had spread throughout the nation. The Gulf, Colorado, and Santa Fe Railroad, which had received the usual land scrip for construction of track, sold certificates for fifty unlocated sections to Eli Stilson and J. I. Case of the well-known manufacturing families in Michigan. Surveyors located the land in the customary checkerboard pattern in Lubbock County in 1878. The following year, when the alternate sections were placed on the market, Stilson and Case acquired them at the two dollars an acre price. Under the Fifty Cent Act, two Illinois speculators named J. S. Keator and W. O. Kulp purchased an adjacent solid block of over one hundred sections. In 1884 they chartered the Western Land and Livestock Company in Iowa, purchased the Stilson and Case block, and gave a first-lien mortgage to Quincy Shaw, a Massachusetts investor who was a cousin of historian Francis Parkman. Controlling interest in the company was sold to Stillman W. Wheelock, a wealthy Illinois manufacturer. Wheelock sent his nephew to Texas to oversee the property, called the IOA Ranch, and employed an experienced cattleman to stock and fence the two-hundred section ranch. Caught in the disaster of 1886–1887, the company lost money on its cattle and was unable to sell its land for the amount of the mortgage, the state having reduced the price of school land to one dollar per acre. Wheelock continued to pour money into the venture until his death in 1894, when the company was liquidated. Soon thereafter, Shaw foreclosed on the mortgage and sold the court judgment at a discount to a San Antonio banker. Virtually everyone involved lost money.

The story was the same throughout West Texas as the cost of ranching caught up with the profit. Countless ranchers went bankrupt, and scores of big ranches were broken up. The few who survived began to adapt their operations to the closed range. They thinned their herds and imported purebred bulls to upgrade their stock to better beef producers. They cross-fenced their pastures and grazed a realistic number of cattle, in most of West Texas an average of one animal to twenty acres. They added wells and windmills so that their cattle would not walk off fat in getting to water. They even planted feed crops to provide winter forage. For health they fed, doctored, and dipped their animals. And they adopted the ancient practice of castrating bull calves to produce better beef and to control breeding.

The extension of railroad lines into West Texas enabled ranchers to ship cattle from nearby points. A line to Fort Worth was completed in 1881, and ever after that city has been known as a cattleman's town. Between 1880 and 1882 the Texas and Pacific was laid across the central plains, the Edwards Plateau, and the Trans-Pecos regions to join the Southern Pacific. The Fort Worth and Denver built across the Panhandle in 1887, and at about the same time the Gulf, Colorado, and Santa Fe penetrated central West Texas. Soon feeder lines and short lines, such as the Roscoe, Snyder, and Pacific, were constructed to the major terminals.

The Panic of 1893 shook down the industry again, and a few more ranches went under. But thereafter the industry stabilized. By the turn of the century most of the ranches had been reduced to the size that could be handled by one family living and working on the place: six to ten sections. There were then and there remain today, however, several very large enterprises. Their substantial financial backing enabled them to survive droughts and depressions, and most of them later profited enormously from the discovery of oil.

11

Recovery and Reform

Economic Developments

Introduction The last quarter of the nineteenth century brought not only the close of the frontier and the ensuing cattle boom but also a remarkable growth in the economy, especially in commerce and the beginning of industry. Texas began to change from an almost completely rural and agrarian state to a modern industrialized complex of metropolitan areas. To be sure, this metamorphosis was not wrought overnight nor even in the last twenty-five years of the century, but the foundations were laid and the effects noticeable by 1900.

The period experienced two major recessions in the wakes of the Panics of 1873 and 1893, the formation of labor unions, the vigorous growth of the Patrons of Husbandry, the establishment of the Farmers' Alliance, the first thrusts of the Populist Party, the passage of reform legislation, the tripling of the state's population, and the usual phenomena associated with rapid expansion, not the least of which was the construction of an exten-

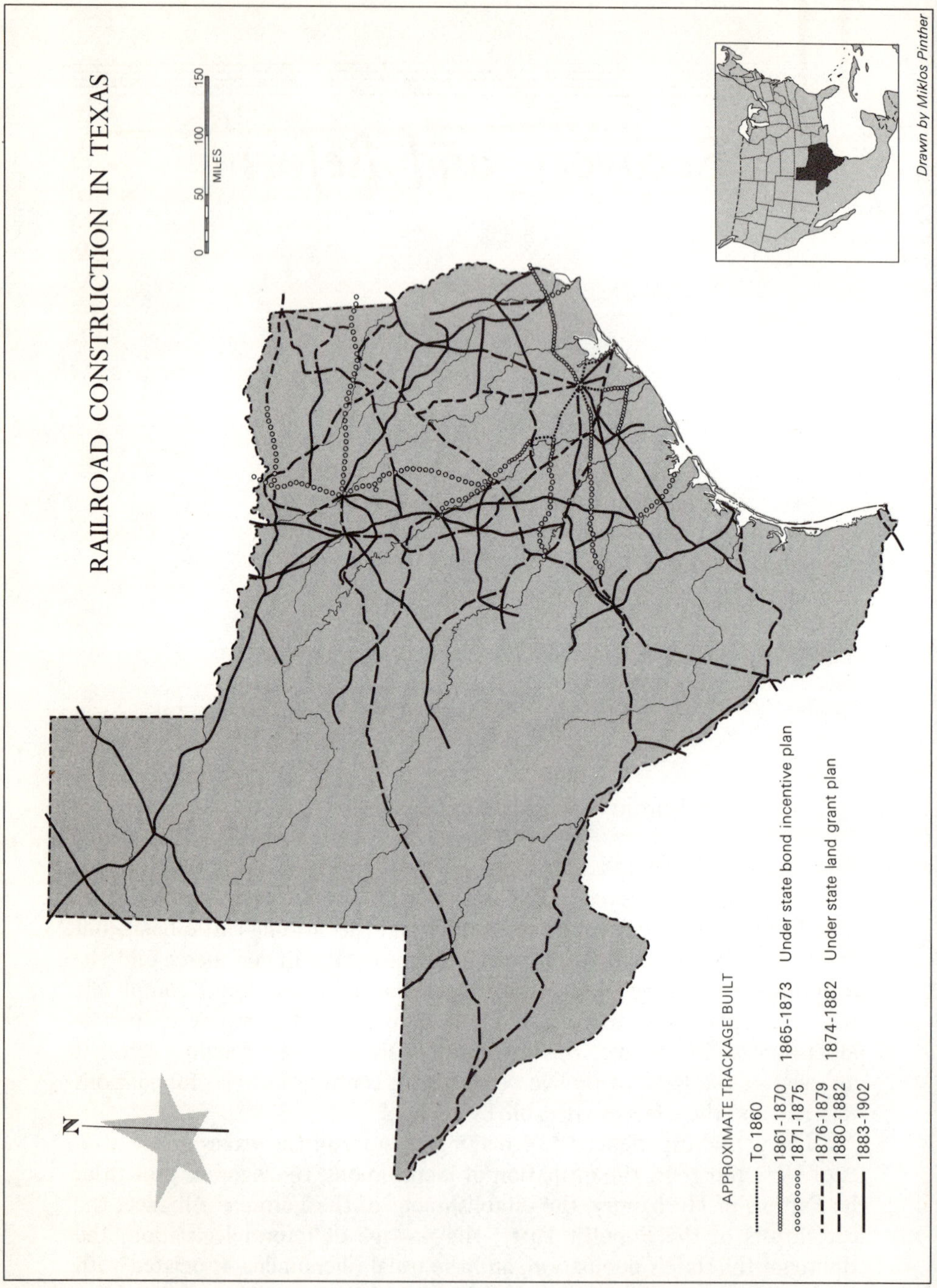
RAILROAD CONSTRUCTION IN TEXAS
0
50
100
150
MILES
N
APPROXIMATE TRACKAGE BUILT
To 1860
1861-1870
1871-1875
1865-1873
Under state bond incentive plan
1876-1879
1880-1882
1874-1882
Under state land grant plan
1883-1902
Drawn by Miklos Pinther

sive network of railroad lines. In 1870 Texas ranked twenty-eighth among the states in miles of track; in 1904 it ranked first.

Railroad Construction It was this great railroad network that underlaid the rapid development of the sprawling state. And had it not been for public aid to construction together with bonuses and special inducements, much less track would have been built and that at a much slower rate. At first public aid took the form of direct state bonuses and of county and city bonds given directly to railroad companies. In 1852 the state legislature granted eight sections per mile of track to the Henderson and Burkville Railroad; in 1854 a general law increased this bonus to sixteen sections.

Construction was at a standstill during the Civil War, with little progress during the first years of Reconstruction. The Constitution of 1869 forbade land grants to railroads, but the Twelfth Legislature overrode Governor Davis' objections and granted bonds to three companies. The bonds were declared unconstitutional, and later a special land grant of twenty sections per mile of track was issued to these companies.

In 1873 the Democrats rammed through a constitutional amendment permitting grants of land to railroads, and the new Constitution of 1876 authorized grants of sixteen sections per mile of track. In all, the state issued patents for over thirty million acres to railroad companies. But, as pointed out in the previous chapter, the companies did not profit greatly, if at all, from these bonuses because they were required to locate and survey the land in the unoccupied public domain in a checkerboard pattern and to dispose of it within eight years. This often meant dumping the land at a price less than the cost of surveying.

More beneficial to the companies were the subsidies by communities along the proposed routes. Railroad promoters used every trick at their command to persuade towns to make direct grants and bonuses, but little persuasion was necessary because most towns were desperately eager for rail connections. Townspeople united to provide depots, rights of way, terminus facilities, and even outright cash bonuses. If a town did not, the railroads usually bypassed it, and it was quickly learned that the railroads had the power of life and death over communities. For example, Jefferson on Caddo Lake was a thriving river port where connections were made for Red and Mississippi river traffic. In 1870 it ranked second to Galveston in volume of commerce. When the falsely secure town refused to give the aid required, the Texas and Pacific built instead through Marshall. Stunned Jeffersonians watched in disbelief the almost dizzying decline of the town's trade and consequently of its population. Similarly, Washington-on-the-

Brazos and scores of other stubborn communities became virtual ghost towns as the life-giving iron rails kept clear of them. On the other side of the coin, Houston, even before the Civil War, had recognized the vital necessity of rail connections for commercial growth. San Antonio, though it tried desperately, was late to get a railhead. Fort Worth and Dallas vied eagerly for connections and thrived on the commerce brought by the railroads. In West Texas such prosperous little cities as Abilene, Sweetwater, Colorado City, and Midland were born as the Texas and Pacific built westward.

The T. and P. was perhaps the greatest of the early lines in Texas. It was chartered by the federal government in 1871 and authorized to construct a line from East Texas to San Diego, California. Work on the tracks began at Marshall in 1873 under the great engineer Grenville M. Dodge, but progress was slow because of the Panic of 1873. The line reached Fort Worth in 1875. Railroad magnate Jay Gould obtained control of the company in 1880 and began building toward El Paso.

A dramatic construction race ensued between his line and that of Collis P. Huntington, dynamic master of the Southern Pacific, who was pushing his line eastward from Yuma, Arizona, under a special authorization from congress. Gould and Dodge plunged westward frantically as Huntington's construction crew rolled toward Texas. The two lines met in 1882 at Sierra Blanca, eighty miles east of El Paso, and made Texas' first transcontinental rail connection. By special agreement both companies shared the trackage from Sierra Blanca to El Paso. Huntington purchased the Galveston, Harrisburg, and San Antonio, and increased his system by a connection from Sierra Blanca to San Antonio through the Big Bend.

In all, the Southern Pacific acquired over thirty operating lines in Texas, and its Sunset Route to California from New Orleans became one of the best-known lines in the nation. Other great systems established during this period were the Katy (Missouri, Kansas, and Texas), which built south from the Red River to San Antonio; the Forth Worth and Denver; the International and Great Northern, which connected Laredo with Arkansas and after many vicissitudes became part of the Missouri Pacific system; and the Santa Fe, which by purchases and construction controlled nearly four thousand miles from the Panhandle to Galveston, its principal Texas operating company being the Gulf, Colorado, and Santa Fe.

Texas had in 1870 less than four hundred miles of track, by 1873 more than sixteen hundred miles, by 1880 more than thirty-two hundred miles, and in 1900 almost ten thousand operative track miles. The great period of construction that began in 1876, when the constitution authorized land grants to railroads, ended in 1882, when this provision was abrogated. Approximately half of the railroad trackage in Texas was built during this time. In 1877 more miles were built in Texas than in any other state, and in the peak construction year, 1878, more miles were built in Texas than the total built in the rest of the nation. Continued construction brought Texas to the position of first in the nation in miles of track, a not surprising rank in view of the size of the state.

The construction of all this track was an economic boon, substantially benefiting associated industries, especially the East Texas lumber industry. A great number of board feet in massive crossties formed the underpinning for the ten thousand miles of rails. And an additional forest went into the construction of bridges, depots, livestock pens, corrals, and freight yards. Railroad construction was the principle reason for the beginning of industrial development.

Industrial Developments The chief characteristic of early Texas industry was its reliance upon raw materials, an unsophisticated exploitation or extraction of a finished product from nature. Far and away the most important of these simple extractive industries were the milling and lumber industries. Both had dominated the industry of the state from the earliest times. But more advanced manufacturing such as furniture making, clothing manufacture, and ceramic production, though rare, was not nonexistent. John S. Spratt, the historian of the economy of this period, refers to early industry as "migratory" since most shops moved from one source of raw material to another. According to Spratt, the migratory industry settled down to a permanent basis during the last quarter of the nineteenth century.

In 1870 the total value of manufactured products, including custom and repair work, in Texas was just under $12,000,000, less than one-fourth of the value of farm products in the state and only two per cent of the national value of manufactured goods. At that time a mere 2,400 shops, employing only 8,000 wage earners, one per cent of the population, represented all Texas could muster in the way of industry. Galveston was the leading manufacturing county, with a gross product value of $1,200,000, and flour and grist milling, the state's dominant industry until 1890, accounted for approximately twenty per cent of the total product value. In 1870 there were 533 flour and grist mills scattered across the state in almost every county; in 1900 this number had dropped to 289, although the value of their output had increased nearly 600 per cent—a testimony to the importance of rail shipping. In 1880 the total value of manufactured products in the state increased to $20,000,000, almost twice that of 1870. Three thousand shops paid over $3,000,000 in wages to 12,000 employees. This was not a great increase over 1870 in comparison with the growth in population and the magnification of industry in the nation, but it was a start. The next decade witnessed an almost 300 per cent growth. Although the number of establishments increased to only 5,200, almost double the number in 1880, the capital invested in manufacturing plants increased over 400 per cent that decade, from $9,000,000 to $46,000,000. The value of products jumped three and a half times, to $70,000,000, and the total wages paid, to three times as many employees, rose 500 per cent to $15,000,000.

At that time, 1890, lumbering replaced flour and grist milling as the first-ranking industry. The pine forests of East Texas had long supplied a steady basis for the sawmills and planing mills developed during the period of the Republic. The production of pine lumber was focused at Orange and Beaumont, where in 1870 yearly production topped one hundred million board feet. The forests of East Texas covered an estimated 68,000 square miles and had a potential yield variously estimated to be between 70 and 300 billion board feet. Although during the heyday of the lumbering business the exploitation of the forests was wasteful, reseeding practices were begun sufficiently early to insure a continuing foundation for the lumber business. Today three large national forests in the region further promote forest conservation.

Lumber enjoyed a symbiotic relationship with railroads. Railroad construction had given it its impetus; by 1900 the railroads obtained more revenue from the shipment of lumber than anything else. Over six hundred Texas mills sent their products all over the nation and to many foreign countries. After 1900 the number of mills decreased, although the output did not, as the major operations grew and consolidated. Texas' first multimillion dollar corporation, according to one historian, was the Kirby Lumber Company, chartered in 1901, whose mills were capable of producing half as much as all the others in Texas combined.

The census of 1900 reveals that industry had more than doubled during the preceding decade. The number of plants had increased over 200 per cent to 12,000; capital invested had doubled, to $90,000,000; wages paid had increased to $20,000,000; and the total value of products had risen to $120,000,000. During the three decades, 1870 to 1900, industrial income in Texas increased from one-fourth agricultural income to one-half, and it increased from two per cent of the national total to nearly ten per cent. This growth was significant, but nothing to compare with the development of the next century.

In 1900 lumbering remained the state's first-ranking industry, but that year the manufacture of cottonseed oil and cake displaced milling in the second rank. The development of this industry reflected not only the growth of the cattle business but also the depletion of natural forage, for it had been discovered that cottonseed products made an excellent food for livestock. Until this time cottonseed had been regarded as a nuisance, a waste to be disposed of. The gross value of cottonseed oil and cake was so negligible in 1870 that it was not listed on the census, but the gross value jumped to $14,000,000 in 1900, when there were 103 mills in the cotton-growing regions of the state. Besides lumbering, cottonseed production, and flour and grist milling, the leading Texas industries in 1900 were railroad car construction and repair, cotton ginning, liquor and malt distilling, foundry and machine work, wood planing, and ceramic production. By 1900 Galveston County had fallen to sixth place in manufacturing, behind Harris, Dallas, El Paso, Bexar, and Tarrant. But the state was still basically rural and agrarian, and farming was the means of subsistence for the great majority of people.

Farming Farming during the last quarter of the century involved complicated factors: the move from the humid eastern regions westward to the marginal subhumid areas; the increase of tenancy; the development of new crops, plant varieties, and farming technology; the shift from self-sufficiency to dependent specialization, especially in cotton; and the early use of the machinery that heralded twentieth-century agriculture. It is impossible to single out the most significant of these factors.

The farmers' frontier followed hard on the heels of the cattlemen's frontier and climbed the Caprock onto the High Plains before the beginning of the new century. This movement carried farming into subhumid regions, which because of insufficient rainfall were often hostile toward it. The soils, however, were for the most part deep and fertile, and the fields were easy to open because of the absence of trees and rocks, conditions particularly true of the High Plains. To survive the low rainfall, farmers turned to the techniques invented in the last part of the century called dry farming, described in the preceding chapter.

Because of the generous purchase terms from the state, most of the West Texas farms were operated by the owners, many of whom had come from tenant farms in the eastern part of Texas, where farm tenancy was increasing. During the period the proportion of farms operated by tenants increased from one-third to one-half. There were two types of farm tenants: the cash renter and the sharecropper. The cash renter bore all the risks of the crop himself, besides investing funds in the operation. Little wonder that the tenant who paid rent in shares of the crop (usually one-third of the grain crops and one-fourth of the cotton) outnumbered him five to one. Despite its obvious advantage to a poor man, tenant farming, especially sharecropping, has widely been considered an evil. But the problems were not so much in tenancy itself as in its conditions such as credit extended from owner to tenant and pressure from the owner toward the greater profits of specialization in a single crop.

There was no single cause for the increase in tenancy, which continued into the next century. One was the exhaustion of the public domain, which made it impossible for a poor man to move west to homestead. Another was the depression of the nineties, which precipitated a movement from the city back to the farm. Another was the increase in population without a corresponding increase in industrial and commercial employment. Others were the overextension of credit, the high interest rates, and the falling farm prices with consequent foreclosures that converted some owner-operators to tenants. And in part it was the development of commercialized farming.

The cause of the shift from subsistence farming to one-crop specialization was much less complex. Pioneer farmsteads were virtually self-contained units producing most of the family's needs. The development of rail transportation made possible a specialization in agriculture: it not only broadened the farmer's market potential but also helped convert him into a consumer of goods. Cotton was the big money crop, as it had been since the 1840's. Enabled to purchase many of the items he formerly had to produce for himself, the average farmer began putting more acreage into the cash crop. Cotton production grew by leaps and bounds, increasing from a total value of $10,000,000 in 1870 to over $100,000,000 in 1900. This represented an increase from a total of 350,000 bales ginned in 1870 to 2,500,000 bales in 1900. Despite this fantastic increase in production—1,000 per cent in value, 700 per cent in bales—the price of cotton to the farmer dropped much less drastically. It took very little imagination, therefore, for a subsistence farmer to make the shift to commercial farming. But in the long run he found himself only slightly better off because of a relative increase in prices on nonagricultural products. Some farmers got the feeling, according to one historian, that they were living in a perennial depression. One of the effects, of course, and perhaps the most significant one, of this shift to specialization was that the farmer lost much of his independence. If his cotton crop was poor, or if it failed, or if cotton prices dropped, he was forced to go into debt to survive. Between 1890 and 1900 the number of mortgaged farms increased from 7,000 to 38,000.

Other than cotton, the principal crops in Texas were wheat, corn, oats, and sugar cane. The harvest in all of these increased each decade from 1870 to 1900, although not as phenomenally as with cotton. During this period the number of farms multiplied by nearly six, from 61,000 in 1870 to 350,000 in 1900, and the number of acres in production jumped from 3,000,000 to 20,000,000. Quite clearly, despite the increase in industrial production, Texas' economy was still tied to agriculture, both farming and stock raising. A change was in the offing in the next century beginning with the mighty eruption of the gusher at Spindletop.

Recovery and Protest

The Politics of Recovery According to E. T. Miller, an historian of Texas finances, the financial legacies of the war and Reconstruction periods were "the large growth of expenditures, the great increase in taxation, and the rapid accumulation of a comparatively heavy debt." Once the Democrats had replaced the Radical Constitution with their own rather unwieldy instrument in 1876 and had eradicated the measures of the Davis administration, they adopted the goal of repudiating this financial inheritance. Measures for economic recovery were the main political issues throughout the decade.

But the problems that faced the first Democratic administration under Governor Coke were insurmountable, and the financial situation worsened measurably during his term because of the devastation of the Panic of 1873. An added burden was the expense of the Frontier Battalion, which aided federal troops in defending the frontier. Although Texas was later reimbursed by the federal government for much of this outlay for defense, that did not relieve the exigency of the moment. When Coke assumed office in 1874, there was less than $40,000 in the treasury; tax receipts for the following year were estimated at less than $500,000; and expenditures were projected at over $1,200,000. So critical was the situation that state warrants, uncollectable at the treasury, were passing at thirty and forty per cent discounts. Three expedients were adopted in an attempt to cope with the problem: funding some of the debt with bond issues, increasing the tax revenue, and substituting grants of land for portions of the indebtedness.

These measures apparently met with popular approval, for Coke was reelected in the February 1876 election, which ratified the new constitution. The new legislature immediately set out to increase the general revenue by new procedures of taxation authorized by the constitution. Business taxes were levied in an attempt to tap a source of revenue besides the citizen who owned property. A reform in the method of collecting the general property tax from railroad and telegraph companies, however, resulted in a decrease in revenue. Occupational taxes, authorized by the Constitution of 1876, were placed on a wide variety of occupations. Some of these, such as a two hundred dollar tax on fortune-tellers, were intended to be prohibitive. The occupation taxes were considerably extended later. The Constitution of 1876 also authorized for the support of education a poll tax of one dollar on every adult male. Before the year 1876 ended, this tax was increased to two dollars, half of which was for the general revenue fund. Collection of the tax, however, was difficult, and it generally fell unevenly on owners of real estate.

In the fall of 1876, the legislature elected Coke to the United States Senate to replace Republican Morgan C. Hamilton, whose term expired on March 3, 1877. It had previously replaced James W. Flanagan with Samuel Bell Maxey in 1875. Coke resigned on December 1 to move to Washington and was succeeded by his lieutenant governor, Richard B. Hubbard. Hubbard proceeded along the lines initiated by his predecessor. Although when he left office the public debt had increased, he could claim modest success in reducing the interest rate by substituting six per cent bonds for many of the earlier seven, eight, and ten per cent issues.

Hubbard probably would have been elected to serve a second term if there had not been a deadlock in the Democratic Party Convention of 1878. He, former Governor Throckmorton, and William W. Lang, who was chief executive of the state Grange, were nominated, and each had sufficient support in the convention to prevent a majority vote for any one of them. Confronted with divisiveness within the party and the frightening possibility of a Republican victory if it were not resolved, the convention desperately sought a compromise candidate outside the convention. A special committee chose Oran M. Roberts, former president of the Secession Convention and then Chief Justice of the Texas Supreme Court. He won handily the general election that fall and was reelected two years later, serving as governor from January 21, 1879, to January 21, 1883. He was probably the most significant governor between Pease in the 1850's and Hogg in the 1890's.

Roberts' first inaugural address is one of the longest on record and possibly the most meaningful. He followed that with a series of messages on the necessity for economy in government and several means of achieving it. Most of the legislature accepted his leadership although there was opposition to some of his proposals, especially one favoring reduction in school appropriations. Over the next four years there was a substantial reduction in the public debt, a decrease in the tax rate, a solvent government, and a surplus in the treasury.

Among the first measures passed were a new bond issue at six per cent to refund higher interest bearing paper, which was recommended by Hubbard before he left office; a reduction in the payment of pensions to veterans; a reduction in the percentage of the general revenue allocated to schools from twenty-five per cent to twenty per cent; further reforms in the assessment and collection of *ad valorem* and poll taxes; and several new taxes such as the Bell Punch and Drummer taxes. The soon repealed Bell Punch tax, a levy on the sale of malt and alcoholic beverages, required saloon keepers to ring up the tax on a special mechanism every time a drink was sold. It was laughed out of existence. The Drummer tax was an attempt to gain revenue from out-of-state traveling salesmen, who, Roberts said, enjoyed the benefits of the state without paying for them. It was later declared unconstitutional in the United States Supreme Court. Despite the adherence of both Coke and Hubbard to the pay-as-you-go principles of the constitution, the budget was not balanced under the Democratic regime until 1879, and only then by Roberts' twice vetoing the appropriation bill when the legislature refused to cut the school appropriation. Forced into an extra session, the legislature succumbed to the governor's demands by reducing the school appropriation to one-sixth of the general revenue.

Roberts' most significant contribution to the fiscal operations was not a measure for economy but a proposal that the state release the public domain at minimal prices to any purchaser who wished to buy it. His argument was forceful and logical. In the first place revenue from the sales could help reduce the debt, and in the second place taxes on the property so placed in private hands would increase the general revenue.

As a result two important land laws were enacted in 1879. One, called the Four Section Settler Act, provided for the sale of four sections of school lands—the alternate sections of the railroad surveys reserved to the school fund—to actual settlers at one dollar an acre. The other, called the Fifty Cent Law, placed the unreserved public domain on the market for any purchaser at fifty cents an acre. This second act caused considerable turmoil, and the opposition to it brought about major revisions in the land policy. A loophole in the law permitted speculators to tie up large tracts of public domain on options without consummating the purchase. A courageous land commissioner, W. C. Walsh, stopped this activity by rigidly interpreting some of the wording of the law.

The fifty-cent land was in unorganized counties in West Texas, and purchasers were required to survey and file field notes on it before obtaining a patent. Because of this cost the effective price of the land rose to one dollar an acre. Half the proceeds of the sale were automatically appropriated to the school fund in lieu of the alternate sections. The act, of course, permitted the acquisition of large tracts of contiguous property, which was, as has been pointed out, a boon to ranchers. But many people became alarmed at the possibility of the establishment of large landholding monopolies in the state.

These land acts became a principal issue in the election of 1882. John Ireland, who opposed them, received the Democratic nomination and was elected over a coalition candidate, George W. Jones, who was supported by Greenbackers and Republicans. A drastic revision in the state's land policy followed. A special session of the legislature in 1882 had revoked the general law granting lands to railroads. Then in 1883 the Fifty Cent Law was repealed and the Four Section Settler Act was modified, raising the price and establishing a Land Board to classify the lands before they were put on the market as agricultural, pastoral, or timbered, with or without water. An auction feature was instituted, and the maximum purchase was increased to eight sections. With minor revisions this law remained the state policy until the public domain was exhausted.

Ireland otherwise continued the frugal policies of his predecessor, and in 1884 he was reelected by the largest majority in the state's history up to that time. He urged development of eleemosynary institutions, reform of the penitentiary system, and support of higher education. During his administration, however, the legislature refused to make appropriations for the new University of Texas. His four years in office witnessed several major tumults such as the fence-cutting wars and the strikes of the Knights of Labor in 1885 and 1886.

The Voices of Protest   The labor strikes of 1885 and 1886 were probably the least effective and least significant of the protest movements in Texas during the last quarter of the nineteenth century. Three other dissident segments of Texas society were more vocal and more potent: the frustrated Negroes, who were finding little success in bettering their social and economic position; the ardent Prohibitionists, who believed that alcohol was the root of all social evil; and the bewildered farmers, who were trying to cope with agricultural specialization, increasing tenancy, and falling farm prices and rising consumer costs. These four groups had little in common. Each was responding to different motivations, different evils real or imagined, and different aspects of the social and economic order. Infant labor protested the practices of incipient industry; Negroes feebly protested discrimination; Prohibitionists in a witless guise of temperance protested all drinking; and the heterogeneous mass of farmers protested nearly everything in sight, especially the railroads.

At the beginning of this period not only were the farmers the major occupational group in the state, but also most Texans were farmers.

Their organization, the Patrons of Husbandry, dominated the reestablishment of the state government after the downfall of the Republicans. But the farmers themselves were divided into social and economic plateaus: the big operators participated in what came to be called the Bourbon Democracy, and the small ones, feeling the pinch of the depression of the seventies, turned to join the first protest movement of the period, the Greenback Party. The national Greenback Party had arisen in the Midwest in 1874 to oppose the resumption of specie as the federal government's exclusive legal tender and to support the continued issuance of paper money. In Texas the Democratic Party opposed the resumption act but would not go so far as to endorse a proposal for an expanded issue of paper currency.

During 1877 Greenback Clubs began to appear in Texas, advocating the national demands for inflation of the currency. This idea temporarily united hard-pressed small farmers, many of them tenants, laborers, and Negroes. By the summer of 1878 there were nearly five hundred Greenback Clubs in Texas. At a state-wide convention in August their delegates nominated W. H. Hamman for governor to contest the candidacy of Oran M. Roberts. E. J. Davis and the Republicans decided to join the Greenbackers in an attempt to wrest control of the state from the Democrats, although a small group of Republicans put forth a weak ticket headed by A. B. Norton. Roberts won over Hamman by almost three to one, and Norton carried less than ten per cent of the vote.

Falsely encouraged by the 55,000 votes Hamman received, the Greenbackers renominated him but lost the support of the Republicans, who named E. J. Davis. Roberts won again in this 1880 contest, but not by as wide a margin: Roberts, 166,101; Davis, 64,382; Hamman, 33,721. The voices of protest had polled nearly forty per cent of the popular vote but had in the process discovered that the Greenback Party could not unite their efforts. Fusion came in 1882, when both Greenbackers and Republicans endorsed an Independent candidate for governor, George W. "Wash" Jones, a man of Greenback principles who was then serving in the United States Congress. It was the closest election since the election a decade earlier which had returned the Democrats to office. Jones appealed for support to all elements of dissent, including the recently organized Farmers' Alliance and the Knights of Labor. He polled 102,501 votes against Ireland's 150,809.

Perhaps the voices of protest were too strident for the period of returning prosperity; perhaps the objects of their protests were too fragmented; perhaps the fusion of Republicans and Greenbackers as independents was too awkward. Ireland and the Democrats won easily in 1884 over Jones as an Independent and Norton as the Republican nominee.

The Republican Party suffered the beginning of a serious schism. Davis had died the preceding year, and several factions were struggling to dominate the party. Norris Wright Cuney, a remarkable Negro leader from Galveston with control of most of the Negro element in the party, had favored continued alliance with the Greenbackers. The Norton faction bolted the state convention and held a rump "straight-out Republican" convention to nominate a full slate of officers. The next decade saw the Republicans divided into white and black corps, with Cuney the master of the party machinery.

The voices of protest sang in a dissonant chorus of a half-dozen groups in 1886: the Democrats; a minority of disaffected Democrats; the Republicans; the Grand State Farmers' Alliance; the Prohibitionists; and the Antimonopoly Party. The Democrats won, with Lawrence S. Ross as governor, but the party would never be the same again. Conservative, Bourbon, former Confederate elements ceased to control the conventions, and the party, as a matter of survival, began to absorb into its platforms enough demands of the protest groups to dominate the elections. For this reason a brief review of the background and development of these groups should prove helpful.

The Farmers: The economic problems of the farmers have been previously discussed, as has their political influence through the Grange. The Grange, however, was not strictly speaking a political party; consequently a number of farmers, especially the poorer ones, found political opportunity in the Greenback Party. A new agrarian organization that appeared in Texas in 1875 was soon to succeed the Grange as the spokesman of the farmers. The first Farmers' Alliance seems to have begun somewhat spontaneously in Lampasas, Wise, and Parker counties. In 1879 it was reorganized as a State Alliance at Poolville in Parker County, and by 1886 it claimed three thousand lodges in farming communities throughout the state. That year the state-wide convention of the Grand State Alliance at Cleburne altered the Alliance from a fraternal and benevolent group to a politically oriented behemoth. The Alliance excluded Negroes, opposed alien land ownership and speculative futures trading in agricultural products, and demanded currency inflation, prison reform, enforcement of labor contracts, recognition of labor unions, and establishment of a bureau of labor statistics and an interstate commerce commission. This 1886 program, with its many demands of national scope, burst like a grenade over the Texas political scene, even though the Alliance did not nominate a slate of candidates.

Labor: Labor organizations had begun to appear in Texas before the Civil War, lapsing comatose during the conflict and appearing with renewed vigor during Reconstruction. In 1866 a group of longshoremen organized the Screwman's Benevolent Association, which was followed in 1870 by Norris Wright Cuney's Negro Longshoremen's Association. By that year locals of the International Typographical Union had been formed in such Texas cities as Galveston, Houston, and Austin. These groups were not particularly turbulent and were loosely, if at all, affiliated with national organizations. But in the ensuing decade, the Knights of Labor, then the strongest national labor organization, began to operate in Texas, especially among railroad workers. In 1885 this organization boasted from seven or eight thousand individual members to around thirty thousand, including many Alliance clubs which strictly speaking were not part of the vertical, industry-wide organization of the Knights but which sympathized with their goals. Other labor organizations had entered the state, including the United Mine Workers in 1884. The decade of the 1880's was one of labor strife and strikes in Texas, as in the rest of the nation. From 1881 to 1886 one hundred strikes were called, closing the struck establishments a total of 405 days and involving 8,124 workers, who lost an average of 708 days each. The most dramatic of these strikes was the "great southwest rail strike" against the Gould lines in 1885-1886. The largest was a strike of fifteen hundred longshoremen in Galveston in 1885. The most significant was probably the "Capitol boycott" against the firm constructing the Texas statehouse. The first and one of the longest was a strike of fifty draymen in 1880. And the most curious was the "cowboy strike" of 1883, in which some three hundred cowboys in the Texas Panhandle who had never heard of organized labor went on strike against seven ranches for a simple increase in wages. Although none of these strikes was especially effective, the totality of labor unrest, supported as it was by the Farmers' Alliance, became a significant factor in future Texas elections.

The Negroes: The Negroes' social and economic status appeared to have worsened after the return of Democratic control. The depression of the seventies had made it difficult for most to achieve any degree of economic success and had kept the vast majority bound to tenancy and manual labor. Furthermore, that the Negro population of 1890 was almost double what it was in 1870 tended further to depress the Negroes' condition. There was a shift of Negro population westward from deep East Texas to the blackland prairies of Central Texas, but apparently few Negroes filed on school lands or preempted quarter-section homestead tracts, probably more because of a lack of even the small sums required than because of apathy on their part or discrimination by the General Land Office. Although during this period no laws were passed restricting even indirectly their right of suffrage, there was a decline in Negroes' political influence partly because of an apathy arising from the improbability of Republican victory but more because of a decline of approximately ten per cent in the proportion of Negroes in the total population.

The Prohibitionists: Like the labor movement, the Prohibition movement in Texas was rooted in the 1850's, and like labor it did not gain much strength until 1870, the time of the organization of the United Friends of Temperance and its juvenile affiliate, the Bands of Hope. And, also like labor, it became a powerful voice in the 1880's, after the establishment of the Women's Christian Temperance Union. The vehement emotionalism and clever semantics of articulate spokesmen gave the Prohibition movement a broader and more heterogeneous base than any of the other protest movements. For this reason, perhaps, first the Grange, then the Greenbackers, and finally the Alliance supported some form of Prohibition legislation. In 1886 a state-wide Prohibition convention in Dallas adopted a platform and nominated a slate of candidates. The platform piously included a plank invoking the blessings of the Almighty Creator, demanded that the legislature submit to the voters a state-wide Prohibition amendment, and enlisted the aid of the Alliance by denouncing all "futures" operations. E. L. Dohoney, whose chameleon nature had run the political gamut from Unionist to Confederate to Greenbacker, was the Prohibitionists' gubernatorial candidate.

The Politics of Reform

The Beginnings of Reform Thus the election of 1886 promised to be lively. Could the Democrats sustain their hold on the state government against the mounting tempo for change? Not without changing. The Democrats wooed Alliance votes for their candidate L. S. Ross by nominating for attorney general the young James Stephen Hogg, who had great strength with the East Texas farm vote. Nothing, of course, is ever really that simple in modern politics: Ross' Civil War career made him the most popular man to campaign for office in Texas, and Hogg's selection as attorney general was partly due to the astute political sense of George Clark. The Democrats won the contest, and Ross was reelected in '1888, but his administration was dominated by Hogg and a legislature that responded to at least some protest demands.

The first was the submission to the electorate in 1887 of a Prohibition amendment. Both wet and dry girded for a bitter contest. The *Texas Christian Advocate* and the *Texas Baptist Herald* led the Prohibition fight, which received assistance from such politicians as John H. Reagan, Sam Bell Maxey, and David B. Culberson. Interestingly, James S. Hogg was one of the leaders of the "antis," as were George Clark and Roger Q. Mills, a prominent Texas congressman. The amendment was defeated amid wild accusation and vituperation, 220,000 to 129,000. The total vote was substantially larger than the vote cast in the gubernatorial election the preceding fall, and the Prohibitionists' vote was the largest they were able to muster for more than twenty years.

Although Prohibition failed, the pulse of reform still beat strongly. In the national congress John H. Reagan introduced the Interstate Commerce Act shortly before his elevation to the United States Senate by the Texas legislature in 1887. The same legislature discussed, but did not act on, antimonopoly, antitrust, and railroad regulation. Its successor, however, passed in 1889 the nation's second antitrust statute, a much less effective measure having been passed by the Kansas legislature a scant four weeks earlier. Aimed chiefly at railroad rate-fixing associations, the Texas act provided a broad base for all types of antitrust litigation by defining trusts as combinations of capital, skill, or acts of persons or corporations for the purpose of restricting trade, limiting production, or controlling prices. This important statute was sustained by the United States Supreme Court, which struck down a later Illinois statute. It is worth noting, too, that Reagan introduced a bill in the United States Senate for a federal antitrust act on the same day that the Sherman Antitrust Bill was introduced.

Under Attorney General Hogg the Texas antitrust act became a lethal weapon (as well as a means to personal political success). Using it along with a constitutional proscription against monopolies, recently passed insurance legislation, and earlier feeble railroad regulations, he ruthlessly flayed corporate abuses in the state and occasionally scourged business firms unnecessarily. Since he won most of the actions he instigated, his image became that of a champion of the common people against business, although in fact he was much more a champion of law and its enforcement. His earliest moves were against insurance companies operating in Texas contrary to Texas statutes: in February 1887 he sent a list of them, given him by the insurance commission, to county and district attorneys in a famous "circular letter" urging them to file local actions and promising support. Soon the insurance world was agog with the flurry of activity that rid the state of scores of undercapitalized, insolvent, or illicit companies. Insurance Commissioner L. L. Foster estimated that the people of Texas were saved at least one million dollars during Hogg's four years as attorney general.

Hogg's successes against insurance companies were offset somewhat by his handling of the Willis investigation and his loss of the Drummer tax case before the Supreme Court. In 1885 Judge Frank Willis had heard the celebrated Grass Lease Cases, in which ranchers were charged with violating enclosure laws. Judge Willis's charge to a jury of cowboys and cattlemen predetermined the verdict of not guilty on the grounds that the ranchers' renewals of their grass leases had been legal. The legislature thereupon undertook an investigation, and Hogg assayed the condemnation of Willis. His accusations of the judge were so vituperative and his language so unrestrained that he lost the support of a number of his friends, including George Clark, and utterly alienated the stockmen of West Texas. Since the legislature neither vindicated nor condemned Willis, Hogg stood the ultimate loser. His unsuccessful defense before the United States Supreme Court of the Texas occupation tax on traveling salesmen, the Drummer tax, was a disappointment to him, but his losing was in no way the result of either pyrotechnics or incompetence. And the loss did not discredit him with the voters, for it fell in the middle of the 1888 campaign but both he and Governor Ross were reelected.

A partial reason for the victory was the successful fulfillment of Texas' demands that the federal government reimburse the state for the cost of defending its own frontier. These claims included not only the expense of the Texas Rangers and the Frontier Battalion but also the value of cattle and other property lost because of Indian depredations. A substantial settlement of one million dollars permitted Ross' administration to reduce taxes while increasing expenditures, a situation that could not help but bring him popularity at the polls.

Ross took the limelight briefly after his inauguration to put down the Jaybird-Woodpecker War in Fort Bend County. The struggle for control of the county in the 1888 election between the Jaybirds (regular Democrats) and the Woodpeckers (Republicans) broke out into violence. Three men were killed and several wounded before Governor Ross himself rode into the town of Richmond at the head of volunteer militia forces and quelled the rioting in August 1889.

Before the election Attorney General Hogg had shifted his attention to railroad companies, and during his second term they became his principal targets. He first enforced Texas laws requiring companies to comply with the terms of their charters, especially as to the number of their incorporators and the counties they were authorized to serve. In 1888, by threatening to sue for cancellation of its charter, he forced a small operating line of the Southern Pacific in East Texas to repair its roadbed after a storm and to resume service. The same year he similarly forced the Texas Trunk Railroad to resume operations on thirty miles of abandoned track in Kaufman County. At that time he wrote, "The purpose of the State is to *compel* railroads to do their duty towards the public." That statement was backed by the argument that both the state and individual communities had made substantial contributions to the construction of the lines and that the companies were therefore obligated to operate trains on them in accordance with their charter commitments.

Failure to maintain service was only one of the railroad abuses the attorney general found. More important, he believed, were rate fixing and monopolistic pooling of interests. For self-protection competing lines had formed the Texas Traffic Association shortly after the marriage of the Gould-Huntington interests in Texas. Soon the Association came to dominate the fixing of freight rates in the state. In 1888 Hogg induced the Texas Supreme Court to issue an injunction for dissolution of the Association. But the member lines reformed as the International Traffic Association with headquarters outside the state, and they were able to operate with immunity, although with less effectiveness, for several years thereafter.

Hogg also attacked the methods by which some railroads were disposing of the bonus lands awarded them by the state, and he forced others to dispose of their land as the alienation provision required within a prescribed time. He tangled with railroad magnate Jay Gould over the issue of operating receiverships for lines that were in bankruptcy. Hogg contended that lines chartered by Texas should go to receivers appointed by Texas courts; Gould fought for federal receivership, especially for his East Line subsidiary. After considerable litigation Hogg won this fight too.

"Hogg and Commission" As the election of 1890 approached, two things became apparent: Hogg would be a leading contestant for the governorship, and regulation of railroads would be the chief issue. Hogg advocated the establishment of a state railroad commission for such regulation, and a strong proposed amendment to the constitution was put before the electorate in 1890. "Hogg and Commission" drew support from the Farmers' Alliance and other protest groups, and railroad regulation was so popular that every political convention that year endorsed some form of state control of railroads. But Hogg had made powerful enemies: George Clark, Charles Goodnight and most of the ranching interests in West Texas, the Capitol Syndicate, Jay Gould and practically all of the railroad interests, and indeed the greater part of the corporate business world. Nonetheless, he managed a clear victory at the Democratic State Convention in San Antonio, and in the November election the people of Texas adopted the amendment and elected Hogg with a mandate to establish the railroad commission.

The next step, the actual creation of the commission by statute, was up to the legislature. Anticommission forces, although they had failed at the polls, prepared to kill the commission bill in the legislature. Had it not been for astute maneuvering by the new governor, they would have succeeded. The three-man Texas Railroad Commission was created on April 3. Governor Hogg then appointed John H. Reagan, who resigned his seat in the United States Senate, to the chairmanship, and appointed L. L. Foster, the crusading insurance commissioner, and William P. McLean, a conscientious district judge, to the other two places.

The appointment of Reagan was a master stroke because he enjoyed a reputation for honesty among all classes of Texans. Furthermore, he was competent to withstand the pressures emanating from railroad companies to defeat the incipient commission in the courts in a last-ditch fight. In August 1892, before the commission had begun to function effectively, railroad attorneys won from a federal court an injunction restraining the Texas agency. Reagan appealed to the Supreme Court, which two years later validated the constitutionality of the Texas statute. By the time of his retirement in 1903, he had made the commission one of the most powerful agencies in the state and one of the most respected railroad regulatory bodies in the nation.

With the railroad commission fighting for its life in the courts, the election of 1892 became something of a free-for-all. Primarily in the efforts of James Hogg, the Democratic Party had responded to the voices of protest, but for many of the disaffected these efforts had not gone far enough toward reform. Now a new element joined them: the conservatives who believed the Democratic Party had gone too far. George Clark, who had placed himself at the head of the opposition to Hogg, determined to form any kind of coalition he could to win control of the state government. Party schisms at the time made this seem an imminent likelihood.

The Democrats were torn into three groups: the main body of the party led by Hogg, the conservative element led by Clark, and a discontented group of Alliance men who withdrew from the party to form the Jeffersonian Democrats and to flirt with the newly formed National Peoples' Party, the Populists. The first state convention of the Populists, held in 1891, showed surprising strength. At a second convention in 1892 they nominated Thomas L. Nugent for governor and adopted a platform intended to appeal to labor and small farmers. Nugent, an attorney well known for his sympathy for the farmers, made a strong candidate, and he received much support from the Jeffersonian, also called Skunk, Democrats. Clark and the conservatives had managed to force a further fragmentation of the Democratic Party in the state convention at Houston. When the convention opened, Hogg supporters and regular Democrats rushed in and grabbed every available seat in the spectator sections of the car barn that served as a convention hall. Clark and his followers held their own convention in Turner Hall. The Car Barn Democrats quickly nominated Hogg; the Turner Hall Democrats nominated Clark.

The Republican Party also suffered divisiveness. Cuney's iron control caused white Republicans to revolt and form the Lily White faction of the party in 1890. In 1892 the Lily Whites nominated a slate of candidates, but Cuney and the Regular Republicans held back, promising support to George Clark as a conservative Democrat. It was a strange alliance of former enemies.

Hogg, Clark, and Nugent became the major contenders in the November election, although they were modestly challenged by Albert C. Prendergast, the Prohibition Party candidate, and Andrew J. Houston, the Lily White candidate. The score read: Hogg, 190,486; Clark, 133,395; Nugent, 108,483; Prendergast, 1,605; Houston, 1,322. Hogg entered his second term as a plurality governor, but he did not abate his program for reform; in fact, with the Populist support he expanded it.

This program was customarily referred to as the Hogg Laws, of which the establishment of the Railroad Commission was the most important. Other significant laws were the Alien Land Law of 1891, which gave alien property owners six years to dispose of their holdings; the Perpetuities and Corporations Land Law of 1893, which required all corporations to rid themselves of real estate holdings within fifteen years; and the Stock and Bond Law of 1893, which gave the Railroad Commission authority to supervise issues of stocks and bonds by railroad companies. This last law put an end to watered stock and worthless bonds. The land divestment laws, on the other hand, may have done more harm than good. They were designed to prevent corporate and alien speculation in land, but their principal effect may have been to restrict the flow of outside capital into Texas, and in any case land-owning corporations immediately began to develop legal dodges to circumvent the law.

The End of the Century The last six years of the century were less eventful politically. Largely because of the hardships wrought by the Panic of 1893, the agrarian protest crescendoed, but the discontented elements were bled off from the Democrats into the Populist Party, where they had less effect than they might have had if they had worked within either of the major parties. Furthermore, the machinery and control of the Democratic Party fell into the grasp of the smoothest and most astute politician yet to appear on the Texas scene: the quiet, secretive, and almost self-effacing Edward M. House, who managed affairs with a minimum of disruption or discontinuity.

House, who inherited a substantial fortune at the age of twenty-two, not only had increased it by astute investment to give him comfortable independence but also had thereby freed himself from active business participation. He turned his interests to politics to play an influential role behind the scenes. It was he who managed Hogg's campaign in 1892 and who then wrested control of the party from Hogg in 1894. Early in that election year Hogg offered his support to Reagan as his successor, but House decreed that Charles M. Culberson would be the Democratic nominee. He outmaneuvered Hogg, organized a harmony convention with former Clark Democrats, and nominated Culberson, who was the son of United States Congressman David B. Culberson and who was Hogg's attorney general from 1891 to 1895. Reunification of the Democrats was largely brought about by the startling threat of the hundred thousand votes received by Populist Nugent in 1892. Despite the appearance of candidates from both factions of the Republican Party and from the Prohibitionist Party, Nugent and the Populists ran very strongly in 1894, polling 152,731 votes to Culberson's 207,167.

In 1896 under Cuney's able guidance the two Republican factions united to support the Populist candidate, Jerome C. Kearby, in an all-out effort to defeat the Democrats. The controlling party was also threatened by a new split within its ranks into "gold" and "silver" Democrats, those who advocated a gold standard and those who advocated free coinage of silver. Again House managed harmony. Culberson was renominated, and the Texas Democratic Party pledged itself to William Jennings Bryan and the free coinage of silver. Culberson won the general election with 298,548 votes to Kearby's 238,692. For many years this remained the last serious threat to Democratic control of the state. In 1898, with no difficulty at all, House achieved the nomination of Joseph D. Sayers, who beat his Populist opponent, Barnett Gibbs, nearly three to one. During their short life span, however, the Populists had won a number of local offices and legislative seats and in 1896 had caused the Democrats to build into their platform many Populist demands.

Culberson's four-year administration was an odd mixture of Hogg's dynamic reform programs with his earlier conservatism. Culberson vetoed more legislation than any other Texas governor, primarily in an effort to keep costs down. Yet at least half a dozen important statutes were passed that were truly reform or progressive legislation, for example, the major land act of 1895 and a law attempting to regulate labor relations. A probably more significant continuation of Hogg's policies was the successful antitrust suit that Culberson's attorney general, M. M. Crane, prosecuted against the Waters-Pierce Oil Company. This subsidiary of the Standard Oil Company was based in Missouri and was doing business in Texas in violation of the 1889 antitrust law. Crane won a verdict in 1897 that forced it out of the state, and the decision was sustained by the United States Supreme Court in 1900. Nominally shedding Standard control, Waters-Pierce reentered Texas and became the center of one of the state's greatest controversies a few years later. The Waters-Pierce victory was offset by the loss of the Greer County case in the Supreme Court. Greer County was a Texas county between two forks of the Red River along the 100th meridian. Texas claimed that the North Fork, referred to on early maps as the Main Fork, was the principal channel of the river intended in the treaty of 1819; the Territory of Oklahoma claimed that Prairie Dog Town Fork was the main branch. After a great amount of testimony was heard, the Supreme Court decided in favor of Oklahoma in 1896, and Texas lost the land that was in Greer County.

According to Alwyn Barr's history of Texas politics of this period, the election of Sayers marked a loss of ground for the more progressive leaders of the Democratic Party but did not end the reform urge. Sayers strengthened the antitrust law, vetoed railroad consolidation bills, helped organize relief and flood control, and tried unsuccessfully to ram through a special session of the legislature a true tax rendition bill directed against banks, telephone and telegraph companies, and railroads. As the century ended, all was quiet on the political front.

The flurry of excitement caused by the Spanish-American War did little to disrupt the political somnolence. The nation declared war against Spain on April 25, 1898, to protect American investments in Cuba and to protest the excesses of the Spanish government there. The flamboyant Theodore Roosevelt rushed to recruit from southwestern ranches the regiment of cavalry known as the Rough Riders. Many Texans enlisted and after training at San Antonio followed Roosevelt to Tampa and then up San Juan Hill. The war ended on December 10, 1898, leaving the state undisturbed save for the titillative memory of cowboy-soldiers in slouch hats, blue flannel shirts, and bandana kerchiefs.

Social Developments

Demographic Changes   During the thirty years from 1870 to 1900 Texas' population increased from 818,579 to 3,048,710, raising the state's population from the country's nineteenth largest to its sixth. The decade of greatest growth was the 1870's, when the population almost doubled. The rate of growth in Texas during the thirty years was nearly twice the rate of the nation as a whole. About half the increase in the population during those thirty years came from the excess of births over deaths, and about half from migration to Texas. Most of the newcomers were from the southern United States.

The percentage of rural population declined from 93.3 to 82.9. The percentage of Negroes and members of other nonwhite races (the latter being almost negligible) declined about ten points. The percentage of foreign-born Texans remained approximately the same. Because of the birth of a second generation of foreign-born or mixed parentage, this means that the percentage of persons of foreign stock in the population was increasing markedly, although actual data are not available. People from Mexico constituted the largest group of the foreign-born at that time, but they were considerably fewer than the total of the European-born, among whom Britons were first, Austrians second, and Scandinavians third until 1890, when they were displaced by Bohemians.

That the population was almost completely rural in 1870 is illustrated by the fact that only one of the five most populous counties (in descending order: Washington, Harris, Rusk, Fayette, and Caldwell) contained one of the five largest towns (in descending order: Galveston, San Antonio, Houston, Brownsville, and Jefferson). In the 1880's, however, the growth of the towns was reflected in the county ranking. The largest counties were Dallas, Bexar, Washington, Travis, and Galveston, and the largest cities were Galveston, San Antonio, Houston, Dallas, and Austin. In 1900 the ranks were Dallas, Bexar, Harris, Travis, and Tarrant counties and San Antonio, Houston, Dallas, Galveston, and Fort Worth. Not only had there been a shift of approximately ten per cent to urban dwelling, but there had been a small shift to the larger cities. In 1870 the five largest towns contained just over five per cent of the total population; in 1900 the five major cities contained approximately seven per cent. A more significant change was the movement of the population centers toward the west. By 1900 the axis of population ran from the Dallas and Fort Worth area north through Denton and Grayson counties and south through Waco, Austin, and San Antonio.

Educational Developments The Constitution of 1876 struck down the centralized public education system of the Constitution of 1869 and substituted virtual autonomy in local school boards. But it also provided quite generously for the support of the public schools. One half the remaining unappropriated public domain, all the alternate sections in railroad and internal improvement surveys, and all the funds that had previously been set aside were placed in a permanent school fund, the income from which would be distributed to public schools. Furthermore, all of the one-dollar poll tax and one-fourth of all the occupation taxes were delegated for education. Local taxes and varying proportions of the state *ad valorem* tax were also earmarked by later legislatures for school support.

Nevertheless, the state's pecuniary difficulties during the 1870's made support of the schools rather scanty, and the local control produced a wide spectrum of quality as well as segregation in Negro education. In many areas of a concentration of Negro population there were either no schools or inadequate schools. During the 1880's the situation seems to have improved slightly because of a return of prosperity and because of the demands and platform planks of the numerous protest groups. But in general during this period, lack of uniformity, low standards, and segregation were hallmarks of the Texas educational system.

Somewhat greater advances were made in higher education with the establishment of four institutions supported by the state and several private schools. The first of the colleges, Texas Agricultural and Mechanical College, was created under the terms of the federal Morrill Act, which provided 180,000 acres of land. Texas A&M opened its doors in 1876 with a faculty of six and a student body of forty in a handful of buildings in the middle of a 2,416 acre campus near Bryan. Receiving modest legislative support, the school soon developed into a major southwestern educational institution. It specialized at this time in four-year programs in the agricultural and mechanical arts, a curriculum in which it was a national pioneer. In 1888 the school established the Texas Agricultural Experiment Station System which has proved of enormous benefit to Texas agribusiness. A course in road making instituted in 1890 became the father of its engineering and technological curricula. As did all land-grant colleges, A&M maintained a four-year military training program.

Because Texas A&M was restricted to white students, the legislature provided at the time of its creation for a nearby agricultural college for Negroes. A lack of students, however, caused it to be changed in 1879 into Prairie View State Normal School for training Negro teachers, and it was placed under the supervision of Texas A&M. The school opened in 1885 with a small enrollment and expanded its curriculum in 1889 to include courses in industrial arts.

Another teacher-training or normal school, Sam Houston State Normal School, was established in Huntsville in 1879 for white students. It derived part of its initial impetus from the George Peabody Fund. It became the model for all the later Texas normal schools, which are now part of the four-year college system.

By far the most outstanding achievement in higher education was the establishment of the University of Texas, a major influence in the development of the state although at first it hardly seemed significant. Envisioned by Lamar in 1838 and promoted by a number of educators and statesmen from time to time thereafter, the "university of the first class" became a pawn for politicians. The original fifty-league endowment located in the rich blackland prairies was put on the market to settlers, and the proceeds were for the most part diverted into the general fund. The Constitution of 1876 provided a grant of one million acres of the vacant public lands in West Texas for the school's endowment, but it did not provide funds for current operating expenses. After considerable hassle over the proposed location in 1881, Austin was selected for the main branch and Galveston for the medical branch. The main branch opened in 1883 with thirteen faculty members and two hundred twenty-one students, survived without a biennial appropriation in 1885, and began to develop into a first-class institution in the 1890's. It was divided into an Academic Department, which offered six liberal arts curricula, and a Law Department, headed by former governor Oran M. Roberts. The medical branch in Galveston did not open until 1891, when it replaced an earlier Texas Medical College.

A number of private institutions were established during this period, most of them functioning between the levels of secondary and higher education under the euphemism "academy." Few of them endured. One that did was Texas Christian University, founded as Add-Ran College in Thorpe Spring in 1873 by Addison and Randolph Clark. The school was originally endorsed by the Disciples of Christ, and later transferred to the ownership of that religious body in 1890, when it was renamed Add-Ran Christian University. In 1894 it was moved to Waco with a new name, Texas Christian University, and in 1910 to its present location at Fort Worth. In Waco was the state's oldest and at that time most prosperous university, Baylor University, which had been founded at Independence in 1846 and moved to Waco in 1886 and which was under the auspices of the Baptist General Convention. Another Baptist school, now Howard Payne, was founded in Brownwood in 1889, and a third, now Hardin-Simmons, was founded in Abilene in 1891. The Catholic church developed St. Mary's in San Antonio into a full-fledged college for men and opened two girls' schools: Incarnate Word in 1881 and Our Lady of the Lake in 1896. Trinity University, now located in San Antonio, was established in Tehuacana by the Presbyterian church in 1869. The Methodists established Southwestern University at Georgetown in 1873 and Texas Wesleyan University at Fort Worth in 1891. Many of the other private and church-related schools founded during the period later merged to form other institutions or were taken over by the state.

Charitable education rose with progressivism. After 1856, when the Texas School for the Blind, the Texas School for the Deaf, and the State Lunatic Asylum had been authorized, there was no expansion of the state's eleemosynary institutions until 1883, when the Terrell State Hospital for mental patients was established. It was followed in 1887 by the founding of the State Orphans School and the Texas Blind, Deaf, and Orphan School for Negroes and two years after that by the founding of a third mental institution, the San Antonio State Hospital.

Cultural Developments A number of artists emerged to influence Texas taste. Elisabet Ney, a French sculptress of international reputation, moved to Texas in 1870, with Dr. Edmund Montgomery, her recluse-philosopher husband. They acquired Liendo plantation from the Groce family, where they lived until 1893, when she opened a studio in Austin. For the next twelve years works of true genius came from her hands: statues of Austin and Houston, a tombstone figure of Albert Sidney Johnston, and a startling Lady Macbeth. William Henry Huddle, Henry Arthur McArdle, Robert Jenkins Onderdonk, and Frank Reagh were leading painters of the period. Their works—Huddle's portraits, McArdle's vast panoramas, Onderdonk's landscapes, Reagh's almost impressionistic longhorn cattle—are scattered in museums and collections throughout the state in a testimonial to their contemporaries' appreciation of artistic achievement.

Literary works did not rise to the same level, although Texans were prolific. Most writing focused on Texas heritage in reminiscences and history. The most important of them have become valuable because of their content rather than their literary merit: John C. Duval's *Early Times in Texas* (1890), John J. Linn's *Reminiscences of Fifty Years in Texas* (1883), Hardin's autobiographical *Life of John Wesley Hardin* (1896), Charlie Siringo's *A Texas Cowboy: Fifteen Years on the Hurricane Deck of a Mexican Mustang* (1886), Francis R. Lubbock's *Six Decades in Texas* (1900), and John H. Reagan's *Memoirs* (1906). John Henry Brown, whose education did not include formal training in history, wrote four creditable works on the general history of the state. Mrs. Percy V. Pennybacker, a school teacher rather than a historian, wrote a textbook on Texas history that enthralled two generations of students. A score of lesser lights published useful local and county histories.

Meanwhile, a force was taking shape that would in the next century make a major contribution to the literature of Texas: the history department of the new University of Texas and its offspring, the Texas State Historical Association. George P. Garrison, the first professor of history at the university, established a course in Texas history in 1897, and the same year he organized the Texas State Historical Association, with Oran M. Roberts as president. The widespread interest in the Texas past led to the state's creating in 1876 the Department of Insurance, Statistics, and History, to which was added in 1887 a Bureau of Agriculture. Under its first two directors, Valentine O. King and Ashley W. Spaight, the collection and organization of the state's archives was begun, and the State Library was established. In 1891 Caldwell Walton Raines became the history clerk and ex officio the state librarian, and five years later he published one of the most important scholarly works of the time, his *Bibliography of Texas*. Raines also edited Lubbock's *Memoirs* and the *Speeches and State Papers of James Stephen Hogg*, and he compiled two yearbooks, in 1902 and 1903, which have been of enduring service.

Three Texas writers enjoyed a brief national recognition. William Cowper Brann was a fire-eating editor whose columns gave national circulation to his monthly *Iconoclast* from 1894 to 1898 and brought him death by assassination. William Sydney Porter came to Texas for his health in 1894, suffered numerous vicissitudes including imprisonment, and wrote while in prison the first of the short stories that were to make him famous under his pseudonym O. Henry. Harry Peyton Steger, a graduate of the University of Texas, Johns Hopkins, and Oxford, was a literary consultant for a New York publishing house, where he was the first to recognize O. Henry's genius. A pair of adopted Texans, Alexander E. Sweet and Amory Knox, flashed briefly across the national scene with their humor magazine *Texas Siftings*, which capitalized on the Texas tall tale.

The Texas Statehouse   This entire period was embodied in the building of the Texas statehouse, which interwove ranching, land speculation, labor disputes, reform politics, foreign investments, economic growth, and Texas expansiveness. Envisioning the grandest state capitol in the nation, the framers of the 1876 constitution authorized for this purpose the alienation of over three million acres of the public domain. No action was taken, however, until a fire gutted the old building in 1881. The following year the legislature created a capitol board to dispose of the land and added fifty thousand acres to cover the costs of obtaining an architect.

Competitive designs were submitted, a plan was selected, and a contract for construction was awarded to Mattheas Schnell of Illinois, who agreed to accept the land in payment for erecting the statehouse. That the board had been unable to sell the land and was forced instead to trade it for construction has long clouded the capitol story. The contractor was in effect required to advance the funds for the costs of labor and materials and to await a future sale of the lands for his profits. Schnell turned to Chicago financiers Charles B. and John V. Farwell, A. C. Babcock, and Abner Taylor for financial assistance and transferred to them three-fourths interest in the project. It was Taylor who eventually took charge of the construction when it began in 1883.

A series of frustrations dogged the work. After spending nearly $100,000 to quarry the native limestone required by the contract and to erect a narrow-gauge railroad for transporting it to Austin, Taylor was confronted with the refusal of the capitol board to accept the limestone because of discoloration. Costly delays arose while Taylor and the board tried to arrange an acceptable compromise. Finally the contractor agreed to substitute granite for limestone, and the state agreed to build a railroad to granite quarries near Marble Falls and to furnish convict labor to work the quarries. But this led to further difficulties. Granite, being much harder to cut and shape than limestone, called for more skilled artisans than were available in Austin. Taylor brought in stonecutters from Scotland, but the National Granite Cutters Union immediately instigated a boycott to protest foreign labor. Gus Wilke, the construction foreman, began hiring scab workers. The Knights of Labor then pushed a suit against the contractors for violation of a federal statute forbidding the employment of foreign labor; a minimum fine was assessed against the construction foreman.

Work on the structure was also delayed by almost endless changes in the specifications, some requested by the contractor, some by the capitol board. The bitterest of these disputes arose over the material to be used for the roof. The contract called for copper sheets, but Taylor wanted it changed because the variations in Texas climate would cause too much expansion and contraction of the copper. Hogg, then attorney general and unduly suspicious of the moneyed contractors, forced them to use copper. On the day the building was dedicated, May 16, 1888, a rainstorm blew up, and the roof leaked. The board refused to accept the building, and although Taylor protested the unfairness of it since he had opposed copper from the beginning, the board refused to complete the payments until he reroofed the building with slate.

So costly had the venture proven that the Chicago backers, who had organized as the Capitol Syndicate, had to raise additional funds by floating bonds in England through a London firm entitled the Capitol Freehold Land and Investment Company, which took a lien on the land in Texas as it was transferred to the Syndicate. The total costs of the building, not including interest on borrowed funds, slightly exceeded three million dollars; the Syndicate had in effect paid approximately one dollar an acre for vacant land at a time when much land was selling for fifty cents an acre. Unable to sell the land except at a loss, the Syndicate turned to ranching under the previously discussed XIT brand.

The finished structure was splendid. Second only in size to the national capitol, it rose over three hundred feet from its basement to a magnificent dome crowned by a statue of the Goddess of Liberty. Whether or not the state had robbed itself of its birthright in land, as the peppery land commissioner W. C. Walsh claimed, the people of Texas had received a building in consonance with the expansive spirit of the times.

12

Progressivism and the New Freedom

Progressivism in Texas

Campaigns and Candidates   The measures which reflected the socio-political movement called progressivism began to emerge in Texas quite early in the progressive era and continued to appear from time to time in state legislation long after progressivism had faded from the national scene. Some historians think the progressive movement in Texas fell short of the fulfillment of its mission, but this is true only if the goals are defined in terms of a complete anticapitalism. Other historians hold that Texas led the nation in adoption of corrective adjustments vital to the social and economic betterment of its people during the rampant growth of industrial capitalism.

To sum up a few of the major progressive actions of the nineteenth century might provide a useful backdrop to the early years of the twentieth century. Texas' land policies, despite some faults, were more generous to homesteaders and actual settlers than those of the nation as a whole. Texas' homestead exemption law became a model for many other states.

MAJOR OIL FIELDS
to 1940

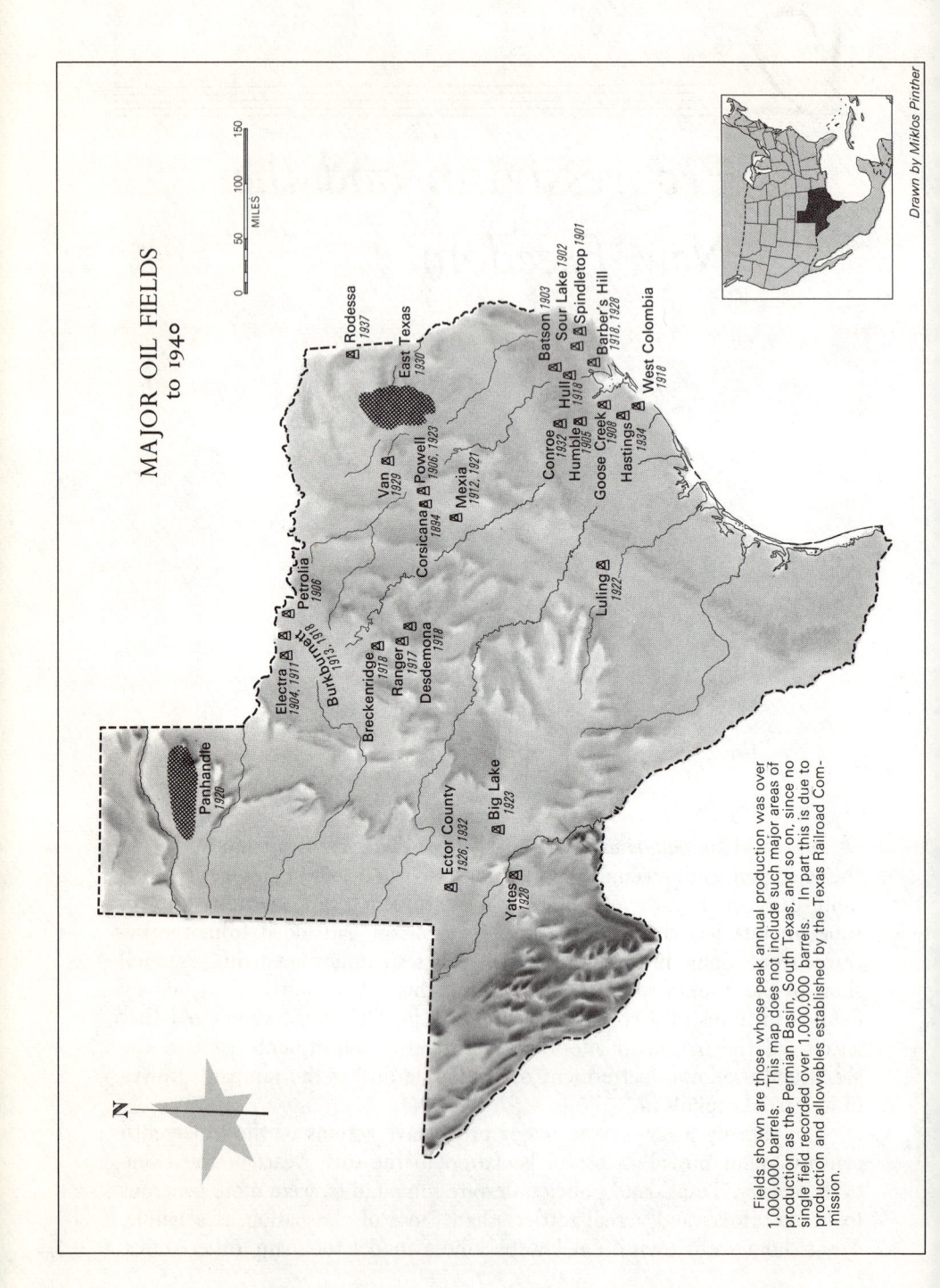

Fields shown are those whose peak annual production was over 1,000,000 barrels. This map does not include such major areas of production as the Permian Basin, South Texas, and so on, since no single field recorded over 1,000,000 barrels. In part this is due to production and allowables established by the Texas Railroad Commission.

Drawn by Miklos Pinther

Texas' antitrust act was the nation's first effective antitrust legislation. Texas was one of the first to attempt railroad regulation, at first by charter enforcement and then by the establishment of a state railroad commission. Texas led all other states in the curbing of wildcat insurance companies. Four important bills introduced by Texas congressmen were the bill that created the Interstate Commerce Commission; an antitrust bill that would probably have been more effective than the Sherman Act; the bill that became the Seventeenth Amendment, which called for popular election of senators; and the bill that became the Eighteenth Amendment, which called for nationwide prohibition (although the progressiveness of this measure may be questioned).

The political leaders during the high tides of progressivism have often been called, somewhat incongruously, conservatives—possibly because of the sharp contrast between their personalities and those of later, more flamboyant politicians such as James E. Ferguson. E. M. House, the principal leader during the progressive era, though not necessarily of the progressive movement, was himself a man of contrasts. The wealthy financier House first backed Governor Hogg, then secured Culberson's election in 1895 and 1897, and continued to dominate state politics for a decade before transferring his master craftsmanship to the national arena. House's behind-the-scenes liberalism, through the influence of his utopian novel *Philip Dru*, was felt, some believe, as late as the early days of Franklin Roosevelt's New Deal.

House successfully managed the nomination and election campaign of Joseph D. Sayers in 1899 and again in 1901. Although Sayers was a Confederate veteran, he was by no means a conservative or Bourbon Democrat. For ten years he was the law partner of George W. Jones, the "independent man of Greenback principles," and he succeeded him in the United States Congress in 1885. At House's suggestion he resigned from congress to win the Democratic nomination for governor from M. M. Crane, who represented railroad and other corporate interests in Texas. Sayers polled over seventy per cent of the popular vote in 1898 and a similar percentage when he stood for reelection in 1900.

House turned next to Congressman S. W. T. Lanham to make the race for governor, and Lanham also won two terms, from 1903 to 1907, by comparable majorities. Although the last Confederate veteran to serve as governor and although a somewhat colorless executive, he could scarcely be called a conservative. He supported numerous progressive measures, and as a congressman for ten years he had represented a heavily Populist district in central West Texas.

House was much less active in the selection of the next governor, although he endorsed the candidacy of Thomas Mitchell Campbell, a long-time member of House's "our crowd." Campbell was actively supported by the former governor Jim Hogg and by the then junior senator from Texas, Joseph Weldon Bailey. This was the first election conducted under the Terrell Election Law (which is explained in the following section) and consequently the first to include a statewide Democratic primary. Campbell received in the primary over twice as many votes as the total cast in the general election of 1906, which incidentally was the smallest vote since Reconstruction. In 1908 Campbell won reelection with nearly seventy per cent of a vote that was average for the period. Campbell is usually considered the foremost—and sometimes the only—progressive governor of the state. His four years in office, from 1907 to 1911, saw the passage of the bulk of the progressive legislation.

The leading opponent of progressivism in the state was Joseph Weldon Bailey, whom his biographer aptly nicknamed "the last Democrat." An attorney, an astute politician, and a highly effective orator, Bailey served ten years in congress, from 1891 to 1901, before his elevation to the senate. He became involved with Henry Clay Pierce, the president of the Waters-Pierce Oil Company, which had been forced out of Texas by antitrust action in 1897. Bailey advised Pierce to reorganize, and in 1900 the company resumed operation in Texas. Litigation in Missouri later revealed that in 1900 a substantial portion of Waters-Pierce stock was owned by the Standard Oil Company, despite affidavits to the contrary. A new antitrust suit was filed in Texas in 1906 and was carried through the courts during Campbell's first term. Texas won the case in 1909, and an enormous fine of more than $1,800,000 was levied against the company, whose Texas property was subsequently sold at auction.

During the hearings it was disclosed that Senator Bailey had received fees of at least $100,000 as counsel for the Waters-Pierce Company. Soon he was also accused of taking legal fees from Standard Oil and the multimillion-dollar Kirby lumber interests. Contending simply that there was nothing illegal in what he had done and that he made his living practicing law, Bailey won exoneration from both the house and the senate investigating committees of the Texas Legislature in 1907, at which time he won reelection to the senate. The Bailey question was put to a popular vote in 1908 to determine control of the Texas delegation to the national Democratic convention. Bailey won the short, bitter campaign, and for nearly a decade pro- and anti-Bailey factions were significant elements of Texas politics. The Bailey question had a marked effect on the Democratic primary in 1910 when Cone Johnson, an outspoken anti-Bailey gubernatorial candidate, was roundly defeated by Oscar Branch Colquitt.

Oscar Branch Colquitt, governor from 1911 to 1915, came to the office with less clearly defined roots in progressivism than those of his predecessors. He had grown up on a tenant farm in East Texas, had been a corporation lawyer and lobbyist, had succeeded Reagan as chairman of the Railroad Commission, and had contended strongly against Campbell in the Democratic primary of 1906. In the period just before World War I, he expressed strong pro-German sentiment, and after the war he served as president of an oil company and head of the Hoover Democrats in Texas. Nonetheless, his administration was marked by a continuation of progressivism, although in his first campaign in 1910 he had promised what he called "a legislative rest."

His strong anti-Prohibition stand in the 1910 election poses something of an enigma, for in that year the Prohibitionists won a referendum that called for the submission to the electorate in 1911 of a statewide Prohibition amendment. Governor Colquitt became a foremost speaker against Prohibition in the ensuing election, one of the bitterest in recent Texas history. Over twice as many votes were cast in the Prohibition election as had been cast in the preceding gubernatorial election. At that time Texas had under local options 167 dry counties, 61 partially wet ones, and only 21 wholly wet, yet the bulk of the population lived in the wet counties. The margin that defeated the amendment was 6,000 votes out of 465,000. But the Prohibitionists did not give up the fight.

Meantime, however, attention turned to the crucial national election of 1912. After a brief return to his many business interests, E. M. House, tiring of state politics, began to take an intense interest in national politics. The idealistic governor of New Jersey, Woodrow Wilson, intrigued him; House took an apartment in New York, contrived a meeting with Wilson, and became—until their break at the end of the war—Wilson's friend, confidant, and adviser. House's part in the nomination and election of Wilson in 1912 has been disputed by several eminent historians, some claiming House's aid the most significant element in Wilson's victory and others claiming it totally inconsequential.

Suffice it to say that a Texas-for-Wilson movement began to form in 1910 under the guidance of former members of House's "our crowd," one of whom later wrote that Texas would have supported Wilson even without House's efforts. In any event, Texas did support Wilson both at the Democratic convention and at the polls in November. In this election William Howard Taft sought reelection as a Republican; Theodore Roosevelt tried an unsuccessful comeback as the leader of the Bull Moose Party; and Wilson ran as a progressive Democrat. House traveled in Wilson's campaign retinue, and after an assassination attempt on Roosevelt, House sent posthaste for his friend, Ranger Captain Bill MacDonald, who for the remainder of the race served as Wilson's personal bodyguard.

Wilson won, and if his cabinet appointments did not reflect the fine hand of Colonel E. M. House, at the least they evidenced Wilson's gratitude to Texas. Albert Sidney Burleson served eight years as postmaster general, and David Franklin Houston served from 1913 to 1920 as secretary of agriculture. House took up temporary residence in Washington.

Progressive Measures At home, where Texas attorney generals continued former Governor Hogg's war on trusts and Railroad Commissioner John H. Reagan won federal court support for Texas railroad regulation, the legislature moved to enact specific progressive measures. One of the most controversial and most often misinterpreted of these measures was the reform of the election laws. In 1901 a constitutional amendment made payment of the poll tax a prerequisite for voting. This was intended as a tax reform because an equitable collection of the poll (or head) tax was difficult. But it excluded from the suffrage anyone who could not or would not pay it, primarily Negroes, poor whites, and Mexican laborers.

An attempt to reform the convention system of nominations was made in 1895. In 1903, subsequent to the poll tax amendment, the legislature passed a statute completely overhauling the election code and modified it in 1905 into the basic form of the present system. This act of 1905, the Terrell Election Law, established primary elections for the nomination of candidates from parties polling over one hundred thousand votes. In general, of course, this law has excluded all but the Democratic Party in Texas. From 1905 to 1918 the convention still made the final nominations on an "instructed" basis, voting by counties. After 1918 a second primary has been held whenever no candidate received a majority. Texas was among the first states to take the nomination of political candidates out of the hands of caucusing convention delegates and place it before the electorate. Clearly of a progressive nature, the Terrell Election Law has been clouded because of confusion of it with the 1901 poll-tax amendment, which was intended as a reform, and the 1923 white-primary law, which was not.

Another governmental reform in which Texas led the nation was the innovation of city government by commission, a direct result of a disastrous Gulf storm in 1900 which swept over Galveston Island killing and injuring hundreds and causing untold property damage. When wind and water had subsided, the enterprising city fathers realized that the old mayor-council form of city government was inadequate to meet the harsh exigencies of rebuilding the city. They applied to the legislature in 1901 for a new charter that authorized a city government by five commissioners. Although it was probably not envisioned at the start, in practice the new form put each commissioner at the head of a separate administrative unit. This proved to be so efficient that the new form of government was soon copied by hundreds of cities throughout the nation. Of Texas cities, Houston secured a commission charter in 1905; five cities received the legislature's sanction in 1907; five more in 1909; and by 1915 over forty Texas cities were following the commission form. A modification emerged in 1913 when Amarillo adopted a council-manager form of city government. In 1912 the Texas Legislature went a step further in democratic innovation by ratifying the "home-rule" act, which authorized any city with a population over five thousand to incorporate and draw up its own charter without submitting it for legislative approval.

Progressive legislation was also passed concerning child-labor restrictions. Thirteen years before the passage of the first federal child-labor act (the Keatings-Owen Act, which was declared unconstitutional), the Texas Legislature in 1903 prohibited the employment of children under twelve years of age in industrial plants where machinery was used and under sixteen in mines, distilleries, and breweries. In 1911 this age limit was raised to fifteen and seventeen years respectively.

Three other labor acts were passed in 1903. One limited the number of hours a trainman could be required to work consecutively. The second required companies to provide vestibules to protect motormen of street railways in inclement weather. The third prohibited a corporation from forcing its employees to purchase particular brands or to buy from company stores. In 1907 the legislature limited the working day of telegraph operators to eight hours, required railroads to provide shelters for work crews, created a Bureau of Labor Statistics, and passed several other minor pieces of labor legislation.

This same legislature enacted the Robertson Insurance Law in 1907, one of the most advanced and controversial of its time. It required insurance companies operating in Texas to invest a minimum of seventy-five per cent of their reserves from Texas policies in Texas real estate or securities. It further required that such securities be deposited in Texas banks approved by the state treasurer. The purpose of the law was twofold: to prevent the flow of capital out of the state and to assure the maintenance of proper reserves. Many companies objected vigorously, and a number argued cogently that returns from investments in Texas land would be inadequate and investment in Texas securities too risky. Nevertheless the law went into effect. One week before it did, twenty-one companies withdrew from the state.

Also in 1907 the legislature replaced the old Department of Agriculture, Insurance, Statistics, and History with a Department of Agriculture, a Department of Insurance and Banking, and in 1909 a Library and Historical Commission. In 1909 the state attempted a guaranty fund system for state banks, which was similar to the much later Federal Deposit Insurance Corporation. But the state system was abandoned in 1927 because it was found to burden conservative bankers with the errors of their more careless competitors.

Numerous efforts at tax reform could be classified as progressive measures. One in 1905 attempted to secure a fuller rendition of property, and another in 1907 attempted to reach by taxation personal property and intangible property, especially of corporations. Even today, however, these largely escape taxation.

One of the most important measures of the time was passed by a special session of the legislature in 1910 to reform the state prison system. Over the years there had evolved many evils in the system, which was basically a sound one. It consisted of several state-owned farms, plants at Huntsville and Rusk where iron ore was smelted, and two correctional schools for juveniles. The two plants operated at a loss, but profits from the farms and from leasing convict labor kept the system as a whole on the credit side of the ledger. In 1909 a special legislative investigating committee found that the prisoners were being mistreated, especially through oversevere punishment. The resulting prison reform act of 1910 provided for the classification and segregation of prisoners, the abolition of the leasing system, the abolition of the demeaning striped garments for all but the most serious criminals, amelioration of severe punishment, a supply of reading matter for prisoners, and, most important, the payment of a small wage to prisoners who worked in the plants or on the farms. It was one of the most progressive reforms of its kind in the country at the time. But the abolition of the leasing of convict labor threw the prison system into deficit. Nearly every subsequent legislature has made changes in the system, some designed to improve the financial situation, some to secure better treatment for prisoners, and some to preserve order in the prisons.

Among other progressive enactments were a new antitrust law, many educational advances, and the establishment of a public warehouse system for farmers to store crops while awaiting more advantageous prices. This last measure, however, did not prove successful.

In 1916 a triumph similar to the Waters-Pierce fine was enjoyed not so much by the progressives as by the Prohibitionists in a case against seven Texas breweries. A voluminous mass of evidence was assembled by Attorney General B. F. Looney, who proved conclusively that the breweries were operating in violation of the antitrust law and that furthermore they had violated the election code by making contributions in elections in which they were directly affected. The breweries forfeited their charters and were fined $281,000 plus costs. The action gave renewed impetus to the Prohibition movement, which was then facing a kind of interdiction by the new governor, James Ferguson.

Jim Ferguson James E. Ferguson, who entered Texas politics in 1914, was to be a major force, and a stormy one, for over a quarter of a century. He was born in Bell County in 1871, left home at the age of sixteen, worked two years as an itinerant laborer in California, Nevada, and Colorado, and returned home to farm and work at odd jobs until after a brief study of law he was admitted to the bar in 1897. He had had virtually no formal education, but he possessed a diversity of talents, not the least of which was business acumen. By the time he announced for governor in 1914 he was president of the Temple State Bank and had business interests in real estate, insurance, and merchandising. But when he announced for governor, he had never held even a minor political office.

His initial campaign for nomination was both tough and effective. Known as an anti-Prohibitionist, he stated that he would run on a platform that would avoid the Prohibition issue altogether, that he would veto any and all liquor legislation, and that he would concentrate on more vital issues, such as relief for tenant farmers, who constituted a very large segment of the Texas electorate. Excited Prohibitionists, flushed with their near-victory in 1911, held a convention and united behind Thomas H. Ball; the anti-Prohibitionists had no choice but to unite also if they hoped to win in the primary. When Ferguson obdurately refused to cooperate and threatened to run as an independent, the anti-Prohibitionists were forced to support him. The primary campaign was a hot one. Ferguson called himself "Farmer Jim" to emphasize his farming background and appeal emotionally to the lower classes. Furthermore, he was obviously not the candidate of the Democratic hierarchy or of any political machine. And his stubborn insistence that there was no place in his program for liquor legislation, either wet or dry, made him appear neutral to many voters who were, as Ferguson sensed, tired of the Prohibition issue. He defeated Ball in the primary by forty thousand votes and won the general election by an overwhelming majority.

Despite his political inexperience, he found the legislature receptive to his program. His proposal during the campaign that a law be passed to limit farm rents and to prohibit the cash bonuses that were sometimes demanded of share renters had attracted national attention and had even evoked a sympathetic story in the London *Times*. Although many critics considered this demagogic window dressing, the legislature responded promptly with the Ferguson Farm Tenant Law in 1915, but it was soon declared unconstitutional.

Other legislation proposed by Ferguson, however, was clearly in the progressive tradition. A revision was made in the warehouse law to make it more effective. Among other improvements in the educational system was a Rural High School Law that provided for consolidation of the inadequate rural schools with a special appropriation to support them. An attempt to reform the court system did little more than increase the number of courts. The first Ferguson administration was successful, but turmoil was in the offing.

At the time of the election of 1916, unsavory rumors of malfeasance were circulating about the governor. He won the primary, however, by over sixty thousand votes and again triumphed in the general election. By uniting forces with Joseph W. Bailey, whom he disliked, he was able to control the Texas delegation to the national Democratic convention. When the next legislature assembled, harmony still seemed to exist despite the rumors, which were increasing in number as well as credibility. Appropriations to education were augmented substantially; eight new colleges were created although they were not all actually established; rural school aid funds were doubled; the child labor law was revised; and other bills such as one creating a state highway commission that were passed appeared to betoken a forward-looking administration.

The need for good roads and a state system of highways had diminished slightly with the coming of the railroads but by 1917 had become more imperative than before because of the spreading use of automobiles. The Constitution of 1876 had restored construction and maintenance of roads to county control; an 1883 amendment authorized a county road tax; and a 1903 legislative act permitted county bond issues for road improvement. The disparity between adjacent counties, and the lack of centralized coordination, however, prevented the development of an adequate highway system. A number of automobile and travel clubs began to appear in the early twentieth century, chiefly the Texas Good Roads Association, which urged the development of state highway programs. When the federal government began making grants to states with central highway departments for the improvement and construction of roads, the pressure in Texas for such a state agency intensified. In 1917 a statute created a department, which after a number of vicissitudes grew into one of the strongest of the state divisions and one of the finest highway departments in the nation.

Even as these bills were working their way through legislative channels, the legislature undertook an investigation of the thickening rumors about the governor's behavior. Apparently to disarm the legislators, Ferguson promised to cease the practices he had been charged with and to reimburse the monies he had been accused of spending improperly. The investigation was dropped, and the legislature adjourned. Trouble flared again almost immediately. Ferguson objected to what he referred to as irregularities in the management of the University of Texas; others said he simply wished that certain faculty members who opposed him be dismissed. President Robert E. Vinson resisted the governor's interference, and in retaliation Ferguson vetoed the biennial appropriation to the university. A mighty protest arose from former students and supporters of the school, who demanded Ferguson's impeachment.

A Travis County grand jury indicted the governor on July 21, 1917, on nine counts relating to the misapplication of government funds. Shortly thereafter the speaker of the House of Representatives in an unprecedented move called the legislature into special session to consider impeachment of the governor. Ferguson either welcomed legislative investigation, as he said, or feared a court trial, as his enemies said, for he endorsed the extralegal special session. The house adopted twenty-one charges against him in August, and during three weeks of sultry summer weather the senate quietly and judiciously heard the testimony. This High Court of Impeachment found Ferguson guilty of ten of the twenty-one charges, including improper use of state monies, attempt to influence certain state officials, improper deposit of state funds in banks in which he had financial interests, and acceptance of $156,000, the source of which he refused to reveal. He was also removed from office and barred forever from holding any other office of honor, trust, or profit in the state of Texas. Fighting to the end the decision of what he called a kangaroo court, Ferguson resigned the governor's office one day before the verdict was rendered, declaring therefore that he was eligible to run again for office and giving him, as his daughter later wrote, "a knot in the end of the rope" by which he could hang on.

World War I and the Twenties

Watching and Waiting on the Border　　When Europe divided itself into hostile camps and the international holocaust called World War I erupted with the assassination of Archduke Ferdinand on June 28, 1914, Texas was involved in an international turmoil of its own with Mexico. The instability of the constantly changing revolutionary governments in hapless Mexico has been mentioned from time to time in previous chapters, as has the basic political dichotomy between Centralists and Federalists, *ricos* and *peones*, upper and lower classes. During a tempestuous century Texas had been the starting point for innumerable revolutions and insurgencies, from Juan de las Casas in 1811, through the efforts of Gutierrez de Lara, the feeble separatist attempt of the Republic of the Rio Grande, to the rise of the arrogant dictator Porfirio Diaz, who also had begun his movement in South Texas. The border was easy to cross, the thinly populated region made evasion of capture simple, and the protective laws of the United States offered refuge to Mexican revolutionaries. Unfortunately international relations were complicated since border ruffians, bandits, and cattle thieves could also cross the border with the same ease.

During the twentieth century, as many Mexican people boiled against the tyranny of Diaz, border trouble mounted. In September 1906 Flores Magon rendezvoused a party of liberal sympathizers in El Paso for an attempt to overthrow Diaz. The conspiracy was exposed, and Magon went into hiding in the United States, but some of his followers attacked Jimenez, Coahuila, hoping in vain for aid from Texas. In 1908 one of Magon's followers, Gilberto Guerrero, who had used El Paso as a base, led an assault on Las Vacas (Villa Acuña) across from Del Rio, later attacking several interior points. But the invasion attempt waned rapidly.

Meantime, Francisco I. Madero, a highly respected landowner of northern Mexico, began to build a much stronger revolutionary movement within Mexico, and after his arrest and imprisonment in a Diaz dungeon he escaped across the border to San Antonio in October 1910 and established his headquarters there. He began a systematic appeal to the American people for aid in the struggle against dictatorship in Mexico. An invasion was announced for November 20, and active recruitment began in Eagle Pass, Naco, El Paso, and Presidio. Diaz accused the United States of selling arms to the Madero supporters, and the entire border seethed with tension. In July that year an armed group of unidentified Mexicans crossed into Texas and killed two Texas Rangers. In November, just before Madero planned to begin his coup, a Mexican citizen was captured and burned alive in the lower valley because he had raped and murdered an American woman. The Madero attack that month fizzled for lack of support, and Madero went under cover, first in New Orleans, then San Antonio, then El Paso. He finally returned to Mexico when Texas authorities issued a warrant for his arrest. The tempo of the revolution beat faster; the border became more unsettled; and President William Howard Taft in March 1911 ordered the mobilization of a full division of United States Army troops at San Antonio to protect the border should the need arise. Early in May 1911 Madero and his revolutionaries captured Ciudad Juarez across from El Paso, and the collapse of the Diaz regime followed with startling haste. Within a month Diaz resigned and went into exile. But Madero's victory was only the starting point for more troubles.

One of Diaz's generals, Bernardo Reyes, slipped across the border into San Antonio in October 1911, denounced Madero, and promptly began recruiting and buying arms in exactly the same way that Madero had done a year earlier. Agents of the Madero government quickly produced proofs of this activity, and Reyes and the sheriff of Webb County were soon arrested. In Laredo, the county seat of Webb County, federal and state authorities found amazing stores of arms, ammunition, and bombs in the possession of Reyes' followers. Reyes himself jumped his bond and fled Texas back to Mexico, his counterrevolution a total failure.

Almost at the same time that Reyes was sneaking out of Texas, the Gomez brothers, disaffected Madero supporters, slipped into San Antonio, where they merged their activities with those of another apostate, General Pascual Orozco. This new movement gained control of the state of Chihuahua in February 1912, and Madero, now president of Mexico, requested permission to send Mexican troops across the Big Bend of Texas to put down the revolution. Governor Colquitt, however, refused for fear of endangering American lives and property. The Orozco rebels, in control of the port of entry at Juarez, began receiving arms and ammunition from the United States in much the same way that Madero had two years earlier. In March 1912 the United States issued a proclamation attempting to halt this arms supply, but it appeared to have little effect.

Mexico soon fell into utter chaos. The Madero government was overthrown in February 1913. Victoriano Huerta claimed the presidency after climbing to power on the shoulders of the Gomez brothers, Orozco, and others, but revolutionaries under Venustiano Carranza forced Huerta to abandon his government and flee midyear in 1914. Almost immediately the Carranza leaders began fighting among themselves, with the result that there was an outbreak of lawlessness along the Texas-Mexican border, especially in smuggling and gunrunning. The involvement of Texas citizens of both Anglo and Hispanic descent prevented any concerted efforts north of the border to check the lawlessness. By midsummer of 1915, however, the raids were linked to a document called the Plan de San Diego, which gave them a more sinister meaning. The Plan de San Diego, ostensibly issued from San Diego, Texas, was a call by the deposed Huerta for a general recruitment of Mexican nationals and Americans of Mexican descent in the border states of the United States to join in an uprising to create an independent republic that would be annexed to Mexico after the Huerta movement was successful there. During July and August of 1915, violence, marauding, and plundering of all kinds became almost daily occurrences in the Lower Rio Grande Valley.

The War Department strengthened its forces at Fort Brown, and several clashes occurred between Mexican and American troops along the Rio Grande—an international outbreak seemed imminent. Venustiano Carranza then used the Plan de San Diego and the border raids to secure the recognition of his government by the United States. His first step was to give assurances of cooperation with American officials in maintaining law and order on the border. There was some evidence and considerable suspicion, however, that he and his generals had instigated part of the trouble. Some abatement of the raids followed, but in September and October new raids broke out. These seem to have originated south of the border: unidentified raiders ambushed army patrols; American patrol planes were fired upon from the Mexican side; a raiding party of eighty armed men crossed into Progresso, Texas; and an attack was made on a railroad train running between Brownsville and San Benito. As the loss of life and property mounted, vigilante committees struck out furiously and sometimes blindly in a series of lynchings. Friction between Mexican-Americans and Anglo-Americans reached disastrous proportions. No one could determine how much of the trouble was inspired by the Huerta Plan de San Diego, how much was outright lawlessness, how much came from the discontented Mexican population of Texas, and how much was instigated by Carranza agents. By October 1915 more than half of the entire mobile force of the United States Army was stationed along the border, with precious little effect. Carranza renewed his assurances of cooperation and replaced his border commander with a new, more vigorous leader. Woodrow Wilson finally recognized the Carranza government as the de facto government of Mexico on October 25, 1915, and within a month the raids came to an end, the result chiefly of impressive activities by the Mexican *rurales*, rural mounted police. President Carranza visited the border in November and conferred with Governor Ferguson, whom he convinced of his sincerity.

But this display of good feeling was only a lull in the storm. Texas suffered slightly from the ensuing Villa raids of 1916 but was fully involved in the effects of the Zimmerman Note of 1917. Pancho Villa, one of Carranza's early followers, had broken with the government and gained domination of Chihuahua, Sonora, and other parts of northern Mexico. His vicious attack on Columbus, New Mexico, in March 1916 caused a retaliatory raid into Mexico by the American Army led by General John J. Pershing. Several raids in the Trans-Pecos region were blamed on Villa, and at one time Villa himself with several of his lieutenants boldly rode into El Paso but without causing trouble. The Pershing expedition had been approved by Carránza, but when it proved unpopular with the Mexican people, Carranza repudiated it. Pershing returned in February after an unsuccessful chase of the Mexican bandit-revolutionary through

Sonora and Chihuahua. With him came hundreds of refugees: Americans, Mexicans, and four hundred twenty-seven Chinese laborers, who were allowed to remain in San Antonio. The publicity given the Pershing expedition served primarily to emphasize the lawlessness along the international boundary and to keep the public temper on edge.

As events in Europe quickened and threatened to bring the United States into the World War, national attention was focused once again on the troubled border lands. In March 1917 the nation learned of the content of the Zimmerman Note, a document in which the German foreign secretary proposed that if the United States declared war, Germany would support Mexico (and Japan) in an invasion of the United States for the purpose of Mexican annexation of Texas, New Mexico, and Arizona. Carranza did not accept the Zimmerman proposal, but a strong element of suspicion lay behind the fact that the United States learned of it not from Mexico but from the British secret service. Public excitement over it was soon eclipsed by the sinking of the *Algonquin* and three other unarmed American merchant ships and by the declaration of war against Germany on April 6, 1917. But American military leaders did not forget the potential danger from the south. Throughout the war the border forts were fully manned, and the boundary was kept under constant patrol.

Texas in the War Shortly after the beginning of the European war, President Wilson sent E. M. House to Europe as his personal emissary to determine whether there was any way the United States might act as a catalyst for conciliation. House visited the leaders of the major belligerent powers, especially in London and Berlin, and returned to Europe again for the same purpose in 1916. His efforts had no effect in promoting peace, but some historians appear to believe that House's obvious pro-British and anti-German views affected Wilson and fed the growing anti-German sentiment in the United States.

In addition to House, scores of other Texans were prominent on the national scene during the war. Burleson, Houston, Gregory, and Love—members of "our crowd"—remained in the cabinet. John Nance Garner, who had been elected to the House of Representatives in 1906, had risen to the chairmanship of the Ways and Means Committee, where all the measures for financing the war began. Garner also served as a semisecret, confidential liaison between President Wilson and congress. During the war Garner visited the White House twice a week for private conferences with the president. As far as the press and the public knew, however, he was visiting Joseph Tumulty, Wilson's private secretary. Tom Connally, later a power in congress, was elected to his first term in the United States House of Representatives in 1916. Garner saw to it that Connally was placed on the Foreign Affairs Committee and several less important committees. Although he was reelected in 1918, Connally chose to volunteer for military service instead and did not take his seat until after the armistice. Sam Rayburn was in his third term in congress when the United States entered the war; his best known work was authorship of the War Risk Insurance Act, which provided $10,000 worth of life insurance for servicemen. Senators Charles Allen Culberson, the former governor, and Morris Sheppard were major figures in the upper house and staunch supporters of the president.

Because of the troubles on the Mexican border and the Zimmerman Note, most of the border forts in Texas had been reactivated or restaffed. Large contingents of both cavalry and infantry spent the war in these posts, from an average of sixty thousand troops at Fort Bliss to the entire Twelfth Cavalry at Fort Brown. Forts Clark at Brackettville, Duncan at Eagle Pass, McIntosh at Laredo, and Ringgold at Rio Grande City maintained active cavalry detachments on patrol along the river. One of the largest border operations during the war was at Camp Marfa, overlooking the town of Marfa in the Trans-Pecos, where were stationed elements of the Sixth Cavalry, Fourth Texas Infantry, Thirty-fourth Infantry, and two battalions of the Pennsylvania National Guard. The largest military posts in Texas, however, were four training camps: MacArthur at Waco, Logan at Houston, Travis at San Antonio, and Bowie at Fort Worth. Through these camps passed most of the nearly two hundred thousand Texans who volunteered or were drafted for service in the army. Fort Sam Houston was the headquarters for military affairs in Texas, and Fort Crockett on Galveston Island was reactivated to provide protection of the coast with two Marine regiments stationed there during the war. An officers' training camp was established at Leon Springs, and several training bases for aviators sprang into existence.

Texas became the principal training area for military aviators during the war because military aviation had had its inception in Texas nearly a decade earlier and the Texas climate offered ideal flying conditions most of the year. The Aeronautical Division of the Signal Corps had been established in 1907, but it had not acquired a plane until 1909 when pilot training began in Maryland. The weather that winter was so unfavorable that in February 1910 the Signal Corps transferred its aviation detachment to San Antonio: a pilot named Benjamin D. Foulois, a small crew of mechanics, and the plane, which was carefully crated and shipped by rail.

Foulois courageously announced to the press that he would make a trial flight on March 2. He had not completed his training under Wilbur Wright, and although he could take off and fly the cumbersome biplane, he had not yet mastered the technique of landing. In the trial flight he crashed the plane on landing. And this was not the last of his crash landings. General H. H. Arnold later recalled, "He would take off time after time and fly successfully, only to come into the field and crash. Then the plane would be repaired while Benny [Foulois] wrote patiently to the Wright brothers, explaining what he thought he had done and presently would receive in the mail an analysis and suggestions for the next flight." A new plane was acquired in 1911, and in it Foulois made the first military cross-country flight, from Laredo to Eagle Pass along the Rio Grande, setting a new world's record for distance traveled in the air. On the return flight startled ducks rising from the river caused a crash landing in the river, which seriously damaged the new plane.

In 1911 congress appropriated money for the purchase of five new planes. Two of these reached Fort Sam Houston late that spring with five new officers who volunteered for pilot training. Two crashes that summer, one of which killed the young George E. M. Kelly for whom Kelly Field was later named, caused operations to be shut down. Flight training was resumed, however, in Maryland in the summer and in Augusta, Georgia, in the winter. All aviation personnel were returned to Texas in the summer of 1913, first to Texas City near Galveston Bay and then to San Antonio, where the San Antonio Aviation Center was established.

During the border troubles of 1915, in the first military use of aviation by the United States Army, two planes with their pilots and ground crews were sent to Fort Brown to fly reconnaissance patrols along the river, where Mexican revolutionaries fired on them. The following year Foulois led the First Aero Squadron into combat in coordination with Pershing's expedition into northern Mexico. Consisting of only six planes in poor condition, it was not successful.

When the United States entered the war, the Aviation Section consisted of only thirty-five flying officers and a relatively small number of serviceable aircraft, but expansion accelerated. The aviation training center Kelly Field was established in San Antonio in April 1917. In May the University of Texas created a School of Military Aeronautics for ground and basic instructions. Its largest class consisted of over one thousand cadets. Together with Kelly Field this formed one of the largest pilot training operations in the world at that time, and San Antonio remained the center of military aviation in the United States until after World War II. Randolph Field, "the West Point of the Air," was opened in

1928, and until 1938 all Army Air Corps pilots received their training in the dozen Texas air bases established during the depression years.

Besides the unique contribution of the development of military aviation, Texas participated wholeheartedly in the entire war effort. On Registration Day, June 5, 1917, over 400,000 Texans registered for the draft. The day was slightly marred by a small protest organization that attempted to capture three central West Texas towns to prevent registration. In a few months the Texas registration reached its total of 989,571 registered Texans. Nearly 200,000 Texans saw active service; 5,171 lost their lives, 1,200 being killed in action in Europe and approximately 1,500 dying of wounds or other causes overseas. Almost half of the deaths occurred in the United States during a devastating flu epidemic that swept across the nation in 1918.

The state government, throwing itself into the war effort, created a State Council of Defense, appropriated money to augment the National Guard and the Texas Rangers, prohibited the forced sale of the property of servicemen for debts, remitted poll taxes for servicemen, and after the war established a memorial sanatorium in Kerrville. Measures on a lesser scale required that every school be equipped with an American flag, that Texas history be taught in all schools, that all instructions be given in English, and that at least ten minutes every day be devoted to teaching "patriotism."

Domestically, Texans went through much the same experience as Americans everywhere. They "Hooverized" food at the request of the Federal Food Administration, observing meatless, wheatless, and porkless days, saved fat and sugar, did without coffee, used substitute foods when possible, and established war gardens. The State Council of Defense spurred usually successful fund-raising drives such as Liberty Loan, Victory Loan, War Savings Stamp, and Thrift Stamp drives. If in some cases, such as Governor Hobby's veto of the appropriation for the University of Texas German language department, Texans were overzealous in their patriotism, they were no different from the nation at large.

After the armistice, when President Wilson made his unprecedented journey to Paris to help negotiate the peace and win acceptance of the League of Nations, he was accompanied by E. M. House, who had already won from Britain and France agreement on Wilson's Fourteen Points as the basis for peace and who, many believe, originally conceived the League of Nations. House served as one of the five American commissioners and took Wilson's place as head of the commission when the president returned to the United States. After the signing of the treaty, House remained in Europe until 1919 as the president's personal representative in London. He returned to the United States in the fall of that year so ill that he had to be carried off the ship on a stretcher. The United States refused to accept the League of Nations. Wilson, having suffered a stroke, could not receive the Texan in Washington, and House never saw the president again. He returned home to Austin and semiretirement.

Postwar Developments The war gave some impetus to Texas industry, which had been growing steadily since the turn of the century. In 1910 the value of manufactured products was more than twice that of 1900, and the number of industrial workers had also doubled. During the next decade oil became the most prominent industry in Texas and in 1920 displaced slaughtering and meat packing, which had been first in 1910. The period before and during World War I saw increases in cottonseed mills, clothing manufacturing, furniture manufacturing, ice and ice cream production, and the building materials industries such as cement, brick, and tile. A small shipbuilding industry got under way in Houston. There was a general expansion of minor industries, but the industrial scene was not basically stimulated by the war.

One of the results, therefore, was that Texas industry could not absorb the thousands of potential workers discharged by the armed services. Texas was probably hit harder by the short depression after the war than were most sections of the country. Because of a sharp reduction in the price of agricultural products at the same time, all levels of the state's economy were affected. Conditions were serious for two to three years before the return of prosperity. In part this caused a new wave of lawlessness across the state in what some historians have called a moral letdown. In the wake of the war came significant social changes such as women's suffrage and Prohibition, most of which had been developing for several decades. In large measure the lawlessness grew out of the Prohibition amendment and the burgeoning oil industry. Social unrest also led to the growth of the Ku Klux Klan and to several labor strikes.

One of the severest strikes occurred from March to December in 1920 when Galveston longshoremen struck for closed shops and higher wages. Disorder and violence raged, and local authorities, unable to handle the situation, called upon the governor for help. After an investigation, martial law was declared. Elements of the National Guard and the Texas Rangers were sent into Galveston to keep the port open and to maintain order. In a special session the legislature passed the Open Port Law, which made it illegal for any person or group to interfere by violence, threats, or intimidation with anyone who was working at loading, unloading, or transporting any commerce within the state of Texas. Friends of labor called it an antistrike law, but others claimed it did not outlaw strikes but merely prevented strikers from forcing other workers to join them. The Open Port Law was used several times against the rising tide of violence by organized labor. In 1926 the Open Port Law was found to be unconstitutional, but by then it had served its purpose.

A second major strike occurred in the summer of 1922 when a national strike of railroad shop workers was called. Several thousand Texans joined in the movement. To protect their property and the workers who replaced the strikers, the railroad companies called on the governor for aid. Trouble broke out in several Texas cities, especially Houston and Denison. The Open Port Law was invoked in Houston, Denison, Sherman, Childress, Cleburne, Marshall, Temple, Lufkin, De Leon, Waco, Kingsville, Gainesville, Amarillo, Dalhart, Texline, Palestine, and Big Spring. Rangers and National Guardsmen were sent to most of those places to maintain order. By the beginning of the following year, control was restored to local authorities. Only Denison had actually been placed under martial law.

The years between the postwar recession and the depression of the thirties have been called the golden era of labor in Texas. Industry expanded, and the general shortage of skilled workers in Texas enabled the working man to make substantial social and economic advances. Membership in the Texas State Federation of Labor dropped from fifty thousand in 1920 to twenty-five thousand in 1927.

There were few significant political developments at the state level before the election of 1924. When Ferguson was impeached in 1917, his lieutenant governor, William Pettus Hobby, assumed the office. He was elected overwhelmingly to a second term in 1918, a noteworthy election because of Ferguson's attempt to run in the primary, because of the new double primary law (although none was needed), and because of women's first opportunity to vote. Except for the Galveston dock strike, Hobby's second term was one of the most harmonious periods in Texas political history.

In the gubernatorial election of 1920, a relative newcomer and an old-timer were the principal contenders. Joseph Weldon Bailey came out of private life to run against three other candidates, most notably Pat Morris Neff, a militant Waco Baptist who had championed woman suffrage and Prohibition. The contest was the first to go into a second primary which Neff won over Bailey by approximately sixty per cent of the vote. Neff, elected in November, was the first Texas governor with a college degree. He later served as president of Baylor University from

1932 to 1947. Still considered one of the best governors the state has had, he won reelection easily in 1922. During his two terms he handled the railroad strike of 1922 and an outbreak of lawlessness caused by an oil boom in Mexia. He also advocated the expansion of the state highway system, the establishment of a state park system, and, unsuccessfully, the need for a new state constitution.

Social and Economic Changes

The Oil Industry Without doubt the most significant development in Texas during the early twentieth century was the explosive growth of the oil industry. Its history involves the discovery and production of crude oil, the building of pipelines and refineries, the establishment of oil-field equipment industries, and the founding of oil companies.

Oil was first discovered in natural seep springs in East Texas, but it had no value other than for medicinal and lubricating purposes. After the Civil War a small field was discovered in Nacogdoches County by drilling below the surface, but the discovery, like those in Brown County in 1878, Bexar County in 1886, and a half-dozen others, made little impact because of the lack of a market and the smallness of production. The first major field in Texas was opened in 1894 when the city of Corsicana, drilling a municipal water well, tapped a major oil-bearing sand.

The actual discovery well was brought in the following year, and in 1896 production was obtained from five wells. Excitement mounted to a fever pitch as every town lot and nearby farm was put under lease. Production rose from 1,450 barrels in 1896 to a peak of 829,554 barrels in 1900 taken from a pool that proved to be about five miles long by two miles wide on the eastern edge of the town. The Corsicana boom is important not only because it was the first in Texas but also because the ingenious operators found new market uses for oil. In 1898 the city of Corsicana began treating the streets with crude oil to keep down dust and to prevent bog holes in rainy weather. In 1901 the Houston and Texas Central Railroad Company began converting their coal-burning locomotives to oil burners because of the ready availability of Corsicana oil. Furthermore, in 1898 J. S. Cullinan, later among the founders of the Magnolia Petroleum Company and of the Texas Company, built in Corsicana the first commercially practical refinery in Texas, which produced illuminating oil and a crude grade of gasoline marketed by the Waters-Pierce Oil Company.

Corsicana was but a prelude. In January 1901, when drilling at Spindletop near Beaumont was stopped for the replacement of a drill bit, an ominous rumble was heard in the twelve hundred foot hole. Suddenly all was bedlam: the well belched explosively, and thousands of pounds of drill pipe, swivels, blocks, and tackle were blown up through the top of the wooden derrick. Next came an eruption of drilling mud. There were a few minutes of quiet, and then a large mass of mud was flung into the air with the sound of a cannon. Then, with a deafening roar, a mixture of mud, gas, oil, and rocks was spewed hundreds of feet into the air. Finally came a steady fountain of black oil. The geyser continued for six days before frantic workmen were able to cap the well. Oil stood in pools all around the location. Not until January 19 was the well finally brought under control, and by that time the estimated seventy-five thousand barrel daily flow had formed a huge lake of oil around the well. Sparks from a passing locomotive ignited this six weeks later and caused a nearly disastrous fire.

The boom that followed this gusher, the greatest then known in petroleum annals, defies description. Within weeks land in the proven field was being sold at prices ranging from $200,000 to $900,000 per acre. Speculation was rampant, and drilling was frenetic. Wells were so close together that one could almost walk through the field stepping from derrick floor to derrick floor. Other gushers blew in, some of which ran unchecked for long periods. Spindletop production topped three and a half million barrels in 1901, and the field produced an incredible seventeen million barrels the following year. This was nearly one-fourth of the total production in the United States. During the next ten years over forty-two million barrels came from Spindletop. Production declined thereafter until 1926, when a new and deeper stratum was tapped. Production in 1927 was over twenty-one million barrels, and the field yielded over more than a million barrels per year until 1934.

The first well, the Lucas Gusher, was drilled into a formation known as a salt dome. Other highly productive salt-dome fields were soon discovered in the coastal plains. Chief among these were the Sour Lake field, discovered in 1902, which peaked at nearly nine million barrels in 1903 and remained over a million barrels per year until 1928; Batson, in 1903, which peaked at ten million barrels in 1904 and stayed over a million barrels per year until 1911; Humble, in 1905, which produced over fifteen million barrels that year and stayed above the million-barrel mark until 1940; and Goose Creek, opened in 1908 with gusher production found in 1916, which peaked at nine million barrels and produced, from a variety of depths, a million barrels per year until 1937.

The fantastic production of the early years brought several developments besides wild speculation. Hundreds of companies were organized, some of which became giants in the field. Among these was the Gulf Oil Company, which was started in 1901 as the Guffey Oil Company with a refinery in Port Arthur. Financed chiefly by the Mellon interests of Pittsburgh, the company was reorganized as Gulf in 1907 with expanded refineries and a network of pipelines reaching as far as four hundred miles into Oklahoma. Another of the Spindletop companies was Texaco, Inc., organized as the Texas Fuel Company by J. S. Cullinan in 1901 and reorganized as the Texas Company the following year. Among the principal investors were former governor James S. Hogg and J. W. "Bet-a-Million" Gates, the former barbed-wire salesman who had made a fortune in wire and steel by that time. The Texas Company built, like Gulf, a refinery at Port Arthur and a network of pipelines also into Oklahoma, and it added an asphalt plant at Port Neches. The Humble Oil Company was organized to develop the Humble Field in 1911 by several operators including Ross Sterling, later governor of the state. The Magnolia Petroleum Company (now Mobil) was an amalgamation in 1911 of several units in Texas, the parent company being the J. S. Cullinan Company of Corsicana.

Texas oil production continued to soar as a dozen other million-barrel fields were brought in elsewhere in the state. Petrolia (1906) was successful not so much because of its production as because of the shallowness and therefore inexpensiveness of the wells and the amount of natural gas. Electra (1904 and 1911) gave rise to the legend about rancher W. T. Waggoner's disgust when he drilled for desperately needed water and discovered oil. The field reached gusher production in 1911, peaked at over eight million barrels in 1914, and remained a million-barrel field until 1950. Powell (1906), although substantial, did not reach million-barrel production until 1923, peaking at thirty-three million in 1924, and producing a million barrels per year until 1931. Burkburnett (1913) began to produce one gusher after another in 1918 and gave rise to one of the wildest booms in Texas. The field peaked in 1919 with over thirty million barrels, but it was rapidly exhausted. Mexia (1912) reached gusher production in 1921, and the resultant boom jumped the town's population from four thousand to forty thousand that year. Peak production came in 1922 with thirty-three million barrels, and the field's yield did not drop below a million barrels per year until 1945. Other fields of over a million-barrel production discovered during this period were West Columbia, Hull, Ranger, Desdemona, Breckenridge, Barbers Hill, Panhandle, Luling, Big Lake, and Yates. All of them brought booms, speculation, prosperity, and personal fortunes.

The Ranger boom, which may have been the greatest, epitomized another aspect of the wild days of the oil industry: the bogus promotion. Hundreds of companies were organized with stock sold to investors all over the country on the basis of prospectuses that were often misleading or totally false. A crusading editor named Don Biggers, who had begun to specialize in oil news in 1918, uncovered dozens of bogus schemes and in 1923 broke the bogus promotion ring wide open by turning his files over to Henry Zweifel, the federal district attorney in Fort Worth. Zweifel estimated that more than one million people had been duped of an estimated $100,000,000 by these fraudulent schemes. Among the score of prominent men implicated and eventually imprisoned was Fredrick A. Cook, who had raced Peary to the North Pole.

The number of real fortunes made from Texas oil, at that time and for decades to come, had a great bearing on the state's development, as did the general stimulus given the economy by every new strike. Only the briefest survey can be made of the concomitant economic impetus.

The manufacture and sale of oil-field equipment and supplies quickly became a major industry. The first wells were usually cable rigs; that is, the holes were punched into the earth by raising with cables and dropping weighted drill stems. After about 1920 most drilling rigs were rotary; that is, the holes were augered through the earth by rotating the drill stem with a mechanism on the derrick floor. By 1920 much of this equipment was being manufactured in Texas. Until the mid-thirties most of the derricks were built of heavy timber produced by the East Texas lumber industry. Houston became a center for the production of pumping equipment and "Christmas trees"—those Rube Goldberg–like arrangements of pipes and valves atop flowing wells.

The building and maintenance of refineries and pipelines provided employment for hundreds of workmen, and railroad traffic was increased markedly by the shipment of oil in specially designed tank cars. The sale of oil products like gasoline, with the advent of automobiles and other gasoline-powered mechanisms, gave economic opportunity to thousands, many of them independent service-station operators. And the millions of dollars of capital investment provided an entirely new base for taxation.

Educational Advances The first quarter of the new century was marked by a remarkable expansion of educational facilities. At the public school level the value of school property increased from slightly over nine million dollars in 1900 to over seventy-two million in 1920. The number of students rose from 708,125 to 1,233,860, and the number of teachers and other professional personnel increased from 15,019 to 31,880, a statistic indicative of a small decrease in the average size of classes. More important, the apportionment of state funds to school districts during the same period increased from $4.50 per pupil to $14.50 per pupil. The amount of local funds in addition to this state support varied from community to community. Yet, despite the increase in facilities, students, and finances, a 1920 survey found that Texas ranked thirty-ninth among the states on the basis of a ten-point index. One of the reasons for Texas' low rank was its extremely poor quality of Negro education. The white schools were substantially better but still nowhere near the top in the nation.

Public support of secondary or high school education was relatively slow to develop in Texas. Although there were a few public high schools in the state before 1900, secondary education did not begin on a large scale until the second decade of the twentieth century. The principal argument for public support of education had been the necessity to provide sufficient education for citizens to vote and exercise other civic duties such as service on juries. Opponents of public high schools claimed that secondary education was unnecessary to achieve this end. Furthermore, it was argued that most Texans could not afford to let their children remain in school three or four extra years and that therefore high schools would benefit only the wealthier families. The fight by enlightened educators through the last years of the nineteenth century was spearheaded by the University of Texas, which served as something of an unofficial accrediting agency until 1917 when the State Board of Education designated a special committee for that purpose. The University of Texas also organized and directed the Interscholastic League, founded in 1910 for high school academic and athletic participation.

In rural areas the problem of secondary education was acute. A rural high school law passed in 1911 during Colquitt's administration created county boards of education and authorized them to consolidate rural districts and establish rural high schools. Part of Ferguson's campaign platform in 1914 was aid to rural schools, and in 1915 he sought and obtained from the legislature a special appropriation for these schools. Another law supported by Ferguson in 1915 strengthened the rural high school law of 1911. A third school law, passed in 1925, broadened the powers of the county boards of education. Ferguson was also at least partially responsible for the passage of one of the most significant educational statutes: the compulsory attendance law. Enacted in 1915, it required children between eight and fourteen years of age to attend school at least sixty days each year. Later statutes have increased both the age limits and the number of attendance days.

Equally important was the twentieth-century movement for uniform and free public school textbooks. A 1903 statute created a special board for the selection of textbooks, and the textbook adoption law was modified and strengthened in 1907, 1911, and 1925. The first free textbook law in Texas, passed in 1911, permitted but did not require trustees to furnish free textbooks from state-apportioned funds. Use of local funds was permitted in 1915, and a constitutional amendment in 1918 provided for free textbooks in all Texas public schools.

The greatest educational advances were made in higher education. More than a dozen colleges and universities and the same number of junior colleges were established throughout the state. At the beginning of the century the state supported only four: the University of Texas, Texas A&M University, Sam Houston, and Prairie View A&M College. There were half a dozen or more small private or church-affiliated schools and four major church-affiliated colleges: Texas Christian, Baylor, Trinity, and St. Mary's. According to a report in 1900 by the state superintendent of public instruction, there were 2,148 college students in Texas.

Considerable expansion occurred at the University of Texas, which established colleges of engineering, education, business, and pharmacy and added a graduate school and a division of extension. Scores of wooden shacks were built to handle the increased enrollment after the war. Many of the shacks remained for years until the discovery of oil on university land in 1923 made possible the erection of new buildings. The discovery well on the two-million-acre university land reserve was a gusher that heralded not only enormous wealth for the university's permanent fund but also prosperity for West Texas.

The Agricultural and Mechanical College of Texas (now Texas A&M University) enjoyed similar growth, especially along technical lines. During World War I more officers in the armed forces were graduates of Texas A&M and its Reserve Officers' Training Corps than of any other school in the country, including West Point.

The normal-school movement for the training of public school teachers swept through the state during the first quarter of the century and left in its wake a Normal School Board of Regents, established in 1911, and six four-year teacher-training colleges: East Texas (established in 1899 as a private school and absorbed by the state in 1917), Southwest Texas (1899), North Texas (1901), West Texas (1910), Sul Ross (1920), and Stephen F. Austin (1923). The state established four other major four-year colleges: College of Industrial Arts for Women (1902, now Texas Woman's University), Texas College of Mines (1913, now University of Texas at El Paso), Texas College of Arts and Industries (1917, now Texas A and I University), and Texas Technological College (1923, now Texas Tech University, the state's second largest university). Two first-class private universities were created during that period: Rice Institute (1912, now Rice University) and Southern Methodist (1915).

By 1925 Texas had as many institutions of higher learning per capita as any state in the union and more than most, a position it has sustained into the present. Tuition at the many state schools was fixed at a minimum, and by the generous support of the legislature and the taxpayers, a college education has been easily available to Texans for nearly three-quarters of a century.

Women, Prohibition, and the New Freedom The Seventeenth Amendment to the United States Constitution providing for direct popular election of senators, instead of election by state legislators, was introduced as a bill in the United States Senate by Texas Senator Joseph Weldon Bailey, who had submitted himself to a popular referendum the year before. It is possible that Bailey intended the bill as a legislative tactic to kill the measure, but it carried and was ratified in 1913. That popular election made any great difference in the selection of Texas senators is difficult to discern. Charles Allen Culberson and Morris Sheppard, both of whom had been originally chosen by the legislature, were simply reelected to their seats by the voters when their terms expired.

Senator Sheppard introduced the bill that became the Eighteenth Amendment to the federal constitution and created the nightmare of Prohibition. The Prohibition movement had gained strength in Texas after its narrow defeat in 1911, especially with the successful litigation against the breweries in 1916 although the election of Ferguson and the reelection of Hobby can be construed as setbacks. Hobby was an anti-Prohibitionist, but it was a special session of the legislature called by him in February 1918 that enacted the first general Prohibition legislation in Texas. This legislature ratified the Eighteenth Amendment, prohibited the sale of intoxicating beverages within ten miles of any military installation, and prohibited the sale, manufacture, or transportation of liquor within the state—a redundancy that the Prohibitionists expected to be declared unconstitutional. It was struck down the following year, but that was of no consequence since by that time congress had implemented the Prohibition amendment with the Volstead Act.

Over twenty-five hundred saloons shut down and probably twice as many private stills sprang into existence. In 1921 Governor Neff, a militant Prohibitionist, warned the legislature that the state was experiencing the worst crime wave in history and urged the passage of more stringent liquor legislation. In 1923 the legislature revised the statutes to make mere possession of one quart or more of an intoxicant *prima facie* evidence of guilt. Neff was still not satisfied. Frequently he sent the Rangers into counties where there were rumors of private stills, and on at least one occasion several county officials were arrested for participation in the illegal activity.

The governor even urged the legislature to provide for the removal of county officials who refused to enforce the liquor laws, but the legislators would not follow him into such a violation of the rights of local jurisdiction.

The success of the Prohibition movement amply displayed the power of women despite their lack of the right to vote, for it was primarily such organizations as the Women's Christian Temperance Union and a host of ladies' aid societies that carried the Prohibition offensive. Concurrent with this movement was the growing demand of women for the right to vote.

Petitions for woman suffrage had been presented to the constitutional conventions of 1869 and 1875, but they had been ignored. In 1893 a group of suffragettes organized the Texas Equal Rights Association as an adjunct of the National Woman Suffrage Association. The organization was soon rent asunder, however, over the question of whether the women should sponsor a state tour by Susan B. Anthony, who, having a mind of her own, came anyway. The suffragist movement was revived early in the new century but functioned only desultorily until 1913. Thereafter a state convention of the Texas Woman Suffrage Association was held annually until after the ratification of the Nineteenth Amendment. By 1918 there was a plethora of local equal suffrage societies in Texas, including two men's leagues for woman suffrage. There was even a National Association Opposed to Woman Suffrage, the Texas branch of which was organized in 1915. This was a women's organization, headed by Mrs. James Wells of Brownsville, with the stated objectives of explaining "the evils which would follow the adoption of a scheme to force upon the Women of Texas the political duties and responsibilities of citizenship."

Women's effort in the war was a major factor in the ultimate success of the movement. In 1915 and 1917 resolutions for a constitutional amendment had not received the necessary two-thirds majority in the state legislature. But in 1918 the same special session that passed the Prohibition measures passed an act permitting women to vote in primary elections. Since Texas was in reality a one-party state, the primary franchise was more important than full suffrage. In 1919 Governor Hobby requested constitutional amendments enfranchising women and denying the right to vote to aliens. It was passed unanimously by both houses and then put before the electorate in the general election, in which women could not vote but aliens could, and it was defeated. But in June 1919 the Texas legislature ratified the Nineteenth Amendment, which received the necessary endorsement of three-fourths of the states in 1920.

Texas was the first state in the South and the ninth in the nation to go on record for the full enfranchisement of her women. But suffrage did not automatically or immediately bring equal rights of citizenship. Women could not serve on juries and were restricted, especially married women, in the control of their own property. Jury service was not extended to women in Texas until 1954 and then only after much debate. The chief arguments against it were women's alleged emotional reactions, women's inexperience in many of the matters that come before juries, the impracticality for mothers of young children to be away from home especially overnight, and the psychological disturbance of separating trial juries overnight because of sex. There is no question that the separation of one part of a jury from another during long trials has changed the jury's basic unity.

A woman's jurisdiction over her own property is closely related to the concept in Texas law, derived from Spain and Mexico, of marital community property. Under Texas codes all property acquired in any fashion, except by gift or inheritance, by either party in a marriage contract becomes the joint property of both. According to the distinguished jurist and specialist in women's rights, Ocie Speer, the community estate begins at marriage with nothing and includes everything that both parties possess at the dissolution of the marriage by death or divorce. Although separate properties can be maintained in a marriage, it is deceptively easy for them to be commingled beyond tracing. Texas law long vested in the husband not only the management of community property but also the management of his wife's separate property. A few gradual changes have been made in community property laws, but basically this situation still obtains. The practicality in ordinary business and professional affairs of having a single responsible party is argued. For example, a merchant whose wife is legal owner of half the stock on his shelves could hardly conduct his business if he did not have the sole legal responsibility for the operation. Nevertheless the laws, at least superficially, disparage women. A married woman cannot buy or sell property or contract a debt without her husband's permission. She can, however, have her disabilities removed by a district court's declaring her a *feme sole* for mercantile or trading purposes. And recently the legislature has permitted married women the legal management of all property they possess separately. The intricacies of the community property concept, however, make it uncertain whether women can obtain equal property rights without destroying the protection afforded them under it.

The New Ku Klux Klan in Texas A strange and baffling social phenomenon arose in the nation in the early 1920's. A paranoid mixture of delusions of grandeur and persecution, it had a loose psychological kinship with the Prohibition movement in that its purpose was to force all humanity to conform to its own credo. It was nativist, racist, and perhaps more than anything else, militantly fundamentalist. For two or three terror-filled years it perpetrated unspeakable crimes against men in the name of God and committed un-American violence in the name of patriotism. It has been called an authentic folk movement, a protector of fundamental Protestantism, a champion of "old-time religion," and on the other hand it has been likened to the Nazi movement in Germany.

Historically it was a revival of the southern Ku Klux Klan of the Reconstruction period: a secret fraternal organization complete with such mystical trappings as oaths, secret handclasps, and unusual titles for officers. But its objectives went much further. The Reconstruction Klan was bent primarily upon subjugation of the Negro; the Klan of the 1920's purposed to impose its own codes upon all of society, and it was only incidentally anti-Negro. It was also anti-Catholic and anti-Semitic. Religious bigotry underlay its entire structure, and it was by no means a southern organization despite its original reconstitution in Atlanta, Georgia. It was particularly strong in Oregon, Pennsylvania, the Bible-belt South, and the old northwest states of Wisconsin, Ohio, Indiana, and Michigan; and to the mortification of thousands of enlightened Texans it reached its greatest extent and influence in Texas.

Kleagles, salesmen of the Klan, brought the movement into Houston in October 1920 and linked it to a Confederate Veterans' reunion. The Imperial Wizard, W. J. Simmons, who was a former circuit-riding preacher, sold "one hundred per cent Americanism" to native-born white Protestants over the age of eighteen at a Klectoken initiation fee of ten dollars per head. The first Texas Klan was organized that month. More than a hundred Houstonians gathered in a field lit by fiery crosses, intoned "Onward Christian Soldiers" and "The Old Rugged Cross," and swore to uphold the principles of the Klan and to obey the Imperial Wizard. With incredible rapidity the Klan spread across the sprawling state. According to historians as well as contemporary observers, the moving force behind the Klan's growth in Texas was not so much its racist proclivity or even its nativism as its condemnation of the alleged postwar breakdown in morality. The popular Baptist governor, Pat M. Neff, decried the sinfulness of flaming youth, petting parties, loose dancing, and other breaches of morality. The Klan enlisted Texans to enforce pure conduct by violence, terrorism, spying, wiretapping, intimidation, and threat.

Before the first Klan year had ended in Texas, more than fifty acts of terrorism by hooded scourges had occurred and countless threats had been issued. A Houston attorney was kidnapped, tarred, and feathered for having the wrong kind of clients (he was a criminal lawyer); a Negro bellhop in Dallas was branded on the forehead with the initials K.K.K.; a woman in East Texas was tarred and feathered and had her hair clipped on spurious charges of bigamy; a Beaumont physician was brutally flogged, tarred, and feathered on the suspicion that he had performed an abortion; a traveling salesman was chained to a tree, threatened with castration, and beaten to a pulp betweeen his waist and his knees. Approximately eighty thousand Texans joined the Invisible Empire to render the Klan's justice upon evildoers. "Texas Klansmen," reported the Houston *Chronicle* on October 4, 1921, "have beaten and blackened more people in the last six months than all the other states combined." And a citizen of Dallas, Hiram W. Evans, became the national Imperial Wizard. Scores of city, county, and even state officials rushed to join the popular uprising against sin, Negroes, and foreigners (for Texas, read Mexican laborers). Sheriffs and city police in a dozen or more communities became leading members. Even one Texas' United States Senator, Earle B. Mayfield, expressed outright support for the Invisible Empire. By the end of 1922 the Klan appeared to be in control of every major city in Texas except Galveston and San Antonio. Time and time again Klan terrorists who were arrested by well-intentioned law officers were "no-billed" by grand juries—or trial juries were intimidated into returning verdicts of not guilty. But by the end of the year, according to Charles C. Alexander in his excellent history of the Klan in Texas, acts of violence began to decrease. The Klan had entered politics in an attempt to control the state government.

In the election of 1922 the Klan block vote was estimated at one hundred thousand. Neff, although not a member of the Klan, was considered by its members as a "friendly neutral." Mayfield, a Klan backer and former member, set out to win Charles A. Culberson's senate seat and succeeded. His major opposition came from Farmer Jim Ferguson, who ran a vitriolic anti-Klan campaign against him. Although Mayfield was the only successful major Klan candidate, the Klan won a majority in the Texas House of Representatives and may have obtained a majority in the Texas Senate. The Klan, in Texas and across the nation, girded itself for the election of 1924, a presidential year.

13

Depression and War

The Depression Strikes

The Politics of Prosperity The election of Klansman Earle B. Mayfield to the United States Senate, which seated him over his write-in opponent George E. B. Peddy, produced torrents of anti-Klan orations in the election of 1924. Alabama's Senator Oscar W. Underwood, campaigning for the Democratic presidential nomination, began his campaign in Texas with a series of powerful speeches against the Klan. Although the Ku Klux Klan was stronger in Texas than in any other state in the union, Underwood and his Texas managers reasoned that an anti-Klan position would give him the majority of the support of the Texas delegation to the convention. Woodrow Wilson's son-in-law, William Gibbs McAdoo, arrived at the same conclusion and made a whirlwind tour of the state denouncing the Klan and its activities. Then Governor Pat Neff, who was believed by many to have endorsed the white-robed moralists, made a surprise speech against the Klan as a preliminary move to secure a favorite-son endorsement in the convention. But McAdoo obtained the support of the Texas delegation, which was called the immortal forty because they voted for him in more than seventy roll calls at the national convention, even after it became clear that the nominee would be John W. Davis.

At the gubernatorial level the principal issue was also the Ku Klux Klan. Klansmen supported Felix D. Robertson, who received more votes than any other candidate in the first primary. But the number of candidates was the largest yet offered the voters, and since Robertson failed to win the necessary majority, there was a runoff in a second primary. Among the aspirants in the first primary were Lynch Davidson, a Houston lumber man; T. Whitfield Davidson, Neff's lieutenant governor; Mrs. Miriam A. Ferguson, wife of the impeached governor; and five others.

Mrs. Ferguson's entry in the race was dictated by Farmer Jim's insatiable desire to return to political power. He attempted in the early spring of 1924 to make a deal with Senator Underwood by offering his support at the state convention in exchange for Underwood's endorsement of his right to be entered on the ballot. When this maneuver failed, Ferguson placed his wife's name on the ticket and began one of the most remarkable campaigns in any state's political history. The couple toured the state, appeared at every gathering they could, and stumped whenever possible. They had two major themes upon which they rendered scores of variations: vindicate "Pa" and destroy the Ku Klux Klan. They were particularly vehement toward the Klan. Usually Mrs. Ferguson, then forty-nine years of age, would make a short speech ending, "A vote for me is a vote of confidence for my husband, who cannot be a candidate because his enemies have succeeded in barring him from holding office." Then Ferguson would launch a tirade principally aimed at the Klan and answer the obvious criticism with a statement that soon became a campaign slogan: "The people of Texas will have two governors for the price of one."

Mrs. Ferguson ran second to Robertson in the first primary and therefore entered the runoff in July, in which she defeated him 413,751 to 316,019, the total vote being the largest yet cast in Texas. Anti-Ferguson sentiment rallied to support in the general election the Republican nominee, George C. Butte, who resigned his professorship at the University of Texas to enter the political lists. The Republicans had polled only 73,000 votes in 1922. Butte received nearly 300,000, but Mrs. Ferguson received well over 400,000 and became the first woman governor of Texas and the second in the nation.

True to their campaign slogan, the Fergusons gave the state two governors, one in office and one in authority. Pa Ferguson established headquarters in the capitol, where most of the executive business actually took place. Little legislation of note occurred during Mrs. Ferguson's term. An anti-Klan statute was passed, but no effective reduction in governmental

DISTRIBUTION OF
FOREIGN-BORN POPULATION
1940

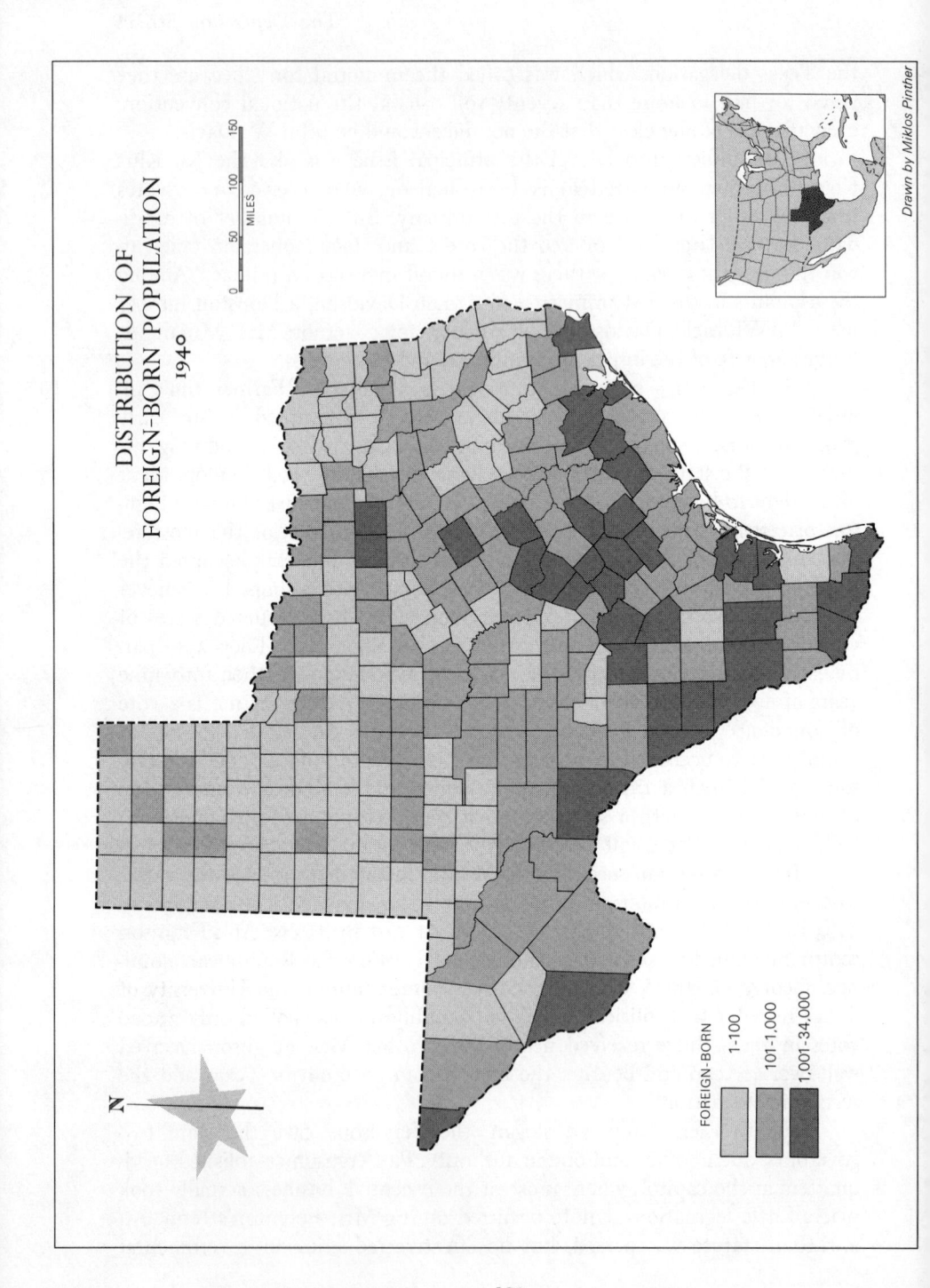

FOREIGN-BORN
1–100
101–1,000
1,001–34,000

Drawn by Miklos Pinther

expenses was made, as the Fergusons had promised. The two most significant events were the scandals that developed over Mrs. Ferguson's pardon policy and over highway contracts. On the recommendations of her husband, Governor Ferguson granted over two thousand pardons in two years, in stark contrast to the ninety-two given by Neff during his four years in office. Ferguson was criticized as narrowly skirting outright bribery in making his recommendations, but no charges were filed and no proof was offered. The Fergusons defended the pardon policy on grounds of economy. The highway scandals brought about Mrs. Ferguson's defeat in the race for reelection in 1926. A young executive in the Texas Contractors' Association, Louis Wiltz Kemp, discovered a curious relationship between Ferguson's office in the capitol and the awarding of maintenance and construction contracts. Ferguson warned him not to publicize the matter or he would be made the "goat." Kemp persisted and was promptly fired. He retaliated by issuing a mimeographed newsletter at his own expense to present facts and figures, which he entitled *The Goat Bleats*. Don Biggers, the journalist who had exposed the oil-promotion frauds at Ranger, used Kemp's data to write fiery editorials, which a courageous editor in Blanco published. The circulation of the Blanco *Courier* jumped fantastically, and Attorney General Dan Moody utilized the exposés in his campaign against "Fergusonism."

In 1926 Mrs. Ferguson received enough votes to cause a second primary, in which Moody defeated her by 495,723 to 270,595. That year, as a result of the large vote polled by George Butte in 1924, the Republican Party held its first state-wide primary, but it received only 31,000 votes in the general election in November. Dan Moody, at the age of thirty-four, became the youngest governor the state had elected.

Moody, a progressive spirit, urged the legislature to embark upon an extensive program of reform and revision in the state government. Only portions of his program were adopted, but many defects in the administrative agencies were corrected. A sweeping revision of the State Highway Department resulted in the foundation of a program of road construction and maintenance that made Texas the acknowledged leader in the nation in its highway system. Similar reforms were made in the education system. Moody had openly charged Ferguson with graft in the awarding of textbook contracts since Ferguson not only was acting clerk of the Textbook Commission but also employed one of the commissioners on the staff of his newspaper. This potential evil was corrected, and, as a part of the revision, a new State Board of Education was created by constitutional amendment. Under Moody's leadership the legislature increased the appropriations for education and tightened the procedures for executive clemency.

Moody easily won reelection in 1928, despite the Ferguson support thrown to Louis J. Wardlaw. But in the general election, the Republican candidate received more than 120,000 votes, in a reflection of the unprecedented stand the Texas electorate took in the national election when it bolted the Democratic Party for the first time in Texas history.

The national convention of the Democratic Party was held in Houston in 1928, the first and only time a national political party has convened in Texas. After a stormy session, the delegates nominated New York Catholic Alfred E. Smith. The Texas delegation voted for Houston financier Jesse Jones and rendered only lip service to the party's choice. Texas Democrats who opposed Smith organized as Hoover Democrats, called Hoovercrats, to support the Republican nominee, Herbert C. Hoover. At issue were bigoted objections to Smith's religion, reaction to his stand for repeal of Prohibition, and spreading belief in Coolidge's Republican prosperity. A spirited campaign caused the Texas electoral votes to be cast for a Republican in 1928. In his bid for reelection that year Senator Mayfield was decisively defeated by Tom Connally, who retained the senate seat for many years to come.

The Crash of 1929 In Texas and the nation widespread prosperity was mounting in 1928. Hoover summed up the attitude of the country during his campaign when he said that America was enjoying "a degree of well-being unparalleled in all the world." Although the American economy had cycled between prosperity and panic in the past and although the general trend had been consistently upward, the boom conditions of 1927 and 1928 were altogether unprecedented. But economic historians later found that credit was overexpanded; industry was overexpanded for the existing consumer markets; agribusiness was overexpanded; the purchasing power of labor was relatively too small; and technological unemployment was growing faster than industry.

These factors did not necessarily precipitate the stock-market crash in October 1929, but they contributed to the extensive depression that followed. The market, too, was overextended. Prices of common stocks had risen sharply on the fever of speculation that swept through every class of America. Purchases were made at minimal margins under the happy delusion that stock prices would continue to rise. A slump in September caused numerous margin calls from brokers, but a blind faith in prosperity prevented all but a few from making personal adjustments. On Wednesday, October 23, a sharp drop in prices started a wave of selling and additional margin calls. Panic struck the stock market the following day, Black Thursday, October 24. Within a matter of hours thousands of Americans were financially wiped out.

Texans in all walks of life suffered in the same proportion as investors and speculators around the country. But since the panic spread first through industry, Texas did not feel the effects of the depression as soon or as deeply at first, for the state's economy still rested on an agricultural foundation. The tragic plight of farmers and stockmen lay a few months further ahead.

Meantime Texas faced the gubernatorial election with little thought of depression or hard times. Fifteen candidates entered the race; eleven names were printed on the ballot; and of these, according to S. S. McKay, seven were major candidates. The two leading aspirants, who went into the second primary, were Mrs. Ferguson and Ross S. Sterling. Mrs. Ferguson stood for election because of the Supreme Court's refusal to permit her husband's name on the ballot. Ross Sterling, a highly successful Houston contractor and oil man, had accepted the appointment from Moody as chairman of the State Highway Department. Supposedly worth over fifty million dollars, Sterling's campaign called for a businesslike operation in the state government. His major plank was a bond issue for the construction of highways. Little was said by either Mrs. Ferguson or Sterling about plans for coping with the economic disaster that awaited the state. Although Mrs. Ferguson topped Sterling's vote in the first primary, Sterling won in the runoff by 473,371 to her 384,402.

Sterling served as governor from January 1931 to January 1933—years when the depression hit the state with its full fury. But neither Sterling nor his legislature enacted any specific relief measures. Rather, in an effort to bolster the sagging state treasury, a few taxes were raised and a few new ones were passed. The only significant depression legislation was the Texas Cotton Acreage Control Law.

Tumbling cotton prices had brought the depression to Texas. In 1931 Texas farmers raised over five million bales, and that year the price of cotton hit a low of six cents per pound: many had farmed at a loss. Throughout the South a demand arose for curtailing the production of cotton. Leaders from six states met in Austin in August 1931 as the Southern Cotton Conference. Nearly every speaker at the conference urged governmental control of cotton acreage. The following month, September 1931, the Texas Legislature took the lead and passed the Texas Cotton Acreage Control Law, which prohibited a farmer from planting more than thirty per cent of his cultivated land in cotton. The legislature hedged on the issue of control by stating that the law was a necessary measure for soil conservation. Soon Arkansas, Mississippi, and South Carolina passed similar laws with the limitation that they would not go into effect until seventy-five per cent of the cotton-raising states had established controls. Thus, prior to federal regulation, Texas was the first and only state to attempt acreage control.

The Texas law was received with mixed comments. Some farmers favored the measure because the only way to raise prices was to limit supply. Others circumvented it, and some objected to it. The antagonism ranged from objections over the thin disguise of the control to objections that it could only hurt Texas farmers unless other states joined in. Perhaps the most serious objection to the Cotton Acreage Control Law came from landowners who rented their farms to tenants. One landlord declared that sixty families of tenants on his property would be unemployed if the law were enforced. Throughout the Coastal Plains in South and East Texas, tenant farming had continued to increase. It was obvious both that many landlords would have to lay off tenants and that many tenants were unequipped for anything but cotton farming. The law was declared unconstitutional by the Texas Court of Civil Appeals in March 1932.

The agricultural depression had struck. The plight of the farmer was serious. Increasing reliance on a single crop with the consequent departure from subsistence operations made farmers particularly vulnerable to the drop in agricultural prices. Conditions worsened during the depression, especially in the plains area, as widespread droughts cut into production. Two results followed: many tenants left the farms to seek employment in towns and cities, only to become part of the growing army of unemployed; many landowners, dependent on farm income, were unable to meet mortgage payments and taxes and faced foreclosure and loss of their land. In West Texas, especially on the plains, a number of ranches had been recently subdivided and sold to farmers on installment purchase plans. The depression and the ravages of the dust bowl spelled ruin for most of these unfortunates. At least two land companies desperately tried to aid the farmers to whom they had sold tracts. Throughout the worst of the depression years neither the Yellow House Land Company nor the Spade lands foreclosed on farms unless the buyers moved away. The Spade lands, operated by the Ellwood heirs, even remitted interest payments one year in an effort to save their farmer-purchasers.

The East Texas Oil Boom The East Texas oil boom saved many farmers in East Texas, tenants and landowners alike, from utter destitution, and it enriched a few. All of Texas benefited to some extent from the oil production in the East Texas field, which was discovered in October 1930, the greatest single oil field in the history of the petroleum industry. With the rapid expansion of the field, a new source of income, if not genuine prosperity, gave relief from the worst of the early depression years. The discovery well was drilled near Kilgore by a persistent wildcat operator named C. M. "Dad" Joiner. In December a second well was brought in, which led speculators to believe that a field had been opened, although neither well was a major producer when compared to gusher production elsewhere. But little did even the wildest dream of the promoters reflect the fantastic production to come. In January 1931 a third well near Longview twelve miles away blew in with small gusher production.

Bedlam reigned. Hundreds of operators, many without resources except their enthusiasm and excitement, began leasing land in the area and spudding wells. By July 1931 over a thousand wells had been drilled, and the year's end saw thirty-four hundred wells in the East Texas field. The estimated production in 1931 was over one hundred million barrels. Peak production was reached in 1933 with over two hundred million barrels—more than all the rest of the state produced that year. A unique characteristic of the field, and a significant one, was that it was almost wholly developed by small independent operators and promoters. At first the major oil companies owned leases on less than twenty per cent of the field because the reports filed by their geologists before the Joiner discovery advised that there was no oil in the region. After the three discovery wells had outlined the field, the major companies still withheld from activity because their geological reports said that the wells were flukes and would be short-lived. Consequently the first operations were a heyday for independent drillers. For example, over five thousand people descended on Kilgore within twenty-four hours. Excitement spawned more excitement. Leasing and drilling increased sensationally during 1931: during one week in October an average of slightly more than one well per hour was brought in.

The spectacular production, though a boon to the depression economy, created enormous problems, especially in marketing. The price of crude oil dropped in nine months from one dollar per barrel to ten cents. Refineries operated by the major companies did not purchase even a small part of the overproduction from East Texas. Some major companies hoped to squeeze independents into selling their leases by refusing to buy crude oil or by reducing its price. There was insufficient consumer market for the products of the refineries if they did purchase the crude oil. And the depression had curtailed the consumer market below its 1928 level.

Aware of the problem, East Texas operators held a meeting in Tyler in August 1931 to seek a solution. A second meeting a week later sent a special committee to Governor Ross Sterling to ask for aid. Sterling issued an executive order on August 17 that required all operators in the field to shut down their wells because of the danger to the entire industry from overproduction in East Texas. In response to threats of violence, Sterling declared martial law in the region and ordered units of the National Guard into the East Texas field. Desperate and anguished independents accused

Sterling, one of the founders of the Humble Oil Company, and General Jacob F. Walters, who commanded the National Guard but who was also an attorney for the Texas Company, of personal interest in shutting down the field. Sterling intended to shut down the field until a system of prorated production could be established. Most of the independent operators, however, believed that the major companies, who controlled the markets, were using proration and politics to force their way into the field. This attitude led to the chaotic conditions that followed.

The field was reopened for production on September 5, and the daily allowable rate was fixed at two hundred twenty-five barrels per well. This was soon reduced to one hundred barrels. The price of crude oil rose, and the combination of circumstances created the oil-field phenomenon of "hot oil." Hot oil was not stolen oil but oil produced illegally beyond the allowable. It was estimated that within a few months after the proration order the amount of hot oil produced was greater than the field's legal production. Because of the secrecy involved in running hot oil, dissatisfaction arose in all ranks. Landowners could not determine whether their royalties were based on the correct amount of oil. Well-owners often found that their "specialists" engaged to run hot oil were pumping more than their instructions authorized and selling it privately.

In February 1932 the state Supreme Court held that Sterling's order declaring martial law was unconstitutional. But the governor maintained troops in the area until December of that year. Control of the field passed from the National Guard to the Railroad Commission. A special corps of investigators was appointed to enforce the proration ruling and check the production of hot oil. Inevitably, with so much money involved, corruption appeared among the investigators. Ernest Thompson, chairman of the Railroad Commission, obtained the assistance of a large force of Texas Rangers in February 1933. A modicum of order was finally achieved by the end of that year.

As hot oil production grew, a market developed for it. During 1931 six independent refineries were established to produce what came to be called "cheap East Texas gasoline." At the height of refinery expansion, there were eighty-seven independent plants in the East Texas field ranging from portable skimming units to half-million dollar industries. An undetermined amount of hot oil was run through these refineries, and the low-priced gasoline found a market all over the Southwest as hundreds of independent trucking concerns developed to move it from the refineries to independent retailers. In 1933 major companies began producing a similar cheap grade of gasoline, and in 1934 the legislature passed a law that required all refineries to account for the oil they processed and to report its sources. This ended the brief expansion of independent operators, but many of them survived and grew into larger firms.

By 1938 more than eighty per cent of the field had been brought under the control of the major companies. The number of wells in the field had increased to over twenty-four thousand, and for many years production from East Texas remained annually more than twice that of any other field in the nation. Appraisal of the effect of the East Texas field on the state economy awaits a major study. But one can assume that the boom conditions, extending through hundreds of independent promoters, drillers, refiners, truckers, and retailers, saved the state from the worst of the early depression.

The Roosevelt Years

The Deepening Depression   In spite of the East Texas boom, Texas despaired at the worsening economic conditions, as did the rest of the nation. Banks failed, businesses closed, businessmen went bankrupt, and unemployment increased. By 1933, 5.4 per cent of the white population and 8.8 per cent of the Negro population were on some form of relief. At first thousands of needy people were aided by friends and relatives. Soon community charities began to share the burden, but such resources were quickly exhausted. Hundreds of unemployed men, many of them unskilled agricultural workers, began to migrate in search of relief or employment. Hitchhiking and "riding the rails" became common. Destitute families made homes in boxcars, caves, abandoned buildings, and even in large crates such as piano boxes. Most of the major cities received this migration in shantytowns that provided only minimal housing for the unfortunates. Citizens looked to government for assistance and blamed Herbert Hoover and the Republican administration not only for causing the depression but also for failing to end it. The shantytowns were called "Hoover Heights"; jackrabbits and armadillos were called "Hoover hogs"; newspapers for warmth by indigent sleepers in parks were called "Hoover blankets." So desperate had many people become that some historians believe the entire nation was on the verge of revolution at the time of the 1932 election.

Just as Hoover caught the blame nationally, so in part did Sterling on the state level. The primary brought forth a half-dozen new candidates and a plethora of promises and remedies. Once again Jim

Ferguson put his wife's name on the ballot, and once again she led the race in the first primary, winning nearly twice as many votes as Sterling. In the runoff all the anti-Ferguson forces combined to support Sterling, but Mrs. Ferguson edged him out, by a mere 3,600 votes out of nearly a million. Since the bulk of the Ferguson support came from rural farm areas, the effect of the depression on the voters is clear. One commentator said, "The voters of 1932 are as rational as the mob who crucified Christ."

Whether or not the electorate was rational, the entire country was looking for a savior to lead it from the morass of the worsening depression. And it was in this role that Franklin Delano Roosevelt first appeared to the people of Texas. In the general election the Democratic vote for Roosevelt was nearly one-quarter of a million greater than the vote for Mrs. Ferguson. A last-ditch effort to stop Fergusonism was made by Republican Orville Bullington, who polled a surprising 317,807 votes (Hoover got only 97,000 Republican votes) against Mrs. Ferguson's 528,986.

One of the reasons for Roosevelt's immense popularity in Texas was the fact that his running mate was the Texan John Nance Garner. Garner was chosen for the vice-presidency not so much because he was expected to return Texas to the Democratic fold but because he was the strongest politician in the Democratic Party. It has been suggested that Garner, who was then serving as Speaker of the House, might have gotten the presidential nomination himself if he had made a serious try for it. Garner and Roosevelt were both men of wealth, Garner having made a small fortune by shrewd real-estate investments and Roosevelt having inherited his. Both men were dedicated to a course of action for relief from the depression. Roosevelt coordinated the ideas of his New Deal cabinet and presented them to congress; Garner by persuasion, cajolery, and a mastery of parliamentary tactics ushered the New Deal into law.

Roosevelt had committed himself to the principles of the slogan "Relief, Recovery, and Reform." It was up to congress to support him. The Hundred Days session of the newly elected congress was probably the most dramatic Washington had ever witnessed. In a whirlwind of legislation, congress spewed out statutes—some of them good, some of them bad, some of them unconstitutional. To effect relief, it pumped money into the economy by providing for direct grants to states and by creating federal agencies to make jobs for the unemployed. To effect recovery, it created the Agriculture Adjustment Agency and the National Recovery Administration. To effect reform, it created a variety of regulatory agencies. Public morale was raised enormously, and in the summer of 1933 there was a temporary upsurge in the economy, falsely heralded as the longed-for recovery. But real recovery was nearly a decade away.

The first New Deal gave way to the second New Deal, which

Roosevelt launched in January 1935 in his message to the next congress. The following year, he and Garner were reelected by large majorities. Recovery was still not in sight, and the New Dealers recommended more pump-priming measures. But they began to meet resistance from reluctant congressmen, especially southern conservatives, and from a rock-bound Supreme Court. Roosevelt undertook a purge of congress in the by-elections of 1938 and a packing of the Supreme Court. Both failed, but the attempt caused a split between the president and Garner. By the time of the 1940 election, Garner was bitterly opposed to a third term for Roosevelt, and he even consented against his personal wishes to let his name be placed at the national convention in futile nomination for the presidency. Garner was not the only Texan to become disillusioned with Roosevelt and the New Deal. Although in 1940 the state did not bolt the party as it had done in 1928, the Texas delegation to the convention was opposed to a third term for Roosevelt.

It would be bootless to attempt to survey the Texas reaction to the New Deal measures during Roosevelt's first two terms. In the first place, public opinion is too categorically divided for any generalization. In the second place, the New Deal's reception and operation in Texas were little different from that in any other state or in the nation as a whole. It is perhaps worth noting that in 1929 the average per capita income in Texas of $462 was above the national average and that in 1939 at $401 it was below the national average. Unemployment, too, rose in Texas between 1933 and 1940. In 1933 slightly more than 100,000 Texas families were on relief. In 1940 more than 200,000 adults were unemployed, and another 111,450 were employed by such federal agencies as the Civilian Conservation Corps on make-work projects. A survey made in Harris County showed that in 1940 thirteen per cent of the population received some form of public assistance.

The New Deal neither ended the depression nor brought recovery, but it did have a profound effect on the lives of the people. The repeal of national Prohibition made local option elections in Texas a vital concern of both wets and drys. The first and second Agricultural Adjustment Acts shook the state's agribusiness to the very core. The Blue Eagle of the National Industrial Recovery Act appeared on hundreds of businesses throughout the state, and its codes were perhaps better adhered to in Texas than in more industrialized states. Thousands of Texas banks closed their doors with Roosevelt's dramatic executive proclamation and reopened under the Federal Deposit Insurance Corporation. Some were closed permanently by federal bank examiners. Hundreds of thousands of Texans found temporary or part-time employment with the Civilian Conservation Corps, the National Youth Administration, the Public Works Administration, and the Work Projects Administration. The Social Security Act touched nearly every adult in the state, and whether they liked it or not, it provided a minimum base for future retirement.

Of all of these federal measures, one should be singled out for attention because it was masterminded by an unusual Texan, Jesse Jones of Houston, the same man the Texas Democrats had nominated for president in 1928. This measure was the Reconstruction Finance Corporation. It had been conceived by the Hoover administration and established by law in 1932. Its purpose was to loan federal funds to such vital segments of the economy as railroads and banks in hopes of checking the spreading depression. Some economic historians believe it was the single most effective antidepression measure the government took. Jesse Jones, then a multimillionaire, accepted a position on the first, nonpartisan board of directors. With Roosevelt's inauguration, Jones became chairman, a position he retained for eight years although he remained the chief power in the RFC until 1945. Roosevelt also named him Federal Loan Administrator in charge of all federal lending agencies, and in 1941 he nominated him Secretary of Commerce. Jones refused to accept unless he could retain his authority as loan administrator. Republican Senator Robert A. Taft supported the unprecedented appointment although he stated, "Mr. Jones already has more power than any other man in the government with the single exception of the president." Later, Henry A. Wallace said of Jones, "Jesse Jones wielded a greater power for a longer period than any human being in the history of the United States."

State Politics Mrs. Ferguson assumed the office of governor for the second time on January 17, 1933, and her husband resumed his role as the power behind the throne. The next two years, however, were much less stormy than any previous Ferguson administration. The open-door policy on pardons was quietly reinstituted as an economy measure. The state's finances were in a deplorable condition, and the state government was operating at a deficit because of the increase in governmental functions and the decrease in tax revenue. Mrs. Ferguson recommended a three per cent sales tax to the legislature, and when this died she recommended a corporation income tax, which also failed. The result was a deficit by the end of August 1933 of over $18,000,000.

The legislature not only failed to balance the budget but also failed to act on a reorganization of state agencies proposed by the Woodruff-Graves committee. This committee of five had been created by the preceding legislature at Governor Sterling's suggestion. Its objectives were to make an intensive study of all state institutions, agencies, and departments and to propose a plan for more efficiency and economy in the government. Most of the actual work was done by the private management firm of Griffenhagen and Associates, whose multivolume report forms one of the most comprehensive studies of any state government. The proposed plan had two principal features: consolidation of the one hundred twenty-nine bureaus and commissions into twenty for an estimated annual saving of about $1,500,000 and reorganization of the institutions of higher education for an estimated annual saving of over $2,000,000. Although several bills were introduced to implement the scheme, none of them was passed.

The legislature did, however, pass a number of constructive measures. The most important of them was a special election for a constitutional amendment to provide a bond issue of $20,000,000 for relief funds and to establish a special agency for administering both them and the federal relief funds available to Texas through various New Deal programs. Other legislation included congressional redistricting, legalization of horse-race gambling and prize fighting, a referendum on the manufacture and sale of 3.2 beer, and the repeal of the Eighteenth Amendment, a measure that carried almost two to one at the polls.

A new phase of Texas politics began with the gubernatorial election of 1934. Fergusonism, Prohibition, and other issues of previous campaigns were resolved or forgotten; new issues and new candidates emerged for the Democratic primary. Seven men were on the ballot, of whom not one was widely known and only one had run before. They brought out a large vote, and an August runoff was necessitated between James V. Allred and Tom Hunter. Allred won, 497,808 to 457,785, and slid into office in the general election in November.

The new governor was from a poor family and had worked hard to become a successful attorney. He was elected attorney general of Texas in 1930 and was reelected in 1932. His gubernatorial platform had included the creation of a commission on public utilities, a board of pardons and paroles, and a modern police system. He advocated a decrease in taxes coupled with an updating of the system of assessment and collection. In messages to the legislature Allred urged an increase in the tax on crude oil among other proposals for balancing the budget, but once again the legislature was apathetic toward any substantial change in the state tax. Perhaps its most significant achievement was the establishment of the Department of Public Safety, which combined the Rangers and the Highway Patrol into a modern and efficient state police force. On Allred's recommendation the legislature submitted to the voters a constitutional amendment authorizing old-age pensions, which was approved in a special election in August 1935. Afterward it took two called sessions of the legislature to pass the pension act.

The pension act added to the popularity of the young, affable governor, who won renomination in the 1936 primary without a runoff and an easy reelection in the November race. Expansion in practically every agency of state government required Allred to ask the next legislature for large appropriations. And because no solution had been found to the tax problem, the state's deficit that biennium was the largest yet. The Dallas *News* referred to the ineffectual legislative attack on the fiscal problem as a "pitiful show of impotence." Allred retired to private practice at the end of his second term, and he was later appointed to a federal district judgeship.

Twelve experienced campaigners and one radio announcer battled for the governor's office in the 1938 primary. Within a few weeks the announcer, W. Lee O'Daniel, turned the campaign into a circus. Without a headquarters, a campaign manager, or any knowledge of politics, he was at first considered a joke by the professional politicians, whom he castigated. But within a few weeks after the campaign began newspaper polls showed him to be the leading candidate, and he quickly became the chief target of all of the opposition.

Startled political savants dug into O'Daniel's background. He was a native of Ohio who had moved to Texas in 1925 as sales manager for a Fort Worth flour mill. By 1938 he was president of his own firm and was marketing a product called Hillbilly Flour. Since 1927 he had conducted a highly popular state-wide daily noontime radio show with three hillbilly musicians. The show's format was simple and homey. It started with the cry "Please pass the biscuits, Pappy," and then Pappy O'Daniel sang country and religious music accompanied by his Light Crust Doughboys. Between songs O'Daniel gave practical advice to housewives, recited poetry, advocated thrift and morality, told stories of heroes, and sold flour. After the show became popular, he bought a bus and toured the state in special appearances. By his own admission he knew little about politics and government and had never voted or paid a poll tax.

How did he come to enter the gubernatorial race? An admirer had written to the radio show asking him to run for governor. He read the letter on the air and requested his audience to advise him. A week later he announced that he had received 54,449 requests that he run. He therefore announced his candidacy on the platform of the Ten Commandments and the Golden Rule. Touring the state in his campaign, he put on free shows and asked the audience to contribute pennies, nickles, and dimes to his flour-barrel campaign chest. It was an amazingly effective technique both as a quasi pledge from voters and as a tool to deride the "professional politicians." "I don't know whether I'll get elected," O'Daniel was quoted early in the campaign, "but, boy, it sure is good for the flour business."

He was elected, winning nomination overwhelmingly without a runoff and romping home with ninety-five per cent of the votes in the general election. He did not get along well with his legislature, perhaps because the members resented the election of a hillbilly musician. But O'Daniel was more than an entertainer: he was a highly successful salesman and businessman, worth a reputed half-million dollars when he became governor. Amid the flamboyance of his performance, carefully designed to create the image of a hick, the new governor advocated a number of sound business principles in government. He had promised an increase in old-age pensions, but the legislature refused to cooperate. He advocated a transaction tax as a thinly disguised sales tax to balance the budget, but he met with no success, and the state's deficit continued to rise. In his 1940 campaign for reelection, O'Daniel pressed the need for a transaction tax so hard that it became, combined with the liberalization of old-age pensions, the chief issue in the election. He won again in the first primary against six opponents, one of whom was Mrs. Ferguson. The fading Ferguson appeal could not compete with O'Daniel's entertainment of the voters.

The 1941 legislature addressed itself with more energy than previous legislatures to the vitally important question of increasing revenue. It rejected O'Daniel's transaction tax and passed after heated discussions the Morris Omnibus Tax Bill, which increased taxes on natural resources and tobacco, levied a new tax on gasoline sales, and taxed the gross receipts of selected businesses such as insurance, telephone, and utilities companies. The legislature also passed a resolution, after the death of Senator Morris Sheppard, that O'Daniel appoint himself to the vacancy. Apparently most of the members preferred him in Washington instead of Austin. The governor, however, astutely appointed Andrew Jackson Houston, the aging son of Sam Houston, who would be no competition for him in the special election. Twenty-nine aspirants filed for the special election, including O'Daniel and a bright young congressman from the Hill Country, Lyndon Baines Johnson, who was known for his staunch support of Roosevelt and the New Deal. The race between Johnson and O'Daniel was very close and the final results were not known until after four days of counting and tabulating. O'Daniel won by a bare 1,311 votes, less than two per cent of the votes cast.

O'Daniel left for Washington and his lieutenant governor, Coke R. Stevenson, succeeded him on August 4, 1941. Stevenson remained in office longer than any man before him and presided over the state during all of the hectic days of World War II, being elected for two terms of his own after he completed O'Daniel's term.

World War II   Sunday December 7, 1941, opened in peaceful worship; it closed in infamy. A ham radio operator in South America picked up the news in Hawaii of the sneak Japanese air attack on the naval base at Pearl Harbor, and he broadcast it to a score or more amateurs in Texas shortly after noon. It appeared to be a hoax, but it was not. National networks confirmed the news in a few hours. Later many newspapers ran extras. Every hour that evening the news got bleaker. The navy's back had been broken: nineteen ships had been sunk, hundreds of men had been killed, shore installations had been bombed.

Senator Tom Connally, the senior senator from Texas, was called to the White House at 9 p.m. that night along with a few other prominent congressional leaders. In the presence of his cabinet, President Roosevelt gave the stark details of the tragedy to the congressmen. Roosevelt addressed both houses the next morning, December 8, just before noon. Connally introduced the resolution declaring war against Japan immediately afterward. Three days later Germany and Italy declared war on the United States. The holocaust had begun.

Actually, World War II had started in Asia with Japanese aggression in 1931 and in Europe with German attacks on weaker nations in 1939. England and France both declared war on the Nazis after their unprovoked and brutal aggressions. In 1940 the United States had committed itself to the support of the Allies by extending lend-lease aid to England, but there had been no thought of open hostilities. Indeed, it had been the policy to remain neutral to the fighting. But with a full-scale war being fought in Europe, the United States made preparations for defense. A peacetime Selective Service Act was passed in 1940, and defense plants were established with support of the RFC.

Even before the fateful attack on Pearl Harbor, Texas had begun its role as a training center for the military forces. The Third Army, which operated all basic training camps between Arizona and Florida, was headquartered at San Antonio. Later the Fourth Army, which readied men for combat and overseas duty, was also located at San Antonio. Fifteen training bases in all were established in Texas, where an estimated one and a quarter million men were prepared for military duty.

Texas was the national center for aviation training during the war. Randolph Field, called the West Point of the Air, in San Antonio had for a number of years been the finishing school for military pilots. Nearby Brooks and Kelly fields supplemented its training, and the Lackland air base was opened in the same region. At the peak of operations there were forty military flying fields in the state, with major training bases located at Lubbock, Midland, Wichita Falls, San Angelo, and San Marcos and with the national headquarters of the Air Force Training Command at Carswell Field in Fort Worth. Besides these Army Air Force operations, the navy maintained major air training bases in Texas at Corpus Christi and at Grand Prairie. Over two hundred thousand men received training in these Texas air bases, including forty-five thousand pilots, twelve thousand bombardiers, and twelve thousand navigators.

Texas was not only a major training area but also a major supplier of men for the armed forces. By the end of 1942 the state was contributing a larger proportion of men and women to the armed services than any other state. In all, nearly three-quarters of a million Texans were in service. The mortality toll was high: 15,764 Texans died in the army, 10,829 of them in combat; 7,258 lost their lives in the navy, coast guard, and marines. Thirty-six Texans received the Congressional Medal of Honor during the war, and Audie Murphy from Denton County became the most decorated hero in the nation. Samuel D. Dealey of Dallas was the most decorated man in the navy. More than one hundred fifty generals were native Texans, including Dwight D. Eisenhower, and twelve admirals came from Texas, including Chester Nimitz. The national commander of the Women's Army Corps was Oveta Culp Hobby, wife of the former governor. More than eight thousand Texas women served in the WAC, and another four thousand served in the auxiliary corps of the navy and marines.

As the war progressed, Texas also became a center for prisoner of war camps, a total of twenty-nine being established in the state. Anti-German feeling, however, never reached the heights that it had during World War I. As in the first war, hundreds of German-Americans, including Admiral Nimitz, served their nation valiantly and patriotically. A side effect of this was to break down further the provincialism of the German communities in the Hill Country.

A far more important by-product of the war, a natural concomitant, was that it accomplished what the New Deal had not: the return of prosperity. Not only did the vast federal payrolls to troops in Texas bolster the economy throughout the state, but also private industry expanded at an enormous pace. Gigantic aircraft factories were built at Fort Worth, Garland, and Grand Prairie. Shipyards were established at Orange, Beaumont, Port Arthur, and Houston. Synthetic rubber plants, boosted by Jesse Jones, were constructed to use by-products of the petroleum industry. And the booming petrochemical industry was born. Munitions plants were scattered in various localities in the state. Steel mills were opened at Dangerfield in East Texas, and the world's largest tin smelter was constructed at Texas City. Old established industries also boomed, such as helium from the Panhandle gas fields and paper products from East Texas wood pulp. Most important, the oil industry expanded to supply fuel for the war machine.

Changes in the agribusiness in Texas occurred during the war. There was a shift toward the use of machinery and toward diversification of crops. Texas had the nation's fourth highest farm income in 1945 and led all the other states in the production of cotton, grain sorghums, cattle, sheep, goats, horses, turkeys, tomatoes, onions, spinach, pecans, and roses. Although the number of farms in operation decreased during the war, total production increased because of the accelerating use of machinery, the total value of which increased during the war years approximately thirty per cent. One aspect of the trend toward diversification was the growth of the livestock business in East Texas. By 1945 there were more cattle on the lush pastures of stock farmers in East Texas than on West Texas ranches.

Full employment and higher wages returned to the state, and in fact one of the biggest problems Texas faced during the war was a shortage of labor. To replace men serving in the armed forces, thousands of women went to work in war plants as riveters, welders, punch operators, and the like. The shortage was especially acute in agricultural laborers. Shortages and rationing plagued the domestic scene. Scrap iron drives were held. Victory gardens were planted. Price ceilings, especially on rental units, were fought. War bonds and war stamps were bought by nearly every family.

State politics ceased to be a major concern. Governor Coke Stevenson, quiet, dignified, and unruffled, grew in popularity, and he was practically unopposed in the elections of 1942 and 1944. But if internal politics were quiet, national politics were not. W. Lee O'Daniel made a stormy race to retain his senate seat in 1942. Against him ran former governors Moody and Allred—the "Gold Dust Twins" O'Daniel labeled them—and to the surprise of most political observers, O'Daniel won again. Another movement began to gather force during this time: the anti-Roosevelt, anti-New Deal Democrats. This group, which called itself the Texas Regulars, began to exercise a wide influence in the state.

When Roosevelt was nominated at the national convention for a fourth term, the Texas Regulars moved heaven and earth to keep pro-Roosevelt electors off the ballot. A Texas court ruling defeated this move by forcing the dissident faction to organize as a separate political party. The Texas Regulars waged a bitter campaign to prevent Texas electors from swinging to Roosevelt, but even with the active support of Senator O'Daniel their showing at the polls was disappointing. The state vote in the general election was more than eight hundred thousand for pro-Roosevelt Democrats, nearly two hundred thousand for the Republicans, and only one hundred thirty-five thousand for the Texas Regulars. Yet the organization became a nucleus of the gathering political storm. Roosevelt died in April 1945, shortly after beginning his fourth term as president. When Vice-President Harry S. Truman became the chief executive, the Texas Regulars turned their ire on him. The brief wartime interlude of political quiet ended.

The Changing Scene

Population Growth   From 1900 to 1950 the total population of Texas more than doubled from 3,048,710 to 7,711,194. The rate of growth was relatively uniform; each decade the population increased approximately 20 per cent. Although some of this increase was caused by migration from other states and foreign countries, a substantial proportion represents a gaining of birth over death rates. The Texas population has grown with the nation and has ranked as the fifth or sixth largest state each decade.

The proportion of white population has gradually increased each decade. In 1900, 20.4 per cent of the population was classed as nonwhite; in 1950 it had decreased to 12.8 per cent. Negroes at first formed by far the greater part of the nonwhite group, an almost insignificant fraction of it being made up of other nonwhite races such as Indian, Japanese, and Chinese. The white population increased during the first half of the century approximately 276 per cent from 2,426,669 to 6,726,534, a 22 per cent greater growth than the total population. But during the same period the Negro population increased only 157 per cent from 620,722 to 977,458. The rest of the nonwhite population increased 546 per cent from 1,319 to 7,202, about half of which came from an increase in the Chinese population.

Equally as remarkable has been the growth of the foreign-born white population, which increased nearly 50 per cent every decade until 1930, when the effect of the National Origins Act of 1924 was felt. The total foreign-born white population of Texas in 1900 was 179,357, approximately 7.5 per cent of the white population. In 1920 it was 360,519, approximately 9.5 per cent of the white population. At that time 69.2 per cent of the foreign-born Texans were Mexicans; 8.6 per cent were Germans; 3.6 per cent were Czechs; 2.2 per cent were Italians; 2.1 per cent were English; 2.0 per cent were Russians; 1.8 per cent were Austrians; and 1.4 per cent were Polish. From 1920 to 1950 there was a decline in the number of foreign-born Texans in each category as well as in the total. The greatest drop, in the Mexican-born population in the decade from 1930 to 1940, will be analyzed later in this chapter.

Despite this decline in the foreign-born population, the number of native Texans of foreign stock—that is, with one or both parents foreign born—increased from 466,651 in 1900 to 655,635 in 1950. The number of persons with one or more grandparents of foreign birth, not enumerated in the census, would probably be four times these figures. The foreign-born population of Texas in 1950 was 4.1 per cent of the white population; the first-generation Americans in Texas made up 9.7 per cent; the foreign-born and foreign-stock population together was 13.8 per cent; the second-generation Americans made up probably about 20 per cent; and all three groups together made up nearly one-third of the Texas white population.

The significance of these data is two-fold. First, Texas is by no means the white, Anglo-Saxon, Protestant state it is often thought to be. It is, rather, one of the most cosmopolitan states in the union. Second, Texas has a heritage of ethnic harmony rather than of racial tension, as is often thought. Unfortunately, two of the major ethnic groups, Negroes and Mexicans, have suffered discrimination and persecution, but the blending of diverse European cultures in Texas has generally been free of trouble. Most of the European immigrants settled in the cities of Dallas, Galveston, Houston, and San Antonio, but many settled in five rural counties: Fayette, Washington, Austin, Colorado, and Lavaca. It is unlikely that any rural area in America has had such an ethnically heterogeneous past or a heritage of such a wide spectrum of peoples. Yet in this region there has never been any serious racial friction or unrest.

There were other significant trends and characteristics of the Texas population: substantial shifts of population from rural areas to towns and cities, a consequent growth of urban areas, and a meaningful population growth in the western portion of the state.

In 1900 the population classed as urban was 520,759, approximately 17.1 per cent of the total. The percentage of urban people in the population grew to 24.1 in 1910, to 32.4 in 1920, to 41.0 in 1930, to 45.4 in 1940, and to 59.8 in 1950. Clearly the shift from rural to urban areas occurred after the beginning of World War II. In 1950 there were 4,612,666 people living in urban communities.

In 1900, 9.5 per cent of the Texas population lived in the ten largest cities, which were, in descending order, San Antonio, Houston, Dallas, Galveston, Fort Worth, Austin, Waco, El Paso, Laredo, and Denison. In 1950, 35.6 per cent of the people lived in the ten largest cities, which then were, in descending order, Houston, Dallas, San Antonio, Fort Worth, Austin, El Paso, Corpus Christi, Beaumont, Waco, and Amarillo. Consequently the population shift was not only from rural to urban areas but was particularly to the larger cities. San Antonio remained the largest city in the state until 1930, when it was displaced by Houston. Previously Dallas and Houston had vied for second place. Beaumont became one of the ten largest in 1910, when Denison was dropped off the list. In 1920 and 1930 Wichita Falls was on the list in eighth and then tenth places. Laredo disappeared from the list in 1920; Wichita Falls was nosed out by Corpus Christi in 1940; and Galveston was displaced by Amarillo in 1950.

In 1900 all but two of the ten most populous counties lay east of the 97th meridian. In 1910 three were west of that line; in 1920 four were west of the line; in 1930 and 1940 five were in West Texas; and in 1950, of the twenty-three counties with population over 50,000, fifteen were west of the 97th meridian, nine were west of the 98th meridian, seven were west of the 99th meridan, five were west of the 100th meridian, three were west of the 101st, and one, El Paso County, was west of the 102nd. There had been a decided population shift to the western part of the state.

The Texas Mexicans There is much misunderstanding, even among Mexicans, of the Mexican population of Texas. It is for the most part not descended from the early Spanish settlers, as is often believed, but is composed largely of relatively recent immigrants from Mexico. In 1850 there were only 4,459 Mexican-born people living in Texas, and about 25 per cent of these resided in the lower Rio Grande Valley counties of Cameron, Starr, and Webb. A recent analysis indicates that most of the Mexicans in those counties had migrated across the river after the Mexican War. Migration to Texas from Mexico quickened in the following decades, in 1880 surpassing slightly the migration from Germany; and in 1900 the number of Mexican-born in Texas reached 71,062.

The next two decades witnessed the truly remarkable increase in the Mexican-born population of the state, which jumped to 124,238 in 1910 and to 249,652 in 1920. Consequently, it may reasonably be assumed that most of the Mexican-stock population of Texas today is made up of first-generation descendants of this massive wave of immigration. They flooded into the border and South Texas counties at an average rate of twenty-five people a day for twenty years. The Mexican-born population of Bexar County increased from 4,752 to 32,934 in those twenty years. In El Paso County it rose from 8,368 to 38,625; in Webb, from 10,755 to 15,140; and in Hidalgo, from 2,366 to 14,601. In 1920 every county had some Mexican-born people living in it, but only in a few of the border counties did they outnumber the native-born population.

Two factors seem to have induced this heavy migration: the revolutionary turmoil in Mexico and the vastly greater economic opportunities in Texas. A few became migrants, following harvests from one place to another, but most settled down to work as laborers on farms and ranches. That they were needed and were encouraged to immigrate is borne out by testimony given in the early 1920's by various Texans before the congressional committees that were shaping the National Origins Act of 1924. Arguments were advanced, some of them rather incredible, that Mexico should be included in the act, that Mexican immigration should be restricted. Agriculturists from Texas and California urged that it not be restricted. When the act was passed, Mexico was excluded, and immigration remained open.

An anti-Mexican attitude, however, was sweeping the country on the crest of the general antipathy of the 1920's to foreigners. So marked was it that in 1930 the Bureau of the Census instructed enumerators that Mexicans, whether Mexican-born or native-born, who were not obviously Caucasian should be enumerated as nonwhite along with Negroes, Chinese, Japanese, and members of other races. The basis for this was reasonable: most of the Mexican-born were of Indian rather than Caucasian descent. But the decision to enumerate them as nonwhites was a departure from all previous censuses, and it was stimulated by prejudice. A mere 3,692 Mexican-born Texans were classified as white on the 1930 census. The total Mexican-born population in Texas was then 266,240, which was a very slight increase over 1920.

Then, during the next decade an astounding thing happened to the Mexican-born population: it dropped nearly 40 per cent, to 159,266. Prejudice, combined with the exigency of depression, seems not only to have closed the border but also to have driven tens of thousands of Mexican immigrants back to their homeland. Mexicans left Texas in the decade from 1930 to 1940 at a rate greater than the rate of immigration between 1900 and 1920. The Immigration Service instituted deportation proceedings against hundreds of indigent Mexican immigrants, and the recently established Border Patrol harried them across the river. Hundreds of others returned to Mexico voluntarily in the face of the mounting racial friction of the 1930's. Although Mexico was not placed under the quota system, immigration was effectively stopped by a variety of regulations, which required the Mexican immigrant to prove his literacy, that he could support himself, and that he had employment. Furthermore, a border fee from fifty cents to ten dollars was levied. The basic reason spurring this exodus is easily understood. The depression had made it difficult to provide relief for citizens, and the additional burden of providing it for aliens was unacceptable. Moreover, with thousands of native Texans looking for work, unemployed aliens were not in the national interest. The result was an inevitable increase in racial intolerance, in discrimination, in mistreatment.

The prejudice that developed toward Mexicans during this decade has had profound consequences. In the first place, as has been pointed out earlier, it caused historians to assume incorrectly that racial friction had always existed between Anglo and Hispanic. It gave the term *Mexican* such an unfavorable connotation that Mexicans adopted the term *Latin American*. It caused a substantial increase in anti-Americanism in Mexico. It caused the Mexican government to refuse to permit the use of contract labor in Texas after the 1942 convention between the United States and Mexico was established, although *braceros* could go to many other states. This was particularly harmful because the war had produced a great need for agricultural labor. Texas was not permitted bracero labor until 1952, and even then Mexico carefully specified that any evidence of discriminatory practices would promptly shut Texas out again.

Unfortunately, the discrimination that had grown to such outrageous proportions against the alien Mexican was also visited upon citizens of Mexican descent. The majority of them had immigrated during the period 1900 to 1920 or were children of those who had. Except for a small minority they spoke little or no English and were illiterate or semiliterate unskilled laborers who were paid extremely low wages. There was little they could do during the depression years to change their situation.

World War II provided enormous opportunities for the Texas Mexican. He proved his patriotism by military service. He found employment at higher wages in defense and war plants. He moved into better neighborhoods and gave his children a better education. Prejudice and resentment began slowly to subside. After the war Texas Mexicans began moving into the middle class. The League of United Latin American Citizens, now nationwide, was organized in South Texas to provide education and social outlets and to fight discrimination. Texas Mexicans have organized politically and have become an influential voice in state affairs. Texas formed the Good Neighbor Commission in 1943 to promote understanding between Anglos and Mexicans. By 1950 over forty communities in the state had adopted Anglo-Latin friendship as a community project. Prejudice and discrimination against Texas Mexicans had by no means ended in 1950. It has not ended now, but it has been greatly decreased.

Industrial Growth Mexican workers were involved in one of the most serious labor disputes in the state's history in San Antonio in 1938. Some twelve thousand Mexicans—men, women, and children—comprised a labor force of pecan shellers. The existence of this destitute group of people, who worked for an average wage of $2.50 per week, had caused the pecan industry to bypass mechanization and rely on the cheap hand labor for a larger margin of profit.

The Pecan Shelling Workers Union was organized in 1933 by Magdaleno Rodriguez, who was described by the county attorney as a "fugitive from justice, a citizen of Mexico, and a labor agitator who betrays his workers." Rodriguez claimed twelve thousand members in his union. The union was financed by the president of the Southern Pecan Shelling Company; in return Rodriguez aided the companies by fighting the adoption of the NRA code in the industry. The NRA effected an agreement with the National Pecan Shellers Association but was never able to enforce it in San Antonio. The effort to do so, however, exposed the deplorable conditions and attracted other labor organizers.

In 1937 Albert Gonsen founded the Texas Pecan Shelling Workers Union, which was brought into the CIO in November of that year. In February 1938, in response to an announcement of a reduction in wages of nearly twenty per cent, the union called a strike. Violence followed. Thousands of picketing strikers were arrested by city police on charges of blocking sidewalks, disturbing the peace, congregating in unlawful assemblies, and carrying signs in public without city approval. Mayor C. K. Quin and Police Chief Owen Kilday accused the strikers of being inspired and led by Communists. The police force, assisted by over one hundred firemen, used tear gas, clubs, and fire hoses to disperse the pickets, one hundred forty-five of whom were arrested. Ten and fifteen dollar fines were hastily levied by the Corporation Court. Since most of the strikers were unable to pay, they were jailed. Eighteen men were crowded into one cell designed for six prisoners; men and women were thrown indiscriminately into the same cells; when ninety men were added to one hundred fifty in a room designed for sixty, the police quieted the ensuing violence by turning a fire hose on the prisoners. The city administration further interfered with the strike by closing, on the grounds that they violated a city health ordinance, the soup kitchens set up to feed the strikers. The National Labor Relations Board and the Texas State Industrial Commission both objected to the city's course of action, as did Governor Allred, who ultimately persuaded the companies and the union leaders to accept arbitration. The board concluded that the "pecan industry in San Antonio is in a perilous plight," with conditions bad for both workers and operators, and recommended a wage increase of slightly more than the decrease that had provoked the strike.

Discord arose again in October when a minimum wage of twenty-five cents an hour was set by the Department of Labor under the Fair Labor Standards Act. Operators responded by simply closing the plants. An estimated eight thousand to ten thousand Mexicans were thrown out of work. After much discussion by operators, federal representatives, and union leaders, the plants agreed to install mechanized equipment and to pay shellers, who were to be trained to operate it, the minimum twenty-five cent wage. The plants reopened with only eighteen hundred workers, but they were earning four and five times the previous wages. Many of the displaced workers found employment as migratory farm workers due to the agricultural upturn then beginning. During 1940 others were absorbed into defense plants.

Within the surge of industrial activity prompted by World War II, the most important aspect, the development of manufacturing, deserves closer examination. As the 1920's ended, petroleum refining, lumbering, and food processing dominated Texas manufacturing. In fact, slaughtering and meat packing had ranked first in 1909 and second in 1919, and in 1929 the expanded classification "food processing" led the list on the basis of value added by manufacturing. With the development of the refrigerated rail car in the 1880's, the Texas cattle industry had attracted meat packers to the state, and by 1895 over four hundred cars of frozen beeves were being shipped each year. Large-scale packing began in the early twentieth century with the establishment of Armour and Swift plants at Fort Worth. By 1940 there were sixty-six meat packing plants in the state and seventy-seven flour and grist mills. With the repeal of Prohibition substantial breweries were developed, especially in San Antonio. Canning plants were installed in the rich fruit and vegetable growing Lower Rio Grande Valley after the turn of the century. Bakeries had been scattered across the state for decades. These and less important operations such as pecan shelling contributed to making food processing the second-place major industry in Texas in 1949.

The decade from 1930 to 1940 witnessed the rise of several new industries: pulp and paper, heavy chemicals, fabricated metal products, nonelectrical machinery, printing and publishing, and stone, clay, and glass. The chemical industry was attracted to Texas because of the variety of raw materials. A major alkali producer opened a plant at Corpus Christi in 1934, and soon other heavy chemical producers moved into the state for the production of inorganic chemicals, especially alkalis and chlorine. The presence of cheap alkali with plenty of pulping wood, natural gas, and water brought paper manufacturers to East Texas. There in 1937 a major pulp producer established a plant, and in 1940 two new plants were built to convert the pulp to paper. Within a few years there were dozens of smaller processors converting the basic paper output to a variety of products such as containers, bags, napkins, and so on. Fabricated metal products such as ornamental iron, sheet metal products, smokestacks, metal window frames, awnings, and venetian blinds developed as a widespread industry. It had a long history of relatively constant growth as had the stone, clay, and glass industry, which was also consumer oriented and widespread throughout the state. The manufacture of gypsum wallboard, a major part of this latter industry, was closely related to the development of the East Texas paper industry. Nonelectrical machinery manufacture became early in the century an important industry because of the petroleum industry but expanded during the thirties to keep pace with the extensive road construction and sulphur mining developments. One of the world's greatest manufacturers of earth-moving equipment, the Le Tourneau Company, was established in East Texas during this period. Printing and publishing have always been dominated by newspaper publishing, but during the thirties several book and magazine publishers began operations that expanded greatly during the following decades.

The Texas industrial revolution began with the building of defense and war plants in World War II. Both established and new industries enjoyed major expansion. Among these were aircraft construction, shipbuilding, and the gigantic petrochemical industry. Aircraft manufacture began with the establishment in 1940 of three small factories, two in the Fort Worth and Dallas area and one in Houston. Near the end of that year North American Aviation began construction of its vast bomber plant near Dallas, and the following year Consolidated-Vultee began building its bomber plant near Fort Worth. By the end of 1943 over sixty thousand people were employed in aircraft manufacture in Texas, and at the peak of production the next year these plants employed eighty-two thousand. The industry spawned such associated enterprises as electronic and engineering firms, which took up the slack in employment after the war when aircraft manufacture was cut back.

At the beginning of the war there were ten shipbuilding firms on the Texas coast with almost fourteen hundred employees. Extremely rapid expansion came at once as the shipbuilding yards at Houston, Beaumont, Orange, and Port Arthur turned out destroyers, minesweepers, Liberty ships, and landing craft. The peak wartime employment in the shipyards of ninety-six thousand fell off sharply after the war to fewer than five thousand in the fifties.

No such dramatic drop occurred in the new petrochemical industry, which was born accidentally in 1940 when an oil company, attempting by fire to eliminate corrosion in a natural gas line, produced unexpectedly a variety of organic chemicals. The Texas Gulf Coast was a natural environment for the new industry because it had the basic petroleum hydrocarbons, fuel in the form of natural gas, and water for cooling. The first organics produced were alcohol and synthetic rubber for wartime use, but postwar production expanded into many synthetics. Among the most important are such fibers as Nylon, Orlon, Acrilan, and Dacron, such automotive chemicals as tetraethyl of lead, antifreeze, and fuel additives, such plastics as styrene and polyethylene, and such miscellaneous synthetic products as rubber, paint, and refrigerants. In the postwar years the more than seventy petrochemical plants built in the state, thirty-four near Houston and Beaumont, produced over eighty per cent of the national supply of petrochemicals.

A postwar industry of importance emerged in the lignite and iron ore area around Daingerfield: steel production. Lone Star Steel began operations there for the War Production Board in 1943 and with a large loan from the Reconstruction Finance Corporation in 1948 embarked on an expansion program, grew further in 1951, and by 1956 had become a major steel producer with more than three thousand employees.

Other metal ore conversion plants have become important to the state's economy. Aluminum production in Texas vaulted from none in 1950 to second in the nation in 1953 with plants in Central Texas and on the Gulf Coast. The only antimony plant in the western hemisphere was built at Laredo in 1930. The only tin smelter in the western hemisphere was built at Texas City in 1942. And the largest refined copper smelter in the nation began operation in El Paso in 1930, where there were also zinc, gold, and silver smelters.

This satisfying industrial growth has not only brought capital investment into Texas but has also maintained a fairly high level of prosperity and furnished employment to thousands of Texans.

14

Flamboyant Texas

Political Affairs

A Period of Controversy For a decade or more after World War II the Texas political scene was punctuated by a series of heated controversies, most of which became directly or indirectly linked with the continuing struggle of the conservative anti-Roosevelt and anti-Truman element of the Democratic Party to retain the control of the party machinery won in 1944. Among these disruptions were the successful attempts of Negroes to break the "white primary rule" of 1923, the attempt of Herman Sweatt to enroll in the University of Texas law school, the Rainey controversy at the University of Texas, the disputed election of Lyndon B. Johnson to the United States Senate, the establishment of the durable conservative regime of Allan Shivers, the bolt of the Texas voters from the Democratic column in the presidential election of 1952, and the revelation of scandals in the General Land Office and in the Insurance Commission.

Homer Price Rainey was an ordained Baptist preacher and a Doctor of Philosophy. He was appointed president of the University of Texas in 1939. Almost immediately he became involved in disputes with the University Board of Regents, primarily concerning board members' efforts to regulate internal affairs of the institution in such matters as the controversial dismissal of several faculty members, the banning of John Dos Passos' novel *U.S.A.*, the rejection of requests for research funds, and a personnel problem at the medical school. President Rainey vigorously defended what he believed were vital principles of academic freedom, but his manner seemed so abrasive and arrogant that the board dismissed him in 1944. He listed sixteen grievances against the board, most of which were controversial, although the major issue was fairly clear-cut. Did the Board of Regents have the responsibility and the authority to control the institution at administrative levels, or was the school an almost autonomous, self-administered agency of the state within the broad policy parameters determined by the board? The issue attracted statewide and even national attention.

After his dismissal, Rainey began a daily radio program and, trading on his credentials as a Baptist preacher, sought to justify his position. Early in 1946 he accepted the entreaties of friends and entered the primary race for governor. There was an element of ambiguity in his numerous talks, for he seemed to combine his desire for reinstatement as president of the university with his ambitions for high political office. Nonetheless, he was the leading contender for the governorship.

Against him were arrayed thirteen other aspiring Democrats, most of whom leveled their political guns at the liberal, pro-Roosevelt target Rainey offered them. Vituperative charges and counter-charges filled the air; the campaign has been called the bitterest in Texas history. According to the highly respected Belden Poll (then known as the Texas Poll), Rainey led the candidates at the end of May, led at the end of June, and at the end of July had even increased his lead. But there was to be a last minute public reaction to the continual outpouring of political bile.

The only major candidate not involved in the Rainey controversy was Beauford Jester, an established political figure, a former chairman of the University of Texas Board of Regents, and at the time a member of the Railroad Commission. His campaign quietly avoided the explosive issues, and he declared, "Beauford Jester is the only candidate in the race who can go to the governor's chair without mud and slime and filth on his hands." To the surprise of many he polled 443,804 votes against Rainey's 291,282, but he did not have a majority, and a runoff was required. Jester defeated Rainey 701,018 to 355,654 in the second primary and went on to an easy victory over the Republican, Eugene Nolte.

Two years later, in 1948, Governor Jester recorded an almost over-

URBAN TEXAS

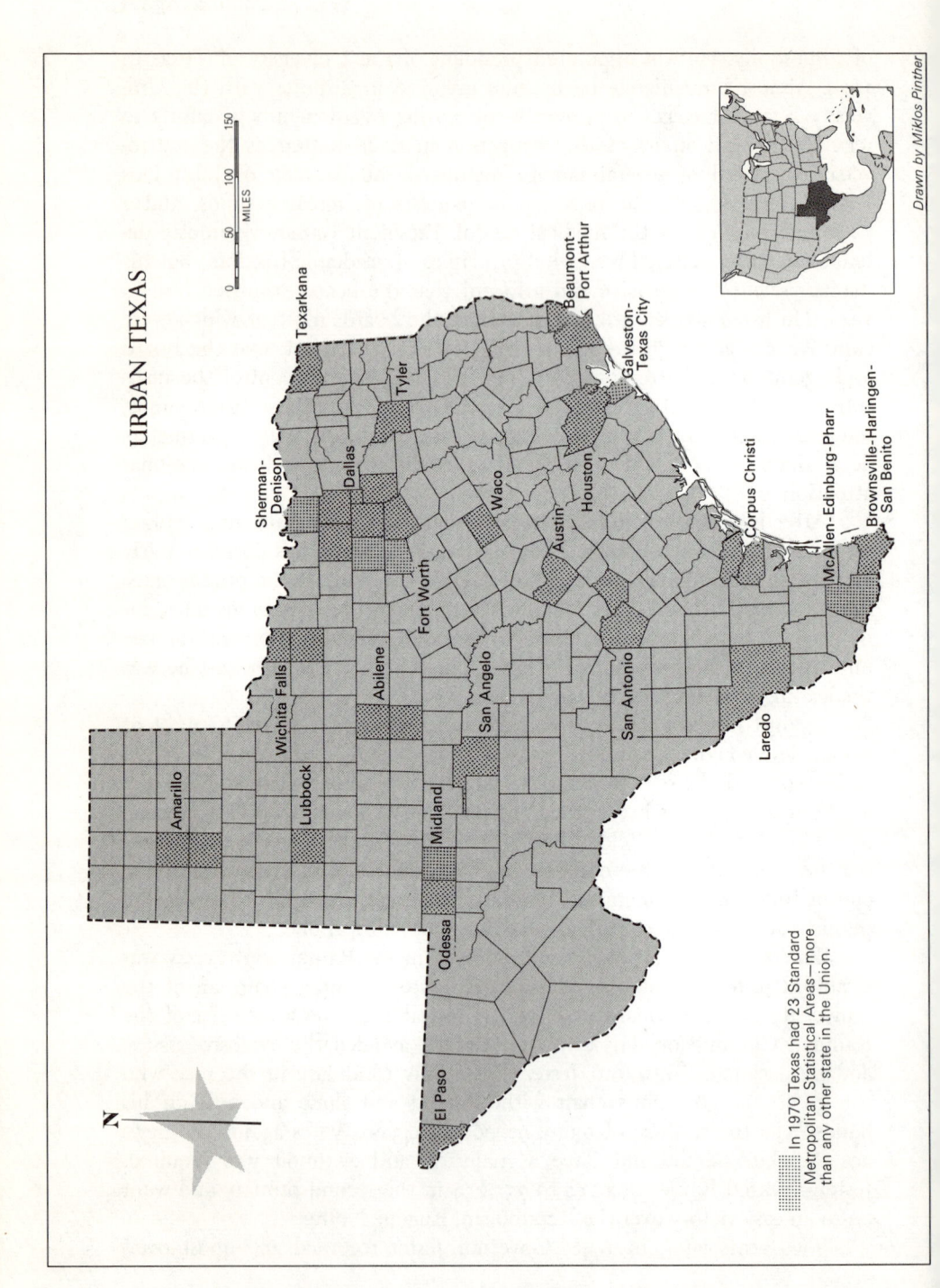

In 1970 Texas had 23 Standard Metropolitan Statistical Areas—more than any other state in the Union.

Drawn by Miklos Pinther

whelming reelection vote in the first primary. But the governor's race was not the exciting one that year: the contest for the United States Senate seat generated almost as much heat as the election of 1946. W. Lee O'Daniel was up for reelection. The very popular former governor, Coke Stevenson, was the first to announce against him; a Houston attorney, George Peddy, was next; the third major candidate to announce was Congressman Lyndon Baines Johnson; and eight minor candidates flung themselves into the scramble, hoping for a chance at the runoff. Late in May O'Daniel announced that he had decided not to run for reelection.

In an early Belden poll, Stevenson led with forty per cent of the vote. O'Daniel, though not a candidate, had fourteen per cent, and Johnson had a mere ten per cent. The young thirty-nine-year-old congressman mounted an intensive campaign. Touring the state in a helicopter (an innovation in American politics), he literally dropped in on hundreds of small Texas communities. He would pause occasionally above a field of cotton pickers to shout ebulliently with a loudspeaker to offset the beat of the blades of the Johnson City Windmill, "Hello down there! This is Lyndon B. Johnson, candidate for the U.S. Senate." Johnson stood for rural improvements, farm-to-market roads, aid to education, higher commodity prices, and a strong military establishment, as well as on his record as a New Dealer in congress. Franklin Roosevelt, he told voters, "was just like a daddy to me." Stevenson said, "I'll keep my campaign down-to-earth," and toured the state in an old Plymouth automobile, buying only five gallons of gasoline at a time in order to make more stops. He made no campaign promises and offered the voters an "open-book" record of his political achievements. Stevenson barely eked out a lead in the first primary. A runoff between him and Johnson provoked such a hotly disputed election that the allegations have not yet faded out of current politics. Johnson continued, in the runoff campaign, to charge Stevenson with inexperience in national and international affairs. Stevenson revised his earlier taciturn tactics and lambasted Johnson as a candidate of labor, a friend of Henry Wallace, and an errand boy of the New Deal.

It was not the campaign that aroused controversy, however; it was the actual counting of the votes. This was the closest major election in the state's history. By midnight of election day the returns showed 470,681 for Stevenson and 468,787 for Johnson. At midnight the next day the returns read 490,285 for Johnson and 489,592 for Stevenson. By noon the following day, Stevenson had recaptured the lead but by only 210 votes; by that evening his lead was down to 119 votes, and there were an estimated 400 ballots still uncounted. Finally, the figures stood 494,330 for Stevenson and 493,968 for Johnson. But this was the unofficial count of the Texas Election Bureau. The official count would be made by the Democratic

State Executive Committee. During the next two weeks, revised county returns began to be reported by the state committee, most of them favoring Johnson. The official canvass gave Johnson 494,191 and Stevenson 494,104, a difference of 87 votes. The official revision from Jim Wells County was to become the focus of attention. It had raised Johnson's total by 202 voters and Stevenson's by only one!

There followed a series of legal maneuvers in which Stevenson and his supporters tried to block Johnson's name from the ballot in the forthcoming general election. Stevenson charged that fraud entered into the revised report from election box number 13 in Jim Wells County. Johnson immediately secured a restraining order preventing a recount of the ballots in Box 13. The Stevenson forces countered by obtaining an order from Federal Judge T. Whitfield Davidson preventing Johnson's name from being entered on the ballot. Judge Davidson also ordered federal agents to collect evidence of frauds in Duval, Jim Wells, and Zapata counties. Johnson's attorneys charged Stevenson with similar irregularities in Brown, Dallas, and Galveston counties. An appeal was made to the Federal Circuit Court to overrule Davidson, but the court decided it could not. Davidson then ordered that all voting boxes in Jim Wells County be impounded. Johnson's attorneys carried the matter to Justice Hugo Black of the United States Supreme Court, who ruled sharply that federal courts had no authority in state elections, especially party primaries.

Johnson's name was entered on the ballot, and Stevenson and his supporters undertook to campaign for the Republican nominee, Jack Porter of Houston, on the grounds that Johnson would not be seated if elected. He was elected by nearly two to one, and although there was some argument in the senate, he was seated. In the years ahead he became Texas' most famous politician.

The unexpected victory of President Harry S. Truman in Texas as well as the nation was almost obscured in the state by the excitement over the senatorial race. It was also little noticed that Truman Democrats had wrested temporary control of the party machinery in Texas from the conservative element. Sam Rayburn was returned to the United States House of Representatives and reelected Speaker.

The Political Career of Allan Shivers   Allan Shivers was elected lieutenant governor in 1946 and again in 1948. Jester died of a heart attack on July 11, 1949, and Shivers served the remainder of his term. The new, forty-one-year-old governor proved himself adept at politics and the operation of the state government. His relations with the special session of the legislature that he was forced to call were harmonious, and he handled himself well before the press and in public.

The gubernatorial election of 1950 brought forth seven candidates in the Democratic primary but no major issues. Shivers won seventy-six per cent of the Democratic votes in the first primary and a term of his own in the general election. A heated campaign for lieutenant governor was won by Ben Ramsey of San Augustine. Shivers now began to build the state's strongest political organization since the days of E. M. House. His widespread nonpolitical appearances during 1949 and his easy election in 1952 gave him great appeal to political supporters at all levels.

The governor assumed leadership of the conservative element in the party and the Texas Regulars who had opposed Roosevelt and the New Deal. This faction quickly fell out with President Truman over the policies of the Fair Deal. By 1951 there were increasing objections to what was believed to be the low standards of ethics and honesty in Washington; to the infamous "five per centers," the influence peddlers; to the acceptance of gifts by public officials; to the civil rights legislation; to the foreign policies that had resulted in the Korean conflict; and to Truman's veto of the tideland legislation, which would have given the state title to its offshore lands. The conviction of Alger Hiss caused thousands of Texans to applaud the often unsavory tactics of Senator Joseph McCarthy in his attack on alleged Communism in the federal government. The general feeling of alarm, although it did not reach hysteria in the state, brought many middle-of-the-road voters into the conservative camp. By 1952 Texas was prepared to bolt the Democratic Party.

Shivers announced for reelection in January and stated his position clearly. "A change must occur in the national trend, not alone for the welfare of Texas citizens but for the benefit of the nation and the world. I want to help fight that battle from Texas ramparts." Attention was focused therefore not upon the state contests but upon the national scene. General interest in politics, as reflected in the precinct convention fights, was the highest the state had ever seen. The principal battles were for control of the Texas delegations to the national conventions and for the senate seat vacated by the retirement of the venerable Tom Connally.

The precinct conventions around the state in May astounded all observers by their size and excitement, especially the Republican meetings, which were usually poorly attended. One columnist labeled 1952 "the year of the amateur" in Texas because the deep interest had brought out so many who usually neither participated nor voted. Shivers and his conservatives won overwhelming control of the Democratic precinct and county conventions, and in the state convention they won an "uninstructed" delegation, which would be free to bargain for a conservative candidate for the presidency. Liberal Democrats who had walked out of many conventions across the state predicted that the "Shivercrats" would not be seated. The Republican conventions fell into the hands of supporters of General Dwight Eisenhower at the county level, but at the state convention a machine-dominated faction refused to seat any but Taft supporters and consequently sent a Taft-pledged delegation to the national Republican convention. Eisenhower's followers claimed that the Texas vote had been stolen and that the Taft delegation would not be seated.

Both national conventions were held in Chicago, and the Texas voters were significant factors in each. In the Republican convention, after much maneuvering in committees, a floor vote of the entire convention seated the Eisenhower delegation from Texas. Their thirty-three votes put the general within nine votes of the number he needed, and a switch of the Minnesota delegation stampeded the convention for Eisenhower. In the Democratic convention the Shivercrats, overrunning every roadblock the liberals erected, were seated, unpledged to any candidate but pledged to support the nominee of the convention. Maury Maverick of San Antonio, leader of the liberals, claimed a moral victory in this loyalty pledge. In the convention Adlai Stevenson represented the choice of the liberals and of President Truman. Shivers with his Texas delegation consistently voted against Stevenson on every ballot, and when the Illinois liberal finally won the nomination, the Texans returned from Chicago dissatisfied.

Shivers won the Democratic primary in the first vote against the liberal Ralph Yarborough and carried with him Ben Ramsey as lieutenant governor, John Ben Sheppard as attorney general, and Price Daniel as United States Senator. These four men and several other Democratic nominees for state office then received the nomination of the Republican convention for the same office (the process has often been erroneously called "cross filing"). The result was unique in Texas election history. Shivers was unopposed for the office of governor and received 1,375,547 Democratic votes and 468,319 Republican votes.

Shortly before the November election Governor Shivers announced his position on the presidential race. He intended to split his ballot and vote for Eisenhower for president, and he urged like-minded Democrats to do the same. Stevenson was not only tainted in Texans' minds with, as the Dallas *News* said, "the corruption, the graft, the debt, the inefficiency, and the scandals of the Truman administration" but also with the unfounded suspicion that he was a Communist sympathizer because of his testimony on behalf of Alger Hiss. The voters of Texas overwhelmingly rejected him and for the second time in the state's history gave Texas' electoral ballots to a Republican candidate. Eisenhower won in Texas by a vote of 1,102,273, which was over three times the vote cast for Hoover in 1928 and approximately fifty-four per cent of the vote cast in 1952.

Shivers' domination of the political scene was complete. In 1954 he sought election to an unprecedented third term, which would give him a total of over seven and a half years as the governor of the state, six years of his own and eighteen months of Jester's. There were three other entries in the primary, including Ralph Yarborough, who forced Shivers for the first time in his career to fight a runoff election, which Shivers won by 775,088 to 683,132.

His third term was marked by insurance and land office scandals, which weakened the political machine he had built. Although he was untainted, he retired to private life in January 1957, but he remained a power in the state as the nominal leader of the conservatives, whose strength waned thereafter as many voters began to shift their political allegiance from the Democratic to the Republican Party.

Legislation and Scandal The Fifty-First Legislature, which adjourned on July 6, 1949, less than one week before Governor Beauford Jester's unexpected death, set a record for holding the longest continuous session and passed some of the most significant legislation in the modern era. No new taxes were voted, but its appropriations together with federal grants totaled over a billion dollars, the highest public expenditures in the state's history up to that time. In its concern with public health, it voted such increases in funds for the support of state hospitals that the governor was forced to veto the second half of their biennial appropriation in order to balance the budget. A State Board for Texas State Hospitals and Special Schools was created to supervise work in the mental institutions and in the state school for handicapped children. A minimum science requirement was established for all medical practitioners, and a licensing system for chiropractors was passed.

The state prison system was thoroughly revamped. Its fourteen installations had been allowed to deteriorate despite—or perhaps because of —an increasing prisoner population. A 1947 inspection exposed the worsening conditions, and a broad plan for improvements was drafted for expanding and modernizing two prisons each year. The Fifty-First Legislature initiated the scheme, and later legislatures followed through with sufficient funds to carry out the program, making it ultimately one of the nation's model penal systems.

Another study in 1947 produced a plan to upgrade the inadequate public education system. The legislature in 1949 passed the important Gilmer-Aikin Law, sponsored by Representative Claud Gilmer and Senator

A. M. Aikin, whose interest in education led to the later Hale-Aikin Commission. The Gilmer-Aikin Law reorganized public education entirely. Teachers' salaries were raised substantially in an effort to attract better qualified people to the profession, and additional increments were provided for years of service and for advanced education. The latter provision led many teachers to return to colleges and universities for summer study as "Gilmer-Aikin co-eds." State funds were provided to all local school districts under a minimum foundation program designed to equalize education throughout the state. The State Board of Education was reorganized to consist of one member to be elected from each congressional district in the state. The board was authorized to appoint a commissioner of education and to establish and supervise the Texas Education Agency, which in turn supervises public education in the state.

The following year, 1950, Governor Shivers was forced to call a special session of the legislature to provide state hospital appropriations for the second year of the biennium. The Fifty-Second Legislature faced the problem of finding funds to keep up with the growing costs of the expanding state government. After a series of deadlocks in committees and once again in an overextended session, the legislature levied a new tax on natural gas and increased by a total of ten per cent the other taxes included in the original Omnibus Tax Bill of 1941. This legislature also passed the first redistricting law in over thirty years in recognition of the urbanization of the state's population.

The next legislature, after much talk about new sources of revenue, resorted to an increase in the same taxes again, leaving the Fifty-Fourth Legislature to face a rather grim financial crisis in 1955. Despite numerous proposals for some form of sales tax, the lawmakers once more raised the levy on gasoline, cigarettes, and alcohol, and despite anguished protests increased the corporation franchise tax to a record high. Possibly the most significant new legislation of this session was the creation of the Commission on Higher Education to coordinate the state's colleges and universities. More than twenty statutes to regulate insurance companies in the state were also passed.

These new regulations were sorely needed. Early in the century, with the establishment of the Insurance Commission and the passage of the Robertson Insurance Law, Texas had been a leader in insurance regulation. But times had changed and obvious weaknesses in the system of regulation had not been patched. The most important weakness was the failure of the state to supervise the issuance of stock by insurance companies. Other corporate stocks had been at least loosely regulated by Hogg's stock and bond law, but insurance stocks had escaped this supervision. Under the antiquated laws and regulations before 1955, an insurance company could capitalize for as little as $25,000 but could offer to the public an unlimited amount of stock in the company. Texas was flooded by insurance stock, and Texans were lured to invest by advertising campaigns that rivaled and occasionally exceeded the promotion of the sale of insurance itself. For example, to sell its certificates, one company calling itself U.S. Trust and Guaranty waged a hard-sell television campaign featuring a famous Washington columnist and a slogan that unquestionably misled some people: "You can put your trust in U.S. Trust and Guaranty."

Among the twenty-seven regulatory acts in 1955 was one that regulated the sale of such securities and several that permitted the Board of Insurance Commissioners to crack down on marginal or corrupt organizations and to investigate the "fitness, competence, and experience" of a company's officers and directors. Another law required a minimum capitalization of $250,000 for all future companies. When the reform move began, there were approximately thirteen hundred insurance companies chartered in Texas and more than seven hundred doing business in the state but headquartered elsewhere. According to one journalist, there were more companies operating in Texas than in all the other states combined. The first move was to force a number of companies into receivership because of inadequate assets. The second was to refuse renewal of licenses in June 1956 to over thirty firms that were too weak to stay in business. The next was to put almost one hundred on a monthly inspection basis and to begin closing them. A fourth was to close several companies operated by speculators and promoters.

The bankruptcy of the Texas Mutual Insurance Company among others kicked off the reform legislation. The action of the Insurance Commission under the new laws closed others, including U.S. Trust and Guaranty, whose president attempted suicide. The company had nearly six million dollars worth of certificates outstanding and owed more than one million in insurance claims that it could not pay. Investigations revealed that nine of the members of the Texas Senate had received fees or other monies from that company, one senator scooping $10,000. A similar operation, under the leadership of a flamboyant promoter named Ben Jack Cage, ran seventy-two insurance and finance companies in a score of states and in several Latin American countries. Called I.C.T., its failure cost Texas investors hundreds of thousands of dollars. It went into receivership, and Cage fled to Brazil. Before the end of that year, 1956, news reporters dug out the fact that the chairman of the Insurance Commission, Garland Smith, had accepted an expensive Hawaiian vacation as the guest of an insurance company.

The next legislature was to open with a fiery investigation of such gifts to public officials and legislators, but the 1955 legislature was concerned with the more important investigation of what has been called "the grandpappy of all Texas scandals," which involved Bascom Giles, Commissioner of the General Land Office, Attorney General John Ben Sheppard, and Governor Allan Shivers. These three men constituted the Veteran's Land Board, established to supervise the $100,000,000 fund created in 1950, in lieu of a veteran's bonus, to help veterans purchase land at a small down payment (five per cent), on long terms (forty years), at a very low interest rate (three per cent). The Veteran's Land Act was one of the most important pieces of legislation in the twentieth century, and despite the scandal which engulfed the program in 1955, it has been of substantial benefit to thousands of former servicemen.

The principal corruption in the program was the practice of real estate operators who bought large tracts of land, subdivided them, and sold them to the Veteran's Land Board for resale to veterans at highly inflated values. Two checks had been built into the program to prevent this: the veteran himself had to sign the purchase papers and to swear he had seen the land before the state consummated the purchase, and the land office required an evaluation from an expert appraiser. But sharp promoters found a means to circumvent the system. Under Giles' instructions all "group sales"— those involving the breakup of a single large tract of land—were to bypass the usual channels and come directly to his office. Many of these tracts, if not most, were appraised by one or two carefully chosen appraisers. These group-sale contracts were then approved by fraudulent entries in the minutes of the Veteran's Land Board, although they were never actually submitted to the board's scrutiny. Furthermore, many of the veteran-purchasers were proved to be either nonexistent or unaware that they had contracted to purchase land. Some even believed that they had been given the land by the state, since the five per cent down payment had been made by a promoter out of his profit. Since the Veteran's Land Act had granted immunity from foreclosure for the first three years, some promoters felt reasonably safe in making these down payments.

The network of corruption was first investigated by DeWitt County Attorney Wiley L. Cheatham, who, with strong suspicion but no proof, brought it to the attention of his father, who was in the state legislature. The two men, unsure of the breadth of the operation or of whom they could trust, took their suspicions to the Texas Department of Public Safety, which went to State Auditor C. H. Cavness, who quietly initiated a routine audit of the land program. Attorney General Sheppard and his assistants participated in these preliminary meetings, lending the vital support of that office to the investigations. Without the aid of the attorney general's office, which was the only agency that could make state records available to grand juries and that could coordinate the efforts of local district attorneys, the investigations would have been severely hamstrung. Meantime, Cheatham gave his story to the editor of the Cuero *Record*, Kenneth Towery, who pursued his own investigation and adroitly trapped Giles himself in an interview, which when published in the *Record* won for Towery the Pulitzer Prize in journalism. Giles resigned from office, and the matter was quickly picked up by Travis County District Attorney Les Proctor and by both houses of the legislature.

Soon hundreds of indictments were obtained from grand juries throughout the state involving scores of individuals. Giles was indicted on more than twenty counts, was convicted of more than a dozen, and was sentenced to concurrent terms of six years in the penitentiary. John V. Bell, a Texas Congressman who had formerly been in the state senate, was indicted for the admitted receipt of over $28,000 in legal fees from the land operation. Estimates vary widely over the total amount of funds defrauded from the state by these promoters, but it probably did not exceed five per cent of the $100,000,000 fund. Governor Shivers and Attorney General Sheppard, who had dived into the investigation, were scrutinized by the legislative committees, who ultimately exonerated them of complicity. However, Sheppard engaged in a bitter fight with Senator Jimmy Phillips, who insisted that the attorney general, even if not a party to the plot, must at least share some responsibility. The publicity persuaded Shivers not to attempt a campaign for a fourth term.

Recent Skirmishes on the Political Fronts

State Politics and More Scandal At the close of his third term Allan Shivers had served in the chief executive's office longer than any other person. His decision not to run again made the election of 1956 something of a free-for-all. Six men entered the race: Reuben Senterfitt, Ralph Yarborough, W. Lee O'Daniel, J. Evetts Haley, J. J. Holmes, and Price Daniel. It was among the most interesting gubernatorial campaigns in modern times, sandwiched as it was between Shivers' repeated reelections and the three-term tenures of the next two governors.

O'Daniel withdrew before the primary election in May. J. Evetts Haley lent the greatest color to the campaign by touring the state with a chuckwagon. Cowboy, rancher, historian, and author, Haley was known for his extreme conservatism, his opposition to integration, and his support of states' rights. Liberals, in a loose organization called Democrats of Texas, hated him with a paranoid passion, which he returned most heartily since he suspected some of them of being Communists. Democrats of Texas supported Yarborough and the moderate element, Price Daniel. Daniel and Yarborough were forced into a runoff campaign, which was heatedly fought and which was narrowly won by Daniel, 698,001 to 694,830. But the intensity of feeling did not end as usual after elections. Daniel was believed by many to represent the Shivers regime, and the Republican candidate, William R. Bryant, unexpectedly drawing a large number of liberal votes, received 261,283 votes against Daniel's 1,350,736.

The new governor was quite familiar with Texas politics. He had been elected attorney general in 1947 on a platform highly critical of the Truman administration, especially because of the "tidelands grab," and he had pledged himself to secure the return of that territory to Texas. In 1938, because of oil discovered in submerged lands, especially off the coast of California, the United States Supreme Court ruled that all offshore lands belonged to the federal government. Because of the terms under which the Republic of Texas originally entered the union, Texas had a special claim to title of its submerged, offshore lands in the Gulf, even though California and Louisiana, which also lost cases before the Supreme Court, might not. Texas believed that its tidelands should be exempt from the ruling, but nothing was accomplished on the matter for several years because of the war. A bill to restore title to the states was passed by congress in 1945 but was vetoed by President Truman. The matter began to attract widespread public attention. In 1948, according to a statewide poll of Texans, the tidelands question was the sixth most important issue; in 1949 it had become first, above such issues as segregation, housing, and the cost of living. Price Daniel rose to popularity by defending the Texas title before the Supreme Court in many months of litigation. When he was elected to the United States Senate in 1952, he introduced a bill restoring the ownership of submerged lands to the states. This bill worked its way through congress and was approved by President Eisenhower, as Eisenhower had promised the Texans he would do. Senator Daniel emerged as the victorious champion of Texas' rights, and it was partly on the strength of this victory that he was able to win the governor's chair.

When Daniel resigned to become governor, the wealthy William A. Blakely was appointed his temporary replacement in the senate, and in the spring of 1957 Blakely lost the special election to Ralph Yarborough, who won by a substantial majority and was reelected to a full term in 1958 and to a second term in 1964.

Scandal broke out again in the legislature during Daniel's first session as governor in 1957. The exposures of the land office and insurance scandals prompted the legislature to undertake an investigation of corrupt lobbying practices, which revealed more malfeasance and a practice widespread among legislators and state officials of accepting gifts from lobbyists. It had become standard for the major lobbyists to give Christmas presents to heads of state departments in Austin. These presents varied in extravagance with the importance and influence of the official. It had also become standard for lobbyists to "feed," that is, to provide members of the legislature with meals, drinks, and occasional entertainment such as hunting and fishing trips. Some lobbyists paid for open breakfast buffets for legislators in Austin hotels, and others financed hotel suites, gave parties, and even loaned boats, planes, and cars.

Far more significant than these petty operations was the conflict of interest that arose when a member of the legislature was a practicing attorney on a retainer from a client whose interests became involved in legislation. Corrupt practice is difficult and nearly impossible to trace in such subtle influence buying. Suppose a hypothetical lawyer from West Texas named John Doe is elected to the legislature, conducts himself well, and is reelected the next year. Suppose then that some major firm or association places him on an annual retainer to represent it in his local area. Suppose that he continues for several years to return to the legislature and that finally someone introduces a bill affecting one of the companies he represents. No lobbyist needs to tell him how to vote: he will lose his cushy retainer if he votes wrong. And naturally after several years of close association with the company, his sympathies are probably sincerely tied to it.

More direct action by lobbyists is much rarer, for example, the payment of "legal" fees to legislators during or immediately before a session of important legislation. Outright bribery is even rarer. But these two forms of corruption were exposed in 1957. The most flagrant was the case of Representative James E. Cox, who was accused of taking a $5,000 bribe from Dr. Howard Harmon, president of the Texas Naturopathic Physicians, for the purpose of defeating a bill that would prevent the practice of naturopathy in the state. Cox at first denied guilt, and when Harmon produced a tape recording of their meeting, Cox defended himself by claiming that he was trying to trap the lobbyist. It was alleged that the naturopaths had spent over $40,000 in lobbying against the bill.

The state capital suddenly was rife with suspicion, accusation, and recrimination. One national magazine called it a "festering of public morals" and stated that in Texas "political morals are at their lowest since 1917, when Governor Jim Ferguson was impeached and convicted on ten charges of misconduct." The lobbying scandals, after the scandals of the previous year, the invective of the 1956 campaign, the contested senatorial election of 1948, and the bitterness of the Rainey campaign, gave Texas a somewhat unsavory image across the nation. Another national periodical's reporter, finding Texas politics "to be frozen at some Paleolithic stage of evolution," likened the state's governmental system to an extinct species. Such rabid criticism is too harsh, of course, but Texas' reputation suffered. Despite the furor, the 1957 legislature failed to enact a lobbying bill, and the next legislature passed only a toothless measure requiring the registration of lobbyists.

Political Battles, 1958–1962 Governor Daniel was not affected by the uproar in the legislature, or at least his political fortunes were not affected. In 1958 he won the primary without a runoff against W. Lee O'Daniel and Henry B. Gonzalez, a rising politician of Mexican extraction who later won a seat in congress. Shivers had established the third-term precedent; in 1960 Governor Daniel determined to run for a third term. The principal issue was taxation, and the governor's principal opponent was Jack Cox, a conservative who advocated a sales tax. These were the only two candidates in what proved to be a bitter contest. Daniel won and fought the strong Republican contender, William M. Steger, in the general election, which Daniel won by 1,627,698 to 609,808 votes. This exceeded the 1952 election for both the most votes cast in a gubernatorial election and the most ever obtained by a Republican candidate. The large turnout of voters was due to the keen interest in the presidential race that year.

Lyndon Baines Johnson, irreverently dubbed Landslide Lyndon by journalists after his narrow victory in the senatorial election of 1948, had demonstrated his astute political sense by becoming the most powerful figure in the senate by 1960 and one of the most powerful men in the country. He decided to become president of the United States. There were many obstacles on the path to the presidency: (1) no Westerner had received a major party nomination in nearly a century because of the lack of electoral votes in those regions; (2) an equally astute and potentially more powerful politician named John Fitzgerald Kennedy was just as determined as Johnson to secure the Democratic nomination; and (3) the Republican incumbent, Dwight D. Eisenhower, was one of the most popular presidents the nation had ever had, and he would give his blessings to his two-term vice-president, Richard Nixon, an experienced politician and a hard campaigner, who would thereby enter the race with an advantage.

Even Johnson's home state, under the leadership of Governor Shivers, had twice voted for Eisenhower. Would Texans support a Republican in 1960? Johnson could count on the support of the Texas delegation to the Democratic national convention, but the question of whether he could carry Texas in the general election weighed heavily in the minds of other delegates. The convention in Los Angeles had elements of a three-ring circus and of high drama. Kennedy and his flexible assistants arrived and claimed a greater delegate strength than Johnson. Despite the slogan "All the Way with L.B.J." there was an irresistible aura of victory surrounding the youthful Kennedy machine. Kennedy supporters thrust the adoption of a liberal-labor platform through the convention channels, causing no little concern to Texas and southern Johnsonites, who wondered how they could present racial integration and pro-labor themes to their constituencies.

The Kennedy bandwagon rolled to triumph on the first roll call. It was a crushing blow to the Texas delegation, which included a tearful Sam Rayburn. The next morning Kennedy invited Johnson to share the ticket with him as the vice-presidential nominee. After hasty conferences with leaders in both camps, the unexpected announcement was made to the packed convention hall.

The Texas electoral vote was to be a critical factor in the general election. Shivers organized a group called Democrats for Nixon, and many conservatives branded Johnson a left-wing liberal and northern socialist. An awkward political situation existed. On the national level Johnson and Texas leaders in congress cooperated with the liberal element of the Democratic Party; on the state level they worked closely with the moderate conservatives. The situation became more difficult for the Democratic nominees because the liberal Americans for Democratic Action scorned Johnson as a reactionary conservative, because a few fundamentalist Protestant ministers decried Kennedy's Catholicism, and because vitriolic racists warned Texans against the integration plank in the platform. Further indignant criticism of the ticket arose because Johnson's name appeared on the Texas ballot twice: as a candidate for the vice-presidency and as a candidate for the United States Senate, for which he was due for reelection. He had received the nomination in the Democratic primary in the spring, before the results of the national convention could have been anticipated.

As the summer turned to fall, the campaign in Texas intensified. A vehement crowd in Dallas hissed and spat at Senator and Mrs. Johnson. Both presidential candidates visited Texas and spoke to large audiences. Election day came and went, but so close was the tally that final counts were not completed around the nation for nearly two days. The late votes from boss-controlled Cook County, Illinois, and some South Texas counties of political disrepute were significant factors in the ultimate victory of the Kennedy-Johnson ticket. In Texas, the Democrats totaled a vote of 1,167,932 against the Nixon-Lodge vote of 1,121,699, a difference of only 46,233 votes. Johnson, incidentally, received a substantially higher majority of votes for reelection to the senate than he did for the vice-presidency.

Upon Johnson's resignation from the senate seat, Governor Daniel once again appointed William A. Blakely to serve until a special election could be held. It was Blakely who had taken Daniel's vacated seat in 1957 but who had been defeated in the special election by Senator Yarborough. The special election in the summer of 1961 ran wide open, but the resurgent Republican strength carried into the senate young John G. Tower, a political science instructor from Midwestern University. Texas could no longer be considered a "safe" Democratic state, and Republican Tower won reelection in 1966.

As Price Daniel's third term drew to a close, he decided to try for a fourth term, but he lost the support of powerful influences in the party. Worried Democratic leaders sought a strong candidate who could break the vestiges of Shivercrat domination and could shake the growing Republican grip on the Texas voters. They found him in John B. Connally. Connally had been a political manager for Johnson since 1938, had been especially effective in the 1960 campaign, and had been rewarded with the post of Secretary of the Navy. Connally resigned the post to return to Texas to slay the GOP and the liberal Democrat dragons.

The 1962 elections proved to be a tough test for Connally. Six strong candidates entered the primary: Connally; the incumbent, Price Daniel; Marshall Formby, distinguished West Texan; Edwin A. Walker, retired army general and spokesman for the extreme right wing; Will Wilson, attorney general and one of the state's most talented and respected jurists; and Don Yarborough (unrelated to the senator), a young man supported by labor and the liberal Democrats. All six contenders received a respectable number of votes. Walker received the smallest, 138,387, no mean figure. Connally received the most, 431,498, and Yarborough, with 317,986 votes, edged out Daniel and entered the runoff. There Connally won a narrow victory of 565,174 to 538,924 votes.

Alarmed conservatives turned to make an extreme push to defeat Connally in the general election. Jack Cox of Breckenridge, who as a Democrat had run a close race against Daniel in the primary two years earlier, switched his affiliation and ran as a Republican against Connally. The results were startling: Connally received 847,038 votes; Cox received 715,025; and Jack Carswell, a nominee of the states' rights Constitutional Party, received 7,135. Connally had won, but he had by no means slain the opposition.

Governor Daniel bowed out of office gracefully. In his farewell address to the legislature, he gave a fourteen-point summary of the achievements of his six-year administration. They included significant advances in both public school and higher education, the construction of over forty dams and reservoirs by the new Texas Board of Water Development, "the largest highway construction program in the history of the state," the establishment of the Texas Youth Council for the prevention of juvenile crime, reform and improvements in the penal and eleemosynary institutions, extensive reforms in the insurance codes, and a lobby registration law. The governor did not emphasize that, besides the political battles, his administration had been marked principally by the continued struggle to make the state's income match its mounting expenditures. In all probability the most significant legislation of the Daniel era was the passage in 1961 of a limited sales tax of two per cent. It took eight months, endless debate, and two special sessions of the legislature. And even after the legislature had finished in mid-August, Governor Daniel was so dissatisfied with the bill that he refused to sign it. But because of the time element he allowed it to become law without his signature, and the new levy became effective on September 1, 1961. The sales tax, which allowed many exemptions such as food, drugs, and some wearing apparel, was the first basic change in the state's tax structure for over twenty years, and it was perhaps the most meaningful change in the state's history.

A Texan Becomes President The assassination of President John Kennedy happened in Dallas, a city dominated by millionaire business and industrial leaders, a city where segregationist Edwin A. Walker lived, a city that housed the headquarters of the conservative group Texans for America, a city that had sent one of the very few Republicans from Texas to the United States Congress, a city where a throng had recently booed, hissed, and spat upon United Nations Ambassador Adlai Stevenson and vice-presidential candidate Lyndon B. Johnson—in short, a city branded in the public eye as reactionary and racist. The world was quick to fix an irrational stigma of guilt upon Dallas, which continues to enshroud it despite the clearly demonstrated fact that the assassination might have happened anywhere.

An equally irrational belief is that behind the assassination must lie a reactionary plot or, on the other hand, a Communist conspiracy involving Cuban revolutionaries and demented left-wingers. Anti-Johnson Texans have even secretly pondered the possibility of the assassination as a coup d'etat. Three shots or four shots, one assassin or two assassins—dozens of questions have been raised in a score of books, hundreds of articles and feature stories, and thousands of debates, reviews, and commentaries, despite the most massive investigation and public report on any incident in history. The Warren Commission Report, in 26 volumes, 17,815 pages, the work of a hasty but thorough investigative commission headed by the Chief Justice of the United States, was released on a worldwide basis, ten months after that fateful day in November of 1963, in order to allay suspicions of conspiracy. It would be incredible if the conclusions of the Warren Report were wrong, yet its publication seems to have stimulated rather than to have dispelled the rumors.

At 11:40 on the morning of November 22, 1963, President John Kennedy and his party arrived in Dallas after a triumphal visit to Houston. They traveled in a motorcade through downtown Dallas amid the enthusiastic cheers of thousands of well-wishers. The president's open car swung onto Elm Street and started down a gradual descent just after 12:30. To its right loomed a gray brick building called the Texas School Book Depository; to its left stretched the open spaces of Dealey Plaza, where a crowd of admirers had assembled; to its front rose a railroad overpass. As the president waved to the crowd, shots rang out. He reached toward his neck, stiffened slightly, and lurched forward in the seat of the limousine. In front of him, Governor Connally turned from the crowd to the president, was struck in the back by a bullet, which traveled through his body and spun him around onto his wife's lap. Another shot carried a bullet into the president's brain. He fell onto Mrs. Kennedy's lap.

The lead cars in the cavalcade drove to nearby Parkland Memorial Hospital, where the president died. Vice-President Johnson, who had been riding in the third car and had followed the presidential limousine to the hospital, immediately left under close guard for the presidential plane. At 2:28 that afternoon at the airport he was sworn in as President of the United States by Judge Sarah T. Hughes in the presence of Mrs. Jacqueline Kennedy and other members of the party, and the plane left for Washington.

A numbed nation sat before television sets as national networks flashed the news of a desperate search for the unknown assassin or assassins. At 12:45 Dallas police broadcast a description of a suspect who had been seen fleeing from the Texas School Book Depository, from which some observers said the shots had been fired. At 1:15 patrolman J. D. Tippit apparently spotted the suspect, stopped him, and stepped out of the car to question him. Tippit was shot four times and died instantly. At 1:40 the desperate suspect was seen entering the Texas Theatre. Within minutes the Dallas police had surrounded the building, turned on the house lights, and arrested Lee Harvey Oswald, who drew his pistol and futilely struck at the arresting officer. A formal charge was lodged against him the next afternoon for the murder of the president. On Sunday, November 24, Oswald was to be transferred from the city jail to the Dallas County jail. As television cameras relayed the scene to millions of Americans, a man darted from the right of the cameras, paused within a few feet of Oswald, and shot him through the abdomen with a .38 calibre revolver. Oswald fell and died soon afterward without regaining consciousness. His killer was Jack Ruby, a nightclub owner in Dallas. Ruby was tried, convicted, and sentenced to death, but he died before the sentence was executed. He had deprived the world of a trial of Oswald, had brought scathing condemnation to the Dallas police force, and had left behind him a legacy of doubt and confusion that may never be resolved.

Governor Connally recovered from his serious wound, and with his mentor in the White House and his popularity booming, Connally's control of the state's politics was assured. He easily won renomination in the primary in 1964, again defeating Don Yarborough and this time without a runoff. In the general election in November, his Republican opponent took less than a third of the total votes.

The interest in the 1964 election, however, was not the gubernatorial race. Lyndon B. Johnson had secured the Democratic nomination for the presidency with liberal Hubert Humphrey of Minnesota as his running mate. He faced a Texas that had voted Republican in the presidential race in 1952 and 1956 and had nearly given victory to Nixon in 1960. Perhaps because of Connally's sure control, perhaps because of association with Kennedy and a burdensome feeling of guilt on the part of some Texas voters, perhaps because of the extremist posture of Barry Goldwater, the Republican nominee, Texas voted 1,663,185 for Johnson and 958,566 for Goldwater. Johnson was returned to the White House for four more years by a national majority. It would be bootless to recount in this history of Texas his handling of problems and the cycles of his popularity or to assess him either as statesman or politician. Beyond any doubt his prestige and his power became greater than any other Texan's.

Johnson might have won a second term, but he chose not to run. The election of 1968 culminated a struggle of conservatives and Republicans in Texas to carry the state for a reborn Richard Nixon. Again the vote was very close, in Texas as in the rest of the nation. Again Cook County, Illinois, and a scattering of Texas counties were late reporting returns. The final tabulation showed that Nixon had lost the Texas electoral vote by less than one per cent, but he moved into the White House with a slim national majority. Texas stands on the threshold of becoming at last a two-party state. Although state politics remains in a state of flux, both parties are maturing, and the tumult of the postwar period appears to have ended.

In the gubernatorial race, Connally, who had won a third term in 1966, declined to run again, opening the contest to a broad spectrum of candidates. Moderately conservative Lieutenant Governor Preston Smith of Lubbock became the first West Texan to hold the office of governor. As Connally left office he could view as major achievements a revision of the sales tax that had broadened its scope and increased revenue substantially, a reorganization and upgrading of the state's system of higher education, a reorganization of several state agencies such as the state mental health activities, a major revision of the state's penal code, and the creation of the Texas Tourist Bureau to develop the state's historic and recreational potential.

Although it was a federal rather than a state negotiation, another accomplishment of this period was the final settlement of an ancient boundary dispute with Mexico over the Chamizal, an area between the twin border cities of Juarez and El Paso. The capricious Rio Grande during flood stages and by natural deposition of silt had changed its course southward of the boundary fixed in 1852. The problem was exceedingly complex, and almost innumerable conventions, agreements, and other negotiations were made between the United States and Mexico from 1884 to 1963. In 1911 an international arbitration convention reaffirmed the boundary of 1852 and awarded the disputed territory to Mexico. The United States, refusing to abide by the decision, claimed that it was contrary to international legal principles concerning river boundaries. Negotiation continued until 1963, when President Kennedy insisted that the United States settle the matter to Mexico's satisfaction. It was agreed that a new concrete channel would be cut for the river in approximately the 1852 course so that Mexico would have four hundred thirty-seven acres north of the later channel of the river. At the same time, Mexico transferred to the United States the one hundred ninety-three acres of Cordova Island, which had extended like a sore thumb more than a mile north of the river into downtown El Paso. In 1968 the final settlement was reached and construction of the new channel completed.

Social and Economic Developments

Civil Rights in Texas The rights of Negro citizens in Texas, conferred upon them by Reconstruction, the Fourteenth Amendment, and the activities of the Radicals, eroded away during the last quarter of the nineteenth century primarily because the Negroes were ill-prepared either by education or occupation to exercise, maintain, and protect those rights. A mere ten per cent of the Negro population was literate in 1870, and at that time virtually all Negroes, male and female, were unqualified by training or background for any employment other than unskilled agricultural and domestic labor. It seems likely that most, though by no means all, of the earlier discriminatory practices visited upon black people were socioeconomic rather than racist.

As was discussed earlier, until the turn of the century Negroes sustained a voice in Texas politics, in approximate proportion to their numbers, through the Republican Party and the leadership of such men as Norris Wright Cuney. Racist discrimination became evident toward the end of the century when Jim Crow laws legalized the customary practice of racial segregation. Negroes had for generations maintained their own churches, had begun to organize their own fraternal and benevolent groups, and had even developed separate labor unions and farmers organizations before 1900. Under provisions of the Constitution of 1876, separate school facilities emerged in the local school districts, and the state attempted with little success to provide higher education at Prairie View. The literacy rate among Negroes rose slowly until by 1919 it reached eighty per cent.

By that time there had been a small shift in occupational status. Approximately sixty per cent of Negro workers were engaged in agriculture, thirty per cent in domestic work, and ten per cent in skilled or semiskilled occupations. A small beginning, about one and a half per cent of the Negro population, had been made in the development of a Negro business and professional class, but at the time of World War I Texas had the lowest proportion of any state of Negro urban employment to Negro population. In short, at the time of the first war the typical Negro was literate, had attended for a few years an inferior segregated school, was employed in unskilled labor in a rural environment, and was accustomed to discriminatory segregation and treatment at every level of his life.

It is often stated categorically that the Terrell Election Law of 1905 disfranchised Negro voters by creating the primary election system and establishing a poll tax as a requirement for voting. It is highly unlikely that this was the intent of the law, which was considered in its time a progressive measure to take the nomination of candidates out of the obscurity of smoke-filled hotel rooms and to put it in the hands of the voters. The difficulties of collecting the poll tax before the election law was passed have been discussed in a previous chapter; the new measure was an attempt to facilitate collection and to make the tax fall equitably across the entire male population. Nevertheless, whatever the election reform's intention, it effectively disfranchised not only many Negroes but also anyone who did not choose to vote as a Democrat or who failed to pay the poll tax: thousands of poor whites, Mexican Americans, and foreign-born.

The 1920's visited a reign of racist terror and reaction on Texas as well as on the rest of the nation, as witnessed by such things as the National Origins Act, the rise of the new Ku Klux Klan, and the classifica-

Flamboyant Texas / 378

tion of Mexicans as nonwhite on the census of 1930. In Texas, as noted earlier, the principal aim of the Klan was pseudomoralistic; only incidentally was it racist, but when it was it was unspeakable. During this period Negroes were disfranchised, for all practical purposes, in 1923 by the white primary law, which prohibited Negroes from voting in the Democratic primary. Jim Crow segregation was enforced everywhere more rigidly. Railroad and bus companies created segregated waiting rooms, sanitary facilities, drinking fountains, seating sections, and restaurant and public dining rooms. It was virtually impossible for Negroes to sleep in Pullman cars, to stay at any major hotel, or to live in a white section of town. The development of "niggertowns" as appendages of white communities had roots in the past and was a natural economic movement. By the 1920's, however, city ordinances and subdivision restrictions began to establish the legal frameworks that created Negro ghettos. A few communities, especially during the early depression years, posted on their boundaries signs reading, "Nigger, don't let the sun set on you here!"

Figures on lynchings and race riots indicate that racial problems may have peaked earlier, but the twenties showed a marked resurgence. From 1882 to 1936, the time of the last Negro lynching, three hundred forty-five Negroes had been hanged by vigilante groups in Texas. Every year, from 1889 to 1922, at least three were hanged. The peak occurred in the late 1890's: twenty Negroes having been lynched in 1895 and twenty-three in 1897. But in the year of the Klan, 1922, sixteen Negroes were lynched. In 1906 one of the nation's most publicized race riots occurred in Brownsville, Texas, when a group of Negro troops stationed at Fort Brown wounded the chief of police and killed a white barkeeper. In response to a conspiracy of silence that prevented federal investigators from determining the underlying facts, three Negro companies were charged with the assault, and one hundred sixty troops were dishonorably discharged. Perhaps the worst race riot in Texas history happened in Houston in 1917 when a clash of Negro soldiers and white citizens ended with seventeen whites killed and thirteen Negroes executed for murder. In a 1919 riot in Longview several whites and blacks were killed and the Negro section of town was burned. The same year Marshall experienced a racial outbreak. In 1943 violence in Beaumont killed two and injured several. Considering all the explosive factors involved, however, Texas has had a minimum of racial trouble, particularly during recent years when there have been such extreme outbreaks in other parts of the nation.

Rectification of racial inequality began during the twenties when the pressure began to be unbearable. In 1924 Dr. L. H. Nixon, a Negro from El Paso, was refused the right to vote under the 1923 white primary law. He filed suit and with the help of the National Association for the Advancement of Colored People took the case of *Nixon versus Herndon* to the United States Supreme Court, which declared the Texas law unconstitutional in 1927. The Texas legislature then transferred control of primaries to the state executive committee, which acted to bar Negroes from voting. Again Dr. Nixon carried the case through the courts, and again, in 1932, the United States Supreme Court ruled the Texas law unconstitutional. Faced with the indisputable evidence that any law that barred Negroes from voting would violate the Fourteenth Amendment, the Texas Democrats excluded Negroes from party membership. In *Grovy versus Townsend* in 1935 the Supreme Court upheld the right of a voluntary organization to determine its own membership. A case brought before the court from Louisiana in 1941 opened this decision to question, and in 1944 the court ruled in the Texas case of *Smith versus Allwright* that Negroes had the right to participate in primaries because these elections were manifestly a part of the election process. Although futile challenges in Harrison and Fort Bend counties were made later, Negroes have had the right to vote in party primaries since 1946. In 1966, for the first time in seventy years, two Negroes, one of them a woman, were elected to the Texas legislature from integrated districts in Houston.

During most of the disfranchisement period a bloc of about five thousand Negroes were allowed to vote in Bexar County, especially in local elections, because of a tightly controlled machine developed by Charlie Bellinger, a powerful Negro underworld figure, who delivered these votes to the political bosses of San Antonio. According to some reports, Bellinger controlled the city government there from 1917 to 1935.

Educational integration has been, when compared with other southern states, relatively smooth in Texas. Negro schools, although inadequate, have been provided since Reconstruction. In 1919 the legislature established a County Training School for occupational training in each county with a large Negro population. These were much better attended than the traditional high schools. In 1948 the Gilmer-Aikin Law contained special provisions for the advancement of Negro education. Meantime, privately funded Negro schools and the Prairie View university undertook higher education for Negroes.

Integration of education began at this level when Herman Marion Sweatt, denied admission to the University of Texas law school, filed suit, and won admission by a Supreme Court decision in 1950. In 1952 a Negro was admitted to Del Mar municipal junior college in Corpus Christi. In 1954 Wayland Baptist College became integrated. In 1955, under special condition, a few Negro undergraduates were admitted to the University of Texas. The following year several other state colleges began integration. At Texas Tech the registration forms simply dropped the blank for re-

Flamboyant Texas / 380

questing the student's race. The school had been established in 1923 exclusively for whites; when asked by reporters the number of Negroes attending the college, officials were conveniently unable to say since the registration forms did not include that information.

The Kansas case of *Brown versus Board of Education* opened the rest of the educational system to Negroes. A high school in Mansfield in the Fort Worth–Dallas area was the first school in Texas to attempt integration, as the result of a suit brought in a federal court, but an irate mob prevented its integration in 1956. Governor Allan Shivers sent Texas Rangers to the community to stop trouble and to urge the transfer of Negro students to other schools.

Racism and integration became political issues of high import in 1954 and 1956. According to D. B. Hardeman, writing in *Harpers Magazine* in 1956, Shivers welcomed the racial issue to bolster his 1954 campaign. The governor was quoted as saying, "If we bow down to the Supreme Court decree, if we artificially and arbitrarily enforce the mixing of white and colored children in the classroom, we are going to blight the education of whole generations of children of both races. While I'm Governor, this is not going to happen." The attorney general attempted to bar the NAACP from the state on grounds of barratry, and during the testimony the Communist connections of some of the founders received widespread publicity. Consequently the gubernatorial campaign of 1956 was rife with intolerance and racism. A referendum containing three proposals to block the 1954 integration decision was carried in the general election by nearly four to one, but no enabling legislation resulted.

The Texas public quickly began to accept legal integration as an accomplished fact. By the close of 1957, one hundred twenty-two school districts had become integrated, and ten years later approximately half of the Negro school children attended integrated schools, while only four out of eleven hundred seventy districts maintained mandatory segregated schools. In effect, however, the physical separation of residential areas segregated most schools in most of the larger communities. Some gerrymandering of district lines seems to have occurred, and federal agencies have threatened to deny funds to such school districts.

Inroads have been made in this and other areas of discrimination and segregation. Jim Crow laws have been abolished, separate dining, seating, and sanitary facilities in public places have disappeared. In 1917, in the case of *Buchanan versus Worley*, the Supreme Court ruled that city ordinances establishing white and black sections of communities were unconstitutional. A later decision rendered invalid the racial restriction entailment of lots in real estate subdivisions. But complete integration cannot occur until the socioeconomic barriers are removed by the slow process of

Negro education. Despite strident demands for "freedom now," the most obvious fact of Negro history has been the accelerating social, economic, and political betterment of the race. Much of this progress has resulted from the shift of the Negro population from farms to cities.

Texas Today The number of Negroes living on farms declined 47 per cent in the decade 1940 to 1950 and 70 per cent in the following decade. In 1940, 17 per cent of Texas farm residents were Negroes; in 1960 this figure had declined to 13 per cent. A corresponding decrease occurred in the percentage of Negroes to the total population of Texas, which dropped approximately 3 per cent each decade from 24.7 per cent in 1880 to 12.8 per cent in 1950. The decline from 1950 to 1960, however, was a slight 0.3 per cent to 12.6 per cent of the total Texas population.

In 1960, with a total population of 9,579,677, Texas ranked sixth among the states of the union. Latest estimates, in 1965, placed Texas fifth, with 10,552,000 people. The following table illustrates some of the population characteristics of the state in 1960:

Total population	9,579,677
White population	8,374,831
Negro population	1,187,125
Indian population	5,750
Foreign-born	298,791
Foreign stock (foreign-born plus native-born with one or both parents foreign-born)	1,082,468
Urban population	7,186,011
Rural population	2,393,666

The nation from which the greatest number of foreign-born have come to Texas is Mexico. In 1960 the total Mexican-born population was 202,315; the total first-generation Americans with Mexican-born parents was 453,208. Most of these people lived in Bexar County, El Paso County, and the lower Rio Grande Valley, but there was scarcely a county in the state that did not have a few persons of Mexican stock. Germany furnished the second largest number of total foreign stock, 110,008. Czechoslovakia was third with 35,900, England was fourth with 34,528, and Canada was fifth with 28,125. Sixth was Italy with 26,996. Natives of nearly every nation in the world lived in Texas in 1960, and eighteen nations had over one thousand natives in the state. They were the six named above and Scotland, Eire, Sweden, the Netherlands, France, Poland, Austria, Hungary, Greece, the U.S.S.R., China, Japan, and the Philippines. It will be a surprise to many that the U.S.S.R. furnished 3,472 Russian-born residents of the state and that 16,533 were of Russian stock. The people of foreign stock were scattered in every county in Texas, but a slightly higher percentage than that of the total population lived in urban places.

Seventy-five per cent of the total Texas population lived in places classified as urban. Most of these urbanites lived inside the twenty-three Standard Metropolitan Statistical Areas; in fact, eight out of ten Texans lived in these areas. Standard Metropolitan Statistical Areas are defined by the Bureau of the Census as distinct metropolitan areas for statistical purposes. Texas has more than any other state and contains some of the fastest growing ones. The three of these with the greatest population estimates in 1967 were Houston, including Brazoria, Fort Bend, Harris, Liberty, and Montgomery counties, at 1,766,315; Dallas, including Collin, Dallas, Denton, Ellis, Kaufman, and Rockwall counties, at 1,415,170; and San Antonio, including Bexar and Guadalupe counties, at 869,123. Of the twenty-three Standard Metropolitan Statistical Areas, Corpus Christi, Midland, and Beaumont led in assessed property valuation per capita. Beaumont was the first in manufacturing values per capita, followed by Houston and then Dallas. In retail sales per capita, Lubbock led, with Odessa and Midland a close second and third. Dallas was the leader in wholesale sales per capita, followed by Lubbock and then Houston.

The decline in rural population was accompanied by a decline in the number of farms but a substantial increase in the size of each. The average value per acre increased to over $120, and the estimated average value of land and buildings in 1966 for the average farm was $97,900. No figures are available on the average value of equipment per farm, but the increase in the amount of farm equipment in use during the past quarter of a century has been great. Other changes in agribusiness included increased production costs and lower profit margins; increased federal aids, subsidies, and supervision; increased use of irrigation; improvement in pest and disease control, with a nearly complete eradication of the screwworm; increased use of scientific methods and tools; increased use of fertilizers; increased cooperation among farmers in both marketing and purchasing; and a shift of cotton production to the High Plains and of livestock production to East Texas. The livestock and poultry industries have been marked by increases in feedlot finishing, in artificial insemination, and in broiler production.

Recent averages of all Texas agribusiness were $6.6 billion yearly, about $2.5 billion representing gross sale of agricultural products. But in terms of the costs of land, buildings, and equipment, farming and ranching brought the poorest returns for the amount invested of any business endeavor. At least two results have been noticeable: the increase in tenant farming and the purchase of farm and ranch land by wealthy investors for speculative and/or tax purposes. Over the last two decades a class of professional farmer has arisen who may own little or no land but may have $20,000 to $50,000 invested in equipment and may farm six to twenty different farms, either on shares or cash rents. In the last agricultural census the value of all farm products was $2,227,339,392, of which crop products comprised slightly over half and livestock and poultry products slightly less. Texas tied with California as the second largest agricultural exporter after Illinois. Cotton and cotton products comprised the greatest money crop, with feed grain second. The total value of beef cattle on Texas farms and ranches was over $1.1 billion; the value of milk cows was over $700 million; and the value of sheep was just under that figure.

The total value of minerals produced in Texas in 1966 was a record high of over $5 billion. Texas ranks as the leading state in the value of minerals produced. Of these, the five most important in 1966 were petroleum, natural gas, natural gas liquids, cement, and sulphur. Several new oil and gas fields were discovered during the 1950's, but beginning in 1958 the number of new wildcat wells began declining sharply, as did the total number of wells drilled. Perhaps the greatest operations in recent years were in the Permian Basin region around Midland and Odessa.

Service industries such as barber shops, laundries, hotels, and repair shops had gross receipts in 1963 in excess of $1.8 billion. A total of 172,273 Texans were employed in such businesses. Of these, laundry and dry cleaning plants had the highest gross receipts, auto repair shops were a close second, and hotels and motels were third. The most significant changes in the last two decades were a drop in gross receipts of motion picture theaters and the construction of luxury motels throughout the state.

Retail trade in 1963 accounted for gross receipts of nearly $13 billion. Food stores led in sales, automotive dealers were second, and general merchandise stores were third. Wholesale trade that year had gross sales of over $18 billion.

Texas is rapidly becoming an industrial state. The number, variety, and value of manufacturing plants have increased with great rapidity in the past two decades. Value added by these plants in 1967 was estimated to be in excess of $10 billion and has increased approximately ten per cent a year for over ten years. In 1967 sixteen per cent of the total working force was employed in the manufacturing industries. On the basis of value added by manufacture, chemical and allied products ranked first; petroleum and coal products, second; and food and kindred products, third. Next, in order, came primary metal products; stone, clay, and glass products; printing and publishing; apparel and related products; and paper and paper products. Lumber and wood products, for decades the most significant of Texas industries, had slipped to eleventh place, and the chemical industries had risen to first. Of the chemical industries, the manufacture of basic chemicals accounted for seventy-five per cent of the value, and of the petroleum industries, refining accounted for ninety-five per cent of the value. In terms of individual industries, petroleum refining was first, and organic chemicals was second, the two together accounting for seventeen per cent of the total of all value added by manufacture.

The labor force in Texas totaled 4,109,317 in 1966, and the average number employed during the year was 3,976,158. Of these, less than eight per cent were engaged in agriculture, a decline that represents the most significant shift in the past two decades in employment classification. Just under sixteen per cent were employed in the manufacturing industries; less than three per cent, in mining and oil production; five per cent, in construction work; six per cent, in transportation; nineteen per cent, in retail and wholesale trade; four per cent, in finance, insurance, and real estate; nearly twelve per cent, in the service industries; fourteen per cent, in government jobs; and eighteen per cent, in management or executive positions in all classifications.

The increasing prosperity of the state from 1950 to 1965 is reflected in the increase of bank deposits by two hundred fifty per cent, of air traffic by five hundred per cent, of exports by two hundred twenty per cent, of imports by two hundred seventy per cent, of motor vehicle registration by two hundred per cent, and of highway mileage by one hundred eighty per cent.

Among the most dramatic recent developments was the establishment in 1961 near Houston of the National Aeronautics and Space Administration's Manned Spacecraft Center. Among the Center's facilities are the famed mission control center, research laboratories, simulation chambers, training operations, and numerous support, management, and maintenance functions.

The Wheeler-Dealers "Wheeling and dealing" is a venerable East Texas folk expression. It conveys a meaning, an image, that defies definition but does not really require it. A wheeler-dealer is a man who makes deals, not occasional deals but frequent deals. He often earns his living by "putting deals together," by making trades. In Texan lore this is always a very good living: the legendary flamboyant wheeler-dealer is always successful, always wealthy. Amon Carter, Bob Young, Glenn McCarthy, H. L. Hunt, Roy Hofheinz, James Ling, Sid Richardson, Clint Murchison, and Hugh Roy Cullen are some well-known names of wheeler-dealers who kept putting deals together, trading and making more deals, wheeling and dealing until they had created vast empires for themselves. There are thousands more just like them, although less successful and many of them even unsuccessful, and the image of modern Texas as a land of wheeler-dealers consistently recurs in the minds of non-Texans all over the world. But today the image is mixed up with oil, scandals, political reactionaries, and crooks.

The chief relationship between oil and wheeling and dealing is that the money from oil revenues made multimillionaires out of many of the practitioners. And many of them, not surprisingly, have tended to support political conservatism since a socialistic or tightly regulated society is antithetical to their way of life. The legends of their successful deals have emphasized fast and easy trades, light-hearted and even haphazard speculations, and quick big profits. Therefore bogus wheeler-dealers, crooks and con men, have been able to operate facilely within these parameters. The illegal machinations in West Texas of Billie Sol Estes were possible because of the climate of wheeling and dealing, but they were by no means typical.

True wheeling and dealing, the basic aspect of the modern Texan personality, holds absolutely no brief with dishonesty. In fact it depends upon the integrity and mutual trust of the parties involved. It has two primary characteristics. First, the deal or trade is usually made on the basis of oral commitments on which all parties must be able to rely. And second, the deal must be advantageous to all parties or it is not practical. It is not the purpose here to add to the myth of oil-rich Texans with more money than they knew how to spend but to emphasize that free-swinging, constructive financial operations may be the single most significant characteristic of Texas history in the last two decades. Nor has this characteristic been limited to large-scale operations or to financial ones. There are wheeler-dealers in the political world and even in the academic world. This flamboyant era, now drawing to a close, brought a mushrooming growth to Texas in the fifties and sixties.

A Selective Bibliography of Texas History

At first the preparation of this bibliography appeared to be an exercise in futility because of the large number of bibliographies and other guides already available. But as the work progressed, its value became clearer: nowhere else can a student find a subject guide to the voluminous literature covering the entire span of Texas history.

Therefore this bibliography is arranged in six major sections: an introduction with a discussion of general histories and reference works followed by five major chronological divisions. Each of these contains an introductory section analyzing the general works of that period and a topical listing corresponding to the chapter and subdivision titles of this book. A few of the chapter subdivisions are not carried in the bibliography, simply because there are no works available with particular focus on those periods. Also, with only two exceptions, unpublished works such as theses and dissertations are not included. Most of the works listed are readily available; very few rare or out-of-print items have been included. Despite the bibliography's apparent extensiveness—over a thousand entries—it contains only about ten per cent of the published works on Texas and less than twenty-five per cent of the worthwhile books and articles.

Introduction

Bibliographies There are many specialized bibliographies of Texas material and a few general ones. The earliest is C. W. Raines, *Bibliography of Texas* (Austin; privately printed, 1896; reprinted Austin: Gammel, 1934, and Houston: Frontier, 1955). Raines included all works on Texas available at that time. A valuable general bibliography is a compilation by the book dealer William M. Morrison privately printed from his own booklists, *Texas Book Prices* (Waco, 1963).

The most monumental of the Texas bibliographies is Thomas W. Streeter, *Bibliography of Texas, 1795–1845*, 5 vols. (Cambridge: Harvard University Press, 1960). The first two volumes list all works about Texas printed within the state before 1954, the third volume lists Mexican imprints related to Texas, and the fourth and fifth volumes list United States and European imprints. Ernest W. Winkler extends the coverage to 1876 in *Checklist of Texas Imprints, 1846–1860* (Austin: Texas State Historical Assn., 1949), and with Llerena Friend, *Checklist of Texas Imprints, 1861–1876* (Austin: Texas State Historical Assn., 1963).

A few of the more specialized bibliographies and guides follow.

Adams, Ramon Frederick, *The Rampaging Herd: A Bibliography of Books and Pamphlets on Men and Events in the Cattle Industry*. Norman: University of Oklahoma Press, 1959.
———, *Six-guns and Saddle Leather: A Bibliography of Books and Pamphlets on Western Outlaws and Gunmen*. Norman: University of Oklahoma Press, 1954.
Campbell, Thomas N., *A Bibliographic Guide to the Archaeology of Texas*. Austin: University of Texas Press, 1952.
Carroll, Horace Bailey, *Texas County Histories: A Bibliography*. Austin: Texas: State Historical Assn., 1943.
Carroll, Horace Bailey, and Milton R. Gutsh, *Texas History Theses: A Checklist of Theses and Dissertations Relating to Texas History Accepted at the University of Texas, 1893–1951*. Austin: Texas State Historical Assn., 1955.
Connor, Seymour V., *A Preliminary Guide to the Archives of Texas*, Austin: Texas State Historical Assn., 1956.
———, *West Texas County Histories*. Austin: Texas State Library, 1954.

Elliott, Claude, *Theses on Texas History: A Check List of Theses and Dissertations, 1907–1952.* Austin: Texas State Historical Assn., 1955.
Girard, Roselle M., *Bibliography and Index of Texas Geology, 1933–1950.* Austin: University of Texas Press, 1959.
Jenkins, John Holmes, *Cracker Barrel Chronicles: A Bibliography of Texas Town and County Histories.* Austin: Pemberton, 1965.
Kielman, Chester V., *The University of Texas Archives: A Guide to the Historical Manuscripts Collections in the Unversity of Texas Library.* Austin: University of Texas Press, 1967.
Rador, Jesse Lee, *South of Forty: From the Mississippi to the Rio Grande, a Bibliography.* Norman: University of Oklahoma Press, 1947.
United States Works Projects Administration, *Texas Newspapers, 1813–1939, a Union List.* Houston: San Jacinto Museum, 1941.
Winther, Oscar Osburn, *A Classified Bibliography of the Periodical Literature of the Trans-Mississippi West, 1811–1957.* Bloomington: Indiana University Press, 1961.

Reference Works   The most monumental effort in compiling the history of any state was undertaken by the Texas State Historical Association in *The Handbook of Texas*, ed. Walter Prescott Webb and H. Bailey Carroll, 2 vols. (Austin: Texas State Historical Assn., 1952). This is a tersely written encyclopedia of brief yet informative articles on all major events, places, and persons in the Texas heritage. The articles were principally written by professional historians and by graduate students in history, and each includes a brief bibliographic note. Although some of the articles are now outdated or incorrect, the work is of great value. A supplementary volume is in preparation.

H. P. N. Gammel, *The Laws of Texas, 1822–1897*, 10 vols. (Austin: Gammel, 1898), is a remarkably useful reference, made even more so by an index to the laws prepared by C. W. Raines in 1902, which adds two more volumes published by the Texas legislature.

The Texas Almanac has been published since 1857 by A. H. Belo Co., carefully prepared by the staff of the *Galveston News* and later the *Dallas Morning News*. It was issued annually until the Civil War and from 1867 to 1873. It was reestablished in the twentieth century. A listing of these later volumes appears below in the appropriate section.

Journals   The greatest repository of Texas historical writing is the magazine of the Texas State Historical Association, which has been published quarterly since 1897, the first fifteen volumes under the title *Quarterly of the Texas State Historical Association* and from then to the present under the title *Southwestern Historical Quarterly*. All are listed under the latter title in this bibliography. Each volume spans a portion of two years, but only the first year is given here. About fifty per cent of the articles from this quarterly are listed in the following sections.

The *Yearbook* of the West Texas Historical Association, which has appeared annually since 1925, contains a wealth of West Texas history, as does the *Panhandle Plains Historical Review*, issued annually since 1928. Other valuable historical periodical series include *Password*, an annual of the El Paso County Historical Society since 1961; *Texana*, a privately issued quarterly initiated in 1963 by the Davis Brothers of Waco, and the *West Texas Historical and Scientific Society Publications*, issued somewhat irregularly by Sul Ross State College since 1926. The *Southwest Review*, begun as the *Texas Review* at the University of Texas in 1915, is issued quarterly by Southern Methodist University. Primarily a literary magazine, it contains articles of historical interest as well. The *Southwestern Social Science Quarterly*, started in 1920 as the *Southwestern Political Science Quarterly*, also contains articles of an historical nature. The annuals of the Texas Folklore Society, published since 1916, contain little scholarly history but provide the flavor of the Texas heritage.

General Histories There are several general histories of Texas, some of substantial proportions, such as Louis J. Wortham, *A History of Texas*, 5 vols. (Fort Worth: Molyneaux, 1924), but most of these have been rendered out-of-date by research during the past several decades. It is not useful to include them all here, but some have been listed in later sections whenever they are particularly fitting.

The best single-volume history of the state has long been Rupert N. Richardson, *Texas: The Lone Star State* (New York: Prentice Hall, 1943). The shorter third edition appeared in 1970.

The most recent and readable of the general histories is the six-volume *Saga of Texas* series, ed. Seymour V. Connor (Austin: Steck-Vaughn, 1965). Each volume is listed in the appropriate section.

The Spanish Period / Chapters 1, 2, 3

The Spanish period of Texas history has received more scholarly attention than any other era. This is largely due to the work and influence of Herbert Eugene Bolton, whose publications must be admired, despite their flaws. Small errors have not greatly marred the magnificence of his historical contributions. His two surveys of borderlands history bring Texas into perspective in the colonial history of North America. One in the Yale Chronicle of America series, *The Spanish Borderlands: A Chronicle of Old Florida and the Southwest* (New Haven: Yale University, 1921), is highly readable. A second was written as a textbook with Thomas Maitland Marshall: *The Colonization of North America* (New York: Macmillan, 1920). Bolton's *Texas in the Middle Eighteenth Century* (Berkeley: University of California Press, 1915) is a compilation of articles he published earlier in the *Quarterly of the Texas State Historical Association* (now the *Southwestern Historical Quarterly*). *Spanish Exploration in the Southwest, 1542–1706* (New York: Scribner's, 1908) is a compendium of journals of explorations translated by Bolton, and probably some of his graduate students, with perceptive introductions by this great scholar. Other less general works by Bolton are cited in the appropriate subdivisions below.

The first history of Texas, the work of a Franciscan padre Juan Agustín Morfi, was translated by Carlos E. Castañeda under the title *History of Texas, 1673–1779*, 2 vols. (Albuquerque: Quivera Society, 1935). Castañeda also wrote the massive *Our Catholic Heritage in Texas*, 7 vols. (Austin: Von Boeckmann-Jones, 1931–1958). It is often inaccurate but useful if one can check Castañeda's sources.

A more meticulous work on this period is Charles Wilson Hackett, ed. and trans., *Pichardo's Treatise on the Limits of Louisiana and Texas*, 4 vols. (Austin: University of Texas, 1931–1946). This work contains documents, garnered from various Spanish and Mexican archives by the monk Pichardo, in support of Spain's position on the western boundary of Louisiana after the territory's purchase by the United States.

A fine treatment of the Spanish influence on native Americans is Edward H. Spicer, *Cycles of Conquest: The Impact of Spain, Mexico, and the United States on the Indians of the Southwest, 1533–1960* (Tucson: University of Arizona, 1962). Another significant aspect of this period is discussed in Henry Folmer's *Franco-Spanish Rivalry in North America, 1524–1763*, volume VII of the *Spain in the West* series (Glendale, Calif.: Arthur H. Clark, 1953). Useful, despite its being out-of-date, is Hubert Howe Bancroft, *History of the North Mexican States and Texas*, 2 vols. (San Francisco: The History Co., 1890).

Two books by the young historian Odie B. Faulk summarize in readable narratives the entire history of the era: *The Last Years of Spanish Texas, 1778–1821* (The Hague: Mouton, 1964), and *A Successful Failure* (Austin: Steck-Vaughn, 1965), the first volume in the *Saga of Texas* series.

CHAPTER 1 / THE BEGINNING

The Land and the People

Geological Development

Gannett, Henry, *A Gazetteer of Texas*. United States Geological Survey Bulletin No. 224, Series F, Geography, 36, 2nd ed. Washington, D.C.: Government Printing Office, 1904.
Humble Oil and Refining Company, *Texas through 250,000,000 Years*. Museum Notes, No. 4. Austin: Texas Memorial Museum, 1939.
Johnson, Willard D., *The High Plains and Their Utilization*. Twenty-First Annual Report of the United States Geological Service, Pt. 4, and Twenty-Second Annual Report of the United States Geological Service, Pt. 4. Washington, D.C.: Government Printing Office, 1901–1902.
Sellards, E. H., and C. L. Baker, *The Geology of Texas*, 2 vols. Austin: University of Texas Bulletin, 1934.

Topography

Arbingast, Stanley A., and Lorrin Kennamer, *Atlas of Texas*. Austin: University of Texas Bureau of Business Research, 1963.
Johnson, Elmer H., *The Natural Regions of Texas*. Austin: University of Texas Press, 1931.
Kennamer, Lorrin, and William T. Chambers, *Texans and Their Land*. Austin: Steck-Vaughn, 1963.

Early Man

Suhm, Dee Ann, and Edward B. Jelks, eds., *Handbook of Texas Archeology*. Austin: Texas Archeological Society and Texas Memorial Museum, 1962.
Wendorf, Fred, Alex D. Krieger, Claude C. Albritton, and T. D. Stewart, *The Midland Discovery: A Report on the Pleistocene Human Remains from Midland, Texas*. Austin: University of Texas Press, 1955.

The Indians

Atkinson, Mary Jourdan, *The Texas Indians*. San Antonio: Naylor, 1953.
Gatschet, Albert S., "The Karankawa Indians," *Archeological and Ethnological Papers of the Peabody Museum*, vol. 1, no. 2 (1891).
Glover, Wlliam B., "A History of the Caddo Indians," *Louisiana Historical Quarterly* 18 (1935): 872–946.
Newcomb, W. W., *The Indians of Texas*. Austin: University of Texas Press, 1961.
Ruecking, Frederick, "The Economic System of the Coahuiltecan Indians of Southern Texas," *Texas Journal of Science* 5 (1953): 480–97.

Sjoberg, Andree, "The Culture of the Tonkawa," *Texas Journal of Science* 5 (1953): 280–304.
Sonnichsen, Charles Leland, *The Mescalero Apaches*. Norman: University of Oklahoma Press, 1958.
See also other entries under Chapters 1, 2, and 3.

Spanish Beginnings

Charting the Gulf Shores

Bolton, Herbert Eugene, "The Spanish Occupation of Texas, 1519–1690," *Southwestern Historical Quarterly* 16 (1912): 1–26.

Cabeza de Vaca

Bandelier, A. F., ed., and Fanny Bandelier, trans., *The Journey of Álvar Núñez Cabeza de Vaca*. New York: A. S. Barnes 1905; reprinted Chicago: Rio Grande, 1964.
Hallenback, Cleve, *Álvar Núñez, Cabeza de Vaca: The Journey and Route of the First European to Cross the Continent of North America, 1543–1536*. Glendale, Calif.: Arthur H. Clark, 1940.
Krieger, Alex D., "Un Nuevo Estudio de la Ruta Sequida por Cabeza de Vaca a Traves de Norteamerica," Ph.D. dissertation, University of Mexico City, 1955.

The Coronado Entrada

Bolton, Herbert E., *Coronado, Knight of Pueblos and Plains*. Albuquerque: University of New Mexico Press, 1949.
Hammond, George P., *Coronado's Seven Cities*. Albuquerque: United States Coronado Exposition Commission, 1940.
Williams, J. W., "Coronado: From the Rio Grande to the Concho," *Southwestern Historical Quarterly* 63 (1959): 190–220.
Winship, George P., ed. and trans. *The Journey of Coronado, 1540–1542*. Annual Report of the Bureau of American Ethnology, 1892–1893. Washington, D.C.: Smithsonian Institution, 1896; reprinted Chicago: Rio Grande, 1964.

De Soto and Moscoso

Hackett, Charles W., "The Retreat of the Spaniards from New Mexico in 1680 and the Beginnings of El Paso," *Southwestern Historical Quarterly* 16 (1912): 137–68, 259–76.
Hammond, George P., *Don Juan de Oñate, Colonizer of New Mexico, 1595–1628*, 2 vols. Albuquerque: University of New Mexico Press, 1953.

Hughes, Anne E., *The Beginnings of Spanish Settlement in the El Paso District*. Berkeley: University of California Press, 1914; reprinted El Paso: El Paso Public Schools, 1935.
Strickland, Rex W., "Moscoso's Journey through Texas," *Southwestern Historical Quarterly* 66 (1962): 109–37.
Varner, John Grier, and Jeanette Johnson Varner, *The Florida of the Inca*. Austin: University of Texas Press, 1951.
Williams, J. W., "Moscoso's Trail through Texas," *Southwestern Historical Quarterly* 66 (1962): 138–57.
Woldert, Albert, "Expedition of Luis de Moscoso in Texas in 1542," *Southwestern Historical Quarterly* 66 (1962): 158–66.

The Lure of the Conchos

The River of Nuts

Bolton, Herbert Eugene, "The Jumano Indians, 1650–1771." *Southwestern Historical Quarterly* 15 (1911): 66–84.

The Mendoza-López Expedition

Bolton's introduction to Mendoza's journal in *Spanish Exploration in the American Southwest* is especially useful to this entire section.
Connor, Seymour V., "The Mendoza-Lopéz Expedition and Location of San Clemente," *West Texas Historical Association Yearbook* 45 (1969), 3–29.
Kelley, J. Charles, "Juan Sabeata and Diffusion in Aboriginal Texas," *American Anthropologist* 57 (1955): 981–95.

CHAPTER 2 / THE MISSIONARY ERA

The First Mission Wave

Fort St. Louis

Bolton, Herbert Eugene, "The Location of La Salle's Colony on the Gulf of Mexico," *Southwestern Historical Quarterly* 27 (1924): 171–89.
Cole, E. W., "La Salle in Texas," *Southwestern Historical Quarterly* 49 (1945): 473–500.
De León, Alonso, "La Salle's Occupation of Texas," trans. Walter J. O'Donnell. *Preliminary Studies of the Texas Catholic Historical Society*, vol. 3, no. 2 (1936), 1–33.
Joutel, Henri, *Joutel's Journal of La Salle's Last Voyage, 1684–1687*. Reprint of 1714 London translation. Albany: Joseph McDonough, 1906.
Parkman, Francis, *La Salle and the Discovery of the Great West*. Boston: Little, Brown, 1879; reprinted New York: Frederick Ungar, 1965.

De León's Expeditions

Dunn, William Edward, *Spanish and French Rivalry in the Gulf Region of the United States, 1678–1702.* Austin: University of Texas Bulletin, 1917.

———, "The Spanish Search for La Salle's Colony on the Bay of Espíritu Santo, 1685–1689," *Southwestern Historical Quarterly* 19 (1915): 323–69.

Phares, Ross, *Cavalier in the Wilderness: The Story of the Explorer and Trader, Louis Juchereau de St. Denis.* Baton Rouge: Louisiana State University Press, 1952.

The First Missions

Clark, Robert C., "The Beginnings of Texas—Fort Saint Louis and Mission San Francisco de los Tejas," *Southwestern Historical Quarterly* 5 (1901): 1–26.

———, *The Beginnings of Texas, 1684–1718.* Austin: University of Texas Bulletin, 1907.

Hatcher, Mattie Austin, "Description of the Tejas or Asinai Indians," *Southwestern Historical Quarterly* 30 (1926): 206–18.

Terán de los Rios, Domingo, "The Expedition of Don Domingo Terán de los Rios into Texas (1691–1692)," trans. Mattie Austin Hatcher. *Preliminary Studies of the Texas Catholic Historical Society,* vol. 2, no. 1 (1932), 1–67.

The Second Mission Wave

The Ramón-St. Denis Expedition

Blake, R. B., "Locations of the Early Spanish Missions and Presidio in Nacogdoches County," *Southwestern Historical Quarterly* 41 (1937): 212–24.

Bolton, Herbert Eugene, "The Native Tribes about the East Texas Missions," *Southwestern Historical Quarterly* 11 (1907): 249–79.

Espinosa, Isidro de, "Ramón Expedition: Espinosa's Diary of 1716," trans. Gabriel Tous. *Preliminary Studies of the Texas Catholic Historical Society,* vol. 1, no. 4 (1930), 1–24.

Ramón, Domingo, "Captain Don Domingo Ramón's Diary of His Expedition into Texas in 1716," trans. Paul J. Foik. *Preliminary Studies of the Texas Catholic Historical Society,* vol. 2, no. 5 (1933), 1–23.

The Alarcón Expedition

Chabot, Frederick C., *San Antonio and its Beginnings.* San Antonio: Artes Gráficas Printing Co., 1936.

Hoffman, Fritz Leo, "The Mesquia Diary of the Alarcón Expedition into Texas," *Southwestern Historical Quarterly* 41 (1937): 312–23.

Spell, Lota M., ed., "The Grant and First Survey of the City of San Antonio," *Southwestern Historical Quarterly* 66 (1962): 73-89.

The Third Mission Wave

Reoccupation by Aguayo

Hackett, Charles W., "The Marquis of San Miguel de Aguayo and His Recovery of Texas from the French, 1719-1723," *Southwestern Historical Quarterly* 49 (1945): 193-214.

Peña, Juan Antonio de la, "Peña's Diary of the Aguayo Expedition," trans. Peter P. Forrestal. *Preliminary Studies of the Texas Catholic Historical Society*, vol. 2, no. 7 (1935), 1-68.

Canary Islanders

Buck, Samuel M., *Yanaguana's Successors*. San Antonio: Naylor, 1949.

Pedro de Rivera

Murphy, Retta, "The Journey of Pedro de Rivera, 1724-1728," *Southwestern Historical Quarterly* 61 (1957): 125-41.

The Indian Dilemma

Richardson, Rupert N., *The Comanche Barrier to South Plains Settlement*. Glendale, Calif.: Arthur H. Clark, 1933.

Wallace, Ernest, and E. Adamson Hoebel, *The Comanches, Lords of the South Plains*. Norman: University of Oklahoma Press, 1952.

The Fourth Mission Wave

The Establishment of Nuevo Santander

Bolton, Herbert Eugene, "Tienda de Cuervo's Inspection of Laredo, 1757," *Southwestern Historical Quarterly* 6 (1902): 187-203.

Scott, Florence Johnson, *Historical Heritage of the Lower Rio Grande*. San Antonio: Naylor, 1937.

The Western Missions

Allen, Henry Easton, "The Parilla Expedition to the Red River in 1759," *Southwestern Historical Quarterly* 43 (1939): 53-71.

Bolton, Herbert Eugene, "The Founding of the Missions on the San Gabriel River, 1745-1749," *Southwestern Historical Quarterly* 17 (1913): 323-78.

Dunn, William Edward, "The Apache Mission on the San Sabá River," *Southwestern Historical Quarterly* 17 (1913): 379–414.

―――――, "Apache Relations in Texas, 1718–1750," *Southwestern Historical Quarterly* 14 (1910): 198–274.

―――――, "Missionary Activities among the Eastern Apache," *Southwestern Historical Quarterly* 15 (1911): 186–200.

Friend, Llerena B., "Old Spanish Fort," West Texas Historical Assn. *Year Book* 16 (1940): 3–27.

Reeve, Frank, "The Apache in Texas," *Southwestern Historical Quarterly* 50 (1946): 187–219.

Simpson, Lesley Byrd, ed., and Paul D. Nathan, trans., *The San Sabá Papers*. San Francisco: John Howell, 1959.

Sjoberg, Andree F., "Lipan Apache Culture in Historical Perspective," *Southwestern Journal of Anthropology* 9 (1953): 76–98.

Weddle, Robert S., *The San Sabá Mission, Spanish Pivot in Texas*, Austin: University of Texas Press, 1964.

Renewed Activity on the Coast

Bolton, Herbert Eugene, "The Beginnings of Mission Nuestra Señora del Refugio," *Southwestern Historical Quarterly* 19 (1915): 400–4.

―――――, "The Founding of the Mission Rosario: A Chapter in the History of the Gulf Coast," *Southwestern Historical Quarterly* 10 (1906): 113–39.

―――――, "Spanish Activities on the Lower Trinity River, 1746–1771," *Southwestern Historical Quarterly* 16 (1912): 339–77.

Dunn, William Edward, "The Founding of Nuestra Señora del Refugio, the Last Spanish Mission in Texas," *Southwestern Historical Quarterly* 25 (1921): 174–84.

Oberste, William H., *History of Refugio Mission*. Refugio, Texas: Refugio Timely Remarks, 1942.

The Transfer of Louisiana and the Shift in Spanish Policy

Brinkerhoff, Sidney B., and Odie B. Faulk, *Lancers for the King: A Study of the Frontier Military System of Northern New Spain, with a Translation of the Royal Regulations of 1772*. Phoenix: Arizona Historical Foundation, 1965.

Kress, Margaret K., trans., "Diary of a Visit of Inspection of the Texas Missions Made by Fray Gaspar José de Solis in the Year 1767–1768," *Southwestern Historical Quarterly* 35 (1931): 28–76.

Solis, Father Gaspar José de, "The Solis Diary of 1767," trans. Peter P. Forrestal. *Preliminary Studies of the Texas Catholic Historical Society*, vol. 1, no. 6 (1931), 1–42.

CHAPTER 3 / SPAIN'S LAST YEARS

Reorganization

East Texas

Bates, W. B., "A Sketch History of Nacogdoches," *Southwestern Historical Quarterly* 59 (1955): 491–97.
Bolton, Herbert Eugene, "Spanish Abandonment and Reoccupation of East Texas, 1773–1779," *Southwestern Historical Quarterly* 9 (1905): 67–137.

The Provincias Internas

Thomas, Alfred Barnaby, *Teodoro de Croix and the Northern Frontier of New Spain, 1776–1783*. Norman: University of Oklahoma Press, 1941.
Vigness, David M., "Don Hugo Oconor and New Spain's Northeastern Frontier," *Journal of the West* 6 (1967): 27–40.

The New Indian Policy

Bolton, Herbert Eugene, *Athanase de Mézières and the Louisiana-Texas Frontier, 1768–1780*, 2 vols. Cleveland: Arthur H. Clark, 1914.
———, "Spanish Mission Records at San Antonio," *Southwestern Historical Quarterly* 10 (1906): 297–307.
Haggard, J. Villasana, "Spain's Indian Policy in Texas," *Southwestern Historical Quarterly* 43 (1939): 479–85.
Harper, Elizabeth Ann, "The Taovayas Indians in Frontier Trade and Diplomacy, 1719–1768," *The Chronicles of Oklahoma* 31 (1953): 268–89.
———, "The Taovayas Indians in Frontier Trade and Diplomacy, 1769–1779," *Southwestern Historical Quarterly* 57 (1953): 181–201.
———, "The Taovayas Indians in Frontier Trade and Diplomacy, 1779–1835," *Panhandle-Plains Historical Review* 26 (1953): 41–72.
Loomis, Noel M., and Abraham Nasatir, *Pedro Vial and the Roads to Santa Fe*. Norman: University of Oklahoma Press, 1966.
Moorhead, Max, *The Apache Frontier: Jacob Ugarte and Spanish Indian Relations in Northern New Spain*. Norman: University of Oklahoma Press, 1968.
Richardson, Rupert N., *The Comanche Barrier to South Plains Settlement*. Glendale, Calif.: Arthur H. Clark, 1933.
———, "The Culture of the Comanche Indians," *Texas Archeological and Paleontological Society Bulletin* 1 (1929): 58–73.
Wallace, Ernest, and E. A. Hoebel, *Comanche: Lords of the South Plains*. Norman: University of Oklahoma Press, 1951.

Spanish Colonial Life

The Missions

López, José Francisco, "The Texas Missions in 1785," trans. J. Autrey Dabbs. *Preliminary Studies of the Texas Catholic Historical Society*, vol. 3, no. 6 (1940), 1–24.

McCaleb, Walter F., "The Attitude of Spanish in Texas toward the Indians," *Southwestern Historical Quarterly* 1 (1897): 126–27.

Walters, Paul H., "Secularization of the La Bahía Missions," *Southwestern Historical Quarterly* 54 (1951): 287–300.

West, Elizabeth H., ed., "Bonilla's Brief Compendium to the History of Texas," *Southwestern Historical Quarterly* 8 (1904): 1–78.

The Settlements

MacLean, Malcolm, "Journey of a Jacket: An Incident of the Texas Frontier in 1735," *Southwestern Historical Quarterly* 53 (1949): 68–70.

The Cattle Industry

Faulk, Odie B., "Ranching in Spanish Texas," *The Hispanic American Historical Review* 45 (1965): 257–66.

Texas in 1800

Faulk, Odie B., "A Description of Texas in 1803," *Southwestern Historical Quarterly* 66 (1962): 513–15.

Guice, C. Norman, "Texas in 1804," *Southwestern Historical Quarterly* 59 (1955): 46–56.

Alarums and Excursions in the Wings

Spain's New Neighbor

Cox, I. J., "The Louisiana-Texas Frontier during the Burr Conspiracy," *Mississippi Valley Historical Review* 10 (1923): 274–84.

Garrett, Julia Kathryn, "Dr. John Sibley and the Louisiana-Texas Frontier, 1804–1814," *Southwestern Historical Quarterly* 45 (1941): 286–301; 46 (1942): 83–84, 272–77; 47 (1943): 48–51, 160–61, 319–24, 388–91; 48 (1944): 67–71, 275, 547–49; 49 (1945): 116–19, 290–92, 399–431, 599–614.

Haggard, J. Villasana, "The Neutral Ground between Louisiana and Texas," *Louisiana Historical Quarterly* 28 (1945).

The Independence Movement in Mexico

Haggard, J. Villasana, "The Counter-Revolution of Béxar, 1811," *Southwestern Historical Quarterly* 43 (1939): 222–35.

Filibusterers and Patriots

Cox, I. J., "The Early Settlers of San Fernando," *Southwestern Historical Quarterly* 5 (1901): 142–60.
———, "Educational Efforts in San Fernando de Béxar," *Southwestern Historical Quarterly* 6 (1902): 27–63.
———, "The Founding of the First Texas Municipality," *Southwestern Historical Quarterly* 2 (1898): 217–26.
Dabbs, J. Autrey, ed. and trans., "Additional Notes on the Champ d'Asile," *Southwestern Historical Quarterly* 54 (1950): 347–58.
Dabney, L. E., "Louis Aury: The First Governor of Texas under the Mexican Republic," *Southwestern Historical Quarterly* 42 (1938): 108–16.
Faulk, Odie B., "The Penetration of Foreigners and Foreign Ideas into Spanish East Texas, 1793–1810," *East Texas Historical Journal* 2 (1964): 87–94.
Faye, Stanley, "Commodore Aury," *Louisiana Historical Quarterly* 24 (1941): 611–97.
Garrett, Julia Kathryn, *Green Flag over Texas*. New York: Cordova Press, 1939.
Hatcher, Mattie Austin, "Joaquín de Arrendondo's Report of the Battle of Medina," *Southwestern Historical Quarterly* 11 (1907): 220–36.
———, "The Municipal Government of San Fernando de Béxar, 1730–1800," *Southwestern Historical Quarterly* 8 (1904): 277–352.
Henderson, Harry McCorry, "The Magee-Gutiérrez Expedition," *Southwestern Historical Quarterly* 55 (1951): 43–61.
Jarrett, Rie, *Gutiérrez de Lara, Mexican-Texan: The Story of a Creole Hero*. Austin: Creole Texana, 1949.
Ratchford, Fannie E., ed., *The Story of Champ d'Asile*. Dallas: Book Club of Texas, 1937.
Walker, Henry P., ed., "William McLane's Narrative of the Magee-Gutiérrez Expedition, 1812–1813," *Southwestern Historical Quarterly* 46 (1942): 234–51, 457–79, 569–88.
Warren, Harris Gaylord, "The Origin of General Mina's Invasion of Mexico," *Southwestern Historical Quarterly* 42 (1938): 1–20.
———, *The Sword Was Their Passport*. Baton Rouge: Louisiana State University, 1943.
West, Elizabeth H., ed., "Diary of José Bernardo Gutiérrez de Lara, 1811–1812," *American Historical Review* 34 (1928): 55–77, 281–94.

The Adams-Onís Treaty

Brindley, Anne A., "Jane Long," *Southwestern Historical Quarterly* 54 (1950): 211–38.

Brooks, Philip Coolidge, *Diplomacy and the Borderlands: The Adams-Onís Treaty of 1819*. Berkeley: University of California Press, 1939.

Stenberg, Richard, "The Western Boundary of Louisiana, 1762–1803," *Southwestern Historical Quarterly* 35 (1931): 95–108.

The Beginnings of Anglo-American Settlement

Miller County

Manning, William R., "Texas and the Boundary Issue, 1822–1829," *Southwestern Historical Quarterly* 17 (1913): 217–61.

Marshall, Thomas Maitland, *A History of the Western Boundary of the Louisiana Purchase, 1819–1841*. Berkeley: University of California Publications in History, 1914.

Strickland, Rex W., "Miller County, Arkansas Territory, the Frontier that Men Forgot," *Chronicles of Oklahoma* 18 (1940): 12–34; 154–70; 19 (1941): 37–54.

Moses Austin

Bacarisse, Charles A., "Why Moses Austin Came to Texas," *Southwestern Social Science Quarterly* 40 (1959): 16–27.

Hatcher, Mattie Austin, *The Opening of Texas to Foreign Settlement*. Austin: University of Texas Bulletin, 1927.

Mexico and the Republic of Texas / Chapters 4, 5, 6

The years 1821–1846 have probably been more thoroughly researched than any other major period in the history of Texas or of any state in the union. Source materials are readily available. Among the most important publications of correspondence are:

Adams, Ephriam D., *British Diplomatic Correspondence Concerning the Republic of Texas*. Austin: Texas State Historical Assn., 1918.

Barker, Eugene C., ed., *The Austin Papers*, 3 vols. The two-part volume one was published as the second volume of the *Annual Report of the American Historical Association* for 1919 (Washington, D.C.: Government Printing Office, 1924). Volume II was published as the *Annual Report*

Bibliography / 402

of the American Historical Association for 1922 (Washington, D.C.: Government Printing Office, 1928). Volume III (Austin: University of Texas Press, [1927]).

Barker, Nancy. There is now in preparation an important collection of French diplomatic correspondence relating to Texas.

Binkley, William Campbell, ed., *Official Correspondence of the Texan Revolution, 1835–1836*, 2 vols. New York: Appleton-Century, 1936.

Connor, Seymour V., and Virginia H. Taylor, eds., *Texas Treasury Papers*, 4 vols. Austin: Texas State Library, 1956.

Garrison, George Pierce, ed. *Diplomatic Correspondence of the Republic of Texas*, 3 vols. Washington, D.C.: Government Printing Office, 1908–1911. Published in the annual reports of the American Historical Association.

Gulick, Charles Adams, Jr., ed., *The Papers of Mirabeau Buonaparte Lamar*, 6 vols. Austin: Texas State Library, 1920–1927.

Williams, Amelia W., and Eugene C. Barker, eds., *The Writings of Sam Houston, 1813–1863*, 8 vols. Austin: University of Texas Press, 1938–1943.

Winfrey, Dorman H., and James M. Day, eds., *Texas Indian Papers, 1825–1916*, 4 vols. Austin: Texas State Library, 1959.

In addition, the journals of the Texas Congress are in print, including journals of the secret sessions of the senate. Memoirs and reminiscences are available, and many are listed here, under the topics where they have the greatest focus.

Several histories were written by contemporaries who either lived through or received firsthand accounts of the period. The earliest of three important histories is Henderson King Yoakum, *History of Texas from Its First Settlement in 1685 to Its Annexation in 1846*, 2 vols. (New York: Redfield, 1855; reprinted Austin: Steck, 1935). Yoakum not only talked to men who had personal experience with the major events, but also found and cited documentary sources for most of the salient points in his work. Several generations of scholars have found Yoakum's history readable and reliable. Francis W. Johnson, one of the leaders at the siege of Béxar and the farcical Matamoros campaign, spent most of his life collecting material for a history of Texas he never finished. The dean of Texas historians, Dr. Eugene C. Barker, with the aid of Ernest W. Winkler, edited Johnson's work in the first volume of Francis W. Johnson, *A History of Texas and Texans*, 5 vols. (New York: American Historical Society, 1914; revised and reissued, 1916). John Henry Brown, who was a boy during the Texas Revolution, later became acquainted with the major Texans and wrote several important historical works. His *History of Texas*, 2 vols. (St. Louis: L. E. Daniell, 1892–1893), is especially valuable for this period. There are nearly a score of other Texas histories by contemporaries of less significance, but they are characteristically flamboyant and some are disparaging. Abolitionist Benjamin Lundy's *The War in Texas* (Philadelphia: privately printed, 1836; reissued 1837) is very derogatory. William M. Gouge, *The Fiscal History of Texas, Embracing an Account of Its Revenues, Debts, and Currency, from the Commencement of the Revolution in 1835 to 1851–52* (Philadelphia: Lippincott, 1852), is an unfavorable study of the way the Texas debt was handled.

Later scholarship includes the monumental work of Hubert Howe Bancroft, *History of Texas and the North Mexican States*, 2 vols. (San Francisco: The History Co., 1890). Bancroft employed field men to gather documents and ghost writers to author much of his history. But the scholarship is valid, the footnotes extensive, and the treatment objective. Despite errors and more recent advancement of knowledge, the work remains valuable.

A truly definitive study of Texas' relations with the Centralist-Federalist dichotomy in Mexico has not been undertaken, but an excellent survey of this relationship, and the latest and most readable work on the Mexican period, is David M. Vigness, *The Revolutionary Decades, 1810–1836*, the second volume of the *Saga of Texas* series (Austin: Steck-Vaughn, 1965). George Lockhard Rives, *The United States and Mexico, 1821–1848* (New York: Scribner's, 1913), surveys the principal events in the diplomatic relations of the two nations but fails to examine Mexican actions in terms of the constant political flux. Nor does he thoroughly consider American diplomacy in Whig-Democratic differences. Eugene C. Barker's study, *Mexico and Texas, 1821–1835* (Dallas: Turner, 1928), is better. A student interested in this relationship should read Henry B. Parkes, *A History of Mexico* (Boston: Houghton Mifflin, 1938), in connection with this kaliedoscopic period.

The best survey of the events of the Texas Revolution is William C. Binkley, *The Texas Revolution* (Baton Rouge: Louisiana State University Press, 1952). Binkley edited the two-volume *Official Correspondence of the Texas Revolution, 1835–1836* mentioned previously. Andrew Jackson Houston, a son of Sam Houston, wrote a somewhat idolatrous work, *Texas Independence* (Houston: Anson Jones, 1938). Among a half-dozen contemporary accounts, the best is C. Newell, *History of the Revolution in Texas* (New York: Wiley and Putnam, 1838; reprinted Austin: Steck, 1935).

The history of the Republic of Texas has attracted many people. Attorney and amateur historian Clarence R. Wharton produced the quite readable *The Republic of Texas* (Houston: C. C. Young, 1922). William Ranson Hogan, *The Texas Republic: A Social and Economic History* (Norman: University of Oklahoma Press, 1946), is both scholarly and entertaining. A total picture is presented if it is read in conjunction with the excellent study by Stanley Siegel, A *Political History of the Texas Republic, 1836–1845* (Austin: University of Texas Press, 1956). The latest book on the Republic, Seymour V. Connor, *Adventure in Glory*, the third volume of the *Saga of Texas* (Austin: Steck-Vaughn, 1965), is based almost wholly on contemporary and original material and presents several new interpretations of minor events of the period.

The romance of the proud little Texas Navy has been reflected in a number of excellent works:

Dienst, Alex, *The Navy of the Republic of Texas, 1835–1845*. Temple: privately printed, 1909.
Douglas, Claude L., *Thunder on the Gulf, or the Story of the Texas Navy*. Dallas: Turner, 1936.
Hill, Jim Dan, *The Texas Navy in Forgotten Battles and Shirtsleeve Diplomacy*. Chicago: University of Chicago, 1937.
Wells, Tom, *Commodore Moore and the Texas Navy*. Austin: University of Texas Press, 1960.

The serious student should examine topical studies of the period. Among these, the following have been selected as examples that reflect different aspects:

Binkley, William Campbell, *The Expansionist Movement in Texas, 1836–1850*. Berkeley: University of California Press, 1925.
Carter, James David, *Masonry in Texas: Background, History and Influence to 1846*. Waco: Grand Lodge of A. F. and A. M., 1958.
Lathrop, Barnes F., *Migration into East Texas, 1835–1860: A Study from the United States Census*. Austin: Texas State Historical Assn., 1949.
McKitrick, Reuben, *The Public Land System of Texas, 1823–1910*. Madison: University of Wisconsin Press, 1918.
Miller, Edmund T., *A Financial History of Texas*, Austin: University of Texas Bulletin, 1916.
Webb, Walter P., *The Texas Rangers*. New York: Houghton Mifflin, 1935; reprinted Austin: University of Texas Press, 1965.
Williams, Elgin, *The Animating Pursuits of Speculation: Land Traffic in the Annexation of Texas*. New York: Columbia University Press, 1949.

There are perhaps a hundred good biographies of men and women of the time. Some of the best ones are listed below.

Barker, Eugene C., *The Life of Stephen F. Austin, Founder of Texas, 1793–1836*. Nashville: Cokesbury Press, 1925; New York: Da Capo Press, 1968.
Callcott, Wilfred Hardy, *Santa Anna: The Story of an Enigma Who Once Was Mexico*. Norman: University of Oklahoma Press, 1936.
Christian, Asa Kyrus, *Mirabeau Buonaparte Lamar*. Austin: Von Boeckmann-Jones, 1922.

Copeland, Fayette, *Kendall of the Picayune*. Norman: University of Oklahoma Press, 1943.
Cravens, John Nathan, *James Harper Starr, Financier of the Republic of Texas*. Austin: Daughters of the Republic of Texas, 1950.
Estep, Raymond, *Lorenzo de Zavala, Profeta del Liberalsimo Mexicano*. Mexico City: Porrua, 1952.
Frantz, Joe B., *Gail Borden, Dairyman to a Nation*. Norman: University of Oklahoma Press, 1951.
Friend, Llerena, *Sam Houston, the Great Designer*. Austin: University of Texas Press, 1954.
Gambrell, Herbert Pickens, *Anson Jones, the Last President of Texas*. Garden City, N. Y.: Doubleday, 1948.
——————, *Mirabeau B. Lamar, Troubadour and Crusader*. Dallas: Southern Methodist University Press, 1934.
Green, Mary Reva Maverick, ed., *Samuel Maverick, Texan*. San Antonio: privately printed, 1952.
James, Marquis, *The Raven*. Indianapolis: Bobbs-Merrill, 1929, 1953.
Roland, Charles P., *Albert Sidney Johnston, Soldier of Three Republics*. Austin: University of Texas Press, 1964.
Sexton, Irwin, and Kathryn Sexton, *Samuel A. Maverick*. San Antonio: Naylor, 1964.
Wisehart, M. K., *Sam Houston, American Giant*. Washington: Robert B. Luce, 1962.

A list of topical studies with sharper focus on the particular subdivisions in Chapters 4, 5, and 6 is given below.

CHAPTER 4 / THE MEXICAN YEARS

The First Colony

Stephen F. Austin

Bacarisse, Charles A., "Baron de Bastrop," *Southwestern Historical Quarterly* 58 (1954): 319–30.

The Mexican Revolution

Manning, William R., "Texas and the Boundary Issue, 1822–1829," *Southwestern Historical Quarterly* 17 (1913): 217–61.

The Old Three Hundred

Bugbee, L. G., "What Became of the Lively?" *Southwestern Historical Quarterly* 3 (1899): 141–48.
Moore, R. W., "The Role of the Baron de Bastrop in the Anglo-American

Settlement of the Spanish Southwest," *Louisiana Historical Quarterly* 31 (1948): 606–81.

Colonization under the Republic of Mexico

Legal Structure

Ashford, Gerald, "Jacksonian Liberalism and Spanish Law in Early Texas," *Southwestern Historical Quarterly* 57 (1953): 1–37.
Bacarisse, Charles A., "The Union of Coahuila and Texas," *Southwestern Historical Quarterly* 61 (1957): 341–49.
Barker, Eugene C., "The Government of Austin's Colony, 1821–1831," *Southwestern Historical Quarterly* 21 (1917): 223–52.

The Empresario Contracts

Henderson, Mary Virginia, "Minor Empresario Contracts for the Colonization of Texas, 1825–1834," *Southwestern Historical Quarterly* 31 (1927): 295–324; 32 (1928): 1–28.
Rather, Ethel Zivley, *De Witt's Colony*. Austin: University of Texas Bulletin, 1905.

The Fredonian Rebellion

Parsons, Edmund Morris, "The Fredonian Rebellion," *Texana* 5 (1967): 11–52.

Colonial Life

Barker, Eugene C., "Descriptions of Texas by Stephen F. Austin, 1828," *Southwestern Historical Quarterly* 28 (1924): 98–121.
Bertleth, Rosa Groce, "Jared Ellison Groce," *Southwestern Historical Quarterly* 20 (1916): 358–68.
Burnam, Jesse, "Reminiscences of Captain Jesse Burnam," *Southwestern Historical Quarterly* 5 (1901): 12–18, 164.
Douglas, Claude Leroy, *James Bowie: The Life of a Bravo*. Dallas: Banks Upshaw and Co., 1944.
Hatcher, Mattie Austin, *Letters of an Early American Traveller, Mary Austin Holley*. Dallas: Southwest Press, 1933.
Holley, Mary Austin, *Texas*. Baltimore: n. p., 1833; reprinted Austin: Steck, 1935.
Menchoca, Antonio. *Memoirs*. San Antonio: Yanaguano Society, 1937.
Red, William S., *The Texas Colonists and Religion*. Austin: Von Boeckmann-Jones, 1924.
Robinson, Duncan W., *Judge Robert McAlpin Williamson, Texas' Three-Legged Willie*. Austin: Texas State Historical Assn., 1948.

Sánchez, José Maria, *Viaje a Texas en 1828-1829*. Mexico City: Coleccion de Papeles Historicos Mexicanos, 1939.
Smithwick, Noah, *The Evolution of a State*. Austin: Gammel, 1900; reprinted Austin: Steck, 1935.
Visit to Texas. New York: Goodrich & Wiley, 1834; reprinted Austin: Steck, 1952.

The Change in Mexican Policy

Terán's Recommendations

Morton, Ohland, *Terán and Texas: A Chapter in Texas-Mexican Relations*. Austin: Texas State Historical Assn., 1948.

The Law of April 6, 1830

Barton, Henry, "The Anglo-American Colonists under Mexican Militia Laws," *Southwestern Historical Quarterly* 65 (1961): 61–71.
Houren, Alleine, "Causes and Origin of the Decree of April 6, 1830," *Southwestern Historical Quarterly* 16 (1912): 378–422.

The Later Colonies

Barker, Eugene C., "The Influence of Slavery in the Colonization of Texas," *Southwestern Historical Quarterly* 28 (1924): 1–33.
Oberste, William Herman, *Texas Irish Empresarios and Their Colonies*. Austin: Von Boeckmann-Jones, 1953.
Rister, Carl Coke, *Comanche Bondage*. Glendale, Calif.: Arthur H. Clark, 1955.

Political Chaos and Confusion

Anahuac and Velasco

Barker, Eugene C., "The Battle of Velasco," *Southwestern Historical Quarterly* 7 (1903): 326–28.
Parmenter, Mary Fisher, Walter Russell Fisher, and Lawrence Edward Mallette, *The Life of George Fisher, 1795–1873*. Jacksonville, Fla.: H. & W. B. Drew, 1959.
Rowe, Edna, "The Disturbances at Anahuac in 1823," *Southwestern Historical Quarterly* 6 (1902): 265–99.

The Convention of 1833

Winkler, Ernest W., "Membership of the 1833 Convention of Texas," *Southwestern Historical Quarterly* 45 (1941): 255–57.

Chapter 5 / The Texas Revolution

The Outbreak of Resistance

The Downfall of Federalism

Almonte, Juan N., *Noticia Estradistica Sohre Tejas*. Mexico: Ignacio Cumplido, 1835.
Casteñada, Carlos E., "Statistical Report of Texas by Juan N. Almonte," *Southwestern Historical Quarterly* 28 (1924): 177–222.
Cleaves, W. S., "Lorenzo de Zavala in Texas," *Southwestern Historical Quarterly* 36 (1932): 29–40.
Estep, Raymond, "Lorenzo de Zavala and the Texas Revolution," *Southwestern Historical Quarterly* 57 (1953): 322–35.

Resistance in Texas

Barker, Eugene C., "Journal of the Permanent Council, October 11 to 27, 1835," *Southwestern Historical Quarterly* 7 (1903): 249–78.
―――――, "Proceedings of the Permanent Council," *Southwestern Historical Quarterly* 9 (1905): 287–88.
Bennett, Miles S., "The Battle of Gonzales, the 'Lexington' of the Texas Revolution," *Southwestern Historical Quarterly* 2 (1898): 313–16.
Donaldson, Nanna Smithwick, "Concerning the Gonzales Cannon," *Southwestern Historical Quarterly* 5 (1901): 356.
Grayson, Peter W., "The Release of Stephen F. Austin from Prison," *Southwestern Historical Quarterly* 14 (1910): 155–63.
Ward, Forrest E., "Pre-revolutionary Activity in Brazoria County," *Southwestern Historical Quarterly* 64 (1960): 212–31.

The Federalist Rebellion against Tyranny

The Organization of Provisional Government

Brown, John Henry, *Life and Times of Henry Smith, the First American Governor of Texas*. Dallas: A. D. Aldridge and Co., 1887.
Steen, Ralph W., "Analysis of the Work of the General Council of Texas, 1835–1836," *Southwestern Historical Quarterly* 40 (1936): 309–33; 41 (1937): 225–40, 324–48; 42 (1938): 28–54.

The Siege of Béxar

Austin, Stephen F., "General Austin's Orderbook for the Campaign of 1835," *Southwestern Historical Quarterly* 11 (1907): 1–55.

Crimmins, M. L., "The Storming of San Antonio de Béxar in 1835," *West Texas Historical Assn. Year Book* 22 (1946): 95–117.
Garver, Lois, "Benjamin Rush Milam," *Southwestern Historical Quarterly* 38 (1934): 79–121, 177–202.

Confusion in Texas

Barker, Eugene C., "The Texas Revolutionary Army," *Southwestern Historical Quarterly* 9 (1905): 227–61.
Smith, W. Roy, "The Quarrel between Governor Smith and the Council of the Provisional Government of Texas," *Southwestern Historical Quarterly* 5 (1901): 269–346.

The Fall of the Alamo

Bonham, Milledge L., Jr., "James Butler Bonham: A Consistent Rebel," *Southwestern Historical Quarterly* 35 (1931): 124–36.
Dobie, J. Frank, "Jim Bowie, Big Dealer." *Southwestern Historical Quarterly* 60 (1956): 337–57.
Frantz, Joe B., "The Alamo," in *Battles of Texas*. Waco: Texian Press, 1967.
Lord, Walter, *A Time to Stand*. London: Longmans, Green, 1962.
Shackford, James Atkins, *David Crockett, the Man and the Legend*. Chapel Hill: University of North Carolina Press, 1956.
Tinkle, Lon, *Thirteen Days to Glory, the Siege of the Alamo*. New York: McGraw-Hill, 1958.
Williams, Amelia, "A Critical Study of the Siege of the Alamo and the Personnel of Its Defenders," *Southwestern Historical Quarterly* 36 (1932): 251–87; 37 (1933): 1–44, 79–115, 157–84, 237–312.
Williams, Robert H., Jr., "Travis—A Potential Sam Houston," *Southwestern Historical Quarterly* 40 (1936): 154–60.

The War for Independence

The Convention of 1836

Kemp, Louis Wiltz, *The Signers of the Texas Declaration of Independence*. Houston: Anson Jones Press, 1944.

The Loss of South Texas

Davenport, Harbert, "The Men of Goliad," *Southwestern Historical Quarterly* 43 (1939): 1–41.
Day, James M., "Goliad," in *Battles of Texas*. Waco: Texian Press, 1967.

Miller, T. L., "Fannin's Men: Some Additions to Earlier Rosters," *Southwestern Historical Quarterly* 61 (1957): 522–32.
Scarborough, Jewel D., "The Georgia Battalion in the Texas Revolution," *Southwestern Historical Quarterly* 63 (1959): 511–32.
Smith, Ruby Cumby, "James W. Fannin, Jr. in the Texas Revolution," *Southwestern Historical Quarterly* 23 (1919): 79–90, 171–203, 271–84.

The Campaign and Battle of San Jacinto

Barker, Eugene C., "The San Jacinto Campaign," *Southwestern Historical Quarterly* 4 (1900): 237–45.
Charlton, George L., "Vince's Bridge, Question Mark of the San Jacinto Campaign," *Southwestern Historical Quarterly* 68 (1964): 342–51.
Connor, Seymour V., "The Battle of San Jacinto," in *Battles of Texas*. Waco: Texian Press, 1967.
Dixon, Sam Houston, and Louis Wiltz Kemp, *The Heroes of San Jacinto*. Houston: Anson Jones Press, 1937.
Filosola, Vicente, *Evacuation of Texas* . . . (a translation). Reprinted Waco: Texian Press, 1965.
Henderson, H. M., "A Critical Analysis of the San Jacinto Campaign," *Southwestern Historical Quarterly* 59 (1955): 344–62.
Lane, Walter P., *The Adventures and Recollections of General Walter P. Lane, a San Jacinto Veteran*. Marshall, Texas: News Messenger Publishing Co., 1928.
Presley, James, "Santa Anna in Texas: A Mexican Viewpoint," *Southwestern Historical Quarterly* 62 (1958): 489–512.
Santos, Richard G., *Santa Anna's Campaign against Texas, 1835–1836*. Waco: Texian Press, 1968.
Tolbert, Frank X., *The Day of San Jacinto*. New York: McGraw-Hill, 1959.
Winkler, Ernest W., "The Twin Sisters' Cannon, 1836–1865," *Southwestern Historical Quarterly* 21 (1917): 61–68.

A Brief Analysis of the Causes of the Revolution

Barker, Eugene C., "Land Speculation as a Cause of the Texas Revolution," *Southwestern Historical Quarterly* 10 (1906): 76–95.
Casteñeda, Carlos E., trans., *The Mexican Side of the Texas Revolution*. Dallas: Southwest Press, 1928.
Dillon, Merton L., "Benjamin Lundy in Texas," *Southwestern Historical Quarterly* 63 (1959): 46–62.
Lowrie, Samuel Harman, *Culture Conflict in Texas, 1821–1835*. New York: Columbia University Press, 1932.
Shaw, Elton Raymond. *The Conquest of the Southwest*. Berwyn, Ill.: Shaw Publishing Co., 1924.

Chapter 6 / The Republic of Texas

The Establishment of Stable Government

Problems of the Ad Interim Government

Binkley, William C., "The Activities of the Texas Revolutionary Army after San Jacinto," *Journal of Southern History* 6 (1940): 331–46.

Muir, Andrew F., "Tories in Texas, 1836," *Texas Military History* 4 (1964): 81–94.

The Election of 1836

Richardson, Rupert N., "Framing the Constitution of the Republic of Texas," *Southwestern Historical Quarterly* 31 (1927): 191–220.

The Question of Recognition

Rather, Ethel Zivley, "Recognition of the Republic of Texas by the United States," *Southwestern Historical Quarterly* 13 (1909): 155–256.

Stability

Connor, Seymour V., "County Government in the Republic of Texas," *Southwestern Historical Quarterly* 55 (1951): 163–200.

Later Political Events

Winfrey, Dorman H., "Mirabeau B. Lamar and Texas Nationalism." *Southwestern Historical Quarterly* 59 (1955): 184–205.

⸺, "The Texan Archive War of 1842." *Southwestern Historical Quarterly* 64 (1960): 171–84.

Domestic Affairs

Problems of National Defense

Shearer, Ernest C., *Robert Potter, Remarkable North Carolinian and Texan.* Houston: University of Houston Press, 1951.

Wells, Thomas, *Commodore Moore and the Texas Navy.* Austin: University of Texas Press, 1960.

Wilcox, Seb. S., "Laredo during the Texas Republic." *Southwestern Historical Quarterly* 42 (1938): 83–107.

Financial Affairs

Frantz, Joe B., *Gail Borden, Dairyman to a Nation*. Norman: University of Oklahoma Press, 1951.
Muir, Andrew F., "Railroad Enterprise in Texas," *Southwestern Historical Quarterly* 47 (1943): 339–70.
Nichols, Ruth G., "Samuel May Williams." *Southwestern Historical Quarterly* 56 (1952): 189–210.
Porter, Eugene O., "Railroad Enterprises in the Republic of Texas," *Southwestern Historical Quarterly* 59 (1955): 363–71.
Williams, Elgin, *The Animating Pursuits of Speculation*. New York: Columbia University Press, 1949.

The Establishment of Colonies

Amsler, Robert W., "General Arthur G. Wavell: A Soldier of Fortune in Texas," *Southwestern Historical Quarterly* 69 (1965): 1–21, 186–209.
Amsler, Robert W., ed., "A Prospectus for the Wavell Colony," *Southwestern Historical Quarterly* 56 (1952): 543–51.
Barker, Eugene C., "General Arthur Goodall Wavell and Wavell's Colony in Texas," *Southwestern Historical Quarterly* 47 (1943): 253–56.
Biesele, Rudolph L., "The First German Settlement in Texas," *Southwestern Historical Quarterly* 34 (1930): 334–39.
―――――, *The History of the German Settlements in Texas, 1831–1861*. Austin: Von Boeckmann-Jones, 1930.
―――――, "The San Saba Colonization Company," *Southwestern Historical Quarterly* 33 (1929): 169–83.
Braunfels, Prince Carl Solms, *Texas 1844–1845*. Houston: Anson Jones Press, 1938.
Cohen, Henry, "Henry Castro, Pioneer and Colonist." *Publications of the American Jewish Historical Society*, no. 5 (1896); reprinted Galveston: n.p., n.d.
―――――, "Settlement of the Jews in Texas," *Publications of the American Jewish Historical Society*, no. 2 (1894), 139–56.
Connor, Seymour V., *The Peters Colony of Texas: A History and Biographical Sketches of the Early Settlers*. Austin: Texas State Historical Assn., 1959.
―――――, "A Statistical Review of the Settlement of the Peters Colony, 1841–1848," *Southwestern Historical Quarterly* 57 (1953): 38–64.
Eagleton, Nancy Ethie, "The Mercer Colony in Texas, 1844–1883," *Southwestern Historical Quarterly* 39 (1935): 275–91; 40 (1936): 35–57, 114–44.
Haas, H. E., "A Brief History of Castro's Colony," *Southwestern Historical Quarterly* 12 (1908): 80–81.
King, Irene Marschall, *John Meusebach, German Colonizer in Texas*. Austin: University of Texas Press, 1967.

Roemer, Ferdinand von, *Texas, with Particular Reference to German Immigration and the Physical Appearance of the Country.* Translated by Oswald Mueller as *Roemer's Texas.* San Antonio: Standard Printing Co., 1935.
Tiling, Moritz, *History of the German Element in Texas from 1820–1850.* Houston: privately printed, 1913.

Indian Affairs

Armbruster, H. C., "Torrey's Trading Post," *Texana* 2 (1964): 112–31.
Daniell, Forrest, "Texas Pioneer Surveyors and Indians," *Southwestern Historical Quarterly* 60 (1956): 501–6.
Greer, James K., *Colonel Jack Hays, Texas Frontier Leader and California Builder.* New York: E. P. Dutton, 1952.
Gregory, Jack, and Rennard Strickland, *Sam Houston with the Cherokees.* Austin: University of Texas Press, 1967.
Henderson, H. M., "The Surveyors' Fight," *Southwestern Historical Quarterly* 56 (1952): 25–35.
Mann, W. L., "James O. Rice, Hero of the Battle of the San Gabriel," *Southwestern Historical Quarterly* 55 (1951): 30–42.
Muckelroy, Anna, "The Indian Policy of the Republic of Texas," *Southwestern Historical Quarterly* 25 (1921): 229–60; 26 (1922): 1–29, 128–48, 184–206.
Sibley, Marilyn McAdams, "The Texas-Cherokee War of 1839," *East Texas Historical Journal* 3 (1965): 18–33.
Vigness, David M., "Indian Raids on the Lower Rio Grande, 1836–1837," *Southwestern Historical Quarterly* 59 (1955): 14–23.
Warren, Harry, "Colonel William G. Cooke," *Southwestern Historical Quarterly* 9 (1905): 210–19.
Waugh, Julia Nott, *Castroville and Henry Castro, Empresario.* San Antonio: Naylor, 1934.
Winfrey, Dorman, "Chief Bowles of the Texas Cherokee," *Texas Military History* 2 (1962): 210–21.
Winkler, Ernest W., "The Cherokee Indian in Texas," *Southwestern Historical Quarterly* 7 (1903): 95–165.

Other Domestic Programs

Connor, Seymour V., "Land Speculation in Texas," *Southwest Review*, Spring 1954, pp. 138–43.
Konwiser, Harry M., *Texas Republic Postal System.* New York: H. L. Lindquist, 1933.
London, Lena, "The Initial Homestead Exemption in Texas," *Southwestern Historical Quarterly* 57 (1953): 432–53.
Muir, Andrew F., "The Free Negro in Harris County," *Southwestern Historical Quarterly* 46 (1942): 214–38.

_____, "The Intellectual Climate of Houston during the Period of the Republic," *Southwestern Historical Quarterly* 62 (1958): 312–21.
Newsom, W. L., "The Postal System of the Republic of Texas," *Southwestern Historical Quarterly* 20 (1916): 103–31.
Schmitz, Joseph William, *Thus They Lived: Social Life in the Republic of Texas*. San Antonio: Naylor, 1935.
Schoen, Harold, "The Free Negro in the Republic of Texas," *Southwestern Historical Quarterly* 39 (1935): 292–308; 40 (1936): 26–34, 85–113, 169–99, 267–89; 41 (1937): 83–108.
Stenberg, Richard, "Jackson's Neches Claim, 1829–1836," *Southwestern Historical Quarterly* 39 (1935): 255–74.
Winkler, Ernest W., "The Seat of Government of Texas," *Southwestern Historical Quarterly* 10 (1906): 140–71, 185–245.

Foreign Relations

Texas in the Family of Nations

Adams, Ephriam Douglass, *British Interests and Activities in Texas, 1838–1846*. Baltimore: Johns Hopkins Press, 1910; reprinted Gloucester, Mass.: Peter Smith, 1963.
Blake, Clagette, *Charles Elliot, R. N., 1801–1875, a Servant of Britain Overseas*. London: Cleaver-Hume Press, 1960.
Brown, Alma Howell, "The Consular Service of the Republic of Texas," *Southwestern Historical Quarterly* 33 (1929): 184–230, 299–314.
Denton, Bernice B., "Count Alphonso de Saligny and the Franco-Texienne Bill," *Southwestern Historical Quarterly* 45 (1941): 136–46.
Edwards, Herbert R., "Diplomatic Relations between France and the Republic of Texas, 1836–1845," *Southwestern Historical Quarterly* 20 (1916): 209–41, 341–57.
Kossok, Manfred, "Prussia, Bremen, and the 'Texas Question,'" *Texana* 3 (1965): 227–69.
Laurent, Pierre Henri, "Belgium's Relations with Texas and the United States, 1839–1844," *Southwestern Historical Quarterly* 67 (1963): 220–36.
McClendon, R. Earl, "The First Treaty of the Republic of Texas," *Southwestern Historical Quarterly* 52 (1948): 32–48.
Maissin, Eugene. *The French in Mexico and Texas, 1838–1839*. Salado, Texas: Anson Jones Press, 1961.
Marshall, T. M., "Diplomatic Relations of Texas and the United States, 1839–1843," *Southwestern Historical Quarterly* 15 (1911): 267–93.
Moraud, Marcel, "The Diplomatic Relations of the Republic of Texas," *Rice Institute Pamphlet*, vol. 43, no. 3 (October, 1965), 29–54.
Schmitz, Joseph William, *Texan Statecraft, 1836–1845*. San Antonio: Naylor, 1941.
Worley, J. L., "The Diplomatic Relations of England and the Republic of Texas," *Southwestern Historical Quarterly* 9 (1905): 1–40.

Mexican Relations

Bell, Thomas W., *A Narrative of the Capture and Subsequent Suffering of the Mier Prisoners in Mexico*. De Soto County, Miss.: R. Morris & Co., 1845; reprinted Waco: Texian Press, 1964.

Binkley, William C., "The Last Stage of the Texan Military Operations against Mexico, 1843," *Southwestern Historical Quarterly* 22 (1918): 260–71.

―――――, "New Mexico and the Texan Santa Fe Expedition," *Southwestern Historical Quarterly* 27 (1923): 85–107.

Carroll, H. Bailey, ed., "George W. Grover's 'Minutes of Adventure from June, 1841,' an Account of the Texan-Santa Fe Expedition," *Panhandle Plains Historical Reivew* 9 (1936): 28–42.

Carroll, H. Bailey, "Steward A. Miller and the Snively Expedition of 1843," *Southwestern Historical Quarterly* 54 (1950): 261–86.

―――――, *The Texan-Santa Fe Trail*. Canyon, Texas: Panhandle Plains Historical Society, 1951.

Falconer, Thomas, *Letter and Notes on the Texan-Santa Fe Expedition, 1841–1842*. New York: Bauber & Pine, 1930.

Gailey, Harry A., "Sam Houston and the Texas War Fever, March–August, 1842," *Southwestern Historical Quarterly* 62 (1958): 29–44.

Green, Thomas Jefferson, *Journal of the Texian Expedition against Mier*. New York: Harper & Bros., 1845; reprinted Austin: Steck, 1935.

Hendricks, Sterling B., "The Somervell Expedition to the Rio Grande, 1842," *Southwestern Historical Quarterly* 23 (1919): 112–40.

Kendall, George Wilkins, *Narrative of the Texas Santa Fe Expedition*, 2 vols. London: Putnam & Wiley, 1844; reprinted Austin: Steck, 1935.

Lindheim, Milton, *The Republic of the Rio Grande*. Waco: Morrison, 1964.

Loomis, Noel M., *The Texan-Santa Fe Pioneers*. Norman: University of Oklahoma Press, 1958.

McCaleb, Walter Flavius, *Santa Fe Expedition*. San Antonio: Naylor, 1964.

The Mexican Soldier, 1837–1847: Military Organization, Dress, Equipment, and Regulations. Mexico City: Nieto-Brown-Hefter, 1958.

Nance, Joseph Milton, *After San Jacinto the Texas-Mexican Frontier, 1836–1841*. Austin: University of Texas Press, 1963.

―――――, *Attack and Counterattack, the Texas-Mexican Frontier, 1842*. Austin: University of Texas Press, 1964.

―――――, ed., "Brigadier General Adrian Woll's Report of His Expedition into Texas in 1842," *Southwestern Historical Quarterly* 58 (1954): 523–52.

Stapp, William Preston, *The Prisoners of Perote*. Philadelphia: G. B. Zieber, 1845; reprinted Austin: Steck, 1935.

Vigness, David M., "Relations of the Republic of Texas and the Republic of the Rio Grande," *Southwestern Historical Quarterly* 57 (1953): 312–21.

Winkler, Ernest W., "The Béxar and Dawson Prisoners," *Southwestern Historical Quarterly* 13 (1909): 292–324.

Wooster, Ralph A., "Texas Military Operations against Mexico," *Southwestern Historical Quarterly* 67 (1963): 465–84.

Annexation

Friend, Llerena, ed., "Contemporary Newspaper Accounts of the Annexation of Texas," *Southwestern Historical Quarterly* 49 (1945): 267–81.
Jones, Anson, *Memoranda and Official Correspondence Relating to the Republic of Texas, Its History and Annexation*. New York: Appleton, 1859.
McLemore, R. A., "The Influence of French Diplomatic Policy on the Annexation of Texas," *Southwestern Historical Quarterly* 43 (1939): 342–47.
Middleton, Annie, "The Texas Convention of 1845," *Southwestern Historical Quarterly* 25 (1921): 26–62.
Smith, Justin H., *The Annexation of Texas*. New York: Barnes & Noble, 1911.
Smither, Harriet, "English Abolitionism and the Annexation of Texas," *Southwestern Historical Quarterly* 32 (1928): 193–205.
Stern, Madelene B., "Stephen Pearl Andrews, Abolitionist, and the Annexation of Texas," *Southwestern Historical Quarterly* 67 (1963): 491–523.
West, Elizabeth Howard, "Southern Opposition to the Annexation of Texas," *Southwestern Historical Quarterly* 18 (1914): 74–82.

Statehood, War, and Reconstruction / Chapters 7, 8, 9

There is no adequate general survey of the period of early statehood. Ernest Wallace, *Texas in Turmoil* (Austin: Steck-Vaughn, 1965), the fourth volume of the *Saga of Texas* series has, however, a splendid coverage of the period from 1849 to 1875. One of the older general histories of the state particularly useful for this period is Dudley Wooten, *A Comprehensive History, 1685–1897*. 2 vols. (Dallas: W. G. Scarff, 1898).

There are a number of works on the Civil War period. Although none are definitive or outstanding, three are quite good:

Ashcroft, Allan C., *Texas in the Civil War: A Resumé History*. Austin: Texas Civil War Centennial Commission, 1962.
Farber, James, *Texas, C. S. A: A Spotlight on Disaster*. New York: Jackson, 1947.
Henderson, Harry McCorry, *Texas in the Confederacy*. San Antonio: Naylor, 1955.

Among the reminiscences and memoirs of the period, two are outstanding:

Reagan, John Henniger, *Memoirs: Wth Special Reference to Secession and the Civil War*, ed. Walter F. McCaleb. New York.: Neale, 1906.
Lubbock, Francis R., *Six Decades in Texas*, ed. C. W. Raines. Austin: B. C. Jones, 1900.

For the period of Reconstruction, Charles William Ramsdell's great work, *Reconstruction in Texas* (New York: Columbia University Press, 1910), has long been standard. It does not, of course, reflect the emendations of later revisionist historians. Nor does W. C. Nunn, *Texas under the Carpetbaggers* (Austin: University of Texas Press, 1962).

Works with more particular focus are listed below.

CHAPTER 7 / STATEHOOD

Early Years

The Mexican War

Barton, Henry W., "Five Texas Frontier Companies during the Mexican War." *Southwestern Historical Quarterly* 66 (1962): 17–30.
Brent, Robert A., "Nicholas P. Trist and the Treaty of Guadalupe Hidalgo," *Southwestern Historical Quarterly* 57 (1953): 454–74.
Fuller, John D. P., "Slavery Propaganda during the Mexican War," *Southwestern Historical Quarterly* 38 (1934): 235–45.
Fulmore, Z. T., "The Annexation of Texas and the Mexican War," *Southwestern Historical Quarterly* 5 (1901): 28–48.
Holland, James K., "Diary of a Texan Volunteer in the Mexican War," *Southwestern Historical Quarterly* 30 (1926): 1–33.
Moore, A. W., "A Reconnaissance in Texas in 1846," *Southwestern Historical Quarterly* 30 (1926): 252–71.
Nortrup, Jack, "Nicholas Trist's Misson to Mexico: A Reinterpretation," *Southwestern Historical Quarterly* 71 (1967): 321–46.
Reeves, Jesse S., *American Diplomacy under Tyler and Polk*. Baltimore: Johns Hopkins Press, 1907.
Sellers, Charles, *James K. Polk, Continentalist, 1843–1846*. Princeton: Princeton University, 1967. The second volume of a projected three-volume biography.
Smith, Justin, *The War with Mexico*, 2 vols. New York: Macmillan, 1919.
Stephenson, Nathaniel W., *Texas and the Mexican War: A Chronicle of the Winning of the Southwest*. New Haven: Yale University Press, 1921. Volume XXIV of the *Chronicles of America* series.

The Boundary Controversy

Baxter, S., "Texas and the Peace of Guadalupe Hidalgo," *Scribner's* (1878), pp. 868–78.

Binkley, William C., "The Question of Texan Jurisdiction in New Mexico under the United States, 1848-1850," *Southwestern Historical Quarterly* 24 (1920): 1-38.
Bowden, J. J., "The Texas-New Mexico Boundary Dispute along the Rio Grande," *Southwestern Historical Quarterly* 63 (1959): 221-38.
Cox, I. J., "The Southern Boundary of Texas," *Southwestern Historical Quarterly* 6 (1902): 81-102.
Dugan, Frank H., "The 1850 Affair of the Brownsville Separatists," *Southwestern Historical Quarterly* 61 (1957): 270-87.
Goetzmann, W. H., "The United States-Mexican Boundary Survey, 1848-1853," *Southwestern Historical Quarterly* 62 (1958): 164-90.
Hine, Robert V., *Bartlett's West: Drawing the Mexican Boundary*. New Haven: Yale University Press, 1968.
Neighbors, Kenneth F., "The Taylor-Neighbors Struggle over the Upper Rio Grande Region of Texas in 1850," *Southwestern Historical Quarterly* 61 (1957): 431-63.

The Compromise of 1850

Hamilton, Holman, *Prologue to Conflict*. Lexington: University of Kentucky Press, 1964.
Neighbors, Kenneth W., "The Expedition of Robert S. Neighbors to El Paso in 1849," *Southwestern Historical Quarterly* 58 (1954): 36-59.
————, ed., "The Report of the Expedition of Major Robert S. Neighbors to El Paso in 1849." *Southwestern Hstorical Quarterly* 60 (1956): 527-32.
Spillman, W. J., "Adjustment of the Texas Boundary in 1850," *Southwestern Historical Quarterly* 7 (1903): 177-95.

The Settlement of the Texas Debt

Gouge, William M., *The Fiscal History of Texas*. Philadelphia: Lippincott, 1852.

Political Developments

Biesele, R. L., "The Texas State Convention of Germans in 1854," *Southwestern Historical Quarterly* 33 (1929): 247-61.
Blount, Louis Foster, "A Brief Study of J. Pinckney Henderson Based on His Letters to His Brother David, 1835-1856," *Southwestern Historical Quarterly* 34 (1930): 181-202, 271-92.
Coyner, C. Luther, "Governor Bell's Record: A Correction," *Southwestern Historical Quarterly* 13 (1909): 325-27.
————, "Peter Hansborough Bell," *Southwestern Historical Quarterly* 3 (1899): 49-53.

Gary, Hampson, "General J. Pinckney Henderson," *Southwestern Historical Quarterly* 49 (1945): 282–86.
Sherman, S. H., "Governor George Thomas Wood," *Southwestern Historical Quarterly* 20 (1916): 260–68.
Wooster, Ralph A., "An Analysis of the Texas Know Nothings," *Southwestern Historical Quarterly* 70 (1966): 414–23.
_____, "Membership in Early Texas Legislatures, 1850–1860," *Southwestern Historical Quarterly* 69 (1965): 163–73.

The Frontier

Exploration

Bender, A. B., "Opening Routes across West Texas, 1848–1858," *Southwestern Historical Quarterly* 37 (1933): 116–35.
Erath, Lucy A., "Memoirs of Major George B. Erath," *Southwestern Historical Quarterly* 26 (1922): 207–33, 255–80; 27 (1923): 27–51, 140–63.
Greenwood, C. L., "Opening Routes to El Paso, 1849," *Southwestern Historical Quarterly* 48 (1944): 262–72.
Martin, Mabelle E., "California Emigrant Roads through Texas," *Southwestern Historical Quarterly* 18 (1914): 287–301.

The Indian Problem

Benedict, J. W., "Diary of a Campaign against the Comanches," *Southwestern Historical Quarterly* 32 (1928): 300–10.
Biesele, R. L., "The Relations between the German Settlers and the Indians in Texas, 1844–1860," *Southwestern Historical Quarterly* 31 (1927): 116–29.
Crimmins, Martin L., "Colonel George Croghan and the Indian Situation in Texas in 1847," *Southwestern Historical Quarterly* 56 (1952): 455–57.
_____, "Colonel Robert E. Lee's Report on Indian Combats in Texas," *Southwestern Historical Quarterly* 39 (1935): 21–32.
_____, "Fort McKavett, Texas," *Southwestern Historical Quarterly* 38 (1934): 28–39.
Foreman, Grant, "The Texas Comanche Treaty of 1846," *Southwestern Historical Quarterly* 51 (1947): 313–32.
Koch, Lena Clara, "Federal Indian Policy in Texas, 1845–1860," *Southwestern Historical Quarterly* 28 (1924): 223–34; 29 (1925): 19–35, 98–127.
Olmsted, Frederick L., *Journey through Texas*. New York, 1857; reprinted, with notes by James Howard, Austin: Von Boeckmann-Jones, 1962.

Expansion of the Frontier

Bender, A. B., "The Texas Frontier." *Southwestern Historical Quarterly* 38 (1934): 135–48.
Crane, R. C., "Some Aspects of the History of West and Northwest Texas since 1845," *Southwestern Historical Quarterly* 26 (1922): 30–43.
Crimmins, Martin L., "Col. J. K. F. Mansfield's Report of the Inspection of Texas in 1856," *Southwestern Historical Quarterly* 42 (1938): 122–248, 351–87.
―――――, ed., "Freeman's Report on the Eighth Military District," *Southwestern Historical Quarterly* 51 (1947): 54–58, 167–74, 252–58, 350–58; 52 (1948): 100–9, 227–34, 349–53, 444–47.
Day, James M., *Jacob de Cordova, Land Merchant of Texas*. Waco: Texian, 1962.
Fornell, Earl W., "Texas and the Filibusters of the 1850's," *Southwestern Historical Quarterly* 59 (1955): 411–28.
Jones, Billy Mac, *Health-Seekers in the Southwest, 1817–1900*. Norman: University of Oklahoma Press, 1967.
Shearer, Ernest W., "The Callahan Expedition, 1855," *Southwestern Historical Quarterly* 54 (1950): 430–51.
Tyler, Ronnie G., "The Callahan Expedition of 1855: Indians or Negroes?" *Southwestern Historical Quarterly* 70 (1966): 574–85.

The People of Texas

The Population

Connor, Seymour V., "A Statistical Review of the Settlement of the Peters Colony," *Southwestern Historical Quarterly* 57 (1953): 38–64.
Rijebian, Ermance V., "La Reunion: The French Colony in Dallas County," *Southwestern Historical Quarterly* 43 (1939): 472–78.
Wooster, Ralph A., "Foreigners in the Principal Towns of Ante-Bellum Texas," *Southwestern Historical Quarterly* 66 (1962): 208–20.

Social and Cultural Aspects

Arneson, Axel, "Norwegian Settlements in Texas," *Southwestern Historical Quarterly* 45 (1941): 125–35.
Banks, C. Stanley, "The Morman Migration into Texas," *Southwestern Historical Quarterly* 49 (1945): 233–44.
Bollaert, William, *William Bollaert's Texas*, ed. William Eugene Hollon and Ruth Lapham Butler. Norman: University of Oklahoma Press, 1956.
Bracht, Viktor, *Texas in 1848*, trans. C. F. Schmidt. San Antonio: Naylor, 1931.
Christensen, Thomas P., "Danevang, Texas," *Southwestern Historical Quarterly* 32 (1928): 67–73.

Dworaczyk, Edward J., *The First Polish Colonies of America in Texas*. San Antonio: Naylor, 1936.
Friend, Llerena B., "The Texan of 1860," *Southwestern Historical Quarterly* 62 (1958): 1–17.
Gaillardet, Theodore Frederic, *Sketches of Early Texas and Louisiana*, trans. James L. Sheppard III. Austin: University of Texas Press, 1966.
Jones, Billy Mac, "Health Seekers in Early Anglo-American Texas," *Southwestern Historical Quarterly* 69 (1965): 287–99.
Linn, John J., *Reminiscences of Fifty Years in Texas*. New York: D. & J. Sadlier, 1883; reprinted Austin: Steck, 1935.
Reinhardt, Louis, "The Communistic Colony of Bettina, 1846–1848," *Southwestern Historical Quarterly* 3 (1899): 33–40.
Renick, Dorothy W., "The City of Kent," *Southwestern Historical Quarterly* 29 (1925): 51–65.
Schmidt, C. F., "Viktor Frederich Bracht: A Texas Pioneer," *Southwestern Historical Quarterly* 35 (1931): 279–89.
Schmitz, Joseph, "Impressions of Texas in 1860," *Southwestern Historical Quarterly* 42 (1938): 334–50.
Schmitz, Joseph William, *Texas Culture in the Days of the Republic, 1836–1846*. San Antonio: Naylor, 1960.

Economy

Transportation

Briscoe, P., "The First Texas Railroad," *Southwestern Historical Quarterly* 7 (1903): 279–85.
Connelly, Thomas L., "The American Camel Experiment: A Reappraisal," *Southwestern Historical Quarterly* 69 (1965): 442–62.
Davenport, Harbert, "Notes on Early Steamboating on the Rio Grande," *Southwestern Historical Quarterly* 49 (1945): 286–89.
Fornell, Earl, "A Cargo of Camels in Galveston," *Southwestern Historical Quarterly* 59 (1955): 40–45.
Lammons, Frank Bishop, "Operation Camel: An Experiment in Animal Transportation in Texas, 1857–1860," *Southwestern Historical Quarterly* 61 (1957): 20–50.
Lesley, Lewis B., "The Purchase and Importation of Camels by the United States Government, 1855–1857," *Southwestern Historical Quarterly* 33 (1929): 13–33.
Mahon, Emmie Giddings, and Chester Kielman, "George H. Giddings and the San Antonio-San Diego Mail Line," *Southwestern Historical Quarterly* 61 (1957): 220–39.
McKay, Seth Sheperd, "Texas and the Southern Pacific Railroad, 1848–1860," *Southwestern Historical Quarterly* 35 (1931): 1–27.
Muir, Andrew Forest, "Railroads Come to Houston, 1857–1861," *Southwestern Historical Quarterly* 64 (1960): 42–63.

Santleben, August, *A Texas Pioneer*. New York: Neal, 1910; reprinted Waco: Morrison, 1967.
Williams, J. W., "The Butterfield Overland Mail Road across Texas," *Southwestern Historical Quarterly* 61 (1957): 1–19.

Slavery and the Plantation System

Barker, Eugene C., "The African Slave Trade in Texas," *Southwestern Historical Quarterly* 6 (1902): 145–58.
Curlee, Abigail, "The History of a Texas Slave Plantation, 1831–1863," *Southwestern Historical Quarterly* 26 (1922): 79–127.
Fornell, Earl W., "The Abduction of Free Negroes and Slaves in Texas," *Southwestern Historical Quarterly* 60 (1956): 369–80.
―――――, "Agitation in Texas for Reopening the Slave Trade," *Southwestern Historical Quarterly* 60 (1956): 245–59.
Wooster, Ralph A., "Notes on Texas' Largest Slaveholders," *Southwestern Historical Quarterly* 65 (1961): 72–79.

CHAPTER 8 / SECESSION AND CIVIL WAR

Secession

The Constitutional Issue

Boucher, Chauncey S., "In Re That Aggressive Slaveocracy," *Mississippi Valley Historical Review* 8 (1921).
Ramsdell, Charles W., "The Natural Limits of Slavery Expansion," *Southwestern Historical Quarterly* 33 (1929): 91–111.

Secession Sentiment in Texas Politics

Dunn, Roy Sylvan, "The KGC in Texas, 1860–1861," *Southwestern Historical Quarterly* 70 (1966): 543–73.
Sandbo, Anna I., "Beginnings of the Secession Movement in Texas," *Southwestern Historical Quarterly* 18 (1914): 41–73.
Steen, Ralph, "Texas Newspapers and Lincoln," *Southwestern Historical Quarterly* 51 (1947): 199–212.

The Mounting Tempo of Secession

Bridges, C. A., "The Knights of the Golden Circle," *Southwestern Historical Quarterly* 44 (1940): 287–302.
Friend, Llerena, *Sam Houston: The Great Designer*. Austin: University of Texas Press, 1954.
Gage, Larry Jay, "The City of Austin on the Eve of the Civil War," *Southwestern Historical Quarterly* 63 (1959): 428–38.

———, "The Texas Road to Secession and War: John Marshall and the Texas State Gazette," *Southwestern Historical Quarterly* 62 (1958): 191–227.
Maher, Edward R., "Sam Houston and Secession," *Southwestern Historical Quarterly* 55 (1951): 448–58.
White, W. W., "The Texas Slave Insurrection in 1860," *Southwestern Historical Quarterly* 52 (1948): 259–85.

The Secession Convention

Oates, Stephen B., "Texas under the Secessionists," *Southwestern Historical Quarterly* 67 (1963): 167–212.
Sandbo, Anna I., "The First Session of the Secession Convention of Texas," *Southwestern Historical Quarterly* 18 (1914): 162–94.
Winkler, Ernest William, ed., *Journal of the Secession Convention of Texas, 1861*. Austin: Austin Printing Co. for the Texas Library and Historical Commission State Library, 1912.
Wooster, Ralph A., "Analysis of the Membership of the Texas Secession Convention," *Southwestern Historical Quarterly* 62 (1958): 322–35.

Military Affairs

Early Offensives

Colton, Ray C., *The Civil War in the Western Territories*. Norman: University of Oklahoma Press, 1959.
Crimmins, Martin L., "An Episode in the Texas Career of General David E. Twiggs," *Southwestern Historical Quarterly* 41 (1937): 167–73.
Hall, Martin Hardwick, *Sibley's New Mexico Campaign*. Austin: University of Texas Press, 1960.
Kerby, Robert Lee, *Confederate Invasion of New Mexico and Arizona, 1861–1862*. Los Angeles: Westernlore, 1958.
Mitchell, Leon, Jr., "Camp Ford: Confederate Military Prison," *Southwestern Historical Quarterly* 66 (1962): 1–16.
———, "Camp Groce: Confederate Military Prison," *Southwestern Historical Quarterly* 67 (1963): 15–21.
Oates, Stephen B., *Confederate Cavalry West of the River*. Austin: University of Texas Press, 1961.
Pool, William C., "The Battle of Dove Creek," *Southwestern Historical Quarterly* 53 (1949): 367–85.
Rippy, J. Fred, "Mexican Projects of the Confederates," *Southwestern Historical Quarterly* 22 (1918): 291–317.
Watford, W. H., "Confederate Western Ambitions," *Southwestern Historical Quarterly* 44 (1940): 161–88.

The Defense of the Coast

Barr, Alwyn, "The Battle of Calcasieu Pass," *Southwestern Historical Quarterly* 66 (1962): 59–67.
──────, "Texas Coastal Defense, 1861–1865," *Southwestern Historical Quarterly* 65 (1961): 1–31.
Cumberland, C. C., "The Confederate Loss and Recapture of Galveston," *Southwestern Historical Quarterly* 51 (1947): 109–30.
Fitzhugh, Lester N., "Saluria, Fort Esperanza, and Military Operations on the Texas Coast, 1861–1864," *Southwestern Historical Quarterly* 61 (1957): 66–100.
Jones, Allen W., "Military Events in Texas during the Civil War, 1861–1865," *Southwestern Historical Quarterly* 64 (1960): 64–70.
Shook, Robert W., "The Battle of the Neches, August 10, 1862," *Southwestern Historical Quarterly* 64 (1962): 31–42.
Tolbert, Frank X., *Dick Dowling at Sabine Pass*. New York: McGraw-Hill, 1962.
Trexler, H. A., "The *Harriet Lane* and the Blockade of Galveston," *Southwestern Historical Quarterly* 35 (1931): 109–23.
Young, Jo, "The Battle of Sabine Pass," *Southwestern Historical Quarterly* 52 (1948): 398–410.

Texans at the Other Fronts

Anderson, John Q., ed., *Campaigning with Parsons' Texas Cavalry Brigade, C. S. A.: The War Journals and Letters of the Four Orr Brothers, 12th Texas Cavalry Regiment*. Hillsboro, Texas: Hill Junior College, 1967.
Chilton, F. B., comp., *Hood's Texas Brigade*. Houston: n. p., 1911.
Fitzhugh, Lester N., comp., *Texas Batteries, Battalions, Regiments, Commanders, and Field Officers, Confederate States Army, 1861–1865*. Lancaster, Texas: Mirror Press of Midlothian, Texas, 1959.
Jeffries, C. C., *Terry's Rangers*. New York: Vantage Press, 1961.
Oates, Stephen B., "Recruiting Confederate Cavalry in Texas," *Southwestern Historical Quarterly* 64 (1960): 463–77.
Rose, Victor M., *Ross' Texas Brigade*. Kennesaw, Ga.: Continental Book Co., 1960.
Ulmer, J. B., "A Glimpse of Albert Sidney Johnston through the Smoke of Shiloh," *Southwestern Historical Quarterly* 10 (1906): 285–96.

Domestic Affairs

State Politics

Estill, Mary S., ed., "Diary of a Confederate Congressman, 1862–1863," *Southwestern Historical Quarterly* 38 (1934): 270–301; 39 (1935): 33–65.

Gcise, William R., "Missouri's Confederate Capital in Marshall, Texas," *Southwestern Historical Quarterly* 66 (1962): 193–207.
Holliday, Florence E., "The Powers of the Commander of the Confederate Trans-Mississippi Department, 1863–1865," *Southwestern Historical Quarterly* 21 (1917): 279–98, 333–59.
King, Alma D., "The Political Career of Williamson Simpson Oldham," *Southwestern Historical Quarterly* 33 (1929): 112–33.
Miller, E. T., "The State Finances of Texas during the Civil War," *Southwestern Historical Quarterly* 14 (1910): 1–23.
Vandiver, Frank E., "Letters from the Confederate Military Service in Texas, 1863–1865," *Southwestern Historical Quarterly* 55 (1951): 378–93.

The Military Board and the Effort to Finance the War

Ashcraft, Allan C., "Confederate Beef Packing at Jefferson, Texas," *Southwestern Historical Quarterly* 68 (1964): 259–70.
Delaney, Robert W., "Matamoros, Port for Texas during the Civil War," *Southwestern Historical Quarterly* 58 (1954): 473–87.
Vandiver, Frank, "Texas and the Confederate Army's Meat Problem," *Southwestern Historical Quarterly* 48 (1944): 225–33.

Union Sentiment in Texas

Elliott, Claude, "Union Sentiment in Texas, 1861–1865," *Southwestern Historical Quarterly* 50 (1946): 449–77.
Havins, T. R., "Administration of the Sequestration Act in the Confederate District Court for the Western District of Texas," *Southwestern Historical Quarterly* 43 (1939): 295–322.
Smyrl, Frank H., "Texans in the Union Army, 1861–1865," *Southwestern Historical Quarterly* 65 (1961): 234–50.
————, "Unionism in Texas, 1856–1861," *Southwestern Historical Quarterly* 68 (1964): 29–42.

Domestic Hardships

Davis, Edwin Adams, *Fallen Guidon: The Forgotten Saga of General Jo Selby's Confederate Command, the Brigade that Never Surrendered, and Its Expedition to Mexico*. Santa Fe: Stage Coach Press, 1962.
Hill, Lawrence F., "The Confederate Exodus to Latin America," *Southwestern Historical Quarterly* 39 (1935): 100–34, 161–99, 309–26.
Nunn, W. C., *Escape from Reconstruction*. Fort Worth: Leo Potishman Foundation, 1956.

CHAPTER 9 / RECONSTRUCTION AND REACTION

Reconstruction

Presidential Reconstruction

McCaleb, Walter R., "John H. Reagan," *Southwestern Historical Quarterly* 9 (1905): 41–50.
Ramsdell, Charles W., "Texas from the Fall of the Confederacy to the Beginning of Reconstruction," *Southwestern Historical Quarterly* 11 (1907): 199–219.
Roberts, O. M., "The Experiences of an Unrecognized Senator," *Southwestern Historical Quarterly* 12 (1908): 87–147.

Congressional Reconstruction

Elliott, Claude, "The Freedman's Bureau in Texas," *Southwestern Historical Quarterly* 56 (1952): 1–24.
Miller, E. T., "Repudiation of State Debt in Texas since 1861," *Southwestern Historical Quarterly* 16 (1912): 169–83.

Radical Rule

Dimick, H. T., "The Bonfoey Case at Marshall," *Southwestern Historical Quarterly* 48 (1944): 469–83.
Holland, J. K., "Freedman in the Legislature," *Southwestern Historical Quarterly* 1 (1897): 125–26.
McConnell, Weston Joseph, *Social Cleavages in Texas*. New York: Columbia University Press, 1925.
Miller, E. T., "The State Finances of Texas during Reconstruction," *Southwestern Historical Quarterly* 14 (1910): 87–112.
Norvell, James R., "The Reconstruction Courts of Texas, 1867–1873," *Southwestern Historical Quarterly* 62 (1958): 141–63.
Russ, William A., "Radical Disfranchisement in Texas, 1867–1876," *Southwestern Historical Quarterly* 28 (1924): 40–52.
Singletary, Otis A., *Negro Militia and Reconstruction*. Austin: University of Texas Press, 1957.

Reaction

The Election of Coke

Wheeler, T. B., "Reminiscences of Reconstruction in Texas," *Southwestern Historical Quarterly* 11 (1907): 56–65.
Wood, W. D., "The Ku Klux Klan," *Southwestern Historical Quarterly* 9 (1905): 262–68.

Coke and the New Constitution

Ericson, J. E., "Delegates to the Texas Constitutional Convention of 1875: A Reappraisal," *Southwestern Historical Quarterly* 67 (1963): 22–27.
McKay, Seth Shepard, *Seven Decades of the Texas Constitution of 1876*. Lubbock: Texas Technological College Press, 1943.
Ogletree, D. W., "Establishing the Court of Appeals, 1875–1876," *Southwestern Historical Quarterly* 47 (1943): 5–18.

Lawlessness

The Aftermath of War

Dohney, E. L., "Arrest of R. L. Robertson in 1865," *Southwestern Historical Quarterly* 12 (1908): 317–19.
Ford, John S., "Fight on the Frio, July 4, 1865," *Southwestern Historical Quarterly* 1 (1897): 118–24.
Singletary, Otis A., "The Texas Militia during Reconstruction," *Southwestern Historical Quarterly* 60 (1956): 23–35.

Feudin' and Fightin'

Sonnichsen, Charles Leland, *Ten Texas Feuds*. Albuquerque: University of New Mexico Press, 1957.

The Texas Rangers

Douglas, Claude Leroy, *The Gentlemen in the White Hats, Dramatic Episodes in the History of the Texas Rangers*. Dallas: Southwest Press, 1934.
Durham, George, as told to Clyde Wantland, *Taming the Nueces Strip: The Story of McNelly's Rangers*. Austin: University of Texas Press, 1962.
Sonnichsen, C. L., *The El Paso Salt War*. El Paso: Texas Western College, 1961.
Webb, Walter Prescott, *The Texas Rangers*. Boston: Houghton Mifflin, 1935.

The Late Nineteenth Century / Chapters 10 and 11

The best single volume covering this period is Billy Mac Jones, *The Search for Maturity* (Austin: Steck-Vaughn, 1965), the fifth book in the *Saga of Texas* series. The best coverage of the politics is Chester Alwyn Barr, *Texas Politics, 1876–1906* (Austin: University of Texas Press, 1971). Other works of great value to the political history of the period include:

Farrow, Marion Humphreys, *The Texas Democrats: Early Democratic History in Texas.* San Antonio: Naylor, 1944.
Moreland, Sinclair, *Governor's Messages: Coke to Ross, 1874–1891.* Austin: Texas State Library, 1916.
Winkler, Ernest W., *Platforms of Political Parties in Texas.* Austin: University of Texas Press, 1916.

The last quarter of the nineteenth century witnessed two major recessions as well as economic recovery from Civil War and Reconstruction. Edmund T. Miller, *A Financial History of Texas* (Austin: University of Texas Press, 1916), is a great aid to the understanding of the economy of Texas at that time.

Literature of the frontier and of the cattle industry is itemized in the appropriate categories below.

CHAPTER 10 / THE FRONTIER

Indian Wars and Buffalo Hunters

The War Years

Ewing, Floyd F., "Suggestions for the Observance in West Texas of the Civil War Centennial," *West Texas Historical Assn. Yearbook* 36 (1960): 33–40.
Haley, J. Evetts, "The Comanchero Trade," *Southwestern Historical Quarterly* 38 (1934): 157–76.
Matthews, Sallie Reynolds, *Interwoven: A Pioneer Chronicle.* Houston: Anson Jones, 1936; reprinted El Paso: Carl Hertzog, 1958.

The Postwar Decade

Barton, Henry W., "The United States Cavalry and the Texas Rangers," *Southwestern Historical Quarterly* 63 (1959): 495–510.
Bierschwale, Margaret, *Fort McKavett, Texas, Post on the San Sabá.* Salado, Texas: Anson Jones, 1966.
Carroll, H. Bailey, "Nolan's 'Lost Nigger' Expedition of 1877," *Southwestern Historical Quarterly* 44 (1940): 55–75.
Ellis, L. Tuffley, ed., "Lt. A. W. Greely's Report on the Installation of Military Telegraph Lines in Texas, 1875–1876," *Southwestern Historical Quarterly* 69 (1965): 66–87.
Haley, James Evetts, *Fort Concho and the Texas Frontier.* San Angelo: San Angelo Standard Times, 1952.
Havins, T. R., *Camp Colorado: A Decade of Frontier Defense.* Brownwood: Brown Press, 1964.

Leckie, William, *The Buffalo Soldiers*. Norman: University of Oklahoma Press, 1967.
Porter, Kenneth Wiggins, "The Seminole Indian Scouts, 1870–1881," *Southwestern Historical Quarterly* 55 (1951): 358–77.
Rister, Carl Coke, *Fort Griffin on the Texas Frontier*. Norman: University of Oklahoma Press, 1956.
―――, "Significance of the Jackboro Indian Affair of 1871," *Southwestern Historical Quarterly* 29 (1925): 181–200.
Simpson, Harold B., et al., *Frontier Forts of Texas*. Waco: Texian Press, 1966.
Wallace, Edward S., "General Ranald Slidell MacKenzie—Indian Fighting Cavalryman," *Southwestern Historical Quarterly* 56 (1952): 378–96.
Wallace, Ernest, *Ranald S. MacKenzie on the Texas Frontier*. Lubbock: West Texas Museum, 1964.
Whitehurst, A., "Reminiscences of the Schnively Expedition of 1867," *Southwestern Historical Quarterly* 8 (1904): 267–71.

The Buffalo Hunters

Gard, Wayne, *The Great Buffalo Hunt*. New York: Knopf, 1959.
―――, "The Mooar Brothers, Buffalo Hunters," *Southwestern Historical Quarterly* 63 (1959): 31–45.
Nunn, W. C., "Eighty-Six Hours without Water on the Texas Plains," *Southwestern Historical Quarterly* 43 (1939): 356–64.
Rister, Carl Coke, "Significance of the Destruction of the Buffalo in the Southwest," *Southwestern Historical Quarterly* 33 (1929): 34–49.
Sandoz, Mari, *The Buffalo Hunters*. New York: Hastings House, 1954.

The Rise of the Cattle Industry

The Antecedents of the Boom

Dobie, J. Frank, "The First Cattle in Texas and the Southwest Progenitors of the Longhorns," *Southwestern Historical Quarterly* 42 (1938): 171–97.
Love, Clara M., "History of the Cattle Industry in the Southwest," *Southwestern Quarterly* 19 (1915): 370–99.

The Era of the Great Trail Drives

Bell, James G., "Log at the Texas-California Trail," ed. J. Evetts Haley, *Southwestern Historical Quarterly* 35 (1931): 208–37.
Gard, Wayne, "The Impact of the Cattle Trails," *Southwestern Historical Quarterly* 71 (1967): 1–6.
―――, "The Shawnee Trail," *Southwestern Historical Quarterly* 56 (1952): 359–77.

Herrington, George Squires, "An Early Day Cattle Drive from Texas to Illinois," *Southwestern Historical Quarterly* 55 (1951): 267–69.
Sanderlin, Walter S., ed., "A Cattle Drive from Texas to California: The Diary of Milt Erskine, 1854," *Southwestern Historical Quarterly* 67 (1963): 397–412.
Shelton, Emily J., "Lizzie E. Johnson: A Cattle Queen of Texas," *Southwestern Historical Quarterly* 50 (1946): 349–66.
Skaggs, Jimmy M., "The Economic Impact of Trailing: One Aspect," *West Texas Historical Assn. Yearbook* 43 (1967): 18–30.
―――――, "John Thomas Lytle: Cattle Baron," *Southwestern Historical Quarterly* 71 (1967): 46–60.

The Spread of the Cattle Kingdom

Havins, T. R., "Texas Fever," *Southwestern Historical Quarterly* 52 (1948): 147–62.
Hollon, Gene, "Captain Charles Schreiner, the Father of the Hill Country," *Southwestern Historical Quarterly* 48 (1944): 145–68.
McCallum, Henry D., "Barbed Wire in Texas," *Southwestern Historical Quarterly* 61 (1957): 207–19.
Rippy, J. Fred, "British Investments in Texas Lands and Livestock," *Southwestern Historical Quarterly* 58 (1954): 331–41.
Schreiner, Charles, III, "The Background and Development of Brahman Cattle in Texas," *Southwestern Historical Quarterly* 52 (1948): 427–33.
Utley, Robert M., "The Range Cattle Industry in the Big Bend of Texas," *Southwestern Historical Quarterly* 69 (1965): 419–41.

Frontier Settlement

The Advance of the Frontier

Biggers, Don Hampton, *From Cattle Range to Cotton Patch*. Abilene: Abilene Printing Co., 1905; reprinted Bandera, Texas: Frontier Times, 1944.
Holden, William Curry, *Alkali Trails, or, Social and Economic Movements of the Texas Frontier, 1846–1900*. Dallas: Southwest Press, 1930.
―――――, "Frontier Journalism in West Texas," *Southwestern Historical Quarterly* 32 (1928): 206–21.
―――――, "West Texas Drouths," *Southwestern Historical Quarterly* 32 (1928): 103–23.
Madison, Virginia, *The Big Bend Country of Texas*. Albuquerque: University of New Mexico Press, 1955.
Rayburn, John C., "The Rainmakers in Duval," *Southwestern Historical Quarterly* 61 (1957): 101–15.

Frontier Conflicts

Conger, Roger, "Fencing in McLennan County," *Southwestern Historical Quarterly* 59 (1955): 215–21.

Gard, Wayne, "The Fence Cutters," *Southwestern Historical Quarterly* 51 (1947): 1–15.

Holden, William Curry, "Law and Lawlessness on the Texas Frontier, 1875–1900," *Southwestern Historical Quarterly* 44 (1940): 188–203.

The Closed Range

Burton, Harley True, "A History of the JA Ranch," *Southwestern Historical Quarterly* 31 (1927): 89–115, 221–60, 325–64; 32 (1928): 29–66.

Connor, Seymour V., "Early Land Speculation in West Texas," *Southwestern Social Science Quarterly* 41 (1962): 354–62.

Duke, Cordia Sloan, and Joe B. Frantz, *6,000 Miles of Fence: Life on the XIT Ranch of Texas*. Austin: University of Texas Press, 1961.

Eaves, Charles Dudley, "Charles William Post, the Rainmaker," *Southwestern Historical Quarterly* 43 (1939): 425–37.

———, "Colonization Activities of Charles William Post," *Southwestern Historical Quarterly* 43 (1939): 72–84.

Gracy, David B., II, *Littlefield Lands, Colonization on the Texas Plains, 1912–1920*. Austin: University of Texas Press, 1968.

Haley, J. Evetts, "Grass Lease Fight and Attempted Impeachment of the First Panhandle Judge," *Southwestern Historical Quarterly* 38 (1934): 1–27.

———, *The XIT Ranch of Texas and the Early Days of the Llano Estacado*. Chicago: Lakeside, 1929; revised, Norman: University of Oklahoma Press, 1953.

Havins, T. R., "The Passing of the Longhorns," *Southwestern Historical Quarterly* 56 (1952): 51–58.

Holden, William Curry, "The Problem of Hands on the Spur Ranch," *Southwestern Historical Quarterly* 35 (1931): 194–207.

———, "The Problem of Maintaining the Solid Range on the Spur Ranch," *Southwestern Historical Quarterly* 34 (1930): 1–19.

Lea, Tom, *The King Ranch*, 2 vols. Boston: Little, Brown, 1957.

McCallum, Henry D., and Frances T. McCallum, *Barbed Wire*. Norman: University of Oklahoma Press, 1965.

Pearce, William M., *The Matador Land and Cattle Company*. Norman: University of Oklahoma Press, 1964.

Rickard, J. A., "Hazards of Ranching on the South Plains," *Southwestern Historical Quarterly* 37 (1933): 313–19.

Sheffy, Lester Fields, *The Franklyn Land and Cattle Company, 1882–1957*. Austin: University of Texas Press, 1963.

Stephens, Ray A., *The Taft Ranch: A Texas Principality.* Austin: University of Texas Press, 1964.
Williams, J. W., *The Big Ranch Country.* Wichita Falls: Terry Bros., 1954.

CHAPTER 11 / RECOVERY AND REFORM

Economic Developments

Introduction

Spratt, John S., *The Road to Spindletop: Economic Changes in Texas, 1875–1901.* Dallas: Southern Methodist University Press, 1955.

Railroad Construction

Armstrong, A. B., "Origins of the Texas and Pacific Railway," *Southwestern Historical Quarterly* 56 (1952): 489–97.
Clark, Ira G., *Then Came the Railroads: The Century from Steam to Diesel in the Southwest.* Norman: University of Oklahoma Press, 1958.
Everett, Donald E., "San Antonio Welcomes the 'Sunset'—1877," *Southwestern Historical Quarterly* 65 (1961): 47–60.
Peterson, Robert L., "Jay Gould and the Railroad Commission of Texas," *Southwestern Historical Quarterly* 58 (1954): 422–31.
Rayburn, John C., "Count Joseph Telferner and the New York, Texas, and Mexican Railway Company," *Southwestern Historical Quarterly* 68 (1964): 29–42.
Reed, S. G., *A History of Texas Railroads.* Houston: St. Clair Publishing Co., 1941.

Industrial Developments

Acheson, Sam, *35,000 Days in Texas: A History of the Dallas News and Its Forbears.* New York: Macmillan, 1938.
Dugas, Vera, "Texas Industry, 1860–1880," *Southwestern Historical Quarterly* 59 (1955): 151–83.
Henderson, Dwight F., "The Texas Coal Mining Industry," *Southwestern Historical Quarterly* 68 (1964): 207–19.
Jones, Robert L., "The First Iron Furnace in Texas," *Southwestern Historical Quarterly* 63 (1959): 279–89.
Lasswell, Mary, *John Henry Kirby: Prince of the Pines.* Austin: Encino Press, 1967.
Merchants Association of New York, *The Natural Resources and Economic Conditions of the State of Texas.* n.p., 1901.

Reese, James V., "The Early History of Labor Organizations in Texas, 1838–1876," *Southwestern Historical Quarterly* 72 (1968): 1–20.
Spratt, John S., *The Road to Spindletop: Economic Change in Texas, 1875–1901*. Dallas: Southern Methodist University Press, 1955.
Stephens, A. Ray, "D. A. Orviss: Texas Merchant," *Southwestern Historical Quarterly* 65 (1961): 32–46.

Farming

Hunt, Robert Lee, *A History of Farmer Movements in the Southwest, 1873–1925*. n.p., n.d.
Smith, Ralph, "The Farmers Alliance in Texas, 1875–1900," *Southwestern Historical Quarterly* 48 (1944): 346–69.
―――――, "The Grange Movement in Texas, 1873–1900," *Southwestern Historical Quarterly* 42 (1938): 297–315.
Waller, J. L., "The Overland Movement of Cotton, 1866–1886," *Southwestern Historical Quarterly* 35 (1931): 137–45.

Recovery and Protest

The Politics of Recovery

Ramsdell, Charles W., ed., "Memoirs of a Texas Land Commissioner," *Southwestern Historical Quarterly* 44 (1940): 481–97.
Wooten, Dudley G., "The Life and Services of Oran Milo Roberts," *Southwestern Historical Quarterly* 2 (1898): 1–20.

The Voices of Protest

Allen, Ruth, *Chapters in the History of Organized Labor in Texas*. Austin: University of Texas Bureau of Research in the Social Sciences, 1941.
Martin, Roscoe C., "Greenback Party in Texas," *Southwestern Historical Quarterly* 30 (1926): 161–77.
Smith, Ralph, "The Co-operative Movement in Texas, 1870–1900," *Southwestern Historical Quarterly* 44 (1940): 35–54.

The Politics of Reform

The Beginnings of Reform

Martin, Roscoe C., *The Peoples Party in Texas*. Austin: University of Texas Press, 1933.

Potts, Charles S., "Texas Stock and Bond Law," *Annals of the American Academy of Political and Social Science*, 1914.

Hogg and Commission

Cotner, Robert Crawford. *Joseph Stephen Hogg*. Austin: University of Texas Press, 1959.

Crane, M. M., "Recollections of the Establishment of the Texas Railroad Commission," *Southwestern Historical Quarterly* 50 (1946): 478–86.

Norvell, James R., "The Railroad Commission of Texas: Its Origin and History," *Southwestern Historical Quarterly* 68 (1964): 465–80.

The End of the Century

Billington, Monroe, "Red River Boundary Controversy," *Southwestern Historical Quarterly* 62 (1958): 356–63.

Casdorph, Paul Douglas, "Norris Wright Cuney and Texas Republican Politics, 1883–1896," *Southwestern Historical Quarterly* 68 (1964): 455–64.

Chapman, Berlin B., "The Claim of Texas to Greer County," *Southwestern Historical Quarterly* 53 (1949): 19–34, 164–79, 404–21.

Hare, Maud Cuney, *Norris Wright Cuney: A Tribune of the Black People*. New York: Crisis, 1913.

Madden, J. W., *Charles A. Culberson*. Austin: Gammel's Book Store, 1929.

Proctor, Ben H., *Not without Honor: The Life of John H. Reagan*. Austin: University of Texas Press, 1962.

Richardson, Rupert N., *Colonel Edward M. House: The Texas Years, 1858–1912*. Abilene: Hardin-Simmons University, 1964.

―――――, "Edward M. House and the Governors of Texas," *Southwestern Historical Quarterly* 61 (1957): 51–65.

Social Developments

Demographic Changes

Kerr, Homer L., "Migration into Texas, 1860–1880," *Southwestern Historical Quarterly* 70 (1966): 184–216.

Educational Developments

Battle, W. J., "A Concise History of the University of Texas, 1883–1950," *Southwestern Historical Quarterly* 54 (1950): 391–411.

Bragg, J. D., "Baylor University, 1851–1861," *Southwestern Historical Quarterly* 49 (1945): 51–56.

Ferguson, Dan, "Forerunners of Baylor," *Southwestern Historical Quarterly* 49 (1945): 35–50.

Roberts, O. M., "History of the Establishment of the University of the State of Texas," *Southwestern Historical Quarterly* 1 (1897): 233–65.
Thompson, E. Bruce, "William Carey Crane and Texas Education," *Southwestern Historical Quarterly* 58 (1954): 405–21.
Vandiver, Frank E., "John William Mallet and the University of Texas," *Southwestern Historical Quarterly* 53 (1949): 422–42.
Vinson, Robert E., "The University Crosses the Bar," *Southwestern Historical Quarterly* 48 (1944): 281–94.
Wolfskill, George, "William Carey Crane and the University of Texas," *Southwestern Historical Quarterly* 54 (1950): 190–203.

The Texas Statehouse

Allen, Ruth A., "The Capitol Boycott," *Southwestern Historical Quarterly* 42 (1938): 316–26.
Rathjen, Frederick W., "The Texas State House," *Southwestern Historical Quarterly* 60 (1956): 433–62.

The Twentieth Century / Chapters 12, 13, and 14

The leading historical works on the twentieth century are Seth Shepard McKay's studies of politics. These books have not received the attention they deserve, but they are objective and definitive. *Texas Politics, 1906–1944: With Special References to the German Counties* (Lubbock: Texas Tech Press, 1952) is the most useful. *W. Lee O'Daniel and Texas Politics, 1938–1942* (Lubbock: Texas Tech Press, 1944) was an earlier compilation and is more detailed. *Texas and the Fair Deal, 1945–1952* (San Antonio: Naylor, 1954) is remarkably objective. *Texas after Spindletop*, written with Odie B. Faulk (Austin: Steck-Vaughn, 1964), the sixth volume of the *Saga of Texas* series, summarizes all three works and brings the content up to 1964.

Ralph Steen, *Twentieth Century Texas: An Economic and Social History* (Austin: Steck, 1942) offers a broader view with less emphasis on politics, although the work shows a keen grasp of the essential political events up to World War II.

Other general works of value to a history of the politics of the twentieth century are listed below:

Adams, Frank C., ed., *A Centennial History of Politics and Personalities of the Democratic Party, 1836–1936*, 4 vols. Austin: Democratic Historical Assn., 1937.

Benton, Wilbourn E., *Texas: Its Government and Politics*. Englewood Cliffs, N.J.: Prentice-Hall, 1961.
Casdorph, Paul, *A History of the Republican Party in Texas, 1865–1965*. Austin: Pemberton, 1965.
Gantt, Fred, Jr., *The Chief Executive in Texas: A Study in Gubernatorial Leadership*. Austin: University of Texas Press, 1964.
Gantt, Fred., Jr., Irving O. Dawson, and Luther G. Hagard, Jr., *Governing Texas: Documents and Readings*, 2d ed. New York: Thomas Y. Crowell, 1970.
MacCorkle, Stuart A., and Dick Smith, *Texas Government*, 4th ed. New York: McGraw-Hill, 1960.
McClesky, Clifton, *The Government and Politics of Texas*. Boston: Little, Brown, 1963.
Marburger, Harold J., *Texas Elections, 1918–1954*. Austin: Texas State Library, 1956.
Patterson, Caleb Parry, Sam B. McAlister, and George C. Hester, *State and Local Government in Texas*. New York: Macmillan, 1948.
Soukup, James R., Clifton McClesky, and Harry Holloway, *Party and Factional Division in Texas*. Austin: University of Texas Press, 1964.
Utecht, Byron C., *The Legislature and the Texas People*. San Antonio: Naylor, 1937.

The venerable *Texas Almanac and State Industrial Guide* (Dallas: A. H. Belo) has been issued in this century for the years 1904, 1910, 1912, 1914, 1925–1928, and biennially thereafter, and is of incomparable value for contemporary factual and statistical data. Earlier years of the century are similarly treated in the yearbooks of the Department of Agriculture, Insurance, Statistics, and History (later the Department of Agriculture). The most outstanding of these are the *Yearbook for 1901* and *1903* edited by C. W. Raines.

Almost a plethora of works treating Texas tradition and social, cultural, and economic developments includes:

Bainbridge, John, *The Super Americans*. New York: Doubleday, 1961.
Fuermann, George, *Reluctant Empire*. New York: Doubleday, 1957.
Goodwyn, Frank, *Lone-Star Land: Twentieth Century Texas in Perspective*. New York: Knopf, 1955.
Nordyke, Lewis, *The Truth about Texas*. New York: Thomas Y. Crowell, 1957.
Perry, George Sessions, *Texas: A World in Itself*. New York: McGraw-Hill, 1942.
Peyton, Green, *The Face of Texas*. New York: Thomas Y. Crowell, 1961.
Phares, Ross, *Texas Tradition*. New York: Holt, 1954.
Schoffelmayer, Victor H., *Texas at the Crossroads*. Dallas: A. H. Belo, 1935.

Works of value to a history of the twentieth century with more specific focus are listed below under the subdivisions used in the chapters.

CHAPTER 12 / PROGRESSIVISM AND THE NEW FREEDOM

Progressivism in Texas

Campaigns and Candidates

Acheson, Sam Hanna, *Joe Bailey, the Last Democrat.* New York: Macmillan, 1938.
Adams, Frederick Upham, *The Waters-Pierce Case in Texas.* St. Louis: Skinner & Kennedy, 1908.
Alvard, Wayne, "T. L. Nugent, Texas Populist," *Southwestern Historical Quarterly* 57 (1953): 65-81.
Anti-Saloon League, *The Brewers and Texas Politics.* San Antonio, 1916.
Cocke, William A., *The Bailey Controversy in Texas.* San Antonio: Cocke, 1908.
Davenport, J. H., *The History of the Supreme Court of the State of Texas.* Austin: Southern Law Book Publishers, 1917.
George, Alexander L., and Juliette L. George, *Woodrow Wilson and Colonel House: A Personality Story.* New York: John Day, 1956.
Ivy, H. A., *Rum on the Run in Texas.* Dallas: Temperance Publishing Co., 1910.
King, C. Richard, "Woodrow Wilson's Visit to Texas in 1911," *Southwestern Historical Quarterly* 65 (1961): 184-95.
Kittrell, Norman G., *Governors Who Have Been and Other Public Men of Texas.* Houston: Dealy-Adey-Elgin, 1921.
Link, Arthur, "The Wilson Movement in Texas, 1910-1912," *Southwestern Historical Quarterly* 48 (1944): 169-85.
MacCorkle, Stuart A., "The Pardoning Power in Texas," *Southwestern Social Science Quarterly* 15 (1934): 218-28.
Seymour, Charles, *The Intimate Papers of Colonel House,* 2 vols. New York: Houghton Mifflin, 1926.
Simmons, D. E., ed., *Statewide Prohibition Handbook.* Houston: 1911.
Smith, Arthur D. H., *Mr. House of Texas.* New York: Funk & Wagnalls, 1940.
Texas Merry Go Round. Houston: Sun Publishing, 1933.
Winkler, E. W., *Platforms of Political Parties in Texas.* Austin: State Publishing Co., 1916.

Progressive Measures

Tinsley, James A., "The Progressive Movement in Texas, 1900-1915," Ph.D. dissertation, University of Wisconsin, 1953. I have avoided listing unpublished material in this bibliography, but, because of the dearth of publications on the progressive era, this one is included.

Weeks, O. Douglas, "The Texas Primary System," in Frank C. Adams, ed., *Texas Democracy*. Austin: 1937, pp. 531–34.

Jim Ferguson

DeShields, James T., *The Fergusons, "Jim and Ma": The Stormy Petrels in Texas Politics*. Dallas: Cockrell Publishing Co., 1932.

Lomax, John A., "Governor Ferguson and the University of Texas," *Southwest Review* 28 (1942): 13–21.

McCaleb, Walter F., "The Impeachment of a Governor," *Outlook*, October 10, 1917.

Nalle, Ouida Ferguson, *The Fergusons of Texas; or "Two Governors for the Price of One."* San Antonio: Naylor, 1946.

Ogg, Frederic A., "Impeachment of Governor Ferguson," *American Political Science Review* 12 (1918): 111–15.

Steen, Ralph W., "The Ferguson War on the University of Texas," *Southwestern Social Science Quarterly* 35 (1955): 356–62.

Stewart, Frank M., "Impeachment in Texas," *American Political Science Review* 24 (1930): 652–58.

World War I and the Twenties

Watching and Waiting on the Border

Batchelder, Roger, *Watching and Waiting on the Border*. Boston: Houghton Mifflin, 1917.

Briscoe, Edward Eugene, "Pershing's Chinese Refugees in Texas," *Southwestern Historical Quarterly* 62 (1958): 467–88.

Cumberland, Charles C., "Border Raids in the Lower Rio Grande Valley—1915," *Southwestern Historical Quarterly* 57 (1953): 285–311.

―――――, "Mexican Revolutionary Movements from Texas, 1906–1912," *Southwestern Historical Quarterly* 52 (1948): 301–24.

Hinkle, Stacy C., *Wings and Saddles: The Air and Cavalry Punitive Expedition of 1919*. El Paso: Texas Western Press, 1967.

Niemeyer, Vic, "Frustrated Invasion: The Revolutionary Attempt of General Bernardo Reyes from San Antonio in 1911," *Southwestern Historical Quarterly* 67 (1963): 213–25.

Texas in the War

Barrett, A. P., "Texas and Air Transport," *Texas Monthly*, February 1929, pp. 151–61.

Clark, James A., with Weldon Hart, *The Tactful Texan: A Biography of Governor Will Hobby*. New York: Random House, 1958.

Giles, Barney M., "Early Military Aviation Activities in Texas," *Southwestern Historical Quarterly* 54 (1950): 143–58.
History of Texas World War Heroes. Dallas: Army & Navy Publishing Co., 1919.
Pool, William C., "Military Aviation in Texas, 1913–1917," *Southwestern Historical Quarterly* 59 (1955): 429–54.
_____, "The Origin of Military Aviation in Texas, 1910–1913," *Southwestern Historical Quarterly* 58 (1954): 342–71.

Postwar Developments

Billington, Monroe, "Red River Boundary Controversy," *Southwestern Historical Quarterly* 62 (1958): 356–63.
Gracy, David B., *Littlefield Lands: Colonization on the Texas Plains.* Austin: University of Texas Press, 1968.
Menn, Alfred E., *Texas As It Is Today.* Austin: Gammel's Bookstore, 1925.
Neff, Pat M., *The Battles of Peace.* Fort Worth: Pioneer Publishing Co., 1925.
_____, *Messages of Pat M. Neff.* Austin. A. C. Baldwin & Sons, 1921.
Rogan, Octavia F., "Texas Legislation, 1925," *Southwestern Political and Social Science Quarterly* 6 (1925): 167–78.
Shirley, Emma Morill, *The Administration of Pat M. Neff, Governor of Texas, 1921–1925.* Waco: Baylor University Bulletin, 1938.
Smith, Genevieve, "Two Colonization Projects," *Bunker's Monthly*, September 1928, pp. 335–44.
Sterling, William Warren, *Trails and Trials of a Texas Ranger.* Corpus Christi: privately printed, 1961.

Social and Economic Developments

The Oil Industry

Cooper, Able Wheelis, "Electra: A Texas Oil Town," *Southwestern Historical Quarterly* 50 (1946): 44–48.
Hill, Robert T., "The Beaumont Oil Field, with Notes on Other Oil Fields of the Texas Region," *Journal of the Franklin Institute* 154 (1902): 143–56.
House, Boyce, *Oil Field Fury.* San Antonio: Naylor, 1954.
_____, *Roaring Ranger: The World's Biggest Boom.* San Antonio: Naylor, 1951.
_____, "Spindletop," *Southwestern Historical Quarterly* 50 (1946): 36–43.
_____, *Were You in Ranger?* Dallas: Tardy Publishing Co., 1935.
James, Marquis, *The Texaco Story: The First Fifty Years.* The Texas Co., 1953.

Jeffries, Charlie, "Reminiscences of Sour Lake," *Southwestern Historical Quarterly* 50 (1946): 25–35.
Larson, Henrietta, and Kenneth Wiggins Porter, *History of Humble Oil and Refining Company*. New York: Harper & Bros., 1959.
Rister, Carl Coke, *Oil! Titan of the Southwest*. Norman: University of Oklahoma Press, 1949.
Thompson, Craig, (*Since Spindletop: A Human Story of Gulf's First Half Century*. Gulf Oil Co., 1951.
Warner, Charles A., *Texas Oil and Gas since 1543*. Houston: Gulf Publishing Co., 1939.
———, "Texas and the Oil Industry," *Southwestern Historical Quarterly* 50 (1946): 1–24.

Educational Advances

Eby, Frederick, *The Development of Education in Texas*. New York: Macmillan, 1926.
———, *Education in Texas: Source Materials*. Austin: University of Texas Bulletin, 1918.
Evans, C. E., *The Story of Texas Schools*. Austin: Steck, 1955.
Lane, J. J., *History of Education in Texas*. Washington, D.C.: Government Printing Office, 1903.
Payne, John, "David F. Houston's Presidency of Texas A & M." *Southwestern Historical Quarterly* 58 (1954): 22–35.
Rutland, Robert. "The Beginnings of Texas Technological College," *Southwestern Historical Quarterly* 55 (1951): 231–40.

Women, Prohibition, and the New Freedom

Grantham, Dewey W., Jr., "Texas Congressional Leaders and the New Freedom, 1913–1917," *Southwestern Historical Quarterly* 53 (1949): 35–48.
Taylor, Ann Elizabeth, "The Woman Suffrage Movement in Texas," *Journal of Southern History* 17 (1951): 194–215.
Woolford, Sam, "Carrie Nation in Texas," *Southwestern Historical Quarterly* 63 (1959): 554–66.

The New Ku Klux Klan in Texas

Alexander, Charles C., *Crusade for Conformity: The Ku Klux Klan in Texas, 1920–1930*. Houston: Texas Gulf Coast Historical Assn., 1962.

CHAPTER 13 / DEPRESSION AND WAR

The Depression Strikes

The Politics of Prosperity

Allen, Lee N., "The Democratic Presidential Primary Election of 1924 in Texas," *Southwestern Historical Quarterly* 61 (1957): 474-93.

The East Texas Oil Boom

Boyle, Robert D., "Chaos in the East Texas Oil Field, 1930-1935," *Southwestern Historical Quarterly* 69 (1965): 340-52.
Hart, James P., "Oil, the Courts, and the Railroad Commission," *Southwestern Historical Quarterly* 44 (1940): 303-20.
Harter, Harry, *East Texas Oil Parade*. San Antonio: Naylor, 1934.
McDaniel, Ruel, *Some Ran Hot*. Dallas: Regional Press, 1939.
Mills, Warner E., *Martial Law in East Texas*. University, Ala.: University of Alabama Press, 1960.

The Roosevelt Years

The Deepening Depression

Allen, Edward, *Leading the Lawmakers: Sam Rayburn*. Chicago: Encyclopaedia Britannica, 1963.
Beane, Wilhelmina, *Texas Thirties*. San Antonio: Naylor, 1963.
Connally, Tom, as told to Alfred Steinberg, *My Name Is Tom Connally*. New York: Thomas Y. Crowell, 1954.
Dorough, C. Dwight, *Mr. Sam*. New York: Random House, 1962.
Dunn, Roy, " 'New Deal': Made in Texas by a Texan," *Texas Parade*, April 1961, pp. 7-8.
James, Marquis, *Mr. Garner of Texas*. Indianapolis: Bobbs-Merrill, 1939.
Jones, Jesse H., with Edward Angly, *Fifty Billion Dollars: My Thirteen Years with the the RFC (1932-1945)*. New York: Macmillan, 1951.
Maverick, Maury, *A Maverick American*. New York: Covici-Friede, 1937.
Timmons, Bascom. *Garner of Texas: A Personal History*. New York: Harper & Bros., 1948.
―――, *Jesse H. Jones: The Man and the Statesman*. New York: Holt, 1956.

State Politics

Ashburn, Karl E., "The Texas Cotton Acreage Control Law of 1931-1932," *Southwestern Historical Quarterly* 61 (1957): 116-24.

Douglas, C. L., and Francis Miller, *The Life Story of W. Lee O'Daniel*. Dallas: Regional Press, 1938.

The Changing Scene

The Population Growth

Hamilton, C. Horace, *Farm Population Changes in Texas during 1938*. College Station: Agriculture Experiment Station, 1939.

The Texas Mexicans

Cauley, T. J., "Mexican Immigration," *Texas Monthly*, August 1929, pp. 50–62.
Kingrea, Nellie Ward, *History of the First Ten Years of the Texas Good Neighbor Commission*. Fort Worth: Texas Christian University Press, 1954.
Scruggs, Otey M., "Texas, Good Neighbor?" *Southwestern Social Science Quarterly* 43 (1962): 118–25.
Smith, Genevieve, "The Mexican Element in Texas," *Bunker's Monthly*, July 1928, pp. 108–19.
Texas Good Neighbor Commission, *Texas: Friend and Neighbor*. 1961.
Weeks, O. Douglas, "The Texas-Mexicans and the Politics of South Texas," *American Political Science Review* 24 (1930): 606–27.

Industrial Growth

Allen, Ruth C., *East Texas Lumber Workers: An Economic and Social Picture, 1870–1950*. Austin: University of Texas Press, 1961.
Caldwell, Edwin L., "Highlights of the Development of Manufacturing in Texas, 1900–1960." *Southwestern Historical Quarterly* 68 (1964): 405–31.
Day, James M., "The Chisos Quicksilver Bonanza in the Big Bend of Texas," *Southwestern Historical Quarterly* 64 (1960): 427–53.
Dealey, Ted, "The Dallas Spirit: The Last Fool Flight," *Southwestern Historical Quarterly* 63 (1959): 15–30.
Lasswell, Mary, *John Henry Kirby: Prince of the Pines*. Austin: Encino Press, 1967.
McKnight, Tom L., "Aircraft Manufacturing in Texas," *Southwestern Social Science Quarterly* 38 (1957): 40–50.
Maxwell, Robert S., *Whistle in the Piney Woods: Paul Bremond and the Houston, East and West Texas Railway*. Houston: Texas Gulf Coast Historical Assn., 1963.
"Revolution in Texas," *Look*, August 4, 1959, pp. 23–24, 27, 29.
Sibley, Marilyn McAdams, *The Port of Houston: A History*. Austin: University of Texas Press, 1968.

Walker, Kenneth P., "The Pecan Shellers of San Antonio and Mechanization." *Southwestern Historical Quarterly* 69 (1965): 44–58.
Warner, C. A., "The Oil Industry in Texas since Pearl Harbor," *Southwestern Historical Quarterly* 61 (1957): 327–40.

CHAPTER 14 / FLAMBOYANT TEXAS

Political Affairs

A Period of Controversy

Duckworth, Allen, "Democratic Dilemma in Texas," *Southwest Review* 32 (1947): 34–40.
Weeks, O. Douglas, "Republicanism and Conservatism in the South," *Southwestern Social Science Quarterly* 36 (1955): 248–56.
————, *Texas Presidential Politics in 1952.* Austin: University of Texas, Institute of Public Affairs, 1953.

The Political Career of Allan Shivers

Bartley, Ernest R., *The Tidelands Oil Controversy: A Legal and Historical Analysis.* Austin: University of Texas Press, 1953.
Hardeman, D. B., "Shivers of Texas: A Tragedy in Three Acts," *Harper's Magazine,* November 1956, pp. 50–56.

Legislation and Scandal

"A Cleanup in Texas," *Business Week,* July 14, 1956, pp. 70–72.
Dorries, W. L., "An Appraisal of the Texas Veterans' Land Program," *Southwestern Social Science Quarterly* 36 (1955): 176–84.
Dugger, Ronnie, "What Corrupted Texas" *Harper's Magazine,* March 1957, pp. 68–74.
Fowler, Dan C., "Scandalous Years in Texas," *Look,* November 15, 1955, pp. 65–72.
"In Texas: Probes Outshine Bills," *Business Week,* March 26, 1955, pp. 98, 100, 102, 104.
"Texas Tightens the Screws on Its Insurance Companies," *Business Week,* July 23, 1955, p. 68.
"Those Texas Scandals," *Saturday Evening Post,* November 12, 1955, pp. 19, 81, 86, 89.

Recent Skirmishes on the Political Fronts

State Politics and More Scandal

Weeks, O. Douglas, *Texas in the 1960 Presidential Election.* Austin: University of Texas Press, 1961.

Political Battles, 1958–1962

"Penny Gains New Stature in Tax Debut," *Dallas Morning News,* September 1, 1961, section 1, p. 1.
"Price Daniel," *Dallas Morning News,* January 10, 1963, section 1, p. 8.
Still, Rae Files, *The Gilmer-Aiken Bills: A Study in Legislative Process.* Austin: Steck, 1950.

A Texan Becomes President

Branyan, Robert L., and R. Alton Lee, "Lyndon B. Johnson and Art of the Possible," *Southwestern Social Science Quarterly* 45 (1964): 213–25.
Carter, Douglas, "The Trouble in Lyndon Johnson's Back Yard," *The Reporter,* December 1, 1955, pp. 32–35.
Provence, Harry, *Lyndon B. Johnson: A Biography.* New York: Fleet, 1964.
Report of the Warren Commission on the Assassination of President Kennedy. New York: Bantam, 1964.
Sherrill, Robert, *Accidental President.* New York: Grossman, 1967.

Social and Economic Developments

Civil Rights in Texas

Duggar, Ronnie, "These Are the Times: On Being a Southern Liberal," *Commentary* 37 (January 1964): 40–45.
―――, "Texas Christians Stem the Tide," *The Christian Century* 74 (July 1957): 912–15.
Hall, Charles E., *Progress of the Negro in Texas.* Washington, D.C.: U.S. Bureau of the Census, 1936.
Lightfoot, Billy Bob, "The Negro Exodus from Comanche Country," *Southwestern Historical Quarterly* 56 (1952): 407–16.
Olds, Greg, "Integration in Texas," *The Texas Observer,* October 28, 1966.
Rechy, John, "Jim Crow Wears a Sombrero," *Nation* 189 (October 10, 1959): 210–13.
Sargeant, Frederic O., "Economic Adjustments of Negro Farmers in East Texas," *Southwestern Social Science Quarterly* 42 (1961): 32–39.
Skrabanek, R. L., and J. S. Hollingsworth, *The Nonwhite Population of Texas.* College Staton: Agricultural Experiment Station, 1966.

Texas Today

"Connally Signs $33,000,000 Tax Bill," *Dallas Morning News*, May 11, 1963, section 1, p. 5.

Garwood, W. St. John, Harry Ransom, Allan Shivers, and E. B. Germany, *Texas Today and Tomorrow*. Dallas: Southern Methodist University Press, 1961.

Gregory, Gladys, *The Chamizal Settlement: A View from El Paso*. El Paso: Texas Western College, 1963.

Hundley, Norris, *Dividing the Waters: A Century of Controversy between the United States and Mexico*. Berkeley: University of California Press, 1960.

Kopkind, Andrew, "Connally's Texas: A Report from the Gray Place," *The New Republic*, November 20, 1965, pp. 9–12.

Oates, Stephen B., "NASA's Manned Spacecraft Center at Houston, Texas," *Southwestern Historical Quarterly* 67 (1963): 350–75.

Peters, Donald W., "The Rio Grande Boundary Dispute in American Diplomacy," *Southwestern Historical Quarterly* 54 (1950): 412–29.

The Wheeler-Dealers

"Final Arguments Heard in Estes' Trial," *Dallas Morning News*, March 26, 1963, section 1, p. 12.

Nevin, David, *The Texans: What They Are and Why*. New York: William Morrow, 1968.

"Splitting to Grow Faster," *Business Week*, February 13, 1965, pp. 75–76, 80, 82, 87.

"Swinging Lingo," *Newsweek*, January 23, 1967, pp. 78–80.

Tolbert, Frank, "The Incredible Houston Dome." *Look*, April 20, 1965, pp. 96, 98.

"Wheel-Deal in the Central," *Time*, March 8, 1954, p. 88.

Index

Abilene, Kan., 251, 254
Abilene, Tex., 235, 270, 292
Abilene Man, 5
ad interim government, 116, 123–28, 135–36
Adaes Indians (*see also* Los Adaes), 8, 28, 29, 30
Adair, John, 255, 256
Adams, John Quincy, 66, 153
Adams-Onís Treaty (1819), 60, 66–69, 289
Add-Ran College, 292
Adelsverein, 139–40
Adobe Walls, Tex., 241, 243, 248
Agreda, Sister Maria Jesus de, 16
Agricultural Adjustment Acts (U.S.), 339
Agricultural Experiment Station, Tex.

Agricultural Experiment Station (*cont.*) (*see also* Texas Agricultural and Mechanical College), 291
agriculture, 175, 226, 267, 271, 272, 274, 315; Anglo-American, 79, 85, 86, 90, 96, 183–85; arid land methods, 259–60, 261, 264, 266, 273, 334; cattle ranching and, 249–57, 259, 260, 261, 275, 382 (*see also* cattle industry); Civil War and, 208; depression (1930's) and, 333–34, 337, 338; Ferguson and, 305–306, 338; mechanization of, 346, 352, 353, 382; Mexican labor in, 350, 351–53; Negro labor in, 228, 230, 376, 377, 381 (*see also* slavery); population changes and, 182, 290, 382, 384; prehistoric, 4, 5, 6, 8; pro-

agriculture (*cont.*)
  test movements of the nineteenth-century in, 278–79, 280, 285, 287; schools of, 291; Spanish, 33, 38, 50, 51, 52, 53, 54–55, 56, 57; Tejas Indians and, 24, 25; warehouse system in, 304, 306; wealth (1960's), 382–83
Agriculture, Texas State Bureau of, 294, 303
Agriculture, Texas State Department of, 303
Agua Dulce Creek, 114
Aguayo, Marquis de San Miguel de, 31–33, 55
Aikin, A. M., 363–64
Ais Indians, 28, 47
Aix-la-Chapelle, Treaty of, 42
Alabama Indians, 84, 142
Alamán, Lucas, 89, 92
Alamo, The (Mission San Antonio de Valero), 29, 31, 33, 37, 51, 57
Alamo, battle of the, 110–12, 116, 117, 118, 125; veterans' land grants and, 137
Alarcón, Martin de, 29–30, 55
Albany, Tex., 252, 253
Albion (vessel), 90
Albuquerque, N.M., 15, 130, 197
Aldama, Ignacio, 63
Alexander, Charles C., cited, 327
Algonquin (vessel), 311
Alien Land Law of 1891 (Tex.), 287
Alien and Sedition Acts (U.S.), 186
Alleyton, Tex., 180
Allred, James V., 341–42, 346, 352
Almonte, Juan N., 69–70, 100–101, 111, 156–57
Alvarez de Toledo, José, 64
Amangual, Francisco, 61–62
Amarillo, Tex., 13, 303, 316; population changes, 348, 349
American (Know Nothing) Party, 164–65, 190
Amichel, 9
Ampudia, Pedro, 159
Anadarkos, 141
Anahuac, Tex., 42, 92–94, 103, 122
Anda y Altamirano, Father, 38–39
Angelina River, 14, 32, 141
Anglo-American settlers, 60, 66, 119,

Anglo-American settlers (*cont.*)
  120–22; Texas colonization by, 70–72, 73–87, 88–94, 101, 173, 174, 182, 189
annexation, 66–67, 106, 118, 122, 126, 127, 129–30, 146, 159, 161, 162, 170, 194, 368; Joint Resolution of, 154–55; process of, 156
Anthony, Susan B., 324
Antimonopoly Party, 280
Antitrust Act (Tex.), 145
Apache Indians, 18, 19, 38, 55, 57, 168, 246; Spanish alliance with, 39–40, 41, 43, 44, 51; Spanish efforts to suppress, 34–36, 44, 48–50
Appalachian Mountains, 43, 58
Aransas Bay, 5, 6
Aransas Pass, Tex., 182, 250
Archaic Stage (of man), 5, 6, 8
archeology, 4–7
Archer, Branch T., 106, 127
Argall, Samuel, 247
Arizona, 12, 18, 181, 270, 311; cattle and, 253, 255; secession of, 196–97
Arkansas, 7, 61, 69–70, 148, 218; Civil War and, 200, 203, 204, 231; cotton production controls and, 333; railroads and, 270
Arkansas River, 13, 35, 60, 61, 67
Armijo, Manuel, 150
Armour packers, 353
arms industry, 204, 345, 353, 354
Arnold, H. H., quoted, 313
Arredondo, Joaquín de, 64, 71–72, 84
Arrington, George W., 238
Arroyo Hondo River, 61
Aten, Ira, 263
Athapaskan linguistic group, 18
Aury, Luis, 64–65, 173
Austin, John, 93
Austin, Moses, 70–72, 73
Austin, Stephen F., 68, 73–76, 94, 120; colonies of, 78–79, 80, 81, 82–83, 85, 91–92, 145; election of 1836 and, 127, 128; imprisonment of, 100, 103, 132; Mexican revolution (1821) and, 76, 77–78, 80; San Felipe Conventions (1832) and, 95, 96, 97, 99; Santa Anna dictatorship and, 99, 100, 103; Teran and, 89; Texas independence

Austin, Stephen F. (*cont.*)
  issue and, 106; Texas troop command of, 105, 107
Austin, Tex., 1, 4, 34, 166, 170, 180, 236, 281; art in, 293; capitol building in, 176–77, 257, 281, 294–96; Civil War surrender and, 210, 215, 231; constitutional conventions in, 154–55, 216; construction of, 146; cotton conference (1931), 333; Democratic conventions in, 164, 224; establishment of, 146; population changes, 290; secession convention (1861) in, 193–95; university in, 292
Austin College, 177
Austin (vessel), 134
Austin County, Tex., 173, 207, 348
Austin-Williams Colony, 91–92
Aztecs, 9

Babcock, A. C., 295
Bagdad, Mexico, 204, 205
Bahía del Espíritu Santo, *see* Fort St. Louis
Bailey, Joseph Weldon, 300, 306, 316, 323
Baird, Spruce M., 161
Baker, Cullen, 231–32, 235
Baker, Moseley, 115, 116
Balboa, Vasco Núñez de, 20
Balcones Escarpment, 3
Ball, Thomas H., 305
Bandera, Tex., 252
Bands of Hope, 282
Banks, Nathaniel P., 199–200, 203, 213
Bank of St. Louis, 70
Baptist General Convention, 292
Barbers Hill oil field, 319
Barker, Eugene C., 119–20; quoted, 71
Barnhardt, George, 144
Barr, Alwyn, 289
Barrett, T. H., 200
Bass, Sam, 235, 236, 238
Bastrop, Felipe Enrique Neri, Baron de, 71, 72, 79, 172
Bastrop, Tex., 83, 103, 113, 116
Bastrop County, Tex., 82, 232
Batson oil field, 318

Baylor, George, 238
Baylor, John R., 196, 197
Baylor University, 177, 292, 316, 322
Bays, Joseph E., 86
Beales, John Charles, 82, 90, 173
Beaumont, Tex., 198, 272, 318, 327, 345, 354; petrochemicals in, 355; population changes in, 348, 349; riots (1943), 378; wealth of, 382
Belden Poll, 357, 359
Bell, John, 191
Bell, John V., 367
Bell, Josiah H., 75, 76
Bell, Peter H., 162, 164, 189
Bell County, Tex., 209, 232, 234, 305
Bellinger, Charles, 379
Bell Punch tax, 277
Benavides, Fray Alonzo de, 16
Bernardo Plantation, 75
Béxar, siege of, 105, 107–108
Béxar County, Tex., 180, 273, 290, 317, 379; population changes in, 349, 381, 382
Béxar Department, Coahuila y Texas, 81, 101, 105
Bibliography of Texas (Raines), 294
Bickley, George, 192
Biddle, Nicholas, 147
Bienville, Jean Baptiste LeMoyne, Sieur d', 26
Big Bend, Tex., 1, 3, 11, 56, 270, 309
Big Bend Cave Dwellers, 5–6
Biggers, Don, 260, 320, 331; quoted, 264–65
Big Lake oil field, 319
Big Spring, Tex., 316
Black, Hugo, 360
Black, Jacob, 69
Black Codes, 217, 229
Blakely, William A., 368
Blancas Creek, 37
Blanco *Courier* (newspaper), 331
Board of Education, Texas State, 321, 331, 363–64
Bohemians, in Texas, 207, 290
Bonaparte, Joseph, 62, 65, 66
Bonham, James Butler, 111
Borden, Gail, 136
border disputes, (*see also* Mexico, border of), 204, 237–38, 307–11, 376

Borden Dairy Company, 136
Borrajo, Father, 234
Bosque, Fernando del, 17
Bosque County, 167
Bowie, James, 94, 105, 107, 108, 109, 121; at the Alamo, 110
Bowles (Cherokee chief), 110, 140–41, 142, 172
Bracketville, Tex., 312
Bradburn, John Davis, 92–94, 122
Brady Creek, 166
Bragg, Braxton, 201
Brann, William Cowper, 294
Brassell, Phillip, 234
Brazoria, Tex., 68, 93, 193
Brazoria County, Tex., 180, 382
Brazos Department, Coahuila y Texas, 81, 101
Brazos River, 4, 14, 75, 79, 91, 101, 123, 167; Clear Fork of, 168; Houston encampment on, 115, 116; Indian reservations on, 168; navigation, 180; trade on, 93, 144
Brazos Santiago, island of, 199, 200
Breckenridge, John C., 191
Breckenridge oil field, 319
Brenham, Richard, 150
Brenham, Tex., 232
breweries, 273, 303, 304–305, 323, 353; 3.2 referendum, 341
Briscoe, Andrew, 103
Britton, A. M., 256
Brooks Field, San Antonio, 344
Brown, John, 190
Brown, John Henry, 226, 293
Brown County, Tex., 171, 232, 235, 317, 360
Browning, Joe, 256
Browning, Samuel, 138
Brownsville, Tex., 159, 200, 204, 237, 310; population changes in, 290; riots in, 378
Brown v. Board of Education, 380
Brownwood, Tex., 292
Brushy Creek, 38
Bryan, Francis T., 166
Bryan, William Jennings, 288
Bryan, Tex., 291
Bryant, William R., 368
Bucareli, Tex., 47
Buchanan, James, 193

Buchanan, Richard C., 219
Buchanan v. Worley, 380
Buchel County, Tex., 161
Buell, George P., 246
Buena Vista, 160
Buffalo Bayou, Tex., 117
Buffalo Bayou, Brazos, and Colorado Railroad, 180
Bugbee, Thomas Sherman, 254
Bullington, Orville, 338
Bullock, Richard, 147–48
Burkburnett oil field, 319
Burkham, Charles, 69
Burleson, Albert Sidney, 302, 311
Burleson, Edward, 107, 113, 143–44, 151
Burnam's Ferry, Tex., 113, 116
Burnet, David G., 91, 96, 112, 115, 116, 206; 1836 election and, 126; 1841 election and, 132; 1866 election and, 217, 218; Santa Anna treaties of, 123, 125; treasury warrants and, 135
Burnett, Samuel Burk, 257
Burr, Aaron, 60
Burton, Isaac, 126
Burton, Tex., 233
Bustamante, Anastacio, 89, 129, 133, 157; Santa Anna and, 88, 92, 94, 125, 149
Butte, George C., 329, 331
Butterfield Overland Mail Company, 179

Cabeza de Vaca, Álvar Núñez, 11–12, 14
Caddoan Indians, 6, 7–8, 14, 17, 25, 51, 172; Anglo-Americans and, 84, 140
Caddo Lake, 178, 269
Cadillac, Lamothe, 27, 29
Cage, Ben Jack, 365
Caldwell, Matthew, 151–52
Caldwell County, Tex., 290
Calhoun, John C., 153, 187
California, 52, 81–82, 102, 159, 187; agricultural exports of, 383; coastal oil lands of, 368; gold rush (1849), 162, 165, 166, 250; railroads of, 270; U.S. invasion of, 160, 161

Callahan County, 138
Camargo, Mexico, 37
Cameron County, Tex., 171, 349
Camino Real, 47
Campbell, H. H., 256
Campbell, Thomas Mitchell, 299–300, 301
Camp Bowie, Fort Worth, 312
Camp Logan, Houston, 312
Camp MacArthur, Waco, 312
Camp Marfa, Marfa, 312
Camp Travis, San Antonio, 312
Camp Verde, San Antonio, 181
Canadian River, 6, 13, 15, 166, 169, 256; Indian battles on, 241, 243
Canadians, in Texas, 381
Canales, Antonio, 149
Canby, Edward, 197, 219, 220, 221
Candelaria, Madame, 111
Capitol Freehold Land and Investment Company, 296
Capitol Syndicate, 257, 285, 296
Caprock, The, 3, 4, 62, 150, 246, 255; farming on, 273
Carlotta, empress of Mexico, 243
Carranza, Venustiano, 309, 310–11
Carson, Kit, 241, 243
Carson, Samuel P., 112
Carson County, Tex., 256
Carswell, Jack, 372
Carswell Field, Fort Worth, 345
Carter, Amon, 384
Cart War (1857), 179
Carvajal, José Maria, 92
Casa Blanca, Tex., 143
Casas, Juan Bautista de las, 63, 173, 308
Case, J. I., 265
Castañeda, Francisco, 104
Castillo, Diego del, 16
Castle Gap, 166
Castro, Henri, 139, 173
Castro Colony, 139, 194
Castroville, Tex., 139, 167, 176
Cator, Bob and Jim, 248, 254
cattle industry, 55–56, 57, 171, 182, 230, 240, 275; buffalo destruction and, 248, 254; cottonseed products and, 272–73; cowboy strike (1883) in, 281; depression and, 333; expansion of, 249–57, 259, 261, 266,

cattle industry (*cont.*)
267, 277–78, 346, 382, 383; fencing and, 249, 260, 262–63, 264–66, 284; feuding and, 233, 234; meat-packing industry and, 315, 353; rustling and, 236, 237–38, 244, 263–64; Spanish, 55–56; trail driving in, 250–51
Causey, George, 248
Cavness, C. H., 366
Centralia Draw, 166
Centralists (Mexico), 87, 89, 92–94, 95; anti-U.S. feeling of, 120, 129, 153, 159; Santa Anna and, 88, 99, 102, 125, 141, 149; Texas independence and, 106, 119, 122, 125, 131, 149, 157
Central Texas (*see also specific place names*), 194, 207, 251, 281; Indians of, 38, 168
Chambers, Thomas Jefferson, 164, 202, 203
Chambers County, Tex., 42, 249
Chamizal region, 376
Champ d'Asile, Tex., 66
Charleston, S.C., 148
Cheatham, Wiley L., 366–67
chemical industry, 353, 383; petrochemicals and, 345, 354, 384
Cherokee Indians, 84–85, 95, 107, 172; Houston and, 109–10, 128, 140–41; Texas expulsion of, 142
Cherokee Treaty, 109–10
Cherokee War, 142
"Chicken War," 30–31, 32
Chihuahua, Mexico, 14, 19, 44, 56, 61, 62, 309; U.S. invasion of, 160; Villa in, 310, 311
Childress, George, 112
Childress, Tex., 316
Chinese, the, in Texas, 311, 347, 350, 381
Chiracahua Indians, 18
Chisholm, Jesse, 251
Chisholm Trail, 251–52
Chriesman, Horatio, 79
Christianity (*see also specific religious groups*), Indians and, 14, 15–16, 18, 19, 24, 25, 27, 28, 30, 36, 39–40, 41, 50–53
Cincinnati, Tex., 180

Civilian Conservation Corps, 339
civil rights (*see also* progressivism; reform movements), 361, 367, 368, 371, 376-81
Civil War, 55, 119, 140, 174, 175, 179; cattle industry and, 250, 254; economic hardships in, 208-11; Indian wars during, 241-43; labor movement and, 280; lawless aftermath of, 211, 230-39; slavery and, 185, 189, 209; Southern reconstruction period, 185, 212-23, 269, 275; Texas battles of, 195-202, 203-204; Unionists in, 205-207, 213; veterans' pensions, 277
Claiborne, W. C. C., 63
Clark, Addison, 292
Clark, Edward, 195, 202, 210
Clark, George, 282, 283, 284, 285; election of 1892 and, 286-87
Clark, Randolph, 292
Clark, William, 60
Clarksville, Tex., 175, 177
Clarksville *Northern Standard* (newspaper), 175, 226
Clay, Henry, 154, 162
Clay County, Tex., 171, 240
Cleburne, Tex., 280, 316
Clovis, N.M., 5
Coahuila, Mexico, 14, 29, 30, 31, 32, 48, 61, 149; Apaches in, 39, 44; Magon in, 308; Texas merger with, 80
Coahuila y Texas, Mexico, 80, 92-94, 101-102, 145; Colonization Law (1825) of, 82, 83, 86; Texas separatist proposals, 95, 96, 97, 99
Coahuiltecans, 7, 8, 172
Coastal Plains, 3, 173, 334
Coke, Richard, 212, 224-26, 236, 275, 277
Colbert's Ferry, 179
Coleman, Tex., 252
Coleto Creek, battle of (Goliad, March 1836), 110, 114-15, 117, 118, 125
Collin County, Tex., 138, 382
Collinsworth, George M., 104
Collinsworth, James W., 132
colonization laws (Mexico): Federal (1824), 81-83; Imperial (1823),

colonization laws (*cont.*) 77-79, 80; State (1825), 82-83, 86, 90; Centralist (April 6, 1830), 87, 88-90, 91-92, 94, 95, 100, 101
colonization laws (Texas), 138
Colorado, 3, 6, 18, 35; cattle industry and, 253, 255, 256
Colorado City, Tex., 270
Colorado County, Tex., 207, 348
Colorado River, 4, 19, 34, 75, 82, 101, 113, 220; Comanche battles on, 144; navigability of, 179, 180; San Jacinto campaign and, 115, 116
Colquitt, Oscar Branch, 300-301, 309, 321
Columbia, Tex., 103, 128, 145, 181
Columbus, Christopher, 7, 9
Columbus, N.M., 310
Columbus, Tex., 75
Comal County, Tex., 140
Comanche Indians, 47, 50, 51, 83, 90, 140, 142-44; Amangual expedition and, 61-62; Apaches and, 35-36, 43, 44, 49, 168; buffalo and, 245, 248; Red River agency for, 240-41; San Saba attacks, 39, 40, 41; Santa Fe expedition and, 150; Texas reservation for, 168; Tonkawas and, 38, 40; U.S. military suppression of, 168-69, 243-47, 252
Comanchéros, 244, 246
Comanche Springs, Tex., 166
commission form of city government, 302-303
Commission on Higher Education, Texas State, 364
Committee of Public Safety, during secession, 194-96
Committees of Safety and Correspondence, 95-96, 103, 104; Permanent Council, 105, 107, 108
Compostela, Mexico, 12
Compromise of 1850, 162-63, 187, 204
Concepción, battle of, 105
Concho River, 4, 8, 11, 16-17, 18-19, 24, 62, 179, 253; explorations, 166
Confederacy, The, 185, 194-95, 202-205, 226; amnesty oaths for, 215-16, 217, 218; cattle and, 250; col-

453 / Index

Confederacy, The (cont.)
  lapse of, 200, 208–11, 212, 215, 230–31; Indians and, 240–41, 243; Lanham and, 299; Unionists and, 205–207
Confederacy, The. Army: deserters, 209, 210, 211, 230, 231; draft resistance, 206–207; Texas movements of, 196, 197–99, 200–202, 203, 224
Confederacy, The. Congress, 202, 205
Confederacy, The. Constitution, 195
Confederacy, The. Trans-Mississippi Military Department, 200, 202, 204, 210, 215
Confederate Conscription Act (1862), 200, 206
Congregationalists, 177
Connally, John B., 372, 374, 375
Connally, Tom, 312, 332, 344, 361
Connecticut, 70, 112, 189, 207
Connor, Mrs. O. C., quoted, 208–209
Consolidated-Vultee Company, 354
Constitution of 1824 (Mexico), 80, 88, 93, 94, 96, 102, 112; Paredes restoration of, 160; Texas Revolution, 106, 107–108, 119, 121, 122
Constitution of 1825 (Coahuila y Texas), 80–81
Constitution of 1833 (proposed), 96
Constitution of 1835 (Organic Law), 106
Constitution of 1836 (Republic), 112–13, 126, 127, 131, 183
Constitution of 1845 (statehood), 154–55, 183, 195, 216, 226
Constitution of 1861 (Confederate), 192–93
Constitution of 1866 (Reconstruction), 213, 215–17, 229, 234
Constitution of 1869 (Radical), 213, 219–21, 222, 224
Constitution of 1876 (present), 225–28, 230, 258, 269, 270, 291, 292; highways and, 306; school segregation and, 291–92, 377; statehouse and, 294; taxation and, 275, 276, 302; woman suffrage and, 324; weakness of, 227
Constitutional Party, 372

Constitutional Union Party, 191, 192
Consultation of 1835, 105–107, 108, 109, 122, 127
Convention of 1832, 95–96, 121, 122
Convention of 1833, 96, 97, 99–100, 121
Convention of 1836, 112–13
Convention of 1845, 155
Convention of 1861 (secession), 192–94
Convention of 1866, 216–17
Convention of 1869, 220–21
Convention of 1875, 226–28
Cook, Frederick A., 320
Cook County, Ill., 371, 375
Cooke, Gustave, 201
Cooke, Jay, 226
Cooke, William G., 150
Cooke County, Tex., 207
Coolidge, Calvin, 332
Copano, Tex., 182
Copano Bay, 90, 126
Cordova, Jacob de, 170
Cordova, Vicente, 141–42
Cordova Island, 376
Coronado, Francisco Vásquez de, 12–13, 14, 15
Corpus Christi, Tex., 4, 159, 250, 345, 348, 349, 379; alkali plant, 353; Civil War and, 198; wealth of, 382
Corpus Christi Bay, 90
Corsicana, Tex., 317, 318
Cortéz, Hernando, 9, 12
Cortina, Juan, 204, 237–38
Cortina War (1859), 237
Cós, Martín Perfecto de, 101–102, 103, 104, 117, 130–31; San Antonio siege and, 105, 107–108, 109, 141
Cottle County, Tex., 256
cotton, 182, 184, 192, 208; Civil War trade in, 204, 205, 231; depression (1930's) and, 333–34; ginning, 273; High Plains cultivation, 273, 382; single-crop farming of, 274, 346
Cotton Acreage Control Law, 333
Council of Defense, Texas State, 314
Council House fight (1840), 142–43
county training schools, 379

Court of Civil Appeals, Texas, 334
courts, 121, 127, 131, 306; Black Codes and, 213, 217; Confederate, 207, 232; cotton production control and, 334; and impeachment of Ferguson, 307; judicial appointments, 220, 225; jury rights and, 216, 218, 325; Ku Klux Klan and, 327; state elections and, 360; states' rights issue and, 186–87
Coushatta Indians, 84, 142
Cox, Jack, 370, 372
Cox, James E., 369
Crane, M. M., 289, 299
Cretaceous period, 2
Cristoval, Tex., 166
Crittenden, John J., 193
Crockett, Davy, 111
Crockett, John M., 202
Croix, Teodoro de, 48–49, 50
Crozat, Antoine, 26
Cuartelejo ranchería, Colo., 18
Cuero Record (newspaper), 367
Culberson, Charles Allen, 312, 323, 327
Culberson, Charles M., 288–89, 299
Culberson, David B., 283, 288
Cullen, Hugh Roy, 384
Cullinan, J. S., 317, 319
Cuney, Norris Wright, 280, 281, 287, 288, 377
Cushing, La., 28
Custer, George A., 215
Customs Act (Texas Republic, 1836), 136
Czechoslovakians, in Texas, 207, 290, 347, 381

Dabbs, J. Autry, quoted, 52–53
Daingerfield, Tex., 345, 355
Dalhart, Tex., 316
Dallas, George Mifflin, 154
Dallas, Tex., 1, 138, 139, 170, 345, 354, 371; lynching in, 192, 326, 327; population changes in, 290, 348, 349, 382; President Kennedy in, 373–75; Prohibition and, 282; railroads and, 270; school integration in, 380
Dallas County, Tex., 138, 273, 290, 360, 382
Dallas News (newspaper), 342, 362
Daniel, Price, 367, 368, 370, 371–73
Darnell, N. H., 226
Davenport, Tex., 69
Davidson, James, 232
Davidson, John W., 246
Davidson, Lynch, 329
Davidson, T. Whitfield, 329, 360
Davis, Edmund J., 199, 206, 220, 230, 237; election of 1873 and, 224; Greenback Party and, 279, 280; Indians and, 244, 245; Obnoxious Acts and, 221, 222, 232–33, 275; railroad subsidies and, 223
Davis, Jefferson, 181, 199, 201, 203, 217
Davis, John W., 329
Davis Mountains, 166
Dawson, Nicholas, 152
Dealey, Samuel D., 345
Decatur, Tex., 207
Declaration of Independence, Texas, 112, 122, 177
Delaware Indians, 141
Del Mar Junior College, Corpus Christi, 379
Del Rio, Tex., 3, 17, 308
Democratic Party (U.S.), 163–65, 192; election of 1844, 154; election of 1873 and, 224, 225, 226; elections (1879–1886), 276, 277, 278, 279, 280, 282; election of 1928 and, 332; elections (1960–68) and, 370–71, 375; Ferguson and, 305, 306, 331, 338; Jaybird-Woodpecker War and, 284; Johnson senate seat and, 359–60, 370; Kansas-Nebraska Act and, 187, 190; Ku Klux Klan and, 328–29; national convention (Houston), 332; Negro membership right, 379; New Deal and, 338–40, 346–47; organization of, 332; railroad regulation and, 285–86; Rainey controversy and, 356–57; Reconstruction and, 213, 216–17, 219, 221, 223, 232, 275; Shivers and, 360–63; split of 1892 in, 286–87, 288; Texas primaries and, 300, 301, 302, 324, 356, 371, 377, 378, 379; Woodrow Wilson and, 301

Democrats for Nixon, 371
Democrats of Texas, group, 367–68
DeMorse, Charles, 175, 226
Denison, Tex., 316, 348, 349
Denton, Tex., 192, 207
Denton County, Tex., 138, 243, 257, 290, 345, 382
Denver, Colo., 270
Desdemona oil field, 319
De Soto, Hernando, 13–14
Devils River, 165, 166
DeWitt, Green, 78, 82, 83, 89, 122, 170
DeWitt County, Tex., 232, 233–34, 366
D'Hannis, Tex., 139
Diaz, Porfirio, 308–309
Dickenson, Mrs. Almaron, 111, 113
Dickson, David C., 164, 165
Disciples of Christ, 292
Dixon, Billy, 248
Doan's Trading Post, Tex., 252
Dodge, Grenville M., 270
Dodge City, Kan., 236, 248, 252
Dodge City Trail, 252
Dohoney, E. L., 282
Dolores (Beale's Colony), 90
Dolores (East Texas mission field), 29, 32, 172
Dolores (Escandón's Colony), 37, 57
Dolores, Mexico, 62
Doniphan, William, 160
Dos Passos, John, 357
Douglas, Stephen A., 187, 191
Dove Creek, battle of, 243
Dowling, Dick, 199
Dred Scott decision, 187, 189, 191
Drummer tax, 277, 284
Duffield, George C., 250
Durango, Mexico, 14
Durst, Joseph, 172
Dutch, the, in Texas, 57, 71, 172, 381
Duval, John C., 293
Duval County, Tex., 360

Eagle Pass, Tex., 17, 36, 57, 167, 246, 312, 313; Madero revolution and, 308
Early-Halsey feud, 234
Early Times in Texas (Duval), 293

Eastland County, Tex., 261
East Texas (*see also specific place names*), 4, 5, 92, 231–32, 250, 301, 384; cattle industry in, 346, 382; depression in, 334; forests of, 272, 353; French in, 23, 28, 29, 30–31; Indians of, 7–8, 51, 95, 109–10, 140, 168, 172, 241; Ku Klux Klan in, 327; land speculation in, 91; Negro population of, 281; oil in, 317, 334–37; paper production in, 353–54; railroads and, 270, 271, 284; secession and, 194; Spanish in, 11, 13, 14, 24, 25, 28, 29–34, 36, 42, 43, 44, 45–48, 51, 54, 172
East Texas State Teachers College, 322
Education Act (Republic of Texas, 1839), 144, 145
education, *see* schools
Education Agency, Texas, 364
Edwards, Benjamin, 84–85, 140
Edwards, Haden, 82, 84–85, 122
Edwards Colony, 82, 84–85, 91
Edwards County, Tex., 17, 41
Edwards Plateau, 3, 4, 8, 179, 266; archeology of, 5, 6; Spanish on, 15, 16, 17, 18, 24, 247
Eisenhower, Dwight D., 345, 362–63, 368, 370
"El Cañon," 37, 41, 43, 44, 51
El Capitan, 3, 179
elections, *see* Texas elections; United States elections
electoral code (*see also* Terrell Election Law; poll tax), 302, 377, 379
El Fortin de San José, 56
Electra oil field, 319
Elliot, Charles, 152, 154
Ellis, Powhatan, 157
Ellis, Richard, 70, 112
Ellis County, Tex., 138, 382
Ellwood, Isaac L., 260, 334
El Paso, Tex., 3, 14, 167, 179, 235, 322; civil rights case (1924) in, 378–79; Civil War and, 196; Madero revolution (1910) and, 308; population changes in, 348; railroads and, 270; smelting in, 355; Texas boundary claims and, 131, 376

El Paso County, Tex., 161, 163, 166, 171, 273; Mexican population in, 349, 381; Salt War of, 234–35, 238
Emancipation Proclamation (1863), 191, 215
Emory, William H., 167
Enabling Act (Texas, 1870), 222
England, 49, 59, 112, 249; American Civil War and, 204, 205, 208; Mexican debts to, 157; Spain and, 36, 42–43, 44, 58, 67; Texas cattle lands and, 255, 257; Texas Republic and, 146, 147, 148, 150, 152, 153, 154; Texas statehouse and, 296; World War I and, 311, 314; World War II and, 344
English, the, in Texas, 57, 172, 173, 174, 290, 347, 381
Epperson, B. H., 164
Escandón, José de, 37, 41, 43, 57
Escoceses Party (Mexico), 88
Estes, Billie Sol, 385
Estevanico, 11, 12
Evans, Hiram W., 327
Evans, Ira, 221

Fair Labor Standards Act, 352
Falconer, Thomas, 150, 175
Falcon Reservoir, 5
Fannin, James W., 105, 109, 111; Coleto Creek and, 110, 114–15
Farías, Gómez, 97, 99, 100, 101
Farmers' Alliance, 267, 279, 280, 281; railroads and, 285, 286
Farragut, David G., 199
Farwell, Charles B. and John V., 257, 295
Fayette County, Tex., 152, 207, 290, 348
Federal Colonization Law, *see* colonization laws
Federal Deposit Insurance Corporation, 304, 339
Federal Food Administration, 314
Federalist Papers (Hamilton, Jay, and Madison), 186
Federalists (Mexico), 88, 89, 92, 93, 94, 308; election of 1832–1833 and, 95–96, 97; Monclova government,

Federalists (*cont.*)
102; Santa Anna defection from, 99, 102; Texas independence and, 106, 112, 127, 149; Yucatan revolt and, 134, 149, 150
Federal Loan Administration, 340
Ferdinand, Archduke of Austria-Hungary, 307
Ferguson, James E., 299, 305, 310, 321, 332, 338, 340; graft charges, 306–307, 316, 331, 369; Ku Klux Klan resistance of, 327, 329
Ferguson, Miriam A. (Mrs. James E.), 329, 331, 333, 338, 340, 343
Ferguson Farm Tenant Law, 306
Field, Richard, 84, 85, 172
Fifty Cent Act (Texas), 265, 277–78
filibusterers, 63–66, 67, 72
Filisola, Vicente, 100, 118, 125–26, 141
Fisher, George, 92–94
Fisher, Henry Francis, 139
Fisher, W. S., 152
Five Million Dollar Loan (*see also* bonds; Texas Republic, financial problems of), 136
Flanagan, James W., 221, 276
Flores, Juan, 237
Flores, Manuel, 142
Florida, 192, 193, 235; Adams-Onís Treaty and, 66–68; Spanish in, 9, 11, 13, 21, 30, 36, 43, 58
Foard County, Tex., 169
Folsom, N.M., 5
Forbes, John, 109–10
Ford, John S., 166, 169, 237; Civil War and, 196, 199, 200, 203, 204
Formby, Marshall, 372
Fort Arbuckle, Okla., 197
Fort Belknap, 167
Fort Bend County, Tex., 284, 379, 382
Fort Bliss, 167, 196, 197, 235, 312
Fort Brown, 167, 309, 312, 313, 378; Civil War and, 196, 199, 200, 204, 206
Fort Chadbourne, 167
Fort Clark, 167, 246, 312
Fort Cobb, 197
Fort Concho, 167, 244, 246
Fort Craig, 196, 197

Fort Crockett, 312
Fort Croghan, 167
Fort Davis, 167
Fort Defiance, 113
Fort Dodge, Kan., 246
Fort Duncan, 167, 312
Fort Fillmore, 196
Fort Frontenac, Niagara, 21
Fort Gates, 167
Fort Graham, 167, 168
Fort Griffin, 244, 245, 246, 252
Fort Houston, 135
Fort Inge, 167
Fort Lancaster, 167
Fort Leavenworth, Kan., 235
Fort Lincoln, 167
Fort McIntosh, 167, 312
Fort McKavett, 19, 167
Fort Martin Scott, 167
Fort (presidio) Nuestra Señora de los Dolores de los Tejas, 29, 30, 32, 34
Fort (presidio) Nuestra Señora de Loreto, 32
Fort (presidio) Nuestra Señora del Pílar, 32
Fort Phantom Hill, 167
Fort Quitman, 167
Fort Richardson, 245
Fort Ringgold, 167, 312
Fort St. Louis, 20–23, 24, 29, 60, 172; as Spanish fort and mission Bahía del Espíritu Santo, 31, 32, 33, 34, 36, 41, 43, 51, 52, 54, 57, 63, 64, 68; as Texan Fort Defiance, 113–14
Fort Sam Houston, 312, 313
Fort (presidio) San Antonio de Béxar, 29, 32
Fort (presidio) San Agustín de Ahumada, 42
Fort (presidio) San Francisco Xavier, 38–39
Fort (presidio) San Luis de las Amarillas, 39–40, 41, 43
Fort Sill, Okla., 245, 246
Fort Smith, Ark., 166
Fort Stanton, N.M., 196
Fort Stockton, 19, 166, 167
Fort Sumner, N.M., 253
Fort Terrett, 167

Fort Union, N.M., 197, 246
Fort Warren, 217
Fort Washita, Okla., 167
Fort Worth, Tex., 167, 192, 292, 293, 320; aircraft and, 354; army training in, 312, 345; meat packing in, 353; population changes in, 290, 348; railroads and, 266, 270; school integration in, 380
Fort Worth and Denver Railroad, 266
Fossett, Henry, 243
Foster, L. L., 283, 286
Foulois, Benjamin D., 312–13
Fountain, A. J., 234
Four Section Settler Act (Texas), 259, 277, 278
Four Sixes Ranch, 255, 257
Fox River, 21
France (see also French, the, in Texas), 20, 30, 42, 59, 314, 344; American Civil War and, 204; Mexican empire of, 210, 215, 243; Pastry War and, 149, 157; Texas Republic and, 146–48
Franco-Texienne Company, 138
Franklin, Tex., 161, 166
Fredericksburg, Tex., 140, 173, 176
Fredonian Rebellion, 84–85, 121–22, 140
Freedmen's Bureau, 218, 219, 228, 229, 230
Freeman, Thomas, 60–61
Freeport, Tex., 4
Freestone County, Tex., 222
French, the, in Texas, 90, 172, 173, 174, 176, 247, 381; Aguayo and, 31, 32; arrival of, 19, 20–21, 23, 24, 25; Lallemand expedition and, 65–66; Spanish Louisiana and, 42–44, 49, 172; Spanish trade and, 26–27, 28, 29, 32, 42, 55, 56; Texas Republic and, 138, 139
French and Indian War (Seven Years War), 42
French Revolution, 62
Frontier Battalion (see also Texas Rangers), 236, 238
Frontier Regiment, 241
Fugitive Slave Act (1850), 187
fur trade, 21, 26, 247

Gachupins, 76
Gaines, Edmund P., 141
Gainesville, Tex., 192, 207, 243, 316
Galicia, 33
Galveston, Tex., 11, 75, 132, 150, 177, 181, 312; *ad interim* government in, 116, 123; Civil War and, 198, 215; Customs House, 136; Freedmen's Bureau, 228; Gulf storm of 1900, 302; industry and, 271, 281; Know Nothing Party in, 165; Ku Klux Klan resistance in, 327; longshoremen's strike (1920), 315–16; medical schools of, 292; municipal commissioners of, 302–303; population changes, 174, 290, 348, 349; privateers and, 64–65, 67; railroads and, 269, 270
Galveston Bay, 4, 42, 85, 91, 92, 135; Civil War and, 198, 210
Galveston Bay and Texas Land Company, 91, 173
Galveston County, Tex., 273, 290, 360
Galveston, Harrisburg and San Antonio Railroad, 270
Galveston *News*, 175
Ganzábal, Father Juan José, 38
Garcitas Creek, 21
Garland, Tex., 345
Garner, John Nance, 311–12, 338, 339
Garrison, George P., 119–20, 294
Gates, John "Bet-a-Million," 260, 319
geology, 1–3
Georgetown, Tex., 293
Germans, the, in Texas, 57, 90, 91, 170, 172; architecture and, 176, 177; Civil War and, 206–207; population changes and, 174, 347, 349, 381; Republic of Texas and, 139–40, 173; Texas secession and, 194, 206–207; World War II and, 345
Ghent, Treaty of, 187
Gibbs, Barnett, 288
Giles, Bascom, 366, 367
Gillespie County, Tex., 207
Gilmer, Claud, 363–64
Gilmer-Aikin Law (Texas, 1949), 363–64, 379

Glidden, J. F., 260
Glorietta Pass, battle (1862) of, 197
Goat Bleats, The (periodical), 331
Goldwater, Barry, 375
Goliad, Tex., 34, 41, 57, 101, 104, 111; Matamoros campaign and, 109, 110; Urrea attack on, 113, 114–15
Goliad, battle (October 1835), 104
Goliad, massacre (and battle of Coleto Creek, March 1836), 110, 114–15, 116, 117, 118, 137, 151
Gomez brothers, 309
Gonsen, Albert, 352
Gonzalez, Henry B., 370
Gonzales, Tex., 83, 104, 105, 107, 152; Alamo battle and, 111, 113; Houston withdrawal from, 115
Good Neighbor Commission, 351
Goodnight, Charles, 253, 254, 255, 256, 285
Goodnight-Loving Trail, 253
Goose Creek oil field, 318
Gould, Jay, 270, 281, 285
Grand Canyon, 13
Grand Prairie, Tex., 345
Grand Saline, battle, 142
Grand State Farmers' Alliance, *see* Farmers' Alliance
Grange, The, *see* Patrons of Husbandry
Granger, Gordon, 215, 228, 231
Grant, James, 109, 114
Grant, Ulysses S., 200, 221, 223, 224–25, 244
"Grass Fight," 107
"Grass leases," 255, 256, 257, 259; fencing and, 262, 263, 284
Grayson, Peter W., 100, 132
Grayson County, Tex., 138, 166, 179, 290
Great Northern Railroad, 270
Great Plains, 3, 35
Greeley, Horace, 223
Green, Tom, 197, 198, 202
Green, Thomas Jefferson, 125, 126, 133, 175, 197
Greenback Party, 226, 278, 279, 280, 282, 299
Greer, Elkanah, 201
Greer, John A., 164
Greer County case, 289

Gregg, John, 202
Gregory, E. M., 219, 229, 311
Griffin, Charles, 218, 219
Griffenhagen and Associates, 341
Grito de Dolores (Hidalgo), 62
Groce, Jared E., 75, 86, 96
Groce's Plantation (Liendo), 115, 116, 293
Grovy v. Townsend, 379
Guadalajara, Diego de, 17
Guadalupe County, Tex., 382
Guadalupe Hidalgo, Treaty of, 160–61
Guadalupe Pass, 179
Guadalupe Peak, 3
Guadalupe River, 4, 34, 39, 41, 52, 104; Irish colonists on, 90; Mexican colonists on, 83
Guerrero, Gilberto, 308
Guerrero, Vincente, 77, 86, 88
Gulf, Colorado and Santa Fe Railroad, 265, 266, 270
Gulf of California, 13
Gulf of Mexico, 1, 2, 3, 4, 7, 20; French on, 21, 23, 30; Spanish exploration of, 9, 11, 36; Texas Navy on, 134–35; tidelands of, 361, 368
Gulf Oil Company, 319
Guthrie, Tex., 257
Gutiérrez de Lara, Bernardo, 63–64, 65, 67, 308

Hale-Aikin Commission, 364
Haley, J. Evetts, 367–68
Hamilton, Alexander, 186
Hamilton, Alexander Jackson, 213, 215–16, 221, 231
Hamilton, James, 147, 148
Hamilton, Morgan C., 221, 276
Hamman, W. H., 279
Hancock, Winfield S., 219
Handbook of Texas, 232, 236
Hanrahan, James, 248
Hardeman, Bailey, 113
Hardeman, D. B., 380
Hardin, John Wesley, 235, 238, 293
Hardin-Simmons University, 292
Harmon, Howard, 369
Harper's Ferry, W.V., 190

Harpers Magazine, 380
Harrell-Higgins feud, 234, 238
Harriet Lane (vessel), 198
Harris, DeWitt C., 103
Harrisburg, Tex., 116, 180
Harris County, Tex., 273, 290, 339, 382
Harrison, Thomas, 201
Harrison County, Tex., 379
Hartford Convention, 187
Hasinai Indian confederation (*see also* Caddoan Indians and specific tribes), 28, 30, 34
Hawikuh (Zuñi pueblo), 12
Hawkins, Joseph H., 73, 75
Hays, John Coffee, 135, 151, 160, 237; surveying by, 165–66
Headright Acts (Republic of Texas), 134, 137–38, 139, 169
Hebert, Paul Octave, 198
Helm, Jack, 233, 234
Hempstead, Tex., 115
Henderson, James Pinckney, 146–47, 153, 155, 163–64; death of, 191; Mexican War and, 160, 161; slavery and, 189
Henderson, James W., 164
Henderson and Burkville Railroad, 269
Hensley, William, 69
Herrera, José, 152–53, 154, 156–57, 159, 160
Herrera, Simón, 60, 61, 63, 64
Hewetson, James, 82, 90
Hidalgo, Father Francisco, 27, 28
Hidalgo y Costilla, Father Miguel, 62–63, 76, 77
Hidalgo County, Tex., 349
High Plains (*see also specific place names*), 3, 4, 13, 62, 246; farming on, 273, 382
Highway Commission, Texas State, 306
Highway Department, Texas State, 331, 333
Hillbilly Flour, 342
Hill County, Tex., 222
Hispanics (*see also* Mexicans, in Texas; Spanish, the, in Texas), 119, 120–22, 350–51; Texas statehood and, 170, 171, 173

Hiss, Alger, 361, 362
Historic American Buildings Survey, 176
Historical Association, Texas State, 294
History of Texas (Yoakum), 175
Hittson, John, 244, 254
Hobby, Oveta Culp, 345
Hobby, William Pettus, 316, 323
Hofheinz, Roy, 384
Hogg, James Stephen, 276, 282, 283–87, 300, 302, 364; Capitol construction and, 295; Culberson and, 288, 289, 299; oil and, 319
Holland, 71, 147, 148, 381
Holly, Mary Austin, 175
Holmes, J. J., 367
Homestead Act (Texas Republic, 1839), 144–45
homesteading, 70-71, 144–45, 170, 223, 228, 230, 264; cattle and, 262; exemption law and, 297; Negroes and, 281; public domain alienation and, 274; water supply and, 260 (*see also* Preemption Act; Headright Acts)
Hood, John Bell, 201–202
Hoodoo War, 234
Hood's Texas Brigade, 201–202
Hoover, Herbert, 301, 337, 338, 340, 363; quoted, 332
Horse Marines, 126
Horton, Albert Clinton, 164
Hospitals and Special Schools, Texas State Board of, 363
House, Edward M., 288, 299–300, 301, 302, 314–15, 361
Houston, Andrew Jackson, 343
Houston, David Franklin, 302, 311
Houston, Eliza Allen (Mrs. Sam), 128
Houston, Sam, 96, 119, 130, 146, 163, 164, 202, 343; Cherokees and, 109–10, 128, 140–41; Civil War and, 196; elections (1836–1841) and, 127–28, 131, 132–33, 144; Know Nothing Party and, 165; Mexican invasions (1842) and, 151, 152; San Jacinto campaign and, 116–18, 125, 128; secession and, 189, 190–91, 193–95, 206;

Houston, Sam (*cont.*)
Texas annexation and, 153, 154; Texas Navy and, 150; Texas Rangers and, 135; Texas troop command, 106, 108, 109, 112, 113, 114, 115, 125, 133, 134
Houston, Tex., 173, 177, 180, 231, 281, 320, 329, 374; army training camp in, 312; as capital, 145–46; Commission charter, 303; Democratic national convention (1928) in, 332; Democratic state convention (1892) in, 287; election of 1873 in, 224; Ku Klux Klan in, 326, 327; Negro executions (1917) in, 378; Negro officeholders (1966) in, 379; petrochemicals and, 355; population changes in, 290, 348, 349, 382; railroads and, 270, 316; shipyards of, 345, 354; space studies and, 384
Houston *Chronicle* (newspaper), 327
Houston County, Tex., 24, 135
Houston and Texas Central Railroad Company, 317
Howard, Charles H., 234–35
Howard, George Thomas, 135, 160, 179
Hubbard, Richard B., 224, 225, 276, 277
Huddle, William Henry, 293
Hueco Phase, 5–6
Hueco Tanks, Tex., 166
Huerta, Victoriano, 309, 310
Hull oil field, 319
Humble Oil Company, 318, 319, 336
Humphrey, Hubert, 375
Hunt, H. L., 384
Hunt, Memucan, 146
Hunter, Tom, 341
Huntington, Collis P., 270, 285
Huntsville, Tex., 195, 208, 292; penitentiary at, 232, 245, 304
Huston, Felix, 126, 133–34, 143–44

Iberville, Pierre LeMoyne, Sieur d', 26
Iberville, La., 27
Icarian Colony, 173
Iconoclast (periodical), 294
Illinois, 139, 187, 189, 191, 265, 295,

Illinois (cont.)
375; antitrust laws and, 283; cattle industry and, 250, 251, 383
Illinois River, 21
Imperial Colonization Law, see colonization laws
Incarnate Word, School of the, 293
Incas, 9
Independence, Tex., 177, 292
Indiana, 139, 189, 326
Indianola, Tex., 139, 179, 182, 199, 250
Indians (*see also specific groups*), 7–8, 252, 254, 347, 381; Anglo-American settlers and, 75, 79, 83, 84, 90, 95, 104, 107, 109–10, 203, 236, 257; Confederate war on, 241–43; epidemics among, 25, 53; French and, 23, 26, 27, 30, 40, 66, 172; Mexican descendants, 350; Spanish and, 9, 11–12, 13, 14, 15, 17, 18, 19, 23, 24, 25, 27, 28, 30, 32, 33, 34–36, 37–42, 43, 44, 47, 48–53, 57, 61, 66, 172; Texas Republic and, 133, 140–44; U.S. military expeditions against, 140, 141, 167–69, 238, 243–47, 248
Indian Territory, 96, 109, 140, 142, 243; cattle industry leases of, 256; reservations in, 167, 168, 240–41, 245, 246–47, 248, 252; U.S. roads through, 167
Industrial Commission, Texas State, 352
industry, 181–82, 267, 271–73, 297; aerospace study and, 384; antitrust laws and, 283, 284–85, 287, 289, 299, 300, 302, 304–305; child labor and, 303; Civil War and, 204, 208, 209; depression (1930's) and, 332–33, 337; labor movement and, 278, 280–81, 289; New Deal and, 339, 352; segregation in, 377; service industries and, 383; strikebreaking of, 315–16, 352; taxation of, 289, 304, 340, 341, 343, 364; World War II and, 344, 345–46, 353, 354
Insurance and Banking, Texas State Department of, 303
Insurance Commission, Texas State, 364, 365

Insurance Statistics and History, Texas State Department of, 294, 303
insurance companies, 283, 299, 303, 343, 373, 384; stock regulation, 364–65, 368
International Railroad, 270
International Traffic Association, 285
International Typographical Union, 281
Interscholastic League, 321
Interstate Commerce Act (U.S.), 283
Invincible (vessel), 125, 126
IOA Ranch, 255, 265
Iraan, Tex., 16
Ireland, John, 278, 279
Irion County, Tex., 166
Irish, the, in Texas, 49, 57, 83, 90, 170, 172, 173, 174, 199; population (1960), 381
Iron Front Saloon, Austin, 236
Isleta, Tex., 18, 56
Italians, the, in Texas, 173, 174, 347, 381
Iturbide, Agustin de, 76–77, 78, 87, 100

Jack, Patrick C., 93
Jack, Spencer H., 100
Jack, William, 93
Jackson, Andrew, 66, 68, 118, 119, 129–30; nullification theory, 187
Japanese, the, in Texas, 347, 350, 381
JA Ranch, Palo Duro Canyon, 255–56, 257
Jaybird-Woodpecker War, 284
Jefferson, Thomas, 59–60, 68, 186
Jefferson, Tex., 178, 269, 290
Jenkins' Ear, War of, 36
Jester, Beauford, 357, 359, 360, 363
Jimenez, Coahuila, 308
Jim Crow laws, 377, 378–79, 380
Jim Wells County, Tex., 360
Johnson, Andrew, 213, 215, 217, 218
Johnson, Cone, 300
Johnson, Francis W., 103, 107, 108–109, 114
Johnson, Lyndon Baines, 343, 356, 359–60, 372, 375; John F. Kennedy and, 370–71, 373

Johnson, M. T., 164
Johnson County, Tex., 167
Johnston, Albert Sidney, 133, 142, 169, 201, 202
Johnston, Joseph E., 166, 195, 200, 201
Joiner, C. M. "Dad," 334, 335
Jones, Anson, 133, 154, 155
Jones, George W., 278, 279, 299
Jones, Henry, 69
Jones, Jesse, 332, 340, 345
Jones, John B., 236–37, 238
Jonesborough, Tex., 69–70, 112
Journal of the Mier Expedition (Green), 175
Journey Through Texas (Olmsted), 184
Joutel, Henri, 23
Juárez, Benito, 237, 243
Juárez, Mexico, 19, 36, 308, 309, 376
Jumano Indians, 8, 15–16, 18, 19

Kansas, 13, 187, 209, 235, 283; cattle and, 251, 252, 253, 254, 264; Indians of, 246; railroads and, 270; school integration in, 380
Kansas-Nebraska Act (U.S.), 187, 189, 190
Karankawa Indians, 7, 41–42, 51, 52, 79, 172
Karnes, Henry, 116, 142–43
Katy Railroad (Missouri, Kansas, and Texas), 270
Kaufman, Tex., 192
Kaufman County, Tex., 285, 382
Kearby, Jerome C., 288
Kearny, Stephen W., 160, 161
Keatings-Owen Act (U.S.), 303
Keator, J. S., 265
Kelly, George E. M., 313
Kelly Field, San Antonio, 313, 344
Kemp, Louis Wiltz, 331
Kemper, Samuel, 64
Kendall, George Wilkins, 150, 175, 261
Kendall County, Tex., 207, 261
Kenedy, Mifflin, 254
Kenedy County, Tex., 254
Kennedy, John Fitzgerald, 370–71, 376; assassination of, 373–75

Kentucky, 58, 59, 92; Civil War and, 201, 210; Peters Colony and, 138, 139; states' rights issue and, 186
Kerr, James, 83
Kerr County, Tex., 207
Kerrville, Tex., 252, 314
Kickapoo Indians, 243, 246
Kilday, Owen, 352
Kilgore, Tex., 334
Kimble County War, 238
King, Amon, 114
King, Richard, 180, 254
King, Valentine O., 294
King County, Tex., 256, 257
King George's War, 36, 42
King Ranch, 180, 254
Kingsville, Tex., 316
Kiowa Indians, 35, 240, 241, 243, 244, 245, 246, 248, 252
Kirby Lumber Company, 272, 300
Kleberg, Richard, 254
Knights of the Golden Circle, 192, 196, 206
Knights of Labor, 278, 279, 281, 295
Knox, Amory, 294
Ku Klux Klan, 219, 315, 325–27, 328–29, 377–78
Kulp, W. O., 265
Kwahadi Comanches, 244

Labor, 271, 272, 371, 383; convict, 295, 304; depression (1930's), and, 332, 334, 337, 339, 350, 377; laws, 289, 303, 306, 315–16; Mexican, 350, 351–53; Negro, 280, 281, 287, 288, 371, 377, 379, 381; occupation percentages (1966), 384; occupation taxes, 275–76; poll tax and, 302; war shortages (1940's), 346
Labor, Texas State Federation of, 316
Labor Statistics, Texas State Bureau of, 280, 303
labor unions, 267, 295; beginnings of, 280–81; segregation in, 280, 377; strikes and, 278, 281, 315–16, 351–53
Lackland Air Base, San Antonio, 344
Lady in Blue legend, 15–16
La Branche, Alcée, 130
L'Archeveque, Jean, 23

Lafitte, Jean, 65, 66, 67, 173
LaGrange, Tex., 177
La Junta, Mexico, 19, 50
Lallemand, Charles, 65–66, 173
Lamar, Mirabeau B., 125, 126, 128, 133, 134, 144, 153, 175; capital establishment by, 145–46; Cherokee expulsion by, 142; election of 1838 and, 131, 132; financial problems and, 136, 147; Mexican Federalist revolts and, 149–50; Peters Colony and, 138; Texas University and, 292
Lampasas County, Tex., 234, 238, 280
Land Act of 1816 (U.S.), 70
Land Act of 1820 (U.S.), 70–71
Land Act of 1895 (Texas), 289
land acts and land policy (*see also* specific acts): cattle industry and, 254, 255, 256, 257, 259, 262, 264; colonization program (Mexico), 73–96; colonization program (Republic), 137–40; Comanche hunting grounds, 240; divestment laws on, 287; freedmen and, 228, 281; Indian petitions for, 140, 141; Mexican laws on, 77–79, 80, 81, 88–90, 91–92, 95, 101; Monclova government and, 102, 103; public domain alienation, 257–59, 264, 274, 277–78, 294–95, 296; for railroads, 180, 220, 222–23, 225, 227–28, 258–59, 265, 269, 270, 278, 285, 291; Salt War and, 234–35; scrip and, 136, 146, 148, 170, 265; Spanish, 69–70, 72, 73, 76, 171; state debt payment and, 275; of the Texas Republic, 90, 101, 127, 129, 134, 136, 137–40, 141, 145, 154, 292; United States, 136, 148, 153, 163, 169–70
Land Board, Texas State, 278
Land Board, Texas Veterans', 366–67, 368
Land Office, Texas State General, 281, 356, 366
Lang, William W., 276
Lanham, S. W. T., 299
Laredo, Tex., 37, 57, 87, 110, 152, 171, 309, 312, 313; antimony production, 355; Civil War and, 199; population changes, 348, 349; railroads and, 270; State Militia post, 167

Laredo, Tex. (*cont.*)
Larios, Father Juan, 17
LaSalle, Robert Cavelier, Sieur de, 21, 23, 31, 60, 172
Las Cuevas, Mexico, 237–38
Las Moras Creek, 90
Las Vacas (Villa Acuña), Mexico, 308
Lavaca County, Tex., 348
Lavaca River, 21, 83, 90
La Villita, San Antonio, 33, 34, 57
law enforcement (*see also specific agencies, e.g.,* Public Safety, Department of): Allred program, 341; Daniel administration, 373; Ferguson pardon policy and, 331, 340; feuds, 233–34; Kennedy assassination and, 374–75; Klan police membership and, 327; labor unrest and, 352; oil frauds and, 320, 331; post-Civil War, 211, 222, 224, 230–39; post-World War I, 315; prohibition and, 323–24; vigilante methods of, 192, 207, 231–32, 235, 308, 310, 326, 378, 380; "wheeler-dealer" culture and, 384–85
Law of April 6, 1830, *see* colonization laws
Lawrence, Adam, 69
League, Hosea, 91
League of United Latin American Citizens, 351
Lea-Peacock feud, 234
Lee, Robert E., 169, 195, 200, 202, 210
Leftwich, Robert, 91
León, Alonso de, 23–24
León, Father Diego, 15
León, Martín de, 82, 83, 122
Leon Springs, Tex., 312
Le Tourneau Company, 354
Lewis, Meriwether, 60
Liberty, Tex., 66, 85, 91, 92
Liberty County, Tex., 249, 382
Library, Texas State, 294
Library and Historical Commission, Texas State, 303–304

Liendo Plantation (Groce's), 115, 116, 293
Life of John Wesley Hardin (Hardin), 293
Limestone County, Tex., 222
Lincoln, Abraham, 191, 192, 193, 195, 210; assassination of, 217; *habeas corpus* suspension by, 228; Reconstruction and, 213, 215, 216
Lindheimer, Ferdinand J., 175
Ling, James, 384
Linn, John J., 293
Linnville, Tex., 143, 144
Lipan Indians (in Texas), 18, 35, 39–40, 41, 44, 49; Mackenzie massacre of, 246
"Little Colony" (Austin's), 82–83, 91
Little River, 167
Lively (vessel), 75, 79
Live Oak Creek, 166
Livingston, Robert R., 59
Llano Estacado, 13, 253
Llano River, 4
Llanorian Mountains, 1, 2, 3
Lockhart, Matilda, 143
Lodge, Oliver Cabot, 371
London, Treaty of, 32
London *Times* (newspaper), 305
Lone Star Steel Company, 355
Long, James, 65, 66, 67–68, 72
Longley, Bill, 235, 238
longshoremen, 315–16
Longview, Tex., 335, 378
Looney, B. F., 304
López, Father Nicolás, 17–19, 247
Los Adaes, 30, 32, 33, 34, 43, 60, 61, 172; capital removal from, 44, 45, 47
Louis XIV, King of France, 20, 21
Louisiana, 4, 7, 25, 26, 27, 40, 78, 218; cattle drives to, 55–56, 249, 250; Civil War in, 199–200, 204, 210; land speculation in, 71, 79; railroads and, 270; secession and, 193; Spanish in, 28, 29, 30, 36, 42–44, 45, 49, 55, 249; tidelands of, 368; U.S. transfer of, 56, 58, 59–60, 154, 187, 249
Loving, Oliver, 253, 254
Lower California Road, 166

Loyal Union League, 219, 230
Loyal Valley, Tex., 207
Lubbock, Francis R., 190, 202, 203, 207; memoirs of, 293, 294
Lubbock, Tom S., 135, 201, 202
Lubbock, Tex., 5, 13, 248, 345, 375, 382
Lubbock County, Tex., 265
Lubbock Lake Site, 5
Lucas Gusher, 318
Lufkin, Tex., 316
Luling oil field, 319
Lundy, Benjamin, 119
Lunatic Asylum, Texas State, 293
lynching, 192, 207, 234, 308, 310; Ku Klux Klan and, 326–27, 378
Lynch's Ferry, Texas, 116
Lytle, John T., 253, 261

McAdoo, William Gibbs, 328–29
McArdle, Henry Arthur, 293
McCamey, Tex., 19
McCarthy, Glenn, 384
McCord, J. E., 203, 204, 241
McCoy, Joseph G., 251
McCulloch, Ben, 135, 143, 196, 201
McCulloch, Henry E., 196
McCulloch County, Tex., 166, 171
McCullough, Samuel, 104
MacDonald, Bill, 301
McGloin, James, 82, 90
McKay, S. S., cited, 333
Mackenzie, Murdo, 256
Mackenzie, R. S., 245–46
McKenzie College, 177
McKinney, Thomas F., 105–106
McLean, William P., 286
McLennan, Neil, 170
McLeod, Hugh, 150
McMullen, John, 82, 90
McNelly, L. H., 222, 233, 236–38
Madero, Francisco I., 92, 308–309
Madison, James, 186
Madison County, Tex., 180
Madisonville, Tex., 233
Magee, Augustus W., 64
Magnolia Petroleum Company, 317
Magon, Flores, 308
Magruder, John B., 198, 200, 203, 210
Manga de Clavo, Mexico, 97

465 / Index

Manila, Philippines, 42
Mansfield, Tex., 380
Mansfield, battle (1864) of, 200
Marble Falls, Tex., 295
Marcy, Randolph B., 166, 167, 168, 245
Mares, José, 50
Marfa, Tex., 312
Marshall, Tex., 269, 270, 316, 378; Conference of Governors, 203, 210
Martín, Hernán, 16, 17
Martin, Wiley, 115, 116
Martínez, Antonio, 66, 71, 75–76, 79
Mason County, Tex., 171, 207, 234
Mason County War, 238
Massanet, Father Damian, 23, 24–26, 28
Masterson, "Bat," 236, 248
Matador Ranch, 255, 256, 257
Matagorda Bay, 21, 23, 25, 29, 32, 34, 36, 65, 83; Civil War and, 198, 199
Matamoros, Mexico, 90, 94, 118, 125, 141; cotton trade, 204; Texan plans to invade, 108–109, 110, 114, 126, 133, 151, 159
Matthews, J. F., 201
Maverick, Maury, 362
Maverick, Samuel A., 107, 234
Maverick County Tex., 90, 171
Maxey, Samuel Bell, 202, 276, 283
Maximilian Emperor of Mexico, 210, 243
Mayfield, Earle B., 327, 328, 332
Medicine Lodge Creek, Treaty of, 244
Medina, battle of, 64, 71
Medina River, 33, 64
Melish's Map (1818), 68, 69
Mellon, Andrew W., 319
Memoirs (Lubbock), 294
Memoirs (Reagan), 293
Menard, Tex., 19, 39
Mendoza, Juan Domínguez de, 17–19, 247
Mercer, Charles Fenton, 139
Mercer Colony, 139
Merritt, Wesley, 215
Mescalero Indians, 18, 35, 49
Mesilla, N.M., 196, 197
mestizos, 53, 54, 57, 62, 79, 172, 173

Meusebach, Ottfried, Baron von, 140
Mexia, Ignacio, 159
Mexía, José Antonio, 94
Mexia, Tex., 317, 319
Mexican Revolutions: (1810–1811), 58, 62–66, 68, 69–72; (1821), 76–77; (1822–1823), 77–78, 87; (1829–1832), 88, 92, 94–95, 122; (1839–1841), 149, 157; (1844), 152, 156; (1845), 159; (1864), 237–43; (1911), 307–309; (1916), 309–11
Mexican War (1846–1848), 90, 129, 156–61, 163, 167, 177, 201, 349–50
Mexicans, in Texas, 83, 87, 89, 206, 309, 310, 349; poll tax and, 302, 377; population changes among, 290, 347, 348, 349–50, 381; white racism and, 327, 350–51, 377–78
Mexico, 9, 18, 94, 206, 207, 325; Anglo-American colonization of, 77–105; army of, 92–95, 99, 110–18, 123, 125–26, 141, 152, 237, 309; border of, 3, 33, 36, 43, 60, 61, 67, 68, 69–70, 125, 148, 159, 160, 161, 162, 203, 236, 237–38, 246, 308–11, 312, 313, 350, 376; Cherokee land petitions to, 140; Christian Indians of, 51, 52; Congress of, 99, 101, 102, 159; colonization laws, 77–83, 86, 87, 88–90, 91–92, 94–95; constitutions of (*see also* specific constitutions), 80, 88, 93, 94, 96, 102, 112, 160; cotton trade of, 204, 205; French government of, 210, 215, 243; German note (1917) to, 310, 311, 312; national debt of, 129, 149, 157, 159, 161; navy of, 134; Pershing invasion of (1916), 310–11, 313; Confederate refuge in, 210, 226, 230; slaveholder plans to invade, 192; slavery abolished in, 86, 183; Texas Republic recognition by, 123, 125, 129–30, 134, 147, 148–53, 154, 156–57, 159; Texas War of Independence and, 103–22; U.S. treatment of Mexican nationals and, 350–51
Mexico City, Mexico, 12, 29, 30, 33,

Mexico City, Mexico (*cont.*)
  96; Austin in (1821), 76–78; Austin in (1833), 96, 97, 99–100, 132; frontier communications of, 48, 56, 63; Perote Castle in, 150, 152; provisional (1821) government in, 76, 77, 80–82; St. Denis in, 27–28; Scott expedition to, 160
Mézières, Athanase de, 49
Michigan, 265, 326
Michler, Nathaniel, 167
Midland, Tex., 5, 270, 345, 382, 383
Midland Man, 5
Midwestern University, 372
Mier, Mexico, 37; battle, 152
Milam, Ben, 82, 85, 102, 104, 107
Milam, Tex., 92
Milam County, Tex., 38
Miles, Nelson A., 246
Miller, Burchard, 139
Miller, E. T., quoted, 275
Miller, James B., 96, 164
Miller County, Ark., 68, 69–70, 79, 148
Millican, Tex., 181
Mills, Roger Q., 283
Mina, Francisco, 65
Mina (Bastrop), Tex., 103
Minnesota, 362, 375
Mission Nuestra Señora de la Candelaria, 38, 41
Mission Nuestra Señora de Guadalupe, 28, 47
Mission Nuestra Señora de los Dolores, 28, 30, 47
Mission Nuestra Señora del Espíritu Santo de Zuñiga, 32, 41, 52
Mission Nuestra Señora de la Luz, 42
Mission Nuestra Señora de la Purísima Concepción, 28, 32, 51, 52–53, 105; relocation of, 34
Mission Nuestra Señora del Rosario, 41, 51, 52
Mission San Antonio de Valero (The Alamo), *see* Alamo, The
Mission San Clemente, 19
Mission San Francisco de los Tejas, 24, 25, 27, 28, 29, 32, 34
Mission San Francisco Xavier de Horcasitas, 38–39, 54
Mission San Ildefonso, 38

Mission San José de los Nazonis (San Juan Capistrano), 28, 34, 50, 51
Mission San José y San Miguel de Aguayo, 31–32, 51, 52
Mission San Lorenzo de la Santa Cruz, 41
Mission San Miguel de Linares, 28, 29, 47
Mission San Sabá de la Santa Cruz, 39, 41
Mission Santísimo Nombre de María, 25
missions, 14, 15–16, 17–19, 50–53; Aguayo expedition and, 31, 32–33; Jesuit, 51; secularization of, 50, 52, 57; *Seno Mexicano* and, 36–42; Spanish-French cooperation in, 27, 28–30; Spanish relocation of, 34, 41, 43, 44, 45, 47, 52
Mississippi River, 4, 13, 14, 25, 178, 249; cattle shipment on, 250, 251, 269; French on, 20, 21, 26; Lafitte and, 65; Spanish Louisiana and, 43, 44, 58, 59, 60
Missouri, 26, 70, 78, 150, 189, 270; cattle drives to, 250, 251, 253; Civil War and, 201, 202, 204, 210; oil industry and, 289, 300
Missouri, Kansas, and Texas Railroad, 270
Missouri Compromise (1820), 187
Missouri River, 60
Mitchell County, Tex., 144, 261
Mobile Bay, 26
Mobil Oil Company, 319
Monclova, Mexico, 17, 36, 101–103
Monroe, James, 59
Montague County, Tex., 40
Montana, 252, 253, 255
Monterrey, Mexico, 36, 76, 86, 160, 205, 210
Montezuma, 9
Montgomery, Edmund, 293
Mooar, J. W., 248, 254
Moody, Dan, 332, 333, 346; reform platform of, 331
Moore, Edwin Ward, 134–35, 150
Moore, Francis W., 132, 175
Moore, John H., 104, 144
Mora Valley, N.M., 244
Moravians, 207

Morfí, Father Juan Agustín de, 48
Morfit, Henry, 129
Morgan, James, 116
Morris Omnibus Tax Bill, 343
Moscoso, Luis de, 13–14
Motley County, Tex., 256
Mound Builder people, 8
municipal charters, 302–303
Muldoon, Father Michael, 86
Murchison, Clint, 384
Murphy, Audie, 345
Murrah, Pendleton, 203, 204, 205, 209; Confederate defeat and, 210, 211, 230
Músquiz, Ramón, 95, 96, 100
Myers, A. C., 248

Naco, Tex., 308
Nacogdoches, Tex., 37, 47–48, 57, 59, 79, 96; Burr intrigue and, 60; cattle drives in, 55–56; Cherokee Treaty (1836), 109–10, 140; Edwards Colony, 82, 84–85, 122; founding of, 47–48; Gaines troops in, 141; Gutiérrez de Lara attacks, 64, 67; Houston as representative of, 132; Las Casas coup in, 63; Mission Guadalupe at, 23, 47; Terán report (1828) on, 87
Nacogdoches, battle of, 94
Nacogdoches County, Tex., 28, 232, 317
Nacogdoches Department, Coahuila y Texas, 81, 101
Nacogdoches Indians, 8, 28
Narváez, Pánfilo de, 11, 14
Nashville, Tex., 92
Natchitoches, La., 32, 48, 49, 50, 68, 73; founding of, 28; Gutiérrez de Lara in, 63, 64, 65
Natchitoches Indians, 8, 27, 28, 29
National Aeronautics and Space Administration, 378–79, 380
National Association for the Advancement of Colored People (NAACP), 378–79, 380
National Association Opposed to Woman Suffrage, 324
National Granite Cutters Union, 295
National Guard, 314, 315, 316; oil field closure and, 335, 336

National Industrial Recovery Act, 339, 352
National Labor Relations Board, 352
National Origins Act of 1924, 347, 350, 377
National Pecan Shellers Association, 352
National People's Party, *see* Populist Party
National Recovery Administration, *see* New Deal
National Trail (proposed), 253
National Woman Suffrage Association, 324
National Youth Administration, 339
Navarro, José Antonio, 150, 173
Navarro County, Tex., 263
Navasota County, Tex., 23
Navasota River, 144
Nazoni Indians, 8, 28
Neches Indians, 8, 17
Neches River, 4, 8, 14, 68; Spanish missions on, 24, 25, 29, 32, 34
Neches, battle of the, 142
Neff, Pat Morris, 316–17, 323, 331; Ku Klux Klan and, 326, 327, 328
Negroes, 11, 12, 57, 111, 172, 348, 361, 367, 371; freedman status of, 149, 212, 213, 215–16, 217, 218–19, 220, 228–30, 278, 376; freedman murders, 231, 235; Ku Klux Klan terrorism and, 219, 325–27; labor unions and, 280, 281, 287, 376; lynching of, 192, 378; military service of, 104, 199, 200, 230, 244, 378; poll taxes and, 302, 377; population changes among, 173, 281–82, 290, 347, 381; poverty of, 279, 281–82, 337, 377; in Reconstruction public office, 221, 222, 226, 230, 377; schools and, 229, 291–92, 321, 356, 376, 377, 379–81; in slavery, 53, 86, 118, 119, 127, 182–85, 187, 189, 208, 209, 212, 213; Texas Blind, Deaf, and Orphans School for, 293
Negro Longshoremen's Association, 281
Neighbors, Robert S., 161, 162, 166, 168
Neill, James C., 107, 109, 110

Neo-American Stage (of man), 5, 6–7, 8
Neri, Felipe Enrique ("Baron de Bastrop"), 71, 72, 79, 172
Neutral Ground Agreement (1806), 61, 84
New Braunfels, Tex., 39, 140, 144, 170, 173
New Braunfels *Zeitung* (newspaper), 175
Newcomb, J. P., 206
New Mexico, 3, 5, 6, 150, 253, 311; cattle industry in, 254–55; Civil War and, 196, 197, 219; Indians of, 8, 12, 13, 18, 35, 44, 48, 50–51, 142, 150, 241, 243, 244, 246; as Spanish province, 14–15, 17, 18, 33, 36, 50, 61, 62; Texas boundary claims and, 130, 131, 161, 187, 189; U.S. annexation of, 159, 161–62
New Mexico Territory, 162, 163
New Orleans, La., 75, 125, 148; Anglo-American fortification of, 60; Civil War and, 199, 206, 210; Mexican revolutionaries in, 64, 65, 66, 67, 94, 308; Spanish government in, 43; Texas cattle drives to, 55–56, 182; Texas provisional government (1863) in, 213, 215
New Orleans *Picayune* (newspaper), 261
New Packet (vessel), 90
New Regulations for the Presidios of the Frontier (Spain, 1772), 44, 45, 48
newspapers (*see also specific journals*), 175, 190, 206, 209, 354; Texas State Printer and, 222
New Washington, Tex., 91, 116
Ney, Elisabet, 293
Nimitz, Chester, 345
Nixon, L. H., 378–79
Nixon, Richard, 370, 371, 375
Nixon v. Herndon, 378–79
Niza, Father Marcos de, 12
Nokoni Indians, 169
Nolan, Philip, 59
Nolte, Eugene, 357
Norris, James, 122
Norris, James M., 241

Norris, Samuel, 84
North American Aviation Company, 354
North Llano River, 17
North Texas (*see also specific place names*), 194, 207, 209, 234
North Texas State Teachers College, 322
Northwest Ordinance (1787), 187
Norton, A. B., 279, 280
Nueces County, Tex., 171, 240
Nueces River, 3–4, 17, 90, 151, 170, 171; cattle ranching on, 249; missions on, 37, 41, 43, 44, 51; Taylor forces on, 159; Union Loyal League on, 207
Nuevo León, Mexico, 14, 48, 61, 149
Nuevo Reyno de la Montaña de Santander y Santillana, 25
Nuevo Santander (*see also* Tamaulipas), 36–42, 48, 63
Nugent, Thomas L., 286, 287, 288
Nunn, W. C., quoted, 232

"Obnoxious Acts" (1870–1871), 221–22, 224, 232–33, 275
Ochiltree, W. B., 164
O'Connor, Thomas, 254
Oconór, Hugo, 49
O'Daniel, W. Lee ("Pappy"), 342–43, 344, 346, 359, 367, 370
Odessa, Tex., 382, 383
O. Henry (William S. Porter), 294
oil industry, 14, 145, 301, 315, 317–20, 331, 336–37, 353; antitrust laws and, 289, 300; cattle lands and, 256, 257; independent producers in, 334–35; Spindletop and, 275, 318; taxation and, 341; tidelands issue and, 368; University of Texas and, 227, 322; war and, 345, 346, 354–55; wealth (1960) of, 383, 384, 385
Oklahoma, 13, 251, 257, 289, 319; Indians of, 35, 169, 241, 244
Old Eight Ranch, 257
Oldham, W. S., 202
Old Station, Matagorda Bay, 83
Old Stone Fort, Nacogdoches, 84

"Old Three Hundred," 78–79, 83
Olivares, Father Antonio de San Buenaventura, 29
Olmsted, Frederick Law, 175, 184
Omnibus Tax Bill (1941), 364
Oñate, Juan de, 14–15
Onderdonk, Robert Jenkins, 293
Onís, Luis de, 66
Open Port Law (Tex.), 315–16
Orange, Tex., 181, 272, 345, 354
Orcoquisac (mission and presidio), 42, 43, 44, 51, 54, 60
Ord, O. C., 238
Orphans School, Texas State, 293
O'Reilly, Alejandro, 49
Organic Law (1835), 106
Orozco, Pascual, 309
Ortega, Father Juan de, 16
Oswald, Lee Harvey, 374–75
Our Lady of the Lake School, 293

Pacific Northwest, Adams-Onís Treaty on, 67
Pakenham, Lewis, 152, 154
Paleo-American Stage (of man), 5
Palestine, Tex., 316
Palmito Ranch, battle (1865) of, 195, 200
Palo Alto, battle of, 160
Palo Duro Canyon, Tex., 13, 246, 248, 255–56
Palo Pinto County, Tex., 169
Panhandle, The (*see also specific place names*), 2, 3, 35, 166, 248, 257; archeology of, 6; farming in, 261; Indians of, 241, 243, 246; railroads and, 270; Spanish in, 13, 15
Panhandle Grass Lease case, 256
Panhandle oil field, 319
Panic of 1819, 70
Panic of 1873, 226–27, 267, 270, 275
Panic of 1893, 266, 267, 274, 287
Panuco River, 14
Paredes, Mariano, 153, 159, 160
Parilla, Diego Ortiz de, 39, 40–41
Paris, France, 148
Paris, Treaty (1763) of, 42, 43, 49, 58
Parker, Cynthia Ann, 169

Parker, Quanah, 169
Parker County, 280
Parkman, Francis, 265
Parmer, Martin, 84, 122
Parrott, William, 159
Parson, W. H., 201
"Pastry War" (1838), 149, 157
Patrons of Husbandry (The Grange), 226–27, 267, 276; political action of, 226, 279, 280, 282
Pawnee Indians, 35
Payne University, Howard, 292
Peace Party, 207
Pea Ridge, battle (1862) of, 201
Peary, Robert Edwin, 320
Pease, Elisha M., 164, 165, 176, 177, 189; as provisional governor, 218, 221, 276; unionism of, 206, 217
Pease River, 169
Pecan Point, 69
Pecan Shelling Workers Union, 352–53
Pecos, Texas, 13
Pecos River, 3, 8, 16–17, 18, 19, 62, 179, 253; surveys on, 165, 166
Peddy, George, 328, 359
Pedraza, Gómez, 88, 94
Penetka Comanches, 168
Penn, William, 244
Pennsylvanian (Upper Carboniferous) Period, 1
Pennybacker, Mrs. Percy V., 293–94
Pension Act (Tex., 1936), 342
Permanent Council (1835), 105, 107, 108
Permian Sea, 1–2, 383
Perote Castle, Mexico City, 150, 152
Perpetuities and Corporations Land Law (Tex., 1893), 287
Pershing, John J., 310–11, 313
Peta Nocona (Comanche chief), 169
Peters, W. S., 138
Peters Colony, 138–39, 170, 173, 189, 194
Petrolia oil field, 319
Philadelphia, Pa., 70, 147, 148, 186
Philip V, King of Spain, 30
Philip Dru (House), 299
Philippine Islands, 42, 381
Phillips, Jimmy, 367
Piedras, José de las, 93–94

Pierce, Abel H. ("Shanghai"), 254
Pierce, Henry Clay, 300
Pike, Albert, 240
Pike, Zebulon, 60, 61
Pilgrim, Thomas J., 86
Pilot Point, Tex., 192
Pinckney Treaty (San Lorenzo), 58
Piñeda, Alonzo Alvarez de, 9, 11
Piper, Edward, 250
Piute Indians, 35
Pizarro, Francisco, 9, 12
Plains Indians (see also specific groups), 7, 18, 35, 40, 41, 51, 140, 215; buffalo culture of, 245, 247–48; destruction of, 241–47; Vial and, 49–50
Plainview, Tex., 5
Plan de Iguala (1821), 77
Plan de San Diego, 309, 310
Platte River, 35
Plum Creek, 144
Plymouth, England, 148
Point Bolivar, 67–68
Poles, the, in Texas, 207, 347, 381
Polk, James K., 154, 155, 159, 160
Ponce de León, Juan, 9
Ponton, Andrew, 104
Pool, Walter, 69
Poolville, Tex., 280
population, 267, 274; eighteenth-century, 56, 57, 58, 172–73; nineteenth-century, 85, 86, 172–75, 189, 281–82, 290; prehistoric, 5; slave, 183, 189; twentieth-century, 347–49, 381–82
Populist Party, 267, 286, 287, 288, 299
Port Arthur, Tex., 319, 345, 354
Porter, Jack, 360
Porter, William S. (O. Henry), 294
Port Lavaca, Tex., 180
Port Neches, Tex., 319
Portugal, 20, 174
Potosi, Mo., 70, 72, 73
Potter, A. J., 253
Potter, Robert, 113
Potter and Bacon Trail, 253
Powell oil field, 319
Power, James, 82, 90, 254
Power and Hewetson Colony, 254

Prairie View State A&M College, 291–92, 322, 377, 379
Preemption Act (1854), 170
Prendergast, Albert C., 287
Presidio Nuestra Señora de los Dolores (Tejas), 29, 30, 32, 34
Presidio Nuestra Señora de Loreto (La Bahía), 32
Presidio Nuestra Señora del Pilar (Los Adaes), 32
Presidio San Antonio de Bexar (San Antonio), 29, 32
Presidio San Agustín de Ahumada (Orcoquisac), 42, 43, 44, 51, 54, 60
Presidio San Francisco Xavier (San Gabriel), 38–39
Presidio San Luis de las Amarillos (San Saba), 39–40, 41, 43
Presidio, Tex., 8, 56, 308
presidios, 26, 28, 29, 32–33, 34, 38, 39–40, 41, 42, 43, 44, 53–54, 56, 57, 60–61
Preston, William, 210
Price, William, 246
Printer, Texas State, 222
prisons, 232, 245, 278, 280, 294, 341, 373; convict labor system, 295, 304; Dallas, 374–75; Ferguson pardon policy, 331, 340; modernization (1949) of, 363; penal code revision (1966), 376; prisoner-of-war camps, 345; strikers in, 352
Proctor, Les, 367
progressivism (see also reform movements; civil rights), 293, 297–307, 331, 363–64
Progresso, Tex., 310
Prohibition, 278, 280, 282–83, 287, 299, 315; brewery trusts and, 304–305; Constitutional Amendment on, 145, 299, 323–24; referendum of 1911 on, 301; repeal of, 332, 339, 341, 353
Prohibition Party, 287, 288
property laws, 325
Protestantism, 86, 174, 177, 348; education and, 292, 293, 322; Ku Klux Klan and, 326
Provincias Internas (Spain), 48–49, 61, 71–72, 89

471 / Index

provisional government (1835), 105–107, 126–27, 141; Matamoros campaign and, 108–109, 110, 141; treasury warrants of, 135–36
provisional government (1865–1866), 213, 215–16
Pueblo Indians, 8, 14, 15, 19; Revolt of 1680, 18, 50–51
pueblos, 6–7, 12, 13, 53, 54–55
Public Safety, Texas State Department of, 341, 366

Quakers, 244–45
Quebec, Canada, 21, 26, 27
Queretaro, Mexico, 51
Quihi, Tex., 139
Quin, C. K., 352
Quitaque, Tex., 244
Quivera, 12–13, 15

Rábago y Teran, Felipe de, 38, 41, 43
Railroad Commission, Texas State, 285–87, 299, 301, 302, 357; oilfield division, 336
railroads, 145, 166, 180–81, 236, 247, 306; agriculture and, 274, 278, 285; antitrust laws and, 283, 284–85, 299; cattle shipment and, 250, 251, 252, 253, 254, 266; federal loans to, 340; labor laws and, 303; lumber industry and, 271, 273; Reconstruction and, 220, 222–23, 225, 269; regulatory commission on, 285–87, 299, 301, 302; segregation on, 378; strikes, 281, 316, 317; Texas Constitution of 1876 on, 227–28, 258, 269
Raines, Caldwell Walton, 294
Rainey, Homer Price, 356–57, 369
Ramón, Diego, 27, 28
Ramón, Domingo, 28–29, 30, 31, 32
Ramsey, Ben, 361, 362
Randolph Field, 313–14, 344
Ranger oil field, 319–20, 331
Rankin, Melinda, 175
Rath, Charles, 248
Raton Pass, 253
Rayburn, Sam, 312, 360, 371
Reagan, John H., 202, 217, 226, 288,

Reagan, John H. (cont.)
293; Prohibition and, 283; Railroad Commission and, 286, 301, 302
Reagh, Frank, 293
Reconstruction period, 185, 212–23, 376, 379; Indians and, 243, 244; reaction against, 223–30, 269, 275, 326, 377
Reconstruction Acts (1876), 213, 218
Red River, 3, 4, 27, 28, 50, 142, 166, 179, 199, 246, 270; Anglo-American exploration of, 60, 61, 167; Apache-Comanche battle on, 35; cattle shipment on, 250, 251, 252, 269; Comanche-Kiowa agency on, 240–41; French trade on, 32, 40, 49; Louisiana boundary, 67, 68, 69; Oklahoma and, 289; Olmsted on, 184; Peters Colony on, 138, 170; Wavell Colony on, 85
Red River County, Tex., 69
reform movements (see also progressivism; civil rights), 146, 147, 160, 192, 275–89
Refugio, Tex., 109, 114
Reminiscences of Fifty Years in Texas (Linn), 293
Republic of Texas, see Texas, Republic of
Republican Party, 191–92, 193; election of 1860, 191–92; elections of 1866–1873, 216–17, 219, 220, 221; elections of 1879–1900, 276, 279–80, 287; election of 1912, 301; elections of 1924–1932, 329, 332, 337, 338; election of 1946, 357; elections of 1952–1964, 361, 362–63, 368, 370–71, 375; Greenback Party coalition, 278, 279, 280; Jaybird-Woodpecker War and, 284; Reconstruction period and, 212–13, 217, 218, 219, 220–23, 232, 376, 377; resentment (1872–1876) and reaction against, 223–30, 232, 275; split of 1892, 287, 288; Texas primary system and, 331
Republican River, 6
Resaca de la Palma, battle of, 160
Reyes, Bernardo, 309
Reynolds, J. J., 219–20, 221

Index / 472

Reynosa, Mexico, 37
Rice, James O., 142
Rice University, 322
Richardson, David, 175
Richardson, Rupert N., quoted, 224
Richardson, Sid, 384
Richardson, Willard, 175
Richmond, Tex., 116, 284
Richmond, Va., 70, 191; Confederate seat in, 197, 198, 203
Rio Grande River, 3, 5, 9, 11, 17, 90, 381; agriculture on, 353; cattle ranching on, 237, 249, 254; Emory survey of, 167; Indians of, 7, 13, 14, 35, 39, 241, 246; Louisiana Purchase and, 60, 67; navigation on, 180; Santa Anna forces on, 113, 118; Spanish settlement on, 18–19, 27, 29, 31, 36, 37, 51, 56, 161, 171; Texas boundary claims and, 108, 118, 123–24, 130–31, 159, 160, 161, 162, 376; U.S. fortification of, 196, 199, 215, 221, 309–10, 312; Woll on, 152
Rio Grande, Republic of the, 122, 149, 308
Rio Grande City, Tex., 199, 312
Rio Grande Colony, 90, 173
Rio de los Nueces (River of Nuts), see Nueces River
Ripperdá, Baron de, 45, 47
Rivera y Villalon, Pedro de, 33–34, 35, 39, 40
Roberts, Oran M., 194, 217, 218, 292, 294; as governor, 276–78, 279
Robertson, E. S. C., 82
Robertson, Felix D., 329
Robertson, Jerome, 202
Robertson, Sterling C., 91–92
Robertson Insurance Law, 303, 364
Robinson, James W., 106, 108
Rockwell County, Tex., 382
Rocky Mountains, 2, 3, 35
Rodriguez, Joseph, 224
Rodriguez, Magdaleno, 352
Roemer, Ferdinand, 175
Roman Catholicism, 20, 90, 99, 173; anti-Catholicism and, 164, 326, 332, 371; as citizenship requirement in Mexico, 78, 82, 86, 120; education and, 292–93, 322

Roosevelt, Franklin D., 299, 338–40, 343, 344, 359; Texas Regulars and, 346–47, 356, 361
Roosevelt, Theodore, 289
Roscoe, Snyder, and Pacific Railroad, 266
Rose, Victor, 111
Ross, Lawrence S., 169, 201, 280, 282, 284
Rough Riders, 289
Round Rock, Texas, 236
Rubi, Marquis de, 43–44, 45, 48, 54
Ruby, Jack, 375
Ruiz, Francisco, 63
Runnels, Hardin R., 165, 190, 202
Rural High School Law (Tex.), 306
Rusk, Thomas Jefferson, 113, 125, 126, 128, 164; death of, 191
Rusk, Tex., 304
Rusk County, Tex., 290
Russians, the, in Texas, 347, 382, 391
Rutersville College, 177

Sabeata, Juan, 18, 19
Sabine Boundary Convention (1837), 148
Sabine Lake, 4, 68
Sabine Pass, 33, 195, 198, 199
Sabine River, 3, 4, 8, 14, 60, 61, 64, 116, 141; Louisiana boundary and, 67, 68, 69
St. Denis, Louis Juchereau de, 27–29, 30, 49
St. Lawrence River, 21
St. Mary's University, 177, 292, 322
Salado, Mexico, 92, 152
Salado Creek, 151
Salas, Father Juan de, 15–16
Salcedo, Manuel de, 63, 64
Saligny, Alphonse de, 147–48
Salt Creek Massacre, 245
Saltillo, Mexico, 23, 36, 63, 94, 100, 109; as capital of Coahuila y Texas, 80, 91, 101, 102
Salt War, 234–35, 238
Sam Houston State Normal School, 292, 322
San Angelo, Tex., 2, 16, 19, 243, 345
San Antonio, Tex., 1, 11, 71–72, 75–

473 / Index

San Antonio, Tex. (cont.)
  76, 85, 101, 170, 179, 236, 240, 362; Alamo battle in, 110–12, 113; California routes from, 166; Civil War and, 196, 197, 206, 231; colleges of, 292–93; Comanche Treaty (1840), 142–43; Cos fortification of, 104, 109; Council House fight, 142–43; Democratic convention (1890) in, 285; Gutiérrez de Lara capture of, 64; Know-Nothing Party in, 165; Ku Klux Klan resistance in, 327; Mexican invasions (1842), 151–52; Mexican Revolution (1910–1916) and, 308, 309, 311; Negro voters and, 379; pecan shellers' strike in, 351–53; population changes in, 174, 290, 348, 349, 382; Rough Riders in, 289; Santa Fe and, 50, 61–62; as Spanish capital, 44, 45, 47, 48, 57, 63, 66; Spanish settlement of, 29, 30, 31, 32–33, 34, 36, 37–38, 40, 41, 43, 51, 54, 172; state militia post in, 167, 196; Texan siege (1835) of, 105, 107–108, 141; Texas statehood issue and, 99, 100; Western Trail and, 252
San Antonio Aviation Center, 313
San Antonio and Mexican Gulf Railway Company, 180
San Antonio River, 4, 29, 31, 32, 34, 75, 170, 171; cattle on, 249; irrigation canals of, 52; Long on, 67–68; Nuevo Santander and, 37, 41, 43
San Antonio State Hospital, 293
San Augustine, Tex., 29, 361
San Augustine University, 177
Sanborn, H. B., 260
Sánchez, Manuela, 27
San Clemente River, 19
San Diego, Tex., 309
San Elizario, Tex., 235
San Felipe de Austin, Tex., 79, 80, 86, 115, 116, 180; Conventions of 1832–1833 in, 94–96; Tenorio and, 103; Texas Provisional Government (1835) in, 105–107, 108
San Fernando Cathedral, 33
San Francisco, Calif., 201
San Gabriel mission field, see San

San Gabriel mission field (cont.)
  Xavier mission field
San Gabriel River, Indian fight on, 142
San Ildefonso, Treaty (1800) of, 59, 60
San Jacinto, battle of, 115–18, 122, 141; veterans' land grants, 134, 137
San Jacinto (vessel), 135
San Jacinto River, 116, 117
San Juan Bautista, Mexico, 27, 29, 36, 57
San Juan Bautista, Yucatan, 134
San Lorenzo (Pinckney) Treaty, 58
San Marcos, Tex., 345
San Marcos River, 39
San Patricio, Tex., 90, 109, 114, 170
San Sabá mission, see Mission Nuestra Señora de la Santa Cruz
San Sabá presidio, see Presidio San Luis de Amarillas
San Sabá River, 4, 19, 39, 41, 44, 61
Santa Anna, Antonio López de, 88, 92, 93, 94, 114, 148; army command of 1846, 160; dictatorship of, 99–103, 122, 130, 149–50; elections of 1832–1833 and, 95–96, 97; overthrow (1844), 150, 152, 156, 157; restoration (1841) to power, 149–50; San Antonio siege and, 109, 110–12, 113; San Jacinto campaign and, 115–18, 122, 123, 133, 141; Texas invasions (1842), 151–52; treaties of Texas with, 123, 125, 131
Santa Fe, N.M., 130, 142, 150, 197; Kearney occupation of, 160, 161; routes to, 50, 60–61, 166; as Spanish capital, 14, 15, 16, 17, 23, 27
Santa Fe County, Tex., 161
Santa Fe expedition (1841), 149, 150, 151, 175
Santa Fe Railroad, 252
Santa Gertrudis land grant, 254
San Xavier mission field, 37–39, 41, 51
San Xavier presidio, see Presidio San Francisco Xavier
Sardinia, 30, 174
Satanta (Kiowa chief), 245
Sayers, Joseph D., 288, 289, 299

Scandinavians, in Texas, 174, 206, 290, 381
Scharbauer, John, 261
Schnell, Mattheas, 295
schools (*see also* specific institutions), 86, 95, 223, 259, 276, 304, 372; appropriations veto (1879), 277; cattle lands and, 255, 256, 262, 265; centralized administration of, 220, 227, 291; Mexican immigrants and, 351; Negroes and, 229, 291–92, 321, 356, 376, 377, 379–81; parochial, 86, 292–93, 322; "patriotic" studies in, 314; on plantations, 183; reorganization (1933), 341; reorganization (1949), 363–64; reorganization (1966), 376; rural high school system, 306, 321; Texas Republic and, 144, 145, 163, 177; textbooks and, 321–22, 331
School for the Blind, Texas, 293
School for the Deaf, Texas, 293
Schreiner, Charles, 253
Scott, Dred, 187, 189, 191
Scott, Winfield, 135, 160
Screwman's Benevolent Association, 281
secessionism, 162, 164, 165, 185, 186–95, 276; Civil War surrender and, 210–11, 215; dissent and, 205–207, 213, 221; nullifications, 215–16, 217
Sedalia, Mo., 250, 251
Seguín, Erasmo, 63, 75, 96
Selective Service Act (U.S., 1940), 344
Semicolon Case, 224–25
Seno Mexicano, 36–37
Senterfitt, Reuben, 367
Sesma, Joaquin Ramirez y, 110, 113, 115, 116
settlement, 172–78, 228, 233, 297; Anglo-American, 69, 70–79, 80–87, 88–94, 118–19; Czech, 207; English, 43, 174; Mexican colonization laws and, 77–78, 81, 88–90, 91–92, 94–95, 100, 101; Neutral Ground Agreement and, 61, 84; Spanish, 26, 29, 30, 31, 33, 36–37, 42, 44, 45–58, 172, 349; Texas Republic inducements to, 134, 136, 137–40,

settlement (*cont.*)
144–45; Texas State frontier, 165–71, 236, 240, 241, 257–66, 277–78
Seven Cities of Cíbolo, 13, 14
Seven Laws, 102
Seven Years War (French and Indian Wars), 42
Seymour, Tex., 252
Shaler, William, 63–64
Shannon, William, 157
Shaw, James, 176
Shaw, Quincy, 265
Sheep War, 261–62
Shelby, Joseph, 210
Sheppard, John Ben, 362, 366
Sheppard, Morris, 312, 323, 343
Sheridan, Phillip H., 215, 218, 219; Indians and, 244
Sherman, Sidney, 117
Sherman, William T., 200, 245, 246
Sherman Antitrust Bill, 283, 299
Sherman, Texas, 177, 207, 316
Shiloh, battle (1862) of, 201
Shivers, Allan, 356, 360–63, 364, 366, 367, 368, 371, 372, 380
Shoshone linguistic group, 35
Shreve, Henry, 179
Sibley, Henry H., 197, 198
Sibley, John, 60, 63, 68
Sierra Blanca, Tex., 270
Siete Leyes, 102
Simmons, W. J., 326
Sioux Indians, 256
Siringo, Charles, 293
Six Decades in Texas (Lubbock), 293
Slaughter, C. C., 254
slavery, 182–85, 208, 209, 213, 215; British abolitionism, 146, 147; free soil issue and, 153–54, 162; fugitives from, 92, 187; land speculation and, 75, 86; Peters Colony and, 139; Southern secessions and, 162, 164, 165, 187–89, 190, 191–95; Spanish and, 9, 11, 14, 53, 56, 182; state emancipations from, 215–16, 218, 221, 228; Texas Constitution on, 127; Texas Revolution and, 118, 119, 122, 130, 146
Slidell, John, 159

Smith, Ashbel, 178
Smith, E. Kirby, 200, 204, 205, 210, 215
Smith, Erastus ("Deaf"), 83, 116, 117
Smith, Garland, 365
Smith, Henry, 81, 106, 110, 127, 128, 135; Matamoros invasion and, 108, 109
Smith, Preston, 375
Smith County, Tex., 232
Smith v. *Allwright*, 379
Snyder, D. H., 254
Solms-Braunfels, Carl, Prince of, 139-40
Somervell, Alexander, 151, 152
Sonora, Mexico, 310, 311
Sour Lake oil field, 318
Southern Cotton Conference (1931), 333
Southern Methodist University, 322
Southern Pacific Railroad, 266, 270, 284
Southern Pecan Shelling Company, 352
South Plains (see also specific place names), 2, 3, 4, 5, 35, 261
South Texas (see also specific place names), 233, 308, 349, 371; cattle ranching in, 55, 237, 250, 253, 254; Civil War in, 199, 206; Comanche raid (1840) in, 143-44; Coleto Creek defeat and, 113-15; depression (1930's) in, 334
Southwestern University, 293
Southwest Texas State Teachers College, 322
Spade Ranch, 255, 334
Spaight, Ashley W., 294
Spain, 20, 30, 36, 289, 325; Florida cession by, 66-68; Louisiana cessions, 42-44, 49, 55, 59-60; Mexican independence from, 58, 62-66, 68, 72, 76-78; Mexican reconquest effort (1829), 88; Neutral Ground Agreement (1806), 61
Spanish, the (see also Hispanics), 7, 8, 9-19, 172, 173; army organization of, 44, 48, 53-54, 60-61; buffalo herds and, 247; cattle branding custom of, 264; colonization

Spanish, the (*cont.*)
methods of, 33, 44, 45-58, 171, 182; French rivalry and, 20-21, 23, 24, 25, 26-27, 29, 30-31, 32, 42-43, 44; sheep ranching of, 261
Spanish-American War, 289
Spanish Fort, Tex., 40
Speeches and State Papers of James Stephen Hogg, 294
Speer, Ocie, 325
Spindletop, 275, 318
Spratt, John S., 271
Spur Ranch, 255
Stafford's Point, Tex., 180
Standard Oil Company, 289, 300
Starr County, Tex., 167, 180, 349
State Colonization Law, see colonization laws
State House, construction of (see also XIT Ranch), 294-96
states' rights doctrine, 186-87, 189, 367, 372; Confederacy and, 203, 205
Steger, Harry Peyton, 294
Steger, William M., 370
Stephen F. Austin State Teachers' College, 322
Stephens, John Henry, 253
Sterling, Ross, 333, 337-38, 340; oil and, 319, 335-36
Sterling City, Tex., 13
Stevenson, Adlai, 362, 373
Stevenson, Coke R., 343-44, 346, 359-60
Stilson, Eli, 265
Stock and Bond Law of 1893 (Texas), 287
Stockdale, Fletcher S., 203, 210-11
suffrage, 212, 217; poll taxes and, 220, 276, 277, 291, 302, 314, 377; school standards and, 321; voter registration issues, 215-16, 218-19, 224, 229, 230, 281-82, 302, 378-79; women and, 145, 315, 316, 324-25
Sulphur River, 231
Sul Ross State Teachers' College, 322
Supreme Court, Texas State, 139, 194, 222, 224, 225, 276; elections to, 227; oil field closure by, 336; and railroads, 285
Sutton County, Tex., 17

Sutton-Taylor feud, 233–34, 235
Swartwout, Samuel, 91
Swartwout, Tex., 91
Sweatt, Herman Marion, 356, 379
Sweet, Alexander E., 294
Sweetwater, Tex., 270
Swenson, S. M., 206
Swift meatpackers, 353
Swiss, the, in Texas, 90, 91, 139, 173

Taft, Robert A., 340, 362
Taft, William Howard, 301, 308
Tamaulipas (Nuevo Santander), 36–42, 48, 63, 83, 237; Mina expedition, 65; separatist movement in, 149
Tampico, Mexico, 9, 36, 89
Taney, Roger B., 187, 189
Taos, N.M., 130, 142, 197
Taovayas village, 40, 50
Tariff of 1824, 187
Tarrant County, Tex., 138, 167, 273, 290
Tatum, Lawrie, 244–45
Tawakoni Indians, 50
taxation, 306, 333, 364; corporate, 289, 304, 340, 341, 343, 364; occupational, 275–76, 284; sales tax proposals, 343, 364, 370, 373, 375; voting and, 220, 276, 277, 291, 302, 314, 377
Taylor, Abner, 295
Taylor, Hays, 233
Taylor, Richard, 200
Taylor, Zachary, 135, 159–60, 161–62
Taylor Bayou, 198
Téhuacana, Tex., 293
Tehuacana Creek, Treaty of, 144
Tejas Indians, 17, 23–24, 25, 27, 30
Telegraph and Texas Register (newspaper), 132, 175
Temple, Tex., 316
Temple State Bank, 305
tenant farming, 273–74, 278, 305–306, 334, 382–83
Tenorio, Antonio, 103
Terán, Manuel de Mier y, 86–87, 88, 89
Terán de los Rios, Domingo, 24–25
Terrell, A. W., 210

Terrell Election Law (Texas), 300, 302, 377
Terrell State Hospital, 293
Terreros, Father Alonso Giraldo de, 39
Terreros, Pedro Romero de, 39
Terry, B. F., 201
Terry's Texas Rangers, 201, 202
Texaco, Inc. (Texas Company), 317, 319, 336
Texans for America, 373
Texarkana, Tex., 14
Texas. Provisional government (1835), 105–107, 126–27, 141; Alamo battle and, 111, 112; Matamoros campaign and, 108–109, 110, 141; treasury warrants of, 135–36
Texas. Provisional government. Permanent Council, 105, 107, 108, 109
Texas, Republic of (*see also specific references*): domestic problems, 133–46; foreign problems, 146–55; government and politics, 123–133
Texas army and militia, 105, 106, 107–109, 110–12, 113, 115–18, 123, 126, 134, 167, 195–96, 222, 240–43, 245
Texas constitutions, *see specific constitution*
Texas navy, 113, 125, 126, 133, 134–35; in Yucatan, 150, 151
Texas state agencies, bureaus, and departments, *see under generic name*, e.g., Agriculture, Department of
Texas elections: 1836–1844, 126, 127–28, 131, 132–33; 1845–1855, 164–65; 1857–1865, 189, 191, 203; 1866–1869, 217, 218, 219, 221; 1871–1879, 212, 222, 224–25, 275, 276; 1880–1888, 278, 279, 280, 282, 284; 1890–1896, 285–86, 287, 288; 1900–1908, 299, 300, 301; 1910–1916, 301, 305, 306, 321, 323; 1920–1928, 316, 317, 327, 329, 331, 332; 1930–1938, 333, 337–38, 340, 341, 342–43; 1940–1948, 343, 346, 357, 359–60, 369; 1950–1958, 361–62, 367–68, 369, 370, 380; 1960–1968, 370–71, 372, 375–76, 379

Texas, University of, 177, 278, 292, 321; Ferguson and, 307; German studies, 314; historical studies, 294; Negroes and, 356, 379; oil and, 227, 322; Rainey and, 356–57; School of Military Aeronautics, 313
Texas (Holly), 175
Texas (Rankin), 175
Texas Agricultural and Mechanical College (Texas A&M), 291, 322
Texas Almanac, 175
Texas Association of Nashville, 91–92
Texas Baptist Herald (newspaper), 282
Texas Boundary Statute (1836), 130
Texas Cattle Raisers Association, 263
Texas Christian Advocate (newspaper), 282
Texas Christian University, 292, 322
Texas City, Tex., 313, 355
Texas Company (Texaco, Inc.), 317, 319, 336
Texas Contractors' Association, 331
Texas Cowboy, A (Siringo), 293
Texas Declaration of Independence, 112, 122, 177
Texas Emigration and Land Company, 138
Texas Equal Rights Association, 324
Texas fever, 250, 251, 253–54, 256
Texas Good Roads Association, 306
Texas Medical Association, 178
Texas Medical College, 292
Texas Military Board (Confederate), 203, 204–205, 208
Texas Military District (Confederate), 196–98, 203, 207, 209–11
Texas Mutual Insurance Company, 365
Texas Naturopathic Physicians, 369
Texas and Pacific Railroad, 166, 266, 269, 270
Texas Rangers, 135, 140, 143–44, 167, 308, 314; Civil War and, 196, 201, 207; fence-cutting wars and, 263; feuding and, 234–35; Frontier Battalion, 236, 238, 247, 275, 284; Frontier Regiment (Norris) and, 241, 284; Highway Patrol and, 341; labor unrest and, 315, 316; liquor law enforcement by, 323; Mc-

Texas Rangers (*cont.*)
Nelly's Special Force, 222, 233, 236–39; Mexican invasions (1842) and, 151; Mexican War and, 160, 166; oil field unrest (1930's) and, 336; school integration and, 380
Texas Regulars, 346–47, 361
Texas Revolution, 83, 92, 97–122, 173, 249; Cherokees and, 109–10, 140-41
Texas Siftings (periodical), 294
Texas Tech University, 322, 379–80
Texas Tourist Bureau, 376
Texas Traffic Association, 285
Texas Trunk Railroad, 284–85
Texas Wesleyan University, 293
Texas Woman Suffrage Association, 324
Texas Woman's University, 322
Texas Youth Council, 373
Textbook Commission, Texas State, 331
Texline, Texas, 316
Thomas, David, 113
Thompson, Ben, 235–36
Thompson, Ernest, 336
Thompson, Waddy, 157
Thornton, William A., 159–60
Thorpe Spring, Tex., 292
Throckmorton, J. W., 206, 207, 216–17, 218, 276; quoted, 194; Indians and, 241, 243, 244
Tiguex pueblo, 13
tin smelting, 345–46, 355
Tippit, J. D., 374
Tobasco River, Yucatan, 134
Toby, Thomas, 148
Tom Green County, 179
Tomlinson's Rangers, 135
Tonkawa Indians, 38, 40, 79
topography, 2, 3–4; Adams-Onís Treaty and, 68–69
Torrey brothers, 144, 167
Tower, John G., 372
Towery, Kenneth, 367
trading posts, 69, 144, 167; French, 26–27, 28, 29, 31, 32, 40, 247
Trans-Pecos region (*see also specific place names*), 3, 5, 19, 163, 181, 261, 312; Indians of, 8, 16; land grants in, 259; railroads, 266; rain-

Trans-Pecos region (*cont.*)
fall, 4; Villa in, 310
Travis, William Barrett, 93, 103, 110–11
Travis County, Tex., 135, 225, 290, 307, 367; secession and, 194, 207
Treasury Department, Texas State, 231, 275, 276, 333
Treat, James, 149
treaties, *see specific treaty*, e.g., Adams-Onís Treaty (1819)
Trespalacios, José, 67–68
Trinidad, Colo., 256
Trinity Bay, 92
Trinity River, 4, 14, 47, 64, 66, 101, 144, 190; navigation of, 180; Ranger camps on, 241; West Fork of, 167
Trinity University, 293, 322
Truman, Harry S., 347, 356, 360; Adlai Stevenson and, 362; tidelands veto by, 361, 368
Tucson, Ariz., 196
Tucumcari, N.M., 150
Tumulty, Joseph, 311–12
Turner, Frederick Jackson, 120
Turtle Bayou, 93
Turtle Bayou Resolution, 93, 94, 122
Twiggs, David E., 196
Tyler, John, 153, 154, 193
Tyler, Tex., 335

Ugartechea, Domingo de, 93, 104
Underwood, Oscar W., 328, 329
Unionism (*see also* secessionism), 205–207, 209, 213, 221; Constitutional Convention (1866) and, 216–17; of Houston, 189, 190–91, 193–95, 206
Union Loyal League, 207
Union Pacific Railroad, 247, 252
United Friends of Temperance, 282
United Mine Workers, 281
United States, 136, 270, 289, 350; Florida purchase, 66–68; Indians and, 140, 141, 167–69, 238, 243–47, 248; Louisiana purchase, 56, 58, 59–60, 154, 187; Mexican revolutionaries in, 62, 63, 64, 65,

United States (*cont.*)
66, 67, 72, 94, 129, 308–309, 310; Mexican War and, 156–61; Neutral Ground Treaty and, 61; New Mexico annexation issue and, 161–62, 163; Pershing invasion of Mexico and, 310–11; slave trade suppression in, 182–83; state highway grants, 306; states' rights doctrine and, 186–87, 189; Texas boundary conventions and, 148, 153, 376; Texas readmission, 213, 215–16, 217, 220, 221; Texas statehood issue, 66–67, 106, 118, 122, 126, 127, 129–30, 146, 153–55, 156, 159, 161, 162, 368
United States Agricultural Adjustment Agency, 338
United States Air Force Training Command, 345
United States Army, 58–59, 60, 61, 64; aviation and, 312–14; camels and, 181; Civil War and, 195–96, 197, 198–99, 200, 201, 203, 206, 213, 215, 221, 230, 231; conscription, 344; Indian suppression by, 140, 141, 167–69, 240–41, 243–47, 248; insurance and, 312; Madero revolution (1910) and, 308; military courts of, 232; Texas roads and, 165, 166; Villa and, 310–11; WAC's and, 345
United States Army Air Corps, 314, 345
United States Army Signal Corps, 312
United States Border Patrol, 350
United States Bureau of the Census, 350, 377, 382
United States Bureau of Indian Affairs, 168
United States Congress: land speculation and, 70–71; National Cattle Trail and, 253; New Deal and, 338, 339; Reconstruction and, 212–13, 217, 218, 219, 220–21, 225; slavery and, 187, 189, 193, 228; Texans in, 111, 128, 145, 164, 189, 217, 218, 221, 223, 276, 283, 299, 311, 312, 323, 332, 343, 346, 356, 359–60, 368, 370, 371–72, 373; Texas Admission Act, 153, 154,

United States Congress (*cont.*)
155, 194; Texas Republic recognition and, 129; Texas revenue debt and, 163
United States Constitution, 127, 185, 186, 187, 316; Thirteenth Amendment, 216, 221, 230; Fourteenth Amendment, 205, 218, 221, 229, 230, 376, 379; Sixteenth Amendment, 145; Seventeenth Amendment, 145, 299; Eighteenth Amendment, 145, 299, 323–24, 332, 339, 341; Nineteenth Amendment, 324
United States Department of Agriculture, 226, 302
United States Department of Labor, 352
United States Department of the Navy, 372
United States Department of War, 160, 181, 244, 309–10
United States Fifth Military District, 218
United States House of Representatives, 311, 312
United States Immigration Service, 350
United States Interstate Commerce Commission, 280, 299
United States. National elections: *1836–1876*, 129, 130, 153–54, 189, 191–92, 193, 212, 217, 223; *1912–1928*, 301, 327, 328–29, 332; *1932–1936*, 337, 338, 339; *1940–1948*, 339, 346, 360, 369; *1952–1956*, 356, 361, 362–63, 375; *1960–1968*, 370–71, 375
United States National Historic Monuments, 32
United States Navy, 65, 134, 344, 345; Civil War and, 198, 199, 204
United States Public Works Administration, 339
United States Reconstruction Finance Corporation, 340, 355
United States Senate, 153, 154, 164, 217, 221, 299; Coke in, 276; Connally (Tom) retirement, 361; Houston seat in, 189, 190, 191; Johnson in, 356, 359–60, 370, 371–72; Ku Klux Klan in, 328; O'Daniel in,

United States Senate (*cont.*)
343, 346, 359; Reagan in, 283; senate elections bill (1913), 323; tidelands issue and, 368
United States State Department, 148
United States Supreme Court: antitrust laws and, 283, 286, 289, 302; Dred Scott decision of, 187, 189, 191; liquor sales tax decision, 277; New Deal and, 339; on occupational taxes, 284; school integration and, 380; tidelands ruling, 368; voting rights and, 379
United States Topographical Engineers, 166, 167, 168
United States Treasury, 162, 163
United States War Production Board, 355
United States Women's Army Corps (WAC), 345
United States Works Project Administration, 340
Upper California Road, 166
Upshur, Abel P., 153
Urrea, José, 126; Goliad and, 110, 114–15, 116
Ursuline Academies, 177
U.S.A. (Dos Passos), 357
U.S. Trust and Guaranty, 365
Ute Indians, 35
Uvalde County, Tex., 240

Valverde, battle of, 197
Van Buren, Martin, 129, 130
Van Dorn, Earl, 169, 196, 197
Van Ness, George, 150
Van Zandt, Isaac, 153
Van Holst, Hermann, 119
Vargas, Pedro de, 51
Varona, Gregorio de Salinas, 24, 25
Vásquez, Rafael, 151
Vehlein, Joseph, 78, 91
Velasco, Tex., 92–94, 180; as seat of government, 123
Velasco, battle of, 93
Velasco, Treaty of, 123, 125, 130, 134
Vera Cruz, Mexico, 25, 26, 30, 33, 89, 125; French attack (1838),

Index / 480

Vera Cruz, Mexico (*cont.*) 149, 157; Spanish attack (1829), 88; U.S. attack (1846), 160
Veramendi, Juan, 63, 75, 121
Vernon, Tex., 252
Versailles, Treaty of, 314
Veteran's Land Act (Tex.), 366
Veteran's Land Board, 366
Vial, Pedro, 49–50
Viana, Father Mariano Francisco de los Dolores y, 37–38
Victoria, Guadalupe, 77
Victoria, Tex., 34, 83, 104, 110, 113, 149, 180; Comanche raid (1840), 143; Vásquez invasion (1842) of, 151
Viesca, Agustín, 102
Viesca (Milam), Tex., 92
Villa, Pancho, 310–11
Villa Acuña (Las Vacas), Mexico, 308
Villa de San Fernando de Béxar, 33, 34, 57
Vinson, Robert E., 307
Virginia Point, Tex., 198
Volstead Act (U.S.), 323
Volunteer Army of Texas, *see* Texas army and militia

Waco, Tex., 144, 145, 170, 177, 232, 292; army training in, 312; population changes in, 290, 348; railroad strike (1922) and, 316
Waco Indians, 35, 243
Waggoner, W. T., 319
Walker, Edwin A., 372, 373
Walker, Samuel H., 135
Walker County, Tex., 222
Wallace, Henry A., 340, 359
Wallace, W. A. "Bigfoot," 135
Waller County, Tex., 75
Walnut Creek, 135
Walsh, W. C., 277, 296
Walters, Jacob F., 336
Ward, William, 114
Wardlaw, Louis J., 332
War of 1812, 70, 187
Warren, Earl, 373
Warren Commission Report, 373–74
War Risk Insurance Act (U.S.), 312
War in Texas, The (Lundy), 119

Washington, John M., 161
Washington, D.C., 146; Cherokee embassy to, 109, 128; Santa Anna in, 130
Washington, Tex., 173
Washington-on-the-Brazos, Tex., 75, 146, 165, 269–70; San Felipe Consultation, 103, 105–107; Texas General Consultation (1836) in, 70, 108, 111, 112–13
Washington County, Tex., 237, 290, 348
Waters-Pierce Oil Company, 289, 300, 304, 317
Water Development, Texas State Board of, 372
water supply, 259–60, 262, 264, 266, 278, 372
Wavell, Arthur, 78, 82, 85, 173
Waxahachie, Tex., 192
Wayland Baptist College, 379
Webb, Charles, 235
Webb, Walter Prescott, 236, 259
Webb County, Tex., 309, 349
Webster, Daniel, 153, 162
Wells, James, 324
West Columbia oil field, 319
Western Land and Livestock Company, 265
Western Trail, 252
West Point Military Academy, 133, 167, 197, 322
West Texas (*see also specific place names*), 1, 2, 3, 4, 233, 238, 253, 299, 385; agricultural methods in, 259–60, 334; Anglo-American colonization of, 82, 90; archeology of, 5, 6; camels in, 181; cattle land speculation in, 255, 257, 259, 264–66, 277–78, 285, 346; Indians of, 7, 8, 15–16, 36, 61–62, 140, 167–69, 240–41, 248; Mendoza-López expedition in, 17–19; population changes in, 349; railroad land grants in, 258, 270, 285; roads, 165–67; Smith as governor, 375; statehood proposal (1869), 220–21; university and grant, 145, 292
West Texas State Teachers College, 322
Wetmore, Alex, 69

481 / Index

Wetmore, George, 69
Wharton, John A., 106, 201, 202, 203
Wharton, William H., 96, 106; the United States and, 128, 129–30, 146
Wheelock, Stillman W., 265
Whig Party, 119, 153–54, 160, 164, 165
White, David, 148
White, James Taylor, 249
White Deer Ranch, 256
Whiting, W. H. C., 166
Wichita County, Tex., 257
Wichita Falls, Tex., 257
Wichita Indians, 35
Wichita Ranch, 257
Wigfall, Louis T., 191, 201, 202
Wilbarger County, Tex., 138
Wilderness, battle of, 202
Wilke, Gus, 295
Wilkinson, James, 58–59, 60, 61, 67, 78
Wilkinson, Jane, 67, 68
Williams, Samuel May, 91–92
Williamson, R. M. "Three-Legged Willie," 103
Willis, Frank, 284
Wilson, Robert, 132
Wilson, Will, 372
Wilson, Woodrow, 301–302, 310, 311–12, 314–15, 328
Wisconsin River, 21
Wise County, Tex., 138, 243, 280
Woll, Adrian, 151–52
woman suffrage, 324–25
women, status of, 145, 315, 316, 324–25; Negro, 376, 379; in wartime, 345, 346
Women's Christian Temperance Union, 282, 324
Wood, George Thomas, 161, 164, 189
Woodruff-Graves Committee, 340–41

Woodsonville, battle (1861) of, 201
Woodward, John, 148
World War I, 301, 307, 311–15, 322, 377; woman suffrage and, 324
World War II, 313, 344–47, 351; industrial expansion and, 344, 345–46, 353, 354
Worth County, Tex., 161
Wright, Claiborne, 69
Wright, Wilbur, 313
Wyoming, 253, 255, 256

XIT Ranch, 255, 256, 257, 263, 296

Yaqui Indians, 50
Yarborough, Don, 372, 375
Yarborough, Ralph, 362, 363, 367, 368, 372
Yates oil field, 319
Ybarbo, Antonio Gil, 47, 84
Yellow House Draw, 248
Yellow House Land Company, 334
Yellowstone River, 35
Yoakum, Henderson, 175
Yorkinos Party (Mexico), 88
Young, Bob, 384
Young, W. C., 197
Yucatan, Mexico, 9, 65, 102, 122, 194; Federalist revolts in, 134, 149–50
Yuma, Ariz., 270

Zacatecas, Mexico, 51, 102
Zambrano, Juan, 63, 173
Zapata County, Tex., 37, 360
Zavala, Lorenzo de, 78, 91, 103, 112, 121
Zimmerman Note (1917), 310, 311, 312
Zuñi Indians, 12
Zweifel, Henry, 320

Counties

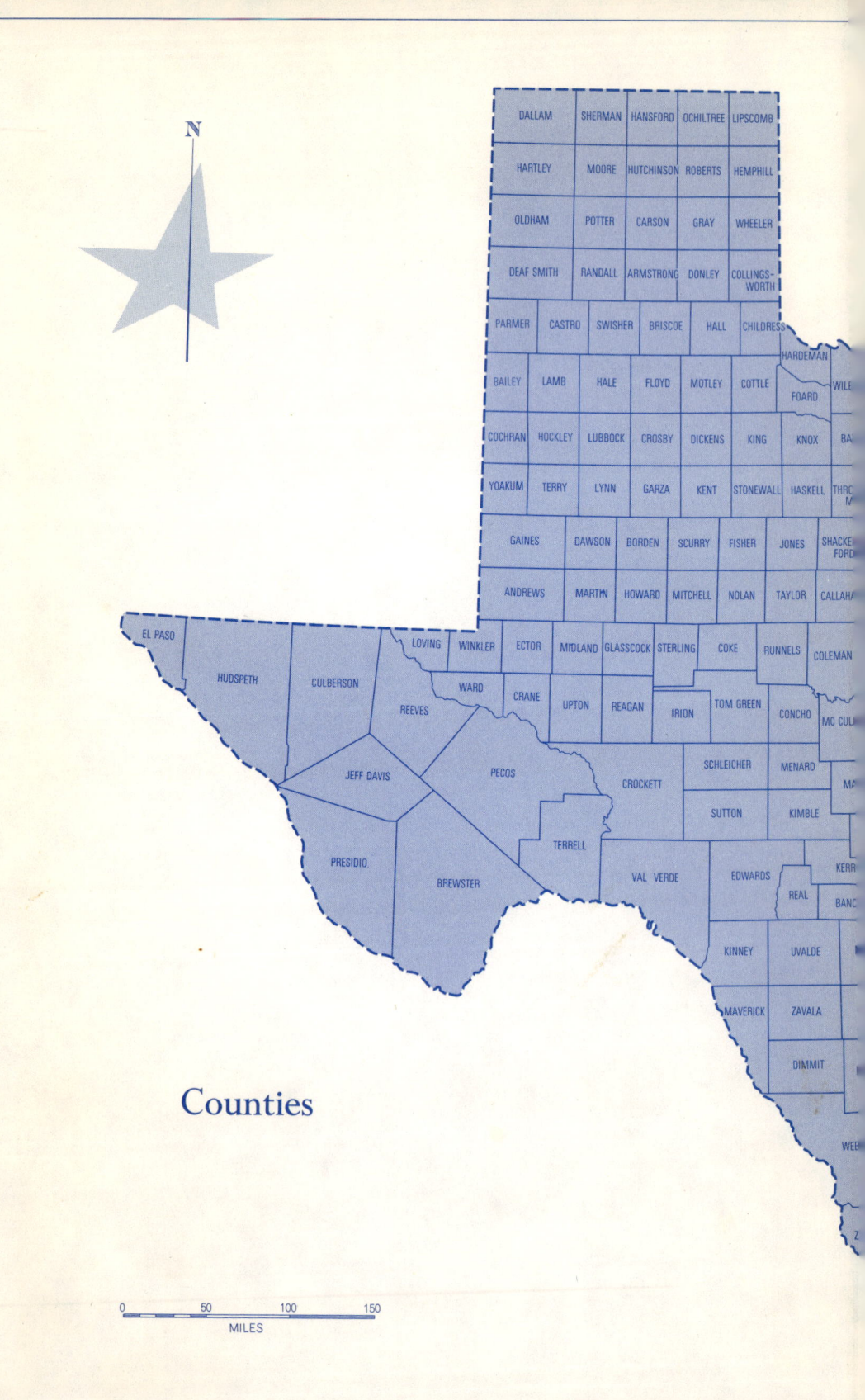

N

DALLAM	SHERMAN	HANSFORD	OCHILTREE	LIPSCOMB
HARTLEY	MOORE	HUTCHINSON	ROBERTS	HEMPHILL
OLDHAM	POTTER	CARSON	GRAY	WHEELER
DEAF SMITH	RANDALL	ARMSTRONG	DONLEY	COLLINGSWORTH
PARMER	CASTRO	SWISHER	BRISCOE	HALL	CHILDRESS
					HARDEMAN
BAILEY	LAMB	HALE	FLOYD	MOTLEY	COTTLE	FOARD	WIL...
COCHRAN	HOCKLEY	LUBBOCK	CROSBY	DICKENS	KING	KNOX	BA...
YOAKUM	TERRY	LYNN	GARZA	KENT	STONEWALL	HASKELL	THRO... M...
GAINES	DAWSON	BORDEN	SCURRY	FISHER	JONES	SHACKELFORD
ANDREWS	MARTIN	HOWARD	MITCHELL	NOLAN	TAYLOR	CALLAHA...

EL PASO

HUDSPETH | CULBERSON | LOVING | WINKLER | ECTOR | MIDLAND | GLASSCOCK | STERLING | COKE | RUNNELS | COLEMAN

REEVES | WARD | CRANE | UPTON | REAGAN | IRION | TOM GREEN | CONCHO | MC CUL...

JEFF DAVIS | PECOS | | | | SCHLEICHER | MENARD | MA...

CROCKETT | SUTTON | KIMBLE

PRESIDIO | BREWSTER | TERRELL | VAL VERDE | EDWARDS | KERR | REAL | BAND...

KINNEY | UVALDE

MAVERICK | ZAVALA

DIMMIT

WEB...

Z...

0 50 100 150
MILES